"...She opens up the sea door,
On the beaches of Exuma Infinite,
And through its floral glow,
We swim the loving moons of affection,
That rise within our souls... "

For Permissions:
clemys@sbcglobal.net or kmmlaw12@gmail.com.

978-0-578-63677-1

Preamble

I stood there at 2:00 A.M. in the wee hours of a magical night, August 6, 2017, in a dense humid warmth, a quiet darkness of the beach with my children, Nate and Kayleigh. For Kayleigh, I knew that this experience would be one that she would remember and draw upon for years to come. I was so grateful. The message was so important. What she had just accomplished on the beach, saving a baby Loggerhead sea turtle, was sacred. She nudged up against me as we stepped towards our car to drive back towards our beach house, and said, "Daddy, that was the most important thing you've ever done for me. Like that baby sea turtle, I fell into a hole, but somebody saved me."

I thought to myself in that moment, yes, you were harmed, you fell "into a hole," but you fought back and you saved you, making that hole ever so temporary. She is raw courage and strength. After what I had seen of Kayleigh's resilience, I didn't worry about this one in this life, for she was battle tested and emerged stronger after this event to which she alluded. I kissed her on her forehead and gave her a half hug and said, "I'm so proud of you, Babygirl, what you just did was epic and amazing. You saved a baby sea turtle, Kakes! You are amazing!"

We were on top of the world. Just over a week later, in the blink of an eye, my little girl was physically killed in a simple, innocent car accident.

*

I was there when she took her first breath in the physical world at 11:09 A.M., May 15th, 2002. I was there when she took her last breath in this physical world at 10:49 P.M., August 17, 2017. And there throughout every day of her magical life on this earthly plain. Present. Every day. For fifteen years, three months and two days – present – an active, honorable, obligated, grateful Father enchanted by his Daughter, and when born soon thereafter, also his Son. That enchantment remains among the four of us, including their sacred

2

Mother, my wife, Jessica. It shall be always. Our love, our relationships, our lights – they transcend all configurations of our souls, whether skinned in a physical embodiment or released upon the wind in our spiritual emergence of true, Higher Life. We are four ropes of light tied together into an unbreakable immortal cord. We are love itself.

Had I known I only had 5,574 days in this physical form with my Daughter - would I have done things differently - treasured more time - made sure I didn't waste moments on petty issues? Not really. There were so few moments of distraction between us. I did not need to suffer through this accident to find the true meaning of life as I had already been living it both within myself and within my family. I have very little to regret. For I was present for it all. I treasured it all. I learned from it all. I engaged it all, with my days filled with Steps 10, 11 and 12 in A.A. and my family as my first priority within my sobriety. I was fifteen years sober when Kayleigh was born. Had deliberately planned to be a Daddy for fifteen years since my first day sober, it being one of the drivers to reconstruct my life from the ground up. I matured beyond my years with one set of priorities in mind – my sobriety and relationship with God, then my sacred relationship with my children, then the amazing relationship I have with Jess, followed by everything else. And everything else is just everything else.

Literally not one of those 5,574 days included missing an "I love you" spoken between us. And not one day has passed since the accident where the same sentiment is not shared between us, vocally, spiritually, emotionally, and sometimes amazingly, still physically, at least for me when I feel her touch me. Quite frankly, during Kayleigh's physical life, I would be surprised if I can find a day when it wasn't spoken multiple times – sometimes seven or eight times a day. It was part of our greeting and our goodbyes, yet not overused or under appreciated. Not one day did she spend an entire twenty four hours without my presence, even in the rare occasion when I was on a business trip, which I avoided like the plague. There was always a few phone calls and videos and FaceTime – sometimes more. I think I spent less than ten days away from her on business, having designed my career to make less money and spend my energy and valuable time with my family. It is simple - I invested in the right asset properly

3

and the result is this – I am a great Father – my children, as a result of having a great Father (and great Mother), are superstars. This is a story, not only of the courageous voice of Kayleigh, but also a story of us - a Daddy and Daughter in love with each other, adorned with heartfelt devotion, respect, butterfly love and unbreakable trust. It, by nature, also weaves Nathaniel and Jess in and through us – these four strings of light bound together in golden love. However, as I continue to write my days with Jess and Nate in the physical bodies we currently occupy, it is not possible to include them in most of this book, lest this book becomes sixty thousand pages long.

When Kayleigh and I were both in our physical bodies, we were effortless, hilarious and content – finishing each other's sentences, knowing which buttons to push or refrain from pushing, almost with an uncanny telepathy, knowing what the other was thinking. Kayleigh was and is my twin – emotionally, in mannerism, in strength and with passion. Now, with one of us on this physical plain and one of us on a much higher spiritual plain, we are effortless, hilarious and content, except when I get in the way with expected grief and despondency that washes in like ocean waves. These pages will demonstrate that, although everything has changed, nothing has changed. We will remain effortless, hilarious, content – if I do my work and stay in that higher vibration, cutting through the daily troubles and struggles and pains and frustrations and abysmal suffering that sometimes collapses the lungs. For the physical death of a child in childhood is a wound that does not heal, particularly as the losses, over time, accumulate. She teaches me new methods of reconciliation, knowing that, through the balancing act of reconciliation, counterbalancing the grief, her Father can live in this physical world, though the horrendous suffering continues.

This book was precipitated by my amazing Daughter's sudden, tragic, accidental physical death. As such, it will prove to be incapable of capturing the entirety of Kayleigh Mickayla Mooney. Out of necessity, this is a collection of snapshots of our relationship, scattered across these pages, like a bin into which art projects by a child are saved by a parent. Several main themes wrap their way and merge through this collection: her unique beauty; her courageous voice as it relates to her empowering recovery from an assault that she refused to permit to define her, and from which she became even

4

more beautiful; her courageous voice as it relates to her unrelated, tragic, accidental death in a traffic accident; and her glorious transition from her young, physical embodiment into her higher truth in her spiritual body of life. She shows us strength, and new found unbridled power to touch us continually and walks with us today in the freedom of pure love and light.

I cannot do all of Kayleigh's life justice and this book is a comparatively insignificant attempt to capture a life as compassionately and wondrously as beautiful as Kayleigh's life was in her physical form, and is in her spiritual embodiment. There is poetry and texts sprinkled throughout the book. Most of the pre-accident pieces are typically first drafts written on my phone in the moment and sent to Kayleigh. Usually at night as I lay in my bed before sleep, Jess beside me reading, I would end my 11th Step each night with the same prayer for our children, and knew that on the other side of the wall, my Daughter lay in her bed, talking to friends, checking her social media accounts. Her little brother, Nathaniel, would also be in his room, likely asleep. My mind frequently drifted towards opportunities to provide my children encouragement, and sometimes, what they facetiously called, "life lessons," while rolling their eyes in my direction. Nathaniel and I have other multiple ways of communion that are sacred to us. For Kayleigh, my Daughter, it was intense conversations about everything, texting, poetry, art, hugs – these were our primary channels. Sometimes these poems and messages were stream of conscience. Sometimes clustered around certain events and my constant desire to be present and support her. The later poems in this book following her physical death are my lifeline to her and to myself, in part, grief work following the greatest pain and tragedy of my life; and partly Kayleigh and I writing together. Further, I do my work in my sobriety, which includes daily 10th Steps, which are to be done throughout the day, whenever needed. I do many a day through constant vigilance, and the combination of Steps 4-9 all wrapped up into that constant self-inventory of life in the 10th Step. If I was to add every 10th Step I have done since the accident, this book would add ten thousand more pages. Who has time to read that? I would never! I sprinkle a few of those 10th Steps throughout the book as they were written in raw, real time on those days, representing the hundreds and thousands I have done. Likewise, the dialogue I had and still have with my Kakie is

5

captured, as well, in this volume, with a very small sampling of our thousands of texts, hundreds and hundreds of which I printed after the accident and keep in a sacred book, as well as samplings of poetry and other writings, and our dialogue in quiet times that have been written down, likewise, as she spoke these words and as I translated them onto paper, for she works alongside me, she channels through me, as we continue to build upon our magnificent relationship.

Our special, unique Daddy and Daughter relationship inverted after the accident so that she no longer needs my guidance, but provides me that guidance I once conveyed to her. She channels through me and I offer her my life as a vessel to communicate, my pen as a way to write, when she needs it. She is a co-author of this book, sometimes writing whole sections and sometimes blending her words in and through mine on these pages. Of the two of us, she is clearly the better writer, and I try not to weigh her style down.

This book does not and cannot track all of the very private horrific grief we experienced upon the fateful night of August 17, 2017; the many hurricanes of wailing, crying, sobbing, breaking down, nightmares, sleepless nights, sleep-full days, lack of food, stunned, horrified and tormented moments; cannot account for all of the cherished memories and the rush to collect and preserve every video and digital photo, every art project, every note she ever wrote, every important Kakie item; cannot account for every new memory after her physical death or all of the spiritual highs and lows of this transition. It cannot attest for all of the fear and all of the courage, or all of the anger cast and gratitude expressed towards the Universe and God. All of the despondency and all of the joy. All of the fantasy, fictional and depressing thoughts. All of the moments I have felt like a hyena in a metal box, circling the same four metal corners in hopes of finding a way out of this nightmare to escape from its grasp and run to her. All of the moments of intractable, immeasurable grief. I am robbed every day and each day for the rest of my life of Kayleigh's magnificent physical presence and all that she would have been and all she would have done in her physical state. This is a fact. No walking down the aisle. No finishing up on her lessons learning how to drive. No driving us to Jekyll Island. Proms. Curfews. College. Graduations. Jobs. New cars. Cats. Boyfriends. Life. Grandchildren. It takes my breath away, this shear panic and horror of the frequency of the realization that my Babygirl, the strongest girl I've ever known, does not get to do anything further in her physical life.

If not for her ability to walk with us daily and prove that her life continues at a much stronger resonation of light, I wouldn't see and feel and experience that she gets to do much, much more. While some have everyday challenges and may complain about their hard day, I take a deep breath and think, "If I asked you to trade places with me, you'd scurry for the door. I know hard days." While they continue to complain about their hard days or having to go out of their way to take their kids to a store or to practice, I think to myself simply, "you get to," and sometimes, "you get to, so shut the hell up and go be with your child!" In the meantime, while we are stuck in our human shells and limited in our capacity, Kayleigh saves another girl; redirects another victim of sexual violence towards a survivor mentality; whispers in a young girl's ear not to go down that hallway; directs her little brother; holds her Mother's hands in meditation; runs her fingers through her Father's hair; touches the hearts of those she loves with courage. She gets to save others and shift the human mosaic of the world. And I am her witness and help write her documentary. I get to watch her miracles.

I am heartbrokenly aware that my Daughter's physical life, glimpses of which I have tried to capture in this volume, was cut short as it was attempting its brilliant ascent. Our lives, however, are not our physical bodies. And death ends a physical life, but not a life, and certainly does not end a relationship. Kayleigh's life simply transitioned out of her physical embodiment and elevated into her spiritual embodiment. Whether she is in her physical body or her spiritual body she is still Kayleigh, just much stronger now in the latter. And so Kayleigh and I commune – in my 11th Step of A.A. in the morning, night and throughout the day – in moments I take to grieve or celebrate her physical or spiritual life; when I need her guiding voice, during intentional meditation, and as I listen to her and walk in her light in our Daddy-Daughter time that has never ended. It actually grows deeper for I have to try harder to remain in contact with her. There is a magnificence that co-exists with this unthinkable, unimaginable tragedy and that magnificence is that she is here with me in her spiritual body of light and continues our work together,

7

affecting thousands in a positive way. She is my guardian. She is powerful. She is amazing. She is alive, filled with God's light, one thousand times stronger than her Father and one thousand times stronger than she was on that fateful day when her physical life transitioned and her spiritual body emerged from her human shell.

I live the greatest gift tucked into the greatest pain, and know, very clearly, we do not belong to this world. I have an audience with God. He holds my hand. He whispers this secret in my ear. And I am special. For I know something few know. I've seen the keys to the kingdom. And they are awash in the galaxies that spin in my Daughter's hands.

Kayleigh, I grieve horribly your physical loss in my life. Grief has no end, evidence that love as well, has no end. We meet daily under our own "One Tree Hill." I celebrate unafraid and unabashed your current life and your brilliant soul that guides me daily on my continuous journey of life. Desperately, I miss you physically, Kakes, but grow with you daily as I daily reconcile this tragedy into our new configuration and also as you continue to learn better ways to cross the wind to communicate with me. I watch you grow, just as I watched you grow from a baby to a toddler to a young child to an older child to a tween to a teenager to a beautiful young, near woman. You speak to many people directly, in many ways, and certainly you speak directly to me. Often, you also speak indirectly through me. I am your pen and will be your persistent channel and advocate. Your courage is unmatched in my life. Teach me your loving ways. I Love you, Sweetheart. Your Daddy is in love with you. Your Daddy is here. Your Daddy is.

*** *She Is....24/7/FOREVER* ***

Kayleigh's Voice (She IS...)

She told me to write this book, several times. A meditation. A soulful journey of mindfulness. I actually jotted down the words I heard her speak just days into this suffering, one of the clearest messages of my life: "Daddy, write a survival guide for yourself and others. One for you and one for people who haven't had this experience (of continuing to feel, see and hear a child's continuance of live after physical death). All of the things in summary that reset your feet. And all the dumb things people shouldn't say ☺ we are helping so many."

Within the first several days following the accident that took my baby's physical life, and having established dialogue with her just moments after she physically passed, she directed me to do several things: (1) knowing I was awake to her and was experiencing her transition in full color, she asked me to find comfort and shelter from the storms and walk in her light, having the knowledge and faith that her presence as my guardian was as real as my breath, and (2) she asked me to tell her story of her courage, represented by her art work, her actions, our texts, and other communications both prior to and following her physical death. She wanted to empower other women, both young and old, in whatever voice each woman chose to use, telling their own courageous story or supporting another in the telling of her own. She also wanted others to know the power of love, the essence of light, and the reality of God's presence that resonates through her, regardless of how one envisions God. She has proven this latter notion resoundingly since her physical death. For her life is not her physical body.

She is like the Moon - the Star of the Sea, glowing full and brightly, reflecting the inspiring light of the sun. She is our guardian, an angel in whose light we walk, filtered from God, through her brilliant soul, showering blessings and light upon us to guide our way. A blazing lantern refracted into thousands of points of light that touched an entire community simultaneously in the days following her physical death. Those thousands of points of light have been multiplied in the thoughts, words and actions of those she has touched and ripples out from those that still toil on this physical plain – those having learned from her example, who have heard her voice or felt her presence, living differently, more directly, deliberately, and following her guiding light.

We, myself, Jessica and Nathaniel, are luckiest among all, having Kayleigh as our Daughter and Nathaniel's sister. We know among all others the powerful impact of her presence, even though many more surely knew and know that impact as well. As the days go by without Kayleigh's physical body in presence, but with her body of light in full, active and current embodiment, the widening circle of those she continues to empower increases. It is quite miraculous.

Dynamic and kind, a compassionate, complex old soul with a tender heart, she was, in her physical life, inquisitive and felt the world around her like it was part of her flesh. Easily hurt, yet quick to heal, she frequently rallied behind people when they were down, ready to lend a hand, provide words of encouragement and a sweet smile. She was fully accepting of others, regardless of their hang ups, their views, their personal choices, their sexual preferences, their politics. It is frequent, even today, that people tell us that when they were down – Kayleigh was there; when they were confused – Kayleigh was there; when they were jaded and alone – Kayleigh was always there to lend an ear and provide a presence of compassion, caring and love. Imagine this girl with these qualities, now shed of the confines of her humanity and shining brighter than a million suns; offering her courage through her voice and example and continuing to display the raw beauty that is Kayleigh Mickayla Mooney in an even more complete way. She is elevated. She is light.

"She Is"

She is as she always was,
And is as she always is,
A compassionate light,
A magnificent young woman,
Tucked into human life,
With a passion more expansive,
That the shell that held her tight,
A brilliance in spirit's laughter,
A thousand moons bright,
Transcending across both worlds,

Where her love, enhanced, ignites;

And she swims in her mother,
And she flows in her Father,
And she grows in her brother,
As if she was still physically here,
Though she is not,
She is,
Her soul dances on the edges of the eyes,
And penetrates the day in ways that can't be denied,
Always with warmth and empathy,
A rainbow enhanced with sunrise,
She is amazing,
Watch her dance,
She is amazing,
Hear her angel voice,
She is amazing,
She is alive,
She is amazing,
My spirit guide.

*

The Best of Me

Above and beyond being my favorite girl in my life, Kayleigh is my muse. She always has been. I wrote to her fifteen years before she was born, and occasionally through those years before she was born. Between the time Jessica began developing Kayleigh in her sacred womb and through about six months old I wrote three volumes of poetry for or about her. Through her life my writing, though slowed at times by the pressures and distractions of life, continued unabated. These writings supplemented the daily presence we had with each other as I raised the kids, cried and laughed with them, spent my days thinking about her and her brother, and engaged at their levels at each stage of their young lives. For Kayleigh, she was a girl whose Father wrote her constant poetry. She gushed with joy at its notion as it became part of her days at every age.

In my writings I celebrated her successes and offered sympathy in hard moments, usually as a little extra encouragement after an earlier talk, laugh, cry or hug. Above all, Kayleigh knew that her Daddy wrote poetry to her and about her, and she was only too quick to share her reality with other girls in her peer group, realizing at a young age, and to her amazement, that our situation was quite unique. There were not a lot of Fathers in her peer group who wrote poetry to their daughters, which she found to be quite odd. This fact accelerated her fondness and excitement in receiving each new piece her Father took the time, energy and love in creating specifically for her. Consistently finding ways to encourage her and enhance the deep connection between us, and to celebrate all she was teaching me about me, I sent this to her several weeks before she physically died, somewhere in mid-July, 2017. It remains one of my favorites:

"The Best of Me"

I give you my gold,
My liquid light,
The balancing poles,
That equate my life,
The best of me,
The best in spite,
Of the rest of me,
That rests and fights;

I give you this light,
That flows from this soul,
It sparks lightning white,
In a heartbeat that glows,
Its streams fill with memories,
Of life's fields and roads,
And leads to your spirit,
Where the best of me grows.

There was no way for me to know when I wrote this, that several weeks later, I would be using the second stanza in her obituary. It wasn't even a thought as I sat in the funeral home twelve hours after her tragic physical death, picking out cards, writing an obituary, beginning to frame a eulogy and making arrangements for her service. Yet there it was.

This poem is about an imperfect human, a Father, who was consistently present with his children, who knew his self-worth and value, who understood clearly his truth, who was offering on a daily basis to his children his love, his light, his gold and sometimes his mistakes. It is about that Father knowing that his children were a mirror of his own light and his children were yet a brighter light than himself. Within his children the best of a Daddy grows. And thus I sent this poem at about midnight via text to my little girl tucked in her bed on the other side of the wall from my bedroom, while she lay in bed checking her Instagram account and chirping with other teenage girls. Her text back to me several minutes later confirmed her thankfulness and resonation of love.

Like many of my poems to her, sent in a manner unknowing that I would suffer her tragic physical death, the words have taken on multiple meanings in the aftermath of this tragedy. Perhaps she now sings these words to me. To you. One new meaning is that the streams are not just our memories together on the physical plain, in her physical body, but now also reflect the reality of new memories we create daily together, even though I am still in my physical body and she is now in her body of light.

*

The Funeral 08/22/2017

I will never forget the overwhelming wave of chaotic, shocked, yet deeply loving energy that rushed over me as we stepped under the threshold at the main entrance of the church to the sound of a family member, an opera singer, singing Kayleigh's favorite song, "Hallelujah." For a moment the pallbearers adjusted before entering the main church. Kayleigh's cousins and I stopped the funeral director momentarily so that I could place a small Loggerhead sea turtle figurine on top of my Daughter's casket. The size of my open hand, the turtle itself seemed to be so tiny compared to the ocean of wood upon which it was set. Kayleigh and I had purchased the tiny figure from one of the little shops on Jekyll Island, Georgia, just twelve days prior.

I held my wife's arm to physically support her and wrapped my other arm around my beautiful son, Nathaniel. A sea of one thousand faces awaited our arrival, packed shoulder to shoulder in the church, and some, finding no seating, standing in the doorways and out in the parking lot and side gardens – the hour at hand of which no parent wishes. Father Patrick nodded and then began the procession as we slowly passed these thousand mourners, gathered in a collective spasmodic shock from Kayleigh's sudden, innocent, accidental death. I caught eyes with friends and family who could only stand at their pews and stare at us, powerlessness etched in their eyes, longing to lunge from the pews and embrace us; collared in their empty stances, none envious of the task that lay before us. It was our show – a show nobody wanted and into which nobody dared to intervene, which is exactly the way Kayleigh and I wanted it.

I am six feet two inches tall and typically am looking eyeball to eyeball or lower to others in any room. In this church, however, on this sacred day, each person in the crowd to my left and right seemed to be blending and stretching liquidly twenty to thirty feet tall. The pure energy and collision of grief and love seemed to stretch the electric crowd to the ceiling. I felt like Moses walking on dry land with huge waves held back on either side, curving outward from everyone's feet, curving upward through all of their bodies and stretching upward ad rounding up towards a single middle point on the distant embroidered painted ceiling of the church. It was awful, magnificent, loving and so very sad as I parted this sea of faces gathered in honor of my beautiful, amazingly wonderful Daughter – a procession no parent ever wants; an event that never exists until you've been there.

This was a moment of pure, unthinkable heartache. A moment of unconditional devotion and love. A moment of other worldly strength and conviction. The roles were reversed on me – the natural order of life in disarray and never to be controlled, wrestled or reversed back into its proper order no matter how hard the denial would come. I had planned my happy, healthy, vibrant Daughter's funeral - me, the bearer of the family's emotional luggage. I was walking behind my Kakie's casket, watching the sea turtle atop glide towards the front of the church and the magnificent altar. The front row. The participants. The readers. The family. God.

Kayleigh's spirit resonated and swirled in passionate light and love throughout the church. I felt her presence very clearly, her warmth and strength unmistakable; embracing each and every person there; a light hug, laying her head on shoulders; spreading her light about the crowd. We were only five days into her new configuration, but also five days of experiencing her life in spirit. It was already very familiar to me, as if she and I had waltzed in this dance for thousands of years together. She held me as I held her Mother and Brother. She beamed from ear to ear across her angelic face, pleasantly surprised by the massive crowd that had gathered to honor her life and her soul. Every teenager wonders about age appropriate subjects like life and death; who will be at my funeral; will people love me, remember me. She had her confirmation – over a thousand; all crushed; all crying; all saddened in total disbelief. This was the shock of the tragedy portrayed in Thornton Wilder's "the Bridge of San Luis Rey."

"She Dances in a Sea of Stars"

She wears galaxies for her gowns,
Liquid light – liquid gold,
And rainbow stars like glittering fabric,
Spiral forth from her sparkling soul –

She dances aloofly on the winds aloft,
And presses her feet like rose petals soft,
Upon my fields of earthly firmament,
Leaving a trace of a heavenly scent,
Where, with her, the hours of my days are spent.

*

Father Patrick 08/19/2017

We are a family of rich variations in ethnic culture and religious backgrounds. All told, Kayleigh and her brother, Nathaniel, are, from their Father, largely Irish Catholic and slightly German Catholic, and from their Mother, Polish Jewish, Lithuanian Jewish, English Church of God, Scottish Presbyterian and Kickapoo Indian. Kayleigh and Nathaniel are a Daughter of the American Revolution and a Son of the American Revolution, as well as the proud descendants of one of the Fenian Brotherhood's leading members in Cleveland in the 1800's. Their ancestors were chased out of Poland during anti-Jewish pogroms; were part of one of the first Connecticut English Christian settlements; were displaced from their homelands when assigned to a reservation and forcibly relocated as a dispossessed Native American people; and sent guns and money to Mother Ireland to fight a rebellion against foreign British oppression. Religiously, with Kayleigh's untimely death, it tied together her Catholic and Jewish faiths.

Particularly, Jessica grew up in a secular Jewish home. As Kayleigh entered her teenage years, she prepared for her secular Bat Mitzvah, just as her mother had done. She enjoyed the process thoroughly several lovely women, including Rifka and Danny, guided Kayleigh and her friend Lilly through the process. Kayleigh also attended a Catholic private high school, Beaumont, and developed a relationship through Catholicism, with her own thoughtful touches, with God.

The challenge, gallantly taken by Father Patrick, whom Kayleigh loves, was to organize, to my wishes, a ceremony in our Catholic parish that was inclusive of Kayleigh's Jewish heritage. A progressive priest, a true shepherd of his flock, passionately grieved with our family and tied together this delicate, gentle and profound event, honoring Kayleigh in a manner that she enjoyed quite thoroughly. She arranged for Patrick. It is who she picked. She was so pleased.

As he toiled to piece this prayer, this funeral together, he was inspired with a particular reading. He came to the house on Saturday, just thirty six hours after the accident and sat with us in our living room.

16

He explained his struggles and the solution that he found; a reading that tied each piece together.

It was very warm – mid August in Cleveland. There was no wind in the atmosphere and very still. We have twenty five windows collectively in the first floor of the house – all were open. As Pat began to read, as if a small yet radiant windstorm was unleashed in the room, as the drapes over the living room windows began to lift and swirl about in the wind; filling the entire first floor with its gentleness from end to end. As Pat ended the reading, the drapes lay low and the wind evaporated, leaving the room as silent as it had been just a minute earlier. Jess and I looked at each other, as I was already beginning to wrap my mind around Kayleigh's new life, and looked at Pat and said, "She likes that one."

He smiled, having just felt the moment, even if he could not fully embrace or understand it – he knew it was what it was – that Kayleigh was present. We had just experienced one of her first little miracles. Joy attempted to creep into the spaces of the tension of our plight. I took a deep breath.

As he left our house, he told us later, significantly, that he started humming a song that he never hums; that he continued to hum this song through the afternoon on Sunday, when the significance of why it was in his mind became abundantly clear; a song by Phil Collins, "You'll Be In My Heart." We did not mention this song to him. He had not thought about it for years, yet here it was stuck in his head. Warmth in the light of the days.

*

Daddy's Eulogy 08/22/2017

As I sat there in the front row of the church, closest to Kayleigh's casket, just to her left, I knew there were one thousand people in the church, and standing in the parking lot listening, who were looking to the grieving Father, for guidance, direction, or just fearing what a dumpster fire it was going to be to have me stand up at the podium and try to eulogize my baby.

I was so exhausted, this being the fifth day since the sudden shock of death of a vibrant physical life. The altar stood in golden silence in front of me as Father Patrick sat down; two enlarged poster photos of Kayleigh, and two others of the four of us when they were little, adorned the altar, along with a painting the kids and I made years earlier. As I stood to step forward, I took a sip from my Pure Leaf Unsweetened Black Tea I snuck into the church, and stepped to Kayleigh's casket. Running my fingers slowly atop the length of the wood, in disbelief and utter silence, I leaned down and gently kissed the coffin above where her face lay inside. Immediately, several things occurred. First, I felt empowered and infused with Kayleigh's light which stripped from me all exhaustion. Secondly, I glanced over to the painting that she, Nathaniel and I had created for Jess' Christmas present of 2005, and found new meaning in the piece. And lastly, and most instructively, I clearly heard Kakes' resounding voice in my right ear, which was closest to the casket, say to me, playfully, and sweetly, "Daddy, suck it up! You can do this! You have ten minutes to explain to these people, some of whom don't know me, what my life was all about and how wonderful I am!"

I stepped to the podium and glanced out to a sea of faces. A full section was filled with girls from Beaumont School. Friends. Family. Work mates. Hundreds from Alcoholics Anonymous. Seemingly hanging from the rafters and bulging out of the doorways at every entrance. Mourners. Supporters. Love.

I began by relaying my new found meaning to the 2005 Christmas painting, intentionally focusing my first few moments in a sacred manner directly to Nathaniel. It was to my right, next to a poster sized photo of Kayleigh glancing up into the sun outside of our house – a picture I had taken on her 15th, and last, birthday, just three months earlier in May. The painting we created is orange and yellow across its face, with blue hand prints down the left side and green hand prints down the right. Kayleigh's were on the left and Nathaniel's on the right. Down the middle was a poem I had written about my babies. It was a Christmas gift for Jess when Nathaniel was eleven months old and Kayleigh was three and a half. I explained to the crowd that I had told the kids that day, in particular the older child, to stay on their side of the painting when I helped them press their painted hands into the canvas. And Kayleigh proceeded to immediately smudge right across and hit one of Nathaniel's prints, blurring and smudging her color across his. I reacted that day and told her, "Kayleigh! Stay on your side!" Then I felt sad that I had overreacted – these are the moments of raising kids. We moved passed that moment within thirty seconds and permitted the mistake to become part of the texture of the canvas and I let it go at that.

From the podium I caught eyes with Nathaniel and said, "Nathaniel, now this painting has a much different meaning as her handprint has washed over yours – she is telling you that she will always be with you and her hand will always be in your hand as you walk your way through your life. She is always with you."
He nodded uncontrollably, sobbing, acknowledging the message, as obscure and abstract as it was to a twelve year old in the depths of losing his entire world.

Then I turned back to the crowd. I told them that I was so tired, but as I stood up and ran my hands over Kayleigh's coffin, and as I kissed Kayleigh's coffin, I heard her very clearly, her voice centering me and infusing within me incredible strength, and telling me, "Daddy, you can do this. There are a thousand people here today and some of them don't know me. You have ten minutes to demonstrate to these people who I am. You can do this. Suck it up, Daddy."

There was a surprised pressure release in the crowd, a collective gasp, a chorus of quiet, subdued and embarrassed laughter, as if air was released from an overstressed balloon. I then looked up towards Heaven, knowing she would channel through me, knowing she was standing at the podium with me in her body of light, and said out loud, "Ok, Kayleigh, let's do this." Then I said the following:

"THERE ARE PEOPLE ALL OVER THIS CITY GRIEVING FOR KAYLEIGH AND HER LIGHT IS SO STRONG THAT SHE IS TOUCHING EVERYBODY AT THE SAME TIME. SHE IS AMAZING. For anybody struggling with their faith, or who don't want to believe this, I implore you to open your mind and open your heart and understand – this is not a WAS, this is an IS. Kayleigh IS amazing. She IS here right now. Kayleigh IS.

Nobody in this church knows what to say. And that is fine. We stand in Kayleigh's light today. She is at perfect peace and is today a much more powerful soul standing in the light of God and filled with all of our love for her. 3 months ago for her fifteenth birthday we told her an old Sioux proverb - "we will be known forever by the tracks we leave behind" - We are so proud of the courageous tracks of your life that light a path for many to follow.

We wanted to take a few minutes to share with you our Daughter who managed to fill in 15 years what most can't accomplish in a long life. Those who knew her know her loyalty, her laughter, her engagement, her emotional attention to others. We have bins and bins full of Kayleigh creations from art to secret projects to boxes filled with other boxes and her special trinkets.

When I was 16 I picked out Kayleigh's name and always knew I would one day have a Daughter. When I met jess at 24 she loved the name.

Kayleigh was banging on the door and demanded to be born into this world. On August 31, 2001, Jess, who was originally not wanting to have kids, told me that if we were ever to get pregnant then we can try just once, only that night. We went out to eat later that night and Jess said, "The first song that comes on the radio is my song to Kayleigh," and the song by Phil Collins "You'll Be in My Heart" came on the radio. Jess knew she was pregnant. And she was.

Kayleigh is a dynamic and energetic soul. She is a caretaker to the three of us particularly to her brother, Nathaniel, who she cherishes with all of her heart. These two formed a B Club which was an anti-parent club filled with secret maps and plans to steal food from the kitchen in the middle of the night. If something was amiss in the house Kayleigh was directing it. She also was responsible for a steady stream of abandoned cats and dogs that joined our family.

She and Jessica shared the closest Mother-Daughter bond I have ever witnessed. Not only a daughter to Jess but truly her best friend. They knew what the other was thinking and cherished their sacred time together. Kayleigh intertwined perfectly with each of us in her own way.

She was always supportive even from a young age. As a toddler if I struggled with something, whatever it was, she would pull out her pacifier and say, "You can do it, Daddy!" She was my biggest cheerleader. And like her love for Nathaniel and Jess, her love for me was unique and unending.

I want to tell you a few quick stories to help our grieving hearts. I am 30 years sober in A.A. When I was 6 months sober it seemed so impossible and I would cry myself to sleep thinking I couldn't make it. At 6 months sober, and not thinking I could stay sober, as I was half asleep I saw on five straight nights an image of a beautiful blond girl with brilliant blue eyes and I knew then that it was my Daughter and she would say "you can do this, Daddy. You can do this." And then a little more forcibly she would say, "Daddy, you will do this." And I would whisper okay and fall asleep. I emerged from those five days with my sobriety strengthened and I have never looked back.

Last week we were on vacation in Georgia and we went out looking for Loggerhead sea turtle nests hatching. We missed one by a few hours and saw all of the tracks. Kayleigh got a flashlight and checked every ghost crab hole and miraculously found one baby sea turtle far down a tiny hole. She demanded I do my best to help her save it. We dug it up and she set it free watching it make its way to the ocean. Then she said "Daddy, thank you. That turtle was me. Like that baby turtle I fell into a dark hole but somebody saved me."

Friday morning with Father Pat. Father told us he was grieving through connecting a Jewish and Catholic heritage together for this funeral as we wished and came up with a reading he wanted to share. The living room was still before he spoke, but when he started to read, every curtain over every window in our living room blustered with a steady and warm wind. Jess and I caught eyes and I turned to Pat and said, "She likes that one."

She was with us before she was born and certainly will always be with us after she died. She will make sure of it. She will leave little spiritual messages along the paths of our lives. You might not always know at first that it was her. But it will be.

I feel broken, but she will guide me through the dark. She is Kayleigh and if she wants something she's going to get it. What she wants for me and Jess and Nathaniel is spectacular life. And she will participate in it. She wants us to live in her light every day that God gives us. I believe she wants that for all of you as well. She wants you to treasure each other and be nice to one another. She hated when people were mean to one another.

Kayleigh wanted to either be a therapist and victim advocate or go to ROTC - or maybe both. I want you to know Kayleigh found her voice before she died - some of you know - she was attacked last October. She prosecuted her attackers and faced them in court two days before she physically died - and told them that you took something that didn't belong to you and I am taking it back and living a good life. I forgive you and I am moving on in my life.

She wants for us what Kayleigh always embraced - happiness, laughter, love and peace. Be at peace, Kayleigh, our little Kakes, our wise and guiding light.

*

Gladiola Gardens 07/28/2017

As will be conveyed in the following pages, my Daughter, Kayleigh, was raped in October, 2016, by boys she knew in a place that should have been safe and in which an assault should never have happened. The events of which are secondarily etched into my soul, including the details, the circumstances, the horror and the specifics, will remain in the sacredness of Kayleigh's light. This is a story of a then fourteen year old girl and her ability to co-exist with fear and faith, persevering through the fear with courage to affirm that her stoic voice would be heard and would never be silenced. This is not a story about the sickened, soul-less, cowardly deranged individuals that harmed my beautiful girl. This is a story of Kayleigh conquering them.

Much of my poetry and texts and live conversations with her after her sexual assault centered on facing the darkness, healing and rising. This piece is one such poem, written one month before she physically died, tracking her re-emergence from the rape, her healing, her strength, and her renewed esteem and belief in herself. This is the sole meaning of this piece – I sent it to her to remind her that she, in prosecuting, using voice and healing, did something that very few women do at any age, particularly at such a young and tender age; that because of her courage, because she fought back, she stood taller than her friends and peers; she stood tallest in the garden amongst the other flowers, having broken free of the grasp of the trauma from the rape and pushing outward to live an amazing life. That was all that was meant by this piece – to look back and see the hard work and to look to her current life bubbling and overjoyed with life.

As with other works, following her physical death, the meaning blends into new facts; changes color; alters at the edges. The words transform in meaning, just as Kayleigh's physical life and spirit transformed when she emerged from her physical life laying in the street against the curb, in my arms, and empowered in that moment in the release of her spirit into my light, and through me into God's eternal light. I sent this to her after midnight on July 28th, 2017. At her funeral it was the poem on the back of her prayer card, with the intention of letting the crowd know that when Kayleigh was confronted in life with something dark (like sexual assault as an extreme example), she always managed to work through it to tease the darkness into light, rising higher and becoming even stronger and more beautiful, and ultimately standing taller than her peers. No other meaning was intended.

"Gladiola Garden"

In the darkness, in the dirt,
Where the soils filter hurts,
Where the residue of thunder rains,
Seep downward through porous terrain,
Touching seedling tucked in fetal ball,

Hardened by its softening walls,
Until the cocoon no longer holds her gaze,
She yearns for sunshine and sunny blaze,
And breaks the earth enriched, empowered,
And stands tallest in the garden amongst the flowers.

*

Impossible Task 08/30/2017

When she asked me to write this book, asked me if I wanted to write another book with her, I gladly accepted. Yet it was daunting. Seemingly impossible to encapsulate this incredible girl and my undying love for her in a book. It is virtually impossible to reflect on, remember, and catalog the millions of moments, day to day, of Kayleigh's childhood and life. Impossible to do it justice. I needed to pull little snapshots out of my memory, from photo albums, from videos, and, certainly as directed by Kayleigh in these pages.

There were seven childhood bedrooms in four homes. I painted each of those rooms at least once; her room from 4-10 I painted three times. There were four homes – the rental on Bradford Road where she was born, from which we moved as a young family to Nordway Road, until she was almost four, to then Washington Blvd, 3035, for the next ten years, and finally at 14 to Washington Blvd house number two seven doors down. There were fifteen years, three months and two days, lived and enjoyed one day at a time, multiplied by 12 to 18 waking hours depending on the age; and always safety at night, sleeping comfortably in a warm, safe bed, with a loving family of which the four of us relied, loved and cherished.

There were thousands of art projects, thousands of walks in the rain and snow and hail and sleet and sunshine and cold and warmth and stifling heat. Four seasons a year, with each of its splendor. There were rocks and bugs and locust and birds and salamanders; squirrels and mice and raccoons and skunks; dogs and cats; and Broadway Cats; and hundreds of nightly books – from "Where's the Cat" to "Goodnight Moon", to "The Kittens Who Danced for Degas" to all

24

of Sandra Boynton's books, "Where the Wild Things Are," and even the children's book that Kakes and I wrote, "Clemy's Pancake House." I specifically cherish nights when Kayleigh first learned how to read and insisted on taking over the reading so she could read to Nathaniel. Hundreds of stuffed animals; hundreds of thousands of negotiations; thousands of meals of many sorts; millions of laughs, many the likes of rolling laughter, mouths agape, until we cried joyfully; millions of smiles, connections of the eyes and hearts; a billion of love transcending each of our homes, delighting in this magnificent family of four. Genuine light. Beautiful light.

There is no possible method to trace the lines around an eternal soul – it would never suffice, yet, as my favorite lyricist, who was the genesis of her name, once wrote, "Kayleigh, I'm still trying to write that love song..." – these pages will fall short, yet I trudge through its ink, with purpose, intention and devotion; sometimes in my hand, and sometimes in Kayleigh's.

It is true and I accept the natural shortcoming of these pros prior to their completion. My Kayleigh is too big for a book; too much of a dynamo for the single dimension of these pages. My hope is to piece together enough of Kayleigh's light to shine upon the soul of each reader in hopes of getting to know this incredible spirit and the most contagiously loving and tender Daddy-Daughter relationship I could imagine. The result, as it unfolds, will be a completely incomplete rendering of the fullness of our lives together and the incomplete full range view of Kayleigh. However, I certainly know where to begin.

*

So We Begin With Marillion: Summer 1985

In the summer of 1985, between tenth and eleventh grade, while lost among the shiny objects in my world and glued to MTV, a new video appeared by a band I didn't know with the name of, "Marillion," and their song, "Kayleigh." They sounded a little like Genesis and my ear turned to the TV, Genesis being one of my favorite bands. The melody, the tone, the atmosphere and the words that cascaded from the TV – it all transformed me quite deeply.

An hour later I found myself at Record Exchange on Coventry Road and found the M's, and worked my way down the tapes until I found Marillion. I flipped through a cassette called, "Misplaced Childhood," and found on this album track two, "Kayleigh." That night, instead of beer, for usual custom, I drank Marillion.

I devoured the entire cassette, a themed album with resonance of Genesis and Pink Floyd – musical heaven. My ears and soul, a temple to the neo-prog rock brilliance of their music, when in my own life I neared the destruction and collapse of active alcoholism, it was a reprieve from the gangrene that had rifled through my spirit. As I neared the end of my life through this wretched disease, Marillion and other favorites like U2 and R.E.M. lifted me from my cemetery gaze. As if the music itself propped me up and kept me alive, it fueled me with another round of energy to continue to battle the mental obsession of late stage alcoholism with its designs to destroy my life.

But the lyrics – the lyrics were transcending. I studied them closely; the little hooks, the refusal to rhyme, the strong dissonance. It was a kaleidoscope of energy, variant in color and texture that rippled through me. A budding poet, and having experimented with different styles, I began mapping some of Fish's cadence. His writing was brilliant and I wanted to be brilliant. As I secured their other albums and talked to my friends incessantly about Marillion, the song Kayleigh always rose to my conscience. It was perfect poetry – the music it's equal.

Its interpretation can be of a rocky, on again – off again romantic relationship based on Fish's real life experiences. The story could be interpreted as unrequited love; a relationship that has soured; a man dismayed in the loss of his true love; questioning his actions, wondering what went wrong. Although art is interpreted as the interpreter feels and sees and dreams. A larger interpretation for me, based on the facts of my life were this – although not willing to admit at the time that I was already a full blown, late stage alcoholic at sixteen, I did feel the soul pain knowing that I was troubled, irresponsible and sickened, that my behavior was hurtful at times, and

26

that I would continue into adulthood, marriage and fatherhood a mess – with my children as alcoholism's hostages, therefore, whom I just knew I would have someday. I feared their disappointment and the shame of letting them down by giving them a broken cradle into which they would be born, in effect, into a "Misplaced Childhood."

Thus, and its full significance did not strike me until after I sobered up, the song led me to proclaim at sixteen, "When I have a daughter, I'm naming her Kayleigh." My alcoholism continued to chew up those around me, until I sobered up on June 28, 1987, just days from death, 18 and ½ years old, with a debris field behind me of someone who drank for forty years. Emerging from the wreckage of my life were very few recognizable assets – one of which was the constant reminder in the chambers of my soul that I would one day have a daughter, in particular, and her name was Kayleigh. Once sober, I reshaped a new meaning to the song - as I would need to stay sober, not just for me, but for her Mother and for Kayleigh and for any siblings she may have. She was such a strong spiritual presence before she was born, I would later joke with her and Nathaniel, that I couldn't see her little brother standing in spirit behind her because she was so big and loud. These were the first glimpses of Kayleigh coming to me years before her physical birth on May 15th, 2002. This song became my motivation to make sure I did not end up as the words in the song nor in the failed relationship it represents. Rather, I would use this song, inapposite, to create successful relationships around me, including someday with my children, ensuring that the sadness in this song would not visit upon my future children and future wife. It's so me – a backwards meaning and warning.

Throughout her physical life she knew this story and relished in the fact that she had impacted me in so many ways years before she was born. I vowed when she was born that Kayleigh would be "my prefect poetry," And when Nathaniel was born, that he too would be that perfection. We listened to the song many, many times over the years and I explained the context into which I placed my stamp. She clearly understood my promise to her – to ensure we did not become the song – one of our many ties that bound us together, as Fish sang, "*do you remember chalk hearts melting on a playground wall…*"

*

6 Months Sober; Christmas, 1987

I sobered up on June 28, 1987. Entering a spiritually dead and emotionally bankrupt world, with the thieving mental obsession of alcoholism cursing me to return to the first drink. I shook, filled with the gangrene of the soul. I struggled with the triage of A.A.'s first responders selflessly supporting me and attempting to transmit to me the tools of my survival and salvation in sobriety. Begrudgingly, I began working my way through the 12 Steps and their sole intended purpose – the removal of the mental obsession which otherwise prevents one from staying sober. Only through the 12 Steps the crux of the disease of alcoholism was removed and I was restored to sanity, subject to continuous living and breathing of Steps 10, 11 and 12.

I struggled horribly, the vacillations seemingly endless, like a square rowboat in a category five hurricane. And sometimes I felt stable. And sometimes not. And sometimes I did my work. And sometimes not. Then came the Christmas season of 1987 and the untenable fear of not surviving, as I was not doing my work. I feared I would not be able to stay sober. Here I was, turning nineteen, sobered up at eighteen, having developed the deadly disease of alcoholism twice as fast as the founder of A.A., Bill Wilson, and potentially having to stay sober for another seventy years. Overwhelmed, my sleep suffered as my mind raced uncontrollably night after night. Then Kayleigh appeared.

I remember this so clearly, thirty years later. Half asleep, my eyes closed, staring at my eyelids, and studying the blackish, reddish dulled shade of the nighttime on my eyes. Head spinning for weeks. Four hundred serenity prayers incessantly to no avail. Then silence struck me and behind closed eyes a vision came slowly into view, at first fuzzy, and then becoming clearer. A radiant image of a tall, skinny beautiful girl with long blonde hair and a faded light blue dress, with sparling blue eyes and the gentlest expression on her face. She was somewhere in her early teens. It was Kayleigh. I knew it was Kayleigh. I said that to myself, and said her name aloud, and spoke both out loud and also in my head to her.

Kayleigh? I asked myself, trying to draw her image clearer. I felt a slow wave of peace flow about me. Entranced, I focused for the first time in days. I reached out to her in an audible whisper, "Kayleigh, I can't do this. It's too hard."

She replied softly, "you can do this. You can do this."

"Sweetheart," I responded, now in my full speaking voice, "no, I can't. I don't know how to do this. I don't know how to continue."

"You can do this," she said again, with further encouragement.

"But Kayleigh, I don't know if I can."

"You will do this," she said lovingly, but now in a firmer voice, "you will stay sober. You must."

I knew then what she was conveying - that if I didn't stay sober, then she would never be born. Or if I didn't stay sober, she would still be born but then my alcoholism would destroy her.

"Okay, okay," I said sheepishly, not clearly believing the path forward. With a few breaths I settled in and tried to fall asleep – nearly complete with this dangerous twenty four hours.

I started falling asleep with her image in my eyes and her voice in my soul. I knew I had better stay sober, and also, that I could stay sober if I learned how to do "the hard." If I didn't, her warning was clear - either she would never be born, or she would be born anyway into a troubled alcoholic home full of pain and tension. For me. For my future wife. For Kayleigh. For any siblings she would have. I stayed sober that night. That next night I dreamed about her again - actually off and on for the next five days. I would say, each of those five nights, whispering, "Ok, Kayleigh, I will stay sober." And I would fall asleep sober. After the fifth straight night of her coming to me to save my human life, I emerged from my sobriety stronger than ever and I have never looked back. The panic settled down in the fluidity of my early sobriety and I embarked on changing my life.

I was well aware of the miracle afoot when it happened. I kept it close to me. I told a few about it in the ensuing years. I told Jess when I met her six years later. I could not see beyond Kayleigh's image in time nor space to also see Nathaniel but there is no doubt that he was there, quietly standing with his sister, waiting his turn to be born two years and nine months after her. He was no less as powerful a soul as his sister, but as the oldest, she spoke for both of them. She was very clear. She was very firm. Courageous. Infectious. It was her credo and has been for all of these years, "you can do this…you can do this."

Fifteen years later, in May of 2002, I held my baby girl in those first days of her physical life and told her the magnificent story about her saving her Father's sobriety fifteen years earlier. She stared into my eyes. She smiled. She pooped. She spit up formula. She cried for me to burp her. And she locked her eyes again into mine - proud of me for the work I had done to stay sober – conveying the immortality between us.

When she was actually old enough to understand the story, I told her again. Somewhere around five or six years old. She knew from then on that she had saved her Father's life and told friends, who knew of my sobriety, that she had done so, repeating my story frequently. Even up to the final weeks of her physical life, she would jokingly remind me that she saved my early sobriety and therefore saved my life, and therefore, I owed her. And I thanked her as I always did.

I told this story at Kayleigh's funeral and subsequently, friends in A.A., who I had supported or sobered up. They in turn gave me an additional gift, by thereafter explaining to me that they owed their sobriety, not to my intervention, but to Kayleigh! When they had sobered up, I was sober and I helped them sober up. Had Kayleigh not come to me at that critical juncture of my early sobriety, I would not have stayed sober to be able to help them sober up. Therefore, Kayleigh played an instrumental part in their own salvation. In thirty years I have touched or worked with thousands of recovered alcoholics. Each, in part, was touched by Kayleigh's spirit in this ever expansive miracle. She came to me in my dreams and in my critical time of need fifteen years before she was born. How many thousands have been impacted by this enlarging miracle as time passes?

*

Six Year Later – Conveying Miracles to Jess 1993

I could not wait to tell Kayleigh's mother. I finally knew who she was to be in 1993. Once we fell in love – once I knew who Kayleigh's mother was, I told her about the miracle at six months of sobriety; that Kayleigh had come to me and saved my sobriety. I also could not wait to tell Kayleigh when she was old enough to understand.

So it was in 1993 that I said to Jessica, "so, she saved my life. She really did. She came to me five or six nights in a row and pushed me through that dark time. So we are going to have a little girl and her name is Kayleigh."

To which Jess responded, "Um, that's a sweet story, but you're an idiot because I'm not having any kids."

I smiled, knowing that it was already ordained. Yes, she would be a mother and Kayleigh would be her first born. I knew it. It was already written. I could not see Nathaniel yet, who is just as joyous, perhaps standing in line behind his sister in my mind's eye. Yet I couldn't help myself, a character trait or defect, depending on one's perspective – to insert the last word: "Yes, yes you will," I said and laughed, "I'll just let you sit with this one. You'll come around."

*

You'll be in My Heart 08/31/2001

Until August 31st, 2001, Jessica never wanted to have children. Having been together since 1993, this was an issue that would emerge – we remained open minded – I would be open minded that the answer may well be no, and she would be open minded that maybe she would grow into wanting to have a child. With that, we built our relationship, matured, married. She always knew of my premonition – my miracle with Kayleigh – her name already picked out, her imminent entrance into this world. And then came August 31st, 2001.

She was at an after work get together with some workmates. It was 8 o'clock. I was sitting on the couch watching TV with our cat, Sheba. I was more interested in my nachos and cheese dip than anything else in that moment. Then Jess stepped into our little rental house, dropped her purse on the floor, kicked off her heels, turned off the TV and said, "Well, I'm going to give you one chance. Literally one chance. If we are ever going to get pregnant and have a baby, it'll have to be tonight."

I may have still been chewing that last chip as I catapulted from the couch and backed her playfully towards our bedroom, where we consummated her offer. It was a magical moment – one I knew was not about sex, nor making love to my wife, but one moment for the ages where we came together as two souls to merge our light into a third.

An hour later we proceeded to go out to dinner afterward and as we sat down in our car Jess said, "When I turn on the radio, whatever song comes on, that is going to be my song to Kayleigh." As she turned on the radio and turned up the volume we heard the familiar sound of Phil Collins' voice singing "You'll Be in My Heart." Jess was flush with joy and said, "Kayleigh! That's our song," as she patted her belly.

Looking back on this now, it still does not seem strange that we knew, by the time we got into the car that August night that, not only was Jess in the process of becoming pregnant, but also that it was a girl. There was no doubt in that fact and we began talking to Kayleigh in that exact moment. She was pounding on the door to enter this world. She was arranging the timing of her entrance. She pored through her Mother's heart and gave her that last little push for Jess to believe that she was meant, not only to be a mother, but to be Kayleigh's mother. As with me in my early days of sobriety, her light illuminated her Mother, though Jess did not understand that at the time. Kayleigh spoke in her spirit voice and Jessica heard her.

Years later, as Father Patrick neared the end of Kayleigh's funeral, time quickened at a frantic pace as I stared down to the open doors so far away at the back of the church. I knew that as soon as the ceremony concluded, as soon as I stood on the outside of the church door, a new hell would begin – day after day, minute after minute, second after excruciatingly long second of living each breath of each day for the rest of my life without my Daughter physically in this world. At forty eight, physically losing my baby at fifteen, and knowing perhaps forty years of life awaited me on the other side of that awful door, I did not want the safety of this timeless ceremony to end.

Then came the first few cords of an African beat from the organ, the beginning of "You'll Be in My Heart." The cruelty of the new reality punished me as I burst into tears, watching Father Patrick begin to direct the pallbearers to their positions. I took Jess by her left arm, and Nathaniel by his right, wrapping my arms around both as we began the longest, and saddest walk of our lives. In my head, looking at the door at the far end of the church that led to the rest of our lives, I said to myself, "No! No! No! No! Go back! Let's go back! Kayleigh!"

The words of the song, sung by a beloved member of the family, cascaded through the church, reverberating on the chandelier of tears of a thousand people who had crowded together to pay tribute to my Babygirl. Not half way down the aisle, Nathaniel's body gave out as he began buckling beside me, wailing, broken and tormented in his inescapable sadness. I held him up as the full weight of his body fell upon my arm to hold. Then Jess, almost fainting, stepping down the aisle like she was tip toeing on delicate fields of clouds, seemingly coming in and out of consciousness from the grief, also let gravity pool her weight into my arms.

In front of my, Kayleigh's coffin – a sea turtle figurine atop the shiny wood. The same feeling about the crowd I had felt on our entrance to the church returned as we existed – the crowd on either side of me seemingly twenty to thirty feet tall and curving upward toward the ceiling. The door at the back of the church, like a mouth agape and preparing to swallow us, approached at a steady pace, until we were under its sway and washed down its throat. Kayleigh's casket was placed in the Murphy's hearse, and Jess, Nathaniel and I closed the car doors to our Honda Pilot and took the first breaths post funeral. We were obliterated and began the horrible process of contending with such a tragic physical loss to someone who means the world to each of us - one day at a time, one hour at a time, one grueling century long second at a time.

*

Kayleigh's Birth and My Poetry 05/15/2002

I was there for her first breath. Of course I was there. I cut her cord. She lay on my naked chest. This is my mission, empowered in my sobriety. I was built to be a Father. I planned and trained and prepared for fifteen years in my sobriety for this day when I would finally hold my little girl. The day had come. I was a rock, battle tested and sturdy. I would do exactly the same thing for my baby boy, placing these two above all others in an impregnable sacred status.

As Jess pushed at 11:09 A.M. on that May 15th, and Kayleigh entered the physical stage of her existence with us, letting out a piercing, sweet cry, I called her name from where I stood holding her Mother's leg, "Kayleigh!"

Blind, outside of her Mother's sacred body but a few seconds, and hearing my voice, she turned to it and set her face aiming over towards me. A thousand years together. Fifteen years of sobriety in preparation. More than nine months of reading to her through her Mother's skin. Talking to her throughout the days over those nine months. Beginning to guide her in my excitement when Jess was in her first trimester – yes, I was a little over excited, but I was a budding Father, the most sacred relationship a man can own.

Jess held her first, as should be the case. I was like a little boy waiting to hold a puppy and couldn't wait to lay on the bed beside Jess, my love, and hold our little Kayleigh. She rested her tiny head, capped in a cotton hat and swaddled tightly in tiny cloth, just under my chin. She moved to the breath in my chest as if we were one, falling asleep

34

in her Daddy's arms – something she would do through her early years until she was too big to fit comfortably on my chest.

"May 15th, 2002"

Her cry, it fills initial breath,
As she swims beneath the moon,
From warm liquid to the air,
Not nearly home like Mother's womb,
I called out her name,
In her first seconds in this room,
Turning blindness into faith,
Scanning for my face –

I held you swaddled in new cloth,
And watched your tiny hand,
Reach around my two fingers,
Reach around a grateful man,
As you suckled my pinky,
So sacredly the trust,
You fell asleep in my arms,
In the warmth of Father's love.

*

The Ever Change Summer 2002

My world would never be again as it had never been, now that she had arrived. The soul that warned me about my sobriety fifteen years earlier, the girl who professed that "you can do this," that many sober days ago, was here finally in my arms. Sacred. Brilliant. Familiar.

That first summer on Bradford Road we blossomed into a family. I took half of the feedings, half of the middle of the night checks, half of the changings, and the three of us took daily walks. I raced home from work early and daily played with my baby. I took naps beside her and made silly faces. I held her closely and vowed my undying love to her, knowing the significance in my relationship was not only

35

about being her Father, but also being the example that would help shape the type of men she would date and the quality of man she would one day marry.

We planted flowers along the back porch, twenty feet cross of Morning Glory. When they bloomed late in summer, Kayleigh would stare at them over our shoulders, awash in a brilliant sea of purple.

"A Mouth of Flowers"

Weaving flocks of Morning Glory,
Cascading the garden gates,
Midnight blue and opal white,
The sun, its golden flakes,
Catch in crystal morning dew,
Cling to petals, silky gowns,
Drawing in on eternity,
And walk her sacred ground,
Baby's voice permeates,
With new life's unique sounds,
She glances with her sky blue eyes,
A kaleidoscope of purple bells,
A mouth of flowers,
A mouth of purple shells.

*

A Childhood of Art Projects Everywhere

We started painting together on canvas before she was nine months old – me pressing her hands in poster paint and she swishing her hands around on old scraps of paper. Green. Blue. Red. Yellow. In combination – gray.

We have some hilarious pieces in our collection. I saved all of it, so that she and her brother could share their pieces with their own children someday. We painted, drew, and colored whatever we could get our hands on. I have over four bins of art saved, plus two other long containers filled with the canvas art. Some pieces hang in our house.

My most significant brainchild with art was putting one of my shirts on her at the age of 11 months, it fitting like a dress two times the length of her body. She wasn't even walking yet. With pacifier in her mouth, her Father's shirt covering her entire body, I lay out a two by three foot canvas on the kitchen table, with an assortment of colors. Her little hands, awash in pastels and reds and blues and greens and yellows, flowing across her canvas. She would overwork one spot and it would turn gray and she would laugh. I asked her if she wanted to retain some of the color and she confirmed that she did. So we came up with a solution.

"Ok, Babygirl, when you get the paint on your hands and you're ready to paint, put your hands on the canvas and as you start painting I'll count to 3. When I hit 3 lift your hands off of the canvas." I demonstrated for her. She understood.

She doused her hands in pinks and whites, and making eye contact with me, let me know she was ready. As she started to paint I said, "1, 2, 3 – ok lift!" She pulled her hands off of the canvas, thrilled with the result. We did this again and again for the next five or six years. When Nathaniel was old enough, I taught him the same trick. He too started art on canvas at 11 months old – for Jessica's Christmas present in December, 2005, which has become a treasured part of our family folklore.

After congratulating her and adorning her with pride for the completion of this first canvas piece, I set it in the basement to dry and sprayed it the next day with a gloss coating to hold the color over time. We dated it. We hung it for her in the house. Then we bought more canvas. Then her brother was born and he too contributed to our art museum. It filled my walls in my legal office at Cleveland Clinic.

Pens. Pencils. Crayons. Markers. On any surface. I saw chalk the other day at this writing at our old house at 3035 where she drew a delightful game ten years ago across the bricks on the house along the driveway. Mostly, however, her favorite surface was canvas. She moved on from poster paint to acrylics which she used the rest of her life. We have so many with names like, "Love for Mommy," "Moon Bright and Mommy," and "Night Dreams."

As Kayleigh matured through her childhood and into her tweens, and beyond, so too did her artwork progress and change. By her 13th year, she bonded with her Grandpa Stu as they each were trying their hand at more sophisticated canvas paintings. Now she was tackling natural scenes, human faces, flowers, rivers, forests, mystical creatures and an entire new swath of colors. Weekly we visited Michael's and stacked up on paints and canvas. Paint brushes, with a tendency of leaving them out and not washing them, were a steady purchase. No matter. She was being creative. It was one of her most cherished outlets. A few dollars here and there – more worth it than me wasting money at lunch during my work hours.

She transitioned at 13 to more solo and concentrated art. No longer would we lay on the floor in the old computer room at 3035 and get paint on the cats and the carpet together. Now she wanted a little space to hone her craft. Like making us a surprise, excited to then present her creations with us.

All of this was also life therapy, a way to express feelings and emotions. Art. Creativity. Daddy -Daughter time. Enrichment – to enrich my children's lives beyond all expectations. Love. Light. Together or separate it was the art of life. She was a mature artist by the time the assault occurred at fourteen and she naturally turned to her comfort and began painting her experience, her recovery, the explanations of which are expressed later in this text.

*

Baby and Toddler Years - Music

I wrote a bedtime song to her and put it to a tune and began singing it to her when she was one year old. It goes as follows:

"It is time my little Kayleigh,
To go off to bed,
It is time my little Kayleigh,
To lay down your head,
There are dreams to be dreaming,
Filled with rainbows and butterflies,
But first my little Kayleigh,
You must waive goodnight..."

She loved it, night after night, for nearly a month until she figured it out – when Daddy sings to me this song, at the end of the song, he goes downstairs and I have to go to bed, alone. This is Kayleigh to whom I refer after all. Once that realization occurred, she would have none of it. After this realization, as soon as I started singing it, she turned that pretty face into a frown and began to cry, prompting Daddy to stop singing. That one went into the box of great intentioned ideas that didn't quite work. It is quite a full box!

After that debacle, through that second year, I pulled out my bag of tricks. I would sing her songs that I knew that didn't mention her going to bed. I was getting very well versed in the baby songs and can sing all of them still. Though she loved these baby songs, they were limiting. She needed something more unique at times to mix it up; something I could really animate and get my voice around. Enter, R.E.M., "Life's Rich Pageant," one of the greatest albums of all time. Being an R.E.M. disciple, it also was exciting to show off to my baby in those intimate moments.

It just is what it is – I love R.E.M. I made several pilgrimages to Athens, GA in my early 20's; ate at Weaver D's; roamed the streets and Peter Buck's club. I studied Stipe's lyric writing. On my trips as a young man back and forth from Cleveland to Charleston, SC, I would start with Chronic Town and cycle my way through all of their tapes in my old jeep as I trucked twelve hours down the highway, singing R.E.M. at the top of my lungs without doors and top and dancing in my seat while I drove. On another trip it was U2. On another, Marillion. They are all a part of my bloodstream.

With Kayleigh and Nathaniel it started with "Swan Swan H." I just started singing it to Kayleigh, having bored with some of the baby songs. Any respectable parent would have done the same. So I did. All the way through the song. She was mesmerized and asked for more. So I sang "Superman." Then she went to bed.

The following night it was the "Flowers of Guatemala" and "Cuyahoga," which wasn't enough for Kakes, so I reverted back to "Swan Swan H," to which, afterward, she would frequently say, "now the udder one, Superman." I understood her garbled words, and so, I sang that again. And again. And again. Every night. (Boys, there is no way you would ever have imagined where your songs would end up when you originally wrote them. They were woven into the tapestry of Kayleigh Mickayla Mooney's soul night after night from the age of one through about seven. Six years of "Life's Rich Pageant." If that doesn't put me on another level as a Father, nothing will.)

Still, I would revert to classics between us, including "Sugar Plum Fairies" accompanied by my dancing fingers to the beat of the song on her cheeks, nose, chin and forehead, making my hand fly like a fairy up and down to the music and watching her eyes mesmerize to the movement of my hand, that, clearly in her eyes, was not a hand, but a glittery fairy with sparkles and rainbows flowing around in the air above her face.

Along with the music, I put hundreds upon hundreds of enchanting glow in the dark tiny stars on her ceiling to make it look like she was in the middle of a vast galaxy, including hundreds on the four blades of her ceiling fan. When we would turn off the light and turn on the fan, the lights would spin and we would both stare into the galaxy and fall asleep together. I think I fell asleep 90% of my life alongside Kayleigh or Nathaniel during their early childhood years, only to wake an hour or so later to drag myself off to my room or downstairs to sit with Jess. Always kissing whoever's cheek was resting up against mine – my little girl, my little boy, either sleeping, having fallen off to sleep in the safe presence and comfort of their Father, who laughed and played with them through the evenings, who sang them to sleep – who fell asleep beside them, understanding the obligation of and grateful for the gift of fatherhood and blessed for each moment. It was my opportunity, my job, to become the texture of the world all around; to bring them to another world. And I did.

*

You Saved Dinkie's Life 09/2003

We never quite knew how. We had never brought you down from the second floor after putting you to bed. Your room overlooked the backyard. You were barely walking yet, sixteen months old, September, 2003. Still in a crib with five pacifiers – one in your mouth, one on each foot and one in each hand, rubbing them along your cheeks.

That evening, as I drove up our dark driveway, pulling in from the street from the right, and pulled into the backyard, I noticed Dinkie and the neighbor's cat who lived across the street hanging out together in the backyard. As I parked I saw them take off down the other side of the house away from me and towards the front yard. I thought nothing of it.

I came in and called for Jess. She had just gone upstairs to you. I could hear you were upset and garbling through your pacifier. Trying to tell Mommy something. She handed you a stuffed animal kitten that looked like Dinkie. You were shouting "Dinkie! Dinkie! Dinkie!" You were inconsolable. Out of breath. I ran upstairs. You saw me and reached for me.

Intuition took over. I picked you out of your crib. You pointed for the hall. I looked over to Jess and we hunched our shoulders and I began to walk carrying you. At the threshold of your door you pointed to the steps. As I carried you downstairs you pointed to the right around through the living room, the dining room, the kitchen and to the back door. I took you outside into the darkness of night and you pointed to the right for the driveway. At the corner of the house on the drive you pointed to the right towards the street. So I walked towards the street along the house on our driveway. When we came to the front corner of the house, and the front yard came into view, you pointed off about forty five degrees across the yard and to a black balled up figure in the street. Dinkie.

I thought she had caught a bat and was holding it down. I handed you to Mommy and walked over towards her. I called to her. She tried to move and staggered. I looked back over my left shoulder from the tree lawn, hearing a sudden noise, and saw that a car was coming directly towards her. I ran into the street and stopped the car from hitting her. Then I realized that the bat was not a bat but a pool of Dinkie's blood. She had already been hit by a car, just moments ago, when she chased the neighbor's cat from the backyard. Her jaw was hanging from her face. And you, Kayleigh, without words - without seeing or hearing it - without having a vantage point to the front yard, knew that she had been hit by a car, and more importantly, that I needed to get down there immediately to prevent another car from totally running her over.

It was amazing then. We knew you had a special gift of intuition. Honestly, we never could quite put our finger on how you managed that feat. But now we know. You are a guardian angel who was tucked into an amazing human life, and in your infancy, your first few years, so close still to the thin veil of God's cradle before your birth to us, your intuition provided you a window into what you could not see with your blue eyes, but what you could see in your soul. And I listened. And trusted you perfectly as a baby. And responded, following your direction. And through me, you saved Dinkie who continued her physical life after her recovery for twelve more years, in love with you and constantly by your side.

*

Nathaniel's Birth 01/25/2005

I woke you around 7AM on January 26, 2005 with a message, "Sweetie, Hi, Babygirl."

You rubbed your eyes with the back of your pudgy hands and smiled, reaching to me and hugging me. I kissed your warm, soft skin and ran my fingers through your hair. I said, "Guess what, Kakie?"

42

"Was my brother born?"

I nodded, "yep, last night at midnight."

Your face lit up like the sun, a smile from ear to ear, and another smile flowing from your blue eyes. You sat up, your excitement hardly contained. You jumped out of your big girl bed and ran to the bathroom. I waited a minute or so and then you hurried back into your room.

"It's a little cold out, Sweetie, let's put on a sweatshirt."

"Ok, Daddy," you said, and slipped on a soft purple pastel sweatshirt, one of the shirts I bought for you on my lunch breaks as I would march through K-Mart in Solon looking for little things for you. You slipped on a matching pair of sweatpants, grabbed a few pacifiers and jumped into my arms.

"Remember, Sweetie," I said, "we have a present from you to give to your brother."

"Oh," you said, in such a sweet, endearing voice, gracious that we had purchased something that you could present to him. I handed you the bag with a stuffed animal spider within.

We were cognizant that you, little Kayleigh, having been the center of our world, was momentarily going to have to share the limelight with a little brother. We wanted this to be your day too, a day you would remember. Certainly day two for baby boy would only be his to recall in photos and videos. You, however, you were meant for this day. As if you were leaning forward, willing me forward to quickly walk you out to the car, willing the car to hurry to his side. You could not wait to stand in your brother's presence and begin your journey as a big sister.

We grabbed a quick bite to eat and a Sippy cup, popped on your boots and stepped out into the frozen January day, our heartbeats quickening in the excitement. I will never forget looking into the rear view mirror and catching sight of you repeatedly in the backseat, smiling, kicking your feet, moving around anxiously in your seat.

43

Singing a song for your brother, "I'm gonna see my brother – my brother – my brother…"

And then we were there, walking into University Hospital and to the floor and to the room where your Mother was laying, your little baby boy asleep next to her in a clear plastic crib, packed with warm cloth. I held your hand as I leaned down to your level, kissed your head and opened the door to a new world for you. As the door swung open, your Mother raised her head, "My Baby! Hi, Kayleigh!"

You ran to her and jumped on the bed and lay your head on her and kissed her. She ran her hand through your hair and said, "Do you want to meet your brother?"

"Oh, yes!"

"Ok," your Mother said, and adjusted.

You slid off of the side of the bed, holding his present closely. Your eyes could barely see over the edge of the crib. You smiled.

"Hi, Nathaniel," you said softly, reaching into the plastic hospital crib, "I'm Kayleigh. I'm your sister, little boy." You touched his hand with yours and he looked in your direction. You smiled, "I have a present for you, Nathaniel." Then you dropped the present on top of his face – the very soft, very leggy stuffed animal spider. We jumped, a little half worried, half tired, and laughed to each other as we pulled the spider off of his face. To this day he is afraid of spiders…coincidence? I lay the stuffed spider near his head instead of on top of his face. He glanced around at this strange new world. "There, Babygirl, that's a perfect place for your present."

You continued to stare at Nathaniel, laying your tiny chin on the plastic edge of the crib, mesmerized by his beauty and your stature in this world – you were, at last, a big sister. For the next year you would say continuously, "Hi baby. My baby!" as you cared for him and began the impactful influence and sway you had over his life. After a few minutes I tried to get your attention. "Kakes," I whispered, as I pulled a small wrapped present out of a bag you didn't realize I brought with us, "Nathaniel also has a present for you."

"Oh," you said, in surprise, and turned around.

I handed the small package to you and you climbed back into bed with your Mother. Your tiny fingers ripped through the wrapping paper and exposed a six pack of Playdoh. You were so happy. At two years, nine months, you were overjoyed and genuinely touched.

You looked down to Nathaniel and said, "thank you, Nathaniel, thank you so much. I love it, Baby Boy." And that was it. All four of us together finally on this plain. From the outset we were effortless, fluid, joined by golden threads of love and light, a complete four leaf clover. As you ripped into the six colors of Playdoh, and they quickly became one huge blob of gray Playdoh, my life was complete.

*

I Am Present

I thank my A.A. training in part for this attribute; that, and the horror of my alcoholic drinking days that destroyed my life. From the ashes I looked out to the world a defeated, debilitated, different man. It focused me on the task in front of me. It showed me how to stay in the moment. It taught me the great lesson of priority and so it became very simple: my sobriety and relationship with God, keeping me spiritually fit, is always first. When Jess and I found each other, she became first behind my sobriety. Knowing children would come, when they did, they became first behind my sobriety, followed by their mother, my sweet and wonderful wife. That is the priority. I have a relationship with God to have a relationship with me to have a relationship with my three loves. That is etched in stone. It is immutable. It never waivers. It never fails. From this priority list I live my life.

45

I purposely did not work 80-90 hours a week. I purposely did not work at a big law firm to forfeit my family time. Those lawyers who are in big firms, with nannies, and balking at those last two sentences as if they too have the depth of what I have – they are in never-never-land – there is no way their family life was as close as one in which children literally come before work. I chose the in-house route for better hours to see my children – and not for a quick minute after they were already asleep. They played with me for hours every night. I didn't go on some potential business trips because I did not want to be away from my kids. I spent every day with them that I possibly could. In her entire life Kayleigh only had less than twenty full days without me – one week when I took Nathaniel on a guy's only trip and a few weeks later when the girls went on a girls only one week trip, and maybe five several day business trips. Otherwise, every day of her life she saw me, laughed with me, interacted with me; was occasionally reprimanded by me, respected and adored me, grew with me and felt loved and sacredly honored by me. That does not happen, to the depth it happened with us, if a parent is not consistently and intentionally present. It is not a sacrifice. It is a choice.

*

I Know She's Supposed To Be In Bed, Jess, But…

Jess was much more likely to keep to nightly bedtime schedules. I too was generally consistent, unless there was a full moon. Or a pretty sunset. Or shooting stars. Or an eclipse. Or an owl. Or a raccoon. Or lightning blazing in crazy trails through the sky. Or wind storms that bent the trees in spiritual dances. On those nights, after Kayleigh was tucked away in bed, Daddy would knock on her door and say, "Hey, Babygirl, I want to show you something cool. Let's go outside for a few minutes."

"Okay, Daddy," she would say, and sit up.

Many times I would wrap her in her bed blanket to keep her warm and carry her downstairs and outside, in all seasons. I have memories of doing this at two, three, four, five, six, seven, eight…never wanting

46

her to miss a natural phenomenon. By the time she was five, I would grab both kids, Nathaniel being two. Sometimes he would pass, electing instead to sleep. My night owl, however, my little girl, my twin, she was always ready to roll.

In those earlier years I would stand there in the front or backyard pointing out the moon or the sunrise or scanning the sky for shooting stars with her, seeing the magical glint in her blue eyes, staring up at the sky, a smile from ear to ear, knowing she was supposed to be in bed; knowing she was instead up after hours with her Daddy seeing cool things. This was true on vacation at Jekyll Island as well; walking her in the pitch blackness under a billion stars, searching for sea turtles and shooting stars.

When she was too big to want to be held, I would hold Nathaniel in the same way and watch the very same expression emerge across his beautiful face. Nate's green eyes glowed as he stared to the heavens on these nights. They are so similar in appearance, and somewhat in mannerism, although they are also unique to each other; a perfect set of children, the joys of our lives.

After a few minutes, sometimes more (like thirty, maybe sixty), I would wind down the after bedtime break with Daddy and start them back towards the house. Invariably, when I returned them to their beds, they gave me huge hugs, big kisses, telling me they love me as we did every night, and smiled off to sleep, usually falling directly to sleep. Both of my children carry these memories, these immortal memories in their souls; both still speak of these moments as well. Nathaniel will occasionally bring it up, especially when we are on the beach at night and he sees a shooting star or a bright Kayleigh moon, stating, "Hey, remember when we used to…" Kayleigh thanks me in meditation for these wonderful little trips to the backyard or the beach, sometimes pulling a memory in from the higher vibrations of my breath. Something so simple. So meaningful. So us.

*

Poetry

My Muse, Kayleigh. I have hundreds, maybe thousands of works that I have written for her. Some are lost to time. Some on old drives. Some in books. Some in scrap paper tucked into the bins that now contain the history of her physical life. Even now, I have been tracking her current spiritual life in poetry we write together.

Kayleigh and I would frequently, in her early childhood, write poetry in the round. She would write a line; I would write the next line. It was hilarious and would typically result in some nonsense story that had no connection to reality, the two of us laughing uncontrollably and shaking the house when one of us fell off of the bed. Jess would hear us and smile and relish the joy in her home, having a break from the societally underappreciated stay-at-home-mom work, and knowing she had a partner whose main purpose in life was her children.

Other times I just wrote to her because I write, and mostly because, my babies are my muses. Over time Kayleigh became my primary muse – a Daddy writing poetry for his Daughter, and Kayleigh fawning all over the outpouring of love. Nathaniel, a boy, and with a different yet equally incredible relationship with me, did not respond to poetry the same way, and so he and I would write our own poetry in different ways. For Kayleigh, however, she studied and practiced her own hand at writing. She could write brilliant, sometimes frightful prose as a young seven or eight or nine year old. It showed her incredible maturity and a grip on the world that she was in, tackling scary concepts in stories of vampires and ghosts and goblins and villains. She challenged the vagaries of life and death; of Heaven and Earth. She was raw creativity and it was another vehicle to express herself and her feelings – just as I had hoped.

One particular experience that I treasure was at thirteen on the way to Denver to see my family, and Kayleigh being terrified of flying. On the plane, half way to Denver, in order to distract her I asked her to do some dual writing, coming up with a story of her wedding in the round. Me writing my perceptions of that day, walking her down the aisle, the smell of her hair, her dress, my shaking hands as a Father "giving away" his little girl; and her impressions, with the ice blue color of the flowers and the length of the train on her snow white dress with silver and platinum sparkles. It absorbed an hour of midflight jitters as she permitted herself to be whisked away on a journey to her wedding with her beloved Father. And so we traveled in our souls and deepened our bond, and arrived in Denver safe and sound.

*

B Club

She is the first born. Slightly A-Type. Organized. Control freak. Older sister. Bossy pants. Yet also so sweet in her intentions, feeling a special responsibility as the older of two children. Inclusive in her games with her little brother. So tender in her unconditional love for him. She used to climb into his crib and cuddle with him, caressing his head, and saying over and over, "Hi baby. You're my baby. Hi baby. You're my baby." Rarely did we truly need to go to his rescue, but with any siblings, they would press each other's buttons and sometimes Kayleigh, being older, would get frustrated with the little guy in ways he couldn't quite understand. And sometimes Kayleigh would internalize frustration she could not quite grasp related to Nate. Through it all they, beginning on day one of being very close, grew closer and closer, year after year. Kayleigh was Nate's best friend growing up, and Nate was hers. Their devotion is permanent; their love unshakable.

So it came to be that a secret society emerged from their relationship, hidden from the prying eyes of nosey parents. Kayleigh needed a central authority under which she could manage all of her designs, schemes and activities, drawn up on art paper, napkins, cardboard and the walls of closets. They would meet in their closets in their rooms. We had a large crawl-in closet in our bedroom at 3035 that we cleared out and handed over to the kids. Within a day every inch of the three walls was covered with their activities, including a map showing how to escape from the house and find treasures around the neighborhood. It was hilarious.

There was also an art room, a larger walk-in closet about ten feet long by six wide that we likewise cleaned out and gave them for a clubhouse space. They partitioned the space, hung a sheet between, and had their own space while still being inseparable. This secret society, which had been nameless, began to be called the "B Club." Before the accident I asked Kayleigh where she got this name and she could not remember. It is lost to Nate as well, but there is was, Kayleigh and Nate, mostly Kayleigh directing Nate, in subjects from learning math to science and shoe shopping, to creating businesses and laying out arguments why they should have a dog, to maps of lost treasure around the backyard to secret paths to get to friends' homes, to breaking out of the house when we would visit Jekyll Island to explore the beachfront.

We have the remnants of the B Club in many bins. We find new pieces from time to time, pulling us back into that simpler time when both children were physically alive and actively engaging at a high level on a daily basis with each other. I hold these pieces of paper and cardboard and remember when they did each of these games and club activities; recall the laughter and the expressions on their faces; felt the immensity of the love and happiness I felt for them both as wonderful kids and very close siblings. Effortless.

I recall being kicked out of the room or the next room or sometimes out of the house when Jess and I would joke with them and try to seek membership into their club. We were never admitted. This remained an exclusive club for Kayleigh and Nate, run by and established by Kayleigh for her little brother, with love and affection. Her compassion aside, it also provided her an incredible outlet for her bubbling over artistic, forceful and dynamic mind that pushed the envelope and drove forward every day, smarter and more intelligent with the senses of the world than I ever could have been.

*

Nathaniel

I could write this book just as easily for Nathaniel if this accident had occurred to him instead of Kayleigh. The outcome would be identical. The pain exactly the same. The spiritual highs equal in every manner. These two are certainly their own cloth, but cut from the same bundle. They are similar in many ways, yet very different children.

This boy. How do I describe this boy? Here is a piece I wrote when he was two and a half years old.

"Nathaniel"

You glance and sun when it catches your face,
Outlines a sweetness that is contagious;
You smile and the light about your frame, just a trace,
Hints at your glory - hints at your grace,
Begins to tell the story,
Of little boy with running feet,
Watch the corner he turns,
Little boy with the faith believes,
In all that he learns,
Eyes green and wide with a wondrous sigh,
Watch this little boy yearn,
Stretching, exercising his mind,
With soul from eyes that burns,
Into our hearts,
A chamber internal fills with his grace,
Each time he glances up to you,
With sun catching his face.

*

Amiss, She Directed It

Our home, a wonderful garden of energy, electricity, excitement and laughter that filled the atmosphere like an orchestra. Its conductor – Kayleigh Kakes. Through the seasons and the years I would come home from work to a new environment each day. On the weekends and in the evenings I was her partner in crime creating new and wonderful spinoffs from her games and activities.

Daily she was engaged, and engaged her Mother, Father and her brother, in hours-long fantasies, to name just a few – princess parades, tea parties, dress up, game shows (including the infamous "Messing With Big Boy The Cat"), pet circuses, clay figurine sessions, zombie painting and hiding and waiting for Mommy, cooking shows, spa days for money, America's got talent competitions, practical jokes, chess and backgammon board game marathons, impressions and dive on the bed games, sled-riding in July thunderstorms, brutal pillow fights, throwing the babies onto bed game (while screaming the Genesis song, "I Know What I Like"), gardening together and landscaping the gardens in the backyard, (although Nate gets credit for the stone circle around the garden in the front yard of 3035), fashion shows featuring Diane – Kayleigh's little sister, skateboard parking, hippie dance parties, swing set kill Daddy with the huge ball game, and alas, in the.....BOOMYARD!!! game. Chaos and laughter reigned in the Mooney house; our home, a canvas on which to paint a beautiful childhood.

*

The Anti-Adult at the Family Parties

I honorably admit it. I make no bones about it. In fact, I wear it proudly. It was me, always me. When you were a toddler and then as a little girl with a little brother, and we were at family parties in Cleveland with your Mother's family, I watched you and was aware that you were the only child as a toddler, and one of two very little people once Nathaniel came along, at a party full of adults. You would make your way around the family and enjoyed their company. Yet, with no other kids, how incredibly boring.

It was me always on the floor with you doing art. It was me always pulling you away from the adults to explore in the house. It was me who would whisper to you – "hey Babygirl, do you want to go for a walk down the street and find cool rocks, or travel through the jungle of the backyard in search of exotic flowers, salamanders, birds, acorns" – anything but have to be a little child at an adult party!

It was also my way of spending time with the people I most wanted to spend time with – my Kakes, and when Nathaniel was born, my baby boy too. Not that I didn't have a good time with your Mother and her family, which I did, but, they are adults – how boring!

My job is my job and has always been my job, which is not a job at all, and that is engaging my babies and introducing the world to my babies from my babies' vantage point, which is why I was always on the floor with you two. These are some of my favorite moments of my life and I gave you two a platform that some children don't get, because, quite frankly, their fathers are spending Saturday for six hours on a golf course or at adult parties acting like adults and sometimes not thinking that maybe their kids are bored. It was always my first thought. Therefore, we would leave and explore and make the occasion even more dynamic. Typically on those nights, when I would be preparing for bed, I would pull from my pockets the tiny heart shaped rocks, and double acorns and other little objects you had found on our jaunts. Holding them in my hand, I knew that I had done my job.

*

Never Kill Zone

A life lover. To look at the world from Kayleigh's eyes. You would find yourself low in the grass; down in the dirt; high in the branches; in the surf; under tidal pool rocks; tracking through swamps; finding something new each day. Actually we used to say that - every time we went somewhere where we went a thousand times before, like Shaker Lakes, we would say "ok let's go find something we haven't seen before." And we would. Every time.

Every bug. Every detail. On the tip of her finger rotated slowly. Lady bug. Spider. Worm. Caterpillar. Locust. Butterflies. And save and set free. Never kill zone. Our home is a never kill zone. This included the "hospital zone" too, including a butterfly hurt by our cats and dragged into the house. Kakes nurtured it and put a tiny piece of tape on the wing and set it free, hopeful that it would fly away, which it did. No wonder generations of a certain type of butterfly returned to us every year at 3035 and would inevitably land on her outstretched finger. She whispered to these winged brothers and sisters, into which they found comfort and peace.

*

Don't Forget to Dance

On many evenings I didn't even change my clothes. Loosening my tie, kicking off my shoes. Turning on a CD and looking down to my children with four arms stretched up to me, I was in my Heaven as you pushed your brother aside to jump into the first slot. It was what I was built for. A real Father. A present Father. A Father with priorities that began with his children. In my chosen and natural element. Nothing diverted me from this obligation and this joy. It was a no-brainer. This was my purpose.

We would take turns, but sometimes, I would scoop you up together and start sashaying back and forth, dancing and singing. You would hold your brothers hand, both of you laughing and dipping and going for a dancing ride in your Father's arms. Nightly, some activity like this. Dancing. Singing. Fight club on the bed the four of us. Nerf gun fights. Walks in the light of summer - the dark of winter. Impersonating each other - we have video! Nightly. This is how I chose to end my work day - the best part of my days - on almost every weeknight.

And so it was at four and one; five and two; six and three; by then you were growing quite long and I could no longer dance with both of you at the same time. So I danced with you both one at a time. Seven and four; at about seven you just danced on your feet and I'd scoop you up occasionally for quick burst of spins, your long blonde hair spinning and catching up to your cackling voice.

Throughout it all, on those nights, I'd frequently turn to an old Kinks CD and go right to a particular song and take your hand and scoop you into my arms. One at a time with my loves, it was our atmosphere. It was my message for your lives and mine. It was my reminder of the magnificence that stared up to me from two shining faces - to stop and see what it is we are supposed to see. To engage as we are supposed to engage - "Don't Forget to Dance."

When you were four, five - you'd lay your head on my shoulder while we danced to this song as I slowly rocked back and forth singing this song to you. Your breath upon my neck. Your tiny arms around part of my back. Your little body pressed to your Daddy's chest. Smiling. Always smiling.

You understood. You were so thankful in our dances. Our dances. With your physical death at fifteen, and seeing all the times in the future we won't get to dance together - Father Daughter dances, your wedding, your brother's wedding, on and on, it occurred to me at this writing that, we didn't forget to dance. We danced every day in some way or another for 5,574 days in this physical world together. We engaged. And so we danced - both learning the lesson in those nights when you were a small child.

"Don't forget to dance, Daddy," you say - I hear you now, sweet Babygirl. Tonight. Will you dance with me?

*

Clemy's Pancake House (2007)

She was four and a half years old. Already a veteran singer to Baby Songs, Disney, Baby Einstein, and other toddler musicals, as well as knowing all of "Cats," she and I daily shared the stage singing these songs – sometimes so frequently that sleep avoided my voice still repetitively and annoyingly humming through the night.

On one particular day, while driving, Kakes in her car seat behind me, the track "Oh My Darlin Clementine" began on the CD. After a few lines of singing loudly together, her voice quieted down to silence and I glanced back to see her lip turn upside down and nearing tears.

Turning off the CD, and pulling over, I asked, "Baby, what's wrong, Sweetheart?"

She slumped in her seat and said, "Does this mean that she dies and never sees her Daddy again?"

I thought about the lyrics to "Clementine" and thought, well damn, it does mean exactly that! I turned to her and said, "no, Sweetheart. They're just trying to teach children how to swim."

She didn't buy my explanation. I continued. "Yeah, um, what happened was," I muttered, telling myself to think fast. Then my muttering turned into these words that flowed like a quick river that couldn't be dammed, "after she fell into the river, her Father didn't see her as she floated under water, but around the bend, she popped back up to the surface, but she was out of his view. He thought she was gone forever, but she was okay and floated, all day…down a river from San Francisco to…, uh, L.A., and that's a long river, so by the time she got to L.A., she was really hungry and stumbled ashore…and took her Mother's ring on her finger, and hocked her ring to buy pancakes, and she loves pancakes, so she built a pancake house and became world famous, and so she built thirty more shops and became a self-made millionaire, who then went looking for her Father and found him in that cavern in the canyon and saved him from his failed mining operations and brought him back to L.A. where they lived forever after."

She slowly juggled her pacifier around in her hand, inspecting my words carefully, her eyes clearly showing the processing of my explanation. She studied my eyes. She sighed. And smiled. And said, "okay, Daddy."

That night I wrote the song that is in our book, matching it to the cadence of "Oh My Darlin Clementine," and intended that this is an interactive book that the reader would sing to a child. Inspired by my Daughter's inquisitive and mature soul, it was a masterpiece. After finishing the text, I brought it to my friend, Ken Kula, an artist at Cleveland Clinic, who brought "Clemy" to life in image. With black and white proofs, Kayleigh, Nathaniel, Jessica and I went to Tommy's Restaurant, one of our favorites, with a huge box of crayons and worked through the color scheme for the book over chocolate milkshakes and French Fries. Thereafter we entered the children's book market and for years she signed copies occasionally for children lucky enough to share her journey.

My intentions were several – empower my Daughter; create beauty with my Daughter; teach my Daughter how to dare to dream; empower a feminism spark in my Daughter; and empower other young girls to believe that they can do anything they put their minds to doing. And, it's Kayleigh! It was just fun.

Even now, after her tragic physical death, I love our work on "Clemy" and it remains one of my favorite examples of a Daddy and Daughter adding value, not only to the world, but specifically also between themselves. How many Fathers have written a children's book with their Daughter? Likely not many. She brought out the truth in me. She illuminated my talents. She honed my fatherhood.

The irony of our book, written ten years before her accident, also does not escape me – the original story of Clementine in which a miner's daughter is tragically killed in an accident in front of him. In our book, Clemy obviously doesn't die. In reality, with Kayleigh, she now assumes both roles. Physically she is like Clementine and has been tragically physically killed and passed in front of me. However, spiritually she is Clemy, whose spirit survives the river and continues to watch over her Father for the duration of his life. Certainly not the flower I imagined when the seed of this book was sown. Yet there it is.

*

Jekyll Island

How could I ever encapsulate twenty five vacations to a beach-house over a fifteen year period of time, filled with dozens of activities per day, per week, per trip? In the spring we would go for eight or nine days. In the summer for fourteen to eighteen days. It was a second home. The kids grew up here as much as they did in Cleveland.

Twenty five vacations to your second home on Jekyll Island, in short, reads as follows: Jekyll Island Club Sunday brunch, lunch tea times, breakfast and dinners, swimming in the pool; Dove bars at the café even if we had ice cream in the freezer; Clam Creek - hundreds of visits to the bridge, finding crabs and skates in the shallows; walking the beach hundreds of times and finding shells and treasures; a five foot Blacktip shark swimming passed us at eleven and you never wanting to go in again as it flipped through a wave five feet in front of us (four years later you went back in!); musty mouth crabs along the tidal pool; Jacques within the tidal pool, these baby shrimp we would capture using tiny plastic cups and hold temporarily in a bucket; body fishing in tidal pools - we would flop in the water and displace the fish and the water onto the sand, with the water receding back to the pool and the fish high and dry, we could capture them and hold them in a temporary aquarium bucket; finding Starfish; Summer Waves water slides and the slow motion ocean; Pirates Passage; alligator purses, matching with her brother and convincing him that all the little boys had an alligator purse containing a stuffed animal alligator - he loved it and showed it to everyone proudly - he was five; hiding from hurricanes behind the couches in the Georgia room overlooking the ocean - the "hurricanes" were just thunderstorms and lightning showers, but we called them hurricanes and scattered about in the excited air; building barriers and screaming to the thunder and laughing and falling over crying from the joy; Easter services; Tortuga Jacks; body surfing; laying in the tidal pools; midnight walks; riding horses including Booker, your last horse ride in August, 2017; ghost tours; deer everywhere; alligator tracking; shark fishing; trips to St. Simon for shopping; bracelets and other crafts and art; our last night on the beach each trip with glow lights in the dark; Turtle center visits, every time we went, checking in on the patients, present for turtle releases whenever they synced with our vacations; and, alas, Loggerhead turtle conservation.

Turtle nests were our midnight folly. Years upon years, from the southern end of the island up until the midpoint where the engineer's seawall began, we walked in the dense, magical humidity, scanned with our red lights and carefully stepped across the sands looking for baby sea turtles scurrying to their new life in the sea. This would all culminate for Kayleigh a week before the accident in one of the most magical moments of her life when she finally found a stranded baby Loggerhead, rescued it and set it free on the long beach to scurry to its new home in the ocean. We stayed with "Phil" until he found his way to the water's edge, and with a blessing from Nate, Kakes and I, scurried off to new life.

Kayleigh surrounds him today with a golden light on his daily journey in the sea, awaiting the day when Phil returns to lay her eggs on this very same beach.

"Olividae"

We walk this low tidal plain,
Weaving the salty puddles exploring,
And through the aquatic debris field,
In the rising sun of summer morning,
Searching for treasures the low tide reveals,
In the long exposed ridges of ocean flooring -

You find a shell - the magic shell,
And squeeze it in your tiny hand,
It's glossy coat - like spiraled belts,
Of browns and beige - of sea and sand,
You jump and run and stomp about,
This Father - this one understands,
No common shell but Neptune's gem,
Glows brighter than the sun in her hand.

*

Mommy/Daughter

I knew the time would come. You would switch back and forth. Most kids go through it. I secretly never wanted it to happen, though I knew the value of its purpose. You were Daddy's little girl. You loved your time at home with Mommy as a baby and toddler and just before your school years. You also loved, loved, loved your Daddy and could not wait for me to get home at night, drawing pictures of you crying a river for me while I was away and proclaiming undying love for me.

I would leave in the morning with a kiss, letting you know I couldn't wait to get home after work to play with you. I would beep and roll down my window as I passed the house on the other side of the median strip, you waving in the bay windows of our living room. And then you would play with Mommy and the new baby all day, building an unbreakable bond, frequently checking in with her to find out the time to see when I would get home. Sometimes she would see you struggling to open something and she would ask if you needed help and you would sometimes say, "No! I want Daddy!" I think you were just trying to mess with Mommy sometimes. It is you, after all.

I would arrive at the end of the day and you would jump into my arms day after day, week after week, year after year, Nathaniel by your side, and we would run off, the three of us, and go act foolish, while we gave Mommy a break. It wasn't just functional – I wanted that time each day. Why would I want to deal with adults all day, lawyers in particular, and then go out to business dinners or go golfing all day on my weekends? My down time was your time. The true value in my life resided with my sobriety, and within my spiritual condition, my children and my wife.

Mommy would occasionally get upset and tell me, "I gave birth to her! I carried her! It's unfair! All she wants to do is spend time with you!" I loved it. And then the day came when you started sharing more time between us and then spending more time with Mommy and then you balanced out our time between the two of us. Then I watched an already beautiful relationship with Mommy get even more special and more complete. As you grew through your years into your tween years and into your teen years, Mommy was another anchor for you – both of us providing a different flavor of comfort and support;

together, providing a complete platform. You would find comfort in us in different ways and with different subjects. In the last year of your physical life, you and Mommy found another deep bond in walking at night and talking about your days; therapeutic time for you both; and shooting the shit time as well. You both needed it and its value enlightened you further.

Yet it was the eyes – both of your eyes. That is where I recognized the depth of the relationship. The way you looked into her eyes and the way Mommy looked into yours and Nathaniel's. It was unmistakable. Pure love and trust. How blessed are you in each other. Your Momma loves you so.

*

Nate's Bus Fell In Water

I remember vividly one night that demonstrated your undying love for your little brother; his third parent in a way. We joke about it all the time. You were five and he was two. We stopped on our way to Jekyll in Charleston, WV at a hotel. He had seen a Simpson's episode with me (don't judge me, reader!) and in it a school bus fell in a river and disappeared. Age appropriately for him, it horrified him and he could not understand what happened.

Then bedtime came. Nate, as a little guy spent his days hearing his sister's stories and never quite edged his voice into the mix as strongly as hers. On this night that all changed. We booked two adjoining rooms and put the kids in one room and we stayed in the other with the door cracked. It was not more than two minutes after we kissed you two goodnight and turned on our TV that we heard your sweet little voices.

"Eee-Heee?"

"Yes, Nathan."

"Bus fall in water, member that?"

"Yes, Nathan. Now go to bed," you said, as if you were his mother, in a sweet motherly voice.

"Okay, Eee-Heee."

A minute passed.

"Eee-Heee?"

"Yes, Nathan."

"Bus fall in water, member that?"

"Yes, Nathan. Now go to bed," you said gently again.

"Okay, Eee-Heee."

After an hour of this, Mommy slept with Nathaniel and you came in and slept with me. We were peeing our pants in the other room and were so happy with how patient you were being with him, while you let him have his stage and start telling one of his scary stories. That day Nate really started cultivating his voice and speaking up. You facilitated that – your love and patience and wisdom – it was actually quite simple, yet you were the comfort that gave him a stage on which to speak.

*

Daddy/Kakes

The KMM's. Kevin Michael Mooney and Kayleigh Mickayla Mooney. I was frequently accused of trying to make a mini-me out of Kayleigh, giving her the feminine middle name of my middle name. Truth be told, I was, and I did. A convenient cover story was true – that Mickayla, fit between Kayleigh and Mooney, sounded like poetry. And I did name her after her Great-Great-Great-Great Grandfather, Michael Mooney, who escaped the Irish Famine, the

Great Hunger in January, 1847 and was the only family member to make it to Americay. "We are the future they dreamed of yesterday," was our slogan, inspired by Michael.

And she was named after me – but naming her Kevin would have been too obvious. And besides, her name was set in the stars when I was fifteen. So she took my middle name. Thank God Jess loved it. It is the perfect name for her. This is the only soul who could so elegantly wear this beautiful name. My baby.

We nicknamed her Kakes while singing "Patty Cake" to her as a baby, inserting her name for Patty into Kayleigh Kakes. After her accident, the Georgia Sea Turtle Center named a rare Kemps Ridley sea turtle "Kayleigh Kakes" in her honor. It was a name that lasts through her transition.

Those who know me know the lengths I will go for my children. For them the richness of life enveloped their days. Nate and I have an amazingly unique relationship in its own right, equal to anything I can write about his sister. However, for this text, I am limited to jotting down mostly a few thoughts about me and Kakes. It's simple – I've never seen a stronger Daddy-Daughter relationship. Period. She and I are so alike; so alive; so passionate with our emotions and our souls; intuitive and compassionate; in love with the other. Daddy's little girl – yes, in the classical sense, that is true, but it is much deeper than that. Our bond transcends time and space, dimensions even. It always has for thousands of years.

As a Father of my beautiful girl, I am pragmatic and true. I do not hide behind male dominated immaturity like staring down boys who looked at my Daughter or trying to be tough and dictate who she could hang out with and who she couldn't. There were certain rules growing up with us, yet more importantly, dialogue and truth searching through the lessons of life among us. I would tell them both that I was trying to raise adults, not children, and therefore they had a say in what decisions we were making and I wanted them to think through their situations, troubles, victories and opportunities.

Kakes, as the older of the two children, and the first to hit each new older age, naturally took to learning new skills that she could use and thereafter impart to her brother. I relished in this with her. We consistently had deep discussions about anything. It is the poetry between us, the artistry of our lives. This includes building such a comfort level between us that she literally talked to me about everything in life. Imagine that – a Father earning the right to talk to his teenage daughter about sex, about drinking, about assault. While she also found comfort in discussing intimate subjects with her Mother, and picked at times to go deeper with one of us over the other, she found comfort in both and trusted us to the ends of the earth. It was another seedling to her voice – the permission to trust, to speak, to listen, to be heard.

"My Little Girl"

She danced with glitter rainbows,
Pulling the light from the leaves,
Lifting the colors from thick summer grasses,
With her laughter,
As the ice cream truck jingled - we watched as it slowly passes,
Secure in her butterfly feet,
Tip toeing along the sidewalk,
Where childhood imprinted this street,
Lined with gardens and wagons and grace,
And flowers and fragrance and faith,
With a strong family union,
Curled in Daddy's arms,
Safe from the dangerous dragons,
And safe from uncertainty in life,
And safe from harm -

Sleep my sweet baby, my little baby girl,
For I have you,
I hold you,
Sleep in the cradle of my hands,
For I have you,
You are safe,
As summer glow alights your face.

*

U2 – Kayleigh's First Concert 01/02/2011

Of course, the boys from North Dublin get their just dues in this book. They will not know their impact until they actually read through these pages; how their artistry, their passion, meant for different people and various purposes, could find their way into the fabric of daily miracles and messages through the ethereal channel of love between a Father and his Daughter – both before, and more importantly, after her physical death.

U2 flows in my blood. One of my favorites. I loved their first three albums and their first and iconic live album, "Under a Blood Red Sky." We used to walk the streets of Cleveland Heights with a boombox blasting those four tapes. Then came "Unforgettable Fire," which was a defining moment for me. It was blood. Rich blood. It took my study of U2 to a higher plain, as did those albums that followed. All of these ended up in their childhood, listening to U2 in the car wherever we traveled.

At nine, Kayleigh was exposed to what they looked like, how they presented on stage. Her Aunt Tricia and her boys, along with me and Kayleigh, went to a "concert" video at the Rock and Roll Hall of Fame and watched this concert. She loved it. All of it. What better band than U2 to have as a first concert? Yet, we did not understand, nor could we at the time, that somehow their music would be threaded into our lives, and these four men would be threaded into our lives from afar simply by producing music that my Daughter would one day use to communicate with me from the higher dimension. That sacredness began in Cleveland this afternoon as we watched Bono banging on a drum at center stage to "Love and Peace."

*

Gifts for the Less Fortunate 11/29/2012

We were part of a gift drive through several organizations, including Family Connections, in Cleveland Heights, distributing in total over 600 gifts to needy children collected via holiday gift drive. Our friend Carly organized the drive. Kayleigh and Nathaniel helped to get the drive moving by buying 40 or so gifts for other children. We went shopping and when we got home, we wrapped and labeled the gifts with ages, and by gender, male or female. The papers and the news media picked up the story and the kids and I found ourselves on the news. How awesome was that. Kayleigh was ten and Nathaniel, seven.

We have always conveyed a sense of giving back to the community; to build the community and become an active participant in its success. My kids were in the public schools at this point in time and saw classmates who were in need. It was instilled in our kids, this code of love and tolerance that makes our family great. Kayleigh was the catalyst of the idea, stating that it would be horrible to wake up on Christmas morning and have no presents. Nathaniel weighed in right away. She expressed incredible compassion and asked me, "Daddy, can we use some of our money to buy gifts for people in need?"

Of course. It was necessary. Required in this teaching moment. It just happened to sync up with the drive that Carly was developing and so we dovetailed into that drive. Each of the kids walked through the store with me and picked out gifts for different age groups, for kids in fourth or fifth grade. These includes books, action figures and stuffed animals. My children were rock stars and an example to the community of giving and humility.

*

Blanketing the Homeless I 01/10/2013

You were ten when we started this legacy, wanting to do something in addition to the gift drive. As we approached the backdoor of St.

Malachi's above the Cuyahoga River, a middle aged African American man shuffled out of the shadows where he had been huddling against the protection of the church walls.

"Excuse me," said this man, slumped over from the frigid chill of a Cleveland January blizzard, "are those blankets?"

"Yes," you said and smiled with your bright blue eyes, "would you like one?"

He glowed. His eyes lighting up behind heavy wrinkles earned on the street. She lowered the oversized plastic bag to the snow and loosened the string.

"You can pick any one that you like," you said in both a child's upbeat, idealistic voice of hope, as well as in a mature tone, understanding the gravity of the situation.

He looked in the bag, shuffling among the six or seven blankets in the bag. He picked a black and white plush blanket, pulled it out, unfolded it and wrapped it around his body and up along his face. He placed a frozen hand on your right shoulder and said, "Bless you – bless you."

He looked up to me, acknowledging the tender compassion in my Daughter and smiled to me in gratitude, as if thanking me also for teaching her these ways. In truth, you had asked what you could do for the homeless. You had come up with the idea of covering the homeless with blankets. I had just provided the means to accomplish your goal.

He turned and walked back down the snowy path, compacted in heavy dry ice, back to the church wall where the wind was less fierce, and sat in the snow wrapped in Kayleigh's blanket – a blanket like the twenty others we purchased that day with money we set aside specifically for this purpose.

Instead of remaining out in the snow and distributing blankets one at a time for any who ventured toward us, we dropped the remainder off at the church manager's office, who was busy in the tiny kitchen attempting to feed those that he could. He was gracious, thanking us kindly. A few dozen homeless Clevelanders were the lucky recipients that night of your blankets and associated love and compassion. The anonymity of the gesture did not lessen its impact on you. It actually increased its strength.

We walked back towards the parking lot. We were strikingly aware of how cold it was as we stood and walked about in that wind for all of ten minutes. Our stricken brethren were out in that weather for days.

"Daddy, are they going to freeze to death?"

"Not now," I said, "you may have given them just a few more degrees of warmth that will keep them going through these extremely cold winter nights. You may have saved some lives tonight. You are amazing, Kakes."

"Thank you, Daddy. So are you," you said and paused. "I feel so bad for anyone who doesn't have a home. At least they know that a stranger loved them enough to try to help, right?"

I hugged you. "Did you see the look on that man's face? Did you see his eyes light up, Kakes?"

"Yeah," you said, smiling up to me.

"He is a homeless middle aged African American man in downtown Cleveland who looked into the eyes of a ten year old suburban white girl's eyes, a complete stranger, and your paths may never have crossed, but he found a bond of love and compassion between the two of you. He knows. His heart was forever touched by yours, Sweetheart."

It was twelve below zero. For the third straight day.

*

"My little love, you are like an enchanting bird that perches softly in the window of my soul, gazing in on me with peace and strength, and offering to me your sweet melody so that my spirit breathes deeper and sings much stronger."

*

Sacred Space 05/21/2014

One thing we were certain to teach our children was to respect each other's humanity, to have permission to be human and make mistakes; that it was part of the fabric of being human. How the mistakes or hard moments are handled was the true test of the spirit. It was the next five minutes of adjustment, the half an hour of retreating and gathering of thoughts and returning with a solution that was most important aspect of a hard moment.

One should expect in intimate relationships to have disagreements, confusion, frustration and the like. In well-functioning relationships this can thoughtfully be minimized. With us it was minimal as we all took time to inventory our own behavior and return to the family member with whom we had an issue and work things out. Kayleigh is a dynamic and engaging, assertive soul, much like her Father. We both had practice is this area of overstepping and correcting. One of Kayleigh's lasting treasures to the world was this impeccable compassion and her innate ability to correct her mistakes, to say she was sorry humbly and to move on to correct those mistakes for the greater gold of the person she had affected. This translated in our home with the gifts of little notes and smiley faces and "I love you's" around the house, even when there wasn't any reason for which to apologize.

This text, which I sent to her when she had just turned 12, demonstrates this interchange.

TEXT 05/21/2014:

Daddy: "I love you darling daughter. Let's make sure when one of us has a hard moment to take a minute in a sacred space and get centered. I will help you do that and cheer you on as you push through the hard moments. Can you do that for me too? ☺*"*

*

Beach Walks 08/08/2014

She was 12. It was our 15th wedding anniversary. Like any other day, I planned my Daddy-Mommy time, my Daddy-Son time and my Daddy-Daughter time. It was a brilliant, humid, sunny day in the 90s down on the beach. We had already walked the beach and searched for sea creatures in the tidal pools a few times that day. Later in the afternoon, however, she took me again. One of my favorite activities, with my favorite girl in the world – there wasn't a moment of hesitation.

When we came back to the house and she disappeared with Nathaniel down the hall, I introspectively absorbed our walk and tried to think of how I could not only thank her but remind her of its importance. So I sent her this:

TEXT 08/08/2014:

Daddy: "Kakey. I know how busy your life is. I wanted to thank you for finding time to walk with me on the beach. It meant the world to me! Lov u!!"
    Kakes: "I lov u too!!!!"

*

70

A Sacred Boat 08/29/2014

A poem at the end of vacation for my family, clearly understanding my obligation, opportunity and greatest joy – to steer, with my wife, our children's lives; the decisions we make as adults largely need to be made for our children, a notion stamped on my heart and taken very seriously:

TEXT 08/29/2014:

Daddy: "A Sacred Boat"

"Placid dreams or turbulent scenes,
Dark haunts or refractions splashed in golden greens,
Foamy sea shows hint of caution ahead,
The waves grow as the wind is fed,
Hold on to Heaven with its hope and its latches,
Hunker down safely low the hatches,
As the storm rips the sails,
With gale force slashes –

Now calm and pool like silver reflections,
Give time for repairs and fruitful introspections,
What will we find in the collective story,
When we take an honest inventory,
Of the voyage to date;

She sits with beauty untainted,
Underneath a sky pastel painted,
She the mother of this one,
Our beloved son,
He a luminary who enlightens my soul,
I love this little boy who rides in this sacred boat;

I smile at the whimsy and wonder,
As the cloud line echoes with percussions of thunder,
She the mother of this beautiful girl,
Who was the first to alter our worlds,
She expands the light emanating from my soul,

I love this little girl who rides in this sacred boat;

We clasp as lovers, fingers to fingers,
Embrace each other as the elements linger,
Waves licking the boards just below,
Lapping up against our sacred boat;

It is ours to steer through the precious waters,
With its passengers, our son and our daughter,
And you and me,
This belove family,
It is ours to guide with honor through the growth,
And ensure the love and safety of this sacred boat,
We steer together,
Through every shade, season and shift in the weather,
This, this our sacred home."

*

13th Birthday 05/15/2015

This was my card to Kakes on her 13th birthday:

"My Dear Daughter, Happy 13th Birthday!! Where has the time gone? I'll tell you where! In our hearts! From the moment I laid my eyes on you and held you in my arms, all the way to this wonderful day, you have been a wonderful child. You are now entering your teen years and I have just a few words that will help you enjoy yourself: 1. take your life one day at a time, and 2. treat yourself with loving kindness.

This is a special day, my baby, and you are so special to me. Here's to you and me continuing to do what we've done the last 13 years – living one day at a time, with laughter, through tears, facing frustration and walking through uncertainty, to loving each other in the way we do. To the Best Daughter Ever, Your Daddy Loves you Unconditionally and Forever!! Love, Daddy"

*

Loving Kindness Meditation

And moments like this where I shared coping skills:

TEXT 06/29/2015:

Daddy: "Thanks Kakes for our talk. When you get stuck you can always turn to something like this. You can also just read it when you wake each morning. Or come up with your own. Love you.

Loving Kindness Meditation – I invite myself to peel back the thin film of fear that coats my eyes; that veil of consciousness that blurs the light of my soul; for at my core there resides a strength and compassion offered lovingly by God to me. This most sacred of gifts – God's love and kindness, offered from God to me for the direct purpose of directing that gift to myself.

I offer myself peace and am deserving of peace, no matter my current situation, where I am at, where I am going and where I have been. Loving kindness is loving myself enough to courageously peel back the scales of fear and permit the inner strength to blossom. I hereby permit my inner strength to blossom. Think my thoughts, speak my words and act my actions, God, my everlasting Father and giver of unconditional loving kindness."

*

Tiny Footsteps on the Ceiling Above Me

For a time her room was on the third floor. Above our bedroom. She was keeping me awake. An effortless moment, choosing light over frustration to make my point:

TEXT 07/01/2015:

Daddy: "Go to bed. Stop walking! Rest your pretty head 🖤🖤🖤🖤🖤."

     Kakes: "ok, goodnight! 🖤🖤🖤🖤🖤 🌙🌙🌙🌙🌙"

Daddy: "I have the best daughter. I know you listen to me and let me guide you. You are super smart and creative and gentle and wonderful!"

     Kakes: "Thank you, Daddy. You are the best Daddy ever!"

Daddy: "I hope so. That is where I put my energy. My sobriety. My wife. My babies! 🖤"

     *

Theatre Camp: Evergreen, CO, July, 2015

Five days away from me – the first time you were ever away from me, an hour or so away from where Nate and I were in Littleton with the rest of the family, while Mommy was home in Cleveland. I started texting you within the first hour that you drove off with my sister Mary. I couldn't wait to see you after this week of camp:

TEXT 07/12/2015:

Daddy: "I LOVE YOU!!!!!!!!!!! 🖤🖤🖤🖤🖤"

     Kakes: "I LOVE YOU TOO DADDY!!!!!!!! I MISS YOU🖤🖤🖤🖤🖤🖤"

Daddy: "I MISS YOU TOO AND AM SOOO EXCITED FOR MY BIG GIRL. I'LL SEE YOU LIKE WEDNESDAY OK? 🖤🖤🖤🖤🖤"

     Kakes: "OK LOVE YOU! 🖤🖤🖤🖤🖤🖤🖤🖤🖤🖤🖤🖤🖤🖤🖤🖤🖤🖤🖤"

Daddy: "DID YOU SEE ME CHASE THE CAR WHEN YOU LEFT? 🖤🖤🖤🖤🖤🖤🖤🖤🖤🖤"

     Kakes: "NO!! DID YOU???? 🖤🖤🖤🖤🖤🖤🖤🖤🖤🖤"

TEXT 07/13/2015:

Kakes: *"Make sure to video the whole show"*
Daddy: *"Ok Baby. Can't wait."*
Kakes: *"Me too! We have to do pretty complicated dances near the end and I'm terrified!"*
Daddy: *"Dance like your daddy and you'll be fine.* ❤️"
Kakes: *"LOL pink nightmare"*

*

Constructive Adjustments

Moments like this captured in texts, occurred frequently. In fact I have hundreds upon hundreds of such texts between us:

TEXT 08/15/2015:

Daddy: *"You built great character today that nobody can take away. You are Kayleigh Mooney – a smart, savvy, emotionally loving and wonderful girl. It is your job to make you shine in this world and I am very proud of the young woman you are becoming. Take that to heart especially when you have a hard moment. Dig down within and love yourself enough to know that we all make mistakes and we all have room to grow. TREAT YOURSELF LIKE A JEWEL AND KEEP IT POLISHED. You are the most amazing daughter to have. Love you Babygirl."*
Kakes: *"Thanks!! Love u too* ❤️"

*

TEXT 10/12/2015:

Daddy: *"Remember that you have great inner strength and can do many things in this world that you might feel scared to do. Just one foot in front of the other and believe in yourself. Just was thinking about this. I love you so much."*
Kakes: *"Thank you. Love you too!!"*

TEXT 10/15/2015:

Daddy: *"Just want you to know I'm always here for you. That's it. Out."*
Kakes: *"Goodnight. Love you ❤"*
Daddy: *"❤ My special baby. You are like an amazing sunrise over the ocean."*

TEXT 10/26/2015:

Daddy: *"The best gift you can ever give me is the gift you give to yourself – be brave and selfless, taking care of yourself with strength, self-love and building yourself up. You will face fears, confusion, setbacks and frustration at times and that is ok. It is as it should be. What you do with those challenges is what can help you grow that greatness you have inside. I've never met someone like you – with all of your wonder and light. You amaze me. Take care of that light and be good to Kayleigh. ❤"*
Kakes: *"Thank you so much. You're the best father I could have ever hoped for and I'm glad that you like to hang out with me because I had a lot of fun today at WalMart. I love you ❤❤❤"*

TEXT 11/08/2015:

Daddy: "♥"

    Kakes: "♥ ♥"

Daddy: "YOU JUST REMEMBER – there is nothing as special as a daughter daddy relationship. And I have a brilliant strong daughter – the best ever. Through everything in life – the best."

    Kakes: "Thank you."

Daddy: "And Congrats my love on such hard work today. YOU EARNED A $50 SHOPPING SPREE WITH YOUR FATHER NEXT WEEKEND!"

TEXT 12/07/2015:

Daddy: "How are you today sweetheart?"

    Kakes: "I'm okay"

Daddy: "Create the happiness you want in this world. Step outside your comfort zone and take healthy risks. You are amazing and strong – just under the fear there is courage. Dig down into the courage and shine! You amaze me my little baby."

    Kakes: "Thank you!"

*

The Courage to Speak

At thirteen, as all thirteen year olds go through age appropriate confusion and change, you did as well. With the platform of our family's openness and support you asked for help in teasing through your emotions – this is not something everybody does. But you did. Because you are amazing. I taught you the value of your voice as a toddler; if in moments I became frustrated and yelled at you, I would do a 10th Step and return within minutes and get on my knees, eyeballs to eyeballs and tell you it was wrong for me to have spoken to you that way – that nobody has a right to speak to you that way – that as your Daddy you need to respect me, but as your Daddy, I need to respect you double as much.

With normal adolescence, and feeling the pressures of thirteen, with the changes, and the peer dynamics shifting, I watched you mobilize resources to adjust to the changes. You had always been highly attractive and an authentic friend to so many, that, once the teenage years started, we watched as a few mean girls, jealous of you, tried to marginalize you, which caused you great confusion. I remember you asking me, "Why would anybody want to be mean to somebody else?" In the crux of a thirteen year olds' world, this was a difficult shift. You retained a calm levity about the fluidity of adolescence, much like a nature adult. It was amazing to watch – hearing your youth in your voice tied to an ancient wisdom. Ultimately, they toned down; came back and apologized, and in Kayleigh Mooney fashion, you welcomed them right back into the fold. While the situation developed, however, it was hard, and you took action.

TEXT 12/10/2015:

> *Kakes: "Do you think I could start going to a therapist regularly to talk about issues I have going on? I think it would really help with anxiety and just to talk about things bothering me."*
>
> Daddy: *"Absolutely. Having an extra set of ears is really beneficial. A lot of people do it. Life is complicated. Sometimes having that guidance is really helpful. Mommy and I did it. And I did it early in my sobriety as well."*
>
> *Kakes: "Yeah I just think it would help me with my problems that are too big to talk about to other people. Like some friends leaving me, that's been really hard for me."*
>
> Daddy: *"I hear you sweetie. Yes we will."*
>
> *Kakes: "Okay thank you for listening. Sometime I just feel like I have nobody to talk to."*
>
> Daddy: *"I am always here to listen to you. Sometimes you probably want someone other than your dad to talk to which is ok. 💕 Try to take a deep breath and stay in the moment. A lot of times we get overwhelmed by fears of the future while the moment passes by."*
>
> *Kakes: "Yeah. Thank you for understanding 💕"*

*Daddy: "You are going to be ok even if you feel a bit off right now.
Stay positive and hopeful. You'll get through it. ❤"
    Kakes: "okay thank you ❤ ❤ ❤"*

*

Daddy Not Perfect? My Constant Reminders

Even with your Father, and actually especially with your Father, you
were encouraged to and trusted that you could use your voice. I knew
when you were a baby that our relationship could have a large impact
on the men you chose to date and the man you chose to marry
someday; upon the quality of your self-esteem; upon the strength of
your voice. That is why I always encouraged you to use your voice,
even when you were frightened, and even when it was uncomfortable.
You learned the worthiness of your voice. I took that responsibility
seriously:

TEXT 12/24/2015:
Daddy: "How are you?"
    Kakes: "Pretty good"
*Daddy: "Great. You are awesome and I know you can get
organized and do responsible chores and have fun."*
    Kakes: "Thank you."
*Daddy: "I'm sorry I was harsh. You really deserve gentleness even
when I need to be firm. You are so precious to me and I want us to
grow and laugh and love and have fun."*
    Kakes: "It's okay"
*Daddy: "Thanks. But remember your voice is yours. You get to
stand up for yourself no matter what, even with me."*
    Kakes: "Okay."

*

How Does Kayleigh Respond to An Argument?

She rallies. She appropriately retreats to gather herself. She evaluates the situation. She processes her feelings, which, at thirteen, usually started in a more self-conscious place, and rapidly emerges through the rebuilding of the way she wants to act, think and speak in this world. She was taught and believed that her voice was special, important and vibrant. That she had a right to speak her mind and had the right to apologize if she made a mistake. She knew from us that we made mistakes and we always corrected those mistakes with our kids, rising into a sense of true humility to demonstrate how to be accountable and self-loving at the same time. In essence, giving ourselves permission to be human.

TEXT 01/03/2016:

> *Kakes: "I'm sorry for everything that happened. It's my fault and I'm sorry. Just know that I love you and I'm sorry. Goodnight."*
> *Daddy: "Thank you. You are responsible for your behavior only. I am sorry for mine. I am listening to you and hear you. I love you."*
> *Kakes: "Love you too."*
> *Daddy: " ♥You are so special to me."*
> *Kakes: "Thank you. You are special to me ♥"*
> *Daddy: "You deserve the best in this world. Your voice is powerful and filled with light! Go light up the world!"*

*

Kayleigh Saves an Ovary 02/01/2016

I was just about to open an A.A. meeting, chairing that night. Jess called. Kakes was in excruciating pain and huddled in a ball at home. She needed to get to the ER. There was a snowstorm. Nathaniel would be home alone. I told her I'd be there, hung up and asked someone to sit in for me and exited the building, sliding down Mayfield Road, just on the edges of the tires slipping out from under me – racing to my child's side.

As I picked her up and jumped back in the car, her pain was obvious. As I had done on other drives to the ER (superglue from art project in an eye, bladder infection, heavy flu), I balanced the danger of the road in a snowstorm vs speed of arrival and leaned on speed, continuing to slip down the road, ensuring not to push it too far – ending up hitting a tree would not help her pain. But I was driven and we arrived in one piece and rather fast.

Scans showed that she has a cyst that has wrapped itself around her ovary. It was strangling the organ and, without surgery, the staff could not tell how long the ovary would remain undamaged and alive without its normal blood flow. We had now been at the hospital for four hours; midnight.

"Is my ovary dying?" she said to the doctor, alarmed.

"The only way to make sure it's okay, Honey, is to go in and remove the cyst," they explained.

"Daddy, I don't know if I ever want to have kids. I don't want to lose my ovary. What if I lose this one and then I have an accident and lose the other one and can't have kids?"

"Sweetheart, this is your body and you are right. It is scary and you have to think through it. I know what I want as your Father."

"You want me to have surgery?"

"I do."

"I'm scared."

"Me too, Sweetheart," I acknowledged, "but it sounds like it's not horribly invasive and they have a chance to save your ovary. I think you should take that chance."

"Okay, Daddy," she whispered, staring trustingly into my soul. She took a heavy, panicky breath, "okay."

They prepped her for surgery and then they dressed me as well. It was now 2 A.M. I was dressed from head to toe in blue surgical gowns, fully fitted with mask and hairnet. I was going in with her no matter what. My baby would see me and hear my voice as she went under the anesthesia.

She was already drifting off with the medicine. I stood beside her in her full field of view until she closed her eyes and I told her I loved her. They confirmed that she was under. Then they kicked me out of the room kindly and got to work.

I sat in the waiting area down the hall from the OR, the only person in that entire space. Alone. Tired. Worried. I did what I do. Here is the 10th Step I texted to my friend, Carly:

TEXT 02/01/2016, 2:45 A.M.:

"Ten: Kakes just went under in surgery. I held her hand while they knocked her out. Really out of nowhere and very scary. Selfish? No. Really locked in. Dishonest? Hard not to wander. Resentful? No. Fear? Yes. 5: Sharing with who? You. 6: Willing to have God remove defects? Yes, God I am willing. 7: Prayer? God, please lock me down and keep my eyes and spirit focused. Keep the river clear. 8: Willing to change? Yes I am willing to change something 9: Change? While she is under surgery eat. Breathe. Do ten. Trust God. Hope for best. Hope she doesn't lose ovary. Expect nothing. Positive. 12: turn to help who? Show my guys how we train for these sudden moments by doing 10th Step inventories over and over and over no matter what. Then when it really matters we answer the bell. God bless my baby."

Several hours later she woke up in the recovery room, her Father beside her. It was 4:37 A.M. I kissed her on the head and assured her she had kicked ass; that I was proud of her; that her ovary was saved.

She was delirious and said, "I feel good. I didn't remember the surgery. I forgot to count, but that's okay. My ovary's alive. Love

82

you….they saved my ovary? Was it actually twisted? So the clot is gone? The cyst is gone? And I'm healthy again? Love you…"

I stayed with her as she fell back asleep, vigilantly by her side until 8:30 A.M. when Jess relieved me after dropping Nathaniel off at school, and I went home to sleep. The next time I would see her laying in a hospital bed with her eyes closed would be an hour after her physical death a year and a half from this day.

*

White House 03/14/2016

We were asked to join a dozen federal agencies and departments on the grounds of the White House to explain further our concept of a validated top level domain. I represented my organization along with our CIO and the CIO's business development executive director, licensed owner of a gTLD, along with several other similar validated top level domains were to convene with the purpose of seeing where our brainchild could support initiatives with which the federal agencies were struggling, by presenting to the world a validated web presence that could, by its structure, prevent bad actors from acting in such domains.

In the early afternoon on the day of our departure, Kayleigh suddenly had a recurrence of her earlier pain in her ovary that had put her in the hospital on January 31st. It was now the afternoon on March 14, 2016, and we found ourselves at Hillcrest Hospital ER, awaiting the doctor and an evaluation. I left my office and hurried to meet Jess and Kayleigh, a friend watching Nathaniel at their house.

There was the least moment of hesitation. I would not leave my Daughter's side. I called my friend Joe, our business development lead, and canceled my participation in the trip. Then I told Jess and Kayleigh that I was staying home.

83

"Daddy! No!" Kayleigh said, sitting up in bed, a sad frown on her face, "you've been looking forward to this so much. This is a once in a career opportunity. You can't miss a meeting at the White House!"

I smiled at her and held her hand. "I'm not leaving your side, Babygirl. Yes, it sucks missing this trip, but there will be others."

"Not at the White House!" she said, "Daddy, don't miss this. You have to go!"

There would likely not be another. I knew that. Maybe there would be. Maybe not. I didn't really care. "Thank you, Sweetie, but it's okay, really. I cannot leave town knowing you are in the hospital."

"But Mommy's here. I'll be all right."

I kissed her on her forehead and smiled. I was professionally disappointed - not with Kayleigh in the slightest, but in this unfortunate yet paramount situation coupled with such an important trip. Mostly I was worried about my baby, which eclipses anything else in my world, least of all, work. If they didn't like me missing this trip, they could fire me and I'd work somewhere else - I would not leave my child's side.

We stayed for several more hours when she was finally cleared and we were told she was suffering from the cyst scar tissue following the emergency surgery on February 1st. She would be okay. She was sent home in the late evening. As I drove home I knew my flight had already left, as had Joe's earlier in the evening. It was after 9 P.M.

As I pulled in the driveway, Joe called to tell me that both his and my flight were pushed back and combined into one flight leaving after ten, due to storms that were rolling through Cleveland - the window opened back up to fly to D.C. With Kayleigh safe at home, and with a tight window to drive to the airport and run to my gate, I may make that flight. I kissed Nathaniel, Jess and Kakes and roared off to Hopkins airport, making my flight as the doors were closing, being the last one on in the last seat available. I would after all, make it to my meeting at the White House, which proved to be a career highlight, but showed in my action, as I always have, what always comes first - my family. My daughter. My son. My wife. I would make the same decision one thousand times out of one thousand opportunities. It had always been the case. It will always remain so, regardless of whose house into which I am invited.

*

Over Protective Daddy 05/05/2016

TEXT 05/05/2016:

Daddy: "I KNOW I CAN BE OVER PROTECTIVE OF YOU. MY LITTLE GIRL!!!!! Thank you for being patient with me as I grow up. ♥♥♥♥♥♥"
　　　Kakes: "Thank you for being this protective! It makes me feel safe, even tho sometimes I seem mad, I actually appreciate it so much. I love you! ♥♥♥♥♥♥♥♥♥♥
Daddy: "Thank you. I love you so much! Really appreciate your text ♥♥♥♥♥♥♥♥"
　　　Kakes: "You're the best father I could have ever hoped for ♥♥♥♥♥♥♥♥"

*

Daddy the Drama Queen 05/20/2016

TEXT 05/20/2016:

Daddy: "Thanks. I promise I'll work on giving you more space and not being so intense. What a drama queen! I need a button that sucks the drama out of me that you guys can press"
　　　Kakes: "Thank you lol. And yeah the button thing sounds cool lol. I'm kinda tired. Tomorrow we can do something fun if you don't have plans. Goodnight. Love you ♥"

Daddy: "Yeah. Yea. Yea. Love u my young smart funny intelligent spirited woman."

    Kakes: "love you. You're a great dad. 🖤🖤🖤🖤"

Daddy: "And you're a great daughter. So happy you're mine. 🖤🖤🖤🖤"

*

Teenager Encouraged 05/30/2016

As the nuances of early teen years continued, you retained that spark, that immutable levity about you. As tiny waves popping up and receding when mean girls would snip at you and you would address them, pivot or realign, not unlike many other teenagers as you learned these valuable coping skills. Thank God it only lasted for short bursts of time. You had always been one of the most genuine and most popular kids. You feel the world so deeply that when they started being jealous of your beauty or your gentleness, and started being mean to you, it impacted you deeply. I watched you try new tools and work your way through those situations and become even more beautiful. Always conquering the situations.

TEXT 05/30/2016

Daddy: "Sometimes we experience pain. Sometimes we hold it close til it doubles and consumes us. The trick is to identify it - process it - learn from it - move on. Every human goes through human things. You are no different. And I am not either. Instead of in A.A., if I was to talk to people in a bar about my problems I might eventually find myself drunk. But if I talk to those in A.A. and surround myself with positive people I will get valuable feedback and strengthen my sobriety. Your decision to take care of yourself. My hope as your father is that you will continue to relearn how to reach out and hold yourself up like a jewel and keep that jewel of your soul polished. I love you."

Kakes: "*I will eventually talk. Thank you for that. I love you.*"

TEXT 05/31/2016:

Kakes: "*Lol. I need to find a good way to deal with my problems. Okay goodnight.*"
Daddy: "*I will support you any way I can. I know it seems really hard but you'll find a way. Start with being willing. Then we can use some tools to help you. I see your pain. I am here always.*"
Kakes: "*Thank you. I love you so much. You're the best dad ever* 💜💜💜💜"
Daddy: "*Thanks baby. You helped me grow up some more today. You are the best daughter and really special. Goodnight.* 💜💜💜💜"
Kakes: "*Goodnight* 💜"

TEXT 06/15/2016:

Daddy: "*Here's the process when upset:*
1. *See situation.*
2. *What is my part? Am I being selfish? Dishonest? Fearful? Angry?*
3. *Talk to someone quickly.*
4. *Ask God to remove selfishness, dishonesty or fear.*
5. *Change to unselfish, honest, courageous. Think what that looks like.*"
Kakes: "*Is that the tenth step thing?*"
Daddy: "*Yep shorter version.*"
Kakes: "*Thank you.*"
Daddy: "💜"
Kakes: "💜💜💜💜"

TEXT 06/29/2016:

Daddy: "*You have one job in this world - to love yourself, take care of yourself and let yourself shine. If you learn nothing else from me - learn this. I love you peanut.*"

Kakes: "Thank you. I will love myself."
Daddy: "And I will too. You're the best daughter. Through ups and downs - through everything - love yourself. 🤍🤍🤍"
Kakes: "Thank you. You're the best daddy 🤍🤍🤍🤍"

*

Summer of Fourteen 07/2016

She was fourteen. Filled with modern issues, including technology and social media platform traps, pressures on young girls to grow up fast, to grapple with sexualizing at younger ages, to have to defend themselves emotionally, to be embroiled with mean girls, to feel depressed perhaps while going through bodily and hormonal changes. Also filled with joy and wonder, with art and color and expression, with passion and purpose, with laughter and boisterous joking, with dynamic moments and dreams of a future, with love and light, with family at her core and the spirit of a warrior in her heart. She was fourteen and filled with all of this, flooding into her wise old soul and her experiences to date, along with all of the abundance of a happy and fun life.

Sometimes she just didn't want to deal with stupid people and therefore changed certain friends who were being catty and mean to others. Kayleigh would not discriminate and exclude. She was a bridge builder and a kind friend. Almost everyone who ever met her would attest to this. She is exactly who one would want as a close ally, a trusted confidant, a true friend who was unafraid in providing comfort and compassion, that immortal love and light.

Yet, as with many fourteen year olds, exploring themselves and emerging into themselves, she juggled the strength of self-love with questioning herself with self-doubt; sizing herself up against others. She had always been a little shy and in the summer of fourteen years old, she began addressing that self-consciousness head on. She would vacillate with confidence and lack of self-confidence, picking herself up again and learning new techniques to be a young girl in this modern world. (As a side note – watching Kayleigh and her friends and peers and other girls her age navigate through the barbed wire of today's society was very unnerving. Things must change for our girls). Through it all, we had dialogue. I watched her express her feelings and engage her voice to address these harder moments, emerging a little more confident, with another bridge built, another peer affected in a positive manner, another estimable act upon which she was developing from a dynamic, brilliant child into a bright, brilliant young woman.

*

Palm Island Mother Turtle 08/06/2016

For the first time, we went to a new beach, Palm Island, Florida, on the Gulf of Florida instead of to our family home on Jekyll Island. Each night I wandered out to see if I could catch a glimpse of sea turtles. The kids stayed with Jess this night, while the lightning sparked off in the ink blackness of the ocean over the horizon.

I walked slowly, scanning the darkness and the shadows. I had walked about a quarter mile when I noticed some slight motion in the shadows in the dune line. To my left, two hundred feet away, I saw her pushing back the sand with her flippers. A very large Loggerhead.

I called back to the beach-house. "Jess! Jess! Send the kids! I found a Loggerhead and she's laying her eggs right now!" I said in a heavy whisper, excited, and keeping my distance from the mature female sea turtle.

In the silhouette of the heated August moon I could see the dancing shapes of my children hurrying down the narrow beach as they drew closer. I met them near the water and explained that we needed to leave her in peace while she was laying her eggs or else we could frighten her and trigger her to abort, heading back to the safety of the ocean without successfully laying her eggs.

We watched her from a distance. She was magnificent. Three feet long. Two feet across and very thick. A shadow in the dunes just under dancing sea oat. Her dark form contrasted against the glow of the white sand under the arching moon. After about five minutes, and trying to quiet my kids, I walked them further down the beach as I thought we were still too close during her delicate window. Nathaniel grew bored and decided to run back to the rental and hang out with Mommy. Not Kayleigh. She wanted to absorb it all.

She and I walked the beach further. We checked other nests. Lightning continued to dance off of the clouds over the ocean. A rumble of thunder miles away. Humidity. Darkness. Beauty. A natural spectacle for a Daddy and his Daughter. A moment with my children. My Heaven.

After a few more minutes we looked back through the darkness and saw her lumbering down from dunes. We gently raced back to where the turtle was slowly walking and, while still keeping a distance, we drew nearer to her and took pictures with our turtle safe red light. We also took one video of her returning to the sea, disappearing into the waves. Kayleigh had finally seen a turtle laying eggs, a sea turtle lumbering on the beach and returning to the sea; something she dreamed about since she was a toddler.

*

High School Begins 09/2016

She adjusted well to the challenges of being in middle school, and was battle tested and ready for high school. She had spent the summer of fourteen retooling and enjoying her life, finding higher meaning in her voice. She kept her levity, her sense of humor, her brilliance, polishing her soul and shining bright. Really, every day challenges of life became her learning grounds and she learned quickly and well. We taught each other through those days. She taught me through my adult issues as well, as I tried to figure out next steps with career, where we might want to live, what schools were best fits for the kids, etc. Constant support, back and forth, we provided each other, the four of us. I returned frequently throughout the day to reaffirm my mission of raising empowered adults.

TEXT 08/19/2016:

Daddy: "You Kayleigh"

Push on the corners of life,
Strip the masks from your face,
Get out of the way and sing your life,
For there is light and love and laughter to embrace,
Fear no human vengeance,
For a human is just a human,
Stand and praise your fellows in their journey,
For there are many low faces you've yet befriended,
Ignite the dark corners of your life,
And be the light that was intended,
For you are magnificent,
For you are you."

TEXT 10/05/2016:

Daddy: "You are amazing and full of light. 🖤🖤🖤🖤"
    Kakes: "I love you 🖤🖤🖤🖤"
Daddy: "I love you more 🖤🖤🖤🖤🖤🖤🖤🖤"
    Kakes: "I love you
most 🖤🖤🖤🖤🖤🖤🖤🖤🖤🖤🖤🖤🖤"
Daddy: "I love you infinity most no
backs 🖤🖤🖤🖤🖤🖤🖤🖤🖤🖤🖤🖤🖤🖤🖤🖤🖤🖤🖤🖤"
    Kakes: "I love you infinity and
two 🖤🖤🖤🖤🖤🖤🖤🖤🖤🖤🖤🖤🖤🖤🖤🖤🖤🖤🖤🖤🖤🖤🖤🖤"
Daddy: "Damn! How do I beat that?!"

*

Rape 10/13/2016

Jess called. "Something happened. I'm on my way to pick her up. Her friend said she was raped."

I am a Dad. These words were never to be uttered to any Dad, to any Mom, really to anybody. As we parted that morning I said what I always said to her, "Love you, Baby. Have a safe, happy, healthy day."

It was now approximately 1:30 P.M. I was twenty minutes away. I called ahead and told them to meet me at the door – I was coming. Kayleigh was already home with Jess.

In the car I did what we in A.A. are supposed to do – instead of arming myself, or fomenting enough to permit myself to unleash violence on another, or prepping myself to blast another human being emotionally, I mobilized my tools. Alone, I turned to God and said, "Whomever you are who hurt my Daughter, I do not have time nor space for you in my soul. I forgive you scumbags. I am focusing one hundred percent of my energy and light solely on my Daughter and her well-being. She will need all of my attention."

Then I did a Tenth Step with my friend Carly, telling her in our first words when I called, to just listen and let me get this out, as I wanted to focus my way through it quickly so I could make good decisions in those first few moments of inferno.

I taught Kayleigh many things – how to forgive – how to fight back and defend herself - how to use one's voice – how she was only responsible for how she thought, spoke and acted, and was not responsible for how others speak, think and act – how there were two types of business, her business and none of her business - how to engage with life – how to empower - how fear and courage can co-exist - how to reach out when wounded – how to care for others when they fell. I would watch her, in the ensuing months, utilize all of these life skills many times over.

That first evening, however, we were all stunned. After the detectives left and Kayleigh had determined to prosecute, and then changed her mind fearfully, then screamed herself into prosecuting again, we sat with her on the front porch and listened to the wind. Just sitting. Breathing. I reflected on images of my time in the North of Ireland when I was young, years before the kids were born, during the war; places I had seen, things I knew about – the powerlessness of this situation, of not being able to protect Kayleigh, it was a breeding ground in my mind to stir up images of me doing unnatural things to these subhuman creatures. Then I would pray, knowing that hurting someone else did not help Kayleigh – knowing ultimately, I would never attack someone, only in my mind. I forgave them under my breath, only to find my own freedom. Cursing them. Flailing under my skin until I realized I was off in fantasy land again, which did nobody any good, and a place that did not support Kayleigh in the slightest. I had no real choice or other desire. I would come back. Again and again. To me. To Kayleigh. To Mommy. To Nate.

*

The Show Went On 10/14/2016

"Screw you, bastards," I whispered, feeling a guttural vindication in watching Kayleigh fight back. From the very beginning, Kayleigh owned them. They would have no sway over her life. Twenty seven hours after they violated my child, my child owned them. She was in charge of a critical function on opening night down at the theatre where she and Mommy were performing. She could hide in her closet, and nobody would have a right to tell her otherwise after what has just happened, or she could make some efforts, no matter how minimal under the circumstances, to live her life. A day after the event, if she hid in the closet, well, so be it. Instead, she dressed for the show. I fumbled. And recovered.

"But, Daddy, if I don't go, the show will be canceled. It's opening night."

"Babygirl, they can cancel," I said, "We do not expect you to go, Honey. We can cover for you and we can tell them they need to push the opening back. We can tell them you have the flu. But it's your decision."

"Daddy, I have to go. Everybody's counting on me. I can't let them down," she paused, "and besides, I can't let them win."

"Okay, Sweetheart," I said, barely capable of getting the words out, "okay. Tell us what you need. We can do this. If it's too much, you can leave the theatre. You can always leave and there's no shame in that."

"Okay, thank you, Daddy," She said and hugged me and ran upstairs to get her shoes. One day after an attack, traumatized, wounded, she was leaning into the next wave and daring to live her life. I turned and sobbed on the couch in solitude.

I stayed on that couch that night during the show, staring out the window, watching TV. Worrying about Kayleigh. I wondered how opening night of "The Fall of the House of Usher" was going. I was exhausted just thinking about how exhausted she must have been. I was in the theatre standing beside her, in any possible spiritual way I could muster.

After 11, and a few texts, the car pulled in the driveway. I met her at the door, having already talked to Jess briefly after the show to check in on them. Kayleigh entered the front door, smiled and collapsed in her Father's arms, and cried, "I did it, Daddy. I did it! Daddy, I am so tired!"

We sobbed together as I held her, balancing holding her but not too closely, suspecting that she needed her physical space. She melted into my arms, almost breathing within me for a few seconds, then raised herself and sat beside me in her own space.

"I bet you are tired, Babygirl. I am so proud of you. You amaze me."

"Thank you. I think I want to take a walk with Mommy if that's okay. And then I want to go to bed."

"Please, Kakes, go ahead. I'll see you when you get back."

My two beautiful blondes crossed through the threshold of the front door and disappeared into the night down the street, celebrating their triumph with a vengeance and crying from the weight of the pain each felt in their own stead. I turned to my phone and wrote this poem:

"You Can"

Like drums that echo through thick fields of cloud,
My heart pounds to its internal scream,
Washed in a sea of faces - I lost you in the crowd,
A crowd that collides, and congregates and beguiles and bleeds,
Leaving their dirty prints on you,
My little, little girl,
But I took you to this river,
And you swam in opal streams,
I made for you this river,
Banked with flowers and daydreams,
I slaved for you this river,
To survive you have only to believe –

That you can.

*

She Named Him "Spirit" 10/16/2016

Several days after this brutal rape, Kayleigh, shocked, traumatized, horrified and scared to be alone for more than a half hour, asked me very directly, more in a firm statement of demand, if we could get her a personal therapy dog; that Rosie, the family dog is wonderful, but she needed her own. He sits here at my feet while I write this piece. He, like her, is amazing.

We went that day to the downtown Animal Protective League to look for a dog for her, specifically as a therapy dog. Stepping through the building and scanning each of the cages, no dog matched the light in her eyes. We thought we might get lucky as this is where we found Rosie three years earlier, our lovely blue-tick beagle.

We searched for others and found the Parma Animal Clinic, who has several cages, and a small selection of dogs. One in particular seemed like the one and so we drove over to Parma. As we talked to the workers we could hear one incredibly obnoxious dog that sounded like a wounded hyena high on caffeine.

"My God, the other dogs must hate that dog," I said to her, as she smiled and agreed.

They took us back to the cages and we walked right passed Randy, a dog with a horrible name, which would, in twenty four hours, become the dog known as Spirit. He was jumping up and down, locking eyes with Kayleigh. "Oh, Daddy, can we look at this dog instead?"

I looked at him. God, he looked so much like a mangy street dog, so much so that I thought that other street dogs would seem like hamsters next to him. He didn't look mean as much as he looked experienced; experienced in being beaten, in running, in hiding, with a little shock in his eyes and a longing sadness for love in his desperate bark. "Uh, let's check the one we came here for first, and then if that one doesn't work out, we can look at this dog…this Randy."

She agreed. We saw that other dog. We arranged a meeting in the fenced in yard with that dog, who was nice enough, but was somebody else's soul-mate. After a few minutes of not connecting, Babygirl said to me, with those big blue eyes filled with light, "Daddy, ok, I met this dog. Now let's see Randy!"

I smiled and we asked the workers to switch out the dogs and bring him out. We waited a few minutes as I glanced occasionally at my baby, thinking to myself, what the hell just happened to my baby? Why are we here? Why are we buying a therapy dog? And also thought clearly: she was just raped. She clearly knows what she needs. It is my job to listen. I've always trusted her gut. This dog will help save her and keep her moving through the hard days ahead. Then I heard the gate open and saw this black and brown medium size dog, who looked like Dobbie from Harry Potter with broken angled ears, a big head like a horse, a skinny little butt and a swirly corkscrew tail – a broken mix between a Basenji and a Rottweiler. I thought to myself, uh…no.

She got down on her knees and opened her arms and, of course, he ran right to her and jumped into her lap and started kissing her face. Non-stop. "Oh, Daddy, this is him. This is my dog. This is my baby."

I knew. The sacrifices we make for our children. I didn't try to dissuade her or lead her to look at another. I knew he was the one. We made the arrangements and they placed him back in the cage in the kennel area with the other dogs. As we stepped away from him, he longed for her already and released the most horrendous rapid fire spattering of barking. My God! He was the hyena dog. Of course he was.

As we drove home with him the next day we concurred that his name was atrocious. Randy? She was very happy, laughing and speaking aloud through different names: Shadow; Night; Phil, whatever came to our minds. We laughed some more. Several days after a rape, even though she was deeply traumatized, she found laughter and hope in her new dog.

"Daddy, I love you so much. Thank you so much for doing this for me. He's going to help me reclaim my spirit," she said.

"That's a great name."

She lit up. "That is a great name." she looked down at him and said, "Your name is Spirit. Hi, Spirit. How are you Spirit?" and that was that.

He merged into this family of four and with his new pet siblings, a dog and three cats. He filled the house with magic. He slept on her bed every night, curled up against her while she cried, wept, laughed, loved, smiled, felt despair, shook and conquered her fear and trauma. He helped her reclaim her spirit in his constant unconditional love. Proving the soul within the dog, he clearly understood his mission and set out loyally to brave the waters before them together.

He protected the house with his terrible hyena barking, ironically teaching an already obnoxious beagle how to bark in an even more ridiculous manner typically associated with a beagle. These two trailed the four of us through the house and each night Kayleigh and Spirit retired to her room.

After the horrible accident, Spirit was immediately impacted, lost in the house after her physical death. However, he was very aware of her body of light and constant presence. We would watch him perk up, and clearly knew that she was holding him and talking to him and playing with him and comforting him. After the accident, he became further proof of her ongoing existence, proving that she was alive, as he indicated, like an early warning system, when she was especially active. He would run over to the couch and dive into the pillows, his tail in the air, his nose pushing at the air on the open seat. He would flip on his back and roll around, excited, and run off to her room. They continued, without a day's break. Each day since the accident they still play like this.

*

The Rape after the Rape

Social media – the curse and the channel. The mode of communication for many, particularly the younger generations. It opens the world up and props all upon a stage, sometimes anonymously, sometimes purposely vain. Within days I sensed the traffic online was harming her. I wanted to throw the phone away. Yet, it was her communication channel to those that were supporting her. Unfortunately, it was also a channel for disgusting, immature and sickened people to insult her and push her to the edge. "Whore." "Slut." "Liar." "It didn't happen." "You're making it up." "You brought this on you." These bullying posts started unconscionably.

She was desperate to respond to every single post – defending herself – telling her story, hitting back and blasting anybody that tried to blame or shame the victim. Some of the posts were from old friends – some current friends. It was a heinous crime atop a heinous crime.

She insisted I take no action against the cyber-bullying, and as a cyber-lawyer with many connections, I had already made my plans. She begged me to step back and let her handle the situation. As is the case with our relationship, we did a little of both. We opened a channel to her to make sure she wasn't consuming herself with these messages. We did not shut down her outlet to appropriate support. I did not exacerbate the situation by going after anybody.

Kayleigh never understood why anybody would ever be mean to another – particularly her, since she was genuinely nice and compassionate to all. To absorb this level of hurtful and directed violence, was therefore, beyond unnerving for her. In her fourteen year old brain and experience, she struggled not to look at the latest post, trying not to get sucked into the void. It was too tempting. Too surreal for her. She looked. She responded. She beat back the words. She gathered support from the crowd who likewise started supporting her in posts. She galvanized her voice and fought back, even though she didn't need to, I thought. She thought, however, that she needed to fight. And so she did. And she was right.

The verbal violence slowed to a trickle. Left were only the stupid, spineless and human-less morons whom she knew were worthless human beings. Clearly these types moved on to the next dramatic target and left Kayleigh alone. It frightened me to think these types of kids would parent and vote someday. Others knew the simple truth - that she had been approached by an old friend, whom she trusted. He, with several friends, entrapped her. She did what she was supposed to do – trust a friend; that friend, however, was never supposed to use that friendship to violate that trust, imprisoning her in a space from which she could not escape. Nothing in Kayleigh predisposed her for that moment. They were waiting for a target – any girl. It just happened to be Kayleigh who walked by. Pure horror.

I've done many 10th Steps to relieve my anger for these social media misfits. Kayleigh did her work as well and expressed her anger and frustration and confusion verbally, in writings, in her art. Nevertheless, if the opportunity really presented itself, she was the type of person who would want to convince herself of their humanity, no matter how far buried in their sickness, and would wish to extend a bridge to these cowards. It's just the way she is. She proved this time and time again. She is compassion. She is the bridge builder. She is love. Her Father through these days, well, I needed to write, for I wasn't Kayleigh and there was only a bridge of fire to be built by my hands to these people.

"Costly Meditation"

A day of costly meditation,
Digging through acrid, caustic webbing,
With its blood clots of emotion,
And the film of scabs beginning to generate a catacomb of healing,
In the delicate fabric that stings to the feeling,
The same delicate fabric that sticks to the ceiling,
And peels away only ever so purposely,
Through this meditation,
Both costly and alone.

*

She Shouldn't Have Had To Do This – But She Stood Up

Because she loves herself. She balanced the therapist, meetings with the prosecutors and detectives, being a warrior for women and just being a kid. She managed school, managed friends, managed sickened peers, managed running crew at the theatre and managed to shine brighter and brighter every day. Yes, she struggled from the effects of the assault; yet I watched her learn how to take that pain and start churning it into gold. She processed her feelings as they came up. I did as well. We worked ourselves into a cadence of therapy, family support and letting the steam out through journaling and expressing ourselves and then counter-balancing by laughing and playing and walking and goofing around.

She should never have been harmed. She should never have had to go through recovery from an event that never should have happened. Yet this is Kayleigh. She mobilized. In the midst of the chaos and the recovery emerged a young woman stronger than any I'd known, with the power of a thousand women wrapped up into one. Certain people, in many different venues and situations, under immense stress and pressure, show up and perform flawlessly. All that she had been learning, incorporating, gathering in life; all that she had become, with all of her coping skills and life lessons, all merged and came to bare at once to counteract the most frightful, callous, violating and difficult type of a challenge. She stood up. She empowered.

"My Little Girl"

The worry comes heavy,
Like loose grains in the veins,
Carrying shards of stone,
Picked up along the river banks-

The river it flows and it eats sod and shale,
Devouring landscapes down to the tiniest details,
Relief I beg of you -

The hunters they bay in the thickets like thieves,
Hungered and haggard with tricks up their sleeves,
Laying out bait with a cunning and precision,
Preying upon inexperience and indecision,
Awaiting, barbed spears, and in the rain -

The worry comes heavy,
As the swell of rapids enraged,
In this section of river,
Into which the excess waters of life drained -

But the river it flows - and pulled down into its folds,
Are the rag rock and sediment and plastics and bitter gold,
That swirl in the waters that nourish fertile fields,
My Little Girl - please, along the way, please let us know how you feel,
This, My Love, I beg of you.

*

Kayleigh's Voice of Courage

The origins of the "Voice of Courage" began in our basement where Kayleigh painted out her pain and recovery across canvas, tracking her initial suffering through her enlightenment. She spread her recovery out over canvas through these initial months of healing, a series of which she and I gathered together and called the "Voice of Courage" following the accident. Samples of her art work hang in our house, as well as a copy of the entire set at the Juvenile Court Prosecutor's Office, with explanations for each piece.

"The Voice of Courage #1 Thin Freedom Light"

Freedom from imprisonment;
A closet into which she was abducted,
And where she was raped;
She focused on that light – five feet from freedom.

~ The Courage to Speak ~

This piece is stark, powerless and ugly; an entire canvas of brushstrokes of black and slight strokes of purple and maroon, with a sliver of radiating white on the right hand side starting from a prick of light at the right side top of the canvas and widening as it stretches towards the bottom of the canvas, and then flows to the left towards the left side of the canvas across the bottom. A crack in a door that should never have been opened; a crack of light, her soul, in the darkest moment of her young life.

*

Father, I Am Above All 11/11/2016

So, there is a part of me. As it would rise I would process it through Step 10 and 11. I am far enough down this spiritual path to know, through experiences aplenty, how utterly useless harboring resentments can be – how deadly they are – taking poison and waiting for the other person to die. However, resentments would come at times through the process of the trial, and I would sift through them in my 10th Steps when they would arise.

They would arise. She would ask me, "Daddy, do you want to kill the boys who raped me? Cause I do!" or sometimes she would ask me, more in confusion and slightly confrontational, wondering why her Father wasn't being outwardly vicious, "Daddy, don't you want to kill these boys?"

I would smile and calculate my response. She wanted to hear her Father stand up for her, yet she wanted direction away from the raw emotion of statements such as this.

"I have lots of thoughts, Kakes," I told her, "my biggest concern is taking care of you and loving you. I stand up for you by being here with you. That takes up all of my soul. If I had any extra energy left over, then I'd want to kill them. But they're not worth death. They're not worth even thinking about. So if I ever have thoughts of revenge against anybody who hurt my baby, of which I have plenty, I process it out and turn back to what's really important. You. Me. Us. I love you, Babygirl. And besides, to resent them is to take that poison and wait for the other person to die."

She approved of the answer, knowing her truth. She really didn't want to kill anybody. She just didn't want them to have harmed her. She really didn't want me to attack anybody. She half-heartedly just wanted to hear me irately yelling at someone, threatening someone and causing a scene. Ultimately, she didn't even want that. It was her response from the trauma. Then again…part of her felt what she felt and she had every right to feel whatever it was that she felt. For me, I knew that if I gave myself any time with such fantasies, I would go down a dark road from which I might not return. So I did not, though at times, I felt the guttural anger that can twist a lover of life into a killer in the red rage of heat and justice. Thank God for Steps 10 and 11. I knew my place was with my family.

"A Sniper in a Derelict Building"

Like a sniper in a derelict building,
Whose slow, calm breath forgives the blood he's spilling,
I wait,
Awakened by a vengeance that leaves no stain,
That leaves no marks - and scorcher's pain,
That once has been awoken,
Finds that dark cancerous crack where the heart was broken,
And digs his prickly roots in the carcass of words unspoken,
Fueled by calculated slow, calm breaths,
Nurturing the weapon like a baby to his chest,
Secure in his derelict building,
With a tactical soul turned willing,
For who holds not revenge in the afterglow defiled,
For you thought not well before you hurt my child.

*

The Poem I Never Wrote 11/12/2016

This is the poem that I never wrote for it would be fitting and primary evidence that would lead to my arrest, should the ideation actually materialize into the material world, thumping a dozen bullets through your head and through your chest, and then another - because nobody touches my Daughter, and you touched my Daughter - I would cut you a thousand times and leave your useless body to rot in the desert, if I could - and I could - I really could. But alas, I could not, and therefore you shall live, for I forgive you and I forgive you because I am free and I chose my energy to be reserved for my incredible girl. When these fantasies emerge, they dissipate just as quickly. Supporting my baby with all of my energy is easy - it is who I am and it is what she and I are. If not, you would be dead.

"You Ask How I Feel - This Is How I Feel"

Open wounds - they crackle like burned and bloodied moths' wings,
Singed, charred, and brittle,

Seeping with gurgling flesh that compounds like popping bubbles from the steam,
Pooling and slowly expanding the arteries and the vein lines,
Where the angst and anxiety frolic in the folly,
And fervently cut new jagged paths through the big country of my soul.

*

"The Voice of Courage #2 A Maiden in the Storm"

Her initial isolation, confusion, shame,
Guilt, sadness;
Where fear and courage co-exist,
She was still standing amongst the storms.

~ The Courage to Stand ~

It was quiet; the silence chaotic and unbundled; a thousand electrical charges circulating the room at one time in any direction. As if she stood atop a rock above the water, the fog and smoky remains of the night lurking about her dampened feet; she stood firmly, a gaze in her eyes unbroken. She would not be broken.
Knowing her, the pause was a collection period – a time to lick her wounds – a time to take a breath prior to launching forward with her focus, her passion, her stubborn resistance to surrender to anything. Yet she needed energy to continue and she, though only fourteen, knew organically that she needed this energy that in her current state, she knew she didn't have. And where would she get this strength? Within. With God. And with family.

We cried. We too stood upon our own rocks. For me, a Father, an active Father, head over heels in love with his sweet child, my rock I stood upon was dulled and rounded, sloping towards the cold waters that pulled and hinted and taunted my feet to enter. Within those waters I would find resentment, hatred, retribution, retaliation; perhaps actions much more akin to total destruction of those who so callously and horrifically harmed my beautiful child. Luckily, I knew and felt and believed that all of these roads led me to depths from which I would not return. So I looked over towards my Daughter who stood on her jagged rock, space enough for only one person, and studied her stance. She would not fall in. She would not jump in. She would not be overcome. It was she who was raped. It was she who was so horribly wounded. Yet she would not be give in. Then neither would her Father.

"Throwing Up My Bones"

The edges are disintegrating,
As I throw up my bones,
Sickened by the marrow and this human experience,
That has leeched from me my light,
And licked away my shield,
I step close enough to rage,
And then I simply congeal,
The only way through this is through this,
For now I lay upon the floor,
Holding onto the stomach,
That purges my spirit's meal.

*

Resilience, Recovery

Resilience is defined as "the capacity to recover quickly from difficulties; toughness; the ability of a substance or object to spring back into shape; elasticity; strength." Added to this definition in the wake of her steady and brilliant recovery was Kayleigh herself. She set the standard for resistance and resilience; for empowerment and practical action; for standing firmly through the fear, the ultimate sign of courage – as courage is not the absence of fear, but having fear and walking through it. One of our little phrases was this – "the only way through this is through this" We could not go around it, under it or over it. It could not be avoided. It needed to be pierced and she punched right through the fabric to claim her rightful light.

I was there, physically, present, and present on my phone when we were not in the same room – her companion, her cheerleader, her Father.

TEXT 11/29/2016:

Daddy: "'Where You Find Peace"

Breathe the healing light of the world,
And be the healing light so that others may breathe,
Retreat not into the saturation where the ego displays its shiny
objects,
Do not wallow in the folly and the fabric it deceives,
Rather, it is for you to harness your passionate spirit,
And let the selfish habits, like captured water, drain from open
fingers,
To return to the flowing oceans of the mind,
Where, alas, against your eager wishes, you find peace."

*

"The Voice of Courage #3 the Transition from Victim to Survivor"

Sickened words thrown at her on social media,
Growing and bleeding into self-blame,
Until she turned her back on such messages;
Using her voice and her tears she chose to survive.

~ The Courage to Heal ~
~ The Courage to Prosecute Her Attackers ~

The truth is, with this one, she was never anybody's victim. She was a survivor immediately. And soon thereafter, an advocate. She would not give them that power. Nevertheless, as mentioned, I wanted to throw her phone away. I could not understand why anybody would ever write some of the horrible things that were written for her viewing. Not only was my child raped, but then raped again by her peers who, in their young and immature teenage minds, wrote horrible, senseless things, sometimes trying to be funny and sometimes just viciously. . As if a rapist mentality spread across a small population of youth, shockingly unaware that they were causing now their own assaults upon an innocent, wounded young girl. Each now have been forgiven by both Kayleigh and I because, once again, Kayleigh and I are free and will not permit anybody, particularly people like these, to have any rent free space in our souls. Yet the poison will always live with these people, whomever these people are, who thought it their domain to attempt to character slaughter my Daughter after she was assaulted.

Within a month, she beat back the nonsense and these posts disappeared. Prosecutions were coming. The youth in Cleveland Heights were put on notice that this heinous crime would not go unpunished. Kayleigh was becoming a legend.

"A Thousand Deaths"

Child, the song that sprained your hearing,
It spared no furrow in the fields of my soul,
The words that gained you sorrow,
Raised my angst into defender's role,
The thought that there may be no tomorrows -
Well, that thought crushed the spirit's skull -

As when you were a tiny baby,
In the pillowed, rugged, metal cage of these arms,
In which you felt God's warmth channeled in your Father's charm,
In which you sank in safety's depths,
Rest there, sweet baby,
And let us walk a while,
Until you regain your balance,
And again we see your smile,
For now my arms are heavy yet these arms are set,
For you - I would suffer,
A thousand, thousand deaths.

*

TEXT 12/06/2016:

Daddy: "you can survive anything and everything – you are your own jewel to be nurtured and polished. I love you because you are you. You are so special."
    Kakes: "thank you. I love you so much. Thank you so much for talking. I really needed that 💜"
Daddy: "Good. I am here always. I would climb a mountain and slay a dragon for you!! You did the work and you got the result. Great job. Take those little moments of proof that show you what loving yourself looks like. You will succeed - dare to dream. 💜"
    Kakes: "I really wanna succeed. I love myself, it's just so difficult but I'm glad you're here for me, that'll make it a lot easier for me just knowing you're here for me 💜"
Daddy" Thank you. Believe me I know how hard it is. I was filled with shame guilt remorse self-hatred and pain. It takes time like shifting the sand on a beach day after day until you make a new dune. The big dune in Jekyll overlooking the rock patio used to be about four feet high in 2000. Now there is a whole twenty foot tall and twenty foot deep dune."
    Kakes: "that's true. I'm sorry if I take my anger out on you sometimes. I'm really working on not doing that. It's just hard for me to admit I'm having trouble sometimes. I'm going to really try to talk more when I'm feeling bad about myself."
Daddy: "Thanks. It'll be helpful for you. I think you pick me since you feel safe letting your anger out with me and sometimes you just need to get it out. Let's both remember that. If I can remember that then I won't take it personally and actually help you get out your feelings. Sometimes it comes out sideways. As long as it's coming out that's good. I actually know when you take your anger out on me it's more about you having a hard moment. And sometimes I'm just a dick!"
    Kakes: "lol. We call can be dicks sometimes. I just want you to know I don't mean anything I say when I'm really mad and yelling. I'm so lucky to have you here, I wouldn't change anything because you're the best dad I could have ever asked for. Especially having been through similar situations. I'm so glad I can relate to

someone who understands and has survived all the bad things and can help me get through it. I love you."

Daddy: "The most mature honest things I've ever heard you say. You continue to amaze me. You really have such wisdom. Do you know what makes diamonds? Pressure. You are a strong beautiful diamond. Goodnight"

Kakes: "thank you. I really needed to hear that. I love you so much. Goodnight, sleep well 🖤 🖤 🖤*"*

Daddy: "Sleep well, Texas girl"

Kakes: "lol 🖤*"*

*

Christmas 2016 – Her Last in Physical Life 12/24/2016

TEXT 12/24/2016:

Kakes: "goodnight my wonderful father. I love you so much 🖤*"*

Daddy: "Goodnight my sweet wonderful daughter. You are amazing. I love you so much 🖤*"*

Kakes: "so are you. Ps I love you more 🖤*"*

Daddy: "pss: oh no you don't 🖤 🖤*"*

Kakes: "pssss I love you most. I'm going to bed. I'll see you tomorrow. 🖤 🖤*"*

Daddy: "Can't wait for tomorrow. Love you!"

Kakes: "Me too! Love you too!"

*

***"The Voice of Courage #4 Sunrise of the Tree of Life"* 01/02/2017**

The re-emergence of her spirit through grieving; healing, therapy, family, walks, art – and the reclamation of her sacred womanhood; the regrowth of the roots in her life.

~ The Courage of Self Love ~

This is one of my favorite pieces Kayleigh ever produced. The background is filled with golden yellows merging into blood oranges and deep reds. In the foreground is the Spirit of Woman, a beautiful black shape merging upward from her stance rooted in black clay, from out of the ground, and, as if liquid in her femininity, branches upward on the canvas into a strong tree that bends in the wind but does not break; with new sprouts of life, these tiny leaves that demonstrate the re-emergence of springtime in the beauty of life.

"The Sun Rises In Your Caribbean Blue Eyes, My Daughter"

As the light re-enraged and the shadows receded,
The hopes sparked afire in the badlands defeated,
We see the best of you -

As the flames re-engaged and danced on the embers,
The vision forward is to always remember,
The pains that nested you -

For here is the moment and no moment is better,
For you can stand strong in the most inclement weather,
We believe - we do -
We do believe in you -
We do -

With the rash of the sun birthed in your Caribbean skies,
Your soul burst through morning,
Erupted from your beautiful blue eyes,
I see the rest of you -

And the rest of you is brilliance,
Like the sun with golden wash that sparked the tides.

*

"The Voice of Courage #5 Peace" **01/15/2017**

Having used her voice against horrific violence, having honored herself in the cradle of grace, though the scars remained, and her journey of healing continued, peace, laughter and light grew about her, a forest of promise and self-love.

~ The Courage to Live Empowered ~

The forest of life, full of vibrant trees. Blues and whites, cloudy mist in the thickets, and strong green trees stretching out across the canvas. This was Kayleigh. She did not avoid the assault. She marched through it. It would remain a part of the forest for the rest of her life, but would not be the tree that defined the forest. For the ugly trees are not the forest itself, just a part of the background, a part of the whole. Yet the whole, in its completeness, is magnificent. In its magnificence, the ugly trees sink into the background of the background; into a sacred space; honored, yet not visible to the viewing of passersby.

"Sunset Washed in Thunder Heat"

Flowers cascade in the sky sea,
Wondrous silky petals,
Like rainbowed blankets cover flowing meadows,
Splash across the heavens above me,
With oil paints and the wispy gowns of saints,
The soft white clouds leave behind chalky sediment,
Piercing the brilliant blue hues that fill with thankful eyes,

- These scenes that fluttering spirits conjure in our dreams.

*

"We Only Have This Moment" 01/31/2017

As we range in the fields where tomorrow holds rainbows,
Or rains for its hosts,
As we strain to reveal where yesterday's hidden pain grows,
Or where the sun shines the most,
Lest we forget,
We only have this moment,
We only have this moment.

As we drift off into fantasy for in its colors we find comfort,
Or self-abusive tools,
We rage at the people who wounded us,
Or anticipate future fools,
And we forget,
We only have this moment,
We only have this moment.

Come back and investigate,
Come back and breathe the light,
Come back to the eternity,
In which these moments hold your life.

TEXT 01/31/2017:

Daddy: "Hi my baby. I feel your spirit and its beautiful and warming!! ♥♥♥♥"
 Kakes: "I love you so much! ♥ ♥"
Daddy: "You too! Don't ever question that. Not eva."
 Kakes: "not eva? Ohhhh eva like ever but eva – I get it"
Daddy: "git it."

*

TEXT 02/06/2017:

Daddy: "I have a daughter. A genius. A sweet soul. A passionate crusader. A human – with strengths and weaknesses and joys and

113

pains. But through it all I have a daughter – like no other – who can stand on her feet even when her feet hurt and offer such a warm, beautiful light to her family, friends and the world. You inspire me to reach for greatness. Thank you for being my teacher ♥♥"

Kakes: "awwww thank you. I love you so much! ♥♥♥♥"

*

Rise Again 02/10/2017

Let me take you where the soul aglow strikes the darkness like a beckon of light from which the shadows retreat. It was here in this early winter, just months after Kayleigh's assault. She had adjusted her footing in a new school. Made new friends. Reconciled old friends. Was engaged in counseling. Journaling. Creating emotive and important art. In the midst of a prosecution of her assailants, becoming the bell of the prosecutor's office, these men and women falling in love with this courageous young woman who refused to permit her voice to go unheard. Other children took notice of Kayleigh's example; several daring the take the stand and testify against molesters and rapists.

By this point, it was here that we clearly noticed that she broke through the grips of the initial tension created by the rape and the after effects of potential threats to silence her prosecution. Against even these threats, which frightened her deeply, she still stood her ground. To have soul-less street thugs post threats and speak retribution in the orbit of these young teenagers was both atrocious and the hallmark of cowards.

Fools. This is Kayleigh Mooney. We knew it would be only a matter of time before trial convicted them of their heinous crime, or they took a plea, frightened of facing her in court. No matter. Kayleigh has deeper work to do and she took solace in that work at 2989, daily engaging her life. Playing. Laughing. Crying. Shaking. Strengthening. Maturing. Healing. Becoming more beautiful than she had already been.

"To Rise Again"

The poison pocked the crystal lakes that pooled beneath the skin,
She swallowed a thousand tiny knives to slay her conscience,
And kill the blizzards of thoughts her mind kept trapped within -

Unveiled - it dragged its tongue of folly, ragged and webbed,
Across her brow where the sweat droplets moistened her head,
With purpose, intention and the dream of the dead -

Yet the next morning light raged alight in her eyes,
Just barely, just barely, and just hours alive,
Where the wounds festered and with thoughts that linger of the end,
She stepped forward - to rise again.

*

"Father's Blossom" *02/17/2017*

Swim in God's light,
Bathe in the crystal fountains,
With golden tides to hold you,
Embrace the fullness of the air,
It is there to craft and mold you,
In its brilliant atmosphere,
It is there to console you,
In the spirit that we share,
It is peace - and empowerment,
As your soul breathes - repair,
And be the completeness God intended,
After shedding human skins,
Swim in the light of eternity,
That blossoms on the wind.

TEXT 02/17/2017:

Daddy: "*I can't wait to get to Jekyll Island! And then* 👣 *– I want to walk on a beach with you. Although people are going to start thinking that I traded in my old bag of a wife for a new younger model!*"
          Kakes: "*Bah hah hah!!!!*"
Daddy: "*Don't tell her I called her an old bag please. I will be sleeping outside for a week!*"
          Kakes: "*I won't. Don't worry*"

*

"She Talks To Me" 02/21/2017

Water whisper - chasing bands of brilliant color in the ocean spray,
Raptures in collapse upon the beach in grand display,
The sea - she utters phrases in a spirit's dialect,
Often tonal enough for the ears to inspect,
If only we could shed the chains of our incessant humanity,
With its fragile crystal box of delicate sanity,
While the waves - in song and dance, crash into the conscience,
And breathe across our palms,
She talks to me,
In the rumble churned to silence,
As I walk her sandy face.

*

Nightmare Becomes Healing Time 02/23/2017

She came into our room and sat with me, having experienced a very scary dream about being abducted by aliens; a rather common nightmare, masking the powerlessness of an assault. After all, it was only four months away from that day – a day that was not an event, but an alteration of her life. After some time, a hug, a smile and sharing "I love you," she went back to her room and crawled back into bed. I heard her sigh a few minutes later and I couldn't help myself.

TEXT

Daddy: "I know sweetheart. I think it's a really strong chance it's you working out the trauma."
>   *Kayleigh: that's good. I want get passed it."*
Daddy: "When someone is raped it's a crime of power and being overpowered. What better way to be overpowered than by aliens who can do whatever they want to us. Scary right? So they represent not so much the people but the feeling of powerlessness and being overpowered against your will."
>   *Kayleigh: "ooooohhhh that actually makes a lot of sense."*
Daddy: "and your mind is so creative it can be a double edge sword. When you flitter off into fearful fantasy your colorful creative mind can make clear and vibrant images that are scary. Just like mine!"
Kayleigh: "yes, that definitely happens. LOL! I'm glad I had that realization. Thank you, that made me feel a lot better. I'm gonna try and get some sleep. Goodnight. I love you 🖤🖤🖤🖤*"*
Daddy: "Love you too. Sorry when I seem to get frustrated. I just want to help you so much and don't always know how. You are an amazing kid. God is always with you and so is my soul.   We walk together forever."
Kayleigh: "aww thank you!! I love you and God so much!! 🖤🖤🖤🖤🖤🖤🖤🖤🎸🎸🎸🎸🎸🎸🎸🎸*"*

*

Guys' Vacation – Girls' Vacation March, April 2017

The only time we ever did this, due to your school schedules. Nate and I went snorkeling in Key Largo. You and Mommy, a week later, went to New York City. I hated being in Florida without you, although it was such a great bonding vacation for the boys. Nathaniel and I are as close as you and I. the time with him was precious. Yet, you were not there. It would be no different if you and I got the chance to switch the kids like Mommy and I had planned someday – Daddy Daughter vacation and a Mommy Son vacation. We never did get that chance. If so, I would have missed him with the same passion as I missed you in Florida. We made sure we spent time together before he and I drove off to Key Largo. Once there, I sent you daily texts.

TEXT 03/17/2017:

> Kayleigh: *"I'm sorry I was selfish. I wish we could have done something fun. I feel bad. ☹ I love you."*
> Daddy: *"Thank you sweetheart. Have fun with mommy. 💜 💜 I love you."*
> Kayleigh: *"Can we do something fun tomorrow??"*
> Daddy: *"Yes. I'm not going to see you for ten days which is like forever to me!"*
> Kayleigh: *"I know! It's going to feel like so long. ☹"*

TEXT 03/19/2017:

> Kayleigh: *"👣👣👣👣👣👣"*
> Daddy: *"Just like God always walks with you……so do I."*
> Kayleigh: *"aww thank you daddy I love you!! 👣👣👣 💜 💜 💜 💜"*

TEXT 03/25/2017: (After I showed her a picture of a nurse shark we swam with)
> Kayleigh: *"oh wow that's amazing!! My day has been pretty boring but it was okay."*
> Daddy: *"Miss you. Wish you were here."*
> Kayleigh: *"me too daddy 💜 come home soon."*
> Daddy: *"I can't wait to see you back Sunday at 8pm 💜👣."*
> Kayleigh: *"I can't wait 💜👣"*
> Daddy: *"👣👣👣 💜 💜 💜 💜"*
> Kayleigh: *"👣👣👣 💜 💜 💜 💜"*

TEXT 03/27/2017

Daddy: *"Good! 4 days til li kiss my baby on her forehead. Isn't that shark cool?"*

118

Kayleigh: "awwww it'll fly by! And yes she's beautiful. I can't wait to see her!!
Daddy: "it would be a good beach for you with a friend for sure. So much to do."
Kayleigh: "I can't wait!!"
Daddy: "jet skis. Parasail. Kayak. Longboards. Snorkeling. Sunning. Crystal clear water!!!"
Kayleigh: "I'm glad you guys are having a good time I can't wait to join you!!! The water is so pretty!!"

*

Girls Trip to New York April, 2017

Your school vacation, lagging behind Nate's by several weeks, finally came. Your vacation to New York City was a dream come true. You two, with our friend Johnathan, played the ticket lotteries and ended up seeing Sunset Boulevard, Phantom of the Opera and your all-time favorite, Cats. Along with seeing Billy Joel in concert, restaurants out on the town, and living the New York life for a week, it was an experience you cherished, particularly spending it with one of your best friends, your Momma.

Nate and I continued doing our guy things and I turned frequently to writing, as I do. I counted the days that I was away from you physically, knowing that a full week was a long time. The week away in Florida was bad enough, but having to do it again so soon was doubly hard. I thought about what it would be like when you went to college and secretly, and not so secretly, began dropping hints that I wanted you to be with me forever. I recall saying, "you can't ever leave and have to go to Cleveland State or John Carroll and stay near your Daddy!" I was playing with her, of course, though there was a hint always of truth, wanting my babies with me. Ultimately, I knew the day would come that you would go to college away from Cleveland, move out to another city, and not see me as much and I wished only to help you along with that journey. As with everything else following August 17, 2017, those events I knew would happen, never did and never will.

119

At the time, though, certainly with no way to know that in four months my beautiful, happy, vibrant daughter would be physically killed in a perfect and horrible car accident, I stayed in the moment and wrote you poetry. You are, yourself, poetry. This piece is one of my favorites that I wrote to you while you were away in New York. Like other pieces, it has an eerie dual meaning following the accident. I meant to say in this piece that a long life was still relatively short in the larger life of a soul and therefore we needed to embrace life fully – that you were doing just that – that in a long life you would fill every second with vibrant illumination. I never intended it to sound like your life was short or would be "momentary," but that is what would happen four months after I wrote this.

"*One Moment of Poetry*" 04/12/2017

She flittered through the flack and flux,
She filtered through the haze and musk,
Dainty yet draining her roots in the firmament,
Grasping the soils in this spiritual permanence,
A momentary presence in the physical world,
A moment of poetry - this little girl.

*

An Active Shooter, NYC Subway 04/14/2017

I was sitting with Nate at Granite eating cheeseburgers. The girls were in New York vacationing and seeing plays. I recalled the time Jess and I lived in the city prior to kids and felt nostalgic for a moment, texting this sentiment with Kakes.

TEXT 04/14/2017

Daddy: "tell Mommy - let's move back to NYC I'm in a New York State of Mind"
Kayleigh: "something just happened"

I heard nothing for a few minutes. Then she continued.

Kayleigh: "everyone started screaming to run so we hid. I don't know what's happening."

I sat at Granite with a cheeseburger on my plate in Cleveland, hundreds of miles from my girls. A few minutes passed and she was not answering. Finally, in what seemed like a week, but only a few minutes, I finally got through to my girls. There were loud pops in the subway. Someone had screamed "shooter!" Everybody scattered. A few minutes later, people were now getting off of the floors and feeling like the danger was over, they told me. The police had tackled and arrested somebody. They were shaken.

I would later be told that the crowd in the subway heard a gun and they scrambled in a panic to get away. With a potential active shooter in the tight confines of the subway system at 42nd street, the crazed crowd carried Jess and Kayleigh off in the rush. They ran into a Victoria Secret, the closest store to them, and dove behind the counter. Several minutes later, after not hearing from her, she finally responded that apparently the danger was over. Very appropriately, she was panicky and overwhelmed with emotion, asking not only her Mommy, who was with her, for support, but also her Daddy, her safety.

TEXT 04/14/2017

Daddy: "Breath exercise. The event is over. Now it's just a hangover of adrenaline. You are safe. You are ok. In and out slow breaths with affirmation that you are ok."
 Kayleigh: "Ok"
Daddy: " 🐾God is with you always."
 Kayleigh: "I'll remember that 🤍thank you"
Daddy: " 🤍🐾love you!!!!!"
 Kayleigh: "love you too. I miss you 🤍🐾"
Daddy: "The Footprints Prayer – one night I had a dream...I dreamed I was walking along the beach with the Lord and Across the sky flashed scenes from my life. For each scene I noticed two sets of footprints in the sand; One belonged to

me, and the other to the Lord. When the last scene of my life flashed before us, I looked back at the footprints in the sand. I noticed that many times along the path of my life, There was only one set of footprints.

I also noticed that it happened at the very lowest and saddest times in my life. This really bothered me, and I questioned the Lord about it. "Lord, you said that once I decided to follow you, You would walk with me all the way; But I have noticed that during the most troublesome times in my life, There is only one set of footprints. I don't understand why in times when I needed you the most, you should leave me.

The Lord replied, "My precious, precious child. I love you, and I would never, never leave you during your times of trial and suffering. When you saw only one set of footprints, It was then that I carried you."

Kayleigh: "thank you. I'm going to read that now to calm down. I can't stop shaking and I can barely breathe."

Daddy: "🖤👣"

Kayleigh: "🖤👣 🖤👣"

In was later that night that I heard the full account in detail from Jessica, after she had stepped away from Kayleigh to talk. When Kayleigh heard the gunfire, she immediately and instinctively starting pushing Jessica in the crowd out of the hallway and into the store. She aimed Jessica towards the counters in the stores and tackled Jessica to the floor behind the counter and threw herself over her mother and pinned her down, protecting her mother, and exposing herself to a potential crazed gunman. Jess said that she was shocked and thought, no, no, this isn't right - I need to be sheltering my Daughter, and began wrestling with Kayleigh to try to change positions and push Kayleigh underneath Jess. Jess managed to shelter Kayleigh and held her down until they knew they were safe.

In an instant, with no time to think, Kayleigh Mickayla Mooney sacrificed herself for her Mother. That is who my Daughter is.

*

TEXT 04/15/2017

Kayleigh: *"aww I can't wait to see you. Only a few more days!"*
Daddy: *"I know I can't wait. I've never been away from you this long with both vacations and I DO NOT LIKE IT!!!!"*
Kayleigh: *"I miss you so much!! Let's watch a shark movie when I get back!! Just like old times!!"*
Daddy: *"Yes! I found an absolutely horrible movie called "Sand Sharks." Can't wait to watch with you."*
Kayleigh: *"Me too!!!! I love horrible movies haha!!!!"*
Daddy: *"Me too."*

*

Cats 04/17/2017

I took her to "Cats" at the State Theatre in downtown Cleveland when she was four. She was dressed up as Grizabella and so cute. The crowd fawned all over her as I carried her through the crowd, holding her extra high on my chest so that her head was as high in the crowd as mine. At intermission I almost put her on the stage, where Deuteronomy was sitting staring out to the crowd. I was afraid she would have run over and jumped on his lap, or started acting out the scenes. Ten years later, Jessica and Kayleigh played the theatre lottery and won front row tickets each day to various shows, five days in a row, and she was now seeing "Cats" again - this time on a New York stage. She was so excited. And then she had the surprise of a lifetime.

TEXT 04/17/2017

Kayleigh: *" 🐾🐾🐾 Guess who I met???!!??! You...oops not you haha!!! You're going to freak out when you see this!!!!! get ready!!!!!"*

Then she sent me a picture. And I burst out into a high pitched laugh, full of excitement. There she was, sitting on Deuteronomy's lap, on a New York stage, with the most awe struck expression I'd ever seen on her beautiful face. She had met her bliss. She was in "Cats," just as she had always dreamed in her childhood fantasies.

*

Threads of Spring 2017

It is thread in the fabric of our existence. It is promised in the contract of life, as we march on, sunrise to sunrise, infallible and pliable, intellectual, emotive and utterly human. And it shall come. This new disturbance that tests the will of men and women. When it is, and what it is, we shall only know when it presents itself; and at that juncture, upon its presentation, and the jostling of our attention, when we pull back the veil and peer through that window of time, we shall raise our eyes and our hearts to its challenge; but only if centered through daily preparation, moment to moment, shall we be ready to adjust and adapt and drive home the change required to address the newly developed situation - walking through all of its unknown hindrances and all of its slightly hidden yet abundant promise - and into a new morning we could not possibly dream on in the current landscape of today. When it comes - the only way through - is through. We will then harness the wind and breathe light into our palms.

She and I made a wind chime when she was nine. It broke when she was twelve. It stayed there in a box on the front porch. Then, after the move, in a box in the garage of the new house. Then I fixed it. It hangs in our yard. I sent a picture of it while she was out with her friends in May of 2017 with this note:

TEXT 05/11/2017

Daddy: "When I hear these wind chimes I hear your magical soul. ❦"

    Kayleigh: "aww you fixed it!!!! ❦"
Daddy: "For you."
    Kayleigh: "I love you."

*

TEXT 05/12/2017

Daddy: "IF YOU WANT TO SEE GOD'S STRENGTH IN THIS WORLD – LOOK INTO THE EYES STARING BACK TO YOU IN THE MIRROR. ❦"
    Kayleigh: "AWW THANKS DADDY I LOVE YOU ❦"
Daddy: "you're welcome sweetie. Be gentle with yourself. You are so, so special."
    Kayleigh: "I will ❤ have a great day."
Daddy: "you too. Can't wait to see you and spend time with you. Kayak tomorrow morning?"
    Kayleigh: "maybe. I don't know. But we will definitely do something."

*

My Baby's Fifteenth Birthday 05/15/2017

Sweet sixteen was just a year away. Yet this was her Golden Birthday – the year she would turn the age of the day that she was born – fifteen on May 15th. She knew its significance in our family, but had no idea that we were planning to throw her off and plan a surprise for fifteen rather than sixteen. We always told her we would have a huge blow out for her sweet sixteen. The fact that we changed it up was a perfect set up for a surprise.

We organized some of her friends and Jess took her shopping. While away, Nate, her friends and I worked at a frenzied pace to set up the backyard with balloons, sodas, food, snacks, presents, ribbons and chairs. The plan entailed Jess walking Kakes through the house with us hiding in the backyard, stepping outside and being floored with a surprise. I received the text that they were pulling down the street and everyone took their positions.

As Jess led Kayleigh out of the back door, and pushed her onto the steps, she was hit with a barrage of silly string and a loud screaming volley of "Happy Birthday!" from all who surrounded her.

"I'm so confused! What's happening! What's happening?" she asked over and over, a gigantic, beautiful smile across her face.

"Happy Birthday!" her friends shouted again.

"Wait, what? Thank you!" she said, mouth agape, eyes wide open and shoulders rocking from laughter, covered from head to toe in silly string, hanging from her Roman nose, glossed across the top of her hair like a pink and purple web, and captured in her hands as she tried to prevent it from hitting her face. It was hilarious.

"Oh my God!" she screamed, laughing.

We had a memorable day; placing a ladder on the garage and the girls and Nathaniel climbing up on the roof - I can still see the indentations of the ladder on the soft edges of the garage – a timeless marker on the property of a lovely day where my Daughter celebrated her birthday with close friends, her beloved brother and her parents. They braided her hair; placed a princess crown on her head; fawned all over her. Her Father used trick candles, eliciting a boisterous response from her. During the attempts at blowing out her cake, I snapped a few iconic shots of her, one of which captured her magnetic beauty, both external physical prettiness as well as her immense depth of pure gorgeous spiritual illumination. I used this picture three months later at her funeral, blowing it up into a poster and placing it on the altar. It also adorned the prayer funeral card.

This remains one of my favorite days of my life. I wrote the following related to her magical Golden Birthday.

"A Golden Day for You"

Sprinkling liquid crystals sparkle in points of rainbow light,
That rattle on the canopy with symphonic notes of life,
Catching in the long shafts that form rivers down green stems,
To birth the next generation of radiant precious gems,
As the silent sun blazes in the summer morning sky,
With hues of deep blues as high as they are wide,
Welcoming me as the slumber rains flurry off to the distance,
And the quiet warmth breaks down all resistance,
Ushering in a golden day.

*

TEXT 05/16/2017:

Daddy: "I was just thinking of my life and what was important. One thing that you do very well is to know your truth. Your truth is not negative or gross. Your truth is your light untarnished by anything."
    Kakes: "I love you"
Daddy: "I love you too, Honey. I once knew a man I hated and was disgusted by. That man I love like gold today because I gave him the respect he deserved and he learned how to love himself and take care of himself and now he is almost 30 years sober."
    Kakes: "awwww that's sweet"

*

127

Everyday Life 05/22/2017

TEXT: 05/22/2017

Daddy: "remember you are pure light. Inside, beneath the fear, beneath sadness and painful experiences, you are light. Pure beautiful light."

> *Kayleigh: "thank you. I love you, I'm sorry I was all mad today. You didn't deserve all the stuff I said."*

Daddy: "I know. You get overwhelmed and scared sometimes. I don't even take it personally. I know I help you get your emotion out."

> *Kayleigh: "yes, thank you. I love you so much. Goodnight daddy, sleep well, I hope you dream of rainbows and unicorns. ❤️"*

Daddy: "you too my love ❤️"

*

TEXT: 05/29/2017

Daddy: "you are the best daughter I could have ever have dreamed of"

> *Kayleigh: "aww why'd I just get this! I love you so much! ❤️"*

Daddy: "you did such a mature great job with your card to grandpa. Remember – true happiness comes from loving yourself enough to be of service to others. You really did such a great job of that today. So proud of you and how you are making great choices in life. Please keep moving. ❤️"

> *Kayleigh: "thank you so much, I will keep moving and I'll never stop. I love you so much and that really, really means a lot to me, thank you ❤️❤️❤️❤️🎶🎶🎶🎶"*

*

Kakie's Cheerleader – Finals at Beaumont 06/07/2017

TEXT 06/07/2017:

Daddy: "Yeah Kake! Go get em!! You're going to be great today!
⚘⚘"
*   Kakes: "thank you!! I hope I do okay!! ⚘⚘⚘⚘⚘⚘"*
Daddy: "me too. No matter what I love you and God has you!
⚘⚘⚘⚘⚘⚘⚘⚘. There's an old A.A. saying: "plan the plans. The
results will managed themselves." Just means prepare and then
relax."
*   Kakes: "I like that a lot!! I just finished my math test"*
Daddy: "Awesome. Sounds like you kicked ass."

{later in the day…}

Daddy: "which test do you think you didn't do good on?"
*   Kakes: "theology."*
Daddy: "its ok. Take a deep breath. Nothing you can do about it right
now. Need to focus on the next test. So junk it out of your head and
regroup for the next test. Love you. You can do this. ⚘⚘⚘⚘"
*   Kakes: "thanks. I love you too ⚘⚘⚘"*
Daddy: "I'm your biggest cheerleader. Do the best you can do and
we will all be ok with the results. Breathe sweetheart."
*   Kakes: "thank you so much. I love you!"*
Daddy: "you too baby. Hang in there. You're ok"

*

You Need to Rest Some Times 06/14/2017

I spent my life after work playing with the kids in the yard or in the
house or traveling up and down the street or taking adventures or
sometimes just sitting on the front porch with them. On this particular
night I was having Daddy Daughter time; just the two of us; laughing,
talking about our lives and our dreams. I was in a period of touch up
painting both the internally and externally needed areas. I was hitting

different sections after spending time with my kids and wife, after a day at work.

She could tell I was physically tired, even though my spirits were as balanced and high as normal. She was addressing me with direction and love, touched by and grateful for my ability to pack so much into our lives, but worried that packing that much in was taxing my resources. She would never trade in her time with me, but wanted me to pull back on other activities.

"Daddy you work so hard for us at a really intense job and then you come home and paint rooms and make gardens. And always find time to spend with each of us every day. Literally every day. Sometimes you need to slow down and just sit. I'm worried about you. You need to rest sometimes."

"Thank you, Sweetheart," I replied, more proud of her for her insight, but still touched so tenderly by her concern. She was watching; taking note; seeing what a husband and father should be; charting out her own tasks, which included resting. She knew I meditated every day, which was a form of rest, but wished for more rest for her Father.

"I mean it," she said and got up to go get something to drink inside, "you need to rest sometimes."

*

Renaissance Summer 06/18/2017

It continued, this renaissance of light. I was walking in the shadow of a brilliant girl. My daughter's courage and strength continued to stretch over the mesh fabric of her healing wounds. She was in the midst of a Renaissance, something I would talk to my A.A. guys about – taking that next step in a Renaissance of our lives. My Daughter was standing at the doorway of the next great chapter of her life, having empowered herself to this point. I sent this to her to capture that idea:

"Renaissance 2017"

Fold back the edges,
Unpeeled and prone,
Rip up the flooring,
Where the walls are sown,
Unhinge the staging,
From soil these stones,
For the weather it radiates,
Inside your soul -

Change the lenses,
Change the flow,
Plough the fields,
Release its gold,
Where seedlings spring,
In flourished blooms,
And spirit sings,
Like cardinals swoon -

Pull back the curtains,
And be exposed,
Unfurl these blankets,
Emotionally clothed,
And know this,
What you already know -
Tomorrow awaits you,
And wakes for your soul.

*

Most Proud of My Sobriety 06/21/2017

I caught her many times in the corner of my eye, the way she looked
at me; happy, humble, grateful – in love. Sometimes with a sense of
awe and sometimes, quite frankly, with a grin of frustration. Mostly
fluttering – like butterflies in her heart and butterflies in her eyes for
her Father, the man she loves the most in this world.

There were the superficial things – she was proud that her Daddy was a lawyer and worked at one of the world's premier healthcare systems; that we had a middle class, nice home; we had two nice Hondas; she always had nice clothes and we took two vacations each year in March and August, all a result of the hard work of her Mother and Father. For Kayleigh, these were impressive things, but things. That type of glory was a passing cloud. The true glory lay in the light between our eyes and hearts. That glory, for me, begins with my sobriety; for everything in my life begins with my sobriety and everything ends without it. She knew this credo. She lived in its brilliant rays of life.

Kayleigh, not only understood that, she cherished it and still does through this day and into tomorrow. It is the true gift, besides Nate and Kakes and Jess, of my life and it was sacred. To all of us. To Kakes.

She would tell me she was proud of my sobriety. She would ask me about my drinking days, the events, the feelings, the horror, how I survived, how blessed my days became after I was given the gift of sobriety. She would remind me that she saved me in my early, fumbling sobriety, coming to me when I was six months sober at Christmas time, 1987. She knew that her life could be very different, had her Father not been or not stayed sober; instead destroying the family in vicious alcoholism. She knew she was sacred to me; Nate was sacred to me; Jess was sacred to me; that I was sacred to me. She held me in reverence, not just because she believes I am the world's greatest Daddy, but also in the gratitude she feels in the passion of my sobriety.

TEXT 06/21/2017:

> Kakes: "goodnight I love you and I'm sorry I wasn't in the mood to talk. I was a little sad."

Daddy: "super powerful daughter. Your strength in permitting yourself to cry is an inspiration. Keep inspiring me. 👣"

> Kakes: "thank you. But you're the inspiration here!! 💜💜"

Daddy: "Haha. I'd be glad to be half as strong as you."

Kakes: "you've been sober for how long?? Almost 30 years!!! You're the inspiration here and I love you. Thanks for being here for me ♥"

*

One 06/24/2017

By far one of my favorite videos I possess is one I made a week before the July 2017 U2 concert while we were out driving around. I was sitting in the back seat behind Jess. To get us ready for the upcoming show, I played "One" and clicked on my phone to record it as I started singing it. I called out, "sing it family!"

I panned first over to Nate in the backseat behind Kayleigh in the passenger seat. He played with his hair to the camera and sang along to the beat. Then I panned to Kakes and she looked back at me over her left shoulder and began dancing to the music and smiling at me with that infectious grin. Then I panned over to Jess in the driver seat texting away on her phone while we sat at a red light. She glanced at me and back down to her phone. Then I filmed me singing loudly through the first stanza of the song, "We carry each other, carry each other..."

That's it. Simple. Effortless. We are One. No matter what we face; no matter our physical or spiritual state, we get to carry each other, carry each other...

*

30 Years Sober 06/28/2017

Thirty years sober. A lot of work went into that, daily. Happily sober. Happily married. Happy children who love their parents. For me, knowing that my priorities had positioned my children for success, that success being love and family above all, I had done my job well

133

to date. With a centered and empowered family, a successful career as a lawyer and operational leader, with a bright future ahead of me, my feet firmly below me, I celebrated my thirtieth anniversary sober with my family and my home group, the oldest continuous meeting in Alcoholics Anonymous. I led that night, my wife and children sitting in the audience. The kids had never heard me lead before. It was a special moment for me.

These innocent passengers in this boat, my children, my wife, they were here with me witnessing the greatness of heart that comes with properly working and living the 12 Steps. In particular my kids, as a result of the Steps, I am a great Father. As a result of being a great Father, my children are superstars. And so it is, as it was that night, looking out from the podium at my three loves sitting in the audience that night, the primary beneficiaries of the work that I had done to date, and the work I promised to do until my physical death, my sobriety is theirs; it is not mine and never has been. I have no right to throw it away. No right to harm it. No right to risk it. It is their gift. Theirs.

Yet before my sobriety, in the grips of pain, in the springtime of 1987, I heard for the first time, "Where the Streets Have No Name" from the then new "Joshua Tree" U2 album and it was a nail in my coffin. This song always reminded me of how I felt in that final desolation of full blown late stage alcoholism with Bono's lines, *"...We're beaten and blown by the wind, trampled into dust, I'll show you a place, high on the desert plain, where the streets have no name..."*

*

"What A Summer Night" 07/03/2017

U2. July 3, 2017. Thirty years in the making for me. It was a hot, sultry summer Cleveland night. As the opening band, One Republic, finished their songs, and the sun finally banked off behind Cleveland Browns Stadium, Kayleigh, Nathaniel, my sister Tricia and I settled into our space awaiting U2.

U2 brought the "Joshua Tree" concert through Cleveland in late summer, 1987. I was just months sober. I had tickets to the concert, this being one of my favorite bands. I did not think I would stay sober though, and begrudgingly, passed on going to the concert. It was many a good decision in my early sobriety safeguarding my fledgling life. Then time and life took over and, to my chagrin and amazement, I never got back to another U2 concert, as much as their impact remained present in my life. That held true for thirty years until this night, as Bono said as they left the stage that night, "what a summer night!" My 30 years sober anniversary gift – U2 with my children, accompanied by my sister.

They started with "Sunday Bloody Sunday" and ripped into the early set as the crowd in Browns stadium went into a frenzy. With Nathaniel to my right, Kayleigh to my left and U2 off in front of us, I embraced the moment. I sang with my babies through the entire show, holding them often and dancing with them, crazy, loud and freely flowing with the music, particularly the songs that had a deeper meaning for me and my kids, "Where the Streets Have No Name," "Bad," "Pride," "Beautiful Day," "Elevation," on and on. It was one of those nights where I stayed completely in the moment, and as they passed, I let them go, residing in the present second by second as the night became a more magical spectacle as the show progressed. I cried through certain songs, thinking back on the beginning of my journey in sobriety and how far I had come.

Then they played "One" to close the show. I grabbed them both, my arms around their wastes; Kayleigh on my left side and Nate on my right, swaying with their Daddy, smiles draped across their faces. I screamed the lyrics along with Bono. The kids did as well. This was one of the songs I interpreted into our lives – that I promised them I would never become part of the emotional difficult part of the song, and I would always strive to be the positive side of the lyrics – that we would love each other always and carry each other, carry each other…

That night of my life was, at the time, and even now, one of my favorite nights of all – mostly because of my two loves and the ability to share something so amazing with them. That night shall remain a beautiful night, as amplified after the accident, for eternity.

*

We Are the Ones We've Been Waiting For 07/05/2017

I came across a wonderful expression of life and wisdom in a writing by a Hopi elder. It was referenced in a video someone had posted on YouTube in a song by Mark Burgess, known mostly from his time with the Chameleons UK, another one of my favorite bands. The song is "Happy New Life," and the video displayed parts of the Hopi statement throughout. It touched me deeply and I knew immediately that this was intended for my oldest child.

To let her know that she was strength, courage and light, I found the full statement and posted it on her door to her bedroom, after highlighting the sections below in yellow. I told her I was so proud of her and that, above all girls I have ever known, I had never met a girl like her. She was raw courage and delightful gentleness, even when portraying an edgy side, designed to hold her own while protecting that intimate innocence she honored so deeply within. She is magic. She always has been.

With the convictions of those who harmed her already in the books, and nearing the sentencing hearings, I wanted her to know that this was her time. Her hour. Her time to shine, mostly for herself, and secondly, if possible, but not required, for others. She was the leader among her friends. She was the young woman who challenged the odds and the horror stacked upon her by a rape. She used someone else's insanity to become more beautiful and much stronger. She was the one the world had been waiting for.

I am her Daddy. I am her cheerleader. I am her witness. I am her support. And I taped this to her bedroom door. I watched her read it. I watched that smile overtake her silky, sky blue eyes and the corner of her lips rise, knowing that her Father adored her, believed in her, stood with her, and had such faith in her. My little girl – you are the one. You are the one we've all been waiting for.

"WE ARE THE ONES WE'VE BEEN WAITING FOR –*BY HOPI ELDERS (WITH PERMISSION)*

...YOU HAVE BEEN TELLING THE PEOPLE THAT THIS IS THE ELEVENTH HOUR,
NOW YOU MUST GO BACK AND TELL THE PEOPLE THAT THIS IS THE HOUR...
...AND DO NOT LOOK OUTSIDE YOURSELF FOR YOUR LEADER...
...KNOW THE RIVER HAS ITS DESTINATION
...ALL THAT WE DO NOW MUST BE DONE IN A SACRED MANNER AND IN CELEBRATION.
WE ARE THE ONES WE'VE BEEN WAITING FOR."

*

TEXT: 07/20/2017

Daddy: "pull back the curtains, and be exposed, unfurl these blankets, emotionally clothed, and know this, what you already know – tomorrow awaits you, and wakes for your soul."
        Kayleigh: "I love that!! Did you just write it?"
Daddy: "for you 🖤❦*"*

*

Daddy-Daughter Time 07/26/2017

During that last week of work before our trip to Jekyll Island I went through all of the things I would be doing with both of my children. I could not wait. Walking the beach. Swimming. Horseback riding. Searching for sea turtles. Scanning the midnight beach for boiling turtle nests. Dessert at the Jekyll Island deli – Dove Bars. Finding gators at night on the golf course. Shark fishing. Summer Waves water park. Kayleigh driving us all over the island every day (even

137

though she had just turned fifteen – I started her driving lessons at thirteen – nobody tell the authorities!).

There would be Daddy Son time. Daddy Mommy time. Daddy Daughter time. For Nate and Jess, I have other stories in my heart. For the pages of this book, I could not wait for my Daddy Daughter time. She is my favorite girl in any world and to get away from work for two weeks to hang out with my three loves without anybody bothering us was priceless. I wrote this for her days before our trip and sent it to her while she lay in her room talking to her friends.

"Dad and Daughter Footprints"

Beneath blue sky, the sea it sighs,
Cresting purpose - birds of prey,
Above - touch clouds, swoop and glide,
Dignified, and colors catch in the salted foam webbing of waves,
Crystal ice - it melts to the heat of summer day -

We were walking - walking there, there in the light,
We dared the footsteps that tracked through soft white sands,
From morning until night,
The glow it captured us - consuming our words,
And gracing us with a silence that nothing can disturb,
Deep within our hearts,
Where our love is loyal,
It is faithful,
It is graceful,
It is undeterred.

*

Gladiola Garden II 07/28/2017

She survived a rape. Not only did she survive, she thrived. She used the experience to teach and help others, at fourteen and fifteen. She was the most beautiful girl and used the horror of a rape to make herself even more beautiful. Who does that? Kayleigh Mickayla Mooney – that is who.

I watched her mobilize her resources and attack therapy; work with detectives and the prosecutor office; write poetry with me; do art with me and Mommy; play with her brother; take walks with Mommy and sit with me on the couch crying and then catching her breath, breathing deeply and turning her grinning despair into a smile and the compact jewel of a diamond in her eyes. She took the pressure of what she had experienced and made diamonds of her life.

Her peers knew this. The youth that followed her on social media knew this. She was a legend for those who were watching. I do not disparage any woman who has not stepped forward. I speak only facts. Very few women, as we know, factually step forward after an assault, and when they do, it is typically years later. It took Kayleigh thirty seconds to reach out for help and start the grueling process of healing, seeing it through every stage of the criminal justice system.

She had done an amazing job of handling the initial acuteness of the trauma and rapidly regained her footing. She broke free of any lurking situational depression, fear, anxiety, self-blame and defeat. She would not be defeated and therefore stepped forward; fought forward; fell forward and picked herself up again and again in those first few months. She changed the self-blame into knowing she did nothing wrong – that she actually did something right, trusting a friend; that the boy who harmed her had no right to violate her trust and set up the assault. She held them accountable. She used her voice.

In a very short period of time she broke out further from the clutches of the event – an event that in her rearview mirror would always be a part of her, but an event, and the people who perpetrated it, would not define her and would not intimidate her into failing to use her voice. She stood taller than any girl I had ever known. My Daughter, this wondrous soul, this spectacular example of powerful self-love and brilliant strength, stood taller than any other girl, any of her peers, and in fact, in my eyes, any other woman who every walked the treacherous boundaries of this earth. She was a flower and the tallest of the most beautiful flowers in the garden. I conveyed this to her and wrote this to her late one night on the eve of our trip to Jekyll Island,

139

the trip that would prove to be our last with all four of us in our physical state.

*

Jekyll Island 07/29/2017

We arrived. Peace. Letting go of the last portion of the year. Relaxation. A brilliant family of four, isolated in perfect communion from the daily activity and grind of our typical days. For me, with the sentencing hearings coming, with an interview looming and the possibility of moving the family to Jacksonville, I had much on my mind. I took to the beach immediately upon arrival. Jess, Kakes and Nate would join me as they wished, coming and going from the house; sitting on the rocks; going for walks; running through the beach house.

This was my favorite vacation. By far. We had all been strengthened by the empowerment of the last year in the way we banded together, healed and walked through our own fears with the courage to use our voices. All four of us were impacted in our own way and each was provided a sacred cradle in which to process and heal. We were higher in our amplification of life; stronger in our resolve; battle tested and prepared to take on the world. Upon our return, Kayleigh would master tenth grade; Nate would start a new school; Jess and I would deliver the news that we were moving and pack up the house and move, or else stay in Cleveland and continue to flourish and guide our babies towards their adult lives. We let it all hang out and embraced every moment. I sat in my lounge chair in the tide, the waves crashing against my legs in the surf.

"A Soul Is Searching..."

With heart cords - vibrate in rejuvenation,
He burned morning breath on pyres of elation,
Gazing out to waxing, rolling morning sea,
With its glitter waves of purity dying out just under the reach of his feet,

Bleeding days of stress gone by,
Bleeding tears from his feet that fed the salty tides,
Walking the beach he yearns a man's reclamation,
From the fleeting power of the sea - comes a soul's rejuvenation.

*

A Red Flag Day 07/30/2017

I was told not to go in the ocean surf under any circumstances. The day before we left for Jekyll I spent the afternoon with the dentist, digging into a thirty year old root canal that had gotten infected. They sutured the inside of my mouth below my lower teeth and I had wire sutures stretching and bleeding across the front of the inside flesh. I asked. "Under no circumstances, Kevin," he said, "do not risk it."

On day two at Jekyll we had epic waves. I sat on the beach hearing my doctor's voice wobble around looking for a landing. I watched Jess, who is no swimmer, go into the ocean to attempt the waves. Then my Babygirl, who had not tempted the surf for four years, jumped up and said, screw it, and screamed into the surf. I was a good patient for almost fifteen minutes. Jess came back out of the water as I passed her and ran into the surf. For the next several hours, Kayleigh and I battled with the waves, body surfed and had an amazing time. Nate had stayed back at the house playing a video game.

It was a Red Flag day. Yet we were in the ocean. Significantly for Kayleigh, she was in the ocean. When she was eleven, I coaxed her into the surf with me on a day with rolling waves, against her fear of sharks in the brownish, Jekyll tide. Convincing her that I had her and she'd be safe, we stepped out into the surf. Within a minute a five foot Black-tip shark popped up in the wave in front of us, approximately ten feet away. We screamed and ran, laughing, and not laughing, together back towards the beach about ten feet quickly and watched it swim off towards others in the surf. That was the last day in the Jekyll surf for Kayleigh at the age of eleven. Until this day at fifteen.

We have amazing video of this moment as Jess sat on her towel and captured me and my girl playing in the waves. I have a few photos as well that Jess took that day that I taped into my A.A. Big Book showing Kayleigh and I in this high surf, with a caption that reads, "Leaning into the next wave together." I was not going to miss out on spending time with one of my children, and despite the warnings of my doctor, I went in. I always went in. I always will, Red Flag or not.

"Songs of a Beach Wind"

A wind caught dancing in the bending shafts,
Sea oats rooted in sand and crab grass,
Like silky petals abloom and pastel scented,
Flowing like faint rainbows - calm, iridescent,
Through a heavy air amidst a thunder heat,
We hear its chorus and harmonics of peace,
That passes from the ears and the eyes towards the soul,
And vanquishes stress once immersed in its fold.

*

Kayleigh Asked Me About Drinking 08/01/2017

She knew my background, at least the basics, and notwithstanding some of the more specific episodes of the catastrophe of my drinking. She understood since the age of five, for a decade, the disease of alcoholism; the physical craving in the body and the mental obsession in the head. She was always curious how Daddy was diseased and I taught her about that disease. She knew that she was derived from my DNA. She was never worried about herself, but curious to make sure that somehow this was not genetic; that somehow, even if not genetic, that she would not fall down the same path as me. When a topic would dance just beyond her full understanding, she would investigate to see the entire picture. It's what she always did.

She wanted to make sure, if she was drinking and experimenting with her friends, that she wouldn't end up like me. A fifteen year old girl asking her Father to review with her the few experiments she had with

142

drinking! Who does that? At fifteen I had lied a few hundred times about my drinking and would never have asked my parents about drinking at all, hiding it, lying about it, manipulating about it. This is the difference between me as a full blown late stage alcoholic and Kayleigh who would never have developed the disease. She was just a normal kid doing normal fifteen year old experimentation. It was awesome that she asked me about it, yet it was rather ordinary. We talked about everything. Least of all, I had not a worry in the world about Kayleigh and her ability to blaze an amazing trail in her life. She was battle tested, powerful, sure footed and very street smart. That night, while she walked on the beach, I wrote to her:

TEXT 08/01/2017:

Daddy: "Thank you for talking to me about your experimenting with drinking a few times and wanting to make sure you don't go down the same path as me. Just by asking this, you will not go down the same road. I am so proud of you. You are at a pivotal point in your life. A true cross roads. Had I taken the time to feel through this like you are doing I would not have developed the disease of alcoholism. I didn't take the time to walk through this at 15 and now own a fatal disease every day of my life like a gun to the back of my head - every day of my life until I pray I die sober. You can prevent that same fate and I believe you will - by adjusting now and not using alcohol to bury your emotions. I know it's easy to use alcohol to bury feelings and it's hard to feel sometimes – for anybody. I promise you on the other side of any difficulty emerges a brilliant stronger woman who has been tested by fire and has withstood great storms of a young life. You are empowered to take care of yourself. As your dad I pray more than ever you listen to my words like you've never listened before - this is your time. This is your life. This is your soul. Watch well your ways - the results will manage themselves. Love yourself and do not walk the same splintering road that I did that resulted in the death without dying and life without living of alcoholism. Feel your sorrow. Struggle your struggles. Cry your tears. Scream your screams. Laugh your beautiful laugh. And be who God intended. Sweet Kayleigh I have never been more proud. I stand in awe in your shadow."

*

Summer Waves 08/02/2017

Summer Waves is a great example of how the four of us get along with each of the other of us, effortlessly, beautifully. At this water park we did what we normally did - making sure we had every combination of the four of us, switching the kids off with us; sometimes parents on a ride, the kids off on their own. Me and Nate. Then me and Kakes. Kakes with Jess. Then Nate with Jess. Then kids together; parents together again. Effortless.

Kakes and I had a favorite when she was a little girl and we went down our double tube; the yellow white slides; slides we loved, trying to flip high up on the sides as we flew down the tubes; me in front; Kakes feet under my hands. Laughing and screaming. Such a blast. My baby. Then Nate and I hit the slides, particularly his favorite, Pirates Passage; the monster slide. We raced down the blue and red solo slides. We floated in the Slow Motion Ocean. I have a memory of Kayleigh and me swimming all the way out to the deepest part of the wave machine-open pool. We swam out to the rope and just floated together in the slowly rolling waves. Nate soon joined us. Jess, not long behind, floated up in a raft.

On our return to the house, I took to the ocean where I continued to sit in the surf, letting the waves of the sea wash over me and pull from me the stresses of my life. I talked to God. I listened to God. I tried to see the path that lay ahead for the family. I would interview an hour away in Jacksonville several times during the two week trip. I felt fully empowered. Alive.

*

Kake's Statement 08/03/2017

The sentencing hearings were set on two days – August 3rd and August 15th. As we were on vacation for the first hearing, and could not stand in the same room as her assailants to give her statement, we asked Kayleigh if she would want a statement read, authored by her, conveyed by the Rape Crisis Center representative. She very clearly wanted to make a statement and wrote it. It was read to the court by her representative.

Kayleigh Mooney Written Statement: "I want to start this out by saying that you took my life from me. I have a completely different view of the world and now it's not a good view. I'm scared to turn a corner or walk down the street and it's all because you wanted something without taking my opinions or my voice into consideration. I'm now struggling to get that voice back and it's not easy, especially with all of the shame, guilt and self-hate I have because of this. I understand that everyone makes mistakes and that's what makes us human, and I hope and pray that you learn from this situation as well. Every action has its consequences and trusting you caused me to suffer consequences. So now it's your turn. Please look back on this and realize that you violated me and fix it. That's all I can ask of you, forgive yourself, because I forgive you, but never forget. I plan to do the same because it's pointless to hold a grudge and it only makes you miserable which I do not want. Yes, this had a huge impact on my life. I have been healing but at times I really struggle, but nothing lasts forever. Thank you for listening and I forgive you. I also want an apology letter from everyone. Thanks, Kayleigh"

Its impact was made and her voice was heard. The juvenile system, however, is broken and rape and kidnapping charges do not typically carry jail time. The first two sentences were astonishing to us as the prosecutor spoke to me the following day as I walked through the waves up to my knees at Jekyll, hearing the words come through the phone and wondering how I could position this in a manner that would impact Kayleigh's victory in this matter – the victory of using her voice. I was disgusted by their sentences, but once again turned my eyes away from these sub-humans and towards the grace and dignity of my Daughter. I explained my displeasure to the prosecutors, the results of the first two sentences, the shortfall, but also voiced my gratitude that Kayleigh's voice was heard and they were held accountable.

I prayed, gathered my words, and sat with her to convey the sentences. She was furious. "No jail time, Daddy?" she said, "I go

145

through all of this and stand up and use my voice and these assholes rape me and they don't get jail time?"

"I'm really mad too, Honey," I said, "Remember, they admitted to your face their guilt, that they assaulted you. They have felonies on their records. They have been labeled as sexual offenders. Your voice has been heard, even if the court system is broken – they are trying to rehabilitate juveniles like this which is the only reason they didn't get jail time. It is bullshit because these people are beyond rehabilitation."

"That's bullshit, Daddy! They deserve to be locked up!"

"I agree, Babygirl, let's just keep pressing forward. We have two more when we get home on the 15th and you will be in the room for those. Your impact will be heard. Don't forget that the most important thing is that you are you and you used your voice and nobody, not even these scumbags can ever take that away from you."

She had had enough of our conversation, the court system – all of it, and didn't want to talk about it anymore. She left me with a hug and walked off down the beach and processed with her friends. She walked at length on the beach, where she always felt the spirit of the ocean speak to her soul. She came back and sang in the bathroom to make herself feel better. She made a video that she wanted to share with other teenage girls about never giving up, never letting anybody take your voice, and gathering together, the women of the world, to fight forward, to stand together and use their collective voices as one. One strong voice of womanhood that would not be deterred. Never defeated, this is what my Babygirl did with such disappointing news – she made herself even more beautiful.

Then she went and sat on the rocks and stared off to the ocean, just like her Father does. And then she took a deep breath, returned to the house, and told us to get ready for dinner - she was planning a family dinner at a restaurant of her choosing and a family activity to follow. And she did, living to the fullest; refusing any setback, any sickness of others from diverting her from successfully engaging in this moment of her beautiful life.

*

Ghost Tour 08/03/2017

So what did Kayleigh do with uncomfortable, disappointing information? She processed it. Cried and yelled about it. Reconciled it and then moved into the light of her life and made herself stronger somehow through it. That night, instead of hiding under a rock, she took control of the night's activities. She lived.

We had a lovely dinner to be followed by Kayleigh's chosen activity – a Ghost Tour on the island. She arranged the time and the tickets (with my credit card). She ensured we finished dinner at the restaurant on time and boarded the bus with about fifteen other people, none of whom we knew. It was a cross section of Americana on that bus; beautiful people with differences and similarities, of every race, size and attribute.

I have never claimed my family is perfect and we certainly could be irreverent but never in a way that was designed to harm anyone and certainly always refraining our joking to a private setting. Although on this bus, I just couldn't resist. It was private enough – our eyes rolling among us; our texting back and forth privately. They were so cliché. So stereotypical. It was too easy.

We sat at the back of the trolley bus beside a very obnoxious, over the top, deeply southern stereotypical family. One of the girls was sitting in the seat beside me and another on Kayleigh's side – with the four of us in the middle. The girl beside me was wet – literally wet – as if she had just come out of the swimming pool and did not dry off. At all. She was wet and dripping on my seat and my arm like gristle popping off of bacon as she leaned forward to scream and swear at her mother in the seat in front of her, and then collapse back in her seat laughing. The parents were loud as well, and were likewise dropping F bombs loud enough for the other families in the bus to hear. All in all, they seemed like they were good people – just a little unrefined, even for our unrefined standards.

They were having fun, just like us. Yet, the irreverence emerged within our tight family circle, glancing askance at each other with stupid smirks on our faces – clearly egging each other on with eye rolls and gestures as if we were saying, "my God, did you hear what she just said," or "my God this kid smells so bad" or "what are we doing on this bus with this family?" The two instigators started texting each other – the KMMs. It wasn't long before the first poem flew off of my phone in Kayleigh's direction. She read it and chortled loudly. Then another. And a response back to me, which caused me to crash to my seat laughing. The wet girl just thought I was stupid.

We were literally rolling in our seats and hardly able to contain our laughter in our inside, innocent joke, of which they were never aware, which was our intent – never to make fun of someone in a manner they would know, and never harming another. Just between us, make some jokes – some of which were a little dodgy or edgy and meant for an audience of two. Here is just one of those texts, verbatim, from that wonderful night.

TEXT:

"There once was a tour for ghosts,
In a school bus hot as assholes!
With a gingerbread man,
Talking into his can,
And a creepy girl next to Kayleigh with a knife!!"

She blasted a loud laugh at this one. Then showed it to Jess and Nate. Then I threatened my family with a Haiku. Four hooligans lost in folly. And we were.

After the ghost tour, she returned to the glory of the Jekyll rocks in the darkness having defeated the failures of a juvenile court system; having embraced life to the fullest under uncertain circumstances; having lived to the fullest with her three loves. She was empowered. She would not be contained by anybody. I watched from the house and could see her phone off in the darkness of the beach within a perfect blackness of night and under a rising moon. Kayleigh was rising.

Daddy: "*Ok sweetie. I love that you go sit on the rocks. I love doing that.*"

    Kayleigh: "*I love it too!!*"

Daddy: "❤️ *get a good sleep. I have lots of plans to have fun with you tomorrow. You are my baby and I want to spend time with you.*"

    Kayleigh: "*okay!! I love you, I wanna spend time with you too* ❤️❤️❤️❤️"

Daddy: "*sorry I was getting cranky with you earlier today.*"

    Kayleigh: "*it's okay....we're human, we all have flaws and hard moments. I'm glad we can work through it.*"

Daddy: "*me too.*"

*

Then She Made a Video to Help Other Girls 08/04/2017

Still furious from the juvenile court's inability to function on the rule of law, Kayleigh found her empowerment in supporting herself by supporting others. She knows how to heal herself. She also knows the duality of helping others to help oneself. And so she did.

Courageously, she continued to chart out her story – the assault, the confusion, the shame, the anger; the boys, the ring leader who had been a childhood friend and the sadness that he could have targeted her randomly, an innocent, vibrant, smart and outgoing girl – any girl just walking by and it happened to be her; all wrapped up into a video she entitled, "*Trigger Warning – I Was Raped.*" Like the Hopi statement, Kayleigh was leading; she was the one we were waiting for."

*

Night Shark Fishing 08/05/2017

At 10:30PM she came out to the dunes where I was sitting. "Daddy, let's go down to Thorne and go shark fishing."

"Okay!" I said, "We've got some frozen shrimp bait and you just bought that new fishing knife. Let's roll. Is Nate coming?"

"No, I asked him. He never comes shark fishing."

I smiled. "True," I said, "he's just never liked it."

We packed up and drove a few blocks away and parked near the beach access path in the quiet darkness, surrounded by the wild beauty of Jekyll's flowing ocean oaks and Spanish moss. There was barely a breeze on the hot night. The waves were tiny, trickling against the beach. We loaded the lines and began shark fishing, wearing our red turtle lights on our foreheads. I took several pictures of her standing in the surf, her long skinny body silhouetted by the moon rising in the sky behind her.

I had been taking her shark fishing since she was ten, when she caught her first Black-tip and her first Bonnethead, along with some other ocean surf fish. We fished for sharks every vacation to Jekyll and were mostly successful. On this night, we were only successful in spending wonderful time together, having very little bites and reeling nothing in except unfreezing shrimp in the warm waves.

Then fireworks went off in the darkness behind us. Literally. One hundred feet away. We looked at each other like, WTF? We glanced back to see a happy family just being a happy family.

"Yuh think with miles of beach and only us out here, they could find another place to shoot off fireworks?" Kayleigh said and laughed, "my God!"

"No shit," I said, "you wanna call it a night and go see what Nate is up to?"

"Yeah, we can try again maybe tomorrow. I'm wide awake. Let's go do something."

*

Kayleigh Saves a Baby Loggerhead Sea Turtle 08/06/2017

The night, just after midnight, was an average August night on Jekyll Island - sticky, humid, hot, and buggy and still. After shark fishing and hanging out, after midnight came and went, the three of us walked southward from the pavilion stairs under a beautiful, bright moon. Kicking along the dry dune lines, we laughed with each other, played with one another, while scanning the shadows in the dunes for loggerhead nest posts. That was our intention – see a nest hatch.

After a half mile or more, Kayleigh and I came across the nest of our destiny. We tripped across the unmistakable tracks in the feint light - the telltale tracks of new life, scattering down the beach directly towards the surf. One hundred tiny tracks from one hundred tiny sea turtles. With Nathaniel in tow, we followed the tracks cautiously, attempting to see if any remained on the beach, and if so, ensuring that we would not crush them under our feet. At the now dry, high tide line all of the tracks disappeared.

"They hatched three hours ago," I said to the kids, judging the space between the high tide line and where the water was lapping the beach descending the slope towards low tide. The moon would have been directly above the horizon and low at that time. It was now three hours higher and arching off to the southwest.

Nathaniel, consumed by his age, ran off doing spin kicks, laughing, throwing sand. I sat there on my knees at the water's edge mesmerized by the new life of all of these tiny tracks. Kayleigh disappeared from my side, up the beach following the tracks back towards the nest. Bending over, the red light in her hand occasionally flickering on and off. I was curious, and followed my child, busy scurrying across the beach.

151

"Daddy", she said, "we have to check every hole." She learned that reality many years ago on this beach; that ghost crabs dig their holes occasionally near sea turtle nests in order to ambush the babies as they try to scatter to the water. Sometimes they fall into holes on their own. Although she appreciated the subtleties of nature and the natural order of things, she would have none of it.

She must have checked forty, maybe fifty holes on the beach, some of which were ghost crab homes. Some were empty. Some just shadows in the sand. Then she found her.

"Daddy!" she screamed, "Daddy! I found one! It's been pulled down a crab hole! Please help me! Help me!"

I ran to her side and adjusted our iPhone light down the dark hole, the definition of which we could not see with our low, turtle safe red light flashlights. As the shadow danced around in the shaft of a hole, about a quarter in diameter, and the light illuminated two feet down this angled hole, we saw the back tiny flipper of a Loggerhead. I was excited, but cringed defeated.

"Daddy, save it!"

I paused. What could I tell her? "Kakes, God makes a hundred babies per nest because some don't make it to the ocean."

"Mine is going to make it," she insisted, "You have to help me get her out!"

I was afraid it was being eaten, upside down, by a ghost crab. I didn't want her to see that. I resisted. Hesitated.

"Daddy," she begged me, "please help me."

I know Kakie. I knew the significance of the moment. She had never seen a baby sea turtle in the wild, let alone one isolated two feet away from her who would die without her intervention.

"Okay, Kakes," I said, "Let's do it. Put your hand over the hole to stop the dry sand from falling in. We don't want to lose the hole."

She did. I started scooping away the dry sand and making a large space while she protected the integrity of the hole. Together we calculated how to triangulate the hole, how to enlarge the hole as we dug deeper. We spread the shallow excavation about fifteen inches further from the hole and worked the two spaces together. In the dry sand, we lost the hole. We found it. Lost it again. Re-found it. It took more than thirty minutes, and the use of a small stick to re-find the shaft, before I became nervous that I may harm the turtle we were trying to save if I kept poking around. I took a wide sweep with my fingers, digging a few inches deeper. Kayleigh scooped out another handful of sand that I had loosened, as her finger gently touched across the baby's back flippers.

"Daddy! Daddy!" she cried, "Is that it?" Is that it?"

I pulled away a little more sand. "My God, Kakes! Yes it is! Let me get under it and loosen the sand and then you can lift it out."

"Ok," she said and readied herself.

With both hands, my fingers like tiny shovels, I scooped a space three times the turtle's size and loosened the sand around it. Kayleigh reached down into my hands and lifted the tiny Loggerhead Sea Turtle from the sand.

"Daddy! Daddy!" she cried, "it's Okay! It's okay!"

I called Nathaniel up from the darkness to our side while I pulled out my phone. She cradled the tiny creature in her hands, running her finger on its shell, knowing that momentarily we would place it on the sand and stay with it until it crossed the open beach and entered the ocean. I flipped on the video and caught eighteen seconds of Kayleigh that will live with me forever.

I asked, "Kayleigh, what did you just do?"

"I saw a turtle moving around – in a ghost crab hole, and I saved him and now he's alive. He could have died. And you guys just wanted to give up!"

153

She placed her in the sand and began serenading her as she began her walk to the sea. She named her, "Little Phil," and walked slowly behind her. For an hour and a half we held vigil over the tiny creature as it finally made it to the water's edge. I turned my video back on and captured forty nine seconds of footage. The turtle sped up in the water, not a sixteenth of an inch deep. She lowered her head against the water – its first touch of its eyes in the Atlantic.

Kakes cooed. "Oh, did you see that – did you see him just like dunk his head in? You are beautiful Little Phil. Yes there we go! There we go! There we go!"

Nathaniel yelled, "good boy, yeah!"

"Oh he's about to – oh there he goes! There we go! Oh, are you luring him with that?" she asked me as I hung the red light out a few feet in front of the turtle to see if it would follow.

"I am," I said.

"Good."

"You're a fast learner!" said Nathaniel.

"Oh my god she is so cute," Kayleigh said.

"You are adorable," said Nathaniel.

As the baby Loggerhead entered the sea, I turned off my video. We stood there amazed, having been the shepherd to new life in the ocean. Kayleigh was this turtle's full, bright moon, the star of the sea, alight like Stella Maris. She and I embraced. She had magic in her eyes. She was overwhelmed with excitement, love, compassion, and esteem. She knew what she had just done. She knew the courage she exhibited.

I told her several times on the way back down the beach how proud I was – how she inspires me to never give up. I told Nathaniel he was great with his participation as well. But Kayleigh – she was the architect of this incredible moment.

As we neared the parking lot, nearly three hours after we had left the car, she gazed up to me lovingly, and hopefully, and thankfully, and said, "Daddy, that was the most important thing you've ever done for me. We all fall into dark holes but we can be saved. I was that turtle and somebody saved me."

I hugged her again and kissed her on her forehead – amazed at her insight; standing in her light. Knowing all she had accomplished, all she had overcome and walked through over the last year or so. She had not so much fallen into a dark hole as having been thrown into a dark hole. She had been saved. The somebody, however, who saved her, was Kayleigh herself.

"August The 6th"

A warm wind - kiss the neck,
Heating skin that hemorrhage sweat,
And humid haze hung heavy,
The air a cloak deep, thick and wet;

August in its eternity,
Across this atmosphere calmly spread,
My children at my side,
Always at my side,
A night I never, never will forget;

My son in the shadows down near the water,
On the dune line, the steady eye of my Daughter,
In a summer darkness lit by high moon,
The month would prove to end in ruin;

But on this, this August the 6th,
Walking the midnight beach with my kids,
The air wrapped in frenzied laughter, alight,
As we saved a baby sea turtle on this sacred night;

The sky bowed in glory,

155

The future expanded in hope and praise,
Not a hint of the disaster that would come,
In just eleven days;

But on this, this August 6th,
The moment defined the miracle of life for her,
As we saved a baby sea turtle,
And further empowered my little girl.

*

A "Hello, Father" in the Midst of a Brilliant Atmosphere
08/08/2017

Likely our finest vacation together, the four of us hummed along effortlessly. It was our custom – an occasional outburst or hard moment on behalf of one of us, like any family may expect, but mostly, we just hum.

The atmosphere of the trip was calming and filled with love – Jess and I trying to keep up with a tween and a teen. My Daughter had long put the initial trauma of the assault behind her, cleaning up the daily emotions as they came, striving for strength and courage and light and laughter. She was all of that. She was a warrior. I was not worried about Kayleigh in the slightest. She was the safest kid in Cleveland Heights after standing up to her assailants and standing them down in court. That chapter was closing. The next was opening up in its amazement.

My kids played "The Floor is Lava" game in every store that we walked into – WalMart, Flash Foods, restaurants – it was a little much, yet irreverently funny. Always on the verge of raising eyebrows or getting reprimanded by the workers at WalMart, I was aggravated and told them to stop. I look back on that aggravation and realize how absolutely effortlessly we were living – having been challenged and having overcome such a horrible experience – we were powerful, just as we had always been; we were back in our daily living. All four of us. Four equal parts to that four leaf clover

Kayleigh found in the yard when she was two years old, a moment we remember as the time when we sensed that Jessica was pregnant with Nathaniel. And thus we were the Mooney's – proud, unbreakable, kind and full of light.

Jess and Kayleigh rode horses. The kids made videos and blogs. We hung out on our dunes; walked the beaches; slept in the AC and detoxed from the daily grind. We went to Coastal Kitchen for dinners; to the Jekyll Island Clubhouse; shopping on St. Simon's Island and across the shops on Jekyll. I visited my A.A. home group on Jekyll that I had been a part of for twenty five years.

In the middle of the trip I stood in the kitchen staring out to the ocean and Kayleigh entered the kitchen facing me and walked up to me. "Hello, Father," she said, and threw her arms around me.

"Oh, hello Kakes," I said, as I melted in my Daughter's arms, "it's so great to hug you. Just stay here a minute and let me hold you. I haven't held you in a long hug in such a long time!"

She giggled and sank into her Father's arms, knowing that she hugged me almost daily. I couldn't help but thinking how much I loved my little girl, and my God, she has gotten so tall! She is just as tall as me. I am holding a woman. My little girl is a woman.

We stood there rocking gently back and forth and laughing slightly, smiles on both of our faces; grateful in the other and truly feeling that divine spark that we shared. After thirty seconds or so, she slowly stepped back and looked into my eyes and smiled, nodding her head to the side, and kept walking, be-bopping through the kitchen and into the TV room where Nathaniel awaited her. I continued to stare back out the window towards the ocean, feeling the empowerment of the love in this family as constant as the water is to the ocean.

*

If You Listened To Silence What Would You Hear 08/09/2017

Listen to silence, it's cadence of breath, absent long winding antidotes and truncated with capsules of life strung bead by colorful bead along a radiant string of time - touching each other like tiny golden, emerald, sapphire and ruby auras; time expands within its cradle, a horizon bleeds endlessly, while I lose the scales of contemplation, of fabricated thought, of worry and raw emotion in its seeming emptiness; and along its breath, as I listen, and begin to truly hear its life, there in the silence, the time becomes momentous, the time seems full of light and I become those pulsing, illuminated beads of deep color whose purpose need not be known in this perfect stillness - rather, I am as I listen - I am as the silence is - I am timelessness itself in its breath.

"Aqua Opal Seascape"

Blanket of silver sparkles,
Blend with golden crests of waves,
A hundred thousand points of light,
Spread out when ocean sprays,
Aqua opal seascape,
Its turquoise blues ingrained,
My aqua opal sea-dreams,
They wash away life's strains.

*

She Is Like the Moon 08/10/2017

Each day. My routine. My joy; sitting in the ocean on a lounge chair either listening to the ocean and becoming one with the ocean, or listening to music, my iPhone lodged between my shoulders blades and pressed against the chair, permitting the music to encapsulate every cell of my body, to glance across the big country of my soul, becoming the music as it rolled in and out to the feel and texture and the waves as they crashed under my feet and up my legs. It's just my thing; my way of physically permitting the ocean to take my stress away from me one wave at a time – crashing against me and peeling away the stress. I spent more time on this last vacation than any others in the water in this manner.

I had much on my mind. Much of which to let go. Letting go of my own trauma and merging that energy into continuous life; contemplating moving the family to Jacksonville, the worry of which in my life was mostly on that point: how would a move affect the kids if we moved now. I discussed this with God and listened for answers. Much sweat, tears and contemplation drained into the ocean, mostly while my children, who were up into the wee hours of the nights, slept through the mornings while I sat in the ocean. We had already completed a long but empowering ten months, filled with the conquering of an assault but also its trauma and the trauma of prosecution, awaiting just the sentencing hearings to conclude the formal proceedings. She was safe. Likely one of the safest kids in the neighborhood as these sub-humans were terrified to meet her in court; afraid of her, knowing that if you mess with Kayleigh Mooney, you get felonies and go to jail. Ironically, due to her bravery in standing down these thugs, she was very safe. My original theory of moving the family to keep her safe was no longer reality.

One of the bands that I like, Future Islands, has a melody that flows like that of the waves crashing down on the beach – the rhythm of the Atlantic encased within the music itself. I spent many hours in the ocean on that last vacation prior to her death specifically listening to Future Islands. Each time I cycled back to the song, "Like the Moon" I halted my contemplation and turned my light towards Kayleigh. Though generally a romantic song, it like any art, can take on multiple meanings and some of the lyrics resonated with how I interpreted my child; my relationship with my Daughter. I had always likened her to the moon and the representation was a good fit.

She is magical – her light like that of the Moon. It was a theme throughout her life, a constant connection to that mystical celestial fire. The Moon permeates her being. She was conceived under a Full Moon. She was born under a New Moon. She was always radiant like the Moon. We waked her under the great solar eclipse of August 2017. Her funeral was the day of the Feast of the Queenship of Mary in the Catholic Church – Mary, known to the ancients of the church as the Moon – the indirect light to the true source of light.

On one afternoon during our last vacation, I returned from the water's edge to the house and found Kakes and said, "Hey Kakes, this is my song to you, it's called "Like the Moon" and it reminds me so much of you and sort of reminds me about our relationship."

We listened to it several times. She liked it and found its meaning. On August 12th, on the way home from Jekyll, nearing the end of an all-day drive, we listened to it again, somewhere outside of Canton, Ohio, me driving, tears welling in my eyes from the happiness and contentment I felt with the four of us. I looked back to Kakes in the middle row of seats, smiling at me, her figure filling the rearview mirror. I made the "I love you" sign in sign language and she reciprocated with a pleasant smile and the same sign with her hand. Nathaniel in the far back row of seats bopping away on a video game. Jess sitting in the passenger seat beside me. What a family. What a life. I was awe struck. Secure. Empowered. Grateful as we pulled back into our driveway after a great two week vacation, thinking about those days sitting in the ocean and permitting the ocean to strip the layers from my being.

"Sitting In the Sea (Future Islands)"

Sitting, pitching gently in the sea,
While the warm waves lap over me,
Contemplating life,
In a lounge chair in water one foot deep;

Sitting, pitching gently in the sea,
My mind like the summer waves and the humid, choppy breeze,
I have decisions coming due,
With thoughts of how they will affect you, and you, and you,
My Loves,
My Three;

Sitting, pitching gently in the sea,
The ocean's spirit speaks to me,
It brings me intuition,

It brings me to my knees,
Begging for answers,
To life's direction,
I close my eyes and then I see,
As the next wave covers me.

*

August 10, 2017

I returned from my interview in Jacksonville upbeat. I had this job locked up if I wanted it. I talked to Jess during the one hour drive back to Jekyll and I knew they were at the pool. I stopped at home and changed and drove the last few minutes to the pool.

As I walked through the metal gate, walled with lively bushes, the pool beyond came into view. I looked down into the water and found Nathaniel were I expected him. Next to him in the water was Jess. I thought, where's my Kakes? I glanced around the pool deck across lounge chairs and umbrellas. There I saw a long, tall beautiful woman with long blond hair in a leopard patterned bikini laying out on a lounge chair on her stomach. There she is, I thought - my child woman. I smile and thought, she is really quite beautiful - and she has finally arrived. My little girl is not a little girl anymore. She is a woman. I felt such an immense pride looking over to her. She was so vibrant; so full of life; such a joy to be around; a true companion; a mature young adult with grace, dignity, self-love and a warrior's courage.

As I placed my towel on a lounge chair and kicked off my shoes and smiled at Nate and Jess, I continued my musing and thought, most dads are crazy when they dread having a beautiful young daughter, drawn from a reservoir of immaturity or misguided male truncated nonsense of how to protect their girls; coming across controlling, patronizing, dismissive and shielding. Not me. I could not wait to see her flourish as a young woman; challenge herself in an ever evolving fluctuation of innocence blending into maturation; falling in love, out of love; making mistakes; finding her full humanity, including spiritually, mentally, sexually, emotionally and physical intimacy – everything life has to offer – the fullness of experience. I could not wait for the next several years getting her through the rest of high school and college and was fully prepared. I raised her all the way through childhood to get to this place where she would take off as an adult and light up this world. She is ready, I thought, as I gazed across the pool, and she is brilliant; compassionate; dynamic; battle tested. Full of life and love and laughter. And it was all vibrantly true.

A week later I held her in the street as she took her last breath listening to her Daddy's words.

*

Driving Away From Jekyll 08/12/2017

Every time we were on Jekyll, for Kayleigh approximately 25 vacations, we stepped down the dune path to the rock wall and stood looking at the sunrise, always needing to leave around 7 A.M. in order to get home to Cleveland between 7-9 P.M. The night before this last morning, I took the picture that is the cover of this book. We bid farewell to Jekyll and the Atlantic Ocean, not wanting to leave, with our usual farewell, "until the four of us see you again!"

As we drove northbound on I95, we passed the coastal islands and marshes off of the Georgia coast. Off in the distance, unknown to us on that morning, a fisherman found a wounded Kemps Ridley Sea Turtle floating in the ocean; seriously injured due to a boat strike. It would be shipped in the opposite direction, southbound on I95 on that day to the Georgia Sea Turtle Center on Jekyll Island.

As we drove the twelve hours home, it was my habit to scan back into the car and see my babies from time to time. Nathaniel was in the third row playing video games. I made occasional eye contact and flashed him the ALS sign for "I love you," as we always did, plus our sign for "always and forever." Kakes lay down in the second row, listening to music. When we made eye contact a few dozen times she smiled at me and blew me kisses or rolled her eyes, depending on

162

how happy or bored or tired or cranky she was during that long drive. I will always remember her sitting in the middle right behind me and Jessica, talking to us – the third adult in the car, and me catching eyes with her and flashing the same sign, "I love you, always and forever," and seeing her do the same – in her young woman's hand, so far from the little toddler hand that first made this sign so many years before.

We were ready for the next phase of our lives. I was quite sure we were going to get an offer to move to Jacksonville. We would all adjust and come out stronger. Or we would stay put and continue to grow. As the Father, and knowing our kids, and having a partner as amazing as Jess, we were ready for either.

"The Last Morning on Jekyll Island"

A golden haze - emerge in the waves,
Unleash smoky pastel steam,
That streaks across the dawning sky,
As the deep blue of night subsides -

The songs of the water,
Licking the cool morning beach,
Capture the ears in their soothing melody,
If only, as we leave, we could bottle its serenity,
If only we did not have to leave -

Twinkling stars shine over the western marsh,
As the sun breaks horizon's line,
Here, between two worlds, my soul rise,
Bathing my spirit with the beach,
It's sand, its wind, its salt, its reach -

The children, they wave at the sea,
And step away from the rocks with me,
The last morning on Jekyll Island,
Press to memory its beautiful scene...

*

I stood at the podium beside my Daughter, the judge in front of me. The disgusting perpetrator to our right sitting quietly, his attorney trying to manipulate the court system. With a voice that rolled from strength to pain, through tears and cracking, and back to empowering, I said the following words:

"My Daughter has been severely harmed by this crime. My family has been destroyed by this crime. In effect, we may be imprisoned for 30 to 40 years dealing with the fallout of this crime. There can be no leniency. We are troubled by the fact that jail time normally does not follow rape convictions in the juvenile court. Leniency has already been granted by this plea bargain and allowing felony ones to be reduced, in exchange for the boys' admitting their guilt directly to my Daughter. No further leniency is warranted. My Daughter is amazing and my Daughter used her voice to stand up against horrible violence and her perpetrators. She is courageous and years ahead of her time. What message are you sending to her, to thousands of others who will be raped in weeks, months, in the years ahead, if you let rapists, perpetrators like this walk free? It is saying that her voice has not been heard and not honored. That cannot happen. The community demands accountability for this heinous crime and leave no doubt, this was a heinous crime. This family expects accountability. Nothing short of incarceration is acceptable."

I was quite pleased with myself. Then I motioned to Kakes and smiled at her, and the prosecutor said, "Honey, do you want to say anything?"

She shook her head slightly and whispered, "No," even though she had planned on speaking directly to the boys.

"It's okay, sweetheart. You don't have to say anything if you don't want to," I said.

The prosecutor, however, said, "It's okay. Talk into the microphone."

And she, at first sheepishly and frightened, and then straightening her back and taking a deep breath, leaned forward and said, "hi, I'm Kayleigh."

She ran her fingers through her hair to gather her thoughts and bent down slightly in her stance. Then she straightened back up again, looked at me for comfort and support and sighed. She addressed the assailant directly in a very calm, empowered and stable courageous voice, stating, "We were friends and I trusted you and you violated my trust. I want you to know that you took something from me that wasn't yours to take without taking my opinions or my voice into consideration and I've taken my life back and I'm going to keep living a good life. I'm struggling at times to get that voice back and it's not easy, especially with all of the shame I have because of this. But I will succeed. So now it's your turn. I get to hold you accountable. Please look back on this and realize that you made a mistake and fix it. That's all I can ask of you. I want you to know that I forgive you, but never forget. And I want a written apology from all of the boys. That's all. Thank you."

*

Beach Painting 08/17/2017

Thinking back on our recent vacation, the best in a series of wonderful vacations, I sat in my office at Cleveland Clinic and stared outside at the trees. We were just five days away from the beach and I already missed it. In just a handful of hours, unknown to me, my life would be destroyed. My last poem, on the afternoon of the 17th, just hours before the great fracture of my life.

"Beach Painting"

Painting the sands with swaths of water salt,
Painting the dune lines, with sweet grass and straw,
Painting the beachfront - it moves to the melody,
That picks up the pieces dispersed in the heart.

*

Our Last Text 08/17/2017

We had been home five days. I went back to work. Nate was with his friends, and Kakes with hers; the kids enjoying the last week of summer before school started in the next week. I had a 7th and an 10th grader. After being with them both every day for two weeks, I was really missing them during those first few days home. I sent her what would be our final texts, a photo of her hands holding little Phil the Loggerhead Sea Turtle that she saved a week earlier, cast in a heavy red light of the turtle-safe lights we used on the beach that night.

TEXT: 08/17/2017

Daddy: "My baby and her baby."
   Kayleigh: " 🖤🖤🖤🖤"
Daddy: "I need time with you. I feel so far from you since we've gotten home. I need my baby."
   Kayleigh: "I know. We need to spend time together 🖤. Also, I have a question."

*

Our Last Physical Conversation 08/17/2017

It had only been five days since we returned from vacation, but to me it seemed like an eternity. She ran off with her friends she hadn't seen in two weeks and I was busy digging myself out of being away from the office for two weeks. We spent time together each night as we always did, but shorter spurts. It was already Thursday of that first week back. I wanted my Daddy Daughter time and wanted us to make plans before she embarked on this awesome new school year, fully empowered, excited, happy and ready to tackle the next phase of life.

I drove in the driveway at around 6 pm. She had several options that night including going to a pool party, which she really didn't want to do, or maybe stay back at the house and do a sleepover with a bunch of girls.

We talked at 7 PM to try to figure out what we were all doing. I was off to my A.A. meeting, Practical Experience, leaving at 7:30 PM. Jess and Kayleigh and I sat together on the couch going over her options. We had a very sweet and deeply private conversation about her life, about her incredible strength and maturation as a young woman, about her continued recovery from the sexual assault and how proud we were of her. We talked about how she had three big things going on – one, just being fifteen with its challenges of learning how to be a young adult, even though she was years beyond her peers; two, that she was working through her sexuality and evolving into a woman, which was age appropriate; and three, that she was still recovering from a rape, although she had made it through the acute stages, there could still be residual effects we wanted her to be aware of – that we wanted her to continue to take great care of herself and continue to make healthy decisions.

We were uncomfortable with one option that night, and suggested she do something else. She heard us and agreed, though disappointed as she was not permitted to do what she had originally asked to do. She knew that, with us, we would say yes 9 of 10 times. An incredibly sweet and compliant kid, she accepted our decision and drew up other plans that night, which included going to this party of which she did not really want to go. She made arrangements to be picked up. She went up to her room, turned on her music and put on makeup. Around fifteen minutes before I was to leave, I walked up to her door and smiled and said, "Love you."

She smiled, "love you."

She made her way back downstairs and was sitting on the couch at 7:30 pm with Jess. I grabbed my Big Book to go to the meeting, walked over and leaned down and kissed her on her forehead. "Love you, Baby," I said.

She smiled up to me. "Love you, Daddy."

That was my last verbal interaction with her. The next time I talked to her, it was three hours and some minutes later, leaning down to her, my mouth inches from her right ear, telling her over and over, "Kayleigh, its Daddy. I'm right here. You're going to be okay. I love you, Sweetheart. Daddy's right here, Kayleigh. I love you, Kakes. I am right here. Kayleigh, Daddy's right here…"

*

In the Evening I Stood Upon A Mountain 08/17/2017

On August 17th in the evening I stood upon a mountain, the clear warm breath of wind flowing through my soul. A father of two beloved children by my side living out the ends of their childhood days; one already a mid-teen, the other a tween. A beloved wife. My sobriety. A job and a house. Two dogs. Two cats. Respect. Humility. A good life. An amazing life.

On August 18th a mountain stood upon me, its weight compressing my chest; my lungs filled with concrete; the day a journey of a thousand moments of courage and disbelief.

That mountain still stands upon me. I am learning how to shift its weight. My shoulders are adjusting traumatically to its pressure; misaligning my joints; rupturing my spine; punishing me with headaches and heartaches and human aches and horrible sadness.

*

Tragedy and Physical Death 08/17/2017

Jess and I were watching TV when Caroline called at about 10:45 PM, frantically telling me that Kayleigh had just been hit by a car. I asked to talk to her, hearing someone screaming in the background, thinking it was Kayleigh crying. She said she couldn't talk. As I ran

168

to my car I asked where they were and she told me – corner of Euclid Heights Blvd and E. Overlook. I drove the distance in a minute or so. As I quickly slid into a spot and jerked the car into park, I glanced up and saw a few people huddled in the street; red and blue flashing police car lights; kids huddled to my left; others running around frantically. A crowd gathering at the corner.

I ran as fast as I could to her side. There was a girl screaming beside her. I pushed the air where she was to motion to leave and give me space. I wanted Kayleigh to hear only my voice. This is what Kayleigh wanted as well. I would be told later by the two women in the street that they saw me running towards Kayleigh, and by the way I ran they knew it was Dad, and told Kayleigh that her Father was running to her side. I did not know this at the time, but she tried to reach out for me and tried to open her eyes as they fluttered trying to open as I ran to her. A moment later she was laying still.

I threw myself on my knees on the curb and reach down to her. I was afraid to touch her – imagine that – afraid to touch my child for fear that I may further harm her. "Kayleigh, its Daddy. I'm right here. You're going to be ok. I love you, Sweetheart. Daddy's right here, Kayleigh. I love you, Kakes. I am right here. Kayleigh, Daddy's right here…"

She could hear me. One of the women asked her, if she could hear her Daddy's voice, to squeeze her hand. Kayleigh squeezed the woman's hand to acknowledge that she heard me. The woman told her, good girl, Kayleigh, if she could, do it again. Kayleigh squeezed her hand a second time. She looked so peaceful.

As I first ran from my car, across the side road to the main road where she lay, I thought she looked unconscious and assumed we would be able to get her to the hospital and stabilized. I assessed the situation within several seconds that was afforded to me; scanned the crowd, a car fifty feet to me right; a man sitting on a curb; cop lights flashing blue and red; two women with my baby in the street – her head pushed up against the curb, her long blonde hair looking beautiful as it cascaded down her shoulders and lay on the street. There was a track of blood a foot or so away from her gorgeous face from where she struck the street, the impact that would take her life in another minute.

169

I had no idea I had but one minute with my beloved child. One minute – if you had one minute with your child, what would you do?

The right side of her face looked as it always did – simply gorgeous; no sign of trauma; she looked like she was sleeping, clearly not in any pain and clearly unaware that she has been clipped by a car or that she had been thrown to the street, striking the concrete near her left temple. Thank God for the integrity of her face, even on the left side where she impacted the street, which I saw and scanned for hours later in University Hospital. The damage was internal mostly – but at this point in the street, other than the strip of blood, no one would be able to tell that she had suffered any trauma.

She took her last breath in the cradle of my voice. Weeks later I could hear her voice clearly as it was in the street that night, conveying to me, "Daddy, Daddy I have no idea what just happened. I have no idea what's going on. Daddy, you are here. Of course you're here. You're always here. Okay, I am safe. I am with my Daddy. You just said I will be okay. I believe you, Daddy. Okay, okay…"

"Sir," said a fireman gently, "sir, please step back. We have to let the EMT check your daughter."

I stepped back and kneeled. He knelt beside me and placed his hand on my left shoulder. The EMT checked Kayleigh and nodded negatively to the fireman. The fireman, squeezed my shoulder, paused and said, "sir, do you know what's happening?"

I said, "Yes, I know but I don't want to know what's happening."

"Where's my baby?" I heard Jessica suddenly scream. She was one minute behind me in the other car. She came running and cutting through the crowd to me as the medics placed a white sheet on top of Kayleigh. I stood up and hugged Jess. She screamed out loud, "Is my baby dead? Is my baby dead?"

I jumped up, nodded and burst into tears, having to tell my wife, through jagged breaths and immense suffering, "yes."

She wailed in my arms, looking down through the fireman and a police officer, as two other mothers momentarily dragged her away from the sight. It was like the air came exploding out of the whole city. Officers, firemen, EMTs, neighbors, Kayleigh's friends - they were all stunned. Neighbors with hands over their mouths. Wide eyed. Teenagers crumbled on the curbs and in front yards. A few hugs were offered me. A few people didn't dare touch me. Heads draped low. Weeping. Some of the officers were fathers and thought of their own children. Some dared not to stay with me for fear of breaking down in tears. A few others cried openly with me. She was not drunk. She was not a teenage party casualty. She did not throw herself in front of a car and actually was never in front of the car. She did not intend to get hit by a car. She intended only to gather her shoes across the street to come home. Literally, none of her actions or omissions – nothing in her life, literally nothing, led her to this moment. It was arbitrary, unrelated to anything, sudden, innocent and perfectly horrible.

I stepped back to Kayleigh as Jess stumbled away and told the police, "I am going to pray with my Daughter." They stepped aside and I lay in the street with her and cradled her head. I knew somehow the importance of the transition and instead of buckling in the shock and grief, I continued to father Kayleigh, directing her, in my human limits, through the heavenly steps that she so beautifully had just taken. I said, "Babygirl, I already feel your light. You are in the light. Be in the light with God. You just transitioned. I love you so much, Kayleigh! We just inverted our relationship. You no longer need your Daddy to direct you as a teenager, but your Daddy is going to need you to direct him. I have no idea how I'm going to do this. I have no idea what to do, Babygirl. I need you. I know you are here. I know you are in the light. God, into Your hands I commend Kayleigh's spirit."

"Light Passes Through Glass"

The embodiment has fallen,
Your physicality, farewell,
Forlorn the arms with frequent embrace,
When you released from your human shell,
As the eternal light left your eyes,

171

And the life lifted from your face,
Awakened in that sacred space,
As I held you, child, as you passed,
Your soul blazed a trail through mine,
Like bright light passes right through glass.

*

Telling Nathaniel 08/17/2017

He was in the third floor playing video games. It was around 11:30 pm. Jess had come home with one of the woman, Colleen, who was in the street with me. I returned home, having been instructed by the police to meet Kayleigh at University Hospital after thirty minutes or so, giving the hospital time to clean her up.

Two parents stared lifelessly at the other. One child was just physically killed, passing in one of the parent's arms. The second was about to receive information, delivered by his parents, which would utterly destroy his life. We walked up to his room and asked him to sit on the bed with us. He saw the horror in our eyes and asked, almost in a streaming cry, "What's wrong?" I could see in his eyes he knew something had happened to Kayleigh. Subconsciously he may have already been spiritually aware that she had already come home to comfort him and was sitting on the bed with us.

I spoke. "Kayleigh," I said.

"Did the boys kill her?" he screamed.

"No," I said, somehow in a disassociated moment thinking how strange it was that he went right to that fearful conclusion, me knowing that these sub-human boys she was prosecuting didn't have the power to kill Kayleigh. I refocused. "She was hit by a car." I choked on my breath and wept, continuing, "Kayleigh was killed in a car accident."

Nathaniel screamed in a piercing wailing that rattled the atmosphere with sheer guttural anguish. The four of us sat on his bed sobbing together, Nathaniel and Jess unaware of Kayleigh's presence – me sensing her vaguely in the room; all of us devastated. He stammered on and on asking questions through the bubbling tears and abrasive breath. After some time, sensing his needs, I looked into his eyes. He was desperate for direction; for words that would brace for him a road to walk on.

"Sweetheart, I am so sorry what is happening. Please know that Kayleigh is right here, even though she has passed from her physical body tonight. We honor Kayleigh by living in her light. We live with her by living our lives and living in her light."

He nodded. I was unaware whether his twelve year old mind could even comprehend the spiritual, metaphysical notion of what I was saying, even in the best of times. In the worst moment of his life, he just nodded. Nonetheless, in that initial moment where he needed a road, his Father gave him a road, lit by the glorious light of his sister.

*

University Hospital Emergency Room, Room #41 08/18/2017

They led me into the frame of your room, an hour and a half after I last saw you laying in the street where you last lay in my arms; our perfect communion of love and loyalty and total trust in that epic moment in the street. In a way, it was only you and I in the street – two souls, eyes locked eternally together, resisting the chaos, blocking out the rest of the world and focused only on the vitally important doorway of light that God was opening for you.

The physician on staff stepped through the curtain with me and stood by my side. Room #41. She held my hand for a moment as I adjusted my baring I stepped inside. The image I never wanted to witness – one of my children, in childhood, laying physically dead on a table; yet it was the only image in that moment that I desperately wanted to see, wanting only to be with you, to absorb any pain to support my

173

child; to do anything and everything I could do for you; to honor you and continue to be the Father you deserve; to transition with you.

You were wrapped tightly and sacredly in white sheets, tucked under your armpits. Your arms lay outside the cloth. They combed your beautiful blond hair back tightly against your head, and lay your long hair under you. I sat on your right side and stared at my beautiful baby.

I wanted, and didn't want, to see the trauma. I raised myself and slowly kissed your forehead, just as I had done for years when you were preparing for bedtime as a child. I saw the contusion near your left temple – reddish blood clots under your skin. A stitched gash worked its way down your beautiful left cheek bone. Another stitching came across from the left side of your jaw to your chin. Your mouth was slightly open and a few of your lower teeth, that had been so perfectly set a few hours earlier, were slightly crooked. My baby. I was relieved that the integrity of your face was retained – your beauty, even after physical death, apparent. I sat with you for some time just staring at your face, not knowing what to do; should I touch your hair; kiss your face; lay next to you on the bed and hold you. You were talking to me. It was as if it was down a long hallway of light. You were talking but I could not quite hear you.

"Kakie, I know it was an accident, Babygirl," I said, "I am not mad at you, or disappointed, or frustrated with you or blaming you at all. You did nothing wrong. It was not even a mistake. Just a horrible accident. I have nothing but unconditional love for you. The police told me the driver did not see you. You did not see the car. It's not your fault, Sweetheart. It just happened and here we are."

My heart ached for you. My child was struck by a car going thirty five or forty miles an hour. I continued to hear your voice faintly. We were talking to each other. We were communicating in our new configuration. It was humanly stumbling and incoherent, but also, considering we were communicating across two dimensions, in one respect, as clear as glass. We would begin within these first few hours trying on our channels and driving our energy to be with the other.

*

Last Rights 08/18/2017

After an hour or so a reverend finally presented. He covered all denominations. "You are Catholic?" he asked.

"Yes, Kayleigh is Catholic."

"I am very sorry, Sir," he said while he gathered his readings for the three of us. He handed me a Rosary made of children's colorful beads. He read several prayers including "Sacrament of the Sick" and "Absolut., Indulg., Blessing." We recited two Hail Mary's. He blessed her soul and made the sign of the cross over her beautiful face. We prayed together. I wept. I tried to remain present. I did.

With a somber face, but one marked with the confidence that I knew that Kayleigh was in the Kingdom of Heaven, he smiled, not merely for the realization, but also in a firm sadness watching a father suffer the unthinkable. He patted me on the shoulder, glanced lovingly at Kayleigh, and bowed, exiting the tiny room.

*

My Tears in Your Skin 08/18/2017

I held you hand for several more hours, working out the initial struggles I had before me; having quite a dynamic conversation. I held your hand almost the entire time, certainly feeling the lack of bodily warmth on your skin and the soft physical texture of life that had dissipated. I ran my fingers through your hair like I did when you were a new baby, a toddler, a little girl. You were happy. I could sense your tenderness, grace and gratitude; wrapping your arms around me as I ran my fingers through your golden hair above your forehead. You rested your angelic head on my right shoulder.

I wept, wiping my bubbling tears on my arm, soaking my wrists. I made my own sign of cross on your forehead with my tears, which I watched slowly soak into your sacred body. I reminded you how proud I was of your physical life; of who you were and who you are. I breathed from the lungs of a human and shared this air with an angel's breathing in the light of God; the mixture of human and angelic energies filling the room and expanding the bridge between father and daughter.

Several friends, members of A.A., sat in the hallway patiently; sentries; warriors of selfless love. I did not want to leave your side, yet I knew I needed to go home and try to sleep several hours in order to plan your funeral. I told you that over and over, asking you what you wanted; how I should arrange your celebration of your life. I tried to get up several times and sat back down. I was paralyzed between this sacred space and the rest of my life that resided outside of Room #41.

I needed to ask the doctor to stand with me and hold my hand and walk me out when it was time to leave. I could not leave your side. I asked her to give me a little more time and then come to retrieve me. After a few more minutes talking with you and adorning you with my commitment to face a thousand deaths for you, my commitment that I would do whatever it was you wished, I realized that when I left the room, you would be leaving with me spiritually; that your body would be safe, but that you, Kayleigh Mickayla Mooney, your life was not your physical body.

There are two times where I intuitively understood, that once I walked through a door, that my life would be utterly changed. In both cases I did not want to walk through those doors. One would be in four days as we exited the church during your funeral; the other was leaving your side in Room #41.

As I walked from Room #41, I knew that you had already conquered your death and that you are bigger than this world, but also knew that I am not. My grief was so horrific; my wound an eternal blow.

*

8 A.M., A.A. 11th Step 08/18/2017

I laid in bed for only several hours, not really sleeping as much as I was punctured of my energy as if a bomb exploded in the shell of my chest and obliterated my life. My cells were spread across the universe of my life; in pieces. I woke from this destruction on my first morning of this nightmare of the rest of my life, knowing I had to plan my oldest child's funeral. And importantly, I needed to start my day like I started every day over the last thirty years, with my A.A. Big Book open on my lap and the 11th Step.

I called Carly. "I need to do my 11th Step," I cried to her, "will you sit on the phone with me while I do my 11th Step?" I was wailing. She was sobbing along in shock.

No excuses. We do our work. I told that to my guys for years. We opened our Big Books on the phone and turned to page 86 and asked God to keep us sober for this today, reading through the prayers; meditating together; sobbing the entire time. I was less than ten hours into this nightmare, but I refused to dishonor my Daughter by not doing my work. I made a promise to her in the street that I would not use her physical death as an excuse for any failure in my life. My life begins with my sobriety. My day begins with Step 11.

A flood of unfamiliar rushed over me. New words and phrases, I thought. I needed to try new words on, work through phrases that made sense to me. Control and filter the words from others funneling into my ears, knowing somehow the risk of people, some very well intentioned, thinking they needed words, when all I needed was for them to listen. This would all start today, I thought. The wording was important. Very important.

As between Kakes and I, the wording was also important. I did not know consciously at the time, but she was already planting words in my mind, driving my mind towards certain phrases, giving me the ideas that translated into speech. She was in the light. She was here. She didn't die but transitioned – her life was not her physical body. She wasn't far. All of these concepts, concepts no parent truly ever believes they will have to wrestle with fell upon my brain and my heart like a ten thousand page textbook of a foreign language written in font size eight, in invisible ink, upside down and backwards in code and encrypted that you have to learn on the fly with which only days are provided to learn and upon which your life depends.

Kayleigh was present. I knew this. She already learned how to direct certain situations and was arranging the feelings and the color and the direction of this first morning, which I did not understand until later.

*

She Started Making New Contact Immediately 08/18/2017

Kayleigh's miracle, as I call them, began immediately, in the time just before her transition, during the transition and in the full freedom of her higher elevation. In the street she held on until she heard my voice, knowing she was in a desperate condition and knowing her Father would be there. She blasted her light directly through me as she took her last breath and left her physical body, in a golden white explosion of light that I could not see, spiraling and circling about me and embracing me, literally kneeling on the curb alongside me on my right side, her left angelic arm cupping my left shoulder, her head pressed up against the right side of my head, looking down with me at her body.

Those that knew of the sudden tragedy who were close to her all reacted in their own private ways. They did not know this, but Kayleigh has already spread out across the city trying to touch and comfort all those whom she loved. Her very good friend Luisa, after hearing about Kayleigh's physical death, sat alone in her house and sobbed, searching to music for comfort and pressed shuffle on her music on her phone. The first song that played was "You'll Be in My Heart." She conveyed this to us a week later, stating that she never listens to that song. She was unaware of its significance to Jess and Kayleigh when it played several hours after Kayleigh's physical passing. She just thought it was odd. She did not understand its importance until five days later at the funeral when I told the story of the song. She was astounded to hear that particular song was Kayleigh's song. The next chapter of Kayleigh's life was in full swing and nobody quite understood that. However, her spirit twin, her Father knew it.

*

Meditation Second Morning 08/19/2017

I certainly felt you immediately after you took your final human breath. That is clear. However, I could also hear you in the street, but did not quite realize it on that first day. By thirty six hours later, after your initial understanding in your body of light, and adjusting to your million points of light in your new body, I started to faintly hear you in my right ear like you were sweetly calling to me in the house from one floor to another. That second morning, in my 11th Step, I heard the following and jotted it down on the notes in my phone, in essence, beginning this book: "DADDY - IT'S KAKES. I'M RIGHT HERE. YOU'RE GOING TO BE OK. I LOVE YOU SO MUCH. YOU ARE THE BEST DADDY EVER. THANK YOU FOR BEING MY DADDY. THANK YOU FOR BEING THERE WHEN I DIED - I TRIED TO OPEN MY EYES TO SEE YOU! I WAS SO SAFE IN YOUR PRESENCE. JUST LIKE I KNEW I WOULD BE. BE SAFE IN MY PRESENCE DADDY. I'VE GOT YOU...GIVE ME YOUR LIGHT JUST AS YOU ALWAYS HAVE...DADDY I WILL NOT LEAVE YOUR SIDE. YOU CAN DO THIS DADDY AND I WILL LEAD THE WAY. I LOVE YOU. I AM YOUR GUIDING LIGHT. AND I AM AT PEACE."

*

The Memorial I 08/19/2017

It sprung up like wild flowers on the side of a mountain in spring time. A bouquet of purple flowers. Another. A glass vase filled with colorful flowers. Another. Ribbons tied to the telephone poles that she had been standing beside as she stepped out into the street. A steady stream of people she knew began to come to the site where their beloved Kayleigh had been physically killed. I began to see the vast walks of life that encompassed her own; different groups of kids, young adults, parents, merchants. Being a highly evolved and compassionate young woman, who nearly never judged others, she had befriended many.

The teens had already been by. There was spray paint spread across the concrete island separating the converging streets. "R.I.P. Kayleigh" was written along the curb where a day earlier the top of her head lay pressed to the curb and where my knees lay as I held my little girl. "We love you forever, Kayleigh," Was also spread across the concrete in big purple letters. A box of chalk was left at the twin telephone poles for friends and mourners to write her notes on the ground. Several Sharpies were left on that day and people began writing on the telephone poles themselves, these twin telephone poles, standing so closely together, that locked her view to the left of the road on that night as she stepped off the curb. Soon, within days, there was little real estate untouched on the telephone poles from the ground to about seven feet high.

In this catastrophic convulsion of love, a city and thousands of its inhabitants poured forth with confusion and light and love and grief and turmoil and shock and horror and pain. It could have happened to anybody. Everybody knew it. Anyone's child. Nothing in her life led to this moment. She did nothing wrong. She did not see the car, obscured by these twin telephone poles, and the driver, responsible for what is in the road in front of him, did not see her. Neither did anything wrong. It could have happened to anybody. Anybody's child. This time, horrifically, it just happened to be mine – my beloved, incredible Daughter.

"*Guiding Light*"

...And now, my precious child,
I face this not alone,
Nor shall this moment steal,
The union of our souls;

I cannot fathom fracture,
It's depth, its grieving folds,
Its heartache will take decades,
To lessen painful blow;

Yet the wind in your eyes,
So warm and unique,
And when I open up the heart,
I hear your spirit speak;

The moment was so sudden,
In its instant you were gone,
And as that night crept towards morning,
I dreaded that first dawn;

The only silver lining,
The only hope to hold,
Though you had taken final breath,
It also freed your soul;

And I, a grieving Father,
And you, fifteen years old,
The victim of a tragedy,
As you died in the road;

Yet now, my precious child,
You assume a guiding role,
Illuminate your Father's life,
With the omniscience of your soul;

And away deep in the night,
And through the days long,
I will follow streaming melody,
Of sweet Kayleigh's spirit song...

*

Big Book 08/20/2017

Because I must. This is part of the equation of high caliber sobriety. Particularly with the shock of the last several days. Carly had asked what I needed and I said I needed people to listen and I needed to work with new people in A.A. With no map to cover this treacherous ground, she organized a meeting to run through a part of the Big Book. She asked where we wanted to meet and I chose Shaker Lakes as it is a place that Jess and I had taken our children thousands of times for walks and games and nature adventures. It is one of Kayleigh's favorite places.

Carly was with me, as was my friend John who had been with me at University Hospital, and his wife Elizabeth, with several others in the fellowship. We had one dear friend call in from China. We sat over near the footbridge close to Coventry Road on the grass. Sixty or so hours after the worst tragedy of my life, I led a small group through the Big Book, stopping at times to catch my breath or to sob. Listening to the discussion. Turning back to the text. Grounding myself with A.A. and Kayleigh. Somehow. I worked my way through the pages. I showed up.

I felt my baby sitting beside me. Kakie was extremely proud. It was a critical attempt to fight through the worst suffering that a human can endure by walking directly through the suffering and also turning myself to another to be of service.

*

Dear Babygirl 08/20/2017

This below paragraphs are the second real time entry in what became this book as I started to journal and jot things down as well as I could. I knew, even this early in the process, that not only was I fully aware that I suffering an immense tragedy and its complimentary life sucking grief, but I was unconsciously aware that a miracle was afoot. Among the grief, family showing up, preparing my Daughter's funeral, managing the unmanageable, imagining the unimaginable, living the unlivable, I pulled out my phone and wrote a few notes.

Hi, Baby. I have three things that are coming to my mind, all wrapped up in the symbol of the Trinity Cross that we bought for your fifteenth birthday just three months ago that you wore around your neck. In three pieces, I need to grieve, I need to reclaim my life in this new configuration and I need to continue to build my relationship with you on a higher, spiritual plain.

As I wrote this to you, I heard you in my right ear, in a faint but familiar voice, attempting to puncture the crossroads of two dimensions, fighting to work your way through the air to comfort me, "Daddy, don't be ashamed to live and laugh and love. I want you and Mommy and Nathaniel to live - through the grief - I understand your grief and it will be hard, but also you need to reclaim your lives. It will be different now that I am not physically here with you and very sad at times. At other times live. Through the sad and the happy live in my light. I am always with you. I AM ALWAYS WITH YOU. I AM RIGHT HERE!"

*

The Great Eclipse During Kayleigh's Wake 08/21/2017

We set up this day in three stages. The first was just the four of us. We prepared Nathaniel that we would spend time together, just the four of us in the funeral home, with Kayleigh's casket open. He would be seeing her laying there, physically lifeless; her eyes closed, her soul's light having emptied from her shell. She would look different, I explained to both Jess and Nathaniel, due to the light leaving her body. Only I had seen her physically lifeless in Room #41 for hours after the accident. Our intimate time with Kayleigh in that hour are not subject to amplification in this book, but is instead kept in a sacred place among the four of us.

We closed the casket at the end of our intimate time together, the last time we would see Kayleigh's beautiful face. The immediate family gathered together next as we had planned. Only I stated a few words. There would be no stage to provide for others in the family. Jess and I were very keen on directing our Daughter's ceremonies as we saw fit without any straying from the message or convulsions from others. She is ours and this is the path we chose together. These were some of my words that day, "We celebrate Kayleigh today during a solar eclipse - she reminds us that Darkness never blocks out the light completely. Not ever. Kayleigh's light is so bright, like the eclipse, we can't look directly into it. Kayleigh will always show us the way through the darkness."

As the eclipse began, and Kayleigh being the power of the Moon, the family and extended family stepped out into the parking lot and, using special glasses, watched the magical celestial event. I talked to Kayleigh through the entirety of my participation outside, even using my phone to take several spectacular pictures. She bounced back and forth among her family, both her mother's and her Father's, among many people she loved. I could feel her presence as she enlightened the mourners, not wanting us to suffer, but understanding clearly that we were.

The power of the event was mesmerizing in the midst of the worst tragedy of my life. This solar eclipse, named the "Great American Eclipse," was a complete solar eclipse visible across a wide band that crossed the entire United States. It had been nearly one hundred years since a similar total solar eclipse was visible across the United States. The pull of the celestial bodies was intense; the coloring of the air itself a smoky yet ethereal glow. This was Kayleigh's wake, my girl, the Moon; conceived under a full moon; born on a new moon; eclipsing the sun.

*

1,000 Strong, the Wake 08/21/2017

I organically knew I would be seeing hundreds, if not thousands of faces, and likely would be carrying a heavy load. Just before the doors were open to the general wake, I turned to Kayleigh and said,

"My daughter, you lost your physical life, but I didn't lose you. Our relationship has changed. You are now my guide and it is up to me to listen to your soul and follow your light. Guide me sweet Kayleigh. The rhythm of Heaven is dancing on my soul. Talk to me Kayleigh with this gentle light from God."

I felt her presence strongly and could sense, if not clearly, hear her words, "Daddy, you can do this. I am right here."

We sent Nathaniel upstairs with his cousins after the first twenty guests, already exhausted by the experience of standing in a receiving line at a wake for his beloved sister at the age of twelve. Jess lasted only a few minutes longer. It is what it is factually and I do not begrudge her for this. In her distress she was walked upstairs as well. My mother asked if she wanted her to stand with her. I kissed her and said no. I would stand alone and greet one thousand faces all gathered in honor of my Babygirl. I asked my sisters and brother and mother to stand off to the right of me about ten feet away to keep the line moving.

More than three hours later I shook the hand or hugged every guest who came to give Kayleigh their last respects; every single person who honored my child was honored in turn by me. Each person who loved my Daughter and stood in that line more than a thousand deep was loved in turn by me. Kayleigh held my hand, reinforced my legs and layered an iron constitution within my stomach and my lungs. For Kayleigh I stood strongly, proudly, defiantly and, with a broken heart, lovingly. Afterwards, when I was finally able to take a few minutes alone, I wept. And wept. And wept.

*

Initial Transcending 08/21/2017

The unthinkable is the most unbearable pain I never imagined…we are beginning the grieving, continuing to develop this new relationship with her, while trying to piece our lives together in this new configuration where one of the four of us is in a spiritual body.

185

The grief, in time, may swallow me. For now I am locked in, but then thereafter will come the rest of my life.

When she stepped off the curb, she was behind two telephone poles and never saw the car coming and the driver equally did not see her. Just like that, my life was obliterated - but for her strong light it would be much worse. She and I are so incredibly connected and she gets me moving every day the last few days. We have lost no connection, although the channel is strained due to the shock of her sudden physical death and transition into her spiritual body. She is learning her new body. I am learning how to find my child. We are grappling with this together towards the other. I know this. I feel this. I own this. I am this.

It is now nearing midnight on the day of one of my children's wakes, something I never thought I would write. What I learned and felt today - your mission now with us is so much larger than your physical life was with us before your physical death. And your life was expansive. We walk with a purpose. And I have never been so proud. Everything I ever taught Kayleigh and the wisdom I gave her, I am now her novice and she has wisdom I have yet to understand. Our relationship has just inverted and she is my teacher standing with God and watching over me like I have watched over her.

I stand in the sunrise for the beauty of my life and the brilliance in Kayleigh's soul. I am your advocate. I carry forth your voice. You are my guide. Teach me sweet angel - radiant light. Illuminate my path forward. I love you, Kakes, completely.

"When the Ocean Burns To the Ground"

Besieged in a cresting emotional blaze,
A forest fuels a fire,
A tornadic wind spirals it higher,
And explodes in the clouds like a hurricane of fireworks,
A thousand lights dance and trail back to the earth,
After the eruption,
To catch ablaze the fields where once you lay,
In its destructive consumption,
And even the ocean weeps aflame,

As its orange fiery waves crest and collapse upon an ashen beach.

*

Morning of Funeral – Children's Room Upstairs 08/22/2017

I was fully running and controlling this horrific situation as best as I could, advocating, standing for my child. While trying to ensure that Kayleigh's pre-funeral prayer service before her funeral procession from the funeral home was as beautiful as she is, I stood out in the hallway before others gathered. I was talking to my baby. At the far end of the hallway was the room to the right in which Kayleigh's body lay in a closed casket. I just happened to glance up above the doorway into that room and noticed three signs all tucked together.

There was a "Kayleigh Mooney" placard above the door to direct visitors to the right wake as there were several rooms available. There was an exit sign right beside her placard. Above the exit sign another sign read, "Children's Room Upstairs," Directing guests to a lounge area on the second floor. All combined in one collection, one sentence, it read, "Kayleigh Mooney, Exit, Children's Room Upstairs."

I glanced to the Heavens, a tiny smile attempting to penetrate the corner of my wounded lips, knowing the spiritual nature of the message, arranged in such a way that only I noticed it. God was here. Holding her. Kayleigh was here, holding me. On only day five, it was an action in this first batch of re-arrangements that she performed, lining messages up just beyond our literal comprehension; just beyond the vision of our typically narrowed eyes. She was running and controlling this horrific situation as best as she could as well, ensuring to passionately and forcefully penetrate the physical world in a way for us to know that she was present and active and in love with her family. Even in the horrific depths of my trauma, she pushed he way through.

*

Mary Part I 08/22/2017

Those walking with me in these first days after Kayleigh's physical death were witness to some rather spectacular, and sometimes subtle, miracles. Father Pat sent me a text in the morning prior to Kayleigh's funeral, his soul touched with my Daughter's spirit and the significance of her connection symbolically to the Holy Mother.

TEXT: 08/22/2017

"Kevin, I wanted to share some more thoughts for you today. You've mentioned that Kayleigh was conceived under a full moon, and yesterday as we waked her, we experienced a total solar eclipse under a full moon, and today, as we commend her to God in the funeral, the Church celebrates the Feast Day of the Queenship of Mary. Mary, who was referred to by the ancient Church Fathers as the Moon. The moon's light comes not from itself, but is a reflected light, from the Sun. Just as Mary's light and radiance are a reflected light from her Son. She is the Moon and the Stella Maris, the Star of the Sea that guides us home. And I was thinking about the two times in my life that I had been privileged to witness sea turtle hatchings in South Carolina. I was told by a marine biologist friend that the turtles hatch under a full moon, and it's the brilliant light of the moon that guides them to the sea (which is why conservationists are so insistent that beach-front homes turn their lights out at night during hatching season, lest the turtles get confused). I won't be preaching about Mary, the Moon, the Star of the Sea, today because of her explicitly Catholic-Christian connection. But I wanted your heart to rest in these images and this providence. Mary the Queen, who suffered and lost HER child, knows what you are going through. God bless you!"

*

Daddy, I Left You a Stone 08/23/2017

"Daddy, I love you so much. You didn't get a chance to get a prayer glass stone at my funeral. You were so busy at my funeral and did an amazing job, but I wanted you to have one of my stones. I love you so much.

Last night, while you slept, I left a special glass stone by the side of your bed to find when you wake up. I was sitting there on the edge of the bed as you woke up. I made sure you glanced over to your right and your eyes caught the tiny, clear, round stone. You were perplexed. You wondered if Mommy had left it there – if Nate had left it there. You picked it up and rubbed it between your thumb and finger, somewhere in your soul knowing the truth, but logically, in your mind, not quite understanding yet.

You carried it downstairs and asked Mommy if she had left it. Of course she had not, which is what you wanted to hear. You asked Nate the same question and he clearly had no idea what you were talking about. That left only one more person in the house who could have left that funeral stone on the bedside table – Kakes."

You cried out, "Babygirl, you left me a stone. Somehow you left me a stone from your funeral, right next to me while I slept. You are amazing, Babygirl. I love you so much!"

"You sat back down on your bed and sobbed loudly, your shoulders shaking. I wrapped my arms around you, Daddy, and helped you breathe. I love you so much. Thank you for you."

You said, "My baby, you are telling me that you are okay, present and at peace. If you can leave me a stone somehow in this physical world, you are okay and you are powerful. Thank you for the message, Honey, your Daddy loves you so much!"

"Thank you, Daddy, I am hear."

*

FedEx Man Sean 08/23/2017

I gave him a can of Coke. He looked tired and thirsty. It was hot outside. He was delivering flowers. A lot of flowers. Day after day over the last five days. He was surprised. He knew I was the Dad. He picked up on the tragedy on the first day and was vigilant with us, ensuring everything sent to us arrived; frozen food; flowers; other packages.

I would not hear the fully story from Sean until September 23rd when he and I spent some longer time together. Yet on this day, in the midst of my horrific grief, with a pain of which nothing hurts this much, I gave him a Coke. I don't know how, but I did and it touched him.

*

Spirit 08/23/2017

Depressed, he slept on your bed every night since the 17th, looking for you in your physical body, that which he is so accustomed. Sulking in grief. Soaked in sadness. Yet you are not there in your physical body and he is confused. Yet there is something else. Something that he senses that maybe others do not. He knows you. He smells you. He sees in ultraviolet and, likely, he sees you – you in a color that the human eye cannot see but just as present as any traditional color.

On this day, the day after your funeral, with visitors coming in and out of the front door, he escaped. This was a serious problem as he had been a runner, a street dog. My nephews watched him run out of the front door and take a quick left at the sidewalk and literally run up the sidewalk eastward seven houses away. He turned at that driveway and ran into the backyard, a place he had never been, and sat down. The backyard he was sitting in so obediently was our old house, a house we had been away from for five months when we brought Spirit into the family. He went to see Kayleigh who was sitting in our old backyard at our old house, calling him there; coaxing him there, a place he would be safe and where we would be able to secure him.

While this tiny miracle with Spirit was happening, I toiled with this unnatural, new un-normal life as if I made a mountain with my bare hands only to see it fold under the weight of its first test of wind. The attention in these first days is brilliant. And brutal. It is real. It is all for you, Sweetheart. So many people running in and out of our home. Stopping by. Hugging. Crying. It is beautiful but it brings great fear in me – as there will be a time coming shortly - when will it end. When will mourners feel they have done their duty and stop showing up? When will those who are more aware and authentic likewise return to their daily lives? That is when this is going to be really hard, walking around in this world uncomfortably, like a ghost, while others are clicking along obliviously in their lives without this terrible grief. I shudder.

"My Perfect Poetry"

Penetrate my darkness - your spirit music, faith,
Grace me your voice - wind chimes, breathe,
And breath, embraced,
Come to me for I am here - I am awake,
You are my perfect poetry - released upon this fate.

*

Beaumont Mass for Kayleigh 08/24/2017

The school year opened up with a convocation mass. For Kayleigh. Kayleigh was honored as her classmates, now in day one of tenth grade without her in her seat and uniform, wept openly with a scathing sadness. The shock reverberated around the chapel.

There is a tradition at Beaumont, that if you cut through the chapel to get to another section of the building, you have to pull out a glass stone from a jar, pray, and then place the jar in a second jar. The stones were similar to the ones that we passed out at Kakes' funeral.

The President of Beaumont told me she took several of Kayleigh's stones from her funeral and mixed them into the stones in the chapel jar so that girls would occasionally be praying with Kayleigh's stone, in effect, with Kayleigh, without knowing it. I took one of the blue stones and told them, as mass was now over, that I wanted to sit in the chapel for a time alone.

And there I sat, alone in the chapel. Holding a blue glass stone. Otherwise empty handed regarding my Daughter; lost in the moment and wanting to go back seven days and freeze my living there. So much had already been lost; so much suffering had already occurred, and we were merely ending the first week of the rest of our lives.

One of the Beaumont staff, after perhaps fifteen minutes alone, stepped up to me in the front row and sat down next to me, taking my right hand in her hand and rubbing the top of my hand. Her name is Sue. I talked to her, conveying the now familiar stories, apparent miracles, which have made up the first set of building blocks following Kayleigh's death; that somehow Kayleigh was quickly learning how to shoot down heavenly channels to me; that she was actually, literally communicating from her new standing as an angel.

We prayed, me now reaching for her hand. I spoke to Kayleigh aloud, a father reaching for his beloved daughter, telling her how proud I was, how I knew it was an accident, that it was not her fault and that I knew that; that I only had devotion for her. Slowly my voice faded to a whisper. As I struggled to continue, Sue straightened up and she channeled Kayleigh's voice and said, "Daddy, I am here with you and I love you. God is great and has allowed me to be your intercessor and I am here for you. I will never leave your side. I love you so dearly, Daddy. Be strong as you walk this road knowing I am right beside you."

*

The Sentencing – One Week After Her Physical Death 08/24/2017

I was told at the end of the day on the 24th, nine days after Kayleigh held her assailants accountable, and in the epic empowerment of her womanhood, forgave them, that the primary rapist, the boy who she had trusted, was sentenced to 1 year in jail and would receive a 10 year Tier 1 sex offender status, and would be required to write an apology letter to Kayleigh. This in a broken juvenile system that sees no juvenile rapists held accountable with jail.

I held a blank stare. Empty eyes. My soul, in its endless throbbing from the sting of the worst possible event that could ever happen to me, now had to return to this. A blessing. A truth. A spark in the fabric of humanity that the good can be heard and the evil can be punished. She forgave him and so did I. On this day, I fight back the guttural desire to want bad things for him – to want him to be raped, repeatedly, like a million times, in jail, and maybe shanked; no. I will not go down that road. I will not dishonor my baby like that. Kayleigh stood a thousand feet higher than this boy by forgiving him, authentically forgiving him, and so must I. If she, the one who suffered the assault, can lay down the gauntlet of love for me to pick up, then I will pick it up. Whatever will happen in his life, and in the lives of the others, so be it. It will happen and it will be. Good or bad. It has nothing to do with me nor any intention, for I have no intention but my God given right to spiritual neutrality. I am free. I am honoring my Daughter's wishes. I grow with my girl.

And then I heard her voice, just inside my right ear, clearly. "Daddy! Daddy, my voice was heard today. It was really, really heard. Thank you and Mommy for supporting me through finding my voice. I could not have done it without you. I love you, Daddy. Thank you!"

One of the thousands of tragedies of Kayleigh's physical death is the simple fact of her boisterous and abundant life, despite the assault. She processed and pushed through the acute phase of recovery from the assault and she truly, happily lived. Not exactly the way she wanted to due to the assault, but she adjusted, pivoted and walked through it. Her voice was heard. She lived. Really lived. That scales the tragedy even more for us because we know what she overcame. And could see that the pieces were there for a spectacular adult life.

She had her voice fully intact and empowered. She was excited about the future. She was expanding into theatre. Into school. Looking at colleges. Painting. Singing. Maturing through relationships. She expanded an already open dialogue with her parents, learning together as equals.

"Star of the Sea"

And rise, the Moon awakened - its sacred guiding light, afire,
Its glow unveiled the darkness of the beach of its shadowy attire,
She steps forth out from the Moon and places angel's wings within the shallow tides,
Silvery glitter ripples cap the waves and sparkle in the rise,
She is calling for sea turtles to follow her towards the ocean's waters,
Leaning forward gently, my Guardian, my Daughter,
They scamper toward her light,
Toward a new life in the open sea,
As she steps backwards in her silver gowns,
Leaving moon sparkles in the wake as she released,
And as they cross the threshold and swim out under her angel feet,
She returns to the moonlight and watches over me.

*

Active Minefield 08/25/2017

There are one thousand active mines that I can place in the ground and then intentionally step on. And I refuse. What would be tantamount to grief avoidance or a slow erosion of my soul, I resist. What would be my suicide in an installment plan, through self-destruction, shame, guilt and self-pity, I resist.

What if I...put her in a private school in 7th grade; moved her to Jacksonville a month earlier; permitted her a sleepover rather than going to the party at which she physically died; had moved her to Colorado or outside our neighborhood to a gentler suburb. None of these "what ifs" are born in fact and none of these fictions bring my baby back. Further, these "what ifs" are the instrument of my destruction. I resist. I grieve. I love. I grieve. I flail and grieve. I smile. And grieve. And live. And grieve.

Give me the words and I will give you the pen. Channel through me, my Love, and give me the words you want written. The world will hear your lovely voice, both directly from you, and indirectly through your Daddy. Let's write, Kakes, and change the new world. Our partnership is brilliant. We raised an incredible soul. I am overjoyed and at peace with that part of this new reality set. For fifteen years, three months and two days of your physical life you and I, Mommy and Nate, once he was born, lived to the fullest. Just stumbling into our second week of this lifelong tragedy, we are learning our legs and still living, albeit in two different body types now. Let us grow.

*

Mary Part II 08/25/2017

Several days after Kayleigh's funeral I found myself sitting on her bed. I ran my hand over her pillow where she lay her beautiful head at night – just a week or so removed. I stared at the stuffed animals on her bed – the penguin she slept with, the teddy bear at her feet; a lion; a puppy; a tiger. It re-occurred to me that, although she was a young woman five feet ten inches tall, and looked like a young woman, she was still a young girl. My little girl.

I sat back and consumed her entire room. We had moved a year prior so she was only in this room for fifteen months. Still, she had filled it with Kayleigh in only the way Kayleigh could do it. I smiled.

It is a typical fifteen year old girl's bedroom – a little disheveled; magazines stuffed under bed along with high heeled shoes; other stuffed animals and random makeup boxes and bags; trinkets from her childhood on shelves. Clothing strewn into the corner. A bulging closet filled with dresses, sweaters, shoes, shirts and skirts. An overused makeup table, with a three mirror vanity. Her artwork covering one wall of her room. Between her two front windows, what she called her, "Proud Wall," told the story of her pride.

However, on another wall, at the head of her bed stands the wall between her wall and the wall of her parents' bedroom. Although I had seen this wall for some time, and watched the images on it grow throughout the months, its significance reached its pinnacle in this moment. There are likely fifty printed pages of images from the internet that she printed one at a time and taped to her wall. I recalled the first several photos she printed months earlier, right after the assault, and while she was taping them to her wall, I noticed that they seemed to be harsh images; metaphorical images of someone self-harming, slogans of rebellion with an edge, angst, frustration, relationship heartache, escape.

I recall I heard her singing in her room, the music floating down the stairs. A teenager adrift in song. Practicing her pitch. Learning her tone. All was well. Touched, I wanted to see her face and spend a moment with her. I knocked. Opened her door after she said, "come in."

"Hey Baby," I said.

"Hey Daddy," she replied, "come on in."

She was sitting on her floor at the foot of her bed, cutting out images from pictures she had run on the printer; images she had searched for and found on the internet. On her wall beside her bed she had already taped several other images. As I glanced to the images, they frightened me; an artist's pencil drawing of a wrist slit with stars and planets in the wound; an Alice in Wonderland picture with a scary rabbit; a woman's lips with black lipstick; a hand squeezing a rose stem and bleeding.

I am Daddy and I know everything, right? I intervened, but took a breath before I did so, calmly trying to manipulate the situation. "Sweetie," I began, "are you sure you want to put those on your wall?"

"Yeah, I'm sure," she said, smiling at me with that gorgeous smile.

"But they are kinda scary images. Do you want to sleep at night with those images on your walls surrounding you? Your room is a peaceful, sacred place. These pictures aren't so peaceful."

"To me they are."

Hmm. I was failing to curtail her artistic exercise that did not meet my approval. Could I manipulate her in some other manner? Should I just act in a dictatorial fashion and declare she cannot post these pictures on her walls. No, that was never my style. Instead, I tried letting her explain. "I guess I don't understand," I said.

"What's there to understand?" she asked, as if I was an imbecile. "It's simple, Daddy. When I have a thought that is scary, or a really strong feeling from the assault, I go out to the internet and find an image that represents that feeling and print it and tape it on my wall."

Daddy-Knows-Everything still did not quite understand. She looked at me and smirked with her eyes, her lips curling slightly in thought. She could tell she had failed to explain the value of her actions to me. I stood there like a deaf bear.

"Daddy," she said, "if I get them out of me and paste them on my wall, then these feelings don't stay inside me. It's therapy!"

"Oh" I said, her mature logic finally translating. She was nurturing herself through image identification, and processing the emotion or thought by physically pulling it out of her, where she remained unafraid of the thought or emotion once it was removed.

Smart kid. Really smart processing, I thought. I had done my Dad thing and overstepped without appreciating her path and the brilliance of her choices along that path. She was processing a rape. She was processing self-doubt. She was processing self-esteem. She was processing in a way I never dreamed or concocted you could process. I finally understood.

"That's really kind of cool," I said, sitting on her bed. "So, if you have a strong feeling of self-doubt, instead of doubting yourself, you find a scary picture or dark picture and get that feeling out of you."

"Exactly," she said, smiled, and abruptly interjected, "now can you please leave my room?" She turned back to her scissoring of the next image.

I kissed my palm and patted her on the head with it. "Love you, Baby, great job."

"Love you too," she said, as I raised to my feet and stepped through her threshold. So impressed with her.

Nice job, Dad, I remember thinking then, walking out of her room. Once again I stood in the presence of glory; a young woman who was caring for herself in a mature and artistic way, much differently than most fifteen year olds would do. She was vomiting up fear and physically separating herself from those feelings and fears. Literally doing self-therapeutic activity. So much more advanced than anything I could muster. And there it was. On the wall instead of coursing through her veins. The assault did not define her. Random thoughts would not define her. She was free.

What struck me on this day, while mourning her physical loss, was something I hadn't noticed before. At some time in the last few months, she has twisted a hook screw into that wall directly behind and above the headboard, and directly into the images on the wall. From the hook hung her Rosary, given to her by her Grandpa Bill, through me, after his physical death in 2012. The significance is this – at night Kayleigh lay on her bed, underneath her Rosary – protected by God and the Virgin Mary, which physically stood as a barrier between Kayleigh and the images on the wall that had scared her and had been jettisoned from her soul. Her spiritual belief stood between her and her pain. That was powerful.

It was another message from Kayleigh – Daddy, I am free and at peace, just as I was at peace before the accident; I am with God, and with Mary, with whom I share a similar light. I felt a piece of my tension release, grateful for her maturity both mentally and spiritually. She amazed me by this incredible thought process, implemented while she was physically alive, and conveyed to me after her physical death.

"Water Moon"

And midnight shade and shadow moths,
They come to roost in lungs that fret,
And drape the mouth with heavy cloth,
And spread their wings like fishing net,
And drain the gasps that draw on breath,
And thread the soul with fibrous webs,
Yet in the tears, the Moon, it shines,
And fills with light a broken chest.

*

Shells with Father Pat 08/26/2017

Pat and I went to the site. I reached into a bag of shells from one of our trips to the beach and when we arrived at the site, I randomly grabbed a few shells so that each of us could lay down an offering at this expanding garden of flowers and candles and stuffed animals growing across the concrete island at the base of the two telephone poles. We sat on the concrete, while the cars whistled by. The pink chalk on the street still marked clearly where her feet and her head were laying. The gravel they spread on the street to cover her blood was being pounded into the asphalt by the constant rubber of tires.

This type of grief twists and torques the parent mind and mine was no different than others in a similar situation. The grief expands and warps the ordinary; makes gigantic the gentle and basic moments. The doubt. The fear. The feelings. The fear that, in her soul, somehow the pure gentle light of love that she cherished with me had been erased. I was worrying that Kakes did not know the depth of my love for her, based on an old early teenage writing I had just found in her room where she wrote down free thought that included an argument we had that made her sad.

Pat reached into the bag and, without looking, picked out a few shells and began spinning them in one hand around each other. He told me

199

that she and I, this relationship, was a strong relationship. That her writing her words down was like using her artwork to just get her feelings out. He also said that he knew in his soul that this was a terrible tragedy and not in any way on purpose. That she could not have timed it. She was not drunk. That she was big and dynamic. I agreed. Even if she was apparently frustrated with someone at the party and even if she said anything dramatic in the moments prior to the accident, he said, this picture right here on the telephone pole that someone had stapled, it was so vibrant -it was not the picture of a child who killed herself. A girl facing down rapists in court a few days before the accident is not someone who killed herself. I think he wanted to just ensure I was not afraid of this, as one child had wrongly posted on Instagram the night of the accident his assumption that she must have done this on purpose, which was not true, and which caused us great pain and suffering on top of what we were already facing. The boy corrected his statement the next day and apologized. Out of thousands of people, only a few ventured into guessing dramatically and conjuring something self-inflicted, which did not happen.

I told Pat that she had a pleasant look on her face when she physically died – that she was not surprised – that she had no idea she had been hit; that she was not tensed up and expecting an impact but unaware and just walking when she was struck. The mortician told me the same thing in Room #41 – that she knew that Kayleigh had no idea she had been hit, based on her soft facial features.

Pat rubbed his head, staring into the street, continuing to fumble the two shells in circles. He was satisfied that I had faith in the innocence of her accident and returned to the conversation about our relationship. "You two are beautiful together. I would hope you would not worry about that at all. Every father and daughter will have hard moments and you guys had very, very few of them. When it happened she wrote it down because she's in love with you and wanted to make sure you two continue to grow. You two are so, so strong."

Suddenly the two shells clicked together. he and I both looked down into his right palm and realized that, out of hundreds of shells in this bag, he had unknowingly pulled out two white shells that were two sides of the same shell. He smiled, handed them to me, and said, "You'd better keep these. She's telling you that you are one."

The combined shell, two pieces fitting perfectly together as one, sits next to her ashes.

*

Angel in the Sun (In the First Week of the Transition) 08/26/2017

In these first few days following her physical passing, a series of miracles began; spasmodic messages as Kayleigh tried out her new energies. One was from my friend, Vicky, from work. Her daughter, knowing about Kayleigh's tragedy, and during the great eclipse and Kayleigh's wake, took a picture of the sun. What she captured was an amazingly clear picture of what appears to be an angel in white flowing gowns kissing the sun during the eclipse. She brought this to me in a frame. I was stunned.

I thought about the other situations that had already come to pass – Father Pat and the shells; Spirit running to our old house and just sitting in the backyard; after the funeral a warm rain and a rainbow and my thought, that we knew Kayleigh was amazing, but could we have had one of God's favorite angels in Kayleigh this whole time, and my soul hearing God respond resoundingly with a "yes'; the day after the funeral Tricia and I seeing four doves fly over our house; finding a turtle picture Kayleigh had drawn as a child when looking for candles; her friend Annie telling me that she opened her locker and a purple feather fell out of it and effortlessly danced in the air; the current owners of our old house, Chris, finding a birth embroidery and old painting that Kayleigh had made for Jess up in Kayleigh's old room; ur friend Amy finding angel earrings and an angel pin she found just laying on her table in her room, originally given to her after her sister Kate had physically died thirty five years earlier; the day after the funeral alone at site and a stranger came and sat with me, wondering what it is like to be a parent – I told her I wouldn't change anything, even with this tremendous grief in each second, for the joy of Kayleigh's life. I told her, "thank you. Kayleigh brought you to me."

She smiled and said, "No, Kayleigh brought you to me."

Kayleigh is connecting people. All of your light is shining through. None of it is getting stuck in your humanity which has been shed. You are free and at total peace. Empowered by God and the love you share with us all. Like a light exploding and refracting out in thousands of beams you are enlightening an expanse of humanity that ripples out from you. These are those communications of which we were aware. Many more I am sure fell on deaf ears and muted minds.

*

She Was Just Trying To Come Home 08/26/2017

It was so simple. Her shoes and shorts were on the other side of Euclid Heights Boulevard. She wanted to come home to be with me and Jess. We are her safety and her comfort; always have been. No matter what the kids were up to at the party; no matter who upset her or with whom she was angry or afraid; no matter, she would confide in us - one or both of us. It was a steady reliance we came to depend upon. No matter the situation she could always talk to us about it - sometimes she would not and would choose a friend, but she always trusted our council. And treasured that sacredness in our bond.

So it was on August 17, 2017, at a pool party, a house near where multiple streets come together with a main artery and twelve stop signs, in a patchy darkness, with kids running around, feeling like she wanted to come home to her safe environment after someone had frustrated her, that she came to be standing behind two telephone poles that blocked her view to traffic and traffic's view to anybody who might quickly emerge from behind those poles. As she stepped out into Euclid Heights, designing to gather her belongings on the other side of the street to come home to spend time with us, the driver did not see her sudden presence. She and the car collided at the front right bumper, immediately spinning her at her hip and throwing her down head first towards the street on the left side of her head. If she was a second earlier, she would have been in front of the car, perhaps being hit in her hip and legs and thrown off out of the street; a second later and she would have run into the side of the car and bounced off back out of the street. Instead, the perfect strike of a human and an automobile caused her to be spun straight down to the street, causing severe head trauma that would physically kill her just minutes later. She was trying to get her shoes. She was trying to come home.

*

The Georgia Sea Turtle Center and Kayleigh Kakes the Turtle 08/26/2017

Instead of flowers for her memorial, we had requested that donations be made to the Georgia Sea Turtle Center. In those first days, scores and scores of donations poured forth representing thousands of dollars. –Further, a silver lining in our horrible grief, in honor of Kayleigh and her love for sea turtles, emerged as the Georgia Sea Turtle Center named a rare and endangered Kemps Ridley Sea Turtle after her, designating the nameless beauty, "Kayleigh Kakes." She was brought to the center on August 12th, a boat strike victim, the same day we drove home from Jekyll and is being cared for in their hospital and will be released when healthy. They have been humbled by all of the support and donations that have come to the center in Kayleigh's name. My sister in law, Kristen Graham Klein, helped with some of the correspondence and certain thanks go to her for the help in getting this accomplished.

I submitted the following information to the center to post publicly: "15 year old Kayleigh Mooney and her family, from Cleveland, Ohio, have a vacation home on Jekyll Island. She spent her young life enthralled by nature and in particular, sea turtles, spending many vacations learning about and participating in conservation. On August 6, 2017, Kayleigh, with her brother Nathaniel and her Daddy, walked the midnight beach looking for Loggerhead sea turtle hatchling tracks. One nest had released a few hours before and they could see by the light of the moon scores of baby tracks leading to the sea.

Kayleigh, using her red light, proceeded to check every ghost crab hole along the tracks and miraculously found one baby sea turtle two feet down a narrow angled hole. She demanded her Daddy do his best to help her save it. After a half hour of diligently digging they tracked the hole to the sea turtle and set it free, watching it make its way to the ocean. Then she said to her Daddy, "Daddy, thank you. Sometimes we fall into dark holes but we can be saved. That turtle was me. Like that baby turtle I fell into a dark hole but somebody saved me."

The significance of this moment relates to a young woman who had been assaulted, who had used her voice to fight back and emerge from the darkness, like the baby sea turtle she saved.

On August 17, 2017, just 11 days later, Kayleigh was tragically struck by a car and physically killed. Her light, however, lives on forever in her family, friends, and in the sea turtles she desperately tried to save - Kayleigh, the full moon, the Star of the Sea, guides her hatchlings home.

Thank you, Kayleigh, for your light - Mommy, Daddy, Nathaniel."

*

The Four of Us in Our New Configuration 08/27/2017

We have no choice but to move forward in our new, current configuration. We are reconciling this hundreds of times a day. The four of us together – that you, my Daughter, have physically died and were spiritually released. Three of us are here on earth in our physical bodies and you are with God in Heaven as well as walking here on Earth in your spiritual embodiment, in two places at once. That is our current state. The four of us together. Guide us, Sweet Girl, as we continue our walk, the four of us together.

I explained it, somehow through the horror, to Nathaniel just after the accident by writing in on paper like this:

Earth:	Heaven:
(4)	(0) this is where we were
(3)	(1) this is where we are now
(2)	(2) then this
(1)	(3) then this
(0)	(4) until we are all in the same body of light

He understood, as much as his twelve year old mind could manage.

You are never not with us. A guardian angel of the highest order devoted to family and God, flooding us daily with your light to illuminate our way on a daily basis until we are all in the same bodies on the same plain again.

*

Morning Meditation and Intention 08/28/2017

In my morning meditation and grief journaling this am I heard Kakie tell me, "let's walk with a purpose today, Daddy," giving me encouragement to reclaim the shattered pieces of my life, while grieving her physical loss and continuing to develop my relationship with her. She is and always was particularly proud of my sobriety and is watching it closely right now, although it is the last thing that is at risk in me, for drinking following this tragedy was never an option; dishonoring my baby by drinking was never an option; using my child's physical death to then destroy my soul was never an option. Instead of being a subject within my daily 11th Steps, she now participates and directs the dialogue, shifting my mind's eye, my spirit with direction and purpose.

On only this eleventh day in this new configuration, you are accomplishing so much. You are an amazing soul and have shown such strength throughout the years - one of my rocks walking together

205

shoulder to shoulder. I would not be who I am without you. Let's keep walking...show me how to walk, how to see, how to hear...

*

133,700 - Forever Altered 08/29/2017

There are no doubts nor lurking suspicions. One fact, like a constant irritant, rashes my skin. I will be forever broken - mostly now, differently later, but partly always. There is nothing that can change this. Nothing that can swallow the pain. My Babygirl has been physically killed; the event the likes of which ripped my heart from my chest, leaving it there on that road where she took her final breath inches from my face and safe and secure in my light. No. The doubts are non-existent. I am forever altered. A fault line fracture has ruptured through the core of my soul. Its mark will never dissipate though its pain, I am told, though, as I counterbalance in moments, I may potentially be able to pivot enough to breathe. I am not so certain. I grieve you, sweet Kayleigh. I live in your light.

She tells me, already, in meditation in the morning and at night, and throughout the day, frequently – to focus on the 133,700 hours of boisterous laughter and life, not the 50 hours that, by example, represent the collection of little arguments or hard moments that we may have had over fifteen years, three months and two days that clearly did not and do not define our relationship. The 133,700 hours of embracing each other mostly define us. The 50 other hours collectively, a part of our history, but a mere backdrop to the beauty. That is a numeric representation of our relationship, having so few hard moments throughout the years. That is the power of our give and take, our back and forth, our eternal blending of light and love.

*

I Brought You Home Today In a Box 08/29/2017

The title of this piece is so absurd; crass; horrific; brutal truth. Your body, having been cremated, was sacredly handled and your ashes placed within a beautiful Celtic urn; a box with ornate Irish weaves, picked out by your Father. Truly a pretty box, one you would have placed your most prized jewels within.

As I left the funeral home, sobbing, I cradled this tiny box and carried it like a running back who has been told his entire career rested on securing the football on this play. I wrapped my arms around it, flexing my muscles to compactly hold on to you; to ensure I would not drop this box.

The last time I held onto you at this size was the day you were born, holding your fresh body in my arms, in the cradle of your Father, who likewise, held you so securely to ensure I would never drop you. And I never did. Now, your ashes fit into my arms in that cradle and I hate everything that has happened to you, but I am so grateful to be able to care for you. That has not changed and never will. Whatever you need, I am here. What you need right now is safe passage of your ashes home, which I accomplished; another horrifically hard car drive.

Mommy and I, weeping with jagged words and muffled, almost non-human sounds, placed your ashes on a round side table in the dining room, in the center of all of the traffic of the house, right where you should be and want to be. We adorned your box with the tiny turtle and tiny glass pumpkin I bought for you just weeks before to commemorate the saving of your baby sea turtle. I also wrapped your birthday presents from May across the top; two necklaces I bought on a Daddy Daughter birthday shopping spree – your Claddagh necklace and your Trinity Cross necklace, along with a marble Irish Cross figure.

So your ashes are now home, safe under my supervision. Thank God. A relief comes over me, coupled with the horror that my beautiful five foot ten inch tall daughter is now sacred ashes and fitting inside this tiny pretty box. It is your human shell reduced. It will always be a part of you, but it is not your life. As you stand here beside me in your body of light, wrapping your arms around me, hating all that we are going through, you invigorate my faith by reminding me of your present journey of duality – boisterous in the Higher Life with God, and here with God on the physical plain guiding your family of four in the physical world. You kiss your box holding your ashes with such delicate humility. I will surrender my life in the protection of this box, Kayleigh.

*

Well Meaning People 08/30/2017

It began much quicker than I anticipated. Really, really it should never have begun at all. Yet here it was right in my face. The lovely good intentioned – the avoiders – the questionable intentioned – the clueless.

I hear all the time from well-meaning people who have not lost a child, "no parent should suffer the loss of a child," or "it is unnatural for a child to die before a parent," and as they are saying this directly to me, someone who actually has just physically lost a child, I shake my head and think, I am, and I know and you don't!

There are other variation that I am starting to suffer, including, "give time time" and "time will heal all wounds" and "this too shall pass" and "she's in a better place." And I want to vomit.

I am less than two weeks into a lifetime nightmare so let me start there. Kayleigh was in a wonderful place with a wonderful life and a wonderful family and every joy and happiness within her, and her entire hopeful life in front of her. She faced it with dignity and strength and laughter and deep thinking. She was brilliant in her physical form. After her transition, of course she's in a "better place," meaning, she is one thousand times stronger than she was before her transition, now stripped of human hang-ups and the cage of humanity, and wearing the eternal gowns of one million points of light in her brilliant spiritual life. Yes, therefore, she is in a better place, but the place she was in previously was pretty amazing as well.

All of these statements and a myriad of others are meant to build bridges to relate, to support, out of their own uncomfortableness and sometimes with the thought in mind that somehow they need to come up with words of wisdom in order to save this fragile family from itself. We do not need words of wisdom – we need ears of wisdom.

Well-meaning people – stop talking. Just stop talking and listen. More than anything, parents who have lost their child physically in this world need others to listen. To really listen. To let us talk in circles. To vomit emotion. To shake and fall apart without anyone needing to drum up salutations and words of encouragement. I know for me, as I am facing this tragedy one second at a time, and in the middle of this experience, I do not want nor do I need words of wisdom. I don't need mantras and words of advice. I need trusted souls who will listen.

We don't need verbal platitudes or words of encouragement – words of encouragement are a house of cards with no durability – this is a child's physical life, tragically and innocently lost in childhood in a horrible, simple accident. These simple suggestions and unknowingly self-centered intrusions only aggravate the situation and further isolate the grieving parents. They even come across sometimes more like a weapon than they do an olive branch of love. As this nightmare keeps giving, perhaps those around me can reflect for a moment and offer me ears of wisdom. The words I will make myself.

"You Will Never Make Them Understand"

Like throwing air into the sky,
Like wetting the sea as if it's dry,
Like drying the sand on a desert plain,
Like watering the grass in a steady rain;

Ah, they never tell you in a clever way they hear,
Nor that the discomfort is a means to disappear,
So it is, they tell you not a thing for which you care,
Not anything - not any time - not anywhere - beware:

Like applying logic to the illogical mind,
Like offering reading glasses to the man who is blind,
Like screaming at the deaf inches from their ear,
When you know - and you know - that they can't hear;

Ah, and down the winding road, a labyrinth, it tells you,
To chart a course right though it's heart,
It persuades you - compels you,
Yet in the last analysis frustration makes its stand,
In all these vain attempts to make them understand...

...For, unless they too suffer this nightmare,
You can never make them understand.

*

"The Voice of Courage #6 Your Canvas" 08/30/2017

This is the final piece of Kayleigh's "Voice of Courage." It was simply my addition, a full, blank white canvas, to present to her girls at Beaumont, a doorway forward in their lives, with Kayleigh's example guiding them, with these words:

Kayleigh offers you this canvas for your voice;
To support one another, to stand up against bullying,
To refuse to permit sexual violence to go unpunished;

Or to stand as Kayleigh to tell your own courageous story.

~ The Courage of You ~

*

Possum 08/31/2017

I was at the site until nearly 11 PM. When I returned home from being with Kakes, I sat with Jess and Nate in our sitting room. Suddenly, Nate called out, "guys! Look!" He pointed out the window. Outside our sitting room window a Virginia Possum had climbed our tiny tree and stared into our eyes.

Clearly Kayleigh has sent this soul or, perhaps, we guessed, it somehow could be Kayleigh. We went outside and watched it; took pictures of it; talked to it. We looked up the spirit meaning for Possum, which stated, to see a possum indicates that something may not be what it appears to be... one needs to dig deeper and look for the hidden meaning of situations. Possums are born blind and must learn to rely on their other senses to guide them. Possums act as a guide to discovering unseen talents and hidden wisdom and the possum is skilled at uncovering truth. "Virginia Opossum" is known as The Guardian and will give its life to protect those on a spiritual quest.

Then I turned back to my phone and turned to Jess to show her an image I snapped of a possum totem and in my "related" photos on my iPhone were pictures common - only of Kayleigh! They were pictures of Kayleigh's face related to a picture of a possum.

As these events and miracles began to unfold, there was an electric feel to the air, to our souls when we knew it was Kayleigh, and we began to be able to feel and decipher when it was not – sometimes the wind would blow and it was just the wind; and sometimes the wind would blow with a certain current and it was Kayleigh talking. This was clear.

*

Faith and Fear in Co-Existence 09/01/2017

"THERE IS OPPORTUNITY IN THE ECOSYSTEM OF THIS MOMENT TO EMBRACE RADICAL CHANGE BY

211

ACKNOWLEDGING THAT THE TRUE POWER IN THIS MOMENT IS FAITH RATHER THAN FEAR."

I wrote this little treasure on the afternoon of August 16, 2017. One day before Kayleigh was physically killed. Someday God and I are going to have a little discussion about this one and its timing.

This was a message that I conveyed to Kayleigh and Nathaniel on a consistent basis, as well as to my support group in A.A. This writing, the only one on August 16, was wedged between the day prior, where Kayleigh confronted her rapist at a sentencing hearing, and the day after, where Kayleigh was accidentally physically killed in a horrible and unrelated event. And there in the middle is her Father writing a sentence that, on the morning of August 18, my first morning after my baby's physical death, would pound throughout my soul. Stay in the moment. Co-exist with fear. Use courage and faith to step forward. The only way through is through. Mobilize your resources. Do your work. Grieve. Live. Transition with Kayleigh. Courage is not the absence of fear, but having fear and walking through it.

It was extremely difficult to apply this rule, and very easy. It is perfect duplicitousness. It co-exists. Its message will be a lifeline for me as the terror of my life rips new holes in the sails.

*

Conversion of Daddy Daughter Time 09/02/2017

I've converted my Kayleigh time - I would find time each day with her. Now I need to compartmentalize and live my life like I always did and save spots in the day for the two of us to commune - not unlike the way we used to, in a way. Now it is a blending of the physical with the spiritual world, but, regardless, whether Kayleigh is in her physical or spiritual body, it is still Kayleigh and it is still Daddy Daughter time.

"The Rising"

A golden shimmer, swoon,
Its petals unfold in velvet bloom,
Lighting the edges of sea storms raging,
That trail off to horizon with lightening fading,
And it, with star fields only soon,
This magnificent full Moon,
Rises just for you -

It holds your light in liquid gold,
It holds your life, your spirit, soul,
It holds for us remembrance told,
Of Daughter in her grace aglow;

Behold this shimmer, swoon,
Unfold across the sky in silky bloom,
Lighting the beach face and its rolling dunes,
And dance on the tides like one thousand moons,
This magnificence glows,
Your soul, my darling, you.

*

A Father's Light to A Father's Light 09/03/2017

Kayleigh, be with me – let's start our day. For those brief moments
together in the street, you were in the light of my voice, safe,
comforted and secure in love; then you stepped into God's greater
light having been safe in mine. I am so grateful, Kakes, for that
blending between my light and god's light that were a perfect bridge
of transition. I will carry this always. In those brief moments, you
knew you were not alone – you were able to let go in the comfort of
my voice, the cradle of my devotion and love for you. This is the
greatest thing I could ever have done in your life – helping to
peacefully pass your humanness into the spiritual light, with God's
love and strength resonating in the street and granting you an

honored, sacred passage – from your earthly Father, whose love for you is only eclipsed, but barely, by your Heavenly Father.

Every day I will walk here with you by my side – I cannot have you here physically with me anymore – yet I can have you spiritually with me always. I am your Father always, Kayleigh, and if you needed my direction, I am here. Now, in the light of God, you no longer need my direction as a fifteen year old, but I know you are grateful for me and my undying loyalty. I, however, in the inversion of our relationship, my sweet Daughter, need your direction. Your vision, wisdom and light are magnificence which I cannot yet understand – you are my Guardian Angel – my guiding light. We walk together every second of every day, of every century of every life. This is the present step. Help me open my eyes, my ears, my soul, and help me stay awake in the moment. I don't really know how to articulate it that well yet, but I sense the various channels you are building and testing to talk with us and walk with us and be with us; not out of desperation or the feeling of being lost, but out of pure peace and adoration for your three loves, God permitting you and empowering you to be in both places seamlessly at the same time. I love you, my sweet, little baby. And miss you physically horrifically, tremendously. Let's walk, for if I do not, I fear I will enter a death without dying.

*

Speak To Me, Kakie 09/04/2017

Your voice is so ingrained in my mind and soul, like a handprint in concrete. I hear your voice in its human fabric; your pitch, your tone. It's rolling laughter. Its whimper. Its glory. Those are memories now by this span of three weeks of torture. In the interim, I have heard glimpses of your spirit's voice bounce through the atmosphere, roll upon the wind, and penetrate the human physical world in which I am trapped.

Speak with me, Kakie – show me your light. To live with that similar zest for life as I lived before your physical death, knowing that I will never be the same; that I do not resemble my life before the accident. This is the great fracture of my life that will never heal, and I have to bind the canyon sized wound with God's light, your light and my own, through grief reconciliation, weeping, processing, facing down the denial and ultimately, sucking it up and living one day at a time this life, in its new reality, that I do not want.

I have moments where all I want is for this life to speed by me to my own physical death where you can reach across the air with that boisterous smile, and take me by the hand and walk me into the light. That day will come in time. I have no doubts. And then I think of Nathaniel, a little boy already tortured by the physical death of his favorite person. Somehow I need to get him into his forties. Then I can die. Until that day, however, there is much to do in this life – a life I was demonstrating to you how to live prior to the accident. I get to do what I always instructed you to do – namely walking through the pain, through confusion, with self-love and with a purpose. At 15, I watched you walk inspirationally with a purpose. You are my inspiration and I will walk with you by my side, My Love. With a purpose.

I just heard your voice, Kakes, saying, "Daddy, I love you. I am so glad you are my Daddy. I am right beside you. I am not ever leaving your side. The four of us are a great family and we continue to be so. The difference now, I am free and powerful and ever-present with you and God, and I get to guide you with my love and God's love. That is really amazing, Daddy! When you get stuck, and you will, remember that amazement and it will pull you through the dark. Daddy, if the tables were turned, you know you would do everything to be beside me on a daily basis. Well, that's exactly what I am doing – everything I can to be beside you and Mommy and my little brother. I love you guys, Daddy, so much, and am doing my work to learn how to touch you across the wind."

There are no excuses. We do our work. The unthinkable is the most unbearable pain I never imagined....we are grieving, continuing to develop this new relationship with you, while trying to piece our lives together. When you stepped off the curb, you were behind two telephone poles and never saw the car coming. Just like that, my life was obliterated - but for your strong light it would be much worse.

You and I are so incredibly connected. You get to live every day with me. Speak to me, Kakie. I am trying to listen.

*

Denial 09/05/2017

I will honor your light today by living in it. By calling on your direction, by knowing that you are living in God's light, I will honor my beautiful baby. You are right beside me, loving me, encouraging me, hoping for me, instructing me in my direction through my life – one day at a time.

Certainly I haven't slept in a few weeks. However, I could not sleep well last night either, I think because I am going back to work today and I fear I won't be able to have as much one on one time with you once the chaos of life begins today. I have been able to meditate so much with you over the last several weeks. I will, however, take my time with you. My moments – either sadness, grief, emptiness, quietness, gladness, humility. Whatever it looks like – I will sit with you, My Love, where and when I can.

I miss you, Kayleigh, and still can't fully comprehend that you were physically taken from my life. Denial permits the mind to slowly adjust. Otherwise, it would shock the system and stop the heart. Mine is nearly stopped. The house is so dangerously quiet, drained of your incredible energy. Unbalanced. Off balance. Obliterated. The new un-normal is a life I do not like and do not want, but the only one I have. With you with me spiritually, I can face this life one step at a time, but I do not want to – and I want to. I love you, Kakes, and I know you love me too.

The sanctuary of sleep is my safety from the storms of grief. So necessary, but I cannot remain in its harbor. I want to stay and nest. I can dream of you, My Love, or dream of nothing and shut my body down. Right now, in the acute stages of grief it is so vital, but I need to be careful of using it as a crutch. The great sleep escape.

We are all tied up – Nathaniel in particular who is lost in life, lost in school, who doesn't have the tools to focus and whose stress is growing by the day. Kakes, God, please bless this little boy and grant him your peace and light. Show me how to support him, remembering to be gentle.

Today I am hoping to have good moments. God knows I will also have many that are brutal. I will walk in your light, even when I can't breathe.

*

Darkness 09/06/2017

Moments. There are horrible moments, as one might suspect. Sometimes these moments are very close together, one after the other for an entire day; a week, separated with pops of laughter, breaths of calmness. It co-exists, and does not prevail. It shows its lack of color, and fades in the light. It rises, and falls. Not unlike the tides and the waves that come as they are – in their nature, in their curling, foaming faces. The darkness comes, married to its mistress, isolation; they conspire to steal my light.

"I Can't Wait Til I Throw up This Life"

The day I throw up this life,
I will be glad and rejoice in it;

Yes, I will live in a sacred manner,
I will make the sunrise to sunset matter,
Even if I wouldn't rather,
I will through the begrudge,
Through the flowers and the sludge,
Even when I don't want to budge,
I will heave through every day,
Through all the laughter and the pain,

217

Until that joyous moment filled with delight,
When I leave this shell exhausted,
And I gladly throw up this life.

*

Unpredictable 09/07/2017

Good morning, Kakes. Last night was pretty sad for me. I anticipate that frequently and really at an unpredictable rate. I dreamed of your turtle last night – she is beautiful, like you. I was afraid when I woke today that your voice would start fading at some point. It is a terrible thing to fear. I call to you in my 11th Step – and the pets surround me. You are here by my side and you always will be. I love you. I miss you physically tremendously. Sweet Soul, sing to me today.

"This Sea, This Boat, and Me"

Grows inside - this wayward, unpredictable tide,
It pulls us from our blankets,
And sends us scurrying for the safety in our grief,
Arid and with unquenched thirst,
Or stranded out to sea,
Where I realize,
There is no boat to cradle me,
Just the movement of the ocean as it swallows my eyes.

*

Harsh Facts of New Un-Normal 09/09/2017

One of a thousand hard parts of the new un-normal is sinking in – extra money I don't want now that I am not paying for private school; not needing a five bedroom house; not needing a large car for four tall people, etc. It is ugly since I would rather have you, my Baby, and be in debt and working until I was 80 struggling to pay bills and working it out financially in the eleventh hour. But I can no longer have you on the physical plain and can no longer pay for things that you need and I see the extra money only as a curse – only horrific heartache. The reality is that you want me to be smart with my money and do good things with it in your name. I will challenge myself to take your money, invest it and use it for Nathaniel.

I can hear you Kakes, "Daddy, I want you to live a beautiful life. That is what you taught me and that is now what I will teach you. I love you so much and can guide you now. It's really cool! How great is that?! You have to listen to me now! Ha! You can do this, Daddy, you can do this!"

Show me how to walk in your light, Kakes. Teach me how to use my voice more freely and in a strong manner. Show me how to be the channel for your voice. You use your voice by yourself, certainly, but also through me and I want to be your persistent advocate. I will use my tools and continue to open further to the channels and the modalities that you are mastering.

"Daddy, there is no way you were prepared in any way for my physical death. Your sobriety gave you tools most don't have but nothing prepared you for losing me physically. Be gentle with yourself, Daddy, please. This is hard for you and seems unbearable, but it is not. Stay in my light – I will never leave your side. I love you so much!"

Today is a new day full of promise and pain, full of daring and doubt, full of blessings and moments where I may feel my heart will stop beating from the weight of grief, disbelief, denial and a strong desire to not want this life and this road. The "this was not supposed to happen to us" needs to change to "this happened to us." It is cruel. It is unfair. It did strip from the physical world a promising, wonderful young woman. It all sucks. However, Kakes, you now walk with me 24/7/Forever, which you couldn't do before the accident. You now sit with me, you carry me like Footprints and you empower the wind in my sails, sitting by God's side.

Kayleigh, my beautiful girl, I will do my work – I promise you that – and I will keep my channel open to you and God. Footprints, Babygirl, Footprints.

*

But A Month Ago, A Turtle 09/10/2017

How could this be? We were just walking down the beach after midnight. A treasured experience between a Father and his children that would last a lifetime. It was just thirty four days prior and the world was so different then. I want to go back to that place where our four knees ground into the sand while we dug up a stranded sea turtle in a ghost crab hole while your brother ran up and down the beach. I want to go back. Please, God, let us go back.

"A Midnight Moon"

A midnight moon blooms in mystic golden hue,
Grayish blackened stains smeared with darkened blues,
We walked, the three of us,
Across the open beach face just over rolling dunes,
I was there with your brother,
I was there with you -

A midnight moon danced in the glances of your eyes,
You were so awake - you were so alive,
We laughed and played and searched for little signs,
Of baby sea turtles stuck and left behind;

My little girl, my little girl,
How you filled with wonder my wonderful world,
My little girl, my little girl -

A midnight moon graced the waves with splash of light,
Hanging on the sky like a beckon bold and bright,
You saved a turtle and encouraged its new life,
Walking with it to the sea - leading with your own light;

Now little girl, the midnight moon, it hears my cries,
You were so awake - you were so alive,
But now, my little girl, your brother and I,
We walk amiss, alone, without your body by our side;

We know - we know that you are there,
Beside us you are here,
You are so awake - your spirit, so alive,
As we will walk under midnight moon with its mystic hues,
We know that its light is alive - alive inside of you.

*

Nathaniel 09/11/2017

I am a great Father, who watched his oldest child physically die in his arms, and now watch my younger child spiritually and emotionally die in my arms. So much for good things happening to god people – if you do good, good will come back to you in this world. How about – horrible things can happen to great people and great things can happen to horrible people. The world can be arbitrary and not everything may happen for a reason. Sometimes accidents just happen.

His amazing life has been obliterated as he attempts to regain a foothold on his life. My heart aches for this sweet, little boy. He is amazing and one of the two loves of my life. I give him daily triage. I fear for his dreams. I dream in his fears. I cry with his angst. I wrap his tears with my soul.

"Nathaniel's Eyes"

Piercing gold flecks flow and flitter,
Glittering glow, bright white and green,
Sparkle in the basin of your eyes,
Where your soul swims in a scented, steady stream,

A warming light,
That holds the tender rhythm of your voice,
That strums through the waters toward me,
Fill my crevasses, the spaces experience erodes,
With your light,
And deeply shine,
Enlighten the aging wisdom stones,
That have dulled over time,
And look into my eyes,
Into my folds,
With your beautiful soul,
That enhances the beauty in mine.

*

When I Used To Sleep 09/11/2017

Good morning, Kakes. I love you and miss you physically so much. I woke up late today with a heartache and vicious fear that I won't have my sacred time with you in morning meditation as I am up and running. I hate this world now. Yet I know you walk with me and we will find our time, but it's so sacred and so hard to escape from life sometimes to get quiet with you. And then I remember in the shift, I love this world for this world includes you and your brother and your mother.

I have big meetings at work today. I will bring your courage with me and learn from your example and try to relax and be myself – whomever myself is anymore. Truly, if I could eulogize my beloved daughter in front of a thousand mourners in the worst trauma one can experience, then work stress is like quiet air now – there is nothing in this world I can't face.

I did not sleep well last night and had choppy dreams and nightmares of some of the trauma and issues you were resolving, as well as understandable decisions you were making in the confusion of it all. All age appropriate early teenage thoughts and actions, coupled by a serious crime perpetrated against you. It was a lot. It was confusing and you managed it expertly. I am not embarrassed or disappointed in any decisions that you made, as the road was a road of healing with its ups and downs, leading you to the plain of empowerment on which you stood on that fateful day on the 17th. . I have nothing but unconditional love for you and some residual sadness that you had to struggle through a few serious things cast upon you. I can't help but be happy that, although this tragedy has been set upon our doorstep, you were empowered and struggling forward, if struggling still at all, in your life when you physically died.

"Daddy, you are right – I was struggling at times. How could I not, recovering from a rape? You are right – I was struggling forward and doing better and better. I was on top of the world when the transition came. I am so sorry for your pain. This was a total accident and I'm a little frustrated that it happened, even though I am extremely happy. Thank God I was happy before the transition and just transitioned into a larger happiness. Know that I am at a higher peace than the peace I knew and I am right by your side. I will never leave your side, Daddy."

*

Everpresent 09/13/2017

Kakes, good morning, My Love. A bumblebee too big for its own good flew in beside me during my meditation this morning – as you know. Thank you for that. It believes – and so it flies. Remember that? We used to talk about how important it was that the bumblebee can't read for if it could read the literature claims that she can't fly based on the weight of her body. But she can't read. And she believes she can fly. So she does.

You were with me so strongly last night that I could feel the electricity in the air of your light. Above the window for those few minutes, a small reflection of light the size of my hand, just sitting there watching over me – it is you. I knew it immediately, watching over your Father while I was talking to you. I could find no source for the reflection and there were other traces of light reflected on other walls that remained there as your light above the window disappeared – to go check on Mommy and Nathaniel – I knew it. It is unexplainable, but the feeling that comes with the moment is unmistakable. It was almost overwhelming but so beautiful. I felt literally in your light which is where I want to be.

It's just a parent's intuition. I can always tell when you are beside me – when it is not just the wind, but you traveling in it – when it is not just the wind chimes, but you singing through them and using the metal melody as your voice.

Let's walk today, Kakes, and see what we can accomplish together of my life, and in yours. I know you will do plenty on your own as a guardian angel, but know also that through me, My Love, you will do great things. I am in love with you, my sweet Daughter, my Kakes. Thank you for you – for being my Daughter, my baby, my guardian. Today will be quiet. Let us be quiet together today. I walk and live in your light. I love you, Kakie.

"Daddy, you are right again! I am here. I'm really figuring this out! I love you so much!"

*

One Month by Thursdays 09/14/2017

Today is one month counting off by Thursdays. One month of grief, of total destruction of my life. One month of speaking to you on only a spiritual plain. One month absent the texture of your physical voice. One month of extreme heartache and raw suffering, of near death by heartbreak and abysmal sorrow.

Yet we walk for there is no other option. We do this together. As I let go of the physical and embrace you further on the spiritual, which may take a lifetime, I pause often, vomiting up this road; not wanting to be on this road. I grieve and try to reconcile every wave that causes both extreme pain and also healing salts. Yet what can a man do cast upon a roiling sea with tempests of emotional hurricanes closing in on every angle.

I don't know what I am doing. I am struggling to interact with others. I don't know when or how to bring up your physical death and to whom; how to cut the conversation off when I feel uncomfortable or they try to build bridges or are "trying to help" by telling me about their loss of a cousin or a grandfather or a spouse. I want to shoot them in those moments because it is not a teenage daughter and no one compares to you! We are just a month into this transition and already by the dozens I have many who want to relate by making it about themselves and their losses. The psychology of it is fascinating but I don't really care – I don't have time for this nonsense. I do not disparage their losses, but unless it's the physical death of a child in childhood it actually de-minimizes the unique loss that I am going through when they tell me they know what I'm going through because they lost their parent. No you don't. Stop talking to me. Walk away.

My denial moments are no longer safe and I hate them – I know you are gone physically – and when I think – what happened, what just happened – my Daughter is dead? My daughter is gone? My daughter won't be bouncing up the front walkway? My daughter won't make me late for work by sleeping in too late for school? My daughter won't walk down the aisle or walk for graduation from college or high school or even enter tenth grade? What just happened?

I feel powerless. There is nothing I can do to go back to buying a house in 2016 in another city, or sticking you in St. Ann's in 7th grade, or moving to a rental in Brecksville in May of this year, or making different plans the night of the accident – I can't go back. I can't change history. It'll kill me to second guess myself – would you be alive if I moved you to Jacksonville at the end of 9th grade? There are a thousand similar roads that I refuse to go down because they are fruitless and they will kill me and you want me not to enter these one way streets. It will kill me to reverse engineer my steps to a time where the facts would run down a different chain that didn't lead to your physical death. I surrender. Again. And again. With every passing thought. I surrender. I leave these thoughts upon God's doorstep and hand Him a broom to wash it all away. I cannot change the past. I did just about all I could do. I did not kill you. It was a horrible set of circumstances and a car accident. Still, if we lived in another city – would the accident have happened? No. I surrender. I surrender. I surrender.

"Daddy, it is not your fault and not my fault that I was physically killed. It was just a horrible set of circumstances that were out of our control, as you said. That is what has physically separated us – it was nothing you or Mommy did. My God! You two are the best parents ever! Please know that this is just physical separation. I will always be with you and will never, never leave your side. I love you, Daddy. You ran immediately to my side when I was struck. That is you in a nutshell. That is you under pressure. That is you with your little girl. I am so grateful for you – My Daddy! You are mine!"

*

Courage – Standing in Kayleigh's Light 09/15/2017

What does it mean to live in her light? Stand up and face the day. Remember her inspiration in facing difficulties and duplicate her energy and courage. Face challenges like she did. That is what it looks like when I move back into her light. When she was just a child, burgeoning on young womanhood, she was scared and nervous but reached deep inside and found the courage to face down the sexual assault, a trial, facing her peers and starting a new school. The pressure on Kayleigh was enormous and it did take its toll. However she survived. She faced it all. And she thrived in the mission of Kayleigh loving Kayleigh and taking care of Kayleigh. She is synonymous with courage. You are my example, Sweet Daughter of mine. You are the strength of courage itself.

"I Miss the Texture of Your Voice, My Love"

Alas, alone, upon this silent road,
Slugging barefoot across shards of stones,
My soul through the soles of my feet bleed,
I seethe and I grieve –

The isolation, quiet and profound,
Filled with the pain of absolutely no sound,
So loud – I cannot breathe –

I have old movies that capture your chirping little laugh,
I have your toddler days up through the day you passed,
I have the weight of years where I will have no choice,
My ears strain,
My soul strains,
Just to hear your voice.

*

Morning Prayer and Meditation 09/16/2017

The unthinkable is unbearable, but for her guiding light. She has always been one of my primary inspirations and she pushes me every day. I do a morning prayer and meditation and call her with me, knowing she is always by my side. Then I journal and try to grieve, continue my relationship with her and pick up the pieces that no longer all fit together. I break down all the time and am so heart sick and physically broken down, but I live in her light, which gives me comfort. I swing back and forth, ebb and flow, crash and rise, cry and die, and rise again.

"There Is No Thief That Can Alter the Soul"

And now that this "soul thief,"
Of life came to reap,
Replaced her physical presence,
With a hurricane of grief;

It failed to understand,
All that God can see,
And all that she resonates,
Dwells deeply within me;

And it could not understand,
There is no season for thief,
For the soul is indestructible,
Blazes eternally;

And she is a guardian,
Illuminates my feet,
Directing my heart,
When my heartbreak makes me weak;

And I, as her Father,
Know she triumphs in peace,
She has left this physical plain,
With all of its humanity,
With all of its pain,
With all of its hope, laughter and disdain,
To assume her magnificent place,
Radiance in the sky,
As the Star,
The star of the Sea.

*

Back to Moment 09/16/2017

Babygirl, please be with me. Help me enjoy this amazing life God gave me, which you have enhanced with your soul and illuminate further with your light. You are magnificent. You are my beautiful daughter. You are my little love. If I no longer see this world with the potential to contain beauty, there will be no hope for me. Hope with me. Walk with me.

My concentration wanes, losing all focus, lost at times in this forest of grief. Processing acceptance, rejection, values, denial, our spiritual journey together, the horrible "whys" and all of the other exhaustive tendencies, grief and pain that string together moment to moment to moment. The world is in constant motion. I am nearly standing still.

I know, as I continue to heal, my feet will quicken, closely resembling the world's automatic pace. But I want to be meaningful. Purposeful. I can only commune with God and with you in the moment. And the moment is so fleeting, awash with memories of the past and future sadness of all of the things you will not get to do. I ache. I cry. I fight the wind. I scream. I try to run backwards. I try to wake up from this nightmare. And I can't. Nothing works. Nothing brings you back to your physical body. Be the reality in my dreams. How I love and miss you.

"Daddy, I love you, Daddy. I am right here. I will never leave your side. Come back to this moment. You are right I am here. Come back to this moment. I'm waiting to hug you and guide you. Best Daddy ever. Love you!"

"Words Grief Strangled"

I have not found the words,
Not yet, not since the thief,
Stole the light from my eyes,
And brought me grief,
That thunders in tormenting rains,
Enraged within one thousand hurricanes,
That range collectively behind my eyes,
So, no - I've not yet tried,
Not yet, not since this world decried,
That you would be called home,
Passed into the greater light,
In the fracture that turned my flesh into stone,
And my Daughter breathed goodnight,
But not goodbye,
So, no - I cannot write,
I cannot try to try to try,
Not since the heartache strangled me,
In the moment that you physically died –
My Love, my Daughter, I, I may soon...

...But for now I bleed, I seethe, I grieve, I cry.

*

I Am Not Amazed By My Amazement 09/16/2017

I'm not amazed by how amazing you are. I am not discovering that which I did not already know and that which I didn't tell you before your physical death. I knew you were and know you are amazing. I knew your talents and character and spoke to you often about how proud I was of your singing, your dynamic personality and your thoughtfulness. You knew I knew and I knew you knew. We knew this because we talked about your life – often, each step, each age, each day – with both you and your brother. So I am amazed by your beauty and your soul but not amazed that I am amazed by you. It's what I'm used to. It's who you are. My daughter.

I found a particular photo that had attached to it a poem I had written. We were sitting in the grass in April of 2003 at Fairfax Elementary School, over on the tiny hill. We were playing with grass, pulling it, holding it between fingers, studying it, throwing it, laughing belly laughs, and sharing a universe together – I remember the moment, like thousands of our moments, as if it happened several hours ago.

"Know Always" 04/28/2003

Know that I am here with you,
This world in Kayleigh's hand,
A universe upon a fingertip,
A baby's breath sets the grasses dancing,
Whispers of contentment,
The glow of God's own love,
Settles between finger and thumb.

*

Robber of Physical Fatherhood 09/17/2017

Clearly there is something much bigger than the bounds of her life that is going on. Too many things are lining up. Too many seeming coincidences. She is going to impact thousands.

Still, I have been physically robbed of one of the things I do best - being an active Father to Daddy's little girl. I was substantially in sync - able to anticipate her needs - present and active - loving in my ways. She is my twin. I know her so well and she knows me just as well.

Perfectly human in the mistakes I would make and unique in the quickness of correction. Always trying to find new ways to connect and new ways to guide. New ways to apologize and make corrections. I still remember the excitement when she was a toddler when I looked at our physical size difference and clearly noted how intimidating it must be for a man over six feet tall to discipline or apologize to a child two feet tall. So, when the times came, and they did, and I lost my cool or yelled or was frustrated and needed to apologize, I would get on my knees, chopping down my size. Then I would bend my back to get to her eye level and tell her it was wrong that I said whatever I said that upset her; that nobody had a right to talk to her like that; that as her Father she needed to respect me, but as her Father I needed to respect her double. It did not take long for Kayleigh to empower around this notion - that here was Daddy telling her nobody had a right to talk to her like that, not even him.

Easy for me to say, but I know my truth. I know the priority of fatherhood in my life. I was born to be their Father. I had brilliant moments and I had those moments because I anticipated them, planned for them, dreamed of them and put my ego in the backseat and let my children drive. Both of them found great strength in the nurturing and trusting atmosphere that we created for them. For my part, being a Father and their primary male influence, I took seriously my obligation and responsible to train my children to someday be respectful, empowered, loving adults, by example - Kayleigh learning how men should treat her with dignity and respect; Nathaniel learning how he should treat women with that same dignity and respect.

"I Am Father"

I gave them all that I could give,
Wrapped the days in lasting gifts,
Showing them the strength in how to live,
Teaching them the courage to forgive,
But still the darker shadows on the edging persist,
But still the dangers lurk and lead them off by the wrist;

I am Father, Brother, Son,
Husband to my very special one,
Struck down with disease when I was young,
And cornered with no further place to run,
And that is where this was begun,
And in that lens my soul has sung;

The trials, tribulations, tasks,
My faith grovels with the path you've asked,
Sometimes I'd rather hide within the cracks,
But then I hear her pain spread through the house like viral rash,
For I am Father and, Father, I shall always stand,
And take my child by the trembling hand,
I will sacrifice and struggle - I will actualize this man,
And face the days you've asked me to command;

And so I give as I can give,
And so I live as I can live,
Leaving unknown outcomes in your eyes,
And with my children filling mine.

*

One Month 09/17/2017

What a miserably hard day. Nate, Mommy and I struggled through
the hours, knowing we had survived the first moth of painful
separation. Many firsts. We had just forced ourselves to go overnight
on a first vacation in this new configuration, knowing it would help

us when we really went on a vacation. It was awful. I cried off and on the whole time, honoring the tears then picking us back up. We spent the first thirty days holding both of our children in two different ways, very concerned with Nathaniel and working with him on his path.

It was one month also of Jess getting increasingly frustrated and jealous angry with me, although she was also grateful for my connection to you. She knew if I could feel you and hear you, then there was hope that she could too. The trouble is that she did not. As the first thirty came to a close it was apparent that I was on another path towards the spirit, firmly grounded in a belief in God, while Jess, who did not believe in a God, was stuck. As you performed little miracles and worked your way through channels to us, I could sense it and feel it and Mommy struggled to see, feel or believe. It was her time in a perfect hell.

On the one month anniversary evening we drove Nathaniel to go swimming. I turned on my music through the BlueTooth to Future Islands, which is what I listen to in the waves at Jekyll Island. It was on a very low volume so we could talk. After an hour in the pool we returned to the car. My Bluetooth was on and as I turned on the car I expected to hear my music, Future Islands, and at that low volume. Instead, a familiar beat started playing at full volume for the speakers. I recognized the beat immediately and asked Jess "did you put this on?"

She looked puzzled and didn't recognize the song and said, "No." Then her eyes lit up as she realized the song and said excitedly, "is this on your Phone?"

"No," I said.

She glanced around the car in magical circles as if she was being surrounded and trying to catch the head of a meteor flying around her. "Kayleigh!" She screamed, "You finally came!" Her eyes continued to track around the car as the song "You'll Be in My Heart" pounded through the car.

We all three burst into tears as we realized that you jumped my Bluetooth to Mommy's and then found that particular song and then turned the volume all the way up. It was not a song even set to go in her cue. Mommy saw it happen right in front of her eyes - you telling us that you are with God, you are happy and wondrous and as a guardian have the power to reach across and touch us and comfort us with that song that had already been involved in several miracles.

You worked a miracle and we were all taken by happy surprise as we listened to the song blast through the car, crying, driving home. We stopped at the site and marveled at your power. If we had any lurking denial or suspicion, or fear that our minds were tricking us, those vagaries vanished on this night. It was clear from this point forward that you are truly, presently, actively, currently alive – communicating – producing miracles – engaged with your family. None of these miracles bring you back to your physical body, but all of them remind our failing minds that you are here. And our minds fail us often.

That night, after some further contemplation, Mommy turned to me and said, "Kev, if our daughter has the power to do that, and she does; if she has the true power of a guardian angel, then she must be getting that power from something higher. That's it. I'm done. I believe there is a Higher Power and He loves us enough to allow Kakes to be our angel."

And with that, Sweet Daughter, you brought Mommy to God.

"Yes I did. She is so happy. She has been watching you. Daddy, you are living the faith that you taught me. This is why you walk and continue to walk. Use the lessons you taught me so well. Walk how you asked me to walk. Stand up the way I stood up. Be the courage that I found in myself and take the tiny steps to daily reconcile. You taught me that and I healed when I was wounded and lived an amazing physical life. You are a great Daddy. Now let me guide you. We are just beginning. I love you, Daddy."

*

Memories 09/18/2017

Hours melt from your last miracle and the despondency closes the gap. Everything is in such a torpid flux. And everything has come crashing in. Rushing to remember. Panicking to gather all glimpses, all memories, and all pieces of our physical lives together. Back and forth from the physical to the spiritual, from grief to celebration, to horror to horror to horror.

You are in my heart, in my day, in my light. You are outside of my heart in your own living body. You walk beside your frail Father with such strength, love and grace. You whisper to me, and smile on me and encourage me as if I was your child – looking on me the way I looked at you when you were a toddler playing with little toys, with puddles, doing art projects, collecting rocks and salamanders and bugs, swimming, fixing a butterflies wing, or reading to you at bedtime nightly. We were the best Daddy Daughter relationship I'd ever seen and we still are.

The adjustment is so difficult at times, Kakes, with my human mind and emotion getting in the way. I hold the line of faith and love and it guides me through the darkest hours. I know you are here every hour of the day – in each minute, heartbeat, breath and step, just like that song by Innocence Mission I used to sing to you, which was referencing God, but now also relates to you, "You are like the ticket half I find inside my old leaf raking coat…" Like the song, where the narrator is unintentionally dismissive of God, I fall into these holes unintentionally. I mean, my God, you were physically killed thirty one days ago! I need to be nurturing with myself. It is hard.

Shine your light upon me, my Daughter. I love you eternally, Kayleigh, and am so proud of the woman you had become. I am so proud of your spirit and your incredible guiding light and who you are becoming.

As you know I haven't been sleeping, which is really messing up my days and I haven't found the time to write as much as I'd like, which breaks my heart. I will do some more later today, but I at least wanted to write a few paragraphs now to keep the muscle moving. I need my time with my baby, my guardian. Our long walk last night was wonderful. Thank you for carrying me – just like Footprints, Babygirl. I love you.

*

Killed Again 09/19/2017

I have these moments. Never for any particular reason. I will simply have this thought when I realize again that she has been physically killed and there's nothing I can do about it. That I am her Father – her protector – and there was nothing I could do to protect her or save her. Nothing. And I am killed again. In each second. Each minute. Each hour. Each day away from her final breath. Further, there was nothing she could have done. It was so simple. So innocent. So perfect – a pedestrian hit by a car going thirty five or forty miles an hour and the accident scene is less than five feet long – hitting her hip, spinning her directly down to the street? And I am killed again. In each second. Each minute. Each hour. Each day away from her final breath.

"Waves"

Standing in the ocean to my knees,
Feel the constant changing in the sea,
Tides rolling through me...

...Toward the beach...

...The pull sucking backwards at my feet,
While waves of grief of which I've no control,
Slam through the flesh and flood my soul,
With an emptiness of which I'd never known,
And draining my eyes of their salty, water homes,
And then alone,
I know...

…The wave also forced release,
The healing that hurts but edges towards peace,
The peace that has eluded me,
While standing up to my knees,
In this roiling sea,
In this roiling sea,
In this roiling sea.

*

I Am a Father Who Did Not Lose His Child 09/20/2017

I am a child who did not lose his father, yet my Father has physically passed. Both deaths were sudden. Both found me the first family member with my loved ones - arriving at the hospital just after my Father physically died; arriving at the scene of my Daughter's accident and with her as she physically died. I planned both funerals without guidance. Doing the best I could do under traumatic conditions. And these two really love each other. I know Kayleigh was in love with her grandfather, and he in love with her and her brother.

I never blocked from my kids the beauty of their love for my Father. I could have done that easily by conveying to them stories of difficulties that I had with my Father. I never did. Their relationship was too sacred and mine with my Father repaired. And she, therefore, never owned a cloud over his name and loved him totally (i.e., if I was a great dad then my dad must be a really great dad). And he, therefore, with the power of their love, was present in the street with us. I can't prove this ethereal gift, but its fragrance is as certain as there is air to breathe.

Now they are together watching over me. Working up plans. Tying things together.

"A Horse with Broken Ankles"

Like a severely wounded horse standing on four badly broken ankles, its life dependent upon its stance. With no choice but to stand, no ability to lay down, and driven only by the need to learn how to walk on broken ankles while they heal. He stands. He grieves in his troubled steps. He leaves a trail of tears that pock the blood stains shedding from his swollen hooves that leave a crimson trail in the mud. Tracked not by wolves but by the steady storms of sorrow that conspire to weaken his footing, he staggers on, alone, isolated, in a dangerous wood he has not traveled before.

*

Inverse of this Tragic 09/23/2017

"Daddy, thank you for taping that Hopi Leaders speech on my door just weeks before the accident. I read it all the time as I walked into my room. Daddy, you are the one we've been waiting for – I am the one we've been waiting for – we are the "we." I love you and I am here in the river right by your side. Everything we do we do in a sacred manner. I am so proud of you, Daddy, and so blessed that you are mine."

Kayleigh, how blessed am I? In the inverse of this tragic, incredible sorrow and loss is the tremendous gift of your spirit unleashed from its human shell and experience – you literally are here with me every day, guiding me, participating in my life, just like you always did. You sit with me. You walk with me unhindered. You bathe in God's light, love and joy. You transmit that light, love and joy through you to touch me, to illuminate me, to enhance my own light. Yet, still, it seems this will never be enough as I want to hold your physical hand, have you kiss my cheek, hear your human voice singing off somewhere in the house. I want to guide you and maneuver through disciplining you and taking a breath so I don't snap at you and hold you when you scrape your knee, or nurture you when someone hurts you. That is all now in the physical past. Yet, you now get to do that for me. How blessed am I?

"No, Daddy, how blessed am I?"

*

Sean, My FedEx Man 09/23/2017

The same driver has been with us for five weeks. He started showing up the day after the accident. Dropping off flowers. Dropping off meals. More flowers. More meals. Day after day. I could see in his eyes after the first few days that he knew something was fantastically out of the ordinary afoot. He knew tragedy had come to our doors. He was humble. Loving. A servant of peace and compassion. On one of those first days he looked tired and had dropped off so many flowers that I walked over to him and handed him a can of Coke.

Befriended, he became part of the circle of Kayleigh's presence. Once we explained to him what had happened, and he cried with us, his essence drew closer still. He was a beckon of humanity at times when we sat in the front yard staring at the grass, stunned with what has just happened to our family, to our baby, to our lives. And then Sean would drive by to check on us.

On this day he stopped by as he went about making deliveries. He had no package for us, but still came with a delivery. I embraced him and he asked me point blank, "are you writing?"

"Yes, as a matter of fact, I am," I replied and smiled, "that's one of the first things I heard Kayleigh tell me after the accident – which she wanted to write another book with her Daddy."

"Good. I've been praying for you guys and the Good Lord told me that you have a book in you that you're writing about your daughter that is going to affect thousands of lives."

I smiled in my soul now. A messenger. Confirmation of the path I am to take consistent with Kayleigh's strong voice and powerful message. She brought him here to confirm that I heard her, I heard her correctly, and the book was the key. "Thank you, Sean. You have no idea how amazing it is that you just asked me that. I haven't told anybody that I am writing a book. I just started it, jotting pieces down each day in my notes on my phone. It's about Kayleigh and me; our relationship; her voice of courage with all she was able to accomplish; and also about Kayleigh and I never losing contact through the accident. That she is here. She is alive in her body of light. That we are unbreakable. That she is proving what people want to have faith in, that there is a God, that there is a Higher Life, and that sometimes angels are clearly walking among us."

"Good. God wants you to do this with your daughter. This is part of her legacy. Keep writing. I'll check in with you guys soon."

We embraced. He went on his way. I wrote this day's notes.

*

Released Into My Light 09/24/2017

"Daddy, I released into your light, then into God's light. It is amazing, Daddy, as I flew right through your body and soul. Now I get to take God's light and shine that light down on you. How amazing is that?"

You are amazing, Kayleigh. And I adore you with my life and soul. As much as I can know and trust anything in this world, I know and trust this to be true – that you are my guardian – you do shine your light and God's light upon us – you are always by my side and I can rely fully on your direction and guidance. You are pure love and light. How amazing is that?

I take my gentle, tiny steps and breathe in the moment. I do not want to feel like I am ticking off the hours of my life awaiting my own death, although at times that is exactly what I am doing. I want to live as fully as I can. Like a marathon runner who has lost a leg – I can never again run at top speed, but with a prosthetic leg, I can slowly run those twenty six miles, walking and resting from the pain when needed, or permitting someone to carry me that last few miles. I am building that prosthetic leg, forging it with tears, grief, memories, regrets, trauma, hope, nurturing, light, love and your image and your presence in my soul and in the physical world in your new body. I miss you like one would miss their breath. I love you.

*

Angels in Human Skins 09/25/2017

I didn't know that she had been there. My mind captured the essence of the moment, but not all of the particulars in the fast moving, soul crushing chaos of the accident scene. I remember a tall, slender white woman with me in the street – that was Colleen. She would drive Jessica home. But nobody else, other than shadows of people scattering behind me and off in my periphery.

And so it was that I met Angela today, as I stood with my friend, Eric, at the site. Earlier in the day I felt for the first time like I really was vanquished to hell. I was mad at God, wondering why a perfectly timed accident had happened; knowing many are hit harder or with more impactful force, yet survive. But Kayleigh had no chance. The car barely touched her, yet she had no chance. She could have been one second faster and ended up in front of the car, hit and thrown fifty feet and likely survived. She could have been one second slower and ended up running into the side of the car, hurt, embarrassed, but still physically alive. Yet none of that happened. God didn't intervene. That was my notion. God did not intervene with someone as special and genuine as Kayleigh Mooney and that didn't make sense. He had intervened with me after I threw my live away through alcoholism. He had intervened with many, many lesser people than my Daughter. Yet here we were. Why, oh God, did you not intervene with Kayleigh, I asked earlier in the day. And my heart was filled with immovable, solid, cold concrete.

As we stood at the site a tall African American man approached and said, "I'm sorry – I don't want to disturb you, but you are the father of the sweet girl who was hit here, right? My girlfriend was with you in the street after the accident and she wants to say hello but doesn't want to disturb you."

I hugged him and said, "my God, by all means, please have her come see me."

He ran across the street to get her and walked her back to me. I embraced her. In her presence, although at the moment I could not remember her, I knew it to be true. She was in a blank spot in my memory, but there nonetheless.

She said, "I was with you and Kayleigh in the street. I was across the street and had seen a bunch of kids just hanging out and I remember seeing your daughter as she has such beautiful golden blonde hair, and I remember thinking, what beautiful blonde hair. Then I heard this awful collision and looked up and saw commotion so I ran across the street and to your daughter's side. I kneeled next to Colleen and took her hand and I had a good pulse on her wrist. Like a minute later I saw you running over to the site and I turned to Kayleigh and said, 'Kayleigh you're Daddy's coming. Your Daddy is running over to you and almost here.' Kayleigh fluttered her eyes at that moment when I told her that you were coming and tried to open her eyes to look for you, but could not get her eyes to open. She tried to move but could not. She said Kayleigh was clearly aware that you were coming and was there and was trying to see you."

Angela explained further that she kept her fingers on her neck and had a pulse. Unbeknownst to me, there was an officer who now had a pulse on her wrist. They confirmed this with the other.

She continued, "I kept telling her to hang in there. When you got to her side I stopped talking so your voice could take over. I heard you say to her, 'Kayleigh, it's Daddy, I'm right here, Babygirl. You are going to be all right. I love you so much, Babygirl. Daddy is right here. Daddy is right here.' And then I said to her, 'Kayleigh if you can hear your Daddy's voice, squeeze my hand, which she did, so I said, 'good girl, Kayleigh, good girl. Squeeze my hand again,' which she did. Then the paramedics arrived."

She hesitated, wanting to tell me more. I took in the memory and the filler that she was providing me, so overwhelmed that Kakes had tried to reach for me and tried to open her eyes to lock eyes with me. She continued with a second critical piece to this puzzle, and said, "I am a nurse."

My heart jumped.

"I am a nurse and I almost started CPR on her, but I was afraid she might have traumatic brain injury and I didn't want to hurt her so I waited for the EMTs instead."

Three critical pieces were answered today: that Kayleigh tried to reach for me; that Kayleigh knew I was there listening to her Daddy, her safety and comfort, clearly by squeezing Angela's hand a second time; and now, that God actually did intervened. God may have intervened by letting her pass to Him versus being stranded in a vegetative state, wheelchair bound for the next forty years. I asked him earlier in the day why He didn't intervene with my Kayleigh and now God is telling me, through Angela, that God did. She is free of a body she would no longer be able to use. She is such a deep and complex thinker, to be trapped like that would not be Kayleigh. If that had been our road we would have cared for her and tried to do the best we could no matter what and no matter the consequence. But I know Kayleigh and that would not be something she wanted.

As I left Angela's side, I heard God's words, "You see, Kevin, I did intervene. I permitted her to not be trapped in a body she could not use and a brain that would not function. Now she is with you all the time instead of being confined to a bed. I love you and I love Kayleigh. I have blessed you in ways you do not always know."

God, You intervened. Thank you.

*

243

Happy I Am Me 09/25/2017

I am so happy that I am me – that I love myself enough to permit my humanity with little effort; that I am not worried about who may see me if I break down and cry. I sob frequently. My sorrow is immense.

I feel you closely, Kayleigh. The gap between us seems irrelevant and non-existent at times. You are here with me, right beside me. A calm essence. A slightly warmer wind. A peace that prevails, though we are walking through the worst of the worst of nightmares as parents. Spiritually, yes, you are here beside me always. I am so grateful for that reality – that truth. I am trying to learn your channels. For if a parent was told that they could be with their child, why would a parent not break the bounds of Heaven and earth to accomplish that gift? I will stop at nothing.

Yet you are gone – physically and forever. It kills me to write that notion down. That fact. That truth. It will always be a foreign notion. My heart aches endlessly in that realization. It comes to me countless times a day like a storm of disbelief, trauma and sadness. Inevitably, as I slow my breaths and finish a crying session, I step closer to that maturing acceptance – knowing that my sweet little baby, Kakes, is dead – physically dead. There it is again – writing these words – so important – so excruciating – so surreal. You are not coming back physically. Ever. It is harsh. It is unfair. It is cruel. We are the last family that something like this should have ever had happen to them. Yet it is here. It is final. Yet the only piece that is final is the physical part. Otherwise, you are still alive. You see how my mind travels in these concentric circles? I exhaust me, but I am happy I am me.

Yet what else does your physical death mean? It means transition for you into peace and pure love and light. You were living a peaceful, dynamic, incredible life. You did not need to physically die to be at peace – thank God. So you transitioned, from a peaceful, emotionally dynamic life into a peace one thousand times greater than our human capability. Thank God you were both at peace prior to the accident and at peace following the accident – the continuum – your soul, your power, your peace.

"Daddy, I love. You. I am at peace. You are right – I really was before the accident too. I loved my human life! I have a great family. I had everything I could ever want. I am so sorry about the accident. I had no idea. I am here. Let's keep walking. I have so much to show you. You can do this, Daddy. You can do this."

*

A Kaleidoscopic Explosion of Humanity 09/26/2017

Like thousands of shards of broken glass blasting through the lens. Whatever chunks of glass I spit up through the fabric of my soul. Light and darkness. Blending through my breath.

I know you visit me while I sleep. I know you walk with me through my days. I know you hug me when I'm not looking. And you kiss my cheek, my left cheek, although you are usually on my right side, and smile on your Father. I know because you tell me. I know because I know you. I know because our relationship continues unbroken. Love is forever and, my little Love, your love is filled with God's light and love. I miss you, Sweetheart. You are my Babygirl. I am so very proud of you.

There are so many things that are difficult in the new un-normal. So many things that I used to do so naturally - supporting you, nurturing you, directing you, encouraging you, standing beside you in your trials and triumphs. Now I stand empty handed with words collecting in my throat for which no direction is longer needed. That stings horribly. I was made to be a father. It is my calling. My light. And I am a great father. Yet, with you, all of these skills that I was honing have halted, it seems, and will now be wasted as you no longer need my guidance as a teenager. This is a harsh fact. I continue to be your Father, leave no doubt, but it has altered so much, it is hard to get my baring.

With your brother I certainly continue unabated. I was called to also be his Father and, as you, I adore and love him to the ends of the earth. My babies - whom I love equally and uniquely individually, each

245

getting 100% of me to each person's 50%. But with you, my Babygirl, the pressure builds up in me - all the moments where I used to interact with you and catch up to you and catch you when you fell. That world has gone empty and quiet, part of the extreme torture of my broken heart. In the kaleidoscope I see our human lives, a million shards of light, of rainbows, of seashells and restaurants and vacations and sleepovers and silly faces. None of it puzzles together. All of it free floats on an endless sea trapped within a narrow scope of time.

"Silence"

The silence drips slowly,
And echoes in an emptiness,
And beckons me to wallow,
And beckons me alone;

The silence whispers like a hurricane,
Whispers through my burning veins,
Like a rusty chain of nails,
Gauges trail of tears and pain;

There was a day before this grieving,
Your life stood shining with sparkling promise,
Your Father was beside you,
Cheering you forward,
Your eyes blazed with confidence toward,
Your dreams -
Now set adrift I crack at the fringes of grieving,
Your life tragically ended just as it was beaming,
And I, I cry, cry in silence, silently I...

...And silence - it whispers like a hurricane,
Whispers through my burning veins,
Like a rusty chain of nails,
Leaving trail of tears and pain.

*

Up The Walkway 09/27/2017

There are dozens of times a day, and I am well aware of its fiction, where I glance to see you prancing up the walkway. I almost see you. Then my eyes drop and my heart falls off a cliff and the horrible reality of the new un-normal crashes down upon me.

Your physical life ended, you will never walk up our path again. Not ever. I know this mentally. Emotionally not always. It is a trick of the light. As if you are at summer camp or on vacation or in a Turkish prison and the day you are coming home has arrived. It is a quick hope. A push against reality. A snub at the unfair and unapologetic, brutal facts that stare me down. And it is never true and never possible. Your physical life has ended and the new un-normal is not the world I would like to pursue. Yet I have no choice. I sit on our front steps looking down towards Coventry, waiting for you to come marching into view, up the street, looking down at your phone, the wind blowing in your blonde hair.

"A Thousand Deaths"

Child, the song that sprained your hearing,
It spared no furrow in the fields of my soul,
The words that gained you sorrow,
Raised my angst into defender's role,
The thought that there may be no tomorrows,
Well, that thought crushed the spirit's skull -

As when you were a tiny baby,
In the pillowed, rugged, metal cage of these arms,
In which you felt God's warmth channeled in your Father's charm,
In which you sank in safety's depths,
Rest there, sweet baby,
And let us walk a while,
Until you regain your balance,
And again we see your smile,
For now my arms are heavy yet these arms are set,
For you - I would suffer,
A thousand, thousand deaths.

*

I Will Make You My Song 09/28/2017

What am I to do? Stare at the TV. Lay in bed. Let my life drop from my sullen hands. She would not have that. She would not want that. She wants life and love and light. For me. For her. For us. I watched this child live life to the fullest. Abundantly. With pure joy. With hope. With laughter. I watched this child stare down a rape and use her voice to conquer it. Then I watched this same child stare down her own physical death and use her voice to conquer that as well. Now I watch that child use her voice stoically to guide and direct our lives with love and perfect affection.

It is hard. Excruciating at times. Really excruciating. Yet I have no choice but to breathe. To continue. To make value. For me. For her. For Nate. For Jess. For the four of us. I have a voice that, blended in the centuries with hers, is crafted from the same light. Yet not as strong, and I would never claim to be as strong as my children, I too have a voice that is constructed in fabric of courage.

And I have eyes, eyes that see much differently now. Eyes which contain ears. Ears which contain spirit. A spirit that contains eternity. I observe and absorb the vicious waves that crash upon me and knife their way through me. Firmly in my footing. Awaiting the time when the trauma trickles to a flattened sea. Temporarily. In that temporary reprieve, I find time and space and energy to make improvements, reinforce the foundations, clean up the debris of my life, and build my relationship with her and her brother and her mother. And when the waves comes again I will do the same, as much as I can. She inspires me like no other. I will use my voice. The world will hear my voice. The world will know yours.

"I Will Make You My Song"

A Poet, a man with words drift along,
Arranged in a flow like spirited song,

Colored in the shades of brilliant light,
Refracting through the heart of a prisms life,
That you have enhanced with your presence,
That you have kissed with your eyes -

Know this, my Love,
These words cascade like a sparkling dawn,
As we grow in our communion,
As I make you my song,
As we strengthen our union,
I will make you my song,
As you make me yours.

*

The Community, Tommy's and Quintana's 09/28/2017

Six weeks ago, our beautiful 15 year old daughter, Kayleigh, was tragically physically killed, as many in the community know. What the community does not know is the warmth and love extended to us by Tommy and his whole team. Kayleigh has been in Tommy's hundreds of times since she was in a car seat. She and I wrote a children's book, "*Clemy's Pancake House*," the color scheme of which was determined in the third booth at Tommy's. After her physical death, Tommy and his team adopted a sea turtle in her name, "Keel," being treated at the Georgia Sea Turtle Center. I want the community to be aware of their love and commitment to the greater Cleveland Heights family. We love you - The Mooney4.

Likewise, I want to thank Alex and the staff at Quintana's for their love and support during this difficult time for our family. When the accident occurred, an accident that could have happened to anybody, my life instantly ground down to unbearable grief. The day before my Daughter Kayleigh's funeral, Alex opened up the shop and gave me and my son, Nathaniel, private haircuts - his way of loving us and doing a tiny piece towards getting us prepared for a tremendously difficult day. I want the community to know the greatness of this establishment - great because of its people and their love for all of us. Bless you guys – The Mooney4.

*

Voice of Courage (The Book) 09/29/2017

"If I can save one girl, Daddy, please let's. Please take my recovery art and share it with my girls at Beaumont." I heard her clearly.

This is my Daughter. One of the two loves of my life. Amazing girl. Dynamic. An old soul before her time. Complex. Compassionate. Talented. Sweet. Courageous. Having lived an amazing childhood and wondrous life, even through the assault, she touched many and continues to do so day after day. It is her mission through the brilliance of her presence and her voice.

So it was at fourteen, raped by somebody she knew in a place no one would ever imagine a rape could have happened. She did nothing wrong; made no decision against her intuition. She innocently trusted an old friend and that old friend violated her.

Ten months later, after her initial stages of healing and after successfully prosecuting her assailants, in this completely unrelated event, tragically struck by a car and physically killed, she elevated. Standing at a dangerous intersection and wanting to come home, she stepped off the curb of a busy boulevard from behind two closely positioned telephone poles, crossing to get her shoes on the other side of the street. The driver and Kayleigh never saw the other. So simple. So cruel.

The Voice of Courage captures the space of Kayleigh's life through her art between those two points in time - a glimpse of the dynamic strength expressed by my Daughter. She told me to gather specific pieces, guided by her intuitive hand. I listened and pulled them together, writing a little statement to support each piece, as seen through her Father's eyes, not yet being able to channel her words as well as I would be able to in the months ahead. Her Voice of Courage certainly continues to strengthen since her physical death, proving that life is not our physical body, but contained temporarily within a physical body. Life itself, cannot be contained and perseveres through the transition into something higher, something elevated, something so close to God's own light.

*

You Were Free 09/29/2017

I was reminded this morning that you had reset the deck in your young life – that most of your friends were delightful; a few were a little rough on the fringes of your life; and several dangerous, violent people in our neighborhood had crossed your path – those four sub-humans who raped you. I had a fleeting thought that I wish I had gotten you out; as if, if I had gotten you out of this middle class neighborhood, you would have survived the car accident, which has nothing to do with the neighborhood or evil boys or anything.

This is just me resetting facts out of denial, desire, confusion and sorrow - blaming myself for your death somehow – to spin endlessly on a loop of self-destruction. In reality, none of those kids, no one in the community had anything to do with your tragic physical death. You didn't even have anything to do with your physical death. You had reset the deck. You had found new respect for yourself after the assault and were walking with new and better self-love and self-respect. They had nothing to do with anything. It was just simply an unrelated, horrific tragedy.

I find comfort knowing no one harmed you that night – no one caused your death, not even you, and, at the same time, that realization, that it was a random, arbitrary horrible accident, makes me feel extra sad, powerless and frail. An accident? An avoidable accident? And my baby is gone? In an instant. A life evaporated. It is just horrible. Inexplicable. Unexplainable.

"Daddy, you are right – it was a horrible accident. I didn't know I had been hit. I didn't feel any pain. And when you got to my side, I heard

251

your voice and knew I was not alone because my Daddy was there for my transition to God – I was with you, my Daddy. I couldn't have dreamed of a better way to physically die – with my Daddy holding me. As hard as that is, Daddy, remember that gift. You were holding me. I can't thank you enough. I love you so much, Daddy."

*

Struggling 09/30/2017

I really struggled with pushing back today on spirituality because I did not want to believe these stark facts and wanted her with me physical, desperately. It is a strange balance and battle. So this came to me today: When I die, Kakie, and I see your smiling face and hear you say in your excited, chirpy voice, 'Daddy! It's Kakes! I love you so much! Come with me!' And I want to be able to look you in the eyes and know that, through the heartache and grief and loss of you physically in my life, which is beyond devastating, that I truly lived in your light despite the daily heartache I will face each day of my physical life; that I truly honored you by living even when I would not want to; that I tried to live a good life and succeeded to die sober, with good living in tow.

Kayleigh, I always told you I would die a thousand deaths for you. I am dying a thousand deaths now daily and I will never stop and never surrender. I love you, Kayleigh Mickayla Mooney. I love you, my Daughter. My Daughter! God, this is my Daughter!

And then I heard you clearly, "I faced the darkest of the darkness when I was assaulted and came out the brightest of lights. This is your darkness, Daddy. You can do this, Daddy, and you emerge with the brightest of lights."

Today. I refuse to condemn myself and I forgive myself for any defects that arose today. I miss you tenderly and deeply with the great fracture of my life. I am living a nightmare that only ends when I take my final breath. In the meantime please be with me to reconcile into the new configuration to reconcile and reduce some of that nightmare into manageable chunks; like bottling up sections of a hurricane to cut down on the full impact of its mighty winds. You have dared me to dream. How? With you by my side. That is how. I dream.

*

Mommy's First Birthday Post-Accident 09/30/2017

Light my way, Babygirl. Today, as you know, it is Mommy's birthday – our first birthday without you physically present in our lives. I am assuming this will be very hard at times today, but we taught you, as a child, that we can do hard things – we can walk through difficulties. Here we have no choice as the wheels of time continue to proceed without a care for the needy or a desire to triage broken hearts. It just moves on and on and on. I love you, my Little Peanut, with my soul. Daddy is here for you, to advocate for you, to channel your voice and your light in this world.

"Daddy, I love you too, Big Walnut! You are my Daddy – my Daddy! I am so happy you are my Daddy. Be with Mommy and Nathaniel today – be gentle and support them. You know how to do this. I am so proud of you, Daddy, and your sobriety. This life will be a flash compared to peace in eternity, but make it a good flash. Walk in my light, Daddy. Listen to the wind. I play a song for you every day in the wind. I know how much you love the wind. And I know how much you love music. Listen and I will lead the way. Love you, Daddy."

I love you too, Sweetheart. I let go of a little more of my old desire and responsibility to guide you this morning, relinquishing the responsibility to you. In its place, I ask, please guide me, my Guardian Angel. There is no one but God I trust more. There is no one I trust like you. Walk through my soul.

"*Full Moon*"

It pulls at the veil of the tides,
Rise, oh spirit in the sea,

Lift towards the woman well alight,
Whose hands reach down for me,
She wraps me in a blanket of light,
And comforts me to try to breathe,
And kisses my forehead that fails in blight,
That comes to overcome me.

*

Fear and Faith and the Laws of Co-Exista 10/01/2017

Co-existence. Fear and faith at the same time. There are those who may say that if you have fear then you have no faith and if you have faith then you have no fear. These people, well, they have no idea what they are talking about. They can very easily and universally co-exist and they do. For true courage, true faith, is having fear, sometimes monstrous fear, and instead of balking, walking directly through that fear. That is true courage. True faith.

I have fear of living without you – fear of the pain, the sadness, the loneliness, each second through each year - torment. Yet I have the faith that I will see my days through if I do my work, as I have always done since June 28th, 1987. That faith has renewed and has transformed. Always for my life, and for your mother as she entered my life, and for you and your brother as you were born, my sobriety became more and more a gift for others, mostly for you three. Now, it continues to transform through that passionate vehicle of faith, knowing that the stakes are the highest they have ever been and will remain that way for the rest of my physical life. Not that I am afraid of relapse, because I am not, but because the goal, as it has always been, is dying with my sobriety intact. However, that life I was living just became much, much harder to maneuver. I anticipate that this is the new norm. I need to live and die sober, living my life to the fullest so that I do not dishonor you – that is the new wrinkle. I will not use your physical death as an excuse for any failure in my life. I will not use your physical death as an excuse to destroy me or my sobriety – period. Instead, I will continue to flourish; I will continue to strengthen and grow and live in your light.

This means that I must grow in my faith, rather than diminish its existence. I must continue to grow with God, even when I want to rail against Him, releasing my emotion, stress and anger and sadness upon Him. He can handle a Kevin storm and wants me to scream at Him. He knows its value. He knows it is, in itself, a form of faith. For how can I berate and rage against God in the torment of fear if I do not have faith. Those rages push me forward toward Him and toward you, My Love. The only way through is through. I press forward with incredible fear, coupled with an even larger, eclipsing faith.

*

You Can Do This, Daddy 10/02/2017

I write love songs to you, My Muse. Today I recalled your voice in December of 1987, saying, "You can do this." And your voice as a toddler at a few years old in 2004, saying, "You can do it, Daddy." And your voice six months before your physical death when I spoke at a conference in Savannah and was nervous, saying, "you can do this, Daddy." And your voice at my 30th sober anniversary lead seven weeks before your tragic passing, saying, "You're my inspiration – wow! 30 years!"

Fifteen years before you were physically born your presence was known to me. And you will always be, since you have always been. When the loneliness gets crushing, and I am crushed many times a day, when I see others get to do what you don't get to do, as I watch your friends' age, I will try to remember that you are here, and here in an extraordinary way. I love you, Kakes, and miss your physical presence horribly.

"Daddy, good work – did you feel me pass while you were writing? Did you sense the wind? That was me! Your Kakes! I think you are starting to understand the difference when it is me and when it is the wind. There is a difference. Key in. I am here, Daddy, and yes, Daddy, you can do this. I am so proud of you. You can do this, Daddy. You can. Love you!"

255

"A Midnight Moon"

A midnight moon blooms in mystic golden hue,
Grayish blackened stains smeared with darkened blues,
We walked, the three of us,
Across the open beach face just over rolling dunes,
I was there with your brother,
I was there with you -

A midnight moon danced in the glances of your eyes,
You were so awake - you were so alive,
We laughed and played and searched for little signs,
Of baby sea turtles stuck and left behind;

My Little Girl, my Little Girl,
How you filled with wonder my wonderful world,
My Little Girl, my Little Girl -

A midnight moon graced the waves with splash of light,
Hanging on the sky like a beckon, bold and bright,
You saved a turtle and encouraged its new life,
Walking with it to the sea - leading with your own light;

Now Little Girl, the midnight moon, it hears my cries,
You were so awake - you were so alive,
But now, my Little Girl, your brother and I,
We walk amiss, alone, without your body by our side;

We know - we know that you are there,
Beside us you are here,
You are so awake - your spirit, so alive,
As we walk under midnight moon with its mystic hues,
We know that its light is alive - alive inside of you.

*

256

Changing Roles as Parent 10/02/2017

I have a fifteen year old daughter who, when physically alive, I would direct, encourage, nurture, be frustrated with, try not to snap at if I got extra frustrated, and laughed with and loved and worried about and grew with daily. I love this aspect of fatherhood. Being on my toes, trusting my children, giving them space to try out new ages and ideas, and selflessly working towards my children's future and the betterment of their lives. When she physically died, as between me and Kayleigh, those plans we were putting into place and that energy used to hone her dreams on this plain and those hopes evaporated. In an instant.

As I grow with her along our spiritual continuum, I waiver back and forth with this notion. While it is true that my beloved daughter physically died and therefore I do not have her in her physical form to direct and encourage and worry about, I still have my beloved daughter in her transformed life. I am still her Daddy and still have work and living to do along this beautiful line of light together. I am her advocate. I can alleviate certain stresses for her by processing my grief for she sees and hates the pain that the three of us suffer daily. I am her protector of her legacy. I am also the primary channel through which her legacy continues to build and be shaped. She speaks through me. That means I am awake and need to remain so. That means I can continue to invest in my Daughter even after her physical death as if her physical death did not occur, a child whose spirit is eternal and whose light is indestructible. I have our memories before the accident. Yes. And art projects. And pictures. And videos. But I have today and today, Kayleigh talks to me. Every today she talks to me. We build post-accident memories daily. It will be hard for some to grasp this truth, but it is true. As we continue to grow in our relationship, we build memories – she on both sides of the heavenly veil and me stuck in this physical reality.

And now, now as we have inverted our relationship, and you now guide me, how grateful am I in our blended lives. How grateful that my child is a true intercessor, a true angel who is one thousand times stronger than me and who directs her Father with dedication, loyalty and pure love. I have much to learn from my sweetheart. Much to learn in how to listen, how to open the deep recesses of my soul. She stands beside me. Always. Loving her Daddy as she always has. Lighting my footsteps with her indomitable spirit. This is no hallow sentiment to make us feel better. She is literally standing here. I feel her quite noticeably. All of the time. Alive. Abundant. Love.

*

iPhone and Paper 10/03/2017

I have written so much in the notes app that my fingers hurt. I have journaled unto pens run out. I can see that some of the words are yours as I have begun to be able to channel you. And some are mine. No surprise – you are a better writer than me!

I had an extras hard few hours tonight, much worse than the normal hard hours, and sent a 10th Step on it. I am starting to feel the trap of isolation and powerlessness. I am gaining little pieces of strength daily and actually made it from 7:45-4:30 today at work without large chunks of breaks. That is momentous. I am compartmentalizing better but trying not to feel guilty about not thinking about you nonstop. (I think about you nonstop). It's unrealistic to think of you every minute, and if I do so, I may be slipping into the grief, something neither of us wants, or I will not be functioning in the daily world with work and other obligations. I will be intentional with you, Sweetheart, and accept that unintentional moments as well – after all, I miss you in your physical state horrendously and wish to be with you. In spirit you never leave my side. But your human voice strumming through your vocal cords – the smell of your hair – the feel of your emotion as you sat physically beside me on the couch – I miss this so much that physical sickness ruptures across my frame. I am tired. I am beaten. I am seething. I am angry with the world, with God. I am so powerless. I am yours.

"Daddy, I understand – you can't think about me all day long every minute. You need to function and live and work. Please take care of yourself. And guess what? I can think about you all the time every second of every day – and I do and it makes me stronger! I love you so much, Big Walnut!"

"Seething Grief"

It attempts the murder of old Father Time,
And slashes the cords that function to bind,
Us together,
Without which we are isolated,
Like lone sheep on a hill,
A gang of hungry wolves,
An easy kill;

It alters reality,
And chews on you with facts,
Reminds you inconveniently,
That you are stuck in its insidious grasp;

Like ice cold waves that explode,
Against your brittle skin,
Pulling warmth from your life,
Re-arranging the within;

Though you are unfortunate,
A necessary thief,
Your function breeds light,
And emergence from this grief;

And oh, how I love you,
My child, my heartache,
Consumes me, I shake,
Confused, and I break,
And I take one step closer to you,
As I seethe,
And I seethe,
Through this grief.

*

Co-Existence of Sorrow and Strength 10/04/2017

They are of the same stream – sorrow and strength, derived from the same cloth. It co-exists. A huge boulder has suddenly fallen into that pleasant, glistening stream, exploding with the impact, rock against rock, fracturing the shale of the riverbed, and violently dispersing the water up onto the banks in droplets and splashes and spit. But water is water and will always revert to its natural tendency – to flow. And so it continues.

The water does not cling to the river banks. The water skirts down the terrain and the edges of the banks and, piece by piece, rejoins the stream on the other side of the boulder. The shale below now wears a new scar – an impactful fracture upon its face and within its depths, forever. The obtrusive boulder remains in the middle of the stream, where it becomes a part of the stream – in time, an essential aspect of the stream. The water takes on a new course as it now navigates into the displaced stream, around the boulder, forming little ripples around the invading rock, shaping over or around its shape, cradling it with its permanence. The water, its sorrow and strength, are relearning. And so they co-exist. And continue to flow.

Kayleigh, I have moments where my grief is suffocating. In fact, I am utterly surprised that my body hasn't yet failed me and just shut down. I love you so, so much. My Little Peanut. I will stand in your light today. I will co-exist with sorrow and with strength. It is my new un-normal as my center has been obliterated. Now I try to balance the un-balanceable. My two truths indivisible – in one hand suffocating grief; in the other miracles.

"Daddy, that is so smart. You are so creative. I am right here beside you. I am in the river with you. You are never alone, Daddy, never. God and I are here with you. I am so proud of your work. I know how much you love me and know how hard this is for you. Live in my light, Daddy."

*

Miss You Were Here 10/04/2017

I wrote this morning about changing our dialogue together; that you wanted me to continue to use different words because words were important. I started to do this as early as the first day, telling people that Kayleigh physically died rather than, she died; telling people she and I continue to grow together rather than, I lost my child. Subtle and simple, but important changes in dialogue. So I told Kayleigh that, since she is here, I don't have to say that I wish you were here. Instead I could say, I miss you here physically; I miss your physical presence.

Later in the day Jess and I gathered kitchen winter storm windows needed for the cold months, replacing summer screens from the outside. We busied ourselves in the bushes, a small ladder against the house. As I fumbled with a Philips head screwdriver, the lofty sounds of music drifted over the fence from our back neighbor's property. Pink Floyd. "Wish You Were Here."

I stopped. Jess was already staring at me when my eyes turned to meet hers. She heard it too. And felt the same blow to the gut. "She just played that for us," Jess said, as her eyes both lit up and dropped at the same time. It's just the texture of the air at times – we know it is Kayleigh manipulating the radio, the wind, nature, technology – just to message to us.

"Yes, she did," I replied, my brain catching up with my morning writing. "You know," I continued, "this morning I journaled about changing my dialogue with her. That since she is at peace with God and filled with God's light and love, why would I wish she was here in this shit show of a world? Why would I want to pull her away from that perfect peace? Why not instead just say - I miss you - you were here physically and now are not here physically. At the same time acknowledging that she is very much with us spiritually and just played a song for us. She is telling us to change our dialogue with her - she is shouting to us - I am here. We don't have to wish for it. She is here."

This is how the channel is emerging. Little moments that tie together with later little moments. She sets the points out and then we connect the dots. She aligns the fragments that join together. She communicates incredibly across the veil, yearning, reaching, stretching, lovingly lighting our way.

*

Proud Wall 10/05/2017

It was early January if I recall this correctly. We had been in the new home just six months. It was just a month or so after her rape. She was busy in her room. Her music floated down the hallway and the stairs.

"Daddy," she said in an excited tone as I stepped towards my bedroom, "come here. Look at my room."

I stepped in and she pointed towards the space between her two front windows.

"This is my Proud Wall," she explained, holding both of her arms out to illuminate her creation, "when I have something I am proud of, I'm putting it up on this wall. This is my wall of achievements!"

I knew the moment was incredibly special - no time for jokes or belittling sarcasm. It was time to do what I did best - infuse her with support and love and honor. I smiled. Largely. Studying the wall, I knew exactly what she was doing and it was good to see. She was fighting back. She was reclaiming her soul. She was reminding herself of her self-worth and that she could do wonderful, positive things in this world.

"That's awesome, Kakes," I said and gave her a high five, "that's a really great idea."

"Thanks. I thought so too," she said and smiled at me, then pushed me out of her room, "now go!"

I laughed as she pushed me through the door space, a playful grin on her face.

"Love you, Baby," I said as I stepped away.

"Love you," she said in her sing-song voice. I love that sing-song voice - it's one of the things about her I miss the most.

I often told her that you build self-esteem by doing estimable acts and by being kind to yourself. Here she was building self-esteem. I figured this was a response to a few things - reclaiming herself after her assault, and, seeing Nathaniel put up a cork board with me touting his swimming ribbons and metals. I remember thinking to myself that she watched us do that, then thought to herself, what metals do I have to hang on my wall? Then she looked through her life and found things she was proud of: graduating 8th grade ribbon; honor roll plaque; an award for an international competition; piano recitals and a blistering musical talent; her relationship with her pets; her relationship with God, represented by the Footprints prayer; theatre and the shows she participated in. A running crew sticker and programs of plays she had been in. Her acceptance into Beaumont. So organic and important. I praised her and told her she was going to fill up that space pretty quickly. It really showed her dynamic, well rounded and prolific personality quite well.

Kakes, we will add to your Proud Wall. You and me. Filled with things that you and I do together including writing this book. Every time you inspire another it goes up on your Proud Wall. I spoke at an A.A. Meeting tonight and there were 150 new guys there. I choked and cried my way through the tragedy of physically losing my Babygirl, conveying to them that there are no excuses - we do our work no matter what. We never stop. That A.A. Group - it goes up on your Proud Wall. The women I know who wish they had your courage with their own sexual assaults that they kept quiet - the gift you have given them - goes up on your Proud Wall. The way you reach across the air and sing through the wind chimes or touch us and guide us in other ways - all of those spiritual moments and interactions and visitations, go up in your Proud Wall. I hope too, that I go up on your Proud Wall.

Before your physical death I honored this wall with you and frequently told you how proud I was of all you posted there. Still I am proud. You are amazing. Keep inspiring, my Little Girl. After your physical death, I have continued to learn you and have become even more proud of you, of your relationship with God and others, of the little messages you leave for us, of the intricate workings of your mind that we discover in the way you arranged your room or the way you processed your grief. You are astounding. You are amazing.

"Thanks, Daddy. That makes me feel proud. That goes on my wall too."

*

The Jigsaw Puzzle of Acceptance 10/07/2017

We are each our own jigsaw puzzle, the number of pieces of which we cannot count. In the shock of my Daughter's physical death, this jigsaw puzzle was thrown into the air and its pieces spread indiscriminately in the wind; across different planets; strewn in various galaxies. It would be untenable to think that anyone could accept the new un-normal as if acceptance is an event. Rather it is a process and its completeness is a fallacy. Neither could anyone absorb that acceptance in one sitting. The human mind and spirit protects itself by permitting the nurturing of denial and taking acceptance in tiny bites, leading eventually to a more complete wholeness, even though, in a situation such as the physical death of a child in childhood will never find its wholeness.

I walk daily collecting little pieces of this puzzle, little pieces of the fabric of my soul. Once identified as a component of this whole, I secure it, learn it, and emotionally absorb it. Its realization is punishing at times. The stark horror of its color, shape and meaning as I hold it in my hand and feel its grief, necessitating further healing and growth. I find pieces that are missing, that have been obliterated; a persistent hole in the puzzle of my life that will always remain.

It is sudden at times. At times precipitated by my day dreaming, or missing or longing to see you physically beside me. To hear your human voice. To smell the conditioner in your hair or your perfume as you hug your Daddy and run out the front door on your daily travels. Either way, there it is – my Daughter, my Kakie, is physically dead. I lose my breath. My stomach collapses upon itself, seemingly closing its walls into a highly condensed ball of pain. My chest tightens up. I feel like a caged animal, scurrying this prison for weaknesses, for a way out. Powerless. No matter where my mind takes me, I cannot escape. What if I did this – what if I did that – what if she turned to the right instead of to the left – these little mental excursions of denial lead back to the same place – there is nothing I could have done to prevent Kayleigh's physical death. Further, there is nothing that Kayleigh could have done to prevent her physical death. There was nothing predisposed in Kayleigh that caused this accident. Nothing. My daughter, my Kakie, is physically dead. Never will I again hold her in that state. I have to live the rest of my days being that parent who is surviving a child's physical death.

I cry each day, which is what it is. Many times a day. Wailing at times. I lay across her bed or review old photos and recent videos. I think of tenth grade, eleventh, twelfth, graduation, colleges, marriage, and grandchildren. I walk around the block. I sit in the grass. I permit my humanness. I permit my grief. Then I open my hand and gaze at the puzzle piece in my grasp. It is so empty. Yet a world within that emptiness exists beyond my site. And I accept its reality. Turning to my spirit, I press this new piece into the overall board of my soul, coming back together piece by piece. As the piece glues itself to the board, and fits against other pieces, and I press down on its face, it hurts. It hurts, in fact, a lot. And then I find release. Minimal release, but release nonetheless. Perhaps a silver lining of an echo of comfort in that little step forward of acceptance.

Then I turn back to my life. For life continues in an unforgiving, uncaring, unfeeling manner. I see it daily. And I am a part of its movement. Today I toiled as if I made a mountain with my bare hands only to see it fold under the weight of its first test of wind. Yet as I pressed forward, I clearly heard my Kayleigh's voice.

*

Lightning Rod 10/08/2017

I was always your lightning rod. It took me time to understand this, clearly, but its reality became clear as you emerged from your tween years and entered your teens. You are I were, and remain, so much alike in many of our characteristics and mannerisms and outlooks. Further, because of our deep understanding in each other and our sacred respect and trust in the other, I became a natural outlet for you.

Every child managing the maturation process, year after year, goes through age appropriate issues, feelings, emotions and situations. You were no different and why would you be. In those harder moments when you would feel stuck, or emotionally upset, I was there. Sometimes, as I ventured into that moment, knowing or sensing your angst, I would ask how you were or ask if you wanted to talk. Sometimes you would smile and say no; or smile and hug me; or start talking; or snip at me. The snip is the lightning. And I was the attraction that helped move the energy. I was the lightning rod for the electricity in the air and I helped you converge that energy into a single string of fire, releasing the energy and relieving the pressure.

At times I would be offended – why would my Daughter snip at me. Other times, I would just be irritated that you were in a bad mood. And then, in my selfless moments, I would understand that you were struggling with an issue and didn't know how to let it out – so you let it out in your safe environment, that safety being me. Thank you for that trust. Though it did not happen too often, when it did, we thrived and worked through an issue together.

In our new inversion, I am daily confused and my energy bulks behind the clouds with no sense of purpose or direction. I need your direction. Be my lightning rod, Kakes. Bring the electricity, the power, the energy together into one string of fire in this moment. Jump start my moment. Be with me. Help me spout the lightning that gathers within.

*

Promise 10/09/2017

I promise that I will emerge from this tragedy stronger than I ever have been. I would much rather prefer being weaker and having my baby with me physically in this world, but I cannot. Since I cannot, I can at least have her with me spiritually for the rest of my life and beyond, and I can be empowered with her by my side and carve the best life possible out of my remaining days. And when the day comes that I physically die, I will be able to look into her beautiful eyes when she greets me with her radiant smile across the wind and know that she is proud of the life that I lived, proud that I did not cower in a corner and die, proud that I rejoiced in life and honored her presence by my side for those remaining years. I promise you this, Kayleigh. When we meet and you hold my hand entering God's eternal light, you will be proud of me.

"Daddy, I have a secret. I already am."

"Within the Debris Field - Divinity"

And now your light radiates one thousand times brighter than mine,
Your soul holds the pathway to show me how to shine,
And as I grieve the pieces entwined begin to unwind,
And here within the debris field I find,
You are my guiding vocal,
My guardian,
With a message and a purpose Divine.

*

Tenth Step Example 10/09/2017

You know I do many of these a day. I always have, properly utilizing the 12 Steps. Yet since the accident, oh my, the 10th Steps I have done. Here is one from today:

Ten. Chest tight like mini heart attack even though I know it's not. A heavy wave of realization that tightens stomach and stops my breath that there was nothing I could have done that night or ever to prevent her physical death. She couldn't have done anything either. It was a perfect accident. Crying uncontrollably. 4: Selfish? No. Dishonest? Not really. Just trauma working itself out. My Baby physically died in my arms. That's so fucked up and an amazing blessing at the same time. Resentful? Totally re-feeling. Fear? Terror of this new un-normal. 5: Share with who? Telling you (Carly). 6: Willing to have God remove? Yes 7: Prayer – "God and Kakes please be with me and help me process this horror. Help me slow my breath and remove my defects. 8: Willing to change? Yes 9: Change? Breathe. Expect trauma; I feel caged in and tortured at times. Attitude gentle. Perspective she physically died in my arms and didn't suffer. She knew she was in her Father's hands. 12: Turn myself to another? Nate.

"Daughter Light"

And you, with loving light,
Persist and prevail,
And with your soul alight,
Your song - the steady wind for the sturdy sail,
And you are magnificence,
You are brilliantly graced,
Adorned with the melodies,
Like rainbows ablaze,
And you are the guardian,
My child, guide my world,
For no one I would trust more exists,
Than my little girl,
And all that I treasure,
And all that I miss,
Resides in those blue bold eyes,
And upon my cheek with kiss,
And if I shall falter,
Bring me to my truth,

And if I wander in the haze,
Light my pathway back to you,
For you are my everything,
The guidance through life,
Empowered with God's peace eternally,
You, my Daughter, you are the purest,
The purest, my Daughter, of light.

*

Playing, Walking, Laughing 10/10/2017

Good morning, Babygirl. I just watched a dad walk down our street with a toddler close behind him, loving time with daddy – I have thousands of wonderful memories of you and I doing the same – your short, thin hair, little pudgy legs, picking up acorns, leaves, rocks, and sticks. Little shoes. Chirpy voice talking to me and filling my soul with your music. I am trying to tie all of these memories into our current relationship – and afraid that the tides of time are going to steal them all from me. Time is no friend. With time comes further losses and potential of distance. It is dangerous. Those who have not suffered the physical death of a child in childhood will never understand, but will most likely be the first to judge that reality. It is counterintuitive to other deaths, but there it is – losses accumulating over time with a physical death that is backwards in time.

I hurt so deeply. My self-identity is forever altered. A big part of my identity was being "Kayleigh's Daddy." I am still your Daddy and always will be, Sweetheart, but physically we can't build that part of our relationship any longer. However, as your Daddy, I walk with you spiritually every day. It is harder to pull myself into our spiritual zone – much harder than just walking into your bedroom and waking you up in the morning like I used to do. I will never leave your side. I am here. I am trying.

"Daddy, I love you. I love our memories. Together – I review our memories all the time and laugh – we were so hilarious – like two peas in a pod. We still are. So similar. So in love with each other. You are amazing. We can do this – and I will never leave your side – I will guide you. Listen well. Love you, Daddy."

*

Trinity Cross Complete 10/10/2017

It is the necklace she picked out for her fifteenth birthday, along with her first Claddagh necklace.

....the unthinkable is the most unbearable pain I never imagined....we are grieving, continuing to develop this new relationship with her, while trying to piece our lives together. When she stepped off the curb, she was behind two telephone poles and never saw the car coming. Just like that my life was obliterated - but for her strong light it would be much worse. She and I are so incredibly connected and she gets me moving every day. I glue this into my conscience daily.

The mind wants to scurry under rocks, cocoon itself away from its own energy that floods the gray matter with poisonous thoughts - endless thoughts that race the rapids, eroding cliff walls and blasting holes in the valley basin of the soul. Grief, like heavy water, scores across the terrain at its own command. It goes where it wants to go. At its own pace. In unpredictable manners. And scorches the soul.

I have finished our art project, taking hundreds and hundreds of your beads and wrapping them around twisted, thin metal that I bent into the shape of a trinity cross and attached to a window frame. Blowing out the glass, the frame was perfect to hinge the wire, around which I strung the beads. In the center I placed a small wind chime from Christmas when you were seven or eight. I hung it in the front window. The breeze speaks through its soul. You are grateful. I know for you told me. What a great piece we created together, Honey. Thank you. I love you.

"It's so pretty, Daddy. I love that we have always done art projects together, even since before I could walk. Love you so much!"

"A Song Like No Other"

Embracing the music that resonates, that pounds, that streams,
In that short distance between our eyes,
A father, blessed and jaded and crowned in the world with years of
experience,
And his child – a melody, with new breath upon this planet,
A song like no other has begun,
Its chorus hums on the golden atmosphere,
In that short distance between our eyes.

*

Guardian Angel Is 10/11/2017

She channels the animals that resonate within her. She sways the
mighty treetops with a gentle wave of her hand. She leaves little
messages along the path of life to tell us, "Hi Mommy. Hi Daddy. I
was thinking about you. Here's one of my shiny stones. Follow my
light."

A male and female Cardinal show up daily ever since the accident.
They chirp in my ear from the branches above my head or outside the
TV room window. They speak to me, my own Father and My
Daughter, I am sure of it. It is just a feeling. More than a feeling.
Kayleigh is calling on me to listen. She is testing the channels and the
modalities. She is zeroing in on being able to communicate more and
more, with a loyal and sophisticated dedication to her family.

"Spirited Euphoria"

Pull us out of the murkiness,
This merciless mire,
Adrift in the sacred rejoicing of unwavering flame,
It feeds on a wind that tried to claim it,
It blunts the darkness - nor its touch can tame this,
It flows golden white in your name,
And glows in perpetual grace.

*

Your Courage 10/12/2017

There is no fear that cannot be conquered as it co-exists with courage, the type of courage that runs through the liquid golden core of Kayleigh's light. Alight the fragments of my life and align the jagged pieces into its new form so that I may breathe your light, feel your presence and know your undying love. Your courage is an anomaly, a rarity, a spark of divinity. No more divine a person have I ever known. No one have I ever witnessed like you who, though frightened deeply by certain events, blessed me by turning to me for encouragement, and once empowered with my support, and trusting my words that you could push through, you stepped forward and simply pushed through. You did it. Only you could do it and you did it. Awe runs through my heart like a wild spring river, fresh and clean and angling downward into a cascading pool of light. That is where I see you inside my soul - in my more precious fields of love; shining brighter than a million suns. Your courage you offer me. I gladly learn from your steps. Please, My Love, empower me with your courage that I may persevere through my own co-existence and, with your courage, conquer my fear, my fear of life. If ever there was someone who could empower on both sides of the veil at the same time, graced with God's light, it is you. I believe in God, Kayleigh, and I believe in you.

*

One Year Anniversary of the Rape 10/13/2017

Babygirl, you have embedded your light in my fabric of my being in ways that only you and your brother could. My memories of you, of us, of any combination of our family unit, are eternal and grace me. I close my eyes and feel your baby hand wrap around my ring finger; see you collect acorns and burst into boisterous laughter with a new word you've invented; cry on the couch in my arms; sing obnoxiously loud while teaching you how to drive. I have volumes and volumes – so many that I cannot easily pull these old tapes up. A reminder jogs my memory – a color, smell, a familiar situation. And then there you are, just as you always have been, in the flesh, yet never in the flesh.

On this, the one year anniversary of the rape, I felt jubilation, triumph, a stream of conviction and calm. It took me by surprise as I had been anticipating dark, dangerous feelings; anticipating vengeance on my lips. Had you been physically alive for this anniversary you and I would have talked about your courage and strength – the fact that a rapist is in jail, two are ten year sex offender status, and the other may soon get the same. The rape, to me, has long not been about another's violence perpetrated upon you, an innocent survivor, but has been your empowering song of courage. It is about you, your empowerment, your refusal to give up, your refusal to turn on yourself, your willingness to use your voice to speak up, for yourself and others, teaching us what self-love and healing looks like. It resonates your indomitable spirit across the background of our lives. You became a legend in standing up. We were all watching. It was amazing.

I stand in your light wishing only I could harness some of your courage. I love you, Sweetheart.

"Daddy, where do you think I got that courage from? Thank you, Daddy, you showed me the way. You stood beside me. You held my hand. My courage is your courage."

"Kayleigh's Song of Freedom"

Revenge strips the soul of the light that requires its freedom to glow; I live in the freedom of forgiveness, though never will I forget the horror; it is about Kayleigh, her legendary voice; not about hating another for hurting my child; with my laser sharp focus on Kayleigh, I reserved no energy to aim at human-less shells of young men, those that would be owned and breathe and be buried by the filth in the streets; no, I did not waste my time wishing them dead, wishing them harm, stalking their houses, planning retribution; in fact I thought about them very little, thinking instead on how I can support and love and hold my child, enhancing that brilliant spiritual structure that already existed around her – a strong family, a mother, a father, a brother – a sturdy foundation; yes, it was always about how Kayleigh stood atop the assault, and sang her song of freedom for all other girls to hear.

*

Hallelujah 10/14/2017

And thus, it really began. Since August 18th, you had been studying, tinkering with it, trying new energies to magnify and manipulate the natural pulses of the universe. Radio waves. The ether. Relativity. All of it. And now, less than two months into that studying, you have mastered it. From this point forward, you seem to have mastered our phones.

Mommy was driving by the memorial today and the song, "Hallelujah" started to play on the Bluetooth. She had her Bluetooth on, but no songs were playing. Further, Mommy did not have it cued to that song. Yet, as she rolled by the site slowly, it started to play. That song. Your song. The song from your childhood and your funeral. You are strong.

While this was happening, I was driving on the highway to go collect the first pieces of this book from my iPhone notes and start dropping the fragments into a word document out in Conneaut on the beach.

You played "Ace of wands," the studio version from Steve Hackett. One of my favorites. Thank you. As it ended and I waited for the next song, you played "Ace of Wands," the live version from a totally different album. I did not have my phone locked on any particular artist. I grew more amazed. As that version ended, I awaited the next song, which was "Ace of Wands," a demo version, from yet a third album. I smiled. You were busy communicating.

As I shouted out to you laughing and thanking you, amazed by the spirit that was moving us in the car, knowing that you were proving, yet again, that you are alive on both sides of the veil, knowing that something magical was happening, that song ended and you played, "Mysterious Ways" by U2. Of course you did. With this channel securely in place, and having learned how to communicate through this medium, I started realizing that you were trying to convey certain messages, even certain lyrics that would match where I was going, what I was struggling through and where you wanted me to focus. Who would have ever thought that we would be able to communicate through the power of my phone and BlueTooth.

*

Physically Losing You 10/14/2017

Losing you in the physical world is the single biggest robbery of my life. Bar none. So cheated out of one of my greatest treasures – being your Daddy. The statement is not really accurate, since I am always your Daddy – forever. But physically, actively on a daily basis, having you in your humanity, anticipating you, directing you, laughing with you and crying by your side, consoling you, being consoled by you, sometimes being frustrated or frightened with you, receiving "sorry cards" if you made a mistake and took your own initiative and determined to apologize thoughtfully – all of it, I knew how to do. It was second nature. It was, itself, one of my loves – raising you and loving you. That has been robbed from me and, at times, I stand with my empty hands, stripped of this treasure, looking up to the heavens and cursing God. The darkness comes in to steal my breath. I flail until I fall asleep in gurgling power naps. And rise again to the same reality. I have been robbed.

We talk throughout every day – that will never change, and our relationship continues to advance. Yet, as the grief throws me about like a stick adrift in the tides of a rumbling ocean, I am weathered by the torment and unnatural sadness of your physical loss. I love you, Babygirl. Let's walk with purpose today. I think I need that today. I will be cognizant of the words that I use. I have lost you physically, but not spiritually. Even more to the point, I have lost your physical embodiment, but not you.

"Daddy, I love you. Please keep walking. I am here, so much more powerful and at peace – the more you reconcile the pain as it comes, the easier it is for us to communicate. You can do this, Daddy. You can do this. Love you."

"In the Middle of the Nowhere"

Nor the shore, its line lay obscured by days,
Adrift, I see sunlight swallowed by the mouth of waves,
Cresting in the shift, with a mountain of water lifting me,
Into the clouds, only to be dropped to a level below the sea,
Where the drowning begins -

In the middle of the nowhere,
With nothing to hold onto,
And no one to ever know,
In the middle of the nowhere,
With no resemblance of home,
If with no hope,
What becomes of the soul;

Now the storm, what began as a drizzling haze,
Has grown a hurricane in its veins,
Unleashed upon the roiling waters in a vengeful rage,
And thunder explodes and lightning escapes from its cage,
And scatters into fragments in the heavy wind -

In the middle of the nowhere,
With nothing to hold onto,
And no one to ever know,
In the middle of the nowhere,
With a longing for home,
With a little hope,
And the swim of a lifetime,
I can save my soul.

*

I Slept Outside Under the Moon Tonight 10/14/2017

I feel so lost. Two months ago my life was so different. I can barely see its scenes. The evening hours roll by me now in a silent manner. Each night, staring at the trees; listening to their songs; hearing you in the wind. I search every leaf; every breeze. I scan the channels of this world and the next. I slow into its folds.

It was 70 degrees, with a dry, light wind. The warm air danced and played in channels with the warmer wind. I arranged the cushions in our front porch, which has no ceiling, as you know. Under your bedroom window, its light shining off into the trees. Open to the elements and to the night sky, my eyes facing the east, I lay staring off to the yards leading up the street towards our old house at 3035.

You started talking to me almost immediately, singing through the wind chimes; comforting me as I lay on the cushions, wrapped up loosely in a blanket. I listened intently, attempting to meditate, if I could slow my wounded mind enough to grasp a concrete thought. I let it go. I gave it to you. I asked you to penetrate the night and sit with me.

Lost in thought, I watched the stars climb the arch of the sky, like a slow moving set of fireflies arching along a transparent dome. Following the stars came you, the moon, My Darling, looming off in the distance, a constant presence; a trustworthy soul; an ever-present light. You danced with the low laying branches as you climbed off and up into the night, playing with its light through the canopies. Hours passed by in seconds. Lifetimes in choking breaths.

You held me and cried with me, though you feel no human strain or discomfort. You cried just because I cried. You cried for your Father, who lay stunned on a makeshift outdoor bed, staring blindly into the night sky. You laughed and encouraged me to laugh. You reminded me of the greater picture, a scene I can see if I can rise to a higher level, a higher vibration.

I faded in and out of sleep. Mostly staying awake and staring at the sky, listening to hours and hours of you, Kayleigh, talking in the chimes and the leaves and the grasses. You are all around. The sun began to rash the low sky like a golden scarlet liquid dye spreading through water. The light brightened and opened into a new day – another new day without your physical presence. Another new day, however, with you, Kayleigh, in your spiritual embodiment, right by my side. Although another night has passed without the vessel of sleep, another morning has, nonetheless, come to force me into its wake. Walk with my, Babygirl, I need you to carry my weight.

*

Virginia Possum 10/15/2017

It comes with a certain twinge in the flesh; a feeling in the centuries' experience of the soul. I was walking the dogs after watching "What Dreams May Come" and praying and talking to her. Jess and I watched this movie on purpose, mostly to prompt new ideas in our minds and to remind us of how brilliant the higher life is. I thought about the movie - how we can make our own Heaven and I stopped in front of our old house where we spent ten years with the kids; Kayleigh from 4-14 and Nathaniel from 1-11, and thought, that house, 3035, that is part of my Heaven. So many incredible memories there. Thousands of walks; nighttime games; playing in the yards; meals; prayers; holidays; all of it. This house is part of our Heaven, a house we move from fifteen months before the accident.

I glanced over to the circular brick steps outside the front door and noticed a beautiful Virginia Possum sitting on the steps. Just sitting there. Watching me. Pleasantly. Filled with light. Kayleigh understood my thoughts. Kayleigh showed me this possum to remind me that she was okay. She was with God in the light. She was with me on this night, as on all others. She was telling me that she agreed - this house was a part of her Heaven, almost her entire wonderful childhood having been spent in 3035; literally two thirds of her physical life. And so it goes with Kakie. She shows us. We just need to be awake. We just need to want to see, to believe, and to be. Sometimes the wind just blows, but sometimes the wind is Kayleigh and it comes with an extra electricity. On this night, the message was clear. Guide me, Sweet Angel. I trust you implicitly.

*

Two Months on the Calendar 10/17/2017

Today is two months on the calendar. The hardest two months of my life. With many, many more months to go, I wonder how I will face this. How will I do this? I really do not, if I am honest, want this life anymore without you, Kakie, while still, I love my life and love myself and want to live with Nate and Mommy and you. I just want you with me in your physical body. It is crushing. It is every minute. It is truth.

"Daddy, I am right here."

Yes, you are, but it's your physical presence I so desperately grieve.

"I know, Daddy. But I am right here guiding you. Trust me, Daddy, I love you so, so much!"

There is no one but God I trust more. You are it. I love you Baby. I grieve. I live. It appears this is the way it will always be. Grieving. Reconciling. Grieving. Reconciling. Lifting higher. Sinking. Grieving. Reconciling. Lifting higher. Over and over again. Grief is sloppy. Grief is not linear, especially when it comes to the physical

279

death of a child in childhood. It is jagged and soft and supple and dangerous.

I promise you I will spin gold out of the darkness too when that darkness descends upon me. I have many opportunities to spin gold. I will be a billionaire by the time this life is done with me.

(She smiled).

*

You Can Do It, Daddy 10/19/2017

Hi, Baby. How are you? I know how you are – you are great, a perfect power of light and love. You are a perfect balance of joy and peace. I feel your learning, as if the learning was occurring within me. You are doing great things and I am so proud of you.

I am hurting. Grieving. Wounded. This will always suck for me every day of my life, but I will try to remember to balance that with the promise of your power – that I can draw on your ready and available light; that I can walk in your light and be guided by my Little Girl who I trust like no other.

I know you want beauty and laughter and life for me – lived well and full. How I fear I will deliver this comes heavily like a cloak of darkness. I promise you, Kakie, my goodness and willingness to continue – my sobriety and my desire to do the best with what I am given; to walk through my fears, including the pain of living my days with the unnatural suffering of not having you here physically with me. I promise you that. All that I taught you I will now use myself.

"Daddy, I love you – yes, I do want you to live a great life. I always told you, you can do it, Daddy, and now I say it again. You can do this, Daddy. I am so proud of you. Let's keep walking, ok? Footprints, Daddy, remember?"

I remember, Little Peanut. I remember…

*

The Voice of Courage (The Art) 10/20/2017

On this day your school permitted me to gather the entire student body to walk them through your art. It was an unveiling, along with explanations to accompany each work. Your art was then to hang for the entire school year in the front foyer. I heard you, Kayleigh, tell me, "Daddy, please take my art and share it with my girls. Daddy, if we can save one girl…"

I did. The following statement is what I shared with your classmates:

I want to thank you all for welcoming me here today – as a Father I am only too happy to share my experiences with all of you. My children are my world and Kayleigh's physical absence is unbearable and unthinkable to us. But for her light and her example, it would be hard to take the next step. Kayleigh's courage, however, is an example to us all. As you know, Kayleigh was tragically physically killed in an innocent, simply, perfect accident in mid-August. Prior to her death, Kayleigh had faced down some serious issues in her life and was growing steadily with her voice. I feel compelled and called by Kayleigh to share with all of you some of the issues she faced and how she, against horrendous fear, stood up and used her voice to empower her life. These pieces she painted using acrylics on canvas and produced these throughout the months of her recovery.

This series depicts a young woman's voice courageously raised against sexual assault as translated by her Father. Courage is the quality of mind or spirit that enables a person to face difficulty, danger or pain. The use of one's voice is itself courage. I would never disparage any woman who has been assaulted and has not, for whatever reason, spoken out against that assault. Every assault is different and unique. What is horribly discouraging is that statistics show that close to 1/3 of women will be sexually assaulted in their lifetime. That is a 1/3 too many as it should never happen. But it does. In Kayleigh's case, shaken and distraught, she begged not to take any action with the prosecutors but then wanted to prosecute. We encouraged her to take one step at a time with therapy and speaking with us to make that decision as she walked on a healing path. Early on, with our support, and with immense pressure, she found the courage to walk through her fear and chose (1) to use her voice, (2) to heal, and (3) to prosecute her offenders. Always she had the option to stop the process if it became too difficult emotionally and she never did, even though fear would come.

#1 Thin Light - freedom from a prison; a closet where she was restrained and where her sexual assault occurred; the courage to speak. As Kayleigh's Father, the pit of despair I felt on that afternoon when she was held against her will and raped, was the deepest sadness and powerlessness I ever felt. I can never imagine what it was like for her. Kayleigh's first success in her healing was telling us – immediately. Once she did that she opened herself up to herself. That is pure courage. Courage and fear co-exists at times. Even in incredibly scary situations, we have the capacity to walk through the fear. There was a trauma that she faced and you can see it in the fleeting glimpse of freedom in this painting. The darkness prevails throughout – however, she could see a thin light where the rest of the world went on without her, not knowing that she was being assaulted. Isolated, that light was both a curse and her hope – she wanted only to get on the other side of that door.

#2 A Maiden in the Storm – her initial isolation, confusion, shame, guilt and sadness – yet still standing amongst the storms; the courage to stand. I watched Kayleigh in the immediate aftermath of her assault. She felt isolated. Alone. As if no one on earth could relate to her. She was horribly embarrassed and even had trouble speaking to her parents, which is to be expected, and we have an amazing relationship. She really was alone in the fact that this was her unique experience, and not alone with other women who have gone through similar trauma. We acknowledged to her that we did not understand but would stand beside her and support her and die a thousand deaths for her if need be. With such support, and support of professionals, she still painted this piece with only one person in it – the sole maiden being lashed by the storms of life. Significantly, she was still standing.

#3 The Transition from Victim to Survivor – words thrown at her on social media, growing into self-blame that grew over time until she broke free, turned her back on such messages, used her voice and her tears and chose to survive; the courage to heal and the courage to prosecute her attackers. This is both my favorite and the most heartbreaking piece that she produced. She was bombarded on social media, sometimes by friends who wrote that she was making it up; she was an attention whore; she was being dramatic; that she brought it on herself. NO ONE SHOULD EVER HAVE TO FACE SUCH HATEFUL SPEECH, PARTICULARLY AFTER A RAPE. Please do not hide this if you are being cyberbullied. But it happened and my heart broke all over again. Those horrible messages encouraged self-punishment, the march of those voices slowly turning her own voice against herself, as she began to question herself and blame herself. See the, "YOUR FAULT" at the bottom of the painting. However, she finally had had enough and chose to SURVIVE, with a heart and a semicolon. The path forward was clear – she would use her voice courageously both to heal, to confront inappropriate behavior in others and to prosecute her attackers. Once she made that decision she fought back against the social medial bullying and she wiped it out.

#4 Sunrise of the Tree of Life – the re-emergence of her spirit through grieving, healing and reclaiming her roots in her life; the courage of self-love. This stage was beautiful, but not without steps forward and then back, back and forth. The point is she chose with courage to re-root her feet in her life, to ground herself and reclaim her sense of being a woman. There is a sacredness in womanhood and she wanted to re-invigorate her own. And she did. This piece is gorgeous. The emotion, the bright colors, the hope it conveys is consistent with what I witnessed as Kayleigh integrated into Beaumont mid-year last year, as she made new friends, continued to work in therapy, as she worked with the Rape Crisis Center, as she worked with the Prosecutors Office. She was scared in all of these situations. Remember – faith and courage are not the absence of fear – faith and courage are expressed by walking through fear – fear and courage can co-exist.

#5 Peace – having used her voice and honored herself, peace grew like a forest, though scars remained and her journey of healing continued; the courage to live empowered. Soft gentle soul. I see her in this painting. Kayleigh was forever altered by her rape. She had scars she would wear for the rest of her life, even if she had lived to 90 years old. However, when certain scars heal, the skin is actually stronger. That was her goal and that is what occurred. She wanted to come out of her sexual assault stronger than she had been, and she did. Her courage she wanted to share with others someday by being a victim advocate and perhaps becoming a therapist after college. Without really being aware of it, Kayleigh has already become a victim advocate simply by having the courage to speak up for herself. By speaking, she showed courage. By healing, she showed courage. By prosecuting, she showed courage. I have many women friends who have heard Kayleigh's story, who have told me, in confidence, they too were raped and did not speak out or prosecute. They have told me that Kayleigh's courage at fourteen, fifteen years old, was astounding and gave them a new sense of empowerment and a desire for them to stand up. Simply by these women trusting me with this information, demonstrates the impact Kayleigh's voice of courage has had. A final note on this – two days before Kayleigh physically died, she stood in court speaking out against her rapist who stood ten feet from her, and told him he took something from her that didn't belong to her and she was taking it back, that she forgave him and was moving on with her life. A week after her physical death, because she spoke out courageously in court, all of you are a little safer today as he received prison time and sexual offender Tier 1 status for ten years.

#6 Your Canvas – Kayleigh offers you this canvas for your voice; to support one another, to stand up against bullying or sexual violence, or to tell your own courageous story. Speak. Paint. Write. Engage. You are the future. Your voice is golden. Your life is immensely important to all of us. There are many things that I learn from Kayleigh every day, even after her physical death. Most of all was her example of courage. If she was ready to testify in a hostile courtroom against multiple assailants, then how could I not find the courage to likewise testify? If Kayleigh had the courage to heal, how could I not find the courage to reconcile daily myself related to her tragic physical death. If she could stand up for all of you, how could I, her Father, not stand up for you?

With Kayleigh's love – and on behalf of Kayleigh's mother, brother and myself, know Kayleigh's love for you and her mission to share with you her struggles and her triumph, the greatest of which is self-love actualized by never giving up on herself, and empowering her voice to move mountains.

*

Anger Storms 10/21/2017

Hi, Kakie. Good morning. I didn't sleep very well last night, which means I never was able to dream. I was hoping to see you in my dreams. The stages of grief day to day, hour to hour, event to event, are different as I go. Grief, individually, is itself really akin to a fingerprint, unique to each sufferer. What I am finding is that sometimes my unique fingerprints actually change as my grief subverts, alters, explodes, implodes and eclipses the prior day of torment.

I brace myself for the storm of anger and isolation that lay ahead. I have survived hundreds already in these first few months. I am finding, to my horror, there will be many thousands of storms and much more pain ahead. I promise, in each of those waves, I will claw my way through the wind to stand beside you.

I've been feeling really angry at the universe. And by default, its owner – God. How could such an absentee landlordism be tolerable, reasonable or acceptable? How do shitty people continue to walk around living their lives while an innocent child, a dynamic and brilliant child is struck down in a simple, innocent and perfect accident? In childhood!

I think to myself, God, why all of this - she was an amazing child in her physical life, to which everyone was attracted. She was mature beyond her years and a spearhead of genuine love and compassion. Exactly the type of person you'd want leading in this world. Why. A rape? A tragic traffic death? My God. Kayleigh deserved a thrown. I am so frustrated and angry that I can't even funnel the anger yet.

285

It'll come out, the grief, however it comes. It rolls in like an ink black butterfly that, upon loosening its wings, grows beyond the size of an elephant; its silky thick wings wrapping around me and blocking out the light of the sun. It sits on me and deliberately attempts to suffocate me.

I hate not having you here with me physically – not smelling your shampoo in your hair, hearing your chirpy or agitated teenage voice, our space in the car on the way to school - all of it – me saying as I would drop you off at school since first grade, "I love you, Baby. Have a safe, happy, healthy day." And hearing you reply each day, "you too, Daddy. Love you."

I really do not feel the slightest bit of anger with you, for you have done nothing wrong. I spin around in the storm looking for someone to blame for the accident – the driver, who didn't see you emerge from behind the telephone pole, who was driving in the right lane when everyone in Cleveland Heights knows you drive in the left lane as one approaches Coventry due to parked cars; God, for not preventing the accident or distracting you in the opposite direction or making sure your shoes weren't on the other side of the street; anyone who ever upset you; the shadows; life; the air I breathe. Me. Anybody. Nobody. Everybody. It all swirls around in the swelling winds of powerlessness and utter despair. It all becomes a jumble of fantasy and fury. None of it is accurate. None of it is real.

I want you to know that, even if I have hard moments with you, My Love, which I find that I do not, that it will just be me processing feelings and not meaning to be disloyal to you. In fact, if I was to fail to run directly towards the lion king's roar with every ounce of light and every cell in my body, I would diminish myself, and in diminishing me, I would be dishonoring you. I will not do that. I love you.

"Daddy, of course, I never suspected any differently. You're going to feel whatever you need to feel. I'd expect you will have thoughts about me entering the street, as innocent as it was, of not seeing the car, of assuming I'd be safe crossing the street, even though it was so innocent and such a normal thing to do that most people do a hundred times without an issue. It is okay, Daddy. I know you love me unconditionally. Our relationship is so rich and survives anything. After you let those intense feelings out, we will be closer. Each time. So process. And process again and I don't care what it is you process because it all opens you further to me! Love you, Daddy. I am so proud of you."

*

The Only Road 10/22/2017

On the far side of my grief, I will find a bigger, stronger, more profound relationship with you, Kayleigh. You are there, and here - a perfect light, encouraging me forward through the webbing of my human thought and emotion as I try to hold the hindrance of my humanness aside to let my spirit shine. This is not a road I wanted but is the road that is. You are on this road, lighting my delicate steps forward. In that regard, no matter the road, if you are on it, if you are waiting there for me, then I want this road and accept its mystery, misery and miracles.

I know you are making amazing arrangements; you are lining things up. I don't know yet what these things are, but I can feel this happening. I feel it like I feel your breath. Your voice gets stronger each day. I can sense it so strongly. Your presence is a direct blessing from God. I am the Father of an angel. How can I not, although hampered by grief, feel blessed? I love you Sweet Girl.

"Diamonds in Ocean Eyes"

Celestial glitter like diamonds crushed in ocean eyes,
Radiates like silvery Sunrise,
Deep in the soft blue of liquid light;

Healing my wounded soul so viciously brutalized,
So viciously attacked,
A muddy ink poured into purity,
Darkens in obscurity,

A light that scrambles with its spark,
To fight its way through this darkness,
I turn to your strength,
I turn to your eyes,
That radiate like silvery Sunrise,
That awakens the echoes that shed the night,
From my anguished cries.

*

Daddy, You Work Too Hard 10/23/2017

"Daddy, remember I would come to you and tell you that you work too hard and that you needed to take breaks and relax sometimes. Like, you'd be painting the house and cleaning the yard and playing with us and taking us to dinners and adventures but not really taking time for you. Don't get me wrong – my life was literally full of daily journeys and activities with you, which was amazing. You would always make a ton of time for us, never missing a school play or an important date. You would always get to your A.A. meetings and sometimes golf, but you worked so hard that it seemed like you got little time for yourself. I worried about you in those moments and I told you that you needed to sometimes just sit. And I continue to think about you like this. Take a few minutes now and again. Nobody expects you to be superman, particularly now. I love you, Daddy. Breathe in my light."

"Pathway Alight"

And God ensures the path will be provided,
And she ensures the lantern light that alights this path,
It is there already,
Already perhaps,
But I am human, and therefore, I ask,
And ask,
And ask…

…She is the soul in the garden,
She is the gold in my garden,
She is the glow on my garden,
That leads me, leads me home –

And God, He aligns itself the road,
And she, she lines that glittering road,
Flourish me with lightning sparkles,
That paint beneath my feet these pulsing stones,
And they are there already – already perhaps,
But bound in my humanity, I ask,
And ask, and ask –

And she – she is the soul in the garden,
The garden in which I grow,
She is the glow in my garden,
That leads her Father home.

*

Salamanders 10/25/2017

I moved your art supplies in the basement tonight and under the bin were two salamanders. In the house. Under your art suppliers. Where never there was a salamander. Kayleigh, you obviously brought them to us on this night. As I tried to determine the reason, my memories flooded back. You were almost two, a year before little boy was born.

I taught you how to be gentle with animals. Particularly with salamanders. At grandma and grandpa's house, we would be sitting around with all of the adults. I would look at you, a toddler, the only child in the group, and think, she's gotta be so bored. Get her out of here and go explore. Plus, it was the perfect excuse for some great one on one time with my favorite person on earth. "Hey, Babygirl, do you want to go look for salamanders?" I would ask.

Your eyes would ignite and you would pop your pacifier out and say "okay, Daddy!" You never said no.

My Darling, we would walk down the magical path of stones winding through pachysandra in their backyard, leading to seven flat rocks, some of which that season, and every year thereafter, were home to beautiful, spiritually transformative salamanders. One under the first rock. Two or three under the next. We would hold them in our hands. You cradled them with wonder.

When we were done exploring I would tell you that they needed to go back to sleep. I would set them at the edge of the flat rocks in the dirt and they would slither away to go back home underneath. We would walk away to return to the party, and you, looking back over your shoulder, would always say, "Ba-ba-ders..." and making a snoring noise several times. "Ba-ba-ders.... (Snoring-snoring)."

"Yes, Sweetheart, they are going to sleep."

My memories are so vivid - those moments the best of my life.

Then came this night. There were two that I found under your art bin hugging the cold cement of the basement floor. Symbolizing transformation. You transformed immediately as you passed your light into and through mine, letting go into my voice and my touch and my presence, passing that light to your earthly Father and then me passing your light through mine to our Heavenly Father. You transformed in an instant. Me, however, my transformation is slow and grueling and filled with a mixture of oil and water, toxicity and passion. The salamanders meaning includes detoxing from toxicity, transformation and spiritual renewal. You left two salamanders for me to find tonight letting me know that, although you've already transformed into your body of light, I have not, but still, I am not alone. I am always pared with my sweet little girl. KMM and kmm - Daddy and Daughter. I love you, my little Ba-Ba-Der.

*

Cats 10/27/2017

Jess pulled up next to me in the driveway. I had turned the Bluetooth off on the Pilot. "Angelical Cat" played on my Bluetooth from "Cats," Blasting through the Pilot. Then I realized the song wasn't on my Bluetooth since I did not have "Cats" on my phone. I asked Jess if she had "Cats" on her phone and she looked down and it was playing off of her phone on my car. It was on her phone from the other car, where her Bluetooth was on while mine was off in my car. Later that day the Bluetooth turned on and found "Memories" from "Cats" and then it flipped to Kayleigh's favorite song from "The Phantom of the Opera." Her favorite songs from both albums.

It may seem like little but coincidence, or mere technology automatically connecting as it is programmed to do, but it was not. There is an air to the event when it occurs. There is an honest and sincere insistence flowing from my Daughter to implore us to acknowledge and embrace her presence. Absolutely. Thank you, Sweetheart, for the simplicity of songs. You are getting better at manipulating our phones and cars and Bluetooth. We are watching. We are aware. We are amazed. We are so proud.

*

Target 10/29/2017

A thousand visits over fifteen years. Her earliest memories of Target were on Saturday mornings when we would take her to buy a Special Treat for rewarding a good week, her brother soon to follow once we was three. Both of our kids were never tantrum kids in stored, which I am extremely grateful. One reason may be who they are, and perhaps another is the ways in which we creatively worked with them, holding them accountable if we did have issues, and also giving them special incentives. One such incentive for Kayleigh when she was little was working out a wonderful little trick to prevent Kayleigh from having little tantrums that we would sometimes see other kids have when wanting toys in places like Target. Instead of avoiding the toy aisle, we told her ahead of time we were going to go visit her friends in the toy aisle and started our shopping at the toy section. We let her pick out a small stuffed animal on the shelf to watch over in the cart while we went around the store picking out supplies. When we were done, we would tell her she had five more minutes with that stuffed animal and then drive her back over to the toy shelf. During that brief period of time, she would prepare to part with it. She would wave bye-bye to it and place it back on the shelf, smile at us, thanking us, and we would proceed to check out. She was very satisfied with that arrangement, knowing that when she was at Target she would be able to befriend an animal, some of which might be purchased at a later date.

On this day I recalled this gentle arrangement and it made me smile. And then cry. A flood of those one thousand visits rushed forward and blew through me like a vicious hurricane. Art. Toys. Makeup. Clothing. Makeup. Shoes. Makeup. Food. Makeup. Shampoo. Makeup. There was that time when you were ten when there was a sudden tornado warning and all who were in the Target building were rushed down several flights of stairs into their deep basement. I have a photo of you, your big surprised and excited eyes and big smile radiating back at me while we heard the thunder above.

Then I turned down an aisle that had duct tape. Duct tape. All colors. You used to buy duct tape and make little art objects out of the various colors – pretend phones, computers, little trees, animals, figures. I was struck, as I am daily, that I cannot do little things with you we used to do, including walking through Target or making art projects with duct tape. My heart dried without its blood. My lungs tightened without its air. My vision failed with the veils of tears that crumpled my body in the corner of a lonely aisle in the back of Target between car wax, flashlights and duct tape.

"But Daddy, we can do these things still. Find something you like and buy it and take me along with you. We still do things together. We're just on another frequency. On another channel from each other. You can do this, Daddy."

I placed a package of purple duct tape in the cart, wiped my eyes, began to breathe and walked off towards check out.

"The Channel"

She dressed in gowns of flowing white light,
The gold in her long hair like waves crystal bright,
She kissed the wind and the air warmed around me,
Her essence enhanced me, it danced to surround me,
And I falter -

The pain blocks the pathway - it grinds on the soul,
It thieves the crown from the king from his throne,
It leads to meander down meaningless roads,
While she awaits me - with all that I've known,
She awaits me -

She calls for her Father to break through the dark,
To stare at the wind til I notice her spark,
To calm in the heartache enough to hear her,
To see her -

My Love, yes my Daughter, as the ear bends,
I'll try and I'll try again and again,
For this sacred communion requires this union,
Your physical death,
Your death did not this relationship end.

*

You Are the Best Daddy Ever 10/30/2017

Grief changes us; jades our thinking, leading us down paths we acquire only in obscure daydreams and nightmares. It comes with a punishing tongue and an emptiness that fills the space with despair and self–doubt, self-worship, self-destruction and selfless longing for a loved one so deeply loved. It can kill us. Physically, at least. It can strangle the light.

Grief has no familiar path. It holds not the same path for any two survivors. Even two parents of the same child will grieve along a

293

unique trail. Further, the various stages of grief are not linear. Rather, they jag in and out; little pieces of acceptance, anger and retreat, denial and committing to the work that throws up another hairball of torture, and a few more pieces of acceptance, followed by despondency and joy and anger and suffocation. The human psyche cannot take full acceptance in one bite, particularly with the death of a child while still in childhood. Yet grief – grief is entirely different animal, with no predictable voice and no timetable for exhaustion, it calls for me whenever it wants to call; it hides and springs at me; it huddles and curls me up in its warm blanket promising sleep.

So it came to be with me, through all of my initial grief work. Through my openness and my weakened and awakened state, these moments came to me where I illogically questioned the quality of my fatherhood; where I wondered how good a father I am, even though I have always known my truth that I am a great father and have no qualms in admitting this fact; when I would feel like we were being punished but for what – we are a great family that doesn't hurt anybody. Yet the doubt seeped in ten weeks after her death and the depths of that pain were nearly unmatched in this ungodly awful process. I was watching the thoughts like a movie across the face of a barn, knowing the scenes were fiction.

After five days of processing this, wailing over this, reassuring myself and recycling my life with my children, I simply asked them again. "Nathaniel, do you think I'm a good Daddy?" Very much aware that the question itself can be manipulative, self-serving and self-prophetic, I really wanted to know his thoughts.

"Oh course, Daddy," he said as he flung his arms around me and gave me a big kiss on my forehead, "you are the best Daddy ever. You've given us a great life and are always with us. Kayleigh always thought so too. She thinks you're amazing. And so do I. We always will."

I cried and hugged my boy, who was going through his own sorrow and pain and confusion. I reassured him that he was the most amazing son and brother; that his sister was the most amazing daughter and sister. After a bit we resumed our evening and laughed and played, Kayleigh moving amongst us with that gentle smile and her golden soul.

After a bit, as Jess and Nathaniel and Kayleigh and I sat on the couch watching TV, something told me to go drive up to the pool. It was 8:45PM. The pool would close at 10:00PM. I listened to my instinct and drove to the pool. It was empty. I sat in the sauna with Kayleigh. I swam twenty six laps, talking to Kayleigh and my Father, who assured me she was safe, at peace and full of light and love with him in Heaven. He whispered that she was his favorite grandchild and they were full of pure happiness and really enjoying their time together.

I turned to Kakie and could hear her voice telling me, "Daddy, I love you so much. I am at perfect peace. You don't have to worry about that. And you are amazing. I love you."

I returned to the bubbling heat in the sauna and continued to think about the robbery I have withstood and the daily robbery that will come each day until I physically die. Having been robbed of so much, including the fact that I had invested so much in my baby, I had been there every step, had given her constant guidance, and now I could no longer use those skills on the physical plain with her.

A friend who I sometimes would sit with in the sauna came through the doorway into the pool area and popped in. He was happy to see me. We talked openly as we always do. He was a new father. I was joyful of his new journey. He asked how Kayleigh's trial was going, as he knew of it. I told him on August 15th she stood before her rapist in a sentencing hearing, and because of that he was sentenced to jail time and sexual offender status.

Then, as he did not know, I explained August 17th; Kayleigh at a party, innocently hit by car, her friend called me, she physically died in my arms. As I finished my words he jumped across the ten foot long sauna bench and bear hugged me, tight enough I could almost not breathe. His humanity was purity. His love and his sorrow undeniable. "I am so sorry," he said, "but I am so grateful that she died in your arms. That is such a blessing that you were there with her."

He took in the information, staring out to the pool. He had seen me with my kids for a year or so on dozens of occasions. He had heard my proud, happy stories of them. He also had heard, in general, about the assault, as well as her recovery and her choice to prosecute her assailants. He had spoken with my kids in the past in the sauna on previous nights.

"You know," he said, "I have to tell you, I was talking about you to my father a few weeks back and I told him I had this friend who I would see at the sauna who was always with his kids and always talking about his kids. I told him that you reminded me of my Father. He's a great Dad. And you are too. I've seen it. I've heard it. I told my Dad that you are a Dad to emulate – a real example of what a Father is to someone like me who has just had his first baby. And you know, your daughter had courage to do all she did, and she was a soul ahead of her time, partly because of you and the way you teach her and love her. You are a great Dad."

That felt really good hearing that from an acquaintance who had observed factually what I felt in my heart. We parted, he to continue in the sauna, me to return home to see Nathaniel before he went to sleep, to kiss him and tell him I love him.

As I got dressed, I suddenly felt Kayleigh on my left side and heard her sweet voice clearly, speaking in a funny and sophisticated tone, "so, how did you like that, Daddy? See? You are a great Daddy. You are the best Daddy ever."

"Thank you, Kakes," I whispered to myself, thinking, I needed that. As I walked out of the locker room the thought finally struck me - she just did it again. I had needed her and she came. I had been grieving over a difficult part of grieving, self-doubt and self-worth, and she came to vehemently correct it. She had orchestrated a very simple meeting and a message she had delivered her whole life before and after her physical death to me. This time she did it directly through a third party. Then reveled in her own light - so Kayleigh!

Thank you for your miracle on this night, my incredible Daughter. Our walking together on this path enlightens further with each step. I miss your physical presence horrifically. At the same time I am tuning in more and more and know you are always here, just on a different radio frequency. It's my job to tune in. You are the best daughter ever. Love you, Kakie.

*

Halloween Miracle 10/31/2017

Her favorite holiday. Our first Halloween in this new configuration. It took my breath away. Still, I carved pumpkins with the kids. Nate's had a typical ghoulish face. Kayleigh's was a sea turtle, a crescent moon and a star. As the evening passed by, the glow from our jack-o-lanterns cast an orange glow on our front steps. We forced smiles into our lips for Nate's benefit, something we would need to do so that he wasn't constantly consumed with our grief. We balance very specific grief work with giving him breaks, knowing he is constantly wondering about us, worrying about us, taking cues from us. It is terrible.

As the night, now long absent trick-or-treaters, collapsed and folded up towards midnight, I harnessed the dogs and took them for a walk with Kayleigh. Her sea turtle pumpkin I had carved still held its light; the sea turtle, a crescent moon and the star all flashing in the flickering gourd. It was an uneasy night, full of angst and feeling trapped in a life I no longer wanted - a life without Kayleigh physically that would never see the same heights as I had known before her death. This far into this new un-normal I knew this truth – my great life would never be great again. It could be good, but it would never reach that great level it once held so recently. That truth, as hard as it is to swallow, is not unlike a great marathon runner who has lost his legs, but can still walk a good marathon with prosthetics.

It was cold and cloudy - wispy soft, smoky clouds swirled stagnantly against the bluish gray of a Cleveland October night. The moon was crescent, hanging like a beacon of hope, lifting the atmosphere, like the glance in Kayleigh's eyes. I spoke to Kakie out loud and expressed my 11th step prayer, "God and Kayleigh, please grant me the knowledge of your will for me and the power and strength to carry it out."

"Your sobriety," she said as I walked, hearing her clearly in my right ear, where I hear her, "you stay sober. And live a good life. Tune in, Daddy, and hear me."

I was simply in a heavy state of depression on this first Halloween since her physical death, mourning on her favorite holiday and remembering the dozen years I walked her around for trick or treating in a dozen different costumes. I stopped for a moment across the street from home. Then I saw it.

To my left a flash, a bursting shooting star, shot right passed the moon, flying westbound in an open space in my open view above my neighbor's house. It streaked and then broke up into one hundred crackling pieces and dissolved in the night. It was Kakes. I could feel her. I knew she was with me. Her words were more present now - the need to tune in; the ability to see her and hear her with me. I felt her love cascade all around me. The moment knocked me to the ground, the dogs sitting patiently while I wept on the sidewalk.

After a minute on my knees, I picked myself up and crossed the median strip to our house. On the front step her sea turtle pumpkin candle had burned out since I had left just minutes earlier. As if her light in the pumpkin, shining the shape of a turtle, a star and the moon, had jumped from her pumpkin to an actual shooting star in the sky that kissed the moon, she shined and brightly danced across that wondrous space. I glanced down at her pumpkin knowing this was true. Once again, she conveyed her essence to me. This time, in a pumpkin on her favorite holiday, signaling her presence and her desire for me to take the next fragile step.

*

Inspire Me 11/02/2017

You inspire me. You always have, even before you were born. When I wake I pull you into my days, not unlike how I used to do before your physical death. I used to wake you, say good morning, say – let's go embrace the day. As a littler girl you'd smile and pop out of bed, dancing on your tippy toes across the floorboards. As a toddler you'd say, "Okay, Daddy!" as a ten year old, a smile and a "good morning." As a fifteen year old, "ugh! Go away!" and covering yourself with a pillow and telling me to close your door on my way out. Funny child.

Now I do likewise each day, saying each morning, "good morning, Sweetheart. Let's go embrace the day. What do you want to do today? What do you have in store for us today, Kakes? You inspire me."

"Daddy, I am watching you. You inspire me!"

Thank you. I am so grateful that I flooded your physical life with daily messages of encouragement and togetherness. You understood your value as you saw it, as well as how I saw it – incredible, smart, gentle, worthy, dynamic, compassionate Kayleigh, even when you struggled, as everyone will struggle at times, with esteem. You understood at your core. Thank God your life was so full of love and light.

On this today, I am trying, really trying to go out and be ready for whatever you have in store for us – whatever the day brings us. We walk together, Little Peanut. I promise you I will focus on your light and move further into your peace. I go through a thousand machinations a day; suffer and grieve and sob each day; and life myself upon my feet each day many, many times. I will not fail you. I love you!"

*

Needing Daddy 11/04/2017

Hi, Sweetheart. I miss sitting with you on the couch. So simple. So cruel. I felt myself resisting saying I wish you were sitting on the couch mostly because I think I need to change the dialogue in order to continue to change, and also, do I really wish that my child, who is in a higher freedom, at a higher peace and filled with God's light and love in a perfectly safe place, was here still trapped in humanity? Yes! I do! Selfishly. No, I don't, unselfishly. I am trapped. I am powerless. I am stuck in this moment of life.

You are a powerful companion in this family of four. I walk with you every day and miss you physically with a heart sickness constantly. I am proud of my breakthroughs this week. Firstly, even though you don't need my guidance any more (like how to maneuver in relationships or study for a test), you need me more than ever. You need my love, dedication, loyalty, laughter, companionship, my focus, my voice, my effort to tune into your channel. You need your Daddy just like you've always needed your Daddy and I am jubilant in that fact. I struggled for several surreal days in a panic wondering if you no longer needed me since you were now an elevated angel. The answer is yes and always. You need your Daddy. You need me! You need me! Thank God, you do.

Secondly, and it didn't take long for this to unfold in this tragedy - if someone asks me if I have any kids my answer is simple and straight forward, "yes, I have two amazing kids. I have a beautiful son named Nathaniel (and state his age) and I have a wonderful and courageous daughter named Kayleigh (who is, state her current age) who was physically killed in a car accident at the age of fifteen in August, 2017, but who grows with me daily in her spiritual body." And if they are uncomfortable with that answer or their own limited view on life, then so be it. I don't care. I will not fail to speak of you because someone else may feel uncomfortable. That is their business. Not mine.

I make this recording for us because I sat in a meeting at work and a leader asked a group of thirty if anyone had a daughter. I do, but I flinched, due to your recent transition, and expecting him to call on people for follow up interaction. So I sat on my hand. And boiled. Not at him, but with my mistake. It's a natural mistake – not knowing how to answer a sudden question like that, particularly as we are not even three months out from this most horrific transition. But I did. And I never will again.

I am excited to see what you have planned for me today. Kakes, I love you tenderly and completely, My Love.

"Daddy, good work. Of course you were confused. Stay close to me. I am always here. You will get stuck in your humanity and that's okay. Just always come back to my light. I will never leave your side. Not ever. I love you, Daddy."

*

Daddy, You Amaze Me 11/05/2017

What would Kakes say if she was physically here watching me light candles at her memorial? She'd say, 'oh, Daddy that's so kind. I love you. Thank you for loving me.' So, if she would say that if the accident did not happen, why wouldn't she say that now in her body of light? I believe she does.

"Oh, Daddy - I would say so much more! I always knew you loved me so deeply – seemingly more than other fathers loved their daughters. My friends would tell me. You were their favorite. A few told me they wished you were their father. I knew how deeply you loved me, I thought. But seeing you and feeling your love now that I've physically died and can feel its full impact on this side of the veil, you amaze me. You actually loved me much deeper than I could understand or realize and I always knew it was super deep. My God, I am amazed by your love and devotion and it makes me feel so happy and overjoyed. I have the best Daddy ever. I tell everyone here. I brag about you constantly. And they're jealous here too, just like back in my physical life with my friends. I love you so, so much. Know that I will never leave your side."

Kakes, thank you. I struggle with all of these new challenges every day. I can barely breathe. And then I hear your voice and your message. It comes to me in my right ear, about an inch within, and it comes directly through the chambers of my soul – your voice strumming across the big country of my soul. It dislodges the burden momentarily, enough so that I may breathe.

"My Breath"

As if it ferments in a jar on the shelf,
Along with the container holding my body's health,
Nothing more yet something else,
Aging, aging, aging...

My breath, it penetrates a barbed wire fence,
It pays the Ferryman for its moment of recompense,
It halts in the doorway of innocence,
And buckles to its knees,
Enslaved, I gave my blood -

As if it's eyes have years between visits,
Distraught by the barriers and distance,
Oceans, desserts, lakes and ridges,
And wishing its way home,
As it presses out the lungs,
And whispers on the tongue,
My breath,
Though short, I choose.

*

Beaumont Memorial Mass 11/05/2017

Beaumont had a memorial mass today for alumni who passed this year. Another very excruciating moment - seeing women who have lived so long – the class of 58', of 67', of even 88', which was sad enough, and then Kayleigh at the bottom of the list - class of 2020 – in 2017. Each family had a candle and walked the candle up to the altar. In order, after everyone else had passed, they read Kayleigh's name and I walked down the aisle, a candle in my hand, sobbing wildly. Each step is excruciating, and sometimes barbed with extra grief, and flowered with extra love. I will do anything for my

302

children; suffer any pain; embrace every opportunity to honor them and love them. We are now that family that others look at – with compassionate eyes; with sympathy; and sometimes with gratitude that they are not us. We own it. We wear it with dignity. We hide nothing.

After mass ended we went outside into their back yard where they have a pond and trees frame the yard. All of the trees were in full autumn display of oranges and yellows and reds and browns. Literally millions of leaves, all unique their own colors, danced gently in the breeze. Kayleigh immediately drew my eyes to a leaf hanging amongst thousands on the tree nearest the patio. It was the only leaf my eyes could see as she blocked my vision of all other leaves. It was a beautiful golden, orange, red and brown leaf, with a perfect cut out of a heart in the middle – each half of the heart, the missing flesh, aligned along the spine of the leaf. The hole in my heart. The hole in my leaf. My child's physical absence cut out of the leaf. My child's spiritual presence, the heart within the leaf. A leaf, ingrained with the touch of an angel, a feeling of immortality, a breath of the divine.

She is amazing, my miracle worker - always attentive, always finding new ways to reach across the wind and touch our hearts. When I needed it most, she penetrated the wind, manipulated the natural world, and directed me back to her through the grief. The counterbalance. She is ingenious and creative and devoted and unabashed. So proud...at the same time as I express and expect awe in my girl, I miss her so horribly. My soul is really filled with such immense sorrow. But she touches me then and keeps a spark in my next step.

"Rest in My Light"

Scarlet golden floral fields like clouds,
Thousands stemmed across its brow,
Thousands bare themselves in autumnal dance,
By chance,
Or was it guiding light,
Leading my eyes to unveil a precious sight -

She with the energies,
She with the graces,
She imbued with God's wistful embrace,
That warmly leaves its traces,
Upon me,
I saw no other shape in the mesh,
Across the trees changing landscape,
But for this one sunburst leaf,
With a heart carved from Father's grief,
Right through its flesh;

She was letting me know,
Dear Father, I picked this one for your aching soul,
I am here with you in morning's hidden folds,
Come home, Father, home,
And find the peace you seek in my light.

*

The House is So Quiet 11/06/2017

It is one of the nightmares from the nightmare that keeps giving. The house is so quiet. Not only is it absent the noise and the volume of two teens ripping their way through the house, each a dynamic and loud voice, but the extra voice that comes from the combination of your two voices. A third voice used to erupt in the house as your voice and your brother's merged in song and laughter and yelling and talking and whispering. We have lost all three voices in this house – your physical voice is gone; the third voice in combination is gone; and Nate's voice, well damaged, drifts in a vacuum.

It is so wrong. He is not an only child yet he is the only child physically in the house. He is so used to his big sister drifting in and out of his bedroom and the kitchen and the TV room, engaging and embracing each other's company, company each loves so tenderly. Now when Nate cracks a joke or engages and the volume sneaks up slightly, my first thought is, thank God he is engaging and we have to keep him going; following by, the volume is half, we are missing Kayleigh's physical voice. It is a constant sadness, one that will never lift. And it should not. We acknowledge this with him, always the vocal family, working issues out and checking in on feelings. We remind him that we see the absence for him and that we are not Kayleigh; that we can never fill that vacuum that she and he lived in together. We cry with him. We hold our little baby boy.

It is unsettling. It is cruel. It is a consequence of a perfect, simple, innocent accident with no culpability. It is absolutely terrifically horrible. We encourage Nate's voice of courage, as he bravely steps through each of these days, from a life that was effortless, to one he cannot manage daily without breaking down. And so it is with Mommy and Daddy as well, as we break down and stand up and miss Kakes' physical voice and search madly to hear her spirit voice. She never fails us. She is here.

"Connecting the Light Through the Wind"

The gnostic he lulls in a powerless chair,
Refuses to find the oxygen within the air,
He staggers and stumbles and straggles his struggles alone -

We stand before him profoundly aware,
Alight with a faith that swallows the fear,
Gazing across a fracture, face to face, soul to soul -

A tragedy separated her life from mine,
My daughter, her death unleashed the divine,
Her spirit empowered, she hugs me; she smiles in her hold -

Connecting our light is much harder for me,
Tucked deeply in grief and my humanity,
But here I am, awake and never, never alone -

My Darling, my Daughter, we show the skeptic world,
An unbreakable bond of a Daddy and his girl,
For we cross the wind and together, aspired, we glow.

305

*

Come Here, Padray 11/07/2017

And then she was there. I was asleep, though lightly, so aloofly that I was aware that I was asleep. I sensed I was dreaming, but also realized that my dream and waking states, my physical and spiritual states were merging and overlapping. And then she was there.

I spent the day at an analytics conference, speaking twice on a panel, somehow. At lunchtime there was music, at a volume just high enough to hear, pumped into the conference room. U2's "One" began with its rhythmic cords. My heart sank. I recalled forty five days before Kayleigh physically died - I took her and Nathaniel to see the 30th anniversary of "Joshua Tree" at Cleveland Browns Stadium. During "One" the kids, Nathaniel on my right, Kakes on my left, wrapped their arms around me as we screamed out the lyrics to this song. At the time I treasured this moment, knowing it would be a memory for the ages. Its meaning now is much deeper.

I purposely had not listened to U2 since her physical death only because I wasn't quite ready. On this day it forced itself into my ears. I left the conference room and found a quiet space in the wide underground hallways of the Cleveland Convention Center and sobbed. And sobbed. And sobbed. Thus are the triggers upon me, the moment to moment living required. After some time, I turned back to Kayleigh's light.

My wounds seeped through the day from there on. The image of her accident penetrated my mind - my thoughts of what it looked like when the power of the car that hit her spun her beautiful, precious body and the energy threw her body straight down while spinning, her beautiful left side of her head impacting the street, damaged so suddenly, in a shocking, yet light spattering of blood. I lost my breath. I called my sponsor and walked through a Tenth Step. I accepted the traumatic images, once again, then turned back to Kayleigh's light.

When I returned home I remembered I wanted to ensure the card for her Last Rights was preserved in her funeral box. It had been on the mantle since the morning after her physical death. Finding it on the mantle, I kneeled on the floor and lay it on the hardwood to take pictures of the tiny sheet of paper, upon which were written the absolution and other prayers recited for Kayleigh in her Last Rights at University Hospital in Room #41.

I reread the paper, resting on my knees. My mind flooded back to that night; cradling her right hand, running my fingers through her hair along her hairline, talking to her for hours while she lay in her deathbed. I broke down again. Jess joined me on the floor - two adults crumpled into a messy sobbing of bubbling tears, mourning the sudden and shocking physical death of their oldest child. After some time, I turned back to her light.

I fell asleep in the evening four separate times in four separate place, before finally dragging off to our bed. Typical day in the afterglow.

And then she was there. She was wearing a thin, long black sweater, black tights, and a salmon colored top. She was wearing makeup - her hair a darker golden brown shade, darker than her natural color. This was Kayleigh in the winter months, 2017, when she dyed her hair reddish.

"Come here, Padray," she said, a compassionate smile on her face, as she nodded her head slightly to the right. She stepped towards me - like a mother coming to swoop up her crying child, and wrapped her arms around me as if to say, 'you had a hard day - you are now safe.' She embraced me so perfectly and her warmth flooded through me. I collapsed in her arms. I had needed her and she came. In her ever presence - she had presented. In her omniscience - she had shined. In her compassionate love - she had eclipsed the physical world and the universe deep in my dreams.

Reset, awakening to a new dawn, a new day, I arose in her light and continued this journey on this broken, choking road. I greet, begrudgingly, and say hello to her physical death in order to say hello to her spiritual rebirth. It is the only life for me now, one constantly balancing of the duality of these two truths.

*

I've Got You, Daddy 11/08/2017

She affirmed, "I've got you, Daddy. I'm right here. You can do this, Daddy. You can do this."

It came on the heels of several more days of inferno - the waves recede, gather strength and then return, blowing holes in the fabric of my soul. I was standing in her room. It was the early morning of the twelve week anniversary of her accidental and tragic physical death.

I kissed her pillow. I do it every day - several times. I kiss it in the spot where the back of her head used to lay, her beaming face staring up to the ceiling. She'd be tucked into her blankets tightly, up to her neck. It's just what she always did, wrapped from feet to chin, feeling protected and safe in her bed. Her beautiful face and her long blonde hair upon her pillow.

Before she was a tween I spent time with her each night on her bed laughing, reading, coming up with magical stories. These are some of my favorite memories of her over her first twelve years. However, since she was about thirteen, she was obviously changing and our night time routine changed as well. By thirteen, it used to go like this: we would spend time somewhere in the house typically. She would run off and take a shower and get ready for bed. I would know when she was done and dressed and prepping for bed. I would tap on her door and get permission to open her door and step in. "Goodnight, Baby."

"Goodnight."

Then I would lean over and kiss her forehead and say, "I love you."

She would smile. "Love you too."

I know that she isn't laying in her bed in her physical body, but I know she is here every time I reach down and kiss the pillow. She is everywhere where I am. She is present wherever I go. She is more than I am in her body of light.

My mind races. As if I am holding back the ocean, even though these are not my intentions, and even though I tend to be rather open and able to process my feelings and deepest emotions. On this twelve week anniversary I was spinning in my head while kissing her pillow. I caught this automatic activity and stood silently for a moment to center.

"I've got you, Daddy," she said, "Daddy. I'm right here. You can do this, Daddy. You can do this."

She does have me. She, like a flashlight at my feet in a midnight forest, shines the perfect space where next my foot reaches for its step. She is my cheerleader. Encourager. She wants me to live and love, both for the sake of living, but also specifically so that I can live with her. The trauma and its traps can block me from her channel. She was telling me to process; to survive the meat-grinder. To do "hard" - that we can do "hard."

I used "Footprints" to help Kayleigh frame her relationship with God. It is ironic, and full circle, that she now uses "Footprints" on me. Now she carries me. Each day. She has me.

*

Days and Gratitude 11/09/2017

Who would have ever known driving to work in the morning could be so hard. On this day, on my way to work, I was crying. I was telling her I know we are in transition. That we are always together. That it's my primary job to work through the grief. To be grateful for the days we had physically together rather than being ungrateful for the days we don't have together, that ungratefulness is as abundant as the universe. I was in the process of trying to convince myself of this theory to calm my unsettled nerves, when suddenly she flipped songs on the Bluetooth in the car to a song I have on a soundtrack, but never listened to before. Once again she blew me away.

I started hearing a subtle guitar and Elvis Costello singing, "thank you for the days, those endless days, those sacred days you gave me..." She spoke through a song. She sang to her Father the exact words I was thinking in my mind, to a song I had never heard before, by switching the music on me phone through the Bluetooth in my car; something she has mastered in a very short time. If this had happened once, maybe twice, one may be able to discount it as coincidence. Not me. There is a feeling that comes with the miracle. A sense in the wind. A warming chill in the body, knowing Kayleigh's presence is illuminated, stretching towards me, wrapping her light around me. Such is the life of an angel and her love for her Father.

I hear you, sweet Kayleigh. Use whatever channel you can. I will do the same, as limited as I can. I will reach through the air as much as I can and meet you in the brilliant middle of our loving relationship.

*

Sitting on Your Bed 11/11/2017

This pen, it bleeds my emotion, my grief, my love. The strands of light from my soul flow through this tiny channel and enter the physical world, becoming our river; becoming a lifeline; becoming a stronger bond between Father and Daughter; a witness to your voice; an instrument for your instructions.

Kakie, I sit on your bed, looking out from your room as you would do. I feel your peace here, though I know you are not only here, and you certainly are not trapped anywhere, particularly not in your room. You infuse me with your courage – your strength – I can feel you. I can hear you. Your wind chimes sing to me. Your voice comes to me in the wind, and I hear you in my soul. You work your way through electronics. You move the water. You kiss me while I sleep.

310

A journey I did not want, and one I was not prepared for, for who could be prepared for the sudden physical death of a child. This has been thrust upon me, your Mother, your Brother, and you. I am grateful you are safe and at peace, but you were already at peace and didn't need to physically die to be at peace. You knew a greater peace and self-harmony than most will ever understand in a long life. You are my guide through this journey. I ache for you. I will stand up each day knowing you are here and knowing who you are. I love you, Kakes. Let's keep walking.

"Daddy, I am holding your hand. I am sitting here with you. I walk beside you with devotion, and loyalty and love and light. You are my Daddy. I will never not be here. I know you need to hear that. You might need to hear it every new day. That's fine. I will never not be here, Daddy. I love you so much!"

*

Bluetooth Familiar 11/12/2017

My mind is shot. My body is shot. My chest in disrepair. My soul aching. My feet blistered from the jaggedness of this road. I have now, for months, intentionally engaged in mobilizing my resources – therapy at Cornerstone of Hope; one on one counseling; making lists and trying to knock off chores; taking breaks at work; forcing myself to work; doing my Step work; working with new guys; meditation time with Kayleigh; swimming.

During swimming tonight, and a few visits to the sauna, I saw and sat with my sauna friend, Kamal. He told me that, after I had seen him a few weeks back and told him about the accident, that he was overwhelmed with sadness and thinking about Kayleigh non-stop. He said he spent another hour in and out of the sauna alone. No one else was in the pool area. At one point he said he looked up and through the steam of the sauna and thought he saw a glimpse of Kayleigh walk by near the pool – a girl he had seen many times before, tall, blonde, five feet ten inches tall, a skinny, pretty teenage girl. She just walked by – a few seconds at most, disappearing from view from his vantage point as she made eye contact with him, smiled and walked off to the left. He said it was peaceful - like she was showing the world a sign. He didn't know if he would tell me, or how I would accept the moment he said he had. I thanked him and told him that he did likely see her in her body of light; flashing into the physical world at times, in moments when the channel is open, when the dimensions cross. I told him it is not a ghost or a lost soul or any silly antics we see on the Discovery Channel; that it was actually a soul elevated into the Higher Life, beautiful, authentic. And it was Kayleigh.

That lifted me up. At least momentarily, as the wind can shift and thereto can my consciousness, my grief, my pain and the hard road I am on. I jumped into the car and asked her after swimming tonight, "What are we going to listen to?" The Pilot was set to my Bluetooth. I incidentally had her phone in the car as I had gone to the Apple Store to work with them to ensure I could get her photo files on her phone. It had not been in any of our cars since the night she physically died.

As I listened for one of my songs to come on, perhaps a U2 favorite for me and Kakes, something else happened. Arianna played. I thought, I didn't realize I had this on my phone. I forwarded the songs from the button on my steering wheel. Another Arianna song. Forwarded. Another Arianna song. Then I grabbed my phone to try to manually override the songs Kakes was playing, not really thinking much of it in a blurry moment, and turned on Daysleepers, which immediately began to play on the tiny speaker on my phone while Arianna continued on the speakers in the car. Then I stopped and came back to our new reality set. I realized that she jumped the Bluetooth again and was playing music from her phone instead of mine. I heard her laughing as I smiled in recognition, as she pulled me back out of a dull moment and back into her life.

*

Footprints 11/13/2017

Kayleigh, I have a lovely friend at work, named Patty. She does not know our family intimately; has never met you or Mommy or Nate, but has heard about you all as I would freely talk about my family with such pride, both before and after this accident. She told me today she was drawn to a particular store to buy something commemorative for us, not knowing the family, and having never known what was important or significant. She was drawn to a particular item. She said that a voice told her that I really wanted this and had to have this and that it was very, very important. She said she just listened and followed that intuition.

When I opened the box, I saw a bronzed cross with "Footprints" etched into it. I immediately said, "Kayleigh. Kayleigh brought you to this. You wouldn't have known, but I brought Kayleigh to God through 'Footprints.' She wanted an example of something she could tangibly relate to and I showed her 'Footprints.' She immediately resonated with it and asked me to print it for her so she could tape it to her wall. Throughout the last months of her life, whenever one of us needed a little reminder, we would send the Footprints image to the other in a text, reminding the other that we are never alone."

Patty said, "Oh, I am so pleased. I felt driven, do you understand? Does that make sense? Something told her to go to that store and to pick that piece."

"It was Kayleigh. It's just what she does, particularly when things get dark for me. She will always intercede and pull my head out of the mud. Today it was you. She picked you."

"Darkfully"

Alone with this lowness of loneliness,
Wafting in an emptiness,
The broken soul,
In its folds the pain of child's severance,
We know no other recompense -

Lost as the darkness grows,
Lost among the vacant groans,
Lost in the house that I called home,
Lost, it is plentiful,
The feeling of empty pull,

That sucks the air from the lungs meshed in stone;

My girl, this world is full of accidents,
And one has crossed its visit with you,
My girl, my little baby girl! My God!
My shock in losing you so suddenly,
Has turned its eyes and hunt on me,
And tracks me whether daylight or sleeping -

Run for the yesterday,
Run for the time machine,
Run for your life, Father Time,
Run back an hour before your death,
When the air was light and fields were green,
Run to re-arrange the scene,
And swap your beautiful body for mine;

But no,
We cannot turn back the history,
The mindless universe,
And it arbitrary misery,
And so I set my eyes to this awful road,
The darkness, the loneliness, the lengthiness, the heavy load,
And I trudge forth,
The only hope a brilliant torch,
That seems to illuminate my way,
And I stagger in the badlands,
And follow your loving hands,
That pull me through the darkness and the pain,
And I know you are with me every step,
In every moment of every day,
Cheering me forth,
Plotting a steady course,
Yet the grieving blinds my vision, my Darling,
And I grow darkfully submissive in the parting,
Until I turn my heart to your grace,
Until I find myself staring at your smiling face,
That gazes lovingly across the veil of warmth and the wind.

*

The Wrong Questions 11/13/2017

Why my Daughter? Why me? My son? My wife? My daughter was a spectacular and compassionate girl. A really, really good girl, with a little snap to her, and incredible resilience. She was, in her physical life incredibly compassionate, loving and kind; ever accepting of differences; all about family. She was deadly artistic and had a little bit of an edge, mostly to protect that golden innocence within her. So then, why would God take her? Did God take her? God did not. He did not cause the accident. I knew that. But the wrong questions are the first that come up and they are a poison to the mind.

The right questions are selfless and empowering. What did I teach her? What did she teach me? What beauty are we together? What light can I give you, Kayleigh, for you are my Daughter? What path can you illuminate for me? What is our next step, regardless of whether you are in your physical or spiritual body? How do I raise my vibration high enough to see, feel and hear you consistently? I can answer this in summary, the content of which would fill several books. Yet the wrong questions, they not only tie up the mind in unending quibbling and unsatisfactory tethers, they also block me from God, from Kayleigh and from myself. I will work on asking the right questions.

"The Wrong Questions"

My Love, youthful, my Little Girl,
A centerpiece of this sacred world,
Alight,
You were dancing –

My Girl,
Cruelly ripped from my loving arms,
Stripped from this life in tragic harm,
While we were happy, living,
Loving and laughing,
Growing and giving –

Why with the broken heart,
Why this awful tragedy,
Why without warning,
This one, with her majesty,
Why when the earth needs people like My Girl,
Why, she is just a child,
Fifteen years and several miles,
With long empowered life that now forsakes her;

My love, I was laying on the floor wailing for your presence,
I love you –

*

Hi Daddy! 11/14/2017

"Hi, Daddy! Rise and shine! I thought I'd mix things up this morning. What do you want to do today? Love you!"

I love you, too, Sweetie. So happy to hear your voice, Babygirl. I'm not sure – I just want to spend time with you and your brother and mother. I will keep clear and centered so I can stay open and awake with you. I love you so much, Sweetheart.

Every day, my Babygirl, a sacred manner; I will walk in your light with intention and purpose, ensuring our awareness of your presence with us. Every day of my life, since the accident, I have to, I am forced to live without you in your physical body. However, every day of my life I get to have you in your spiritual body of light and I am not going to miss out on my opportunity to be with my girl. You will participate fully in our lives, our days, our moments, both lighted hearted and difficult, just as you always have. You will laugh with us. Cry with us. Make decisions with us. You will be there encouraging us, nurturing us, guiding us gently in ways that only you will know and understand. You will sing our songs and offer new music to our ears. Offer new color to our daydreams and fill our lenses with golden white light. You are an integral part of this family of four.

And I, your Father, promise to refuse to use your physical death for any potential failures in my own life. I will not use this tragedy to create deeper tragedy. I will not use it as an excuse for me not reaching my goals, not performing, not embracing life. I will not dishonor my sweet, strong, dynamic daughter in that manner. Rather, I promise, you, courageous Kayleigh, to hold your light up like a jewel and keep it polished. I will walk with you every day in a sacred manner. Every day. I will walk in your light, and yours in mine, with purpose and intention, with love and dignity, with this unbreakable bond sealed between Father and Daughter in our first embrace on the day you were born. I promise you that.

You want to see a dedicated father? I will stop at nothing for your voice to be heard. Your voice will be heard and you will participate in this world one day at a time. You will be a part of it and play a part in it. This world is not going on without you, Kayleigh Mooney. As long as I am breathing and physically alive I will ensure that your voice is heard. That your spirit is present. That others know this truth. Yet you are not contingent upon me. You are not here because of me. Your voice is not your voice because of me. I am just your channel and can interpret and channel you. Without me, you would be present nonetheless. For you are alive within yourself and touch us in ways that are secrets to God.

*

Walk Through Grief 11/15/2017

Hi Kakie – I feel you with me. I clearly understand and need to walk through my grief. It is a necessary part of the journey that brings me closer to me, to you, to God. I want to get to a place- it won't be like August 16 and our relationship before the accident and your physical death – but to a place where it is even stronger. As amazing as our relationship was before the accident, it feels like it is maturing and strengthening as we walk this road together. In fact, due to the extreme stress and the nature of our current situation, our love has carried through the breach and has proven itself to withstand these

317

tests of two worlds. A silver lining, having your guidance and your presence so pronounced is a lifeline for me.

All that I taught you to prepare for your adult life – how to walk through fear, how to have the strength to take care of yourself – you have handed that right back to me and asked me to do as I have asked you to do. I know there's a part of you that thinks it is hilarious and you relish guiding your Father about. There is the deepest part of you, though, that takes this responsibility very seriously, resonating in the deepest light of your soul, knowing your love for me and wanting me to take each next step of reconciling, if reconciling can be had. As I do this I reconcile into the new un-normal, getting closer to God, to me and to my beautiful companion – you, my Daughter, walking by my side. I love you, Kakie. Keep me upright. Keep me walking.

"Daddy, thank you for your love and insight. You are exactly right – I do love leading you around! I am here. I am your Kakie. I am here for every step. Let's always intentionally bring each other into each other's day. Say it out loud, that with intention and devotion, you bring me into your day and I will do the same. Okay? Love you, Daddy."

"Inches Behind the Wind"

A different radio frequency,
It is I who must tune in,
She is radiant in life,
Just inches behind the wind;

I hear her,
Her voice opening like a flower in morning,
It does not spring open or it would hurt the petals,
We need to nurture our physical petals,
As they unfold to the light,
God's light mixed with her life,
Purity.

*

Forgetting My Truth 11/16/2017

Babygirl, hi, it's Daddy – I woke up today forgetting my truth – the truth that I am a great Father. I saw only my mistakes and thing in hindsight I could have done better. It was a lonely feeling and shameful, and wholly dishonest! After doing a thorough Tenth Step, and listening to Carly's feedback, my truth came back into view, like a ship's sail working its way through the jagged wind in a deep fog. Very few girls (Carly says none that she knows) enjoys the relationship we have – I created a deep and unbreakable cradle of trust, love, support, acceptance and humanity for you – I showed you my mistakes and my humanity – my errors and how to correct them. When you were a little girl, a toddler even, if ever I yelled at you I would make amends to you on my knees, eye to eye, holding you in that respect and majesty. I literally never failed to make amends to you when my humanity got the best of me. Lucky for us, it was infrequent. Lucky for us, we always reciprocated that respect and gentle love with each other. I miss that in the physical world so much.

You watched that – you benefited from it – participated in our interchange. Learned how to likewise make amends. When you were intensely upset, you would turn to me to let it out – your lightning rod. You trusted me so much you literally talked to me about almost everything. If too intimate a subject, and more suited for a woman to woman discussion, you turned to Mommy and in our mutual support you found an incredibly deep love among us. I don't want to ever forget that – I watched how many of the other fathers were with their daughters – and studied them – and then there was me – full of intention from the beginning – present on a daily basis to do what I wanted to do most – not golf for six hours with three other men; not to sit and watch football all day on Sundays with a group of friends. I would instead spend time with my Babygirl and my baby boy (golfing a quick 9 at 6am and being back by 815 when you and your brother would begin to stir). I am so glad you are my Daughter – something I say to you so frequently it comes out of my mouth like a breath.

"Daddy, its Kakes. Where do I begin – you are amazing. You give me true love. You always have. I knew that then, before the accident, and I know it now. Whether you were changing my diaper and making me laugh, or finding rocks in the forest or shells on the beach, or disciplining me because I was a kid making kid mistakes, or even just being there during emotional times – I watched you cry with me freely. I learned to use my voice from you. I learned fear and courage can co-exist, that courage was not the absence of fear but walking through fear. I learned that I was and am the most special girl in the world to my Father. That I am the most special girl to me. Many of my friends never had that, and never will. But I do. Because I was and am lucky enough to have you, and you are lucky enough to have me. We are the K-M-Ms. I am forever indebted to you for shaping me into the young woman I became and into the peaceful soul that I am. Thank you, Daddy, so much. You may have times like this again where you question yourself – know that it is not me complaining, but you processing your humanity. I'm perfectly happy having the best Daddy in the world. Know your truth and that truth is very simple – you were present and loving every day of my physical life – you were present for my soul's transition, sacrificing without a thought of your own feelings just to be focused only on me as I passed into the light; conscious only of supporting me, while knowing it was happening. Daddy! That is amazing! And you have been with me every day since my transition. We are amazing together and always will be. I hope this helps, Daddy. You are my Daddy. Love you!"

*

Three Months 11/17/2017

Three months – a morning's writing seems inadequate. It is so unfair. I am barely able to crawl from bed. Exhaustion burns through my sight. My eyes rust. My voice warps in the cracks of despair that haunt me. The rush of the day already upon me, tortures the stomach and the lining of the heart. I have to rush off to the world that continues as if nothing ever happened. Some people at work have wondered if I'm better yet! How disgusting!

You are more important than the day. I will leave this writing for now because I must rush off to this unforgiving world, but I will find quiet time later to come back to our words. You are the light of the world. I love you so much. As I used to say each day when I dropped you off at school, "have a safe, happy, healthy day – love you."

"You too, Daddy. Have a safe, happy, healthy day! I am so proud of you. One step at a time, Daddy. You can do this."

*

My Light 11/18/2017

I offer you my light. My Love, my presence, my devotion and loyalty – they are yours. You need your Daddy and I am here. I will never not be here. I stood at your memorial site last night and re-affirmed with you that fact and you answered, blustering through the leaves and wrapped your light around me – because you also know clearly, your Daddy needs you, your light, your love, your laughter, your guidance. We have a lot of living to do together – now one of us is still on this earthly plain in a human shell while the other is in Heaven and fluidly with me here on this physical plane in her magical body of light. Your foothold here is firm. The seat of your soul with your Father.

One day we will again fully be on the same plain in the same body types. Until then, and after that, we are together. I will not dishonor you. I will not turn away through my grief. I am and I will offer you my light rather than focusing on you offering me your light. Your light is an effortless, constant truth. Mine I have to work at, only because of the grief and insufferable loss. The losses accumulate. I am starting to feel this more presently. It is horrible. I promise you that I will process this grief and reconcile as I can, My Love. Love you, Kakes. Let's go live today.

"Daddy, I am smiling on you. I hope you can see that. Look at what you do for me. I am so honored. So glad you're my Daddy. I am here too, Daddy. Let's walk, Daddy."

My Creed to you, Kayleigh: I hold my light with purpose, like a polished jewel, and offer this gift of my life to you, my wonderful Daughter, a gift I pray is well empowered and worthy of our love. I dedicate today with intention to your present and to our incredible relationship as it continues to grow. I'm going to start saying something like this to you each night when I sit with you on your bed.

"I love it, Daddy!"

*

Robber of Physical Fatherhood 11/19/2017

Clearly there is something much bigger than the bounds of her physical life that is going on. Too many things are lining up. Too many seeming coincidences. She is going to impact thousands.

Still I have been physically robbed of one of the things I do best - being an active Father to my Daughter. I was typically in sync - able to anticipate her needs - present and active and loving in my ways. I was energized in it. Built for it. Loved every moment. It made me more alive. It was my passion. It still is, however, it is different. I have been robbed of your physical embodiment.

Perfectly human in the mistakes I would make and unique in the quickness of correction, I was typically trying to find new ways to connect and new ways to guide and also new ways to apologize for mistakes. I still remember the excitement when she was a toddler when I looked at our physical size difference and clearly noted how intimidating it must be for a man over six feet tall to discipline or apologize to a child two feet tall. So, when the times came, and they did, and I lost my cool or yelled or was frustrated and needed to apologize, I would get on my knees, chopping down my size. Then I would bend my back to get to her eye level and tell her it was wrong that I said whatever I said that upset her; that nobody had a right to talk to her like that; that as her Father she needed to respect me, but as her Father I needed to respect her double. It did not take long for

Kayleigh to empower around this notion - that here was Daddy telling her nobody had a right to talk to her like that, not even him.

Easy for me to say, but I know my truth. I know the priority of fatherhood in my life. I was born to be their Father. I had brilliant moments and I had those moments because I anticipated them, planned for them, dreamed of them and put my ego in the backseat and let my children drive. Both of them found great strength in the nurturing and trusting atmosphere that we created for them. For my part, being a Father and their primary male influence, I took seriously my obligation and responsible to train our children to someday be respectful, empowered, loving adults, by example - Kayleigh learning how men should treat her with dignity and respect and equality; Nathaniel learning how he should treat women with that same dignity and respect and equality.

What a beautiful and complex dynamo, she is. Larger than life - almost too big for a human life. Cramped into her humanity, an angel too big for her shell. More mature than many at a much younger age. More creative and compassionate than many. My favorite girl in the worlds. My daughter! My daughter! Kayleigh! My God!

"All That I Miss"

All that I resist,
Whether clenched in teeth,
Or wrangled in a fist,
Echoes the empty corridor, remiss,
Wailing, wailing - for all that I miss;

All that will never be,
All that has been wiped away,
All that we dreamed together,
Is now trapped in the yesterdays,
Never to trigger in morning again,
Never, no more, no tender todays -

And I crumble and nearly persist,
And I barely close the day in weakened fist,
I stagger, I falter, I cry at the altar,

All that remains of me amiss,
My darling, daughter - you are everything, all that I miss.

*

The Front Walkway 11/20/2017

There are times, and I am well aware of its fiction, where I glance westward through the trees to see you prancing up the walkway. I almost see you. Then my eyes drop and my heart falls off a cliff and the horrible reality of the new un-normal crashes down upon me. Your physical life ended, you will never walk up our path again in your human feet wrapped in Adidas shoes. Not ever. I know this mentally. Emotionally not always. It is a trick of the light. As if you are at summer camp or on vacation or in a Turkish prison and the day you are coming home has arrived. It is a quick hope. A push against reality. Denial. A snub at the unfair and unapologetic facts that stare me down. And it is never true and never possible. Your physical life has ended and the new un-normal is not the world I would like to pursue. Yet I have no choice. For this is the only road on which both you and your brother are on. This is my new reality. I sigh deeply and catch my breath.

"Yet Not Dead"

A broken sword blade lodged in my throat,
Its rust a red dust collects in my coat,
A splintered arrow deeply in heart's fleshy bed,
Screwed into my core - pointed with obsidian head,
And they ask me to breathe,
And they ask me instead,
Why can't you live,
When you are yet not dead.

*

A Great Father is Not a Perfect Father and a Penny in My Pocket
11/21/2017

Grief is a strange animal that comes to you for comfort and bites your longing hand. It strips you of the will to live and imbues you with the courage to crumble mountains between your angry hands. Grief occasionally comes with dishonest lenses, tricking the emotion, tricking the shade of the day, tricking me into resetting and recasting the facts. It came to attempt to push me to "unknow" certain facts that are apparent and glaring. Namely – the quality of my fatherhood. It seems to be this week's theme. How wonderful.

I spent fifteen years on a daily basis preparing for Kayleigh's arrival, and subsequently, Nathaniel's arrival, through my daily activity in sobriety. I arranged my life to plan for that day when I would become a father. I purposely, as a lawyer, chose to make less money as in house counsel rather than burn the midnight hours in a large firm specifically because I would have more hours at home with my wife, and eventually, with my kids. I tested my path. I made adjustments before their arrival. And when they were born, I continued to live an inventoried life. I continued to test my path and adjust on a daily basis, with the goal of giving my children the greatest gift I can give them – the gift of my strong sobriety one day at a time, and from that, the gift of a great father. And I am a great father. And because I am a great father, my children are superstars. It is all for them.

But on this day, mistakes surfaced. Hindsight came to wipe the slate clean. As in any relationship, particularly a parent and a teenager, are bound to have precarious moments. In fact, that is part of the contract and age appropriateness for the teen to build and develop a separating life from parents, and ultimately also the job of the parent to continue to flex and adjust and grow with their children. That is what I did – how I interacted with Kayleigh at nine was not going to work at twelve. How I disciplined her or directed her or laughed with her at twelve was going to evolve through thirteen, fourteen, fifteen. And so it did.

There is no perfection that grows in our house – nor is it encouraged. There is only the permission to be human and in that permission, the framework for greatness.

*

Kayleigh and Her Grandpa Bill 11/22/2017

I am a father who physically lost his child. I am a child who physically lost his father. Both physical deaths were sudden. Both found me the first family member with my loved ones - arriving at the hospital just after my Father physically died; arriving at the scene of my Daughter's accident and with her as she physically died. I planned both funerals without guidance. Doing the best I could do under traumatic conditions. And these two really loved and love each other. I know Kayleigh was in love with her grandfather. And he in love with her. She would frequently ask if we could go to his gravesite to visit with him. She would be quiet at his grave; somber; respectful; immortal.

Now they are together watching over me. They show up every day – two cardinals. A female cardinal bounces down to the birdfeeder that sits beside the wind chime that Kayleigh has learned to use as a channel for her voice. It is her in a female cardinal form, or sent by her. Regardless, its essence is her. My Father, a male cardinal, sits high in the tree and sings loudly for the neighborhood to hear, singing a song of dedication to his granddaughter in whom he has such great pride. He watches over her. He teaches her. He learns from her. They share their voices; their wind; their light. They are guiding us. They are here.

*

This First Thanksgiving 11/23/2017

Happy Thanksgiving, my Little Girl. Another holiday is upon us. My daily sobbing continues, although one should not take my tears as a sign of weakness or being stuck. For mine are a sign of strength and reconciling. I am learning this new truth, that healing is not possible

326

in the physical death of a child. That this type of death is unlike any other, backwards in time, and uniquely unwavering. I have learned that healing is not the goal - that reconciling is actually the only truth forward, the only path forward and the path incudes all four of us in our new configuration.

I am eternally grateful for your current presence in my life. For your participation in my every day. I grieve the heavy loss of your physical presence – your laughter, your wit, your loudness and boisterous personality. I miss walking passed your bedroom and seeing you put on makeup, pressed up against your mirror; the delicate lines; your artistic flare. I miss our daily activity – whatever it was. I miss learning you as you grew, and adjusting to you month to month, year over year. I miss all that has been robbed from me and you. I ache for you.

At the same time, I have never been more proud and grateful for you and your power – you pass your light to us every day through the wind, through the house, through our souls. You guide us through the grief and laugh with us in gently moments. You are constantly thinking of new ways to reach us, watching us and feeling our ups and downs, ever-present and blossoming as an angel, touching us directly and intentionally. Your love is magnetic and strong.

I offer you what I offer you every day. A reader someday may see these words and think, 'isn't this something he wrote about several times already?' The answer is simply, 'yes!" Today comes crashing into my first moment of consciousness the same way the first moment collapsed into my eyes yesterday. And so it is each and every day. I will do my work, Kakie, and keep my channel open to you. I feel like I am at the very beginning of learning how to keep my channel open. You are my beloved Daughter and I am your Daddy. I am here and love you so much.

"Daddy, I am so grateful. I love our relationship that grows stronger each day. I knew when I transitioned that you would transition with me as much as you could. Keep walking with me, Daddy, and believe. I am here – I will never leave your side. I know that each new day comes with a new need to reinforce this same strength between us. You are my Daddy – my Daddy! I love you so much!"

*

Umm...Daddy, Shush, Mr. Energizer Bunny 11/24/2017

"...and listen. I know you, Daddy. I watch you and watch over you. I lived with you physically for fifteen years. I was raised into the woman I became by you. I am in love with you and know every aspect of your being. Frankly, you talk too much when you should be listening.

You know it's true, Daddy. Just as with God, if you are talking at Him you cannot truly hear from Him. When you slow down then you get direction. The same is true with me, Daddy. Trust me. I'm a quick learner. And I've been with you every step of the way since I physically died in your light on the street. I like that you call it "physically died" because that is accurate and true. I was spiritually released, as you like to say, into God's light, through your light, my Daddy's light. That is also true. I am alive. My soul is filled with light and love and I am with all of our loved ones. Keep walking, Daddy. I am so proud of you.

However, when you get like the Energizer Bunny, you can't hear my direction or my voice. I love that you talk to me so much every day. Please never stop, but you have to also listen. I love that you sit on my bed and that you kiss my pillow goodnight where you used to kiss me on the forehead. I love that. I just need you to slow down and trust me and listen. I am here with you. I am speaking to you and hugging you all the time. It makes me so happy to be able to do this for you and for me. I am truly amazingly happy and I want you to be happy. And I am your angel. It's all true!

I feel the deep strength of your love for me and its equal in grief. As the grief changes we will grow stronger and stronger together. Just shush sometimes and let me sing to you. Just like before my physical death, in any relationship, we all get equal time on the stage. Let me sing to you, Daddy, just like I always did. Knowing I had you as my audience cheering me on and encouraging my voice always made me happy and it still does and always will. I love you, my Daddy. I am here with you. I will never leave your side."

*

Adidas 11/27/2017

When it gets overwhelming I need only to look inward, to my side and upward to the moon. You are like the moon. Sometimes dipping beyond the horizon and sometimes obscured by clouds, yet always present.

Five minutes after I wrote this I looked down at my feet while sitting on the couch in the TV room and one of Kayleigh's black Adidas shoes was laying there. Just lying there at my feet. I looked over towards the front door and found the other, the right Adidas shoe, lined up with another left footed shoe of a different type an inch apart as if someone was standing in them. As if someone had lined them up and tried them on. I asked Jess if she had tried on Kayleigh's shoes and she said, 'no.' Then I asked Nathaniel if he had moved them. He was oblivious. Certainly, no. Her shoes had been under her book bag near the front door for weeks now, in the exact same place. Yet now each was moved - the one paired with the other brown shoe was moved just a few feet away. The left shoe was moved fifteen feet away and was now in front of the couch where I was sitting. I smile. She is here.

"How did you do that," I asked her, "that is so amazing, Kakes. You are an amazing guardian angel and you are learning so much! Always step into my life. It is always welcome. Don't ever feel like it's an intrusion. It's Daddy-Daughter time and whenever you can cross over to spend direct time with me, I beg you, please do. I am waiting with bated breath for moments with you. I miss you so much and my heart jumps when I sense you near. You are always near. Sometimes my humanity gets in the way. Please keep trying to push through my humanity just like you just did. You moved your shoes! You physically moved your shoes!"

*

Walking Through the Everything 11/29/2017

I taught you to walk through the everything. And no matter how hard - you did it. No matter the fear - you did it. No matter the struggle - you always found a way forward. You are my inspiration of how to take instruction from a trusted loved one and apply it with success. You are now asking me to trust my Daughter and apply what I taught you so well. You trusted me. And you succeeded. I trust you. And I will succeed.

Every day is like flying a kite in a hurricane. Hold me when I crumble. Every day is hard. My great grief and trauma is a mirror image of the magnitude of love I hold for you. I refuse not to live. I refuse to destroy my life. I refuse to use your physical death as an excuse for not stepping up and living. It is dishonorable if I choose to permit the grief to swallow me for an extended period of time. It would be dishonorable to turn my back on you. I refuse that. I will never turn my back on you my love. Never. I will bring you with intention into my every day no matter how hard. In my 11th Step in the morning and at night, and all throughout the day I bring you intentionally into every day where you already reside. Alight and full of energy and amazing compassion. You are alive spiritually. You are here. Always here. You are never not part of my life. You enrich my life just as you always have. It is my duty and work to stay close to you. You are always close to me.

I sat with you at the site tonight. You obviously knew this. I write this in case someone else reads this someday. I sat there and relived is all. It takes my breath away. "Baby," I whispered and collapsed again into tears, "I will face anything. Your Daddy is here. I've been doing the breathing exercises you recently taught me in order to help me slow down and be present with you - Breathe Kayleigh's Peace (Inhale) - Release My Grief (Exhale) - but you know that. You do them with me. I do nothing without you. I am forced to live every day now without you in your physical body, but I get to live each day with you in your spiritual body."

"Daddy, you did amazing. I can't believe how incredible you were as I was physically dying. I could ask for nothing more from my Daddy. You were there. And you were awake. And I knew it and trusted you because of who we are and because of you. Thank you, Daddy, for that moment. I knew you would come. I knew it."

*

Channeling U2 (Of Course You Do!) 11/30/2017

You are accelerating. I left work at lunch to go sit alone at Red Robin. I sat down and wrote this poem:

"Gorgeous Kayleigh"

Like a pictorial memory chain,
Links of joy that time attained,
Links of sand that link to grain,
That packs the fluidity of the tide;

Like a series of videos and photo clips,
Strung together - each with a daughter's kiss,
Bound together in a world I miss,
While our new world fills my eyes,
With your light,
With your grace,
With your spirit's smile,
Alight in your face.

As I wrote this last line "Song for Someone" came through the Red Robin audio system. Red Robin radio? That song? I could imagine "Pride," but an obscure song like this one? Nobody plays that, except for Kakes. She is amazing. Then she said, "see what I can do, Daddy? Isn't that awesome. Nobody else in the restaurant knows that an angel just manipulated the technology to play that song! They think it was just the next song up. How awesome is that?! I know you are sad. I'm right here. Hold my hand and sit here until you feel better, Daddy. Just sit with me. I'm holding your hand."

I had gone to Red Robin to write about my interactions with the song, "One." I left work with that in mind singing it to myself and reminding myself that I hadn't yet listened to U2 since she physically died. Not one song. So I was going there to write about our last concert together physically at Browns Stadium in July and got distracted. Then she played that song. And opened a door. Kayleigh just learned how to channel U2. I'm sure the boys never thought that, when they wrote this song, it would be used to open a spirit door someday between a Father and his Daughter. But that is exactly the tool it has become.

"I'm just getting started, Daddy! There are so many messages I have for you in many of their songs! How perfect. U2, Daddy! Our band!"

*

I Don't Get To 12/01/017

I don't get to take you to school anymore, or comfort you when you are upset, or work through teenage issues, or teach you how to drive anymore - I don't get to do these tens of thousands of things with you anymore - all these things people take for granted. All of these things in future days that now will not happen. I do not get to do. Tenth grade. Eleventh grade. Twelfth grade. Daddy Daughter trip to visit colleges. College. First job. First house. A wedding. Grandchildren. Holding my hand while I physically die as an old man. And thousands upon millions of connecting points and subplots and minor interactions all along the way. I do not get any of this with you anymore.

So what do I get to do? Now in this transition, I get to embrace you in the morning, not unlike I always did, but now spiritually. I get to pull me into your prayer and pull you into my prayer and meditation and feel you walk with me every day. I get to turn to you to guide me and teach me and direct my thoughts, words and actions. I get to see and feel your miracles when you cross over the wind and touch us with your happiness, peace and love. I get to watch you mature and evolve. I am seeing things adjust more and more. I can feel your power and competence with your new legs increasing. It is hard to explain, but there it is, as real and true as God Himself.

My current issue is this - I want it all, from both worlds, and I can't have the former anymore. I must accept the unacceptable. I must accept this truth and turn my heart and eyes towards the latter where we continue our amazing relationship - a Daddy and a Daughter in love with each other and walking hand in hand, side by side.

"Daddy, I am here. I am never leaving your side. Love you!"

Love you too, Peanut. And how amazing - you used to be a positive influence in my sobriety but now you are not only a positive influence on my sobriety but you are actually directing my sobriety like a caretaker. You are guiding me through the valley of death. Thank you!

"Daddy, I am."

*

Purity 12/01/2017

"Daddy, remember, I have been shed of my teenage angst and any age appropriate pushing back on my Daddy to create my own space and now what's left is pure love and light in you. There is nothing to push back on. There is no need. I am way above that now. Nothing is blocking my pure love for you. And I don't need my space! I am right here with you always! Looking up to you as I always have, like when I was seven or nine or eleven with pure magic in my eyes for my hero, my love, my Daddy, when you would get home from work and I would jump off the couch and run and jump into your arms. I love you so, so much!! Like the drawing you pasted in your Big Book, that picture I drew for you when I was a little girl, crying a river for you while you were away at work. Like that.

333

Daddy, I see every minute of you days and know how hard it is. You're sitting in this meeting because they need you and trust you. You are a great worker. How about this. You focus on this meeting for the next hour and when you are done I will give you a huge hug."

Thanks, Baby, okay! Okay! Deal. I just wrote down your words on my notes app and I am turning back to this meeting. When I am done I want my hug and then I will find a quiet space and close my eyes and I'm sure you will tell me, 'great job, Daddy!'

You are trying new ways to communicate and touch me. You are amazing and super smart just like you always were. You are supercharged. And I feel that energy and have a moment where the pain is not so suffocating. It is your purity that is pulling me through.

"Daughter Moon"

Don't leave - I pleaded, don't leave,
The unthinkable - believe, no,
Around the edges of the light,
The darkness heaved, it pushed - it pulled,
Oh no!
- Daughter Moon -

I relive that one minute laying with you in the street,
Where you physically died and were spiritually released,
Such emotional contradictions set me on a course,
Of sadness, confusion, of love and light that seeps through my pores,
The pressure gains steam uncharted,
A pain seethes and the steps become harder and harder and harder,
Until the emptiness itself cries - and the heart wrinkles and dries,
Like scuba diving in the desert,
Or parachuting without a sky -

Guide me Daughter Moon,
Guide me Daughter Light,
My Guardian, you surround me,
There is no one more I trust with my life,
My Daughter Moon,

My Daughter Light,
You come to me each day,
Like the moon comes to the night.

*

Homeless Alcoholics 12/02/2017

Good morning, Kakes. We get to do wonderful things today. We get to lead a meeting to a room of homeless people suffering from active alcoholism. We get to write together a book that will prove, I hope, to touch thousands, maybe millions. We get to show the world your unique courage and lay a path for other women to follow. We get to use your voice. We get to feed your puppies and wash your clothes.

Together, Kayleigh, we can do this. I always told you that you had untapped deep resources to persevere, knowing that I too, possessed these qualities. You reached deeply into yourself and you found great strength, having accomplished, even through threats and bullying, what most women who are similarly situated have never attempted. That gift of your strength echoes in my eyes daily. You are a guiding light for millions, My Love.

"Daddy, I love you. Thank you. Now it is your turn to dig deep. You can do this, Daddy. You can do it. I am right here. Right here!"

I dedicate today to your present, current, active life. I love you too, Kakie.

"And, Daddy, I dedicate our today to you. Daddy, I am so proud of you. Keep walking."

*

This Mortal Coil 12/03/2017

I balance the unimaginable with the imaginable - the horror with the happy; the grief with the joy; a physical death with a spiritual release. Yes, my child, a child still in childhood, was physically killed. The words are so hard to say. So hard to write. For the rest of my life I am forced to live without you in your physical body and your physical experience against my will. The strain and grief and frustration and mourning ripples out from that moment for the remainder of my days. Yet if I permit its advance in an unchecked fashion, it will consume all channels of connectivity to my baby. I will not permit that. Whatever I need to do to remain in contact with, and grow with, my Daughter, I will do.

This requires faith, belief, prayer, meditation and raising one's vibration to a higher level and with a higher law. That is the balance. That is the counterbalance. That is the fresh air among the horrors I live without my child's physical body and presence in that beautiful, dynamic, young body. She is here in her body of light and reminds me frequently that I too am a body of light, encased in this mortal shell, this human gasp of life. In that truth, I get to live the rest of my life with my baby beside me in her body of light; alive, vibrant and cascading love in and through us.

She is becoming my lungs and working overtime to keep me breathing. Our light has always merged like this; our eternal core unbreakable, and always strengthening over time. My focus needs to be on this aspect of this un-normal – accepting this harsh duality, and in facing this in full color, I can grow with my Daughter and my Son, both who need their Father, yet in different ways. My job is to find each way in which my kids need me. And I will. And I do.

*

Devotion 12/04/2017

Good morning, My Love. Today I am reminded of the power and depths of my devotion to you and your brother. As the dust continues to swirl on our new un-normal, in a world where three of us are here in physical skins striving for the spiritual, and one of us is in the spiritual learning how to touch us in various ways, including in the physical world, I am reminded of our effortless energy among the four of us. We are a family of four - we do nothing major as a family without the four of us. You are with us for everything and with intention we strive to see you, hear you and feel you.

I know, as much as I can know anything, you are here with me, watching over me, smiling and laughing with me. You continue to amaze me, sweet Kayleigh. Your voice strums in my ears - both from memories before your physical death and our conversations and interactions since you were spiritually released and given the ultimate highest power of peace; the power to reach through the air; the power of the deepest love. Let's go walk and do something beautiful today, Baby.

"Daddy, keep going. I am so proud of you. You are on the right path. Be with me. I am learning new ways to talk with you. I'm testing a few right now. You know me. I will perfect these channels. Nothing stops the Mooney's, right, Daddy? I will find new ways. I love spending time with you."

Me too, Baby. I trust you. Keep pushing. I will too.

"Enhancement"

My Love,
We are the embodiment of sacred light,
That merges together the lightning strands of two souls,
We are reconciling the great adjustment of life,
No severance, nor closure - bare it cold,
For in the transformation our becoming renews,
Our love,
Yours in me and mine in you,
Continues unhindered, unbroken and expansive,
In the aftermath of a changing of worlds,
Our sacred light, our relationship, abloom, increases – enhances,
For me and my little girl.

*

"Cornered Animal" **12/05/2017**

A cornered animal, caged and worn,
The bars of this prison imprinted on his skin,
Like a metal uniform,
The soft haze of summer – a lost photograph,
The torture melted into his face like an iron mask;

When your voice in the warming wind blows –
The last time I held your hand, I reminisce,
Engaged in life, compelled by the tug at my wrist,
We supposed the years of promise await,
Surpass now the laughter in the eyes with this cruel fate;

My Love, I pace the inner perimeter when the breath evades me,
My Love, I race to escape this box which holds my soul enclosed.

*

Meeting with Jen 12/05/2017

"My grandmother will show up," I told Jess before going to meet with
Jen. "She's been my guardian since she passed in 1982." I was
nervous prior to our meeting, having never met this woman, but
having received a recommendation from a friend. Our friend told Jen
nothing of our experience or who we were. She did not know
anything about me. She did not know that I have children, or that one
of my beloved children had recently physically died and passed into
her Higher Life.

Ten seconds into the reading she said, "I need to acknowledge a
grandmother on your mother's side…she is here. She said that the
number ten is important and so is the month of October."

I told Jen that I am the tenth grandchild and her husband, my Grandpa Joe, was born and physically died in the month of October. My Grandma continued to convey messages through Jen, telling her that she was worried about my Mom, who had just received some medical news. After a few minutes further of discussing a possible issue with my Mom, Jen shifted.

"You have a daughter in spirit," she said gently, "and she is here. And Grandma is with her. I feel like Grandma's presence is very strong with her, like she's showing her the ropes and teaching her."

I cried and acknowledged affirmatively that I indeed have a daughter in spirit. "My baby," I cried, and was so happy to confirm what I already knew, that my Grandma was with my Daughter.

"This is very recent," she said, "She is showing me she was young, mid-teens. A delicate age. She is showing me that she is leaning over. Like she is leaning over and…she is folding over and lays down, and does not get up. Does that make sense to you? Like Cinderella. She is showing me Cinderella. Cinderella has lost her shoes. She is going to get her shoes. I don't understand. Does that make sense to you?"

"Yes," I said gently, "my Baby was going to get her shoes across a street when she was struck by a car."

"So, okay," she said in a loving whisper, "then Cinderella has lost her shoes…" She took a deep breath and smiled. "She is really smart. She's a smart cookie."

She continued to do what God has permitted her to do, namely channel a soul for a loved one, this woman who we had never met, who knew absolutely nothing about us or Kayleigh's recent tragedy. I mostly nodded, answering 'yes' or 'no,' but not providing much other information. Kayleigh was not only present, but she was thrilled that we were sitting together, the three of us, and she was indirectly speaking to me through Jen. My Father showed up with Kayleigh, which was not surprising, and hinted that he had been showing up at the house for years as a cardinal, which made perfect sense. Since the accident, both a male cardinal and a female cardinal show up at the house daily. We could feel their souls each day, knowing it was them.

Jen confirmed that, like my Grandma, My Father was spending joyous time with his granddaughter, showing her around, taking walks, spending time in the happiness of Heaven with my Baby. It was further confirmation. It settled me extensively.

There are many parts to this conversation that will remain private, however, another piece to this puzzle came across when Jen said, "Is grandma Catholic? She is showing me Rosaries and one that has attached to it a charm. Like a Baptism charm. She is showing me a charm from a baptism, from your baptism. Did your daughter and your grandmother ever meet in the living?"

"No," I said, "my Grandma passed in 1982 and my Daughter was born in 2002."

"Hmmm," she said, "well, she is showing me that she has something which belonged to your grandmother and it relates to you. And it is a Baptismal charm. Does that make sense?"

"No," I replied, "it doesn't. I don't remember anything like that."

"Well, keep it in the back of your head. It may make sense down the road."

"Ok," I said, tucking this away with about a dozen other insights that Kayleigh was conveying to me. She was clearly speaking to Jen who was translating for me. I could feel Kayleigh's light; her warmth; her embrace. I could almost hear her voice booming across the air in lovingly happy tones. It is difficult to convey this to a reader, however, it is mostly rooted in a deep feeling that rattles and chirps in the sacred depths of the soul. In other words, when the soul is touched in a way such as this, it leaves no doubt as to its truth. Anyone who has not had this experience will never understand and those that have will fully empathize with its majesty.

I recorded the forty five minute session and when it was over, thanked Jen, and returned to my car, where my sister, Tricia, waited for me.

"And?" Tricia asked, with a comforting smile on her face.

I smiled and took a deep breath. "She confirmed everything that I have been feeling with Kakes; everything that Kayleigh has been doing. She confirmed that my Baby is alive, really alive, just on another channel. Everything I've been writing. Everything I've been experiencing. It is all real."

We drove back from the Pennsylvania border to Cleveland, listening to the recording. My sister cried tears of joy hearing the words conveyed from Grandma, my Father and Kayleigh. And so it is.

*

Memories 12/06/2017

It happened again today, several times, and it almost always happens from people who are not parents, and otherwise always happens from parents who have not suffered the physical death of a child. For no parent suffering as I am would ever say such foolish things. It also keeps happening even though I convey constantly that I do not need words of encouragement or platitudes or words of wisdom. I need ears of wisdom. I say this and people nod and then spout some crazy thing they think they should say to a grieving parent as if they need to save me; as if they understand, which they don't. Even with the good intentioned people, they are being quite self-centered in these assertions and it does not help. It is incredibly frustrating.

I cannot stand people saying, "Keep her in your memory," or, "it's so nice that you keep her memory alive" Or, "keep her alive in your heart."

First of all, I don't keep you alive, either inside or outside of my heart. You are alive all to yourself, with me or without me. Secondly, why would I need to try to keep you alive when you are right here beside me in the present, actively and currently alive? You are not alive in my memories for memories are not alive. You are actually alive as I write these words. These odd rituals people have, these strange words of wisdom really need to be changed. Perhaps that is part of our journey, changing the dialogue of death. Perhaps we can convey to the general public that, when a friend or loved one experiences the physical death of a child in childhood, they just need to listen to us cry and vomit emotion and spin in circles until we reconcile the moment, which, if we are trying to stay in contact with our child, we are certainly to do.

Memories of our time physically together for those 5,574 days before the accident, and memories we have been building since your physical death together, the first of which was you letting go of your light into your Father's light laying in the street; all of these are memories. I have our memories of our 5,574 days together on the physical plain. These are like flash drives of old events I replay in my brain. Then we have all of the new moments we are creating together that will become part of tomorrow's memories of today – our present, with me webbed into my humanness and you empowered and spiritually free. We are present with each other on a mutual journey – two individual streams of light joined together by the power of love. But keeping you alive? Keeping your memory alive? What absolutely stupid things to say to me.

"I Offer You My Light"

In this changing, deeply changing of these worlds,
I open the light that crosses the space distanced by wind,
I offer the light amassed in my spirit for my little girl,
I offer the light enhanced by her glory,
Enveloping days yet risen,
And future steps in her story,
As they unfold,
As of yet untold,
Pressed into the firmament just like her baby feet once pressed into these soils;

She is always,
Always present,
Present here -
She is always by my side,
In the space that we share -

Human eyesight - falter faster, see not, nor any,

When before us, not merely memory nor longed for in souls,
She speaks out from across the barrier,
Jeweled with the wind and lined in gold,
She is offering her unhindered light every day,
I pray -
Please help me shed my human ways,
And reciprocate my light, My Love, today.

*

The Resonant Sound of Light 12/06/2017

An unfamiliar sound, that being a frequency far below the human capacity to hear. Yet the sound exists and has been captured on my iPhone on my recording of my reading with Jen. When light makes sound, it hums in a deep, beautiful, lower tone. The resonance of light. Of energy. Of life.

She displaces the air and her love and light and energy resonates as she passes through the air near us or wraps herself around us or speaks to us. The words coming out of her mouth, the energy to make those words, it is all energy. It is pure light. Creating a low humming sound that vibrates moving the molecules in the air that all vibrate against each other. Light, electricity turning into sound. Love, this perfect electricity, is her soul turning into sound. Like she is vibrating the air around her when she passes through and talks to us. It resonates in a deep tone in our own bodies. It hums in the cells of our bodies and we are unaware consciously, yet subconsciously we know. I have captured her voice on the recorder app on my iPhone. When you listen closely, and hear this deep tonal hum, it is amazing. It is my Daughter's voice from Heaven, from the physical world, living in both places as once in her body of light. She is amazing. She loves us so much.

"Look what I did, Daddy!"

My God, Kayleigh, I never expected to pick up the fingerprints of your voice and energy on a recording. My only expectation was to have a record of that glorious conversation where you spoke through a willing and gentle soul with a special gift to be able to translate the communication channel between us. It is the sound of pure gold in its velvet, deep tones of light resonating around my eyes and ears and skin and heart. Bright light. Vibrating molecules. Proving the truth of Heaven and the existence of guardian angels and the beauty of a Higher Life. You are a powerful soul, gifting us with such an expression of your presence. You are showing the world the power of God. The power of love. The magnificence of your light.

The human comes inclined with its self-destructive capacity to doubt, to fog the lens, to deny clear truth and fact because it does not fit within a proper and understandable, predictable format. Unstructured, so rare the experience, that many will look askance, many will be afraid, and many will just simply be blocked from this deeper truth. That is okay. For I am none of those. I am me and my Daughter and I know my truth. Kayleigh is Kayleigh and she and I know her truth. We are. She is. I am. And she has left her humming angelic voice purposely for me to hear four months after her bodily physical death. Rejoice. Rejoice. Rejoice.

"The Sound of Light"

The sound of light, lifts, glowing,
It resonates the air,
Its essence holds a higher life,
That vibrates the wind it wears,
And in the flowing vocals,
If I listen I will hear,
The most beautiful, familiar voice,
My Daughter's presence – here,
Your life, wondrous sound,
Proves itself, purposely, profound,
I lift myself, My Love,
To your higher ground…

*

With Intention We Make New Memories 12/07/2017

With intention, I start the day always with you by my side. You amaze me. I am so honored to be your Daddy. I love the images I have in my mind of you dressed up in gymnastics clothing, with your hair done perfectly and pretty makeup, tumbling across our master bed and telling me you were the fastest and prettiest jumping bean of them all. And I smiled deeply and said, "Yes, Baby, you are." I have a million simple snapshots like this. We love reminiscing. I feel your smile in the telling and hear your laughter in my ear.

Your smile in that moment, at six, as you batted your eyes at me, the recognition from your Daddy, my audience, made you beam. We continue to make memories every day. You are the prettiest, most incredible angel, Babygirl.

"Thank you, Daddy. I love you."

*

Four of Us 12/08/2017

We do nothing without you Kayleigh. Nothing. You engage. You participate. You laugh. You sit by our side. You decorate the Christmas tree and put up Halloween decorations. You sit at the family dinner table. We sit on the couch, the four of us, as we always have. You open presents with us and walk the dogs. You write. You make new art. You help with decisions. You are ever present. You are pure love and light. You are.

There is such a deep and painful passion, but incredible resolve, when this guttural feeling strikes at my core. I want to scream. Part of me wants to die. The other part of me wants to punish the world. I flail. Daily. And I glance around and I see Nate and Mommy, but I do not see you in your physical body and it destroys me. Then I remember this new duality: everything we do in this life now we are forced, against our will, to do without you in your physical body. However, everything we do, we do with you in your spiritual body. We are a strong, family of four. We are conquering the physical death of one of us and marching forward in this new configuration, no matter how hard at times, no matter the challenge of grief.

I will never stop. I will never leave your side. Never. Babygirl, we were so effortlessly balanced prior to your tragic, physical death. We are adjusting. We four are very strong together. We will come up with a new balance. A different balance integrating each of us and each of our light and personality. We are going through a reconciliation into a new configuration and will emerge even stronger.

"Current Configuration"

We, in the crucible of suffering, know,
There is a hidden light in this shadow bowl,
In the torment of a hurricane in my heart, explode,
Yet deep in the debris field,
There is a sacred path that will never erode;

We are sifting through spiked tears and barbed emotion,
We are adrift in a jagged, metallic ocean,
Poisoned of all of our hopes and dreams,
In the great rupture and fracture of our lives,
There is a sacred path leading out from our screams;

For you have increased a thousand fold,
You have transitioned into liquid gold,
You have enhanced in God's perfect elevation,
Linking our spirits in this new configuration;

Everything has changed and nothing has changed,
We are four loving souls that have been re-arranged,
We are three in the current limits of our human station,
While you breathe the universe in our new configuration;

We are a gentle family cocooned in a blanket of love,
Unbreakable, supportive in a mystic vibration,
We rejoice in all that still is and all that still was,
Bound together in this evolving situation,
All of us adjusting,

To this new configuration.

*

A Daughter's Prayer for Father 12/10/2017

Kayleigh, I don't know why we are on this road. There is no rhyme
or reason to it. But it is what it is. And it is horrifying and traumatic.
And it is beautiful to be here with you on this path. I find myself
saying, 'I don't want this path.' Then I think, you are on this path.
And the only way to commune with you is to get on this path and face
its rugged terrain. Therefore, I want this path. It is a never ending
circle. The hamster wheel, as you have conveyed to us, I ride several
times a day. I am really frightened of my life, Sweetie.

"I Pray In Our Poems"

Sparkle, sweet prayers washed in the Ganges,
Spirited stones, like glassy opal pearls,
Warm within my breathing palm,
Where you hold your light to my flesh,
Amongst these beads,
My many storms of anguish - your mesmerizing calm,
You sing along the cracks in my hand,
You kiss my wounds with your healing song,
You hold me sturdy when I falter to stand,
And faithfully, as the sun promised dawn,
You wash me with illumination - in which radiance we belong…

…And whisper me sweet promises of your Sunrise in each dawn…

…You displace the air about me,
You kiss my cheek,
You grace the air around me,
With your compassionate and silent calm…

"Father, my Father,
Fear well, if so, the new journey of your life,

Yet lead with a courage through the blindness of night,
Believe, and grieve and breathe and,
Stay in my light,
My love for you is etched in the book of eternity,
The stars call my name,
And your voice sings with me,
In our prayers that are poems that we write.

"Daddy, it's okay. Cry. Scream, Daddy. I would scream too. I am mad for the pain that you and Mommy and Nate suffer. I know sometimes you will get stuck. You are human. When you get stuck, remember all that you taught me. You led me down the path of prosecuting and I was scared to death. Remember that. I wanted to hold them accountable and at the same time I didn't want to go forward, but I trusted you and you helped me find my voice. I trust you completely. I love you. Now trust me as I lead you down a scary path. I will not lead you astray and you know that. Trust me, Daddy. I've got you."

*

I Hear Your Light 12/10/2017

My Little Peanut, I am still in awe, but not surprised - still shocked slightly, but not really - still filtering through my human mind and all of its trappings, but know that this is true in my soul - you are with me always - you were with me and so present, specific to this writing, four days ago, as was my Grandma and my Father; that your energy and presence was captured on a low resonating frequency as you talked to and through Jen to me. You confirmed everything you've already been telling me. And even bigger - you proved the existence of Heaven, of God and of guardian angels. Even though I did not need this proof, its confirmation was so warming to my heart and mind. Others, too, will benefit from your courage and the way you prove the Higher Life.

When energy surrounds me, and you are pure energy; when love makes its way into my presence, as you do, that pure and powerful energy displaces the air molecules in the room. Even though I could not see that energy, your energy was there. When you spoke it peaked. When you smiled it peaked. When you hugged me or approached me it peaked. It displaced the air in the room, sending millions of molecules bouncing against each other, resulting in a low, humming sound I could not pick up in my ear, but did pick up on my iPhone.

I have your signature on digital audio - pure gold resonating unto swooping deep tones, sweeping deep sounds of love and light. My human mind wants to contain and control and make sense of what the soul tells me effortlessly is truth. I am watching my Daughter transcend Heaven and Earth - these two plains simultaneously. There is never been a more profound moment or experience in my life than hearing my Daughter's voice from the Higher Life. It's just so incredible. I am so proud of you, Kakes, and humbled and honored to be in your presence, and to be your Daddy. I love you, Sweetheart.

"Daddy, I love you so much. Let go of the thinking and just be. It is true, Daddy, and it's really cool. I'm here and I'm not going anywhere. I am your guardian. I am Your Love."

It's just so amazing and it blows me away. I heard the sound of light - hearing the sound of your soul move around me lovingly, expensing energy to be with me and to speak to me; knowing that you did so and do so because you love me. I am so humbled and I never want to lose that connection. I know you love me incredibly - and I, you.

My mind slips occasionally. I know that what I experienced with Jen was a miracle - I know it. I trust she is not a fraud - what she channeled she could not have found out by reading up on you and me, except for your physical death. I believe, and not because I otherwise would desperately want to, but because I watched and felt truth roll forward with you and my Grandma and my Father by my side. I know you are all three here and I know the experience was authentic and overwhelming. Overwhelm me.

"Hi, Daddy! It was me! It was so cool! Thank you for acknowledging me. I am right here. Don't ever doubt it. I am never leaving your side. I love you!"

Love you too, Sweetie. I am never leaving your side either.

*

Michaels 12/10/2017

For Christmas I went to Michael's to get two images of Kayleigh framed for Jess' parents and my Mom and her husband, Dave. They are smaller versions of the two I had framed after Kayleigh's funeral that are hanging in our house. Kayleigh at her fifteenth and final Birthday in her physical state - beaming, happy, full of light and love. It is so unbelievable.

After settling with the framing department I asked Kakes to walk me through the store and lead me towards something special she wanted me to find. She had initiated that path through the store, speaking to my soul and talking in my right ear. I took a breath and began this journey of discovery, believing the discovery would lead to a physical purchase of something meaningful between us. Something for Christmas - this first Christmas without her physical presence. Maybe something for her room.

I worked my way down every aisle, slowly, sometimes spacey and indifferent to the world around me, lost in my thoughts and staring at colorful boxes and merchandise. I am very aware of this rather common practice. Lost in thought. Lost in grief. Lost in spirit. Sometimes with tears slipping across my face, indifferent to any audience and not caring who would see and who would not.

I was walking back in time as I went aisle to aisle. We did this at twelve. We did this at eleven. This from five through ten. We dropped that on the floor. Picked this string of beads over that one. This color paint and that size canvass. Those glow in the dark stars for her room. Supplies for a solar system we made and hug from her ceiling fan. We ruined the kitchen table with that. When she was a toddler we did this. As a baby we picked out that.

Every aisle had different years of her life. I walked up and down every aisle. I realized then, in that magic moment, that I had done literally every art project for every year of a child's life with her displayed on these shelves. There was no section from which I had not purchased something for us to do together.

Glass beads. Figurines. Plastic animals. Sticks. Ornaments. Wreaths. Stickers. Sticker books. Clay. Playdoh. Markers. Colored pencils. Paint. String. Wood. Metal. Bird houses. Jewelry boxes. Wooden letters. Foam balls. Glass balls. Glass rocks. Canvas. Disney books. Coloring books. Painting books. Paint. Paint. Paint. Paint. Paint.

The heavy tears came back to me and welled strongly like a hurricane behind my eyes. Passionate. Grief. Grace. Strength. "Babygirl, look at all that we've done together that filled up your life," I said out loud, yet quietly, "this is the fullness of our relationship laid out in this store."

She whispered back to me, "Daddy, open your eyes. Yes. Look what you did with me. Most girls don't get that chance with their dads. Every aisle. I brought you here today to see all that you filled my life with. With art and creativity and togetherness. With love, Daddy. Our love is so strong. Our relationship is unbreakable. That is your gift today in this store, Daddy."

My discovery was me. My discovery was her. Our relationship.

*

Saoirse, Ceili, Saoirse 12/11/2017

Your music is a melody that melts the most stubborn reserve, which softens the hardest edge, which reminds us of God's intention for giving us the gentle gift of life. To be free in life is to live in selfless parity with life itself. Never taking oneself too seriously. Always keeping your priority of love, family and friends uppermost in mind. Having compassion for all others. Investigating the nature of humanity and turning its deep secrets on their heads.

You didn't use the crime of rape perpetrated against you to further harm yourself. You used it to empower yourself. You could have curled up in a hole and wilted away. Instead you became courage. Your courage came through in your voice. Your voice became pure strength as you conquered your assault. Ultimately, you used the horrible experience to empower yourself, to empower your voice and engender strength and courage in other girls. Your peers were watching. They knew you stood up to those sick bastards. They knew you contacted the police and prosecuted. They knew too that almost nobody your age would ever dare to do that. There were some that had also been harmed, watching from the shadows, who would not step forward. And others who had been harmed that followed your footsteps through the mine field in the safe places where you had placed your feet.

You vowed to regain your footing. You began your healing process thirty seconds after the assault. You went to work at the theatre and put on a show the following night. You visited the hospital for a post rape exam. You began therapy, journaling, walking with Mommy, positive affirmations with me. Around Christmas time, what ultimately ended up being your last physical Christmas, you were sturdy on your feet and pressing forward through the panic and tears and trauma and reliving of the horror - horrors cast upon you by disgusting, wretched garbage of human beings. Those moments would come and last ten, maybe twenty minutes. Then, after the wave would pass, you returned to the laughter of your life; the strength and happy composure that proclaimed you a battle tested warrior of light.

And ultimately, against all logic, you found a deep and sturdy compassion for humanity that led you to forgive your attackers, verbally stating those words of forgiveness face to face with one of them, and in statements read by the prosecutors to the others. Saoirse. Freedom. You attained a state higher than most humans could dream of in a hundred lifetimes. After all that, and your becoming in freedom and strength, as you entered adulthood, young adulthood, filled with a dynamic personality and a joyous disposition, you were cut down physically in a simple, tragic accident? My God, Saoirse, it eludes me.

"Jump Out of My Soul"

My Child, you left that normal evening, smiling,
A Father's kiss upon your brow,
An "I love you," exchange,
Enriching, as time evolves, now,
I awaited the hour when you'd come home,
A frantic call disturbed the summer night,
While your head lay against the curb in that road,
I rushed to hurry to an unthinkable sight,
And lay there by your side,
In my presence you were not alone,
No Father's eyes can bare such a sight,
It fractured all that I had ever known,
And viewed an image I never could have dreamed,
And as your heartbeat took its final toll,
And as your mother screamed,
I wanted to jump,
I wanted to jump,
Jump right out of my soul.

*

My Father's Fifth Anniversary 12/12/2017

Five years ago today you, my Father, had a massive heart attack and physically died. I scurried to plan your funeral in the natural course of life. Four months ago, as you know, my Daughter, your beloved Granddaughter, was tragically physically killed in a horrible car accident. Again, I scurried to plan a funeral - this time in the traumatic, cruel unnatural, out of order, illogical non-nature of life. I was there moments after you passed, Dad. I was there as Kayleigh physically died in my arms. I did Last Rights for you both.

This morning, while doing my 11th Step, I heard a cardinal. I knew it was you, Dad, on this 5th Anniversary of your death. Your physical death. You told Jess through Jen that there was a familiar bird that

353

visits our yard frequently; to remind us of the radiant spiritual release each obtains in physical death and the brilliance of their souls, empowered a thousand fold, as they continue this journey by our sides.

I stepped over to the window where Kayleigh's window art is hanging and saw you – a stark red male cardinal, staring into the window, singing to me. A few moments later, a female cardinal dropped onto the feeder beside you – your Granddaughter who is in love with you and who was greatly and deeply impacted by your sudden physical death when she was just ten. I hear you both as I write this – visiting us on this special day. I see you. I hear you. You are.

I know that you two are together and it makes you both very happy. It makes us very happy, and relieved as well. I imagine you will be spending a lot of time today with family here in the physical as well as in the spiritual realm with God. Walk with me – guide me. I love you both and miss you both.

A side note to you, Kayleigh, as you bounce about the branches with your Grandfather. My Sweet Child, my Kayleigh, I felt you watching over me while I slept last night – like you were wanting me to sleep better and your light was gently pressing me into the bed to help me sleep better. I haven't slept well since the accident. Thank you, My Love.

"You're welcome, Daddy. Yes, that was me. Love you!"

And Dad, you were there when she physically died. I will never be able to repay you for your love you're your presence. Thank you.

*

Grandmother's Charm 12/13/2017

I was on my way to go sit on her bed to write with her. I promised her earlier in the day that my Daddy-Daughter time would be me and Kayleigh writing her book. I made decaf coffee. I was about to turn to go upstairs when I stopped dead in my tracks in the kitchen and she told me very clearly, 'Daddy, go down into the basement and find the small bin (there are twenty large bins and a few small bins in the basement), and search through it and there you will find what you are looking for at the bottom.'

With my computer bag still over my shoulder, I stepped down the basement stairs and walked over to a small white bin resting with the others against the wall. I began looking through the contents. It was Kayleigh's bin, packed by her when we moved a year and a half earlier from the home where she had spent most of her life. Rocks. Clay figures of dogs and mermaids. Jewelry. A washcloth. Small farm animal figurines. Meditation stones. And, at the bottom, a tiny box. I opened the little box, and after catching my breath, held the tiny item in my hand.

One week earlier I had met with Jen, the Seer, and a Reverend who just happened to learn that she could open a channel to make contact with guardian souls and provided her services to those seeking contact. One of the spectacular moments on the reading we did together, which I recorded, captured my Grandmother in the room speaking to the Reverend and the Reverend conveying that communication, alongside Kayleigh, who was also very present, excited and communicating very directly. She conveyed to me many things about me and Kayleigh that she could not have known. In fact, she had never met me before and knew nothing about me and nothing about Kayleigh.

My Grandmother has been my guardian angel since her death in 1982, and frequently throughout the last 35 years I talk to her and feel her presence. In fact, the day before the reading I told Jess that there was no doubt that Grandmother would show up during the reading. And so she did. With Kayleigh.

During the reading, my Grandmother or Kayleigh made a reference to a small coin sized gift, a symbol from Grandmother, with a baby symbol from a baptism. Whose baptism wasn't clear, but clearly there was a connection between the two of them during Kayleigh's life. They were there, on the other side of the wind, filled with love and light, humming in the space about me, adoring me with their unconditional love for me and giving this Reverend nuggets to piece together in attempts to communicate with me.

I puzzled over this reference to a tiny object for a week, searching Kayleigh's room and the china cabinet and dresser drawers. During the week, it seemed as if I had seen this referenced tiny object before, and I began pulling it together in my memory. I thought, after all, that my Mother may have given Kayleigh a small object related to me perhaps five years earlier. I remember it being silver and taped down in a box. Other than that I knew nothing.

The day before this writing, I called my Mother and asked her if she remembered sending Kayleigh a small coin sized object. She could not remember, but it seemed to jog a memory for her that she could not quite pull into view. The ensuing twenty four hours I thought about this message from Kayleigh and Grandmother during my reading, and asked Kayleigh to help me find it.

Then came 9 p.m. on this night, the brewing of decaffeinated coffee, and a promise to Kayleigh to go sit on her bed and write her book. Then she spoke to me and I followed her instructions and I found the tiny object, its tape still across the face of the object. Giddy, I snapped a picture of the front and the back. The front was an etching of a little boy. On the reverse side, the name, "Kevin." I texted my mom and told her, "She just led me to it. What is this? Have you ever seen this before?"

Our ensuing texts are this:

"Oh. It's a charm off my mother's charm bracelet. Amazing."

"Do you know if she got it when I was a baby?"

"Yes. I made a bracelet for my Mom. Charm was on her bracelet."

"Baptism timeframe?"

"Birth to baptism. 2 weeks old buddy!"

And there you have it – in a reading a week earlier, Kayleigh was telling me that my other guardian angel, my Grandmother, had given her my baptism charm through her daughter, my Mother, Kayleigh's Grandmother. Now Kayleigh was with her Grandmother's Mother, now also a guardian angel, and both of them were talking about their Kevin, through a tiny coin with my name on it from my baptism.

Kayleigh, no honest man or woman could bare to challenge the facts of such proof. You are alive. Honey, each event, each day, each interaction, our channel strengthens. Our dimensions merge. I am here, Babygirl.

"Daddy, I am too! Love you!"

*

Thank You 12/14/2017

Hey Babygirl – thank you for your incredible efforts last evening in directing me to my Grandmother's charm from my baptism, and the message of our constant bond and togetherness that accompanies your miracle. Through me you helped find your baptism by intention, your path to God, and then you found your way, sometimes with Footprints, sometimes with courageous steps. Always with God in your heart and hope in your eyes.

That charm is for both of us, worn by my Grandmother, who has long been my guardian angel, who is now joined by my ultimate guardian angel – you! You continue to amaze me. I promised you amazement in the remainder of my days until we are again in the same body type. Please help me with this next twenty four hours. Love you, Baby.

"Love you, Daddy. Have a safe, happy, healthy day – you said that to me every morning when you dropped me off at school, remember?"

I do. I will never forget.

"When the Pain Visits"

Like thick flowing cement coagulating in my stomach, the delicate acid lining fraying, shedding and melting in the cauldron, a soupy mixture of fear, of pain, of anguish, of courage and light, reaching upward with spiky tentacles, puncturing and pulling my lungs down into the fray, shortening the tepid breath that lingers in the thoughts of longing and grief just long enough to force the diaphragm into action; jerking slightly upward as the belly distends, as the lungs fight to recapture their besieged caverns in this crippled, broken cage - I wait. Silence. Then comes a rushing flood of sallow tears running down the body on the inside, carving new paths in the flesh and pooling in the hardening cement, springing the cooling, drying concoction back into fluid liquid once again, only to prod its spinning mixture further on its destructive campaign, that will one day infiltrate and fill every gap and seal my innards in a rocky incapacitated domain.

*

Their Damned Stories 12/15/2017

People just psychologically turn to themselves, either out of pure selfishness, unawareness or truly attempting, though failing, to build a bridge. Today's damn story was a woman telling me that her mom lost a child forty years ago and she is a total basket case, having suffered for forty straight years and not being able to function in this world. Well, howdy do to you - thanks for telling me I should look forward to being all fucked up for forty years. Really, Lady? Know your audience. The only reason you told me your damn story is because you just heard that I physically lost my child four months ago.

Another one told me that her friend lost a child and the surviving child was so broken by the news that that child ended up as a drug addict on the streets. Well, zippety doo-dah – thank you so kindly for telling me my surviving child is going to become a drug addict and live on the streets. Please know your audience. Better yet, keep unsolicited stupidity, the inability to understand how damaging certain words and phrases can be, to yourself. I have asked for no words. From anybody. Not even once since the accident. Why somebody would hear about our story, and then automatically turn to their own story and get lost in themselves, to the detriment of someone like me who is in a constant state of acute grief, is unconscionable.

People are so self-centered. They want to tell their damn stories. For whatever reason. I did not ask for any of their stories. Truthfully, even this early into this nightmare, having to suffer its pain one second at a time, every second of every day, I know what I need and words of encouragement or their damn stories are not it. Really, if they were a little more sensitive, they would actually say nothing. Or just say, "I am sorry. I don't know what to say. I am here to listen." Even if their minds turned to themselves, trying to relate, trying to "help," trying to be relevant to the experience, they should stop, take a breath, think about what they are about to say, and then – say nothing about their story.

"I Am Isolation"

An alien dropped into a foreign land,
I am isolation – I am this man,
And passersby, offer wishes and platitudes,
Secretly hoarding their gold coins of gratitude,
For unless they walk this path,
They cannot understand,
I am isolation,
In the form of this man.

*

She Was Trying To Come Home 12/16/2017

Her shoes, shirt and shorts were on the other side of Euclid Heights Boulevard. She wanted to come home to be with me and Jess and to spend some time with her little brother. We are her safety and her comfort; always have been. No matter the brilliance in her life; no matter if upset or with whom she would be angry or afraid; no matter the emotion or the situation or the dream or the goal, she would confide in us - one or both of us. It was a steady reliance we came to depend upon. No matter the situation she could always talk to us about it - sometimes she would not and would choose a friend, but she always trusted our council. And treasured that sacredness in our bond.

So it was on August 17, 2017, at a swimming party, a house near where multiple streets come together with a main artery with dangerous, fast moving cars and each of the perpendicular streets having their own stop signs, twelve in all,, but none on the main artery where the cars continued to zip by, in a patchy darkness, with kids running around, having earlier in the night dealt with a boy who was bothering her, having released that stress and having returned to her friends, and finally, innocently and simply wanting to go home at 10:45 to go for a walk with her Mommy,, that she came to be standing on a concrete island lined on two sides by these crossing streets and on the third side by the main artery, behind two telephone poles that blocked her view to traffic and traffic's view to anybody who might emerge from behind those poles. As she stepped out into Euclid Heights, designing to gather her belongings on the other side, unaware of an approaching car that was already upon her, her sudden presence startled the driver of the car as she and the car collided at the front right bumper, immediately spinning her at her hip and throwing her down head first towards the curb and the street. If she had taken a step a second earlier, she would have been in front of the car, perhaps being hit in her hip and legs and thrown off out of the street; a second later and she would have run into the side of the car and bounced off of the car and back out of the street. Instead, the perfect strike of a human and an automobile caused her to be spun straight down to the street, causing severe head trauma that would kill her just minutes later.

She simply went out one night with friends and physically died in my arms three hours later.

"All That I Miss"

All that I resist,
Whether clenched in teeth,
Or wrangled in a fist,
Echoes the empty corridor, remiss,
Wailing, wailing - for all that I miss;

All that will never be,
All that has been wiped away,
All that we dreamed together,
Is now trapped in the yesterdays,
Never to trigger in morning again,
Never, no more, no tender todays -

And I crumble and nearly persist,
And I barely close the day in weakened fist,
I stagger, I falter, I cry at the altar,
All that remains of me amiss,
My darling, daughter - you are everything, all that I miss.

*

Daddy, I Made Light! Happy Hanukkah! 12/16/2017

It was a long night, our first Hanukkah after Kayleigh's physical death, with our first Christmas looming in the near future. I was heavy. Slightly blocked. Tearful.

Jess and Nathaniel were in the Pilot. I drove home in the Accord and decided to swing by the Memorial to say hello and see if the batteries in the Christmas wreath had died. We placed in on the telephone pole a few weeks earlier about six feet off of the ground. As I drove down Edgehill, I could see no flashing wreath in the distance, as I could on every other night.

The lights burned out. The batteries are dead, I thought, and confirmed that thought as I approached the fateful intersection. The

361

wreath was dark. No lights. The vases below the telephone pole were half covered in snow. The Irish flags disheveled. The forever flowers blown about in the wind. Cars passing by, a cold wind, spinning snow. I kneeled down in the snow for five or ten minutes and just talked to my baby. I wished her a Happy Hanukkah. I cried. I mourned. I grieved. I collected the dispersed flowers and vases and trinkets that had been left for her by hundreds of people under the wreath that hung on the telephone pole in darkness.

I checked the little box of tea light candles covered in snow to see if any were dry. I checked the lighter that barely flashed a blue flame after a dozen clicks. I determined to try to light two candles in two vases and managed to get them lit. I told Kayleigh, "Kakes, I have to light one for Mommy and Nathan too."

So I did. They were beautiful. Four glowing lights radiating out of glass half buried in a snowdrift. I felt the stillness. The emptiness of her physical absence. I was having trouble feeling her spirit, even though she never leaves my side.

I stood up to step back and get a picture of the four candles, and when I did, I was amazed. The Christmas wreath lights were blazing in their twinkling pattern - flashing white then flashing all colors – red, blue, green, yellow - back and forth. Kayleigh had turned on the lights of the wreath though the batteries were dead.

"Kayleigh, My Love!" I said aloud, "You - you are amazing. Look what you did, Sweetheart. You turned on these lights for me!"

I felt her on my right side as I kneeled back down in the snow and prayed for her and to her, asking her guidance and hearing her remind me that she is my guiding light; that she is always by my side; that I need to trust deeper and deeper that she is present. That she adores me and loves me immensely.

After ten more minutes under the magical lights, I kissed the street where she physically died and was spiritually released. I stood up to walk away and walked away from this sacred sight the way I always do - backwards, never turning my back on this sacred spot, watching the spot on the road where she lay that night as I step away. I glanced up to the wreath again. The lights began to flicker as I walked away, and faded back out, slowly over the next minute as I walked - dimming, dimming, dimming until their light vanished in the night as I stepped off of the concrete island and into one of the side streets. As I crossed back towards my car, still glancing at the wreath, it returned to a perfect darkness – its voice of lights silenced in reverence.

In the car, uplifted and filled with her wonder, I laughed and felt an overwhelming joy. My daughter did that. My daughter, the guardian angel. My daughter, one of God's favorite angels. My girl, who is alive, who is here, who is strong and full of love and light, brought power back to a wreath and illuminated its lights while I was in its midst.

"Daddy, I made light for you," she whispered.

"You touched the battery. You filled them with light. How did you do that?"

"Happy Hanukkah, Daddy. I'm glad you liked it. I love you so much. I am your guiding light. I will never leave your side," she said to me, but would not give up her secrets.

"I love you, my Kakie. You are amazing, Babygirl."

I drove the half mile home, and as I pulled into our driveway, I could still see, still feel her smile, her energy, her perfect presence.

"What We Can See When We Open Our Eyes with Our Hearts"

If the lighting flourished itself with sound,
If in the melody lightning flowers were found,
Would we, the attentive audience, dream ourselves blessed,
As we feel the eyes open up from the chest;

If the lighting, like dancing golden glitter on a turquoise sea,
Opened the waves to unleash the coral fields underneath,
Would we swim in an angel's gift of melodic sound,
If we open the eyes with the heart - what would be found.

*

Brightest of Lights 12/17/2017

You were making a sanctuary of your soul. You embraced the fear and the darkness and emerged the brightest of lights. I was looking at your proud wall today and my eyes landed on your poster for "House of Usher" and it reminded me that a day after you were raped – just one day after, you had the courage and the strength, somehow, to go to the theater and perform your running crew duties at the East Cleveland Theatre. In a blur you did it, telling us that everyone was relying on you. We suggested you need not do it – that they would manage without you, and you said, "No, they need me."

We collectively sighed and off you and Mommy went – Mommy on stage and you behind the scenes working effects, dropping walls, creating smoke, arranging different sets, and creating a masterpiece. Traumatized and shocked, you were, yet you felt if you did not show up, then the show would not have happened that Friday night, which is true. More importantly, that the perpetrators would win – the sickened boys who harmed you would win. You would not allow that.

Anyone would understand when someone in a cast at a community theatre is unavailable due to sickness or another serious ailment and a show is canceled. Yet you showed up, incredibly, through the courage that became your brand after something much more serious than a sickness. It cannot be underestimated. This was not a simple feat. This was epic, dragging your soul, shattered so freshly, down to a theatre and gutting it out.

After the show, you fell into Mommy's arms and cried. Then you embraced me and Nathaniel. You were selflessly proud, brilliantly alive and completely exhausted. I pray I can exhibit such courage in my life. I fear I fall short continually. I love you, Babygirl.

"Thank you, Daddy, for showing me I can be courageous. I struggled with fear at times, but you always held my hand as I walked through the fear. That made it possible for me. You always told me that courage was not the absence of fear, but having fear and walking through it anyway. So I did what you told me and showed me and walked through it. We walk together, Daddy. Love you!"

*

Four Month Anniversary - She Did It Again 12/17/2017

Jess was feeling worried and depressed since she was not feeling Kayleigh coming to her. Her spiritual journey is so fresh and nascent. She questioned why she seemed to be showing up with me but not her.

We were listening to Nate's music in the car through the Bluetooth. We went into a restaurant, asked for a table of four, enjoyed a dinner with the four of us, and then left the restaurant. As I turned on the car, we expected Nate's music to come back on. Instead Kayleigh flipped phones from Nate's to Jess' through the Bluetooth and found "You'll Be in My Heart" which was not in the queue. We blasted this Phil Collins song as we drove home, exactly like we did on the one month anniversary. She did the exact same thing that night three months prior as she did tonight. It is jaw dropping, but now familiar. She has mastered certain communication channels and pressed her light into her family.

My Babygirl is lighting up the universe. Do I wish she was here physically with me; that she hadn't physically died? Of course. But that's not possible. Now instead, she translates Heaven to us who cannot comprehend its majesty. She connects loved ones across the barrier of Heaven and earth, alive on both sides of the veil in her spiritual body of light. She intermediates love and light. She is amazing.

*

Your Courage 12/18/2017

There is no fear that cannot be conquered as it co-exists with courage, the type of courage that runs through the liquid golden core of your light. Alight the fragments of my life and align the jagged pieces into its new form so that I may breathe your light, feel your presence and know your undying love. Your courage is an anomaly, a rarity, a spark of divinity. No more divine a person have I ever known. No one have I ever witnessed like you, who, though frightened deeply by certain events, turned to me for encouragement, and once empowered with your parents' support, and trusting my words that you could push through, you stepped forward and pushed through. You did it. Only you could do it and you did it. Awe runs through my heart like a wild spring river, fresh and clean and angling downward into a cascading pool of light. That is where I see you inside my soul - in my more precious fields of love; shining brighter than a million suns. Your courage you offer me constantly. I sense your deliberate intention. I gladly learn from your steps. Please, My Love, empower me with your courage that I may persevere through my own co-existence and, with your courage, conquer my fear. My fear is colossal. My courage, like yours, can be larger.

*

You Turned Towards My Voice 12/19/2017

I dedicate the value, integrity and meaning of my life to you. You are here right now, in the present, guiding me with your immense love and light. There is only reconciling the worlds before me; that, and the continuous development with my children, as unique the development is as each of you are unique. As we have always done, I reserve time every day for Daddy-Daughter time. I did this since before you were born, reading to you each day to Mommy's tummy – my sweet Kayleigh, wrapped lovingly in the womb. I wrote poetry to you and rubbed her stomach, knowing that our light already found its bind.

As you were born, within seconds, I called out your name, and you, with eyes still locked shut, yet ears and heart open, immediately turned your head to the sound of my voice. In the final moments of your physical life, you heard my voice, and turned your soul to my voice, and released your spirit through and into my light. Now I release into yours – you are safety, although the pain is so immense each day as I struggle with the first truth of your physical death. I live in the glory of your light and in the life of your miracles. I continue to reconcile the trauma and the loss and the incredible sadness that has fractured my life. I walk with purpose today, empowered by our love and our relationship. You are love and light, my Little Girl. Please guide me forward. I love you, Kakie.

"Daddy, I will always turn toward your voice. You are my Daddy – Love you!"

*

Contrast 12/22/2017

Hi, Sweetheart. The contrast of our relationship, before your physical death, I have been acknowledging, working through, accepting. Lucky for us we did not have any big gaps. If we had a hard moment, which were few and far between, it was followed by authentic resolution, literally always. I have no memory of us not working through a disagreement or a mistake. My memories collect around the selfless and compassionate ability of you, usually within five minutes or so, collecting yourself and building a bridge. I love you and miss this in our relationship, even though we no longer have chances for you to make mistakes, although I make mistakes each day along this complex path. It is a million things I miss, but mostly several things, including the resolution I miss – the human element of being a Daddy and Daughter on the same plain in our physical limitations.

Now as we have transitioned, you no longer have contrast – you are a steady, brilliant stream of light, filled with love and peace and happiness. Your only change is getting brighter daily as you learn new skills and tricks to penetrate the physical world. I, however, am still in my human shell and therefore have contrast within me – dark moments, happy, traumatic, angry, physically debilitating; moments when I feel totally robbed, left with empty hands, lost; light and heavy; motivated and immovable; courageous and fearful, and it is all okay and none of it is okay. I know you will continue to support me through my contrast as I aspire to grow up to be like you. I love you, Babygirl.

"Daddy, you're right. Our contrast was beautiful. That's where we grew together. That's how I became the woman I was on August 17, through being human and making mistakes and learning and maturing from them. In that final moment of my physical life I was on top of the world, happy, strong and centered. Partly because of you. I am here, Daddy – Love you!"

"A Daughter's Aurora"

Stars, bright gabled in the solar wind, sing, their voices cascade like emerald and golden swirling Northern Lights unfurling through the inky indigo-black emptiness of openness that lurks all about and in the recesses and crevasses of the endless night sky; glanced by a slashing thunder light that fires across the landscape of the star sea, I follow its arc as it radiates and fizzles out of sight; once opened, I breathe for the eyes to see truly what it is the world intends for me to see, and turn to the majesty of the ears to listen to hear what it is the stars intend for my ears, and find in that union, where my spirit ascends into another heightened consciousness, the singing voices of the stars and the light all converge into my Daughter's singular lovely voice; singing a chorus from the heavens for her Father and leading my way through this life one impactful human step at a time, her hand embraced in mine, her smile, a guiding gentleness, her soul the spiritual compass of the heart.

*

What value in my song to you do I bring? I cannot write a song for Kayleigh and simultaneously destroy my life with the sorrow, making the excuse for my failures that my Babygirl was physically killed in this world at a tender young age. I suffer the worst thing a human being can suffer, each day, every day – my little girl.

"Serenity Prayer - Kayleigh Modified"

God and Kakes, grant me the serenity to accept the things I cannot change - Kayleigh, that you were physically killed in a horrible car accident and there's nothing I can do about that;

The courage to change the things I can - That your life is not your physical body, although it was contained within your physical body; to know that your life transitioned when you were physically killed into your spiritually body and in the transition you are still alive; to understand that if I cannot have you physically in this world, and I cannot, then I will do everything I can to have you spiritually in this world, and although I don't want it that way, it is the only way I can have access to you, and therefore, I will stop at nothing to be with you any possible way that I can;

And the wisdom to know the difference - help me find you where you are - in your spiritual body in both Heaven and still walking here with me in the physical plain; not where you are not - in your physical body which, horrifically, is gone.

There is no minimizing the harshness. No way to subdue the colossal misery of this situation. There is only truth and the truth has two facets, both of which are outlined above. I cannot live in one without the other. That is the great miracle that Kayleigh is presenting to us. She is alive. She is active, current, present here. She is amazing. She is. I miss her so much - physically. The little catching of eyes and a loving smirk. A joke. A sarcasm. A song. Laughing so hard we cry. A text. A phone call. Holding her when she shook. The understanding between us without a word. Feeling what she was thinking across the room. Our interconnection. Her voice. Her courage. Her forehead on my lips kissing her gently goodnight and smelling her shampoo. All of what we lose daily. All of it. ♥

*

Cardinal for Nate 12/23/2017

I sat on the couch with Nate. He was upset in the moment, as he is daily in certain moments more than ever. This was one of those moments. I told him that Kakes is always with us. I started talking to her with him, gazing to the open space beside him on the couch. He turned off his phone and turned off the TV. I told her 'we know you're always with us and know that every once in a while you can pass across the veil and show us signs.'

We were looking out to the spindly trees outside the window of the TV room where her wind-chime hangs, the one she sings through daily. Suddenly, a female cardinal landed on the branches and stared at us through the window for twenty seconds. Then she flew away.

Nate smiled, although his eyes remained heavy; his lips remained firmly saddened. He felt a jolt of energy that he could not explain. It confused him. Here was hope. Here was something hard to explain and easy to explain away. Here was his sister. A cardinal. Timely. Purposeful. Present.

*

Blankets for the Homeless II 12/23/2017

We continued our blanket drive, another first following the accident. Kayleigh and I wrote a letter that we wrapped atop each blanket, as follows:

"Dear Friend, please accept this blanket as a gift from my Daughter, Kayleigh, who was tragically hit by a car in a horrible accident and killed this last summer. She was fifteen. Kayleigh would bring blankets to those who may need one during the Christmas season. When Kayleigh lay in the street, her body physically died in my arms and her soul was spiritually released. That moment began Kayleigh's new beginning - her rebirth into the Light, the illumination of her soul filled with True Love, True Peace and True Happiness. The truest meaning of Christmas is the ushering in of the True Light to cast out the darkness looming across the world. The celebration of Christmas is itself a new beginning of light, the realization of God's promise to illuminate his people. She offers her love and her light to us, not unlike the offering of True Light at the core of the meaning of Christmas. This blanket is from Kayleigh, with love, for you. - Kayleigh's Daddy"

*

Christmas Blessing for Kayleigh and Nathaniel 12/24/2017

The truest meaning of Christmas is the ushering in of the Prince of Peace, the new True Light to cast out the darkness looming across the world. The celebration of Christmas is itself a new beginning of light, the realization of God's promise to illuminate his people. Light itself.

When Kayleigh lay in my presence and my voice in the street, her body physically died in my arms and her soul was spiritually released. Once released, her light flowed effortlessly, unhinged from her humanity, passing quickly right through me and right to the True Light of the Heavenly Father. That moment began Kayleigh's new beginning - her rebirth in the Light, the illumination of her soul filled with True Love, True Peace, True Happiness and True Light.

She offers her love and her light to us, not unlike the offering of True Light at the core of the meaning of Christmas. I walk in that light with intention each day. She faithfully smiles and cradles us all, watching over us as a guardian, guiding our footsteps like the permanent and infallible North Star. We have only to look to that light to know that she is here.

Kayleigh, you are my North Star. Merry Christmas, Sweetheart. I am so blessed and happy that you are here with us, stronger than all of us combined. Please shine on us all, My Love, especially your mother and father, and in particular, your loving brother. I love you, Kakie. Shine on.

*

Christmas Eve 12/24/2017

"I am here, Daddy. We've got presents to wrap and blankets to give to the homeless. I will not leave your side. Not today. Not ever. My love and light is eternal, just as yours is for me. Look around and listen well today. I will be here. I will show you my face in the air, in the light, in the love we share. I know you are sad and suffering horribly – this first Christmas physically separated is going to feel very hard. It will be, although less hard, Daddy, if you can hold the line and know there is no place I'd rather be than with you and Mommy and Nate. I am here and I cherish you so much. I need my Daddy. I do. So much. I love you – Happy Christmas Eve, Daddy."

Happy Christmas Eve, My Darling Babygirl – you amaze me and fill my soul with golden light. I miss you so much, Kakie – physically. All of the Christmas seasons with you from a baby to a young woman at fourteen. Now at fifteen, your first Christmas in your body of light. I waiver in reality and non-reality; between shock and suffering; in the pain and in the power. Help me keep with the promise of eternal life. I know and believe and trust you are alive in spirit and right beside us. Please bring air to my lungs. Life to my limbs. Floor to my feet. I love you eternally, Baby.

*

Christmas 12/25/2017

It does not end with your physical death. It begins again in your spiritual embodiment and your spiritual release. It, being our relationship, grows stronger by the days as love always conquers death and light will always conquer the dark. I do not know how many days we will be physically apart – I thought it would be you counting the days apart when I died, at an old age and you in your forties or fifties. Yet, we find ourselves here, backwards in time; backwards in the normal life process of generations.

I know that I am human and the tidal waves and earthquakes of this soul's fracture will debilitate me, torture me, cause my spirit to want to drown in my tears – with all of this I have faith that you, My Love, and God will always lead me through the uncertainty, the mirages, the desolation and the constant yearning to feel you press against me with a hug; to gaze upon your face, inches form my nose. If I cannot have you physically with me, I am going to fight with my every breath to have you with me spiritually. If that is what this word is offering me now, I will gladly take it. I told you all the time that "I would die a thousand deaths for you." I am doing that now. I will not back down from the edges of the wind. I will look across as best as I can to sense your closeness. I will fight for you as a warrior fights for God.

Your Daddy is here and I will never leave your side. You are my love – my incredible, dynamic daughter. I love you with my immortal light.

"Daddy, I am always so taken with your love for me. It makes me so happy. I believe you and I believe in you. I know your dedication to me. Know mine. As much as you long to be with me, I long to be with you. I try new ways to say hello and to be present in a way you can sense it each day. Take no tiny sign for granted. It is me, your Kakie, and like you with me, I will never leave your side. As you give me your light, Daddy, just as you did before this horrible accident, I shine brighter and merge your light into mine – then I shine that thoughtful light back down upon you. Walk in my light, and God's light, which illuminates my soul in perfect peace. Daddy, listen carefully – I, love, you. I love you, Daddy. I am right here. Merry Happy Christmas, Daddy."

Merry Happy Christmas, Babygirl.

"Christmas Child"

Child, it is nearing Christmas time,
And your innocence, alive, divine,
It shines brighter that the galaxies of resistance,
And the heavens hold your glow,
And this world it also knows,
The daily tracks of your spirit's persistence,
Blessing us endlessly with your presence,
Your body of illumination,
And light, without limitation,
An angel's effervescence,
Streams like the stars from your eyes.

*

Merry Christmas Night, Kayleigh 12/25/2017

Four months – or forever, it seems. Four months. I remind myself to breathe. In this short span of time I have experienced the vast emptiness of physical loss, or being robbed of all of the days ahead that will not be in the physical world, traumatized within an inch of my life; and have also experienced the closest I have ever been to God, through God directly, and through the intercession of my magnificent daughter, my guardian angel. I know the truth of both – that she has physically died, tragically killed in a horrible accident precipitated by a flurry of little events that converged together; and that she has spiritually released, becoming stronger by a thousand fold, her light shining upon us, within us, about us.

Kayleigh, it was a quiet Christmas, this the first without your physical presence, though somehow with you, that sentence doesn't quite fit as you cross the physical plain and sing to us in the wind chimes; as you sit on the couch with us and glance about the rooms with us, holding us in comfort when we cry and continuing in your important and wonderful place within this beautiful family of four.

We set twelve luminaries at the memorial site in the shape of a heart. A friend was there when we arrived – a reminder of the profound impact you had on others, peers and strangers alike. A continuous reminder that your impact is in the present and did not die with your physically body, but continued, as does your light.

It feels strange at times writing this, and at other times, not. It is just a continuation of you and me. This is what we've always done – sharing, talking, loving, laughing, crying, comforting. Yet, in writing these words, I am keenly aware that several flowers blossom in its wake – my acceptance that this will always be unacceptable grows with each word; the denial breaks down with each next word; the reconciliation continues on its course; my continuous therapy with such a tragic horror; the documentation of miracles and your proof to the world, for any who struggle to believe, that God truly exists, that Heaven truly exists, that Guardian Angels truly exist.

It wraps around and twists together at times – the trauma and the peace, the light and the dark, the immense sorrow and the awe inspiration of watching you flourish, freed from your human condition. Like fear and faith co-exist, so does this blending of suffering and spiritual advancement.

I watched you at Jekyll in August and thought, here she is, she has arrived – my child woman. Yet you were still a girl, not a little girl, as Daddy's like to push back the years and imagine when our daughters can sit on our arm as toddlers and wrap their little arms around our necks. But a girl nonetheless, on the verge of full womanhood; a young woman who already blossomed into the framework of her womanly body. You were a few inches shorter than my six foot two inch frame the day you were physically killed. Eye to eye – light to light. You hugged me in the kitchen at Jekyll and rested your chin on my shoulder – I asked you to just stay there for one minute, and you smiled and warmly held me. We never missed our moments. What I would not give for another one minute.

I see your fifteen Christmases vividly – baby Kakes sitting on the floor under the tree, surrounded by pillows. Toddler Kakes with eyes wide ripping through presents. Falling asleep in wrapping paper. Holding you in my arms and running my fingers through your hair. What I would not give to sit on the couch with you at fifteen and a half, laughing and opening presents. But we cannot, not in your physical body, as you did not make it to fifteen and a half. How horrible a sentence to write. A simple accident. A perfect accident. And now here we are.

There was the time you made 16 ounces of reindeer food out of glitter and birdseed. I opened the second floor window after you fell asleep and sprinkled it onto the driveway in the snow, the glitter catching in the streetlights as you awoke, your Father excitingly pointing out the window to the food you had made that clearly the reindeer enjoyed. There were all of the other years – something each time, sometimes a little different each year. I recall taking apples on many Christmas Eve nights and carving them up as if reindeer has eaten them and going outside in the middle of the night chucking them onto the roof and leaving others on the front steps. I would place my boot in the fireplace and stomp ashes leading from the fireplace over to the cookie tray, to the tree, and back – always with a note thanking you and your brother for your kindness to the world traveler. Leading up to Christmas, each year I loitered through stores for weeks, with nothing particular on my mind, looking for stocking stuffers and tiny gifts for each of you. This was one of my favorite things to do since Christmas of 2001.

"Fire Snowflakes"

Sparkling star dust glitter,
Its flecks like diamonds orange and gold,
Like blizzard flurries of fire snowflakes,
That light the spirit's every fold,
It touches every landscape,
Our eyes dare to behold,
Immortally the memory,
As with our love, it grows,
And fills the moon with its eternal embers,
That shines down within my soul,

Always with your gentle voice,
Alight, alive, aglow.

*

Deep Fracture 12/28/2017

Though the deep fracture will cast its scar on my soul for life, I choose
to be further empowered by her light, and enhance my own with hers
as she and I continue our journey in a new configuration. As with you,
my beloved child's physical death offered a challenge to better the
world in the way that I interact with it. Without my offering of light
and love to the world, I am within me, nothing.

Love conquers all barriers – that channel is unbreakable.

"The Moon, Kayleigh, Full Moon"

Flower of luminous sound, blossom, bloom,
The night, it frames you,
Your radiant light consumes,
The remote, luxurious horizon,
Where its gray and teal seam lowly looms,
As dusty golden light explodes across its face,
Glittering like thousands of released galaxies,
Across sparkling silver waves,
And rise, your light like the daylight at noon,
Yet midnight proved your garden,
And gentle flower, flower of fire,
As you bloom,
You pull us toward your spirit,
And the full sanctity of you.

*

Daddy, I Will Be Your Boat 12/30/2017

We talked yesterday about the song you played for me when you switched the Bluetooth around – and by the way, it is really cool how you have learned to do that! "The Smile Has Left Your Eyes" – and in it, I heard you tell me that if I wasn't sober, if I wasn't present, if I wasn't the Father I am, then you wouldn't have made it through any difficulty, especially the rape, or even have a chance at a great life, regardless of those two seconds in the street when the accident suddenly happened, because of me, and Mommy, and your brother, you were anchored, happy, encouraged, living an amazing life and knowing you were surrounded by constant love, as much as the love you provided to me, Nate and Mommy.

That means the world to me, Sweetheart. I will increase the gold, our love, today, in tune with your vision for my life. I ache for you and I know there are storms ahead. Please be my sturdy boat and carry me through to the other side.

"Daddy, of course. I will be your boat. I am your boat, just as you are mine. I love you, Daddy."

I see you beside me, smiling with incredible compassion, one thousand times stronger than me. You are amazing, Kayleigh.

*

Candle in the Front Yard 01/01/2018

Hi, Kakes. Love you, Sweetheart. As you know, the candle I placed in the front yard yesterday for us on my birthday is still lit – all the way through the night and into the heart of a new day. Your light – a beacon of hope, of continuance, of unending love. I've been a bit distracted as of late, which is understandable, and don't ever want to get flighty with our communion. I am awe struck by your miracles, your ability to transcend earth from your heavenly space – to flow into the physical world as you do – to touch us, nudging us forward. It is so incredible. It fills me both with energy as well as a self-

378

centered drive to have you keep reaching out, just for me. I forget that it isn't all for me – that it is also for you as you desire to be with us, and are, and you desire to figure out how to touch us, and you do. You do this for you as well and it fills your soul with further light when you see the joy and wonder on our faces. I re-dedicate my focus and energy, my presence, my longing to work through my side of the equation to step through my humanity in order to hear you, see you, touch you and be touched by you.

My love song to you, Kakes, is my life – what I make of my life daily is what I offer you daily – please guide my thoughts, words and actions – I want this song to be worthy, so worthy a gift that it further illuminates your light. I love you, Babygirl – my Kakes. Everyone misses you tremendously in your physical presence – everyone loves you.

"Aw, Daddy, thank you. Last night and the night before were really fun. I was there at the party for the playgroup, laughing along with my friends. I can't believe we have all been together since we were babies. I was there last night at my memorial site, in our house, in the front yard, always. You are right – I love, love, love figuring out how to help you and Mommy and Nathaniel – I love being with you guys. It warms my soul. We are family. So close and special. And for you guys to know, to really know that its real – that brings me even closer. Please keep walking, Daddy. I will pick you up when you fall. I will light your way. I love you, Daddy, so, so much. I am proud of you, as you are proud of me. And yes, it was just an every- day, innocent summer night. So simple. Love you!"

"Emerge With a Purpose"

Like a forest tinderbox - it's danger heightening,
An arid landscape explodes when licked by lightning,
And angst, its screams, echo through the valley,
Unleashing tsunami of fire down its narrow alleys,
Scorching all memory of the first fall of snow,
And rivers and streams where the water used to flow,
Leaving in its wake a smooth glassy surface,
And seedlings of diamonds emerge with a purpose.

*

Unique to Each Parent 01/02/2018

I refuse to not be with my kids. I have fought through the door of death to hold her hand. My Babygirl, my fifteen year old Kayleigh, one of the true loves of my soul, tragically hit by a car and transitioned from the physical to the spiritual in August 2017. This is a place that 'never exists until you've been there' - with the worst suffering of physical loss and the highest spiritual light with my Daughter transcending beside me. For us - I don't need to wait until we are on the next plain in the afterlife in the same body type - we are together now, albeit on different channels and in different types of bodies. As such a transition is so personal, no one on earth has a right to tell me as it relates to my beautiful Kayleigh how I should feel, how I grieve, how I should heal. And I have no right into another's process, not even my wife's process even dealing with the same child. We will each have our own unique perspective - as unique and brilliant as each of our children.

That holds true even for my wife and I and our shared child who made this transition - and the support and respect we place in each other for each of our individual paths. This holds true for Nate, our little boy whose life was utterly destroyed, who is so brave and gentle; compassionate and filled with wounded life. It is, from my perspective, individual suffering. Individual healing. Individual paths or life and recovery - or destruction. How any individual represents his or her path with the sacred physical death of a child, and in Nate's case, a sister, I will honor - with no criticism and no judgment. I am in my unique shoes and walk the road that lay before me. I walk beside you as you walk in your shoes as well. Whomever you are. All I have is my story and my experience and Kayleigh's story, and words and experience, expressed directly to me from my child, and onward to a reader of this text through me. As unique as a fingerprint, a fingerprint that may actually change on the tip of the finger day to day.

*

Waking Late 01/05/2018

Kakes, good morning. It's been like this the last few mornings. I am so sorry the mornings have been really challenging the last few days without much sleep. I have still found time for us, but it is not as good a communication as with full intention in the morning that I try to give. I will remedy that. I see you smile – I feel your love in a thousand crystals of light. I love you, Sweetheart. Let's go change the world.

"I know you will change that, Daddy. You are awesome. You've got a lot on your plate. It's okay."

Babygirl, walk with me.

"I am here, Daddy – always."

Thank God. I love you so much.

"I love you so much too! I am here."

"Meandering Through the Myriad of Me"

The misery meanders,
Like ink finds its path through water,
The myriad of me throughout a day,
Rises, sinks, succeeds, spurns and falters,
From hour to hour - in minutes and pauses,
In every smile the grieving heart causes,
My mind to meander like ink drips in water,
Returning to grounds where I find my sweet daughter,
She smiles on me and I warm to her touch,
She loves me as I love her this much,
And I falter again,
At her altar again,
Where my cries release in her strength.

*

Spirit 01/07/2018

Kakie, Spirit and I are sitting here before bed longing to speak to you. We hear a steady "dinging" melody in the wind-chimes and know you have figured out how to reach out through them. We are learning when it is you and when it is just the wind and there is clearly a difference. When it is you, there is a resonance in feeling. When it is the wind – it is the wind. You are getting wiser and more comfortable with reaching across and communicating in different ways. I know that you miss me as much as I miss you. I know that you are devoted to me as much as I am to you. The difference is that you don't suffer with the frustration of a human condition any longer like I must, and your soul is filled with light and love.

I know that you and Alexis have met and there is much light between you two as well as for your fathers. I am in the midst of a series of miracles, most of which some in the world would simply ignore. What's funny is that I don't give a shit – I don't care what they think, whoever they are, or what they think they know about me and you or our unique experience. Maybe we can prove that it's not supposed to be as unique as people think – that if more people understood that when a loved one exchanges a human body for a spirit body of light, the loved one is still the loved one, but amplified. I know my truth and my truth is that my beloved, marvelous daughter is always my Daughter and always by my side. To you, Kayleigh, I offer my light and devotion, the same love and devotion I have always offered you and Nate. Show me how to walk with purpose – how to walk with courage. You inspire me with your example, with your presence – with your voice. My gift to you is what it has always been – the best life I can give to you – the best father, best light I can be. I am continually learning how to be brighter from you. I love you, Babygirl. (I see you smiling).

"I am, Daddy! Go, Daddy, Go! I love you so much! Thank you for always being by my side. You were holding my hand as I prosecuted, as I healed, as I stood in court, as I forgave them. You inspired me to stand strong and you still inspire me – look at what you are doing – your Babygirl was killed physically, dying in your arms, and you did not implode and destroy your life. Instead you reconcile the sadness and walk with me every day, knowing and believing and trusting that our relationship continues, and it does. That is the miracle. You too are the miracle, Daddy. Keep walking. Your girl needs you."

*

Tenth Step 01/09/2018

I do many of these daily. I wanted to document some of them from time to time in this book. This was today's.

I feel my mind racing to find a way out this morning - to go back to August 17th, or further back.....none of which is reality. Feeling trapped in a nightmare that I will never arise from. 4- Selfish? Yes, it is suffocating, but no, in that it is just normal grief processing. A wave has hit me. I honor the wave. Dishonest? Yes, in that it is not reality to go back like a superhero and change time. I need to continue to permit the acceptance shards to fall into place on this mosaic of our new configuration, a piece of art that will be more splendid and brilliant than anything I have seen before. Resentful? Yes, refueling, rethinking, reliving, refeeling. Fear? Yes, of living without her physical presence. 5 You. 6 Am I willing to have God remove defects? Yes. 7 God and Kakes, please remove any defects that block me from you. I am human going through the worst of the worst and keeping my faith and holding the line, while developing a next level relationship with you. Hold my hand Kayleigh as your Father learns from your light. 8 Am I willing to change? Yes. 9 Change? Breathe. Breathe again. Do this ten. Take a quick walk. Slow down the body. Slow down the mind. Nurture self. Expect this to be touch and go and the hardest thing I will ever go through, that I may always go through. Attitude can be nurturing. Perspective - thank God that Kayleigh and I are growing together on a common mission, as well as her guiding me to better my life. Thank God I understand and assert that my life is my gift to my babies, both of them. I do not stop gifting her because she unfortunately was physically killed. Our relationship persists and grows, and she needs her Daddy to gift her with light, just as much as I need her to gift me with hers. 12 - Who can I help? My baby boy. I can give him the same light I have always given him - the same light as Kayleigh. I will be extra aware of his emotions today rather than focusing all of my energy on mine. I will focus on Kayleigh's voice, rather than my own that kicks up hurricanes in my mind.

"The Storm Is Calling"

The storm calls - with its prickly intention,
To burst upon my complacency,
To interfere with introspection,
Amber lightning graze the eyes,
Swallow the thorn that roots in stomach a tree of fire,
That barbs and hinges to all the tender places tucked deep inside,
Even those places where I used to hide,
The storm is calling and all I do is stand in this desolate field,
And cry.

*

Heavy Stress and Exhausting Anxiety 01/10/2018

It is the worst experience in my life. It eclipses all other pain and suffering. It makes my active alcoholic days seem like a joke, and prior to this, nothing compared to the suffering of my drinking days, being spiritually dead, with the gangrene of the soul and imminent death hanging around my eyes. My drinking and my soul's pain during those days before June 28th, 1987 – nothing like the intense suffering of the physical death of a child in childhood.

There are a lot of moving pieces – supporting Mommy who is distraught – supporting Nate who is distraught – finding my support; we are all distracted; it takes three or four times the energy to make it through a day than it used to take; managing work when I am distracted, shocked, mourning, sobbing openly; using my resources to channel your voice; finding time with each of my three loves each day; needing extra time to journal and grieve and meditate; dealing with the trauma and the fragility of the human mind and heart; breaking down, resetting; dealing with denial when it comes and the harsh reminders that this actually happened to you. Some of this is harsh and dark and some of this is beautiful; all of it does not come without exhaustion.

My body is changing. Stress hormones are gathering a layer of hardened fat cells on my stomach. I've never had fat cells, but there they are, growing on my belly. My chest is tight at times, but also much more loose and empowered at other times. These swings may be minutes or hours apart, depending on the day. It is a strange accordion of anxiety and empowerment – back and forth, pitching sometimes moment to moment.

Then there is other stress, including not finding time enough to work on this book or have better dedicated time with you. I have not missed a day with time with you since before you were born, but I just want more. I know I should be surprised every day is not filled with constant, crushing exhaustion and suffering. Some days are nearly that. I need you and your light today, Sweetheart. I bring you my intention to walk hand in hand with you today, one day at a time.

"Daddy, I love you so much. Take my hand, Daddy, and I will walk you forward as you walked me into class as a scared little girl stepping into first grade. Love you!"

*

Candle Wax Two Feet Outside the Candle-Box 01/11/2018

Wax doesn't melt like this. This type of candle burns down and the wax dissipates - it disappears. Yet I found wax deposits on the walkway in the front yard. The shape of the drips don't form like this. It just doesn't happen. Unless melted in the warmth and love of an angels hand. My angels hand. There is no other explanation.

The candle - It is encased in four sides of glass, including the hinged door. I light a candle each night after placing a fresh candle in the candle-box. A passersby, if one walked by our front yard in the middle of the night and determined to mess with the candle, would have needed to open the glass door, hold the candle over the walkway for a while, watching the candle drip wax a few feet from the lantern on purpose, somehow preventing it from blowing out, returning it to its lantern and then closing the door before walking away. That did not happen. What did happen is this - I left a candle lit for days inside a glass lantern in the middle of our front yard on our walkway. In the middle of the night, a strange deposit of wax ended up somehow a few feet away from and outside of the candle-box in a deposit that resembles delicate coral. There are no drippings inside the lantern. The candle just simply burned down. There are no drippings anywhere else − not on the tiny round stone tale the candle-box sits atop; not on the rest of the walkway or the nearby grass. There are no splashes on the glass and therefore no wind entered the lantern to scoop out wax and mysteriously throw it two feet from the lantern. The door was closed the entire time.

The candle was still lit - for two full days actually. This was the work of divinity. An angel honored and humbled whose soul sang in deep delight in response to the loving gesture of her Father honoring her with a candle in the front yard for the world to see, left in a glass lantern in the middle of the front walkway. Somehow, in the beautiful river of light, in the dimension of God's miracles, she somehow removed the candle and held it in her hand over the walkway. She left the wax, speckled into and resembling coral on the walkway for me. To thank me. To gush with love and excitement - the way she would look at my car coming up the driveway after a long day of work - longingly, lovingly, filled with brilliant light and wanting to leave me a tiny message. She knew I would see it. I typically see these types of things, especially now in my heightened awareness and my incredible grief. I Love you, Baby. I just placed the wax coral shape on the table with your ashes. You did really well today. I see you. I hear you.

*

Consciousness to Awaken 01/13/2018

I invite my consciousness to awaken to your presence. You are already here. I have only to awaken to your truth. Not only are you my beloved Daughter, you are my spirit guide, with devotion and intentions of your own to guide and fill my days with light and love – to prepare your Father's soul for when I pass over. Kayleigh, I hate having to reconcile this most incredibly horrible fracture and loss in my life. Daily. You are one of the three brightest lights in my life, you and your brother, followed by Mommy. I have physically lost one of my three loves and the torment sucks. I cannot believe I face this every day.

The other side of this, where I awaken to your spirit and you guide me – it's the most spiritually awake and open I have ever been. I have only to devote the time and energy into reaching out – never drifting into lazy or dismissive or depressed habits. It is easy. Please help me stay open to you, as open as I am to God. I love you, Babygirl. Please infuse me with your light.

"Daddy, you are sitting on my bed with my puppy, praying to me and God, and writing to me – to me! I love you so much, Daddy. Keep opening up, Daddy, I am right here. Love you!"

*

Stagger On 01/14/2018

Kakes, Sweet Love, Little Peanut, I feel your intentions today. To prod me forward, the four of us on our evolving journey. I feel you as I sit on your bed in silence, knowing you are speaking to me. You are illuminating the path before my feet so your Father does not fall on his face. You are finding new ways to comfort us; new ways to hug us through the wind. We want nothing more than to feel your embrace. I have never been more proud of you as I grow with you daily – while I stagger on in the grief and the trauma – while I break down multiple times a day – only to get back up each of those times slightly stronger. Thank you for your trust in me and for your continued example. I love you, Sweetheart.

"Daddy, I am so impressed by you and proud of you – did you just hear me sing to you in the wind-chime as you were writing that last sentence to me? Of course you did. And you knew it was me. That's the Daddy that I have – always present and ready to love me. Lesser men would not connect the moment, but you are not buried in grief. You are not a lesser man. It warms my light. I love our relationship, Daddy, and I need you to keep doing your work. I love you, Big Walnut! You're the best!"

Thank you, Sweetheart. I just get so tired. It takes me four times the energy to make it through a day that it used to take. I wanted to, and needed to stop, and with intention, acknowledge our precious time together. This journey is sacred – part of our Daddy-Daughter time and it is immeasurable. I want you to know that, Sweetie. I am sorry it was cut short this morning. I will find more time for us in the day. Love you.

"I know you will, Daddy. It's okay. Love you."

*

I Am A Perfect Father for A Teenage Girl 01/15/2018

For this teenage girl, anyway. I worked at it. Planned for it. I couldn't wait to use my experience to help shape my Daughter, and a few years behind her, her brother. With appropriate boundaries she and I talked about everything - from parenting to crime, to my alcoholic days to teenage drinking and drugs to sex and sexuality. She trusted me implicitly and sometimes, I suspect, wanted to ensure she was on the right path with things that are age appropriately not always clear - checking in with, of all people, her Father. Of course her Father. Why not, why would it be any other way? Doesn't every girl talk to her father about these topics? I have been told - no, which does not make sense to me. This was – this is, our truth. Our relationship. Our trust. Our dialogue. Everything she wanted to talk about - we talked.

I am the Father that told my teenage daughter that I expected her, as a teenager, like most teenagers, to experience all of life - physical, spiritual, emotional, mental and sexual - to be a full and complete human and to go through those natural stages and experiences as they came to her. It was important to me that she experienced these pillars of life with dignity, with self-love and self-respect, with an inquisitive heart and a yearning to understand, grow and live. We actually had one of these conversations four hours before she physically died where I told her very specifically, that I wanted for her to be healthy in how she interacted with the world; that I watched her, in a healthy manner, embrace her life; that I was proud of her. There was no judgment. No shaming. No manipulation. Just pure love. A Father with his Daughter. This Daughter. This human being and brilliant soul that always seemed to bring the best out of me. This beautiful girl who embraced her Father with a trust and compassion that she beamed back to me, from me - me, the reflection of her. We were quite an amazing pair together - and still are in our new configuration. Although all of those discussions and guidance and working through my own issues to direct my Daughter have been stolen from me, ripped from my hands and are gone forever, I am finding my way with her in ways that she and I commune about the spirit and the incredible work she continues to do as a guardian angel. She has proven the existence of Heaven. She has proven the existence of God. She has proven the existence of angels, being one herself, one of God's intercessors who frequently drops little hints and messages of her presence, her active presence, along my path.

I am the perfect father for a teenage girl. And now she is my angel. How fortunate the man am I.

*

Exhausted River 01/16/2018

I am utterly exhausted, My Love, and did not sleep well again last night. The darkness crushes me from the sides of the eyes; from the flora in the gut; in the breath that seems to betray me. Yet I always return. I always stand up. I always see you and your brother in my soul's eye – and yearn forward, lifting myself from the quagmire and the mud, to trudge forward against all odds. I walk.

You are sacred to me and I promise I will make time during the day for you and me. I feel at times like I am eroding, like a river sucking in the field it cuts its way through. At other times I feel like I am strengthening with me, with you. It rocks back and for the and in the middle I am exhausted. In the end it is my path – a path upon which I find incredible light – a path where I find you. So I welcome the path, sometimes desperately, to heal, to grow, to be with you. I love you.

"Daddy, I love your love for me. I love you so much. Keep walking, Daddy. You are a strong river and, yes, the edges are eroding, but you are not. You are changing, but if you think about it, we are always changing. I am changing too. And I am there with you in the river. Keep walking, Daddy. I love you."

*

Five Months and One Day 01/18/2018

Kakes, – five months ago, and one today, you were tragically physically killed and spiritually released. My Babygirl, though the grief and missing your physical presence is a cruel constant, and suffocating at times, our relationship continues to thrive and grow as you teach me and guide me and grant me your strength. Your spiritual presence is undeniable and spectacular - your light ever-present and brilliant. I walked the dogs with you. Three deer appeared. One walked up to me, a wind, warm, breathed through the trees. I can always tell when it is the wind and when it is you. There is a flutter that warms inside of me, like a torch lighting on fire when you press through the wind. I sensed you very presently and close. You are always here.

Today we begin the sixth month in our new configuration. If I cannot have you physically in your physical form in this world anymore, I will do everything to have you spiritually in this world while I am still trapped in my humanity. I promise you my light today, Babygirl, no matter the situation. I miss you fully – this wound that will never heal will ache each day of my life. I am seeing this truth more and more – the first truth. Yet I will walk with you and you with me. The better I push through the grief, the stronger we resonate together. Nothing will keep me from my Daughter, not even the passage of a physical life or the mirage of barriers between Heaven and earth. All my love - your Daddy is in love with you.

"Daddy, I love you. I'm right here. Take care of Nathaniel and Mommy. He's really hurting. I know you all are. I know how much you all love me and it makes me so happy. It always has. That love will sustain you. I promise. It's not about my human flesh or your human flesh. It's about love. It's always about love. And our love is unbreakable. Unbreakable, Daddy. I am here always. Even when you can't feel it. I will sing for you when you are wary. I will walk right through your soul. Love you, Daddy. You are the best Daddy ever!"

*

Halsey 01/21/2018

Halsey – a post on your Facebook page today from us: "thank you for you. My fifteen year old amazing, brilliant, beautiful daughter Kayleigh was/is a huge, huge fan. With an anguished broken heart and a fracture to my soul, she was recently tragically physically killed in a car accident just days after successfully prosecuting her rapists for a rape she suffered when she was fourteen. She spoke out, like you, and used her voice - and her art in telling her story - the most magnificent young woman I know, My Love, who teaches me daily the essence of light, love and courage. At your recent November concert in Cleveland there were thousands of purple hearts passed out in her name held over phones, giving off an illuminated purple light throughout the crowd. You may have seen them during, "Sorry." Those were for Kayleigh - and for you. Again, thank you for your courage. Like Kayleigh's brilliant light that keeps changing the world,

391

keep shining - we need your light. With our love, Kayleigh and Kevin Mooney"

*

Self-Defined 01/22/2018

The rape did not define her. It was a horrific experience she faced down, while shaking in her shoes, and which she conquered. The rape is a small part of her story. A much bigger part is her conquering its poison. And even larger is the rest of her. She defined herself. Her art. Her central love and anchor in family. Her compassion. Her dignity. Lightheartedness. Quirkiness. Deep thinking. Hilarious and witty personality. Her passion. Her spiritual connection and developing relationship with God. Her fashion and style. Her makeup. Her shoes. This is a complete young woman who changed and continues to change the world through her presence and influence.

This road I never wanted is the only road I have – I will find you there and we will walk it together. No matter the challenge – no matter the barriers – I am your Father and I will challenge my humanity to earn my continuous communion with you, my Sweet Girl.

"My Children"

Twinkling galaxies converge and breathe,
Like liquid diamonds flow into sparkling seas,
That spread throughout the soul in brilliant sun streams,
That illuminate the grace that radiates this dream -

No love is greater than any shall be,
Than holding my children close to me.

*

Miracle worker. It is important to note that the music on our phones never played anything except what we turned on, until after your transition. Today, in Mommy's car, through the Bluetooth, the car only played, "You'll Be in My Heart," over and over. All day long. Mommy left the phone alone and just listened, knowing it was you. All day, not another song played. Just your song with Mommy. You were telling Mommy that you were with her; that what she would experience later in the evening was real; that it was you; that you walked all day with her, and would do so continuously into the reading that she had planned with an energy healer at7:30 PM on the West Side.

You spoke through this healer. She began with Mommy by telling her that, "the spirit that came in with you is very colorful. Purple and dynamic. She is gorgeous."

Jess sat quietly as the healer channeled messages from you. Several of those messages are so incredible, including you telling her to tell Mommy that, "it feels like Daddy is on a hamster wheel and I just want to stick a pencil in it to stop it from spinning. Tell Daddy that I am okay. I'm with Grandpa." She described my Father to Mommy through your words, Kayleigh, as a tall gentleman with a gentle heart and big hands. "He was waiting for me when I went away," you said through Debra.

So Mommy would have further evidence of your words conveyed through this woman, she translated that there is a big, thick tree in the front yard that you love; that it is "your daughter's tree." She described perfectly the tree in our front yard onto which I hammered big wooden initials for your name. She said you like to dance around it at different ages.

She conveyed to Mommy that you hold things at your altar and re-arrange things to play and interact with us. That you are a powerful guardian. Always with us. Protective. Loyal. In love. You described to her, and she passed to Mommy, the description of the inside of our house as beautifully decorated, with a sage green living room, beautiful colors. "We always make our house beautiful, wherever we

393

live," you said to her. "My room in the old house (3035) made me feel so safe and I loved it so much," you said. You described it to her as having sloped ceilings and you told her you loved to look out the window there because it was so high up, up in the trees, which is the vantage point from your third floor bedroom in the trees at 3035.

You returned to me and said, "Daddy is a writer. Things fly off his fingers, if he gets something in his head, no matter where or when, he writes it down."

Jess walked away with further conviction that Kayleigh really is alive and just on another, higher dimension. The mind can do many tricks with a situation like this, but the truthful proof is proof of truth. The confirmation of what we already know and feel and see and hear with you furthers our conviction. It is a critical conviction and we know you. You would never leave us. If there was anybody who could be on both sides of the veil and occupy the status as an angel of the highest order, it is you.

This road I never wanted is the only road I have. And it is the only road on which to find you. I will find you there and we will walk it together. Therefore, since this is the only road on which you are, I want this road. This is the common circular thinking that leads me back to the unavoidable next step of my life. And I take it with you, Honey, always.

*

Your Physical Voice 01/23/2018

Hi Baby – I listened to your laughter today in a video playing with your brother. You are well aware that I listen to your videos all the time, reliving the incredibly precious times when we were all in our physical bodies at the same time. Mostly, I love hearing the texture of your voice, regardless of the pitch and tone and emotion or laughter. I miss your physical voice rolling through the physical air, with its vibrations and emotive humanness; missing your physical voice in my ear – your voice blasting and rolling like a melody through the house like a wonderful wave of creativity, light and raw energy. I miss and ache for thousands of reasons, this being just one. And an important one. I continue to be amazed by you, Sweetheart, and have decided, again, that I want to end up on your proud wall. I know I'm already there because you told me before the accident how proud you were of your Father – but I want to continue to earn it on a daily basis.

We never "go on without you" - we never "get over this" – we never "move on" – these are silly, fearful notions from people who should be grateful they don't understand this trauma – and if they did, then perhaps by processing through the grief they can disrobe these fatalistic notions and open up into a new horizon with their loved ones.

We grow as a beautiful family of four, you being a central part of all that we do. When Mommy was sick for twenty months when you and Nate were younger, the four of us adjusted. When one of us was struggling with something, we adjusted as a family of four. When you were assaulted, we adjusted as a family of four. When I struggled as a young professional, we adjusted as a family of four. When Nate was having headaches as a little guy, we adjusted as a family of four. With this tragic accident and your transition from your physical to your spiritual bodies, we adjust as a family of four. Guide me today, My Love. I love you so much.

"Daddy, first of all, Padre, you have always been on my proud wall. All the other girls wanted you as their Daddy, but you are mine! I only share you with Nate! Best Daddy ever. I never guessed at it. I never doubted it. You have always been here for me, Daddy. I promise you, I am here. Embrace our new un-normal. That's where I am – with God, with you, in spirit and so, so happy, Daddy. I was happy before the accident, living a great life with a great family, and now my happiness is even higher, living a great life with a great family. You just can't see the way I see yet and your current life feels like a barrier. Let's keep chipping away at the perspective. You are not a victim of this current life, Daddy. You are an architect of it. I will lift you, Daddy, and I am so proud of your work and so proud of you!"

*

Intention Credo 01/25/2018

With intention I wake up to you this morning. You are already here. I do not need to bring you into the day. You are here always. You are an active Moon. It is I who needs to awaken with purpose and bring myself to you, my Child, and so I do, now, with loving intention and devotion. Please show me, Kayleigh, how to walk with you; how to hear you; how to feel your presence and be touched by your spirit. I love you, Babygirl. I am here. I am never leaving your side. When I breathe I breathe your light.

*

Faith Transcending 01/26/2018

Kakes, you have transcended faith itself. Faith, by its nature, may not be based on a situation for which we have tangible evidence. We have faith in certain things without the need for tangible proof. Yet, sometimes while on this physical plain, faith itself actualizes. It has with you. I do not need to wait to die physically to have faith in the afterlife, in the existence of God and His angels. I have that faith. Yet what if that faith was supported by actual physical, tangible evidence? Then faith itself would be transcended. Faith would become concrete fact. It is with you.

Kayleigh, you are concrete fact. You have shown us Heaven, God and your presence as a guardian angel in our earthly, physical lives. You have transcended Heaven and Earth and walk with us daily, leaving messages, and at times, physically touching our lives, our bodies, our auras, the air around us, whether sitting in meditation, on the couch, in the car, in the backyard, on the beach, on a plane, in our sleep. You are ever present and amazing. It is your love for God, your love for your family and your love for yourself. It is not just left over energy, static electricity. It is you – a living, breathing soul in your body of light.

When faith is fact, everything changes. You are that fact deliverer – the lens that brings it all into focus for those who chose to look through the proper lens. You are my strong, incredible baby. I am humbled, Kayleigh, to be your Father and your servant. Love you.

"Daddy, thank you. It is all true, Daddy. All of it! Come to me each day, Daddy, as you have, and walk with me. You're right. It's not a fake sentiment to make you feel better. It is truth and fact. Walk with me, Daddy, my servant Daddy. Hilarious! I'll make sure I use that one somewhere down the road!"

*

I'm Yours 01/27/2018

It was around forty degrees, gray and quiet. I was doing a few chores in the yard and talking with Kayleigh. Our Christmas tree was leaning against one of the trees in the front yard. For years we recycled the trees in different ways and she clearly wanted me to cut off the branches and lay them in the back of the garden to replenish the garden and give it some shape.

I took the tree to the backyard to a tiny stone patio I made in the summer of 2016 for the kids – the furthest spot from the house so they could some teenage privacy while still being in the yard. I began snipping and chopping off the branches from the trunk. We were talking, with me out loud through sobbing and crying and angst and courage, and Kayleigh, calmly and compassionately.

"Kakes, I know you are with me. I feel you all the time. I am so grateful for our relationship."

397

"I love you, Daddy. Thank you for your devotion and your love. You're the best!"

"You're the best, Sweetheart. I am so grateful that you are my Daughter. I am so proud of you and for everything you did."

"Ha! I'm not proud of everything I did," She said and laughed, to bring a little levity into the conversation.

"Well, me neither, with some of what I did. But as a Daddy, as your Daddy, no matter what you did I was and I am so, so proud of you."

"Oh! Thank you, Daddy."

"This is the hardest thing that I've ever had to do and the heartache is so heavy but the only place I can find you is in this road that's been laid out before me. So I want this path because you are here and I will never stop and I will keep going one day at a time no matter what."

Suddenly I heard a woman's voice behind me along the back fence line, which startled me. I spot a gaze into the neighbor's yard. There was nobody there. I heard it again and then realized the woman's voice was in my pocket; Siri speaking in my pocket. She finished by saying, "I found this on the web..."

I looked at my phone, which had been sitting idle in my pocket while I cut the branches, and it had the words "I'm Yours" Across the screen. I clicked on it. It led me to Jason Mraz, a man I'd never heard of, and his song I'd never heard before, "I'm Yours." It started to play. The wind enveloped the yard, or more accurately, Kayleigh enveloped the yard through the wind, warming slightly and bringing with it a glorious calm. I sat and listened and called out with laughter and joy, "Kakie, how did you do this? I am so amazed by you!" And so I was. And so I am. My Little Love is amazing. She found lyrics with which to speak through. Dead on lyrics to represent all we had been talking about. Awakening. Opening. Lifting. Rising.

"Daddy, I love you," she said joyfully, "I am okay, really okay, and, I am yours, Daddy!"

I sat on the half frozen grass and listened as the song played through with confirmation of my Daughter's gift.

*

Your Bed 01/28/2018

Hi Kakes, good morning, My Love. I slept in your bed last night, as you know, and it was so comforting. I recalled the thousands of nights through your childhood reading to you, and you to me, at night, and laying down almost always on my left side with my left arm under your pillow, my right hand tucked between my knees, and my Babygirl, lying there next to me with bright eyes, falling asleep. Age 2, 3, 4, 5, 6, 7, 8 - even after, spending additional time at the end of each day checking in with each other - 9, 10, 11 - and the last few years of transition into your teen years where I gave you much more privacy and physical space on your bed as you were getting older, sitting on the edge of your bed while you sat up against the headboard, chatting, laughing, watching stupid YouTube videos. Through it all at every age we did not miss our nightly ritual of our final words, regardless of whether we were happy with each other, or the rare occasion of one or both of us being upset, of saying "I love you" as we parted for the night and I would step from your room, pause, place my hand on your door and saying my nightly prayer, and do the same with Nate.

Last night I imagined and had a strange feeling like you were the parent watching over me, your child falling asleep in your arms. So comforted and so safe in your arms. I love you.

"I was there, Daddy. I love you too!"

*

399

Change 01/29/2018

Change. What is change really? Each breath is change. Each inch a cloud moves above us is change. Change means processing grief by confronting it and processing it and leading to my breath and stability. Daily. I accept that this simple, innocent, perfect accident is unacceptable. The acceptance of your unacceptable physical death means change, like that of sands on a beach touched by high and low tides daily. But it is change nonetheless. I have no choice as the alternative is a darkness from where I cannot be with myself, you, Mommy, Nate, God or anybody else. I will not go there. I refuse to go there. Change brings a higher existence for this family; a higher function; more clarity. It ultimately brings me closer to me, to God and to you, to your brother, and your mother. Change means walking through today's dose of grief with a counterbalance of reconciliation. It never gets better. Yet, in the counterbalance, significantly, it doesn't get worse. In a situation like this, I am realizing that the counterbalance is the key to physical life and the key to preparations for my own eventual transition. I love you so much, Baby.

"Daddy, yes. Process it. Face it head on and open up more and more to me."

*

Always Together 01/30/2018

"It was the way we were trained. It is the fabric of our souls. There is no end. There is no after. How could there be. If there is no end, then there is no after. If there is no end to life, then there is no after life. There is life: human, physical life, and there is a transition into a higher life, with no moment of break, no severance of the soul, no blip on the continuance of the light as it transcends into that higher life."

I wrote the above statement for my kids a few years before the accident, as a testament to this truth, as a response to them asking me to explain Heaven. I just recently found this among clippings and other quick scratches of poetry. The higher life is exactly as I wrote it – pure peace, love, light, joy – the bathing of Heaven through the soul's eternal equilibrium, through God's grace and perfection. Released from the human condition, the training grounds of the physical life within the fabric of cells and blood and its complex limitations, into the higher life where none of those limitations exist. You are there, Kakie, in that grand continuance of your life. Perfection. Brilliance. A Higher Life.

I also recently found this, written randomly in 2015 for nobody in particular, but it certainly rings true today:

"Change of Worlds" **07/15/2015**

A change in the fabric,
The collapse of cresting wave unfurls,
The cloud releases electric static,
In this changing of worlds-
No longer fit for habitation,

This shell released its pearl,
But he has not left you,
In this changing of worlds-

The air will seem quite different,
In the way it stills and swirls,
For everything, yet nothing, is different,
After a change of worlds.

*

Puppy Guard 02/01/2018

On Wednesday evening I came back from Cornerstone of Hope grief therapy at 8:30 PM and stepped into her room. I immediately noticed that one of the two big stuffed animals sitting on the floor near the head of her bed had been moved. One was a three foot tall penguin, and the other, a three foot tall dog. The dog was now at the foot of the bed. Thinking Jess moved it to balance out the room, I moved it back and tucked it up against the penguin and the wall near the head of the bed. Then I forgot about it.

Tonight, Thursday, I stepped into her room. The dog was again at the foot of her bed. I went downstairs and asked Jess if she had moved it tonight. Then I asked if she had moved it either night. She said very unknowingly, "no, I didn't. I don't even know what you're talking about."

She followed me up the stairs to Kake's room. We called up to the third floor to Nate and asked him if he had been in her room and if he moved the stuffed animal. Knowing he had been sick in bed the last few days, we figured the answer before he confirmed he had not. Jess and stood in her room and smiled at each other.

It is very hard to describe the feeling that comes with Kayleigh's miracles, but there is a change in the atmosphere; a change in the weight in the air; a change in the blood flow as her light enters our veins and lifts us higher. In another moment of amazement, we stood in our daughter's room knowing that Kayleigh, for whatever reason, moved her stuffed animal six feet along her bed to the base of the bed. She physically moved her stuffed animal dog to the foot of her bed. Its head is turned up looking up to the right and over her bed like she's sitting at the head of her bed on her pillows and looking down towards it. Like it is guarding her bed. The penguin, incidentally, is gazing over her bed in the same manner, from the head of the bed and looking left up to the middle of the bed. She is so amazing. And so gentle and cute. It's just awe inspiring and miraculous. She moved a big physical object. Twice. On two consecutive days.

Of course I wanted to move it again just to make sure my eyes were not tricking me. I did not. My baby clearly wanted these two stuffed animals at either end of her bed for a reason and I was not going to change course on her. We flowered her with love as we sat on her bed and cheered her on, encouraging her to continue to press through on both sides of the veil. We are walking with a miracle maker. We are humbled by our daughter who continues to learn her angel's trade, filled with gentleness and God's power.

Postscript to particular readers: if you are the type of reader who takes this entry, or entries like this, as if it is wrong, or impossible, or ghostly, or any other immature concept like that, please do us all a favor and stop reading this book. You will not understand the full context of the higher life and the wondrous beauty of the life of a guardian angel. I ask mostly that you keep always my Daughter, Kayleigh, in a sacred manner, and her angelic abilities in an estimable place, even if your mind cannot seem to understand her uncorruptible power gifted to her by God. Thank you.

*

Look to the Moon When You Are Lost, She Holds All Power...
02/01/2018

Today was quite a busy day between us. Tonight, nearly six months after your physical death, I found another wonderful Kayleigh-ism, written into the baseboard in your bedroom behind your comfy chair. A message written, presumably, before August 17th, but knowing you - who knows - it could have been last night.

It is clear what you wrote and intended and meant when you marked the board with this sentence. There are so many implications and cross-references and strings of light in this tapestry that, collectively, help write the colors of your existence. You are the Moon, or like the power of the spiritual context of the Moon. We know that. Mary, to the ancients of the church, is The Moon. Her power, that indirect light from the True Light, envelops you, shines through you, encapsulates all that you are. You are like the Moon; in a humble way, and emulating Mary, inspired to be sacred like Mary. You knew that sacredness before the accident and know it still. You are my baby; a young girl, a sister, a daughter, a friend, a guardian angel in the glorious pantheon of graced souls.

And so it was, as I was sweeping the edges of your room tonight after we talked to you about the amazing re-arrangement of your stuffed animal, that I moved your chair near the closet. My eyes were caught by a twelve inch stretch of words scribbled out inches from the floor on the baseboard. I lay on the floor and recognized your handwriting immediately and ran my finger across the words, written by you before the accident. It was in a minute of higher feeling, lifted up by your stuffed animal movement, yet as is customary, also coming at a concurrent time of suffering and pain. I read the words as if you were sitting with me proclaiming them to me, *"Look to the Moon if you are lost. She holds all power."*

Another sign from you. To follow you – an intercessor imbued with God's direction. To gaze towards you, the Moon, when I am lost, which I am frequently. To know that you hold that ultimate power in custody for God. That you are, as an intercessor, an extension of that truth and the answer. That you are, as a guardian angel, indirect light to the Direct Light. That God has gifted us with your ability to guide us, permitting the glory of that status in our blessed family.

"I promise, Babygirl," I cried, tears running down my face, yet rejoicing in our communion, so strong I could almost feel the flesh of your body of light against my frame in a warm embrace. "I hear you, Sweetheart. I see you in your words. I feel you so strongly. I will always follow you, Babygirl."

*

Live 02/02/2018

You desire us to live. You live - right now, in spirit, your spiritual body of light. Your soul and your mind and your personality all wrapped up together in golden white light. Filled with God's beauty and love, you are an incredible, creative, strong and passionate guardian angel. My Baby! I am so very proud of you as you read these words over my shoulder as I write them. You sometimes take over and run the words through my fingers. I am starting to sense when you write through me and when I am writing.

I feel your smile beaming - your soul flutter, knowing how proud your Daddy is - knowing my love and devotion. You frequently gushed with love for me and with me before the accident. That has only changed in that you now gush even more, now freed from your human condition. That amazes me and sustains me and stabilize me. You are amazing, Kayleigh Mickayla Mooney - my Sweet Girl. I ache for you. I miss you tenderly in your physical state. I am in awe of your eternal beauty. I love you.

"Daddy, first of all - of course I gush over you. You are My Daddy and you are the best Daddy ever. I will always be with you. You watch me - you'll see great things, Daddy. Look what I've already figured out how to do. I am learning quickly. Love you."

*

Who You Are 02/02/2018

You are not the two seconds in the street. You are not the four minutes of the rape. You are the light that passed through me as you physically passed in the street. You are the ten months of recovery from the rape. You are the three minute statement in court directly face to face with your rapist forgiving him. You are eternal light.

You will dictate to me our growing relationship. I will then turn to the world and dictate to the world our relationship, and if some in the world don't understand, I do not care. I am not trying to open any hearts or change any minds. I am trying, through this book, to just write out your voice as it unfolds.

There is nobody in Heaven or on earth that I trust more than my Babygirl. Lead me, Sweetheart. You are the most compassionate of the four of us, followed very closely by your brother. You are the deepest thinker of the four of us. And now, with a distinct advantage, you are the omniscient; alight.

I was built to be your Daddy. And I was built to go through this transition with you - nothing prepared me for this in my life and everything gave me a sense of who I am in order to be able to have been locked into you in that transition moment. I am your Daddy.

405

Yours and your brothers. I was built to transition with you and to help your brother continue through this transition. That is remarkable. Our physical presence together in the same body type ended at fifteen. Writing these words makes me want to vomit. It is cruel. It is wrong. It is unnatural. Way too short. But our relationship continues unabated. Through the transition. I am with you. I stand with you. I love you. I am your Daddy. I am your Daddy…

*

Less Limited 02/03/2018

Kayleigh. I love your name. It is so perfectly you. There is no other true Kayleigh to me in the world. We have had a very cool week. Please help me continue on the right path. As you learn how to continue to cross from Heaven to the physical world on Earth, please teach me how to open from the physical world into the spiritual. I am limited as I am stuck in my human form, but can be less limited as I continue down this road. Please help me see, hear and feel - help me stay focused on your vital sixth sense of God and Kayleigh consciousness. You truly are the most amazing girl ever and I add new incredible items to your proud wall every day.

I do like the bumper sticker idea you gave me in meditation this morning and it is hilarious:

"MY GUARDIAN ANGEL DAUGHTER CAN TRANSCEND HEAVEN TO EARTH AND THEREFORE CAN KICK THE SHIT OUT OF YOUR HONOR STUDENT"

It is so you. I love you, Babygirl. A little despondent today, but I also feel balanced enough to breathe and walk and exist and live. It washes over me a hundred times a day, back and forth. It is normal. It is not unhealthy. I am reconciling. I am growing with you. I know there co-exists unselfishness and selfishness to wish the accident had never happened and thereby having you with me physically today. Yes, I want you here desperately in your physical body, at fifteen and nine months old. Yet also, I would not wish to pull you away from the Higher Life. How could I. it is so powerless. Let's walk.

"I love it, by the by. I hear you about your sadness. I understand. But remember, I am really, really safe and happy, Daddy. Don't you want me to be safe and happy? Of course you do. That is what you have always provided me and always wanted for me. I lived a happy and strong physical life. It's different than how we expected on August 16, but the results are the same - I am happy and I'm with you all the time! That makes me really happy! I don't have to miss you while we are apart and I am at school because I am instead with you all day at work. We do this one tiny step at a time, Daddy. Love you!"

*

Outside Edge, Inside Light 02/04/2018

Such a brilliantly complex kid. I sometimes would get tripped up. Sometimes in my own shortcomings I would not give that complexity its space, getting irritated like any father would at a teenage daughter. Yet at other times I bit my tongue, took a step back and honored your space and your individual pursuit of you. In those moments I excelled. In those moments you shined.

You are a kid who wanted to do good and proceeded to do good; who wanted to feel happy and, as a byproduct of living the right type of life, was happy; who wanted the world to see your beauty and your beauty was contagious. I recall when middle school began and several mean girls started ranging against certain girls, it stunned you. You could not believe that anybody would be mean, for no reason, to another. And then one of these mean girl bullies targeted you and it really broke your heart. On your heals, you learned quickly how to push back, but you also learned that a little armor was required. On the outside, you presented a thin shield and tried to put up some rougher edges, just to protect the sanctity you are inside. That outside persona protected you when the world seemed mean and dispiriting. And it, the world, in those moments when the world seemed like a terrible place, or people in it seemed like terrible people, really affected you. It made no sense. And you tried to make sense of it. It hurt you and you felt hurt. So you threw up some walls and some edges to protect the rainbows and glitter. To protect the brilliant light that you nurtured inside. Outside images were not always inside reality. Most people are like this in one way or another and you certainly had your own voice in the matter.

It was quite easy to see what you were doing. You were so smart with it, and the edge was, well, was not really an edge at all. You had your own flair; your own fashion; your own style. Almost everybody who knows you would comment on how cool you were; how amazing your makeup was done; how outgoing and fantastic you were; how you were a judgment free zone, a truly accepting person. I watched this transition from childhood to middle childhood in middle school and was very proud of you. I recall vividly when some of the mean girls bullied your very dear friend and she had only you to go trick or treating with. Your choice was to go with her, and absorb some of the bullying and isolation that was coming her way, or ignore her and go along with the gang. It was never an option. You and she enjoyed an amazing Halloween, as you ignored the bullies in the crowd. That represents you perfectly. An edge to protect yourself; an inner sanctity of innocence that was never tarnished.

*

The Light - Always With Light 02/05/2018

She was alight in many pictures throughout the years. An iridescent light surrounded her - radiating from her. Around her beautiful face and washed through her hair. Auras are difficult to ascertain around an individual, but not so with Kayleigh. Hers was visible for those willing to see. She was an angel packed into the confines of a human life and human body. Slightly uncomfortable as an evolved soul packed into the limits of a human life, yet always divine. Now she is that same angel freed from that confine - awakened to God's light that has always been hers. She shines unhindered. She is teaching the world about the beauty of love by transcending death itself.

"Thank You, Daddy, For Being My Daddy"

Daddy, there is Daddy!
You have come, of course, you have come;

Let me hear your voice,
For I can no longer see you,
Let me hear your light,
It leads me to truly perceive you,
Your love illuminates this night,
In the moment when I most need you,
Unaware of what has happened to me,
But in your voice - there is only comfort,
Your words breathe across my ear,
Washing away any seedlings of fear,
You told me I would be okay,
You told me you loved me,
That you were right here by my side,
There is no sense of panic and no alarm,
You lay out an atmosphere of calm,
And held me as I sang your song,
...And died in my Daddy's arms....

...Thank you, Daddy, thank you.

*

Present, And Specks of Light on Nathaniel 02/06/2018

Thank you for your continued intervention in our lives. Two times yesterday for sure you intervened and that was only the times that we were really aware. I know you are present. Come sit behind me, beside me, in front of me, with me. Lead your Daddy toward you today.

"I am here, Daddy. Keep searching."

I feel you. A warmth. A slight pressure on the side of my head. A kiss upon my forehead. A light drawing out from my third eye or from the top of my head. You are gloriously strong and gentle, awake and full of spiritual life. Last night you showed yourself as specks or points of light hovering about your baby brother, whom you live so tenderly. Captured last night as we pulled up in front of our old house, it was amazing. It was very dark outside. We stopped and stared at the house, me with tears welling as they do daily when I pass the house you two grew up in.

We noticed that my Dad's tree seemed to have grown, noticing its height on this night and commented to Nate that it looked about nine feet tall. He disagreed. So we stopped and I told him to stand next to it and I'd take a picture. I took two. I could vaguely sense either Kayleigh jumping out of the car with him to take a picture with him and Grandpa Bill's tree, or, Kayleigh whispering something to me - it is subtle sometimes and I don't always catch it in the moment.

When we drove the seven houses to our new house we looked at the images. We enlarged them. We were astounded once again. Like a loose halo around his head there were tiny white dots, like tiny fires surrounding him. Across his chest and on his legs were several other dots of light. These were not reflections from my Dad's tree adorned with Christmas lights. Nor were these a camera trick from the iPhone. Neither did I use the flash on the camera. These were little sparkles of light, as if she was standing next to him in our old yard. These were not visible when I took the picture yet appear very clearly in these photos. Kayleigh was here. There was no extra light to catch. It was you. We showed Mommy and the three of us erupted into a collective cheer for you.

She has told me in meditation that she can show herself in her physical form, even though we can't quite see her, composed of one million points of light draping down her long blonde hair, merging with her long whitish gold gowns and enlightening her angelic face. A few of these powerful lights penetrated the physical world, surrounded her brother with protective, endearing light.

We used to say a prayer together every night with slight variations for each of us, generally as this: "God, please put a golden shield of protection around Kayleigh and Nathaniel..." That golden shield is real. That golden shield is love. That golden shield is unbreakable and eternal. Now, that golden shield is Kayleigh.

We had another: "God, please help Kayleigh and Nathaniel shine brighter than a million suns..." I believe that each of us, though sheathed in human skins and human experience, shines somewhere inside this brightly. When we are released from this constrictive human chamber that light explodes effortlessly upon loved ones in its full magnitude and glory. Kayleigh is as bright as a million suns. Kayleigh is a blanket for us of a million suns. Kayleigh, reflecting and refracting God's light through her pure soul, is our guide. Kayleigh is.

You are here. Here now. I walk humbly in your graceful light, My Darling. I love you.

"I love you too, Daddy. That was me! You saw me! I exerted myself with my light. I am always with my baby brother. Tell him I love him. I am worried about him, Daddy. He really needs you though he says he's okay. How could he be? Help him, Daddy. I know you do and you will. You always figure us out. You are a constant to both of us and you have been a guiding light for him in his grief. I know you are tired. I know you all are tired. I promise, you are on the right path. Keep walking. Love you."

"Growing Light"

Dear Father, breathe the scent of Heaven's light,
Lavender radiance - petals sing,
Dear Father, peacefully, still the mind and you shall see,
Aglow, wispy blaze - it captures the third eye's single gaze,
Dwell within the sound of light,
For I am here and I am alive,
Dear Father,
Dear Father,
The love I hold for you withstands all threats of all forms of night,
The love I know in you fuels this light,
This light I grow with you.

*

"Daughter Light II" 02/07/2018

And you, with loving light,
Persist and prevail,
And with your soul alight,
Your song - the steady wind for the sturdy sail,
And you are magnificence,
You are brilliantly graced,
Adorned with the melodies,
Like rainbows ablaze,
And you are the guardian,
My child, guide my world,
For no one I would trust more exists,
Than my little girl,
And all that I treasure,
And all that I miss,
Resides in those blue bold eyes,
And upon my cheek with a kiss,
And if I shall falter,
Bring me to my truth,
And if I wander in the haze,
Light my pathway back to you,
For you are my Everything,
The guidance through life,
Empowered with God's peace eternally,
You, my Daughter, you are the purest,
The purest, my Daughter, of light.

*

The Heaviness the Visits Lessen 02/08/2018

It just got real heavy again in the last hour. I don't want to convey in these writings that somehow this doesn't happen. It happens multiple times a day. A lot of these writings are me attempting to walk through grief. When these troubles come, she quickly tries to pull me back on the path she is on - not the path she is no longer on, focusing on where I can find her, in her body of light, and not where I cannot find her, in her physical body that is gone. I drift longingly backwards as if she's off at college and I can't wait for the semester to end so I can hold her in my arms physically again and smell her hair and hear her warm giggle. My God. My God. A simple, innocent, perfect accident.

I never want her to stop visiting me and I fear sometimes that she will visit me and get an overwhelming reaction from me mixed with joy and deep sadness, and she will think, I don't want to hurt Daddy with deep sadness so maybe I should stay away. Kayleigh I know you are hearing me think this as I write this and you are able to read this while I wrote this. Know this: your visiting me sustains me. Yes, it causes me to miss what we were on the physical plain, but I miss that already so it doesn't add any angst. It also provides me incredible comfort on this plain knowing you are with me spiritually and our relationship continues to grow. So when you see me cry or see me getting overwhelmed, it is not because your visits prompt that reaction. Your visits prevent those reactions mostly. Your visits reconcile the loss. So please continue to visit as its magic outweighs any longing that may be associated with it.

"Tears"

Shadowed sheets or freezing rain,
A howling wind stirs with pain,
Waning, weathering, eroding,
This man's earthly coating,
Weakening the framing,
Discoloring, salt staining,
Burn the towers down with waterfalls,
Bury the rooms, the walkways, the ruined halls,
Flooded with this sorrow, this sadness enraged,
Touched by the sharpened blades of spinning hurricanes,
That feed across my oceans as I call out your name,
Flurried in the blizzards of loss.

*

Just Now 02/08/2018

You amaze me, my Love. I heard you just now, Kayleigh. You said that we were the best Daddy-Daughter combination you've ever seen. That the relationship, this incredible relationship, did not end with your physical death. Rather, it enhanced and continues to enhance. Now, instead of physically and effortlessly sitting on the couch in two physical forms together, where we most like would not, but we might, take time for granted, now we have to work in a different manner. You told me that you have to work at learning how to penetrate the physical plain to be with me. You have done this incredibly. Your loyalty like a shield of light surrounding me. And I need to focus and center and try to push into the spiritual world, which is not easy, encased in this human life. But I yearn and so do you, which adds light to our relationship, the best Daddy-Daughter combination I've ever seen too.

I listen to you. I trust you. I take your messages clearly as opportunities and as direction from the soul I trust the most in any world. I love you, Babygirl. Keep talking to me. I will keep listening. I will keep learning. I will transcend the spiritual world. I am a warrior and nothing will stop me from being with both of my children.

"Daddy, keep writing. We have an important story to tell. You can do it, Daddy! Love you! Also, I love when we have Daddy-Daughter time. Let's always make sure we do this, many times a day. Love you!"

*

Family 02/10/2018

If there's one person in this family who understood the value of family more than the other three of us it was and is you. We all understood and lived by that creed - family was first in everything we did. Yet there was one of us who would be thoughtful enough, on a very frequent basis, to express that sentiment, not only physically through our words and laughter and smiles, but also through writings. It was you who would leave little messages. It was you who drew pictures about family. Throughout the years a note here, a drawing there - all focused on one thing: how much family meant to you and means to you.

The day I came home from work and you came over to me and hugged me and said you had something for me - an experience that I had gotten used to - set me in our usual manner to sit and focus on the thing that was causing you so much joy in seeking my audience.

"I made you a bookmark for your Big Book," you said proudly and smiled at me.

I looked in my A.A. Big Book and found a bookmark, measured to the exact size of the book's pages, and filled with tiny thumbnail images, one inch by one inch photo copies - of Mommy, Nathaniel, you and me. You drew several hearts on the bookmark and wrote just one word: "family."

You made this for my A.A. book so that every day I opened my book, as I did and do twice a day, I would see this beautiful bookmark and its message - not much different than the message you sent me from Heaven fifteen years before you were born. That message is simply, "Daddy, you can do this." The new translation was a little deeper here at ten years old and I knew it immediately - that family was the greatest gift derived from my sobriety and without my sobriety there is no family. Once again, you were reminding me of the incredible work I had put into my sobriety and reminding me of the incredible work in my sobriety that still lay ahead. At ten you conveyed that message. Ten years old.

I've had that bookmark for six years now at this writing and still see it daily. I am still reminded of its message daily. I still kiss it and nourish the strength of your word and take it to heart every time I open my Big Book. You are amazing. We are an amazing family now on a different configuration, but a strong family of four nonetheless. Without my sobriety there is no family. Without my sobriety I cannot love through my humanness to be in touch with you on the other side. I will cherish my sobriety, Kayleigh, as I always have, as a condition precedent to everything else in my life, including the most important thing to us besides my sobriety - this magnificent family. Thank you for your constant reminders. Family. Family.

"Not Alone"

Not alone, no, not I,
A seam in the air - its veil defied,
Dwelling within the soul - vacant in eye,
She was triumphant and sings while we have crumbled and cried -

Change is upon us - chancing the known,
She is about us - this luminescent soul,
She kissed my forehead - embracing my frame,
She whispered direction to walk through the pain -

No, I am not here facing anything alone,
She with her wisdom - and love,
From which this light has grown,
Engages me - expanding her glow,
Illuminating the every chamber of every inch of my soul.

*

Losses and Gain 02/11/2018

I have physically lost you in this world. I have spiritually gained you in this world and the next. It is still you and still me. It is still our relationship. While I continue to reconcile your physical loss, the final reconciliation point being my physical death, I grow with you through intention and effort and clarity where I can find it. You played that "Amazing" song by the Cocteau Twins yesterday, which I used to sing to Big Boy, and hum to you. Thank you. I hear you. I am humbled. Please keep trying and learning. And be patient please. It is such an intimate subtly at times that most people, not knowing our relationship, would not be able to catch. But I do. I know you.

See? The wind-chimes just started to sing while I am writing with you. Coincidence? For the faint at heart. Not to me. You are here, My Love. Sing. I love, love, love, love your voice.

"Thank you, Daddy. I love singing. Do you really love my voice? I was getting pretty good before the accident, wasn't I? You keep singing too, My Daddy, and keep watching my videos. I love doing that together. Pet Spirit for me. Love you!"

*

Identity for Father 02/12/2018

I was built to be her Father. Built to be Nathaniel's as well. It Was part of my self-worth - my willing and happy sacrifice as a Father, my devotion to molding and shaping my babies, with their inherent goodness and light into incredible people. Part of my identity touching base with her encouraging her guiding and directing her. It was a muscle so frequently used it became part of the daily machinery. Intentional and deliberate. I loved those opportunities. I lived for them. Now that's gone. I need to continuously invert it so she can guide me.

I take many times a day, sometimes just minutes, and sometimes longer meditations, to be alone with Kakes. She is starting to work her way through the dimensions in various channels. It is other worldly, this connection, yet it is also so familiar and logical that it is as common to me as my breath. I felt her touch my hair tonight. It was like electric fingers gently running through my hair, but not touching my scalp. Again, it came with a feeling, knowing that it was her. I was sitting. Nothing was resting against my head. Nothing was touching my hair. Except for my amazing daughter.

*

Present 02/14/2018

We hear people say, "she lives on in your heart," or "keep her memories alive." Both of these sentiments, although good intentioned, miss the mark of reality and are frustrating to hear because it represents people speaking at us, instead of listening to us. It is true that Kayleigh is indeed present, however, not in my heart only. She is present even without my heart. She is present wherever she wants to be present - in my heart - outside of my heart - in Heaven - here sitting beside me. She does not need my heart to be present. She is...all by herself.

And her memory – keep it alive? My volumes of tens of thousands of memories of her physical life are a living testament to our love. All of the memories we share since the accident are witness to the raw and immaculate continuation of our relationship without pause. I guess the notion is, "you have your memories - keep them close at mind." I guess. I have my memories from both albums - before and after the accident, and make new memories with Kakes every new day. But again - I don't need to solely rely upon my memories before her passing. I have an ongoing, current, active relationship with Kakes right here and right now.

Again, the words are very important, particularly in a sacred situation like this. Perhaps, Kayleigh, you can help retrain the way the world uses these words improperly. Or, even better, maybe you can remind people who haven't suffered as we have, that we don't need words of wisdom; we need ears of wisdom. We know what we are going through and how to manage this, because we have no choice and are forced to face the most incredible odds and pain and suffering every second of every day. I will structure our doorway with thoughtfulness, using the right words as its frame through which I can engage in spiritual obedience, reputation of the same basic ideas, to grow deeper and further with you, My Love.

My Valentine on this day, as you are each year, I love you.

*

Transformation 02/15/2018

Physical death is transformation of life - the spark, the light - the mind, emotion and spirit continue on like nothing in time has disturbed it. And so it is with you, My Darling - I know you. I feel your soul with me. You work miracles. I move into your light with intention and devotion - My Love, I miss your physical presence with my every ounce of love and embrace your spirit in its totality on the spiritual as well as this physical plain. You amaze me. I love you, Kakes.

"I love you too, Daddy. It was really fun walking in your dreams last night. Let's do that again! Love you!"

*

Today Is Six Months 02/17/2018

Broken heart. I am really struggling. Sleep is off. Work is off. My Daddy-Daughter time is off. I am watching Jessica crumble. I am watching Nate fall apart. I am seeing myself dissolve in the mirror. This is what has become of us at times in the harsh consequence of such a tragedy.

It is not your fault, Sweetheart. Please know this. We all know you never intended any of this and it was a true and simple accident. We also know that you didn't even make a mistake. Stepping off the curb to come home was not a mistake and I am proud of that step. What happened just after that moment was the accident. We all know you desperately wish to be with us and that you are here in the ways that you can be. Please help us re-invigorate and take reconciliation in hand one step at a time. I hate everything that has happened to us, but I love what you've done with it. Your transformation is epic and brilliant and I am so proud of you. (I feel you touching my hair as you do to remind me of your presence, as I edit this).

I will slow down today and watch for you and hear for you. Intently, I am awake, through the grief and the horror, the processing of trauma and the need to continue to function in a life that has been obliterated of its familiarity. I love you.

"I love you too, Daddy, so, so much. I am here. Slow down. Breathe. You can do this. You can."

"Six Months on This Sea"

Pitch and roll on hungry waves,
In this swirling engine of a hurricane,
With this seething, grieving soul,
That feeds the ocean with its pain,
Above a graveyard of ships, I breathe,
Mine has somehow been sustained,
Six months on this sea,
Six months on this sea -

There was no ocean with this name,
With no choice but this pursuit,
All the storms and the heavy blows,
With no charts to help me through,
Someday I dream a sturdy land,
And there I will find you,
But will I be subdued,
Will I be subdued -

Daughter Dear, I travel on,
With your presence on my sleeve,
As I stagger on these waves,
And bleed across this sea,
I grieve for you, Darling,
I grieve as I gasp in disbelief -
Six months into many more years,
And many more the tears,
Many more the tears.

*

Don't Forget to Dance Part II 02/17/2018

On the six month anniversary of your physical passing, I downloaded "Don't Forget to Dance" and promised you that we would dance together that night. True to my word, I gathered my headphones and went to your room. Spirit lay on your bed. I pet him and closed the door. Your tiny Christmas tree, which I have had lit since early December, set a colorful glow in your room.

I found our song and hit play, tucking my phone in my pocket and holding six year old Kayleigh in my right arm, extending my left arm out to hold your tender hand in mine. I close my eyes and we danced this night in your room.

As I sway back and forth, muscle memory took over quite quickly and naturally. I dipped with the music and spun as you loved to spin, laughing and throwing back your hair. I could see you in my memory. I could feel your presence in my arms, tucked up against your Father securely, safely, gently. You can present at any age. Tonight you were a little girl with her Daddy.

You rested your head on my shoulder half way through the song, just as you used to do, letting go of my hand and wrapping your right arm around my neck. I placed my left hand between your shoulders and continued to sway and dance to the music. It was perfectly lovely having this dance with you, my Daughter, six months after your physical death.

As we neared the end of the song I took your hand again and spun and spun and spun. Your hilarious cackling rattled through the years, passing all understanding and transcending our worlds. Your smile, like the rising sun, beamed and lit up your angelic face. Your eyes - as always - your eyes smiled when looking at your Father. Only this time, instead of looking on your Father with your human eyes as a little girl with butterflies in your heart, you were looking upon me in your angelic form, wise beyond centuries and warmed in the perfect presence of love.

This was our dance. Nobody needed to know about it and nobody needed to see it. I perfectly don't care if anybody does know that I danced with my baby's soul in my arms and don't care if anybody would have caught a glimpse of me dancing, seemingly alone. I was not alone. Hardly. Never have I been more in God's and my guardian angel's presence. I know my truth. I know our light. It was four and a half of the happiest minutes I've had in six months, dancing with my Babygirl as we did years ago. It's still magical, Kakes, dancing with you. Thank you for this wonderful moment. I didn't forget. I never did. Not with you and your brother. Never.

"Daddy, Don't Let the Music Die"

I will play you a song,
Any song you'd like,
Daddy, Daddy, sing along,
And track across your life,
You have gold in the air,
That will never right this wrong,
But may help you, Daddy,
When the grief is heavy and the days are long,
Daddy, oh Daddy -

Daddy, don't let the harmony die,
For in it there is a place for you and me,
It is a place with quilted sunshine,
And rainbows flowing with purity and peace,
That you find in your dreams,
When you cry until you sing,
Sing this song to me,
Sing this song to me,
Daddy -

In this sudden tragedy,
I was ripped from your embrace,
I see the sadness - it collects,
Like jagged pools in your face,
Listen, Daddy, close your eyes,
For my soul - it hasn't died,
Listen as I sing,

Listen as I sing...

...And be the sparkle in my eyes.

*

Convey Direction and Candle Voice 02/18/2018

You are very near. I know you are trying to convey direction to me. I can't explain it, but intuitively I can feel it. Please show me how to be continuously open to further receive your words and see what it is you want your Daddy to see and do. I feel your devotion and love and know that our relationship is growing stronger day by day. We are six months into this new configuration and getting our legs. The intensity is tantamount to looking into the sun. It is blinding and beautiful, the source of all life, the sun within the sun. I am here, Babygirl, and never leaving your side.

"Daddy, good job! Keep coming back to the moment – keep open. You're doing great, Daddy. You can do this. I know you can. I love you so much."

I love you too, Honey. I've learned already that your voice comes in different ways – in the wind; in the wind-chimes; through electronics; in the trees; in candles; through meditation; in water. A thousand avenues for your voice to traverse the heavens to reach my heart. Your voice sometimes appears in the physical world somehow, sometimes an inch within my right ear. Tonight as I lit your candles in the front yard and I swear you appeared in the picture I took of the candle, just after I wrote a poem about you speaking through candle flames. As I snapped three pictures quickly back to back, the middle picture shows the flame cut off midpoint, as if you were moving about it and your energy blocking it from view with your soul's presence.

You are magical. I am so glad I was intentional today – I love my Daddy-Daughter time and my Daddy-Son time; I always have and promise that we will daily have what we daily had, just at a higher level and in a way that makes sense in our new configuration. Come to me in my dreams. I will try tonight to drift deep enough to open my dreams like a doorway for your gracious spirit to pass through. Love you.

"Love you, Daddy. My Daddy!"

*

Poles 02/20/2018

What we are going through, at the poles, are as opposite as one can imagine - the horror of a childhood physical death, followed by the miracle of that child transitioning into a guardian angel and remaining firmly entrenched in our lives. I use to have a center, a center I would explain to people as the results of living a spiritual, inventoried life. Now that center has been obliterated and I've adjusted it to the great balancing act of these very opposite poles; yet the fabric of my spirituality has increased. If we have to have the first situation, a tragic physical death, she clearly understood that we could not survive without the second pole, her spiritual presence. It really isn't rocket science. She is alive. She is in love with her family. She desires to be with her family. So she is. My miracle worker.

"This Is What I Need"

You ask me what I need –

But is it sincere,
Is it an act of kindness,
Or confusion,
Or just acting out of fear,
Is it a drone on the daily tongue,
Without true sentiment we share,
Then in the pause you describe what I need,
And I vacate this atmosphere;

I do not need silver crusted encouraging words,
Nor platitudes for they would be absurd,

I do not desire advice,
For, from such a lack of experience, it would be a curse,
I do not need the blind to see for me,
Nor to be told nothing that is worse,
Than somehow you understand,
When your child has not been ripped from your hand,
No, I do not need these words;

Will you listen - let me talk,
Even if the words wrap in circles,
Will you let the cycle walk,
Will you let me stumble through this,
And break and then collapse,
And let my mind tire after many, many laps,
Will you sit here in the jungle,
Where the wild vines grow within, without, above and beneath,
For if you are willing to sit here and listen,
This is what I need.

*

Hey, You Who Haven't Suffered the Physical Loss of A Child - Stop Giving Me Advice 02/21/2018

In our modern social media world every time most people see a platform, they think it is a natural stage for them to voice their self-centered opinions, occasionally on topics they know nothing about. The modern man and woman never seemed to find a platform they couldn't use. Case in point – a man, not married and having no children, telling me that, "this too shall pass," that, "I need to move on," that, "things will get better." No and No and No. And a woman, married with children, who has not experienced the physical death of a child, telling me, "You will heal in time," that, "your living child needs you," that, "everything happens for a reason." No and Yes, but both of my children are living and both need me, and No.

This is intolerable. Anyone who hasn't gone through this needs to just listen. We are the unfortunate, but also the unfortunate experts, and also, are the fortunate few who are living a miracle. It is strangely fascinating watching people think that they need to give me words of wisdom, like they have to dig into their reservoir of zingers and say something profound in order to be on the same plain as me with this - mostly people who have no clue and haven't gone through this horror. Number one, you are not on the same plain as someone like me, unless your child has physically died in childhood. And I am sorry for the loss of your grandmother or your father in the natural course of life, but that is not nearly the same thing. There is no bridge. Do not build one. It is not welcome. It is not reality. It can only serve to build, in its place, a chasm.

"Another Father with His Girl"

I see a father with his girl,
The center of his world,
They coo and they laugh,
As the love about them stirs,
Don't take it for granted,
I never did, Sir,
I live with no regrets,
As I try to live without the physical state of my girl -

I see a life that was occupied,
With an effortless, effervescent light,
We engaged in each day,
In a range to fill a hundred lives,
We were two of the same,
If in a twin I could delight,
I live with such loss here,
Since my Daughter lost her life;

Rest your head on my arm,
On my shoulder, on my lap,
Where we cry with each other,
And fall to floor with heavy laugh,
Rest my soul, pretty Darling,
In those moments when I gasp,
Longing for you near,
Longing for you here,

For I am very well aware,
That your physical body is gone,
But you, you are still here.

*

Wind-chimes 02/21/2018

A dusting of golden white light charged in the air at the tips of your angelic fingers, like a wand waving slowly throw the wind-chimes and sparking in this physical world. You move the tiny metal bars and sing to us through their melody. Clearly it is you. Yes, at times it is just the wind. Sometimes it is a mixture of the wind and you, as you channel and travel through the vehicle of its gentle breeze. Yet at other times, when the night is still, when no wind, not even a faint whisper eclipses the yard, the wind-chimes sing in your voice. An angel's song of permanence. Of presence. Of guarding her family. Of love and pure devotion, reminding us frequently – that, "I am here and I am in love with you and I will never leave your side."

*

Passion 02/22/2018

You need me more today than you ever have. We are in a relationship. If I am blocked then the relationship is blocked. If I am stuck in despondency the relationship chokes. If, God forbid, I stopped doing my work, resulting in relapse, our relationship dies. The logic in all of this is simple: just as you did prior to the accident, you need your Daddy as I need my Daughter. We love our relationship. We build that fortitude. For that relationship I fight. I kick. I scream through the darkness. I persevere through immeasurable pain and odds that refute logic. I have cried every day for over six months. I have fallen down every day for over six months. I have given you a great father every day over the last six months. I have picked myself up and trudged forward.

When I work through the pain and feel empowered in the passion, I sense your works. You are placing a jigsaw together seamed with love and light around the edges of every piece. You are preparing something magical and incredible for us. You are. I feel it and I feel you in the air about me. Surrounding me. Protecting me. Reaching out to me. Telling me to trust you - that if I do, I will be amazed. There is no one I trust like you. Amaze me, my Little Girl.

*

Full Potential 02/22/2018

Your death ended your physical life here but did not end your spiritual life; rather, your death released your spirit to its full potential. And while I struggle with a million challenges and I dream to turn back the clock and re-arrange events to preserve your physical life with me, underneath it all, in my core, I know that you are continuing to actualize and you are reaching your soul's complete potential. I see you strengthening every day. I hear you strengthening every day. Your voice grows with light. Your soul glows with love. Your essence permeates the air about me like it is the air itself, for me to breathe and ingest and use to push through to another hard minute, minutes that flow glacier-like across centuries in the deadly plain of one second; each second.

"Yes, Daddy, my full potential," you say, cheering me on through our writing and the perspective I continually reconstruct to keep me moving in a balanced path. It would be easy to lay down and die - so easy, it would make my loved ones frightened to know - I imagine it from time to time, fantasizing its release from this horror and horrible pain. It is not a suicide thought. Or a thought of escape. It is peaceful. It is the thought of transition into fullness. Yet it is a mere mirage until it isn't. A misguided fiction I derive from the grief, not wanting to live this life without you physically and not wanting to suffer all of the days before me, absent my Daughter's physical body by my side.

I see a twenty something year old girl walking her dog. She looks like you. I see a toddler in a cute blue and pink dress. A little Kayleigh-Kakes. I see a child getting a driver's license, going to a dance, walking to the store, buying a bikini, graduating high school, talking on her phone, going to college, getting married, having a baby. All around me, a million people who get to do what you do not get to do. Many of whom don't know how lucky they are.

Then I come back to the bigger picture, which is not the easier picture, acknowledging that almost everything about this situation sucks. There is one silver lining. It sits on the horizon like a thin veil of faded light an hour before sun up on the ocean, setting its mystic glow on the distant waters and slowly blooming upon the sea. This silver lining rises and expands and explodes into morning, a fiery sun that warms the faces of early rising beachcombers.

On the morning of your physical death that silver lining grew, and through the ensuing days, more and more powerfully. As you learned how to balance in your new state of being; as you learned how to cross the air to jostle the edges of the physical world about us; as you mastered your wings - you rose and your light exploded across our faces just like the sun, to forever be our warmth and our sustenance. And it continues just like the prayer we said together a few thousand times since you were a toddler, "God, please help Kayleigh shine brighter than a million suns." The prayer we said at night for each of us I recite again now in the depths of my grief. Carry me through, my love, on a prayer that radiates like the sun across a summer's brilliant sea.

"Endless Days"

I've got a spark in my hand,
A tiny universe,
A realm of the spirit,
Into which I am immersed,
It dreams itself golden,
Like lightning strikes a wave,
This electric stream,
Crosses frontiers I cannot save -

I've got a photo in my hand,
A memory of grace,
She was laughing and lighthearted,
With a glow upon her face,
It dreams itself spoken,
As if arranging future days,
This electric stream,
Crosses this frontier where I've sheltered to pray...

...Where she touches me with endless, endless days.

*

Jekyll Night Walk 02/23/2018

Some of my most cherished memories, spending time with my favorite people at my favorite place - my kids, at night, in the heat of summer, the stars above me, a humid breeze, on the beach. Jekyll.

Nathaniel had trailed into the house with Mommy. It was Daddy-Daughter time. Two lounge chairs in the dunes, just fifty feet from the backdoor of the house. A quiet Atlantic breeze. Salt and sand scents drifting about us. A humid rash of heat. The rattle of the warped oaks behind us. The sound of the ocean rolling against the engineer wall fifty feet further down the dunes and in front of us. Peace. My Heaven with my favorite girl in the world.

After we talked for a long while you wanted to go for a walk by yourself and told me I could just go inside. You wanted to be alone on the beach, not because we were having a hard moment, and not because you didn't want to be with me, but because we had just spent some great quality time together and you felt the magic of the night and wanted to own it. It was your time. Midnight. Your beach.

"Okay, have a nice walk - do you want me to go with you?" I asked.

"Thanks. No, I'm okay. You can go inside, Daddy. You don't have to worry about me."

"I always worry about you, Sweetie."

"I know you do, Daddy," she said and smiled, "but I'm a big girl. I'll be okay."

I thought about my Baby, ten months after a rape, walking on the beach at night, alone, and running into three or four drunk boys. Granted, there are almost never three or four drunk boys on this desolate stretch of Jekyll Island. In fact I have never seen that in twenty five years on Jekyll. It is a safe beach. But still - this is my Daughter.

She stood up, leaned over me and kissed me on the forehead. "Go inside," she said and ran her fingers through her hair.

"Love you, Baby," I said as I stood up, "Have fun."

"Thanks, Daddy," she replied. "I'll be okay."

I smiled. Then I walked off in the darkness towards the house and looked over my shoulder, watching her walk off down to the right around the dunes and walking south on the beach. As she turned the corner of the large dune I stopped and continued to watch her, fully intending on staying on the dunes and ensuring she was safe. Her iPhone illuminated her position as she continued her journey alone.

I watched her iPhone sway back and forth in the darkness. She walked away from me as I stood there with my chair in front of me. She would not be able to see me in the shadows from there. I sat back down and turned the chair in her direction. I could tell that she had only wandered two or three hundred yards and climbed up atop the rocks.

I laughed. She was so cute. Finding her bliss but being safe about it, staying within striking distance of the house in the event she ran into trouble. I was relieved, but really, not frightened. Just conflicted. If she had walked five miles she would have been safe. Yet here she was within site in the darkness.

I sat with God, listening for direction on our next steps as a family. I meditated and relaxed, doing what I love to do at the beach at night. The stars were plenty and the humid air was perfect - just almost hot enough to stifle you into sweating, but not quite. Perfection. August. Georgia.

A half hour into my sitting alone I called her, pretending I was at the house. I hid the light of my phone, but watched her phone faintly light up in the distance.

"Hi, Daddy!" She said.

"Hey, Baby, whatcha doin?"

"Just sitting on the rocks and checking YouTube and stuff."

"Oh that's great, Sweetheart."

"Yeah, it is beautiful out here. I love it."

"Great, Kakes. Me too. It's so awesome spending time on the beach at night. Have fun. When do you think you'll be back?"

"I don't know. Maybe another hour or so?"

"Okay. Whenever. You're a young woman now. Have fun."

"Love you."

"Love you."

I continued my meditation. It was wonderful. Occasionally I glanced down into the darkness. She was still there sitting on the rocks.

An hour later, I noticed the phone shine again, moving around. I could tell she was climbing back up from the rocks and likely coming home. I confirmed the little light from her phone moving down from a height and making her way back to the sandy plain behind the rocks. I backed my chair up in the darkness closer to the house and watched a few minutes. She was definitely coming home. I didn't want her to bust me.

I laughed and scurried back to the house with my chair, leaving it on the back deck as I entered the house and ran over to the couch and turned on the TV, awaiting her return.

Maybe ten minutes later, I heard her walk in the back door. The door closed. She was safe. And none the wiser of my hanging back in the dunes to ensure her safety. She sat with me and smiled.

"How was your walk?" I asked.

"It was great," she said, her face beaming, her smile from ear to ear and lifting up her apple cheeks.

"I'm happy to hear, Sweetheart."

"Me too," she said, smiled and bounced off to bed, "goodnight, Daddy. I love you so much."

"I love you too, Peanut."

*

Intention 02/24/2018

My intention is to demonstrate my love for you. You certainly know my love for you as well as my undying devotion. It is effortless for me really – it is part of my DNA as your Father. To get creative with our time together is nothing I haven't done before, actually, even before you were born. Now I am in the crux of a strange tradeoff. When you were physically alive I had those tangible interactions of emotion, physical, spiritual and mental, but limited time with you and the spiritual aspect of our lives contained within the shell of our physical, human lives. Now, with that container gone for you, I do not have those physical moments (although sometimes you penetrate the physical world), but your soul has been unleashed and I have your spirit with me 24/7/4EVER. That is significant.

When you were a child and I was at work I would typically only get a few hours with you physically a day. Now I get no hours with you physically, which devastates me daily, but I get all day of this relationship spiritually. The relationship grows along that significant line. I am your Father, you, my Daughter. Now, you are also my guide as I walk this earth where I used to be your guide. Grant me your spark of motivation. We grow and we transform. We trade places. Yet at the core one thing remains and never changes – our light, our love, our dedication, our resolve. I resolve to love you, and will never be thwarted from that light. I love you, Sweetheart.

"Love you too, Daddy. Well said! I am so proud of you for understanding all you understand. Most people don't, but you do. It is a testament to how much you cherish and love me which makes me so happy. I shine amazingly bright, but somehow, you add a bit more to that brightness. I am so lucky you are my Daddy."

*

Baby Moon 02/25/2018

Hey Kakie, how are you girl, today? How are you, Baby Moon? I sit in the backyard at ten o'clock at night at the end of February on a warm, unusual night under a moon almost full - spending my time just thinking about you. Always thinking about you. Always thinking about you. Just like two Canadian Geese that I see on occasion; one wounded, and the other, which never leaves his side. You and I travel, though my wings are wounded and I am tired with lesser strength. You never leave my side.

You are beautiful tonight. Your light is magnetic. Radiant. Alive. Thank you for our talk tonight. Thank you for wrapping me in your wind. I felt you. I sensed you. I saw you.

*

If I Was Your Child 02/26/2018

If I was your child I would be the luckiest child in the world. I know we have inverted, but I don't know how to be the child in our relationship. I am your Father. My job is to protect you and guide you and nurture you and help you grow up with structure. I always told you that I wasn't raising children to be children. I was raising children to be adults and I gave you a thousand lessons that you cherish deeply. Now it is your turn, but I need to learn how to be your child and let you take care of me. If it is anything like you being my child, then I am going to feel constantly loved and supported. That is exactly what it is. Thank you.

"Your Voice"

The candle light - your voice,
Its tongue of flame in dance, it speaks,
Your fire and your laughter,
On warm wind, its fuel, feeds,
Through the darkness blaze, a path,
I have heard the flicker breathe,
Throwing golden light like lightning palm reeds,
To cushion my wary feet,
I am listening, my Love,
Darling, I believe.

*

Why Hello 02/27/2018

Why hello, Daughter. This morning is calm. There is nothing that should rattle my life after what we've been through. Yet, I am still human and will feel threatened and rattled from time to time. My perspective has changed, but the rattle will come. It is how I weather it that has amplified. In those moments I turn to you and God to slow me down, direct me, and empower me with your light to re-stabilize my eyes. This is nothing I ever wanted, but it is as it horrifically is, and since it is, and you and I have a chance to be together only if I do my work, my God, Kakes, I am going to do my work. Nothing stops me from being with both of my children.

"Why hello, Father. Thanks, Daddy. You can do this – keep pushing. Keep relaxing. And taking breaks. You know I get worried about you. I always have. I love you so much. Let's together go have a great day."

*

My Sobriety 02/28/2018

My sobriety is yours. You helped create it and shape it. I stretched it and honed it partly for you and your brother. You both own a piece of it. A large piece of it. It is yours. It is not mine to destroy or threaten or risk. It is not mine to ignore or damage. It is your jewel which I polish daily as a gift to you, and to your brother, and your mother, and ultimately, to God.

"Daddy, your sobriety means the world to me. Thank you for always being there for me. I see how strong your sobriety is and always has been. Keep going, Daddy, you can do this. Love you!"

*

Fear of Not Real 03/01/2018

It happens. Of course it happens. I am human and I am tucked into this human brain and human mind and human emotion and human experience. We are pre-programmed to deny the existence of anything outside of our senseless egos. Some of us struggle less with this than others. Others live a life vacant of this light. Some are illuminated.

Then some horrific tragedy like the one my family is experiencing happens and it shakes you to the core, bending your eyes, fraying your resolve, testing your faith. I have been fortunate to date in that the random thoughts of doubt and fear and anger have not rooted into tall trees. I have been able to have these natural seedlings occur and then pull them and process them out of my garden. Yet some continue to persist.

I see miracles and I bathe in them. I see Kayleigh and feel Kayleigh and know Kayleigh is right beside me. She flashes into the present and leaves little messages. Then a few days go by and I slip into doubt or fear or confusion. Seedlings, really. But they bother me. I feel sad and ashamed when they arise, when a weed grows in my garden. Then I nurture myself and remind myself that what I am going through is both unique and real; that her miracles are really just that, miracles; that her life is just that, her life – current, present and active.

This is really happening. It is not a series of statements we say to make ourselves feel better like a boy whistling in the dark to pretend he isn't scared. It is quite amazing and true. Authentically true. Kayleigh is alive. More alive than she was the night she was physically killed and spiritually released. Her mind. Her emotion. Her soul. Her being. Everything that makes up my Daughter, except for her physical body and physical human emotional hang ups, is wrapped together into a stream of perfect light. God's light. Angelic light. Divinity. She IS. She always has been. She always will be.

Then my human mind says, subconsciously, really? Yes, really. Regardless of whether I struggle and regardless of whether I believe or not, she persists and grows spiritually and holds me with her presence every day. Probably laughing at me. Always nurturing me. Always protecting me. She is my Babygirl and she is in love with her Father.

In the first six months since Kayleigh's physical death I have seen exactly six full months of miraculous angelic presence. She visits as a cardinal. A possum. She talks through the wind-chimes. She blows warmly in the wind - the type of wind that we know is her, slightly warming than the wind on which she comes. She plays with the

Bluetooth and switches out to shuffle to the perfect song for the emotion of the moment. She placed a rock by my bed. Moved her stuffed animals. Moved her shoes. Talked through four intuitive healers directly to us. Speaks in my right ear. Has begun to touch my hair and my forehead. I have faith. I believe. I cherish this every miraculous step of our journey. I get spoiled by this activity perhaps. I just am so overwhelmed by the shock of this daily grief and the counterbalance of Kayleigh's presence, it sometimes causes me to stumble. The mind can't always make sense of it, and when it can't make sense of it, the mind wants to question that which it does not understand. And after all of that my mind slips into, really? Yes, REALLY!

"Daddy! Daddy, you're hilarious. I'm right here, Daddy. I'm never leaving your side. Trust me, Daddy. I know it's really hard to comprehend. But trust me. I am alive and well and in love with you. I am never leaving your side. Love you!"

*

The Conflicting Sides of the Same Coin 03/02/2018

The story which we are writing has a horror on an unimaginable scale; grief from your physical death in childhood; the worst possible thing that the world could throw at me. Yet, it also conveys an extraordinary peace of spiritual incredibleness, imbued within your beauty. I live the worst of the worst and the best of the best at the same time, always, without fail, and without untangling one from the other. It is fluid, co-existing.

On one side of this coin of my life I absorb the daily punches of severe torture and grief; a wound that will never heal and one that is not meant too – how could it. For the loss is backwards in time and the losses accumulate over time. A daily pain that I reconcile through contact with God and you, through Steps 10, 11 and 12, through journaling, crying, wailing, screaming, meditating, swimming, sitting, running, collapsing, singing and sometimes just being stunned. The counter-balance keeps the weight off of my chest just enough to breathe and function and live. The counter-balance is you.

On the other side of this coin of my life is you, my lovely Daughter, pounding on the wind and calling through the space just within my right ear to ensure that I hear you and feel you and sense you. You are a calming force in the midst of chaos. You are a healing ointment to this wound that never heals, alleviating the torture in the counter-balance. Your miracles counter-balance me. Your voice counter-balances me. Your current, daily presence counter-balances me. You save me in my current state, a state that has changed so drastically since the accident, I hardly recognize it.

I am the ridgeline of that coin, delicately walking this human life, which holds on each side of the ridge each side of that coin. It is all encompassing and threaded together through the pressures of heat and liquid life that molded this coin together. I am that ridgeline. You, my Darling, are the coin's gold. I love you.
"A golden shield of protection, Daddy. Remember our prayer to God we said each night when I would go to bed through my physical life, ever since I was a baby, and into my teenage years. I am now your golden shield of protection, Daddy. Love you!"

*

I Found A Strand of Your Hair 03/03/2018

I sat on your bed tonight at midnight, sitting here like I do every night. Sometimes I do my Eleventh Step prayer and meditation with you on your bed, and sometimes we just sit and talk. Tonight I lay down in the spot where you used to lay and my eye was caught by a golden silver reflection on one of the pillows near my feet.

Your hair. Golden blonde beautiful hair. Just one string. Weaving about the corner of the tiny pillow, it glanced delicately in the light, this last piece of your physical body. The only part of you that I can physically hold. One strand of beautiful blonde hair. I clutched it in my hand, holding it between my index finger and thumb, staring at your string of hair. Wondering - what now. What do I do with this little piece of your hair? I don't want to lose it. Yet where can I put it. The tears flow with the confusion. The sobbing rocks my frame up and down, while I clutch your beautiful blonde strand of hair.

It will always be cruel and this pain will never heal. Particularly with a Daddy Daughter combination like ours, so closely weaved together, yet respectful of each other's individual parts. So devoted and trusting of the other, even in hard moments, knowing the one who had made a mistake always made amends, making the bond more fruitful, more empowered, deeper and true. On a daily basis we were true love. We are true love still.

You are a great companion - you were, in your physical form, so amazing to love and nurture and guide. We laughed. We cried. We cried because we laughed so hard, your eyes closing and mouth wide open as tears spurt from your eyes while we laughed uncontrollably. I miss a million things a day, but laughing until we cry – this I may miss the most.

Now - I laugh. I cry. Quite a lot. At some point every day. You laugh with me, but I cannot hear your expired human voice. Yes, you cry with me, yet I cannot hear your human voice produce new chords and words and sounds and mutters. Yet your voice is not gone. It has transitioned. It has deepened and lightened and expanded. It is courage. Raw courage. It is love. It is light.

We pray a lot. We plan and you guide me in reconciliation. Your fingerprints are all over my days, directing next steps, touching us through the wind, showing up with my Father as cardinals, changing songs on the Bluetooth to match the exact mood we are feeling, redirecting my wayward steps. A great companion - leaving me a strand of your hair to find tonight. I've laid on this bed every day for six months, along with Spirit, sometimes sleeping through the night and always pushing the pillows around with my feet. Yet somehow I find your one string of golden hair on this night, left here specifically for me.

It is a symbol. Everything you do is a symbol. I trust that. Even if it is a representation of just one tiny silver lining, it is still a silver lining. A world can exist within a silver lining. A life can be saved within a silver lining. And it is you. Figuratively and literally. This is your hair. Your physical hair - all that is left of your physical form, except your sacred ashes downstairs in the dining room. You are here. You want me to know that. I know that. I feel you. I watch your splendid angelic activity, catching little glimpses here and there. I am starting to see how you are evolving, page by page in this book, marking miracle after miracle, subtlety after subtlety. You are one thousand times more powerful than your Padray. You are my guide. My love. My Babygirl.

And so I place your hair back upon the pillow at the foot of your bed, not knowing what will come of it. It is your hair and it is on your bed. I suppose I could place it in a tiny plastic bag. I have your brush in a plastic bag. Yet my instinct has told me to leave it here at my feet.

And as I found a strand of your hair tonight, it reminds me of the duality of everything I face - a reminder as this - it churns with pain in my stomach, tumultuous grief and sadness. It reminds me also of your soul's glory, which fills me with strength and faith. There is no gray with this. It is extreme in each side of the lows and the highs. You have physically passed, yet you are still present in the physical world, sparkling on the edges of our senses. One shiny, golden, beautiful breathtaking string of hair. I want to grasp it for eternity. Hold it. Hug it. Kiss it. Merge it against my face like it felt when I hugged you, feeling your hair against my face just a day before the accident. Thank you for your gift tonight, my Kakie. You - your soul, it is alive. More alive than you have ever been.

*

Mommy's Dreams 03/05/2018

Hi Darling. I'm so happy that you came to Mommy in her dreams last night. She literally never dreams, which means it was you. You came to me as well letting me know that the second person to die physically will have the loved one who preceded him or her waiting, jumping up and down, smiling. That is you and what you will do with me. I know. I trust. I believe. Please guide me today, my Love. You are one of the two true loves of my life (with Mommy a close third to you and your brother!). You have galvanized me this morning, when my feet seemed too wary to walk. I woke how I typically wake, with cement poured down my throat. Then I choke. And breathe and rise. With intention I walk with you – both for you to guide me and also just because I want to spend time hanging out with my Daughter. How lucky am I.

"How lucky am I! Thank you, Daddy. Thank you for not giving up. I am here. It is me! It is me! And you know! Yeah, Daddy! Never give up!"

I will never give up, Kakes. Never.

*

Dancing for Degas 03/05/2018

I started reading to you at night tonight. We haven't done that since you were 11 or 12 when we would read a page at a time and trade off. Then we crashed YouTube watching Japanese commercials and hilarious animal videos.

We bought this Degas book when you were two and a half. There are so many books. We never missed a night through your early childhood, merging Nathaniel into the nightly reading before bedtime after he was born. Sometimes together and sometimes one kid per parent, we read in crazy voices and added to the stories. In "Where's the Cat?" We used to pretend to eat the apples off of the tree. My God, the memories.

I will read to you again. It is what we did. It will be what we do. I felt happy reading, Spirit stretched out over my lap as he and I sat with you on your bed. He listened to every word. No one has ever read a book to him before!

But I did. To your dog. To you. The three of us. Magical. Simply magical.

*

March 5th Dream 03/06/2018

I dreamed that there was a woman and a man. They could have been soul-mates - a couple, your mother and I. Or it could have been another kindred relationship similar to the deep and truthful love between you and me.

In the dream the woman suddenly weakened and was dying. A timer, like when a digital picture loads on a phone, spun until it completed the load and she died, disappearing in thin air.

The man was immersed in sorrow and tragic loss. He continued to live, mourning her loss daily until he grew old rather quickly and started closing his eyes, dying. As the timer spun around the wheel and the color filled in, he weakened. When the timer hit twelve o'clock, he closed his eyes and died.

As he did, she reappeared with a huge smile on her face, jumping up and down with joy, and embracing him. The world inverted and instead of him disappearing, they were back together on the same plain, in the same body types, and therefore, could see each other, feel each other, embrace each other and laugh into eternity.

I woke up hoping for that day when I physically die and I see you again, in the same body types, on the same plain. I know. I know. There is a lot of living before that day and my obligation to me and you is to live to the fullest so that I can bring myself into your light with intention daily. That day of my physical death will come. We will be in the same body type again. We will look eye to eye in the same body type again. Laughing. Crying, with intense devotion.

Joking. Embracing eternity together. Together, Sweetheart. My Babygirl, I await that day. In the meantime, we do the same, except in different body types, which makes the contact more difficult, but not impossible. We are the possible. We are the truth. The hope.

I feel you near. You stand within my aura. You hold me while I shake. You lay your head on my shoulder. You feel my body quake. You whisper in my ear, "Dear Daddy, take a breath...I love you. I am here."

"On the Near Side of the Wind"

I have a feeling, surmise,
A boulder in my throat,
A spear in my side,
And a blizzard for my coat,
The frenzy is alive,
In the center of my bones,
This my life can be -

Yet a feeling, arise,
That I am never alone,
There is comfort and calmness,
When she travels through my soul,
Like a million fireflies,
That release like sun unfolds,
This she wants for me -

On the very near side,
So close to her embrace,
Like a veil in the sky,
An inch away from my face,
I yearn and I sense her,
Standing warmly in this space,
This gift she brings to me,
Listen, feel, see...

*

God 03/07/2018

There are moments where you don't even seem to exist, God. A vacant Father. A Father who has abandoned his children. A drunk. Philanderer. Criminal. What you have permitted to happen to my Daughter is criminal, and for that, you are a criminal.

After all that we have been through already - after all that you have asked us to bare - after all we have carried with faith to you - you couldn't have somehow seen to it that the city of Cleveland Heights wouldn't callously rip down Kayleigh's beautiful memorial without telling us, throwing her pictures and vases and their water and candles into a garbage bag? Really? After all we have been through, today, we get this.

The city manager called, having heard that someone at city hall made a decision that six months was long enough for Kayleigh's memorial, and, the memorial, on city property, should be removed. She apologized, telling me they should have talked to us first, which they did not.

I told her that we are good people - really good people, and that if they had told us their intention we would not have liked it, but would have understood. It was well kept. I tended it every several days. It caused no risk to the public. It was a set of vases with flowers burned by winter; a few bows and pictures stapled to the telephone poles that blocked her view of the car and the driver's view of Kayleigh. Honorable. Giving meaning to the community. Permitting people to reflect on life and loss and love. Ripped down with no warning. As if they just threw my baby out in the garbage. As if Kayleigh was garbage. God, if I could kill you in this moment, I would.

I want to tuck her away in my light where nobody else can hurt her or tamper with her. They'd have to go through my soul to get to her and nobody's going to make it that deep alive. But somehow, You do. And You can. So, God, with all we have been through, could You have not intervened?

*

Three Cardinals 03/08/2018

Were they just three random Cardinals? Someone reading this with a skeptic's eye will likely come to that conclusion. We write not for that person, but for the person who is awake. Clearly these were not random backyard Cardinals, but something grand. Mommy and I know this and trust it – we've experienced it daily for months.

You came to us today with my Dad and my Grandpa. To cheer us up – three beautiful Cardinals – three beautiful souls watching over us. It was a great way to wake up today, hearing your spirit voice outside my window, while hearing your Kayleigh voice in my right ear.

The initial moment of waking today was very hard, particularly after what we went through yesterday. It was utterly indefensible that the city, in their shortsightedness, would rip down your memorial that had been bringing joy and communion to hundreds and hundreds of people, and just throw the contents away. Flowers. Glass vases. The water from the vases. Your photos that people placed on the telephone poles. Candles. Stuffed animals. All of it tossed into black plastic garbage bags and thrown in the back of a city truck. There were many reactions I could have had – I took the high road, explained my sadness, told them all they had to do was ask us to start pulling it down and we would have done so.

Once the city workers found your bags, the police brought the contents over to the house; sheepish messengers, clearly embarrassed for the city, and just doing their job. Although they did not say it, they were disgusted that we were handled like this. It was horrible. After everything we've already endured, to have to face inhumane callous actions of a thoughtless city garbage crew was cruel at best. Yet we are bigger and we are better and we are stronger and we persevere.

"I am so sorry, Daddy, this city was so stupid with my memorial and they hurt you so badly. They should have thought through it more. Remember, nobody can touch me. I am free and happy and filled with light and love. The memorial was so special for the last six months and I was always so touched when anybody sat with me at this sacred site. Even without the candles and flowers, it will always be a sacred site. This is where I met Heaven, Daddy, in your arms and in your light, with your permission and in your loving safety. We are bigger. You are right. Thank you, Daddy."

*

Staying Lost is a Choice 03/08/2018

This morning you and my Dad and, this time, my Grandma, perched your spirits in the shapes of Cardinals outside my bedroom window and sang to me. Just to sing.

We prayed. We meditated. I forgave God. You reminded me that God fills your soul with light and love, and if I turn from God, I turn from you. You reminded me that God is not the city of Cleveland Heights administration and did not remove your memorial. Some stupid, callous human did. You reminded me that God did not physically kill you; that your physical body died in a pure accident; that God didn't assault you; that some deranged, psychotic sub-humans attacked you.

Then I drove to work and you changed my Bluetooth and played "Three Little Birds" by Mr. Marley, followed by R.E.M.'s "It Happened Today." What happened today? My Daughter, filled with light, burst back through the physical world to pick her Father up and set his feet again to the firmament.

I am awake, Kakie. I am hurting. I am grieving. I want to fight people. I want to burn down the earth. But I am awake. I find you, not in the intense sadness, but in the choice to pick myself off of the floor and continue our journey. Staying lost is a choice I refuse to take. Fill me with your courage, Babygirl.

447

"If I Burn Down the Earth"

If I burn down the earth,
Reduce its bone to ash,
Will it open up a door,
Will it bring you back,
There's a story to be told,
An angst that doesn't sleep,
It burns within the deep,
Deep inside of me -

These are roads with no hope,
No place I'd bring your soul,
No place where the sun brings,
Its brilliance and its hope,
So I turn from this spinning earth,
With a glowing torch in my hand,
And put out the flames,
That burn down this man.

*

God Again 03/09/2018

Our relationship has shown its resilience. It has been tested nonetheless. One thing we surely agree upon and that is simply the love we have for our children. Regarding Kayleigh, I cannot believe that this was the path you had intended, to watch a brilliant girl have to conquer an assault at fourteen, and a physical death at fifteen. That could not have been Your doing. This was not Your plan. Everything does not happen for a reason. It is not that black and white. Sometimes random, arbitrary accidents happen. Why would it be any other way? You are a father and you wouldn't treat your children that way. You cried with me and Kayleigh in the street. You gave her the power of an intercessor. You are God.

I can meet you on this common ground - I am her Earthly Father and you are her Heavenly Father. Together we are her Fathers and have our own partnership to take care of her and love her and hold her in our light. I can do that with You. I will do my part. I am a great Father. Please, you are a Great Father as well. Let us merge our greatness together in loving this very special soul. And, in so doing, let us match that love that we both have, with the continuous glory in which we hold our son, Nathaniel.

"This River"

There are high caverns shadowed in lowly bruises,
Rivers of acidic sorrow fomenting in the basin,
Irritable rapids and stunting rocks and anxiety abrasions,
And anguish and anger and wailing,
Generalized aggravation,
That crumbles the sturdy sediment on the plain's edges,
Spiking new pains and creating new crevasses,
Where I may be tempted to tuck in and hide,
Yet the holes are acres deep and a mile wide,
Into which I could not shelter even if I tried -

So -
I walk in the river,
I walk in this river,
I drink from this river,
I swim in this river,
I pray to this river,
I pray for this river,
I play in this river,
I cry in this river,
And beg it -

Carry me, carry me away.

*

My Vows to Defend 03/10/2018

My Daughter, my vow to you, is to continue to evolve with an openness and continuous awakening to you; to rise through my human condition in order to commune with you while we are in different body types and in different realms. To give you my love and light. To be your loving Father as I always have been and always will be. To build a sacred temple for you through my thoughts, my words and my actions. You are a strong and vibrant guardian angel who crosses into the physical world to support and direct and love this family of four. I will defend this position in all avenues of my life, with anybody with whom I need to assert myself, for as long as I need to. This is one of my vows to defend. I love you.

My Son, my vow to you, in our path through this human world, I promise to continue to evolve as your Father, remaining present, providing direction through love, laughter, charity, compassion and light, treating you with the gentle dignity that you deserve. I cannot bring your sister physically back to you, yet I can teach you how to bring yourself closer to your sister. She is well alive and brilliant. I will defend this position in all avenues of my life, with anybody with whom I need to assert myself, for as long as I need to. This is one of my vows to defend. I love you.

My Wife, dear Jessica, my vow to you, is my love and light through this life, a life now nearly destroyed with the horrible tragedy that physically stripped our Babygirl from our lives. I offer you my continued patience and companionship, my empathy and my respect for your path with your own grief and reconciliation. I am your soulmate. I will never forsake you. I will defend this position in all avenues of my life, with anybody with whom I need to assert myself, for as long as I need to. This is one of my vows to defend. I love you.

My sacred three, in this incredible family of four, my vow to you is the vow I made thirty years ago - lifelong sobriety. In those shaky moments where the world seems bleak and the steps too frightful or heavy to take, I vow to you to continue down that path, to strengthen my defense against the mental obsession, to feel my life in full color and to emerge at the end of my life, in my final breath, with my sobriety intact. I will defend this position in all avenues of my life, with anybody with whom I need to assert myself, for as long as I need to. This is one of my vows to defend. I love you. I love us, this family of four, regardless of our current configuration. We are unbreakable. We are love itself.

*

To Fall Apart 03/10/2018

To fall apart, and to then stay apart, is to block ourselves from you. If we did nothing with our lives it would diminish your ability to touch us. What you want is our openness and communion, which is also what we so desperately want. You are jumping up and down, smiling, laughing, and engaging. The frequencies of energy you are emanating are love and gratitude; are peace and light; are other worldly. In order for me to hear you, to see you and feel you consistently, I need to resonate with love and gratitude, with peace and light, and be other worldly. You know if anybody can climb a mountain for you, it's your Daddy. I am climbing, though my hands and knees and bloody and bruised and the lungs are full of concrete.

So, and it does invigorate me, I am well aware that you need your Daddy. Differently than you did at fifteen before the accident, which was different than thirteen, and eleven and six. You need me to do my work. You want me to do my work, both for my own benefit as well as our continued path together. I will always do what I can to show up for you, My Love. I never missed a concert and I'm not missing your biggest moments as you penetrate the physical world and walk with us daily. God, please help me walk through the grief, running towards the roar of the lion. Please teach me, Kakes, new and creative ways to sing to you, to open to you, to feel you, to hear you and see you. This is why I live, for this purpose with you in our new configuration, and to do likewise with Nate, Mommy and everybody else. I miss you terribly in your physical form. I love you completely, my beautiful Daughter.

"Do you see my face, Daddy? Smiling. For you!"

*

Two Months Shy of Sixteen 03/15/2018

My Love, we are two months away from your sixteenth birthday. The words we write are hard to fathom. It is very bittersweet. Atrocious. Beautiful. Each year around this time I would be thinking about your next birthday and figuring out how we would celebrate. This year is both so different, yet the same. I am heartbroken in your physical loss and the fact that you physically have no more birthdays; that your physical life did not make it to sixteen! That is horror! How utterly fucked up is that? Yet, May 15 will always be your birthday and we will celebrate you, Kayleigh, on that day, every year, as you continue to age in spirit in our current reality set. You are about to be sixteen. My daughter is turning sixteen, your first birthday in Heaven. We will celebrate.

I love our relationship as its meaning grows and flourishes. It is nearly impossible for me at times to balance it all, but I am getting my feet more firmly rooted, particularly when the big waves hit me. The big waves come daily. I root myself in my love for you and I defy the ocean. Our transition continues to try to test the edges of a love between us that will never die. With each test we get stronger together – whether we are both physically here, bot spiritually with God, or one here and one there, one in this body and one in another type – it doesn't affect the core light of who we are. We are Kayleigh and Kevin Mooney, a Daughter and Daddy who light up our worlds with our love.

So, Babygirl, help me figure out what to do for your first birthday with God. What should I do?

"I want a party! Have a party, Daddy!"

*

Subtly Distracted 03/16/2018

It has been subtle as I have been distracted and busy. And exhausted as the days pile up upon another. So sorry. You are always worth the time and effort, always beyond worthy of any of my light and attention. I hope you do not ever think that, because my effort has been pallid and less intense this week, that somehow it doesn't matter to me. Nothing can be further from the truth. I care so much, My Love, grieve for you so much, and want you with me all the time. I don't want to take your presence for granted and I do not. I need to do better with ensuring sacred time with us.

I hear you frequently and when I do it shifts me from fear and loneliness to a pure uplifting when you intervene. It becomes a working part of my life where I trust and expect to hear your voice and see you somehow cross the physical plain every day. That's the trap I am starting to sense – I feel guilty if I do not stay mesmerized by the fact that my Daughter is a true and powerful intercessor, a guardian angel, who walks with her Daddy each day. I am amazed and I actually have not missed one day together and I never will. I just want more time with my Babygirl and my focus isn't always as sharp to be able to absorb it all. It is so hard to live in both worlds; reaching higher to sense the gates of Heaven and also living in the lower vibrational reality of this physical world. I love you, Sweetheart, and am so proud of you. I just want you to hear it from me that I fatigued; overwhelmed; tired.

"Daddy, write for me. Write this: I, Kayleigh Mooney, love you, My Daddy. So, so much. I am not offended when you live your life and can't quite lift as high as me. You can't in your human form completely, but you try, and that's what is important. You actually lift into the Higher Life, Daddy, many times. Amazing! I am right beside you. The better you live, the deeper we grow. Love you!"

*

St. Patrick's Day - These Harsh Reminders 03/17/2018

This year was the first year, at fifteen, in tenth grade, you were going to go down to the St. Patrick's Day parade without your parents and with your friends. Either I would have driven you and your friends downtown or to the train or one of your friends would have picked you up in a car and I would have watched you with those friends drive off on the Irish High Holy Day. Watching the car curve down the street thinking, "there she goes. Have fun, Baby."

I stare down an empty street, the street you have lived on since you were four.

It was this year. Today. This day that you would have gone to the parade without us. That line is such a harsh line between your childhood and your adulthood - the physical life that was and the physical life that never will be. You were on the verge of womanhood, having matured through your childhood. You were still a child at fifteen for sure, yet no longer childlike. You were a young woman looking with excitement out into your sophomore year, including the excitement about driving and dances and vacations and hitting this parade. And then seven months ago today you were tragically physically killed and spiritually released.

Kayleigh Mickayla Mooney - your name was built for this parade. There's likely nobody else downtown today with such a pretty and purely Irish name. And I don't know what to do. For seven months now I have gone through thousands of firsts and they all suck. This is our first St. Patrick's Day in our new configuration. Should I drive down to the parade and stand there with you. Or should I stay home, knowing that this year is the year you go to the parade without your parents.

I know you will be there. You were so excited about it. Perhaps you will walk in the parade with your Grandpa, my Dad, downtown, and our namesake, Michael. Perhaps you will rest your fingers in the cool winds as they kiss the fields of heather in Tipperary today with our ancestors. Perhaps you will sit with me all day and we will have our own parade. Happy St. Patrick's Day my Irish angel - may God fill further your soul with the purest golden white emerald light on this day.

"Our day is here, Daddy! We are the future they dreamed about yesterday, remember?"

Yes, Babygirl, I do.

*

Guided Meditation - The Park Bench 03/17/2018

Earlier in the day, this St. Patrick's Day, I found a two year old picture of Kakes on St. Patrick's Day and posted it on Facebook. I kept the image with me all day and continued to pull out my phone and look at her. Beautiful girl. Brilliant soul. Charming and wondrous personality. My baby.

In the heat and the height of our grief this day, Jess and I decided to lay down and do a forty minute guided meditation on this quiet Saturday afternoon. Nate played with a friend on his PS4. We adjusted ourselves into prone positions and each had our own headset. We pressed play at the same time and closed our eyes, listening to the same guided meditation.

As the minutes went by and I sank deeper into relaxation, which is needed sometimes in order to open up enough to deeply commune with a guardian, I listened to the narrator take us to a grassy field with a path leading off into a peaceful place. To my right, as I walked upon the grass, quite pleasantly and suddenly, Kayleigh bounced into view beside me on my right side with a huge smile on her face. She was dressed in the clothes in the picture I had been viewing that day, complete with a tall St. Patrick's Day cloth hat.

"Hey Daddy!" she said, and jostled her face about, widening her eyes, clearly giddy with surprising me.

"Hey Baby," I said to her.

"Daddy, this is how you saw me today so I'm going to stay in this outfit and Irish hat as we walk, ok?"

I just smiled as she clasped her left arm into my right arm and started walking me down the path. It was lovely out in these heavenly gardens and we talked as we strolled along.

"I miss you so much, Kakes, and I am so happy to be walking with you."

"I'm always here with you, Daddy, but you've got to do the work like you are doing in order to see me like this. I know it's hard. I'm so proud of you for trying and coming to me."

"My God, Babygirl, that's all I want."

My mind skipped a little. She pulled me with a quick tug.

"Keep breathing. You've got this. Just stay focused and keep breathing."

I did as she told me to do, as if I had a choice in the matter, and focused on my breathing. The picture cleared even further. We came to the base of a grassy hill and we walked up a stone path at a steep angle to a park bench at the top of the hill. We sat down and she opened her hand forward as if to look into the distance.

"Look, Daddy," she said, "isn't it beautiful?"

It was amazing. Across the frontier, as far as the eye could see from left to right, we looked out over a huge valley of light with the warm sun in the light blue sky beaming out over the entire space. I thought I knew what it was.

"Yep, Daddy. That's Heaven. I come to this spot all the time. It's amazing."

"It is," I whispered, mesmerized by what I was seeing and with whom I was sitting. She was beautiful. An angel who's purpose was to love and support and guide her family. She was in her element. A natural. She laughed. She smiled. She kissed me with her eyes. Then she lay her beautiful head on my right shoulder, as we gazed off into Heaven together, arm in arm, hand in hand.

I was timeless. I didn't care about anything except my baby. I knew the meditation would come to a close, but was reassured that our relationship would not. I would come to her again and she to me. That's who we are. That's who we always have been and always will be. I just enjoyed the moment as we talked about her happiness and security and love and light. She reminded me of the sometimes hard journey in front of me and reiterated my need to trust her, particularly in the twisted pitfalls of grief. She said this several times. Very clearly directing me to remember in those earth shattering moments to trust her completely.

She followed my eyes as I gazed into the light in the distance. She told me that the blinding constant light out in the sky was God. Really. God. I was staring at the face of God and couldn't see a face. I just saw blinding light. She assured me He was always watching over us.

Others came to say hello and stood behind the park bench - my Father, Grandmother, my great-great-great Grandpa Michael. They wanted to say hello, but drifted in and out, knowing this special time was Daddy-Daughter time. The constant throughout the sit was my sweet and lovely Kayleigh, who never stood up from the bench. Her blonde hair warmed on my shoulder as we continued to just sit together.

The time was winding down and the narrator on the guided meditation intruded into our communion and started talking again, to which Kayleigh immediately looked up jokingly, shaking her head, as if she could see the narrator. And as if the narrator was bothering us! We laughed.

"Come on, Daddy," she said and stood up. Taking me by the hand we started walking down the path through the garden and back towards the base of the hill. Then the music and narration suddenly stopped. She looked around and I did too, a little confused. "Uh," we laughed.

I opened my eyes and saw that my phone popped up a window "storage is almost full." I clicked it away and the music began again. I closed my eyes and Kayleigh smiled as if she was saying, okay where were we before your stupid phone interrupted our walk?

We returned to where we had begun at the beginning of the meditation, where I stood when she met me on the road and we held hands for a moment. She embraced me and said, "Daddy, I am so, so proud of you. I love you so much. Trust me, Daddy." She was exhilarated.

"I love you too, Sweetheart," I whispered and reopened my eyes, laying on my bed next to Kayleigh's Mother. Kayleigh stayed glistening in a higher presence with me as I continued on with my day, returning now in my memory to our sit on the park bench frequently, knowing that our time together was real.

*

Permanent Memorial 03/19/2018

Hi, Kakie. I love you, Sweetheart. Today we go talk to the city about a permanent memorial for you at your sacred site. I expect very little from the city. Other than the chief, who has been compassionate and loving, I expect them to continue to fumble about and make mistakes.

I need you and your light this morning so I don't bite their heads off. I will be very clear with my displeasure in their negligent and harmful dismantling of your memorial site, but will handle this in an appropriate manner and with your light uppermost in mind. Empower and sustain me. Fill me with the same golden light that flows through your soul. Empower me to be calm and nurturing and awake to life, to God, to you, my Babygirl. You are pure brilliance. I would walk anywhere you ask me to walk. I trust you like no other. I come to you with an open heart today. Walk through my soul, Babygirl - it is a beautiful land fit for your light.

"Oh Daddy, thank you. I love you too, Daddy. You have always been there for me and I trust you. I am always here for you, Daddy. Trust me. Never doubt that. I will never leave your side. The higher you live, the more contact we have. Remember that. It is about you and God. It is about you and me."

*

My Tears Are My War Paint 03/20/2018

No matter where I go, or who I see, if I have a hard moment, a moment of pure sadness that overwhelms me, or a moment of fleeting grief – in any of these situations I may cry. I cry freely. My whole life I was emotionally intelligent enough not to worry about who saw me crying. I may take emotional shelter from public eyes; may confide in a friend or sniffle away the tears as I turn away from those I may not want to know that I have been crying, particularly in business meetings or work arenas. Mostly, I truly never cared if anyone saw me cry. I knew it showed strength and my humanity. These days are only different in that I have now cried every single day for over seven months. At some point every day, I cry. At some points, every day, I break down. And get back up. And strengthen. And step forward a few more steps before I collapse again.

Now I truly am on a new level and I truly do not care. If I cry and someone is uncomfortable, I don't care. If I cry and someone thinks I am weak or falling apart, I don't care. I hide nothing related to my babies. I hide nothing related to the physical tragic loss of my beloved Babygirl, Kayleigh. Nothing.

On the way to work sometimes it will hit me. I arrive and I will have been crying. Sometimes I get on the elevator and wet strings of tears are still clinging to my face. Sometimes not. Sometimes the skin is puffy or red around my eyes – with that look when you know someone has been crying. And always – I don't care. I have worked my way so far into my humanity and my soul and have crossed so many plains to reach Kayleigh on a level we'd never been on before and am not typically distracted or worried or concerned, or aware, that others may see me. In fact, I say, let them see me. Let them see my war paint. My grief that I wear on my face to designate pure love for my child. My grief that adorns my face like blotches of colorful paint, signifying the prowess of a great warrior. I am a great warrior. I am, just as she is.

So watch me walk down the hall or in my car or in the elevator, or at an A.A. meeting or at the grocery store, or at church or walking down the street, and if I happen to have a hard moment, see me cry, if I cry. See me. See my humanity. It is the best thing that I can share with others on this plain, a glimpse of the magical beauty of my soul. A glimpse of the unbreakable bond that I share with my Kayleigh. A glimpse of Kayleigh herself, in my space, around my aura, in the expressions on my face and in the vibrant war paint of tears that line my cheeks in great strength, courage and love.

"Stomach Tears"

There are times when I cry in my stomach,
And the tears rip the lining like glass,
There are times when I sob in my stomach,
And the wailing nearly cuts me in half,
For the promises and the hope,
In an instant - up in smoke,
We roam,
We roam,
We roam...

But there are no moral victory wins,
If there were caves tucked within,
Into which I could retreat,
And travel no more,
Removing my feet,
And sinking into the sadness,
The sobs of which the stomach shakes.

*

I'll Stand By You 03/21/2018

Your brother, Nate, and I were out driving last night. He remarked, "nine days until Jekyll." He seemed sad. It will be our first trip to Georgia without you physically here by our side. He is such a smart and emotional wonderful boy. He is now thirteen. So young, yet he knows.

I had a flurry of images. You in the middle row of seats in the Pilot. Nate in the third row of seats for the long drive. You two running around in the beach house. Sneaking out at night to the dunes and down the water's edge. Your B-Club. Dove bars at the Jekyll Island Clubhouse. Night hunting for gators. Shark fishing. Laying on the beach. Clam Creek. All of it.

I could tell he, too, was reminiscing or thinking about the future and the loss he was feeling. I could hear it in his voice and see it on his face. Just horrific sadness. I told him that this first trip back to the family beach house was going to be hard. Then I told him, "but she is with us. I know it's hard to feel that sometimes, but she's with us. She's sitting right here in the backseat."

Suddenly, and without warning, the Bluetooth popped on and this song by The Pretenders started blaring through the speakers, a Bluetooth that had been off moments prior. "I'll Stand By You." I showed him the iPhone and the name of the song and told him, "This one was for you from your sister. She is telling you that no matter where you go and no matter what you do, she is always standing beside you."

He cried.

"Faithfulness"

Daddy, don't be frightened,
Do not heavily despair,
For I bring the sunshine,
I sing in the air,
I am all around you,
I am, always, here.

*

Georgia Sea Turtle Center Brick 03/22/2018

Outside the Georgia Sea Turtle Center in Jekyll Island, GA, one of Kayleigh's♥ favorite places, and where a Kemps Ridley Sea Turtle named after her, Kayleigh Kakes, continues to heal, this brick was set today to honor my baby. I cannot wait to get to Georgia to get down on my knees and kiss this stone. I love you and our relationship as it continues to courageously grow, Babygirl.

"I Am the Sea"

And its rush of scree and smoky salt,
Erupts upon its latest fall,
Bursting through the sand and silt,
On hindered soul its temple built;

It slips away beneath its quilt,
Of foaming webs of whitish silk,
Retreating into massive curl,
Beneath display of wave unfurled;

And if you disbelieved its sway,
Just watch it rise and recede away,
For it retrieves itself when weak,
And alters landscape when it speaks.

*

Living Breathing Child 03/23/2018

People think that they can talk about their "living child" and it's a living breathing story. That is true. Yet, I have been the unfortunate benefactor of some people in my life who are so clueless it hurts.

They ignore Kayleigh. They assume she is not here. Yet she is. Nathaniel is a living child in his physical body. Kayleigh is a living child too, in her body of light. For them, with someone whose child has physically died, they check in with you, perhaps once or twice to say something gratuitous, like, 'I'm sorry,' and assume that with the child's physical death, so too the story dies and someone like me doesn't need to talk about my deceased child anymore. It is total selfishness and arrogance on behalf of these who stoop to this level. We all love to talk about our children. I love to talk about Nathaniel. And I love to talk about Kayleigh.

The lines of these relationships with those around me are resetting. The circles of trust tighten. I have been abandoned by some adults who are too emotionally uncomfortable with their own lives that they cannot support me in my grief. I have been abandoned by others who thing that there must be something pathological going on with me since I am not healing. Invariably, these are people who are not parents, and sometimes parents who have never gone through the physical death of a child. I remind them that this type of death knows no healing, only daily reconciling, and they, with no similar experience, smile in patronizing grins. Some are removed from that intimate circle of sharing. Some will never again be a part of my life. I cannot babysit adults. I cannot make anybody be anything. So be it.

Kayleigh is a living breathing soul and her story is living and breathing and much more amazing than her physical life was, as wonderful as it was, as well as anybody else's honor student. My girl passes from Heaven and penetrates the physical world every day. I have never been so proud of her. For my friends and family who I trust with this story, I share.

I grow with you, Kayleigh, unapologetically. Why should I apologize for having a relationship with my Daughter? If it makes someone uncomfortable to talk to them about my current, active relationship with my child who was physically killed and whose life transitioned into her body of light, who really has the problem. Not me. I do not really care what anybody thinks. I grow with you, My Darling.

*

Afternoon Nap and Reiki 03/23/2018

I was over exhausted today and came home, kissed Nate on his forehead, hugged Jess and marched right up to Kayleigh's bedroom and threw myself on her bed to rest. It was 4:30 PM. I asked her if I could lay my head in her lap and have her do Reiki on my head. Within a few minutes my hair gently began to move. She was moving her hand through my hair. I felt her fingers moving through my hair and the hair on my head slowly moving in motion to her gentle touch. I zeroed in on this miraculous interaction and tried desperately to stay in the moment with her. It lasted a few minutes, minutes of pure magic, and put me to sleep until after 7 PM! SHE TOUCHED MY HAIR! She is getting so, so strong.

*

Goodnight Moon 03/25/2019

As I have been doing for some time now, I read to you tonight, just as I did every night of your childhood into your tween years. I lay on your bed talking with you after we finished the book. I walked away towards the door, wiping my eyes, and settling down my emotion, when I saw, out of corner of eye, a tiny white feather drift down across my face and land on my shirt.

*

One in the Physical 03/23/2018

I, as a loving father, desire and want, and also am obligated to give my children my light and my love. My challenge currently is that I have one child in his physical body in the physical world and one child in her spiritually embodiment in both Heaven and the physical world. I need to intentionally be with both. I do this like I've always done this - Daddy-Son time and Daddy-Daughter time. What do I offer my children if I don't offer them my light? And how can I offer them my light if I am handcuffed by immeasurable grief, despondency and unaddressed sadness? I cannot. Therefore, like anything else, the only way through is through. With immense courage I offer you two my light. I will make my life adjustments. I will be with both of my children at the same time, in two different embodiments, in two different worlds. Your Daddy is here.

*

First Time Back To Jekyll 03/24/2018

Anxiety. Grief. Torment. It ripped out my heart from the inside. To return to this house, your second home; your beach; your air and your ocean. The only house in your life that spanned your entire life was this house, having moved several times in your life in Cleveland. But this house, on Jekyll, you have been going here since you were three months old. The last time we were here, you were physically alive. You saved a baby Loggerhead Sea Turtle, a moment that I logged at the time in my soul as an experience that would bring light and comfort to you for the rest of your life. I did not know that your physical life would be only several more days.

And now we are back. And the ocean is the ocean. And the birds are birds. The trees shake in the wind as they always have. The sand. The smell. The sounds. The spirit. The experience. But no Kayleigh, at least not in your physical body. I miss your physical body, your voice, your little smirks, your loud shouts and little whispers; your whimsical nature; your interactions. The house is quiet, emptied of half of the child noise we are used to. I hear Little Boy – his lovely voice streaming down the hallways, yet I hear not yours. The noise is cut in half, just as back in Cleveland. The loudness is cut in half. The laughter cut in half. The shouting cut in half. The energy cut in half. He wanders around the house, lost, haunted by his memories; overwhelmed, yet not wanting to show it as he thinks he needs to be strong for his parents, even though we talk to him constantly about

465

his need to feel what he feels and express what he needs to express. We sit and sob with him. He longs for you as your parents long for your physical arms.

There is nothing more important to you than family. I know you are here with us even though, out of our element driving down here, and having to face this first time back at the family beach-house, I've been distant for some reason. I just haven't had the normal space I usually get to talk with you. I will reset as we suffer; will regain footing as I fall.

I miss you so much and the despondency is also blocking my path. I need to meditate and open up an awakened soul once again. This is so hard. So hard, Babygirl. I take a lounge chair and walk down the rocks to the water's edge, place the chair in the water, place myself in the chair, and sob.

*

Where Will I Hide Your Ashes 03/26/2018

You were an angel tucked into human clothes. There was light always escaping you - lining your aura; shining upon the space about you. I see it in pictures at all ages. An angel tucked into a human condition of which you are now free.

Before we left for vacation, I was forced to struggle with very complex issues, like, 'where will I hide your ashes?' Never a sentence I ever imagined I would ever have to utter, but perhaps the most important sentence I own. I staggered around the house, having fantasies of someone breaking into the house and not knowing what your ashes were, and stealing them and breaking them open, finding no jewels, and throwing them behind a garage. I literally almost lost my breath thinking through that. I would need to be thoughtful and careful, not even telling the people watching the house where I would hide you. How horrible is that? A parent should never have to…many, many things.

For those who have never gone through this, you are extremely fortunate. Please, with anybody in your life who is suffering the physical death of a child, give them your ear, and not your voice; give them your love and let them tackle the new grief and complexity that comes with each new day and each new experience.

*

Whose Cross Is Always Bigger 03/27/2018

St. Philomena is my favorite church. It reminds me of an upside down boat, with its curving beams that arch to the ceiling. Within this beautiful church stands a half-life size and imposing full color crucifix. It inspired awe in me as a child, this raw crucifix at a church we visited infrequently, attending mass instead in our own parish on most Sundays at St. Margaret Mary's.

As I matured into my young teen years a deductive logic unsettled me as I listened and interpreted the priests during mass. I would return to this giant gruesome cross at St. Philomena and stare at it, down to every spatter of blood and think, look what they did to Him. They are human. Oh, but I am human too. My God! Look what we did! Look what I did! And I would turn away in shame because I loved God and would never hurt anybody. My sins put him on that cross? But I am just a boy?!

I shuttered and sank in guilt and shame and fear and hid my eyes from God. Could you imagine a child hiding his eyes from his Father? This was partly the teaching I received and partly the interpretation that I formulated.

Years passed and there my relationship stayed - always loyal yet slightly stunted due to my sins that killed Christ. I loved Him. It forced obedience out of fear. It was confusing. It was a lie.

After my life cratered and I sobered up at eighteen and a half, I found myself struggling with my God who was my salvation, but who may still be upset that I put Him on a cross. I returned to St. Philomena and stood under this haunting cross that cast such a heavy shadow across my soul and my years. I stood there in early sobriety and challenged the interpretation. I intentionally changed the dialogue and stood under that peach painted skinned man on the painted brown cross with the scarlet blood streaming from a thousand injustices, and thought - I didn't do this! That early message was misinterpreted. Christ is a good Father. He doesn't want fear and shame driven obedience. He wants what every good father wants - love and compassion for his children, even when his children act up; even when his children see cannot quite see him.

So it came to pass for me that a new interpretation was born: Christ as a man and as God, as he was tortured from limb to limb and scorched with his nailing to the cross, could have, at any time, used his God powers to relieve the pain, even slightly. He could have pretended to be in excruciating pain on the cross, but otherwise, have been laughing and enjoying a massage internally. He could have smote the soldiers or dropped Jupiter on the earth. He could have done anything and everything to relieve his pain. Yet, since he is a good Father, his focus was solely on his children and he would selflessly face anything on their behalf. So even though he could have prevented it, he had a massive decision and chose to die one hundred percent as a man with the full range of human indignity and suffering that comes with it. Because he loves me, he did that. Because of that, and only that, I am never alone. Never will I have a trial or tragedy in which I need to make such a decision - "now, should I use some of my God powers to relieve my pain or subjugate my attackers?" I will never have to make that immense decision, and therefore, I am never alone. But there is One who did and He did it to show me love. Not to excoriate me with shame and guilt. To shower me with love and devotion.

So when I am in a dark place and my cross is hurting me and the pains or decisions of my life seem daunting, when I feel that eternity of isolation in spiritual confusion or outright disobedience, when I am blistering angry at the world that my perfectly happy, perfectly healthy, sweet little girl was tragically physically killed in a simple and innocent accident, I can always turn to Christ - whose cross is always bigger. He knows my trials and struggles and darkness like nobody else for what He endured was much more than I ever will, and for that I am never alone. In that gratitude I can find shelter, companionship, peace, understanding and love.

*

Tenth Step 03/29/2018

Sitting on beach just now. Three fifteen year old girls just walked by me. This is now my life. She too would have been in a bikini with a confidence and her dazzling youth, looking like a goddess with seven more months of development behind her, a woman, strutting down this beach. 4 Selfish? No. Dishonest? Yes. It is fantasy, harshly, because she has been physically killed. Resentment? Yes, refeeling. Fear? Yes, always. 5 telling who? Texted my sister and friend. 6 willing to have God and Kayleigh remove defects? Yes 7 prayer? God and Kakes, how cruel this path is. Please help me make it less cloudy by being clear and purposeful in this moment. 8 willing to change? Yes 9 change? Breathe. Expect this in my life. Attitude turn to my Babygirl. Perspective I am awake and open to her and she relieves the abyss, the abyss that strikes me one hundred times a day. 12 turn to who? Nate who is hurting.

*

And Here We Have Returned 03/30/2018

It is horror. Excruciating. It is sad. It is grief. It is. It is magic. It is familiar. It is unfamiliar. It is joyous memory. It is love. It is her empty bed; a now quiet beach-house. It is Nate walking through the house, haunted by his memories and seeing his past play out with every step through the house and the dunes, crying for his sister; longing for Kayleigh.

I stayed in Kakes' room, planning to sleep in her bed each night, while Jess slept in our room, and Nate in his. It was amazingly eerie, the pain. So silent as if time was slipping backwards. I sobbed continuously. Then took a breath and emerged, trying to protect Nate from constant sadness.

And so I walked down to the ocean and sat on the beach to do my Eleventh Step, as I have done on this beach since 1996. Just seven months ago I did this each morning on our last vacation - Jess sitting in front of the TV having her coffee; you and Nathaniel tucked into your beds; me with my Big Book on the beach. Everything was secure. My confidence in life was unshakable. I looked out to this family's next chapter with hope and wonder. Then five days later you were physically killed in that horrible accident and my life was forever altered.

Coming back to Jekyll Island for the first time since your physical death is very hard. And very soothing. I could not wait, through these months, to walk with you on the beach at night, your light of the moon holding me in its embrace. I could not wait to sit with you during the day at our favorite beach, your sun warming my face, your wind speaking volumes to me while we spend time together. It is as I thought it would be. I see you. I feel you. You reach across and touch me as only you can, with a powerful dedication and a love for your Daddy like none I have ever seen.

We both say to the other, "I am here. I am right here. I am never leaving your side." This we both trust. You knew my presence on August 17 in that fateful moment. And I knew yours. You know my presence this morning. And so too I hold yours. My Love, let us walk with the wind in our face, a Cardinal's sweet angelic song in my ear and your ocean imposing its force upon the edges. As you wrote during your last physical trip to Jekyll in August, "the voice of the sea speaks to the soul-" now the voice of your soul speaks to the sea and the sea lays down its water in your honor. And I am here. And I am grateful for you.

*

Kayleigh Sent A Text from Heaven! 03/30/2018

I sent Jess a text explaining that I fed Nathaniel muffins, responding to her text wondering what he ate. I hit send and placed my phone on the bed. Walking over to the bathroom, I picked up a brush and started brushing my hair. Then I put a t-shirt on. Then I started brushing my teeth. My phone "dinged" in a manner it is not set to make such a noise. Curious, I walked over to it and picked it up. There across the screen I saw that a text was just sent from my phone while I was on the other side of the room, two minutes after I put my phone down. The text simply stated, *"I love."*

Kayleigh. Amazing Kayleigh. I quickly, and with no regard for proper English and grammar, sent a quick text to Jess explaining that I didn't send that last text to her – that our daughter did – our amazing daughter. I wrote, *"That, BTW, just wrote itself from across the room. I heard it ding. I was away from phone for two minutes. Kayleigh just crossed across my phone I didn't write that"*

Jess received the text in the TV room and ran down the hall to Kayleigh's room where I was staying. She burst through the door. "I don't understand," she said.

"Kayleigh just used my phone to send a text," I responded.

"You didn't send that?"

"No, I was nowhere near my phone. I was away from my phone for two minutes. I was twenty feet away the whole time. Jess, she just sent a text from my phone to yours telling you that she loves you!"

We sat on her bed, our hands pressing into the pillows, joyfully sobbing, a mother and father with their oldest child, miraculously using technology to convey that she was alive, present, current and active. As Kayleigh does, when we needed it most, she pressed across the veil and lifted us up.

*

Aftershocks 03/31/2018

I am steeped in an aftershock with a pure wave of grief. There are daily waves. Sometimes they are tsunamis. This wave is over my head and has blasted through my bones and left me in a debris field high on the dune line. The only thing that I find presently in pulling me through is your steady presence and love. Without that, I would be doomed. My Little Girl, My Babygirl, My adult sized child, I ache for you, missing you horribly each hard step that I take in this life. Yet I know you are here for each step that we take together, and therefore, I must make these steps sacred and make them count. I have total faith in you. Please be patient with me as I naturally grieve your physical loss.

"In the Salty Fields"

Dream, drift and seethe,
On the oceans like fallen tree forsaken,
Weep in the caldron of the sea,
In the salty fields until you have awaken,
And beached in a quiet dereliction,
Exhausted by experience afloat,
And skinned raw red by the friction,
And grief that has you by the throat,
Flaunts your dismal weakened condition,
And taunts you in its deliberate goad,
To subjugate to its religion,
And toss you back into the tidal folds,
Until the salty fields,
Have claimed you as their own.

*

Umm, You Left One of Your Stones for Me 900 Miles Away From Home 03/31/2018

A hurricane rolled across Jekyll Island just after our last visit, just after the accident. It sliced our great dune that protected our house in half, and blocked the entrance off of our dune and to the sandy plain that led to the rock wall and the beach. We were forced, therefore, on this trip to walk through the property of our neighbors to the right and down their path through the dunes.

On this extremely windy day, I spent an hour and a half in prayer and meditation with Kakes on beach. It was the third time that day that I sat for a long stretch talking with her, and played with Nate and sat with Jess in between those intervals. I talked to her about how she is teaching others that God and Heaven and guardian angels truly exist; that she was proving what people wanted to have faith in; that her presence on this side of the veil, as well as her presence in Heaven, was miraculous, but that we are all capable of the miraculous; that the human body is not our life; that life transitions from the physical to the spirit body.

At one point I dropped to my knees, the back of my hands lying in the sand, sobbing; jerking from my shoulders up and down, overcome by the raw and unacceptable pain that we were forced to absorb each day. After fifteen minutes, and knowing Jess and Nate were waiting for me and Kayleigh, I wiped my eyes, took a deep breath, and walked back towards our house through the neighbor's frontage. As I crossed the last part of their dunes, something, Kayleigh, told me to look down. Half buried in the sand lay a miracle – one of Kayleigh's prayer rocks from the batch that we had passed out at her funeral. A smooth, polished, clear stone, one we had purchased together at Joann Fabrics on a weekend for a special treat so many years earlier lay at my feet. The timing was perfect, as the wind would certainly have draped sand over it and obscured it from view in just a few minutes. It lay directly in the middle of the cut in the dune where we walk down to the beach. And it was Kayleigh's stone. She had never brought any of her stones on vacation. Nobody else placed one of Kayleigh's stones on the path that her Father was taking to get to the beach. It was Kayleigh.

Stunned, elated, knowing that I was again caught in a miraculous moment, my spine straightened. My strength returned. My conviction grew. I called out to her with laughter and glee and wonder and ran back to the house after taking a picture of it exactly where I found it and another with it in my open hand. I showed Jess and she raced back to the dune with me, followed a moment later by Nate. We three stood there with Kakes on the open, windy dune, knowing that, despite the fact that this wonderful family of four was suffering the worst tragedy a family can suffer, we were also given the greatest of gifts that a family can receive; our baby, alive, active, current, present. Glory. Hallelujah, Kayleigh. You amaze me.

*

The Only Way Through Is Through 04/01/2018

It is thread in the fabric of our existence. It is promised in the contract of life, as we march on, sunrise to sunrise, infallible and pliable, intellectual, emotive and utterly human. And it shall come. This new disturbance that tests the will of men and women. When it is, and what it is, we shall only know when it presents itself; and at that juncture, upon its presentation, and the jostling of our attention, when we pull back the veil and peer through that window of timelessness, we shall raise our eyes and our hearts to its challenge; but only if centered through daily preparation, moment to moment, shall we be ready to adjust and adapt and drive home the change required to address the newly developed situation - walking through all of its unknown hindrances and all of its slightly hidden yet abundant promise - and into a new morning we could not possibly dream of in the current landscape of today. When it comes - the only way through - is through. We will then harness the wind and breathe light into our palms.

"Where You Find Peace"

Breathe the healing light of the world,
And be the healing light so that others may breathe,
Retrieve not into the saturation where the ego displays its shiny objects,
Do not wallow in the folly and the fabric it deceives,
Rather, it is for you to harness your passionate spirit,
And let the selfish habits, like captured water, drain from open fingers,
To return to the flowing oceans of the mind,
Where, alas, against your eager wishes, you will find peace.

*

Tenth Step 04/01/2018

Another first. I listened to Future Islands "Singles" every day in August before the accident in the surf which helped me struggle with understanding the potential move to Jacksonville or not. I just sat and listened to it in the surf for the first time crying, in particular, the song in August I told her was my song to her, "She is Like the Moon." Then she was physically killed. 4 selfish? No, just grieving and crying. Dishonest? No, this sucks. I did everything right, we made every major decision right, including taking into account everybody before me in making that decision to move to Jacksonville. Then she was physically killed. Resentment? Plenty. Fear? Of living. Of life. She's with me spiritually, but the physical loss horror visits frequently. 5 telling who? Texted support group. 6 willing to have God and Kayleigh remove? Yes 7 Prayer – God and Kakes, after all of these firsts, then what? Then second anniversaries. And third. And fourth. And fifth. On and on. I will not make it if I don't process each of these in the moment and so I do. Please remove my defects in this nearly insurmountable cross I've been asked to bare. My Baby. 8 willing to change? Yes. 9 change? Breathe. Expect such sadness. Attitude, need to turn to my guardian and know that she wishes the accident didn't happen too, but since it did, she will be by my side in a different way. Perspective, I have faith she is here so when these low spots rise I turn to her to find my breath. 12 turn myself to help who? Jess and Nate when I go inside.

"Entering the Sea"

We are on a much larger journey in the full context of your existence. Your physical life was one part of that journey. Now we are on the next brilliant phase of your journey and I need to get further acclimated to it. Part of me is awash in grief and seemingly stagnant. Another part of me is trusting your messages and knowing that if I am awash in grief then I miss out on your spiritual presence. That I need to continue my transition and open with a happy heart to the amazement of my Daughter and what you are currently doing. Getting on your beam. Trusting your words that I can transition fully in our Daddy Daughter relationship. That you desire me fully a part of your life and your mission and that you get super excited when I crash through the darkness of my life and enter the magnitude of your brilliant light. I let go of the edges. I enter the sea filled with your light. Painfully. Fearlessly. Guide me.

*

Tortuga Jack's 04/02/2018

I stood in the parking lot here at this restaurant on the beach while talking to a woman in Jacksonville, a rainbow over the humid ocean, my children and my wife seating themselves outside under the tiki bar for an early summer dinner. It was August 10th - seven short days prior to the accident that would strip your physical presence from my life - forever. Now it is April 2nd and I am back here, alone, working on a book for you, with you, my beloved Daughter.

My stomach shook as I approached the restaurant. The abyss of my pain increased. Another first. Coming back to our restaurant, this time, with you in spirit.

We used to come here, Kakie, you and I, to have Daddy Daughter time. You once drank out of a coconut here and fluttered through our lunch together. You had a great pallet and tried new foods all the time. Mostly you loved the company of your Father and was absolutely in love with her family.

Now I sit in the corner of our restaurant, physically alone, overlooking the bushes on the dunes, and beyond it, your ocean; this spot on the deck where we would love to sit together. I have a glass of water at your place before a physically empty yet spiritually occupied seat. We dine together, communing together.

I talk to you in my heart and head in these moments - I really don't care what other people think but it would look pretty crazy if others, not knowing what I was doing, watched me talk to what they think is an empty chair. I suspect others would ask to sit inside, move away from me or call 911. If they knew what I was actually doing, and they had half a heart, they would cry, stop taking their own children for granted, stop complaining about their opportunities to direct or discipline their children, and know how truly blessed they are not to walk through the valley of hell.

No matter. We are at one of our favorite restaurants and my heart and soul are open. My job is to be your Daddy and I am here. And to be your humble servant and student. I study your signs. I learn from your empowerment. I live in your light. I sip from your water as you smile at me and role your eyes, the light breeze catching your long blonde angelic hair and blowing a few strands across your magnetic blue eyes.

We contemplate our next steps individually and also together, however, most of these steps are intermingled together. For instance, I am not present when you touch one of your friends in Cleveland today or help a young woman in Hawaii have the courage to stand up against her rapist. Yet, for me, you are here as I interact with Mommy and Nathaniel, with work, A.A., strangers, on the beach, in my sleep, on the road, in meditation and here at Tortuga Jack's where you and I have a great lunch together. You are one of two of my favorite little companions. Look at us, Sweetheart, transcending Heaven and earth. Only us - the KMM's.

I miss you physically. I am so happy to build our relationship spiritually. Thanks for a great lunch, Babygirl.

"In A Sacred Manner"

Awaken, this light, a million suns,
Sing my spirit free,
She graced the sky's golden silver waves that raise the seas,
That flow out from me,
The mouth of the heavens in which the stars converge,
Gather great dunes grained by billions of points of light,
Adorned with blonde sea oat fields of peace,
That flow from her golden hair,
Her Moon is blooming,
A resurrection,
Dedication, rest, reflection,
All I do I do in a sacred manner,
For you, my Love,
For you.

*

And Then Nathaniel Fell 04/03/2018

I was listening to Future Islands again, the songs I listened to in the water each day in August contemplating our move to Jacksonville. I needed to do it now - struggling through doing the normal - and wanting to take these tiny steps. She invited me to find the courage to sit in the surf and do what I do. She assured me she would sit by my side.

I did, sitting in a lounge chair in the water, the water up to my knees. I listened. I sang. I cried. I felt miserable with my life. My life had been effortless. Now it was obliterated. I felt overwhelmed by grief and took my headset off and lay it down in the pouch of the chair with my phone and fell to my knees in the surf, sinking up to my chest in the water, hunched over. Sobbing. A wretched mess of emotion. A Daddy wailing for his beloved little girl, gone forever. Asking the ocean to strip the pain from my eyes. Asking why. Cursing the cruelty. The suddenness. The shock. Knowing the depths of her physical loss and all that lay before us day after day. Also knowing her spiritual presence is unshakable. Yet I sobbed uncontrollably for my Daughter, making noises out of my mouth I never thought I could make.

Then she did what Kayleigh does, and Jess and Nate appeared climbing over the rocks to the ocean side of the rocks. Knowing my grief, she sent for Jess and Nate and brought them to me. Jess came all the way down the rocks to the sand. Nate stayed on the rocks climbing around like we've done a thousand times.

I stood with Jess trying to catch my breath, hearing Kayleigh calming me and telling me to breathe her light. My sobbing slowed down, beginning to turn like the tide and move away from the physical and re-engage with the spiritual. She told me she needed her Daddy and needed her Daddy to listen.

Then I heard Nate scream as he fell off of the other side of the rocks for the first time ever, falling down upon the lowest rocks and ripped his toenail off. I scurried over the rocks and picked him up and carried him in my arms, a tall thirteen year old, and all the way back to the house and into the bathroom. I was carrying them both. Thus, reminding me again of my dual purpose - here with Nate and Jess in the physical embodiment; and here with Kakie spiritually, ever connected and ever leading me through the misery of her physical loss. We are a family of four, ever vigilant of the other. We just need to open our eyes and hearts.

"This Valley of Pain"

And I, through this valley of pain,
Painted with a grayish stain,
Beg me at the cuff of Heaven's sleeve,
With fire spark and burning grain,
Embedded with this human chain,
Love, it lashes beach in a steady rain,
As salty tears strike like a hurricane,
I may -

Struggle foot soar and shedding skin,
Stretch the soul when it's wearing thin,
Only to channel rainbows on the moistened morning dew,
Unpeeling the crusted edges of my life,
To find the light I find in you.

*

The Feather 04/05/2018

Having spent some afternoon time on the beach, I woke sprawled out on my blankets in a quieting heat. Jess had left me there asleep. Kayleigh was very present, sitting beside me, the wind blowing through her hair, and asked me a question about the current state of our relationship, reminding me she had come to me fifteen years before she was born; spent fifteen years with me physically; and now has been with me ever since spiritually.

I sat up and said, "Kayleigh, grant me the serenity to accept the heartache that our physical relationship together has come to an end, the courage to accept that this full and brilliant continuation of our relationship in different body types, me in the physical and you spiritually, that this harsh reality is upon us, and the wisdom to know the difference."

As I finished my words my attention was drawn southward down the beach, from which a very steady and warm wind had developed. I noticed at eye level as I sat on my blankets, a tiny white feather, swooping through the breeze directly towards me and more than several hundred feet away. It kept its level while it bounced on the air and the breeze, heading directly towards me. I stared at this white feather as it approached, and at the last moment, lifted my hand. It slapped right against my hands and caught between my middle fingers.

This is the third feather she has left for me this trip and the most profound. As if she was saying, "yes, Daddy, yes! That's it. Move into the next phase with me. I am on the wind, yet, I am still in the physical world. I am here, Daddy. You can do it. You can do it, Daddy!"

I can.

"In A Pleasant Wind"

Midday hush in the oak and brush and golden dunes,
Just the sprinkle of sand smoke against the talking palms,
Daytime shadows cast by the brilliant sun,
And strip of radiant crescent moon,
A rush of warm wind speaks the language of the skin,
It breathes, it thinks, it swirls and it swoons,
It is love itself and the light it brings,
Soothes the deepest wounds,
Listen to her sing,
Listen to her sing;

I know your presence here,
Your intention very clear,
You punch through the thin veil between these two worlds,
Will do anything to hold your Father's hand,
Your spirit conquers every fear,
That could develop within this man,
And so you sing to him,
And he hears you,
In a pleasant wind.

*

Crossroads -Tenth Step 04/05/2018

Crossroads. Kayleigh told me that I need to evolve from our physical life together, since we are not both in physical bodies, and that stage of our relationship is no more, and I need to focus on our relationship with us in two different bodies, and our spiritual relationship, which is upon us. I've known that since August 17th, but its concreteness came through her voice so strongly last night. 4 Selfish? Yes, I don't want to let go, or change. I want to go back to August 16th. Dishonest? Yes, it has been no more in the purely physical since August 17th. Resentment? Yes, against the world; sometimes with God; sometimes just re-feeling. 5 tell who? Text friend in A.A. 6 willing to have God remove defects? Yes. 7 prayer? God and Kakes, please remove resistance to this awful change that continues to strip me of my life for I have no choice but to press forward. Please remove sheltering in what isn't. Our relationship is a ship built to leave the harbor. Show me the way out of the harbor. 8 willing to change? Yes. 9 change? Breathe. Expect unknown on these waves. Expect feeling loneliness on these waves at times. Attitude can be honoring of our new configuration by fully embracing it, for there is no other choice. I refuse to block myself from you. Perspective - MY BABY CROSSES FROM HEAVEN AND WALKS ON EARTH WITH ME AND TALKS TO ME EVERY DAY!!!!!! 12 turn to someone I can help? Baby boy Nate and Jess.

*

Daddy, If the Tables Were Turned... 04/6/2018

Kayleigh, if the tables were turned I would do everything in my power to cross the wind to touch you and Nathaniel and Jess. All the time. I would be using my light to illuminate my three loves, all the time. Literally all the time. Ever present. Non-stop. Who am I, then, to fear or think or lull myself into thinking that you wouldn't do the exact same thing for me? It is a dishonor to you to think that, with as much focus and love and meaning you always placed on this family, you wouldn't be doing the exact same thing - moving spiritual mountains to echo light in our surroundings, touching us, warming us, walking daily as a family of four strengthened by your soul's release. God and Family have always been the most important aspects of your life and that has not diminished - in fact, it has increased in your spiritual release. You can now fully access, cradle and enhance these relationships.

The tables are turned and that is exactly what you are doing. I see it. I feel you. It is the comfort you know I need - the communion that pulls me through the fear sometimes hour to hour; sometimes minute to minute; and sometimes through the centuries that hide in seconds. I hear you frequently and you just today told me, 'don't lose us in the different, Daddy.' We are in the different now and it is forever altered. The landscape is that of a foreign planet I've been dropped upon. You encourage me through the change, these heart stressing revolutionary and epic changes of my life.

Every morning I wake up is unfamiliar ground. The world moves on as if it is not, yet it is a rapid alteration adorned with suffering, trauma and miracles. Trapped in a movie that I can't prevent in replay. Lost of balance. Looking over my shoulder for the sound of your physical chirpy voice. Looking down the street to see you come around the corner. Sitting in the silence. And in my prayer and meditation, I hear you. I sense you. We plan the twenty four hours ahead, spearheaded for me with Steps 10, 11 and 12, daily strengthening and reinvigorating my sobriety and my life's resolve, opening with devotion and intention to my three loves and planning activities with each of you individually, just as I did before the accident, and ultimately doing ten things, by example, a day with each of you.

After the last hurricane hit Jekyll Island our beach was wiped out. Big majestic dunes - cut off like a knife through warm butter - literally a fifty foot long massive dune disappeared. Now, instead of dunes, we sit below a forty foot wide, 18 foot high cliff wall closest to the house on a flat beach where the massive dune once lay, looking out to the protective rock wall that, prior to the hurricane, was uniform in its structure - now it lay scattered; low and spread out with water leaking through, other piles of rocks sit high, little touched by the surges that ripped over the wall. Where you sat on that last trip before the accident has been reduces by five feet, barely holding back the Atlantic.

The beach is still a beach and recognizable as a beach, but it has been forever altered. It can still be beautiful - it can just never be the way that it was. Life is always in constant change and sometimes, unfortunately and sometimes arbitrarily, we cannot avoid horrific change in our lives. Horrific change visited our family and we are a beach that will never be the same. There is a massive empty space where the majestic dune used to sit. Yet different from the physical absence of the dune, Kayleigh, you still sit with me very much alive - just in spirit - and embrace your family in your fullness.

*

A Road for the Spirit to Pass Over 04/07/2018

After writing with you, Kayleigh, this day, and clearly hearing you tell me to listen deeper, I jumped into my car and decided to turn on your singing clips on my video files on my phone. A clip started and I heard your lovely voice for several seconds, music to my soul, before the Bluetooth took over and seemingly randomly picked a song from my playlist, literally jumping from my photo video files to my music files. It was "*Song of the Stars,*" from Dead Can Dance. I knew immediately you wanted me to hear this and truly listened deeply, particularly since you just finished telling me to listen better. You were invoking another part of your soul, that of your Native American heritage, and finding a song and an intentional message to reach across the wind with your light.

In the song the singers sing in both English and in Algonquian. It is about guardian angels in the tribe, stars in the sky with voices of light who lay a road for a loved ones' spirits to pass over at the end of physical life. What is significant is that, your heritage on your Native American side is the Kickapoo Tribe, one of the Algonquin tribes in the Midwest. "*…We are like the wind, wrapped in luminous wings, we make a road for the spirit to pass over…*"

You are getting stronger, your messages clearer. You are learning how to clearly manipulate technology and any other tangible items in the physical world, blending your spiritual dimension into our daily lives; crossing our dimensions, the physical world and Heaven; touching your Father, who can then, touch you. You are brilliant, Little Girl, and so brilliantly alive. Keep shining. Keep teaching me. I am listening deeper.

*

Your Closet 04/09/2018

Hi Baby. As you know, I am sitting in your closet area where you used to sit and sing and text and do makeup. Where you used to cry and where you would retreat when you wanted privacy. I have retreated today, the first day back from vacation. The last time we arrived home from a vacation, you were physically alive and our whole future lay before us. There were things that distracted us in a normal life, but for the most part, we were empowered and ready to roll in life. Battle tested. Firm. Loose and relaxed. Alive. Awake.

Now I sit in your closet surrounded by some of your clothes that I have hung on hangers neatly; the Key Largo shirt I bought you; the special blue dress I bought you during a Daddy-Daughter outing on St. Simon Island; the dress you wore to shadow day at Beaumont; your school uniforms. A hairband with your strands of hair caught in a hair-tie.

Even though we daily have magical moments, like you changing the music yesterday to the "*Song of the Stars*," and it elevated me incredibly, I still have these other grief stricken moments. Daily. I am trying to do my Eleventh Step, my prayer and meditation, my journaling. I have such horrible heartache. I don't know what to do.

"Daddy, its Kakes. You know what to do. Do your Eleventh Step and then walk with me. You can do that. I know you can. You are my Daddy and I am so proud of you."

I am so proud of you, Sweetheart.

"Look around this closet, Daddy, surrounded by little glimpses of my physical life. All provided for by you and Mommy. I had everything I wanted in my physical life, Daddy, most of all, the love of an amazing family. I loved and was loved. I love and am loved. That's what these clothes represent."

You're right, Kakes. Help me stay in that light as I step back to the day.

485

*

Caged Animal 04/10/2018

Circling, circling; looking for that crack in the corner that will let me scratch my way back to you. Everywhere I turn - things I can't have. Things you can't have. Things we don't get to do. Things you don't get to do. You are my litmus test. If I am not in contact with you, then I'm going to be useless to your brother. When I am in contact with you, I am spiritually centered and have much more to offer both of my children on each of the plains where you each currently reside.

I was built specifically to be your Daddy, at every age. I focused my energy in my life towards that goal - I never worked in a law firm because I opted to be home for dinner with you; I took extra care in growing my sobriety and self-inventorying in my constant vigilance of Step Ten; I organized my life around ensuring that each day I had time reserved for you and your brother and your mother - one on one time with you each; I adjusted to what worked at 2 to what didn't at 4 - what worked at 11 that didn't at 12, on a constant evolution of expanding my assets and my support system to support an ever changing young woman and younger brother; I never strayed from my priority list: my sobriety, then my children, then my wife and marriage, then everything else. I was built for you. I am built to continue to grow with you. And I will. And I do.

I find myself desperately, painfully desiring to give advice to you for things I was ready for - 16, 18, 20; high school, driving, college, emotions, spirituality, sexuality, the bumps and bruises and triumphs of life. At the ready as I always have been. And now I cannot use these skills. I cannot advise a young woman who no longer is in her physical embodiment. I am a library full of books with no daughter to enrich, with whom to impart the knowledge that would continue to shape your life.

I have this same duplicate library that I use with your brother. He is a boy and I will continue to help him develop into a loving man. But with you - a Daddy's only daughter - the nightmare keeps giving, and I am left holding these lost opportunities that add up and compile daily in the palms of my wounded hands.

*

What Am I Offering My Children 04/11/2018

The question upon waking each morning is this - what am I offering my children today? Depression? Immeasurable grief? Or my example. My light. My courage. My strength. No matter the current difficulty, I will offer you my light. I cannot promise that it won't co-exist with grief, as it will. But I can work at ensuring that my light wins the day.

This is the question I have been asking since I first sobered up, fifteen years before you were born, knowing that how I lived my life as a young, single man before children would evolve into the man I would be once married with children. So even before you were born I would ask myself in my morning prayer and meditation, what am I offering my children today? Before either of you were born - after you were both born, and now after one of you has physically passed into the Higher Life - always I have the same question.

I trust you, Kayleigh, that you are here - you are ever vigilant - you are alive and well spiritually and offering me light strengthened in your heavenly gains. I will continue to learn from you and do likewise. Love you.

"Daddy, you are light! Just like me! You have always been my guiding light. Shine! You can do this!"

"Always This Family of Four"

And so upon us, constant reconciliation,
Rise daily to this new configuration,
And adjust to this unfamiliar situation,
Tragedy and miracles,

Depression and elation,
Merge like strings into a sturdy cord of light,
That pulls this family of four,
Through each of our four lives.

*

Dear Most of You - You Are I'll Equipped 04/12/2018

In the initial blush of the tragedy, flocks of well-wishers, old friends, new friends, strangers, etc. came forward. There were cards by the hundreds if not thousands; bouquets of flowers; meals; prayers. For the mass of this wonderful outpouring of humanity, the job was at hand and the bell answered. Then they moved on. Within days. Within weeks. I warned Jess that this would happen when she would make a statement to the effect that so many people had our backs in those first few days.

Some believe, based on their own unrelated experience, that when their father died four years ago, they grieved and moved on. When their grandmother died seventeen years ago, they grieved and moved on. So why can't I just grieve and move on, as if something is pathological about my experience. It is so selfish and misguided and uninformed and egocentric of these people, none of whom have suffered the physical death of a child. Reader, if you find yourself thinking in this manner with someone who has physically lost a child in childhood, it is time to shut up and listen. It is time to check your head and start taking direction from somebody who actually knows what they are talking about - namely, the person in your life who is suffering the physical loss of a child. There is nothing like this in the world. Nothing. It does not heal. It is not meant to heal. It gets worse over time as losses accumulate. We can counterbalance, but the truth is drastic and harsh – there is no moving on, which is insulting. Who would "move on" from their child? It is a disgusting idea. There is no healing. That is truth.

The point is, dear Reader, if you find yourself resonating or getting angry with me, please stop pretending that you have answers that can help us. You don't. Stop thinking that we need words of encouragement. We don't. Stop thinking that we are irrevocably broken and we need your enlightenment. Actually that is absurd, and we don't. We, in our grief and through our experiences, are some of the most courageous people you will ever meet. We just need you to say that you love us, that you don't comprehend what we are going through daily for the rest of our lives, and you are here for us. When we breakdown in three months from now, six years from now, fifteen years from now, know that you don't understand and know that it is a natural consequence of seeing all that has been lost daily for the rest of our lives with the physical void of our beloved child who didn't get to do this and that, who didn't go here or there, who didn't get to experience all the things we see others experience with complaints. Ignorance. Callousness. Thoughtlessness.

Then there are those who are generally equipped to support us, who haven't gone through this misery. They are rare. They listen. My sister Tricia is one. She defers to me. She doesn't tell me anything. She asks. She asks what she can do. She asks me how Kayleigh and I are doing. She asks what support I need. She defers. Please listen - she defers to me. Defer to me. It is my child.

*

You Are Alive 04/13/2018

You are very much alive I just can't hold you physically in my arms. I can't audibly hear your human voice like I used to be able to hear. I can't be displaced by your physical human body on the couch sitting with me. But you are here. It is amazing.

You are very much alive. No longer in the mission of a fifteen year old working your way through adolescence and dreaming of the future with hopes and fears and excitement. Now your mission is much larger and expansive. Having matured a thousand fold in your spiritual transformation, you are now changing lives at a steady clip;

guarding your family, lining things up for something big. I feel it. I sense it. I am awake.

We are on a much larger journey in the full context of your existence. Your physical life was one part of that journey. Now we are on the next brilliant phase of your journey and I need to get further acclimated to it. Part of me is awash in grief and seemingly stagnant. Another part of me is trusting your messages and knowing that if I am awash in grief and fear of this life then I miss out on your spiritual presence. I need to continue my transition and open with a happy heart to the amazement of my Daughter and what you are currently doing. Getting on your beam. Trusting your words that I can transition fully in our Daddy Daughter relationship. That you desire me fully a part of your mission and get super excited when I crash through the darkness of my life and enter the magnitude of your brilliant light. I let go of the edges. I enter the sea filled with your light. I am a warrior swinging blindly through the darkness to cut down the barriers to you. I find the light. The light is you. Guide me.

*

"This Is Where I Met Heaven, Daddy" 04/14/2018

Right there. Down from this bench. On Euclid Heights Boulevard, which may sound strange. But a spectacular doorway opened that only I could see. A dimension of love and light that I held in my soul, as you do as well. Its magnificence filled the streets and illuminated the darkness of summer night all around, for miles, centered on my body and my soul and blooming with the light of one million suns. Nobody else, including you, could see it. That was just for me. Yet a doorway opened that you, Daddy, could feel. That's why it was you, Daddy, who was by my side when I passed.

You held me as my breath slowed down. I was so calm in your arms. So safe and protected. I really had no idea what was going on. I didn't even know that I had been hit by a car or that my head had hit the street. All I knew was that my Daddy was with me, comforting me, telling me he loved me, telling me I would be okay. My Daddy, the man I looked up to like no other man, the man who means the world to me, the man I could always count on. And you were there. Of course you were there. You are always there.

And then this brilliant blinding light appeared through this incredible doorway. Right there, Daddy, over there in the street. It is hard to imagine for those still in their physical life, but it is true. Right over there on the site where my physical life ended and my spiritual rebirth occurred, where you held your child as I passed in your arms.

I'm happy the city took the time and energy to help you and Mommy and Nate putting in this bench. And I like that it overlooks directly that spot in the street. Because right there, right there, Daddy, a hundred feet or so away from this bench, in the street, next to the concrete island where my head was touching the curb, where my physical body lay, being held by your voice and your love and your nearness, that is where I met Heaven, Daddy. Right there.

*

My Anonymous Friend at Work 04/14/2018

Kayleigh's funeral stone is in a sacred spot on an altar she has at her home. This is the place where my friend likes to daily sit and pray and meditate. She is a highly spiritually connected, intuitive and a sweet soul. She was sitting quietly, not thinking in that moment about me or Kayleigh. She was just sitting, a candle lit before her, absorbing learning from the heavens. All of a sudden she heard, "Hi! It's Kakes!"

"Oh," said my friend, in a surprised moment, "why hello, Kayleigh." She knew it was my Daughter even though she had never met Kayleigh before the accident. Kayleigh proceeded to talk with her and told her several key pieces of information she wanted my friend to convey to me. She felt an intense overwhelming sense of love emanating from Kayleigh; a powerful, high level, sophisticated, elevated angel.

My friend conveyed the following to me, in Kayleigh's words, "I am worried about my Daddy. Tell Daddy not to worry about me - I am okay. I am really content and happy, just as I always have been. I was really taken by surprise when the accident happened, and I wasn't thinking about anything except coming home to see my family. I didn't even make a mistake. And I didn't want to go when the accident occurred. I didn't want to leave my body, but I know now it was part of my overall spiritual journey."

I listened intently, knowing this was true and authentic, that Kayleigh has channeled my friend to pass messages through to me. She continued, "I could not have picked a greater Father, Mother and Brother and you all made everything in life so special. I tried to pack in all that I could in my life. Daddy, you call me a dynamo, and that's what it was like, packing my life full of love, and not knowing then why I was always so present in the moment, but knowing now that I must have subconsciously known my physical life might be cut short. I am in love, head over heels in love with my family, with my Father, my Mother and my Brother. Al four of us feel the same way and we are such a special family. You all know that but I am confirming it again.

My friend then told me that she could see and hear Kayleigh, that she definitely is an incredibly powerful soul who has learned how to use her powers quickly and always for the betterment of love and light all around. She continued with her own reflections from the messages from Kayleigh, "she will never, never, never leave your side. She shows you daily her power in one way or another because she wants you to be very firmly convicted of her truth and miraculous rebirth spiritually and knows the human mind can play tricks on itself when the soul grows weary or sad. She wants you to rejoice with her and be on the same plain spiritually, as high as you can get. She said you let her be fully her. She also said that Daddy has three books. Something of a reboot of "Clemy," and she wants you to finish the current book you are writing. But there is another."

She paused, took a deep breath, and said, "She also told me, 'people better not mess with my family. They don't know how powerful I am,' but she is saying it, not in a threatening manner. More like, if someone messes with you guys, she is going to be right there protecting you and redirecting people with love and light. She is so wise, Kevin, so compassionate. She is love and light itself. I just wanted you to know."

Kayleigh IS. She IS more than anybody ever has been. She IS more than she was in her physical life and she was simply amazing before the accident. Now she IS even more amazing and I have never been more humbled and proud of her. She IS my Daughter. She IS a guardian angel. She IS ever present, with me forever. Simply, she IS.

*

A Thousand Deaths 04/15/2018

A thousand deaths a morning missing you. Sometimes in those initial moments where slumber fades and new light finds me waking to a new day, the deaths of my spirit compile and compound. I breathe your light and try to rise with a positive attitude, with intention and devotion, with purpose. A thousand heavens sing your name.

"A Thousand Deaths A Morning"

A thousand deaths a morning,
A thousand breaths withheld,
A thousand depths outpouring,
From these tortured eyes expelled;

Ten thousand left if maybe,
I live another thirty years,
Each every day a mourning,
That time will never quite repair;

So I wake up in each new morning,
My Daughter's soul - my spirit guide,
Empowered with her presence,
Though the miles - they are long,
These miles, they are wide,

These miles, they are wounding,
These miles in my eyes.

*

15-3-2 04/15/2018

I see our memories of fifteen years, three months and two days all around and they make me smile. Sometimes I see a daddy and his daughter doing something similar to us - sometimes seeing one of these daddies missing out on an opportunity to be with his daughter - both having the same Kayleigh effect on me. I do feel happy and relieved to know how incredibly intentional I was with you throughout your physical life, which helped to fill your life up with joy and abundance. You are an amazingly developed, mature and wonderful soul, partly because of my intentional parenting. I see some fathers who are selfish, disengaged, shitty fathers who haven't the maturity or the clue what a beauty and value they are missing out on, that we know by having such a strong, engaging bond.

I also see all that isn't - all that will now never be. Commercials of young twenty year olds driving around town launching into adulthood, a beautiful blond teenager girl walk by me who looks like you; college kids; high school kids driving; Kids getting into trouble; young couples in love and planning marriages; young moms with little babies - my grandchildren that will now never be. The list is endless and I see it everywhere. It causes such sadness, this nightmare that keeps giving and giving and giving.

Yet the path has shifted upon golden sand. Those things that were to come in your physical life will never be - replaced with the glory of what is and what will come. I can't always see all that will now be in your magical presence. What is, quite frankly, is amazing - you, a guardian angel, transposing, transitioning, traveling across the spirit world to the physical world - sitting here with me right now as I write this on the couch. That is more amazing. When I let go in the tension of the moment, I see the vast light of reality and honesty of your current life and it eclipses anything you could have accomplished in your physical state. I just wish you lived physically to eighty and then were a guardian angel after that long life! But even then, I would not have witnessed nor seen first-hand the power an angel like you possesses!

With my constant intention, and your eternal devotion to your family, we continue to engage and build this incredible relationship. I quite frankly have never seen a better example of a father and his children, spurred by the 12 Steps and true and continuous dedication - does that make me egotistical or just honestly humble in truth. The answer is simple: selflessness is humility and that selflessness is my credo as a father. I know my truth and that truth made it possible, on my end, to be awake with you before you were born, throughout your physical life, and currently in your higher life. And therefore we continue to grow - partly due to me – and largely due to you.

I see so much that will never be on a daily basis. You show me on each of those days what is. I am starting to balance this duality more and more. Where will I put my limited energy? On you, My Love, and on your brother and Mommy.

"Oh course you will, Daddy. You always do!"

*

A Child's Voice 04/16/2018

And now, with a voice louder and more powerful as the days of her new life unfold, her breath like light that crosses the wind, it's warmth - it kisses my face - her voice, it soothes my soul in its multitude of tones, pitch volume and texture. She knows what I need when I need it. She always shows up because she is already here.

We line fields of gold for our children with our experiences. We do for them so that the world does not do to them without feeling the responsive wrath of their voices. We cannot always protect our children, but we can teach our children how to be protective of their most cherished treasure - their voices, their souls, emotions, dreams and truth. Kayleigh's voice is a derivative of this interchange, this interaction between parent and child, shuffling through the superficial and serious, the simple debris, the chaff, the flack and the silver rainbows of life.

*

Time Does Not Make Anything Better 04/17/2018

That construct, like many shortsighted, but certainly well intentioned statements spoken from a perspective of innocent ignorance, flies in the face of facts before a parent whose child has physically died. Time actually makes things harder for me. The further away I get from her physical life the harder it is to retain a fluid and current status of our physical times, or of our new configuration, together. There is a breath that ever becomes larger as time creeps further away from the time when we were in the same space in the same body types on this physical world together. Talk about not taking anything for granted. Now the stakes are so high. If I flinch, or fail to grow, or fall deeply into despondency, or flail in depression, I will lose contact with my girl. I refuse to dishonor Kayleigh like this. I will never stop. I will never fail her. I will figure out the next step, the hard step, the unusual step, the final step.

*

Eight Months on This Road 04/17/2018

Eight months, one second at a time away from your physical breath, the last of which you exhaled into my light and with my mouth just inches from your ear. I honor our relationship and I honor you today by confronting head on today our current reality - you have been physically killed and spiritually released. I have to say this a million times. It is so hard.

496

You are alive and well, just now in a different dimension. Our relationship thrives when I thrive since when I fall apart I drift away unintentionally from you. You are a constant. Constant strength. Constant love and light. Constant wisdom. Constantly with me, cheering me on, encouraging me and guiding me. What an incredible opportunity to grow with you! Yet I fall and falter and need to be reminded. Constantly.

Me, with my human frailties and weaknesses and a mind that attempts to confine, rather than expand, when I can't quite grasp the logic of a situation; me, struggling through the chaos of my wonderful fifteen year old daughter being physically killed in a simple, innocent accident. Me. Through it all, I remain utterly willing and confident in my ability to be there for my children, on two different plains simultaneously, and awaken to you further and deeper. I love you with all my soul.

"Hi. Here we are. What are we going to do today, Daddy? I'm ready to go live with you. Stay intentional, Daddy. Let's go eat at Los Arcos! It's our favorite. Love you too!"

*

"My Sobriety is Not Mine" **04/18/2018**

The soul, dusty embers, its smoky tail drying in fright,
I'd carved metal memories that twist together the broken trail of my life,
That ended encased in green bottles of choking cold glass,
I was survived by only that which I surpassed,
And blessed with a sober breath,
When my spirit wailed, and ruptured and pined,
I was given my sobriety,
But my sobriety is not mine;

For yours is a sacred field I walk with delicate embrace,
For yours is a sacred place - from the warmth of your hand to the smile on your face,

Illuminate darkness, fill in the basin,
Fill your eyes with the heavens above,
I was given my sobriety so that you may know the deepest love,
For you, I turn to the daily work before the day's rise,
For my sobriety is yours,

-It is not mine.

*

Every Day Rejoice! 04/19/2018

Every day from here on out, from August 17th, 2017. I need to counterbalance with your spiritual miracles and knowing I have never been more proud than now - watching you cross Heaven and earth and touch us. Truly amazing girl. You don't get to go to dances in your physical form, but you get to make the rain dance. You get to dance with the rain. You get to dance with your Father and Mother and Brother. You are the light that catches in the droplets of rain itself; the light that we catch in our eyes.

The world knows your light. The world will continue to know your light. You are alive and well. Why should I not rejoice? In one truth I grieve. In the other I need to rejoice. I hear you, Sweetheart, in your sweet voice, "Daddy, I am so proud of you - Daddy, I love you so much - Daddy, look what I learned how to do!" You are pure energy. Pure magic. Pure love. Why should I not rejoice? You are Kayleigh Mickayla Mooney - pure brilliance. The Moon. My Daughter.

I can encapsulate you within a physical body and call you Kayleigh, but you are much bigger than that. The love you see in my eyes - the love I see in your eyes - it is love. Much bigger than the flesh that contains that love while in our physical forms. Our love is eternal. Immortal. Gifted by God and filled with His light.

You say, "The way you guys have always loved me, always love me. It's that simple, Daddy. That's how we continue to grow."

Our relationship did not die in the street that night. It changed. I promise you I will make it one day at a time in this new configuration, even when it feels ever daunting and impossible. At the end of my life, after I have honored every day of our relationship in its current state, then I will be with you fully in spirit - in effect we will finally be in the same body type again and on the same plain together again and our relationship will take on its new form. A relationship that is always, and over time changes, but remains constant and empowered with our love for each other.

Not only did I not lose this relationship that night, I also did not lose my Daughter. Yes, your body physically died, but you did not die. Your spirit actually illuminated and grew by a thousand fold as you were released from your human condition, unchained from the confines of life, and awakened to a higher purpose, higher life and higher love. So not only are you alive, but you are a thousand times more alive, and as present as you have ever been. I just can't see your physical embodiment because that manifestation of you has died, though you can present yourself in any manner that you want. I see specific days in my memory at different ages and you can transpose that into your image during a meditation. You can present as light, wind, the ocean and pretty echoes through the wind chimes. Your voices are endless. Your ability to appear in different ways infinite. We just have to look. We just have to listen. We just have to open.

What I am experiencing is really quite magical. A real study on miracles. I am living miracles with my Daughter, one day at a time, with a higher vibration and clarity of mind and soul. You have a Father who is in love with you, whose heart aches at the descent of each breath, who longs for your presence and your laughter, who is open and awake and yearning higher towards you. And I have a Daughter who is in love with her Father, who will never leave his side, who longs to dance in the air about us and be a part of everything we do. You are lining things up. Those things are coming. At some point. And they have your fingerprints all over them. It will be magnificent.

*

Stress Is a Dam That Prevents the Flow of Light 04/20/2018

It happens every day to everybody, but with those similarly situated to me currently, more so due to various complex and competing triggers: grief, exhaustion, physical health concerns due to grief and exhaustion, pain and suffering, the energy it takes to go from task to task under grief stricken conditions, shock. It all contributes uniquely to the heightened stress that a survivor of a child's physical death must contend. Total heartbreak. Every day. And the world continues. And largely the world, a non-entity, having no capacity for compassion, doesn't care.

Further, at just the time that someone like me needs a stress reduction, these additional stressors tax our limited and frayed resources. It is miserable. It is cruel. It is, quite frankly, inhuman. Yet it is.

When stress builds, and it can build quickly, it compacts upon itself like unorganized jagged debris: logs, branches, garbage, vegetation, sediment - all clogging together to block the natural flow of the river. However, in this scenario it is the singular critical river of light that connects me to God; me to me; me to Kayleigh. It is a dam that causes me distance within that causes distance without.

If unmanaged, it is harder to hear her voice and be attentive to her needs. When I spin off into resentment, or get lost in the forest for an hour trying to understand why this happened or that didn't happen, or why so and so did this or he or she did that, I squander the current hours. I waste the hours. I lose precious time with my beloved daughter, compounding the fact that it is not always so easy for me to stay high enough in my elevation to feel in touch with her. She is an open channel for me and her light flows nonstop like a river of love; a river of pure liquid gold. Then it hits this dam of stress and explodes against its barrier, and I remain disconnected from her, which destroys me. This is my work. This is on me.

Kakie, I promise you I will manage from day to day, from minute to minute, situation to situation in order to manage and reduce my stress. To remove the debris accumulating in the river of light. I will open a wider channel in the process through which we communicate and laugh and play and grow in our relationship. Although there are times that I am a hyena trapped in a metal box, spinning in circles and trying to find the corner where the metal has a breach so that I can escape to you, I will do my work.

*

Daddy, I Have Learned How to Speak Through the Wind
04/21/2018

"Wind Traveler"

Within the wind there is a traveler,
She calls me with her light,
She calls me by name -

"Father, how I love you, know that I am near,
I am with you, with you always - with you always here;"

This traveler, she speaks across the swooning breeze,
A symphonic orchestra that glows from whispered speech,

"Daddy, do not worry for I am filled with God's light,
I will guide your everyday of every moment of your life;"

Within the wind she travels and has learned to use its flow,
To reach her Father's spirit,
To reinforce his soul.

*

Clear Direction 04/22/2018

Hi, Sweetheart. Thank you for such clear instruction this morning. It was so simple. Do the basic work, relax, embrace the reality of our situation and build with love and light a continuous spire of our relationship's sacred home - Higher into a Higher Life. Your physical death will never be okay; will always be cruel; will never be something I will get over or move on from. I am so happy I understand fully that piece of this - and I accept that some things, though unacceptable, need to be accepted, daily, in whatever form it shows itself.

With that in hand, I also turn to what is - and the "what is" truly is your current, active life in spirit. It unfolds before my eyes. I get to watch you "grow up," but not anymore as a teenager in physical, human clothes and situations, but as a fully functioning life in a spiritual body, maturing daily as a spirit guide and guardian angel. And I get to participate in your journey (a warm wind just flipped these pages and the wind chimes just began to sing in your sweet voice as I write with pen and paper). How amazing are you, My Love? I have always been proud of you, but never as proud as I am today as that pride and awe grows daily seeing the glory of God that flows from your angelic hands. Walk with me, Babygirl (your wind just blanketed me again) and encourage me to do my part if I tire, get lost, get struck with grief or temporarily lose my way. I frequently lose my way in the forest. I promise I will always find my way back to the path to you. I promise you my light, Kakes. I will not fail you. I will not fail me. I love you so much.

"She Is Lining Things Up"

She is tying things together,
She is lining up points of light,
She is engaged in an epic miracle,
That will profoundly change our lives,
She is grace that doesn't ask of much,
Just compassion and love that holds the line,
She is tying things together,
That know no space nor time.

*

The Great Counterbalance 04/26/2018

Without the counterbalance, I'm a dead man. There are two sides to this coin. There is the harsh, horrible trauma of my child's sudden, indescribable physical death. If I live only in its weight, I am soon overcome. It is so heavy. So sticky. So isolating. So pure in its trauma. So perfectly awful.

So I need to flip the Kayleigh coin after I process those feelings of her physical loss. For there is another side to this coin - the side of light and continued life. Her spiritual embodiment blooms on the other side of that coin and provides just enough of the counterbalance to center me again. It is pure light and love and Kayleigh in various forms and freedoms - her wisdom realized, her laughter like a chorus of wind chimes, her love and compassion like a billion stars circling happily in a galaxy of rainbows, and her powers of greatness and gentleness unleashed into this physical world by touching us, sending us texts, leaving us stones; her daily, weekly, monthly anniversaries of being reborn in the glorious realm of Heaven.

She and I - we clearly never wanted this. I clearly never will. Yet I must accept what is versus what is not. What is yesterday is not. What is today is. I have a daughter who needs her Father to give her his light and love today. I did so yesterday and for all the yesterdays of her physical life. In A.A., my group talks about not being able to drive a car today on the gas you used last week. So we daily do our work in Steps 10, 11 and 12 to renew and strengthen day after day, knowing we cannot live off of yesterday's sobriety.

So too must I follow the same regime with Kayleigh if I want to renew and strengthen our relationship. It is up to me, since I am the weaker link, to correct my steps, to struggle and trudge forward, to win the day in the wallows, to yearn to a higher vibration where I meet my baby who cheers for me along the way. As if she is a mother on her knees, arms outstretched to her child, and I am that child taking his

503

first few steps, locked with the eyes that illuminate love and safety and trust staring back at me with encouragement, I yearn in the frailty of my human condition towards her perfection.

Her physical loss is a horrible trauma. Yet her spiritual gain is a tremendous miracle. I live in both for I must. I cannot escape the physical loss. Yet I can miss the spiritual gain. Please, God and Kayleigh, empower me forward so that I do not miss your spiritual embodiment, the moments that you sit with me in the car, at work, on your bed; walking side by side with the dogs or sitting in a sauna; watching TV or singing in the car; eating together now at our favorite restaurants, a glass of water or iced tea at your place setting while I eat my food and while you taste that food through me.

You are the great counterbalance in the present that centers me when the weight of your physical loss comes screaming through each day.

"Soul Storms"

Daddy, I don't have to warn you,
As you know,
There will be times when you seethe,
Times of disbelief,
Times of pure inferno,
When you can't breathe,
When the fires won't cease,
And the winds won't slow,
Where the pains increase,
And the tempest grows,
And then release,
As you let go,
And sink to rise again -

Daddy, as I watch you, know,
You are a brilliance,
In the ways that you love me,
You are resilience,
Holding nothing above me,
You are the courage,
That tells its own story,

You are my anchor,
And I am your mooring,
And I will be waiting,
On every new morning,
To guide you through each day.

*

Find Me in the Shadows 04/27/2018

We have received this message from you several times. Very directly in meditation. From a reverend who we met with who can channel you. In your art. I've heard you tell me this in variations – that, by looking into the shadows, that is where you found you - that you were found in the shadows - by you. Not that you lived in the shadows, but that a shadow fell upon you and you fought it off, ultimately elevating yourself, empowering yourself and finding your true beauty of self.

It has become much clearer to me and no longer is a hunch, but a concrete fact. I now understand what you've been telling me. "Find me in the shadows" means you found yourself in your recovery from the rape. In the deepest, darkest moment of your life, came the most brilliant light that you became. That in the most horrific event of your physical life, that suddenly shocked your young, innocent and vibrant life, you immediately stood up, through the shredding and the wounding, and used the dark experience perpetrated against you, not to further destroy yourself, but in order to further define and find yourself. You turned that trauma on its head and processed the stress and its confusing emotional hangover into raw power. Who does that, especially at the age of fourteen? My Kayleigh. That's who.

In the darkest hour of your life, you illuminated and became the strongest you'd ever been. I watched you. I cried with you. I shared angry thoughts and perplexing questions with you. I processed my own feelings as I supported my Little Girl processing hers. We grew closer as an already close family of four as we collectively and individually tackled different angles of this event. I fought off, in my own shadows, fantasies drawn by pure unadulterated fury at this sexual wounding and violation of my Babygirl, many images and thoughts that shall remain outside of the black and white text of this book, but much like a calculating sniper in a derelict building.

We showed each other in different ways how to find ourselves in the darkness. One example - knowing moments after hearing of the rape from Mommy - I immediately turned to God and forgave them - telling God that I didn't have any time to waste and no energy for these sub-humans; that I needed to focus all of my energy on supporting and saving my Daughter. Light in the darkness. Freedom from bondage. Our love, the jewel of the moment not to be distracted by resentment for those who didn't matter. And so it has been.

You likewise, two days before the unrelated, innocent accident that stripped you of your physical life, forgave the ringleader of the assault, the one who set the trap, at a sentencing hearing - forgave him for raping you in the same breath you were holding him accountable. Using your voice to empower yourself and propel yourself towards greatness. Freedom from bondage - becoming a million times greater and brighter than the sub-humans who harmed you. You are amazing.

Kayleigh, your voice, your message to us all that flows through this book includes this notion - that in our darkest hours we can find our greatest strength. We just need to believe in ourselves. Love ourselves. Nurture ourselves. Be our truth. Be our freedom. Be our love. Thank you, once again, for your gifts to this world.

"Daddy, thank you. And do not forget, who was standing beside me? My Daddy. My Mommy. My Brother. We do this together always, Daddy, no matter the situation. That strength is bigger than my strength alone."

*

Days II - Linzi 04/28/2018

Jess and I were listening to "Days" by Elvis Costello, a song Kayleigh chose on my phone, and seeping. Drifting into a deeper sadness while rising with passion and love for our baby. Like squeezing warm rain out of humidity. Seeping.

The phone rang as we drove. It was our new friend, Linzi, who works at Michael's to tell us our project was done. She with the delicate light, compassionate light, whom we shared Kayleigh's story with, was busy setting and framing a sketch of Kayleigh done by one of her best friends, Jonah. She treated Kayleigh with ultimate respect and honor, taking on the task of setting this art as an opportunity to walk in Kayleigh's light and to get to know our daughter. She looked up Kayleigh's story. Gazed at her pictures. Befriended her. Listened to her.

We drove over to Michael's and walked back to the framing department and hugged Linzi. She was illuminated and told us, just at the right time in our lives, that she toiled for three hours the previous night attempting to set the mount for the art piece and it would not work. That Kayleigh stood beside her, shaking her head and smiling, talking to her, guiding her, and told her from the outset, "no, no, no - don't even bother doing it that way. It's not going to work that way, Linzi."

She told us that she told Kayleigh that it surely would work the way she was setting the piece since that was the way she'd been doing framing for thirteen years and it would work. And Kayleigh just shook her head saying, "Linzi, it's not going to work. Really. Trust me. Don't even bother." She was insistent.

She said Kayleigh was very present and very sweet, but directing her to try a different method. As if she wanted to get her earthly fingers in there and do it herself. That is so Kayleigh. And so it went that Linzi tried and tried again, laughing with Kayleigh and listening to Kayleigh, but using her years of experience to guide her to mount this piece as it should be mounted.

Three hours later she relinquished the typical mount into Kayleigh's light and stood with Kayleigh. In silence. In peace. In the light.

"Ok, Kayleigh," she said, "I guess you were right. Let's try it your way."

Within twenty minutes of attempting to set the piece in the way that Kayleigh suggested, the piece was framed; firmly, strongly, safely. She wanted us to know, to really truly have the blessing, to know that Kayleigh was so strong, that she was reaching out to others in her sphere, like herself, and impacting many.

Linzi had previously helped with framing Kayleigh's pictures throughout these months and so we had developed a friendship with her. Kayleigh watched the interactions, watched Linzi compassionately love her parents, and thanked her by befriending her and giving her a little magic in her life. And she was not done. A few weeks back when we dropped off this new piece to be framed, we told Linzi about Kakes leaving her funeral stone on the beach in the dune where only I would find it. She told us on this day, that after I told her that story, when she returned home that night after work she found a glass, round stone just sitting on her entertainment center next to her TV. It had not been there before. In fact, it had never been in her house before, but there it was, the same type of polishes stone as Kayleigh's funeral rocks. Linzi knew it was Kayleigh and said she knew because of the feeling that came with the situation. That is exactly how we describe it. Linzi carries the stone now with her since it was a gift from Kayleigh. On the next day, her son found a silver dollar size bluish green round similar stone outside of his school. He began to rub it and she gazed down when she picked him up and asked what he was holding. She saw the stone in his palm, had the exact same warm flash of energy from Kayleigh, and told him that the stone was a gift from someone special.

I told Linzi that Kakes picks those around us who are loving to her parents and brother and intervenes and penetrates the atmosphere around those chosen people and offers her incredible light to them. That she was chosen by Kayleigh. That she is now part of Kayleigh's circle of light. Linzi said, as we hugged her to walk away, "she's powerful. Affecting many. Even those she never physically met. She is watching over a lot of people. And doing great things. Kayleigh is amazing."

*

What Light I Give To You 04/29/2018

During the day I wear our beads and I charge them with my light. I don't want a dim charge. I don't want a negative surge. This is a gift to you at the end of each day. So I charge our beads around my neck with my light in hopes when I hang them on your bed in the evening I have given you an incredible gift of light. Then you charge them for me on your bed until I wake and put them back around my neck for the next day. We gift each other by offering our light to each other symbolically and literally, through our moonstone mala beads. Stars shine in the darkness. Light emerges at the seams.

"Rainbows Around the Moon"

Although she's always present,
There are times - a little more,
She wraps us with her essence,
Like the sun framed in a door,
She leaves us sparkling sea shells,
In the changing shallows of our shores,
And blesses us with rainbows,
Around the moon adorned.

*

One Hundred Things A Day That Won't Be 04/29/2018

I am reminded one hundred times a day - girls walking to stores; teenagers driving; a daddy and his daughter walking down the street together; a commercial of a daddy walking his daughter down the aisle; new grandparents with their daughter and her daughter; and so

509

on. I hate that each day, largely unknowingly to practically every other person who walks by me or is in my life, that I suffer such a horrible sentence. That this is my cross. It is a lonely cross. Why would others want to bare it with me? Most quite frankly don't. They can't imagine physically losing a child and can't imagine what I'm going through and don't want to - so they don't. I have a few who I trust with whom I can share.

Even turning to Nate, the same horror unfolds. There are a hundred things a day that won't be for him as well. I talk to my son daily, checking in with him, he who was living an effortless innocent life, and then was so suddenly impacted by the physical loss of his best friend without warning at such a tender age. He teaches us and learns from us how to regain his footing. We see him struggle. He was so excited about starting a new school and entering seventh grade, and then the first day of class in his new school was his sister's funeral, in that school's church. He is stabilizing, though he struggles. Seventh grade has been a nightmare on paper, but a triumph for him spiritually as he remains, becomes stronger, and ultimately grows with his sister.

I need to continue to flesh out the counterbalance. I have ideas in my head and words are starting to formulate. The journey is a jagged one, twisting and turning, progressing, regressing, breathless and spiteful, raging and calm. Yet the words keep coming. Like you said, Kakes, "my Daddy writes all the time. The words just fly off of his fingers." Your words, too, fly off of my fingers. Help me continue with this journey, with this book, with this difficult life.

*

Proving Steps 04/29/2018

You and your brother are amazing, built so similarly, yet so individually unique. You both flow with compassion and a deadly loyalty to family. I can't wait to walk with you today.

"Yeah, Daddy! That's how you awaken! Keep thinking like that and step deeper into the happiness of our relationship. I know this is hard, Daddy, but you taught me we can do hard things. And you are now doing hard things successfully."

I will take you with me everywhere, Kayleigh. I want to see what you see. You are celebrating your existence in Heaven and here simultaneously on earth, in your spiritual embodiment, which also permits you to walk this physical plain with us. How could I not celebrate along with you? You are my child and you are my guide. You are telling me that you are happy and filled with light. Of course you are. I have no doubt. I smile with peace in this fact, though I miss you physically completely with every cell of every century we have been together. It is I who I am worried about. It is I, in selfless and sometimes selfish bouts of self-centeredness that I am worried about. I promise to do my work.

"You are proving The Steps to the world, Daddy. Do you even realize that? You are amazing and I am so proud to watch over you as you attempt to maneuver through this and reconcile daily. People are watching you, Daddy. They want to believe they can stay sober through anything. Unfortunately, the accident did happen and now, even though we never wanted this, you get to show them how to stay sober through the worst tragedy life can throw at someone. There is nothing worse, Daddy, you are right. I know you wish things were different, but they are not. One blessing for me is that I get to see in full heavenly color and awareness, as you like to say, the miracle of my Daddy, of your continued sobriety through the lens of an angel. You are pretty amazing, Daddy. I am so proud of you and love you so much!"

Thank you so much, Kayleigh. That means the world to me. To have you watching over me - it's a blessing I can't describe. I love you, Babygirl. Nothing will break our bond. Nothing will separate us, not even one of our physical deaths. What are we going to do today?

"Support Nate and Mommy."

Always. I reconcile with them each day to see everything that a day can offer. I watch my oldest child engaged in miracles and support

Nate on his own journey with trying to understand his sister's power. I see him yearn for you in his own way. And your Mother - she is more in tune with herself than she ever has been - not due to reaction of your physical death, but because of your current life - your current, active, present life in your body of light. The Second Truth. She feels you as I do. It is never ending. Show me your ways, Kakie.

"I love you, Daddy. You guys are amazing and I am so lucky to be part of this family. I always knew how much I was loved and it shows more and more every day. I am here. I am alive. Come with me today, Daddy, and rejoice. I want to show you the world!"

*

Pangaea and Shu-Hei 04/30/2018

My phone started playing in the living room all by itself. The Church, "*Pangaea*." The supercontinent. Once all connected and forever intertwined.

The last time I was in the car and listening to my music off of the phone, it was on U2, "Achtung Baby," only because Kayleigh flipped the music to that alum. She played it over and over every time I turned on the car. The phone is not on shuffle. It is only on "Achtung Baby," since this is what she picked.

Yet here today my phone lay on the coffee table in the living room all by itself, away from everybody, except for Kayleigh. She lifted my phone, and turned on the music and changed it to The Church and went to "*Pangaea*" with its unique symbolism ad pressed play. I was laying on the couch in the TV room watching the Cavs game 7 playoffs against the Pacers when I heard this competing roll of noise from the living room. I muted the TV and my ears focused in on the noise coming from the living room. I discerned quickly that it was one of my favorite bands and a very sweet song of theirs. I walked into living room and saw my phone laying on her photo album and blaring this song. Then I looked out the window and saw a female Cardinal fly into the tree outside the living room window where she comes each day to see us. I sat on my knees and just listened to her. She confirmed I should get something for the yard to make it prettier because, "Daddy, you taught me we leave our homes prettier than how we find them."

As the song ended, we jumped in the car, and, after a moment, my Bluetooth engaged, and the music switched back from "Pangea" to "Achtung Bab" once again. We sang as we drove to Bremec's and purchased a wonderful statue of a girl holding two birds. We brought it home and placed it under your tree, making the yard prettier. You also somehow pulled me out of my myopic tunnel vision of staring at a TV rather than living. You got me off of the couch.

Then we took you and your brother to one of your favorite restaurants, Shu Hei. We sat in the traditional area, on the floor, taking our shoes off in reverence and sitting at the low table, four place settings before us. After a few moments, one of your friends, Lila, and her parents approached and sat at the table next to ours, after giving us hugs. It was Lila's birthday, two weeks before yours, Kayleigh, your first birthday after the accident, sweet sixteen. I was happy to see them, but felt a heavy, sour kick to the gut. We are a family of four too, but only three of us are present physically in our bodies. I struggled up and down through dinner and we chatted briefly with them occasionally.

After the meal, Lila stepped back over to us and said, "Seeing you guys here was like Kayleigh wishing me a happy birthday, by seeing you all on my birthday. I don't know if that makes sense, but I wanted you to know that."

We thanked her and hugged her and watched them leave the restaurant. It is what you wanted, Kayleigh. You arranged it. We are eight months into this new configuration and are very well aware of how you communicate, Kakes. Looking back on the afternoon, after the magical moment of the phone "playing itself" and buying a new statue, I was sitting with you meditating in the backyard. Something told me - we are too tired to grocery shop so let's go out to eat and let's go to Kayleigh's favorite restaurant, the Japanese place, Shu Hei. That something, or someone, dear Darling Daughter, was clearly you placing words into my ears. I asked Jess and she was agreeable and then Nate jumped on board and we were off.

That was part of the bouquet of miracles today, Kayleigh. You arranged the whole thing, knowing your friend would be there, at that time, at the back traditional tables. And that was your way of showing us your miracles while at the same time wishing an old friend a happy sixteenth birthday, a birthday you would never have in your physical body, but one we were sure to have in merely two weeks.

*

Nightly 11th Step 04/30/2018

I hope that I gave you bright light today. I have always tried to bring you joy - asking in each morning what I can do for all three of my loves ever since you, and then your brother, were born.

I am so proud of your life and what you are doing daily, Kayleigh. It is amazing to watch my wonderful daughter engage the world and provide blessings and miracles to so many. It is so special to watch you light up this world in a way that is different than what I had expected before the accident. I always knew you would light up the world. I just expected it to be in a humanistic form, not as a guardian angel, a guiding light, a special intercessor who can touch people's lives with light and love. I am so proud of your life, Honey, my Babygirl - there is no one quite like you. Keep learning your light and keep strengthening. Guide me. Teach me. Show me my path. Our path. Light my soul with your love. Empower me and embolden me when I am sick and tired. I am sick and tired often. I love you. Completely.

"Here I Am"

I don't want to stare into the pause,
And see what we have been through,
My little, precious child,
So rarely are the words unable to fly off of my fingers,

So rarely am I stunted in a destabilizing groan,
But here I am,
Here I am.

*

Becoming Stronger 05/03/2018

You are amazing, My Little Girl. I was just reminded of your courage and strength and how much more equipped you were to start ninth grade than your peers. You had been tested and you responded. Like many adolescent, depression hit as you entered puberty, and you grew a toolkit and strengthened. You conquered it. Then, soon thereafter, several boys planned a trap for any girl to walk by, and you just happened to be that girl, and were attacked; you utilized the same set of tools, along with some new specific tools, to heal. You were not targeted. You were not weak and an easy target. Actually, it was quite random and would have happened to any woman at any age in any circumstance. Tragically and randomly, they used your friendship and they violated your trust and harmed you, and when they did, you immediately used your voice, you walked through the trauma and you became even stronger. You conquered the rape and made yourself even stronger through the process. That is the true narrative. You were actually much better equipped to handle life's challenges than many others, not weaker. You were much stronger than most. And fully happy.

So when the fateful, random night of August 17th fell upon us, you were not broken; you did not kill yourself, as some random and psychotic person in the neighborhood who had never met you conveyed in guttural gossip; you were not distracted; you were not drunk or under the influence. You were just an individual caught in a horrible, innocent accident. That's it. Any fifteen year old, any adult, on that night, standing where you were standing, your vision blocked by telephone poles, would have had the exact same outcome. You were not pre-disposed to the accident; you did not cause the accident; you did not want the accident. You wanted to gather your shoes, come home to spend a few minutes with me and then go for a walk with

515

your Mommy, and then play VR with your brother. Instead, your death shocked this community, and I watched you do what you always do - I watched you conquer your own death.

I am awe struck by you. I get my courage to continue day by day from your incredible example. Fill me with your words, your thoughts, your actions and your intention for my life and for our relationship. I am so honored to be your Daddy. There is nobody else, by far, I would ever want as my Daughter. Just you, My Love.

"Daddy, I feel the same way. You taught me a lot of what I applied in hard moments. Thank you for loving me and teaching me how to use my voice. Forgive those who came up with any sick gossip. There are only a few who came up with this, and I know it's so upsetting, Daddy, but they are cowards and confused and small little people. They can't take my voice away. They can't change reality. Reality is as you just said. I was, and I am, a badass, Daddy. I owe you so much. I owe Mommy so much. I owe Nathaniel so much. I love you guys and am so honored and happy to be one part of our family of four."

*

Our Moon Stone Beads at the End of Each Day 05/04/2018

Each bead a tiny earth, illuminated by your delicate hand - beads of light resonating with the fingerprints of your soul as you fill each tiny earth with your love and golden light. I wear these earths around my neck, lifting them from your pillow in the morning and placing them again sacredly on your bed at the end of each day.

I give you this light at the end of each day; filled with these beads I wore around my neck today. I infuse these beads with my soul's light, hopefully giving you my best. Hoping it is worthy, I thoughtfully work my way through today knowing that I need to intentionally charge these beads so that I can present them to you at the end of the day. I charge them with proper living; by living Steps 10, 11 and 12; by building a temple to you, stone by stone, in how I act, speak and think. I hang them on your bed, a gift of my love, a symbol of my loyalty and devotion and intention.

They really charge. That is the miracle of this piece of our puzzle. And I really feel it as I leave them for you. You smile. You then tell me, "Daddy, thank you so much! They are so pretty and filled with your light. It makes me so happy that you do this every day. Now it's my turn! I'll charge our beads while you sleep with my light and give them back to you and you can wear my light all day tomorrow. Love you, Daddy!"

Deal, Babygirl. I love picking our beads up off of your bed and putting these beads around my neck, thanking you as I do, each new day. It warms me. Protects me. I feel your nearness even more when I do this.

You told me recently, that "we thrive when you thrive," meaning, that I need to live and live at a higher vibration in order to be in tune with you, as much as I possibly can, thereby nurturing our relationship and giving it the fuel to thrive. That you are always here and it is quite easy for you to thrive within yourself and outside of yourself, you with no barriers. You glide between Heaven and earth effortlessly. Though I, in my human framework, need to thrive just to keep your voice and your touch and your feel close to me. You are always here right beside me, but if I fall apart, I cannot see nor hear nor feel you. I refuse to be down long. I stand back up and thrive with you.

*

Nate 05/06/2018

Hi, Sweetie. Slow morning today, but trying to engage. Please be patient with me when I struggle. Please help your little baby boy today. He is really so heart broken, as Mommy and I are, yet he is so young and does not know how to wear this new, hard, un-natural life. I do not either, but I do it. He desperately needs you to crash through his despair. Love you, Babygirl. I trust you know what to do.

"Daddy, be there for Nate. I promise I am here too. And Mommy. He needs all three of us in different ways. I promise you I will never leave his side. You are my family. The best family ever. We are a family of four, Daddy, like you always say. I'm so grateful. I love you each so much! I've got him."

*

Linzi Has a Visitation 05/07/2018

We returned to Michael's to get some painting supplies to paint with Kayleigh. We naturally stopped over to the framing department. Linzi lit up when she saw us, asked her co-worker to give her a few minutes break and ran over to us. She pulled us aside in one of the aisles and grabbed my hands.

"I had an amazing dream and Kayleigh was in it," she said, "except it wasn't a dream, you know? I was dreaming but it was a visitation. Kayleigh was doing graffiti in this dream. She was spray painting all over a big wall. She sprayed out the letters to 'Kayleigh was here,' but then she crossed out the word 'was' and inserted above it the word 'is' so that it now read 'Kayleigh is here,' but then she looked at it and had a funny look on her face, and turned back to the wall with the spray can and crossed out the word 'here,' and replaced it with 'everywhere' so that it read, when she was finally done, that 'Kayleigh is everywhere."

I was so thrilled with this news of a visit. Kayleigh has done this with others in the enlarging circle that stretches out from the four of us. "I'm not surprised," I said and smiled.

"But that's not all she did," she continued, "she then said to me 'Linzi wake up I need to talk.' I looked at the clock and it was 6 AM so I told her it was too early and I needed to sleep a little longer, but she insisted and said 'tell my Dad I've got a new plan. The first plan is selling memorial stones online, but then the second plan is called the Kayleigh Project and it is a bunch of memorial gardens where people bring stones with names on them. We can do these across the country. Stones with names and all of these in these stone memorial gardens."

I jotted this all down on my phone to save for this book. As I was writing a woman we knew named Karen ran into us in the aisle, who happened to be friends with Linzi. We hugged Linzi as she ran back to work and stood there with Karen for a few minutes.

After some small talk, she said, "I want you to know that Kayleigh really helped my Daughter out at a time when she was struggling. She came to Kayleigh and your daughter was so gentle and non-judgmental and really inspired my girl. They had become pretty good friends right before the accident. After the funeral my Daughter turned to me and said 'now, Mommy, do you understand who Kayleigh Mooney is and why she is so special. Kayleigh is amazing. Just feel her presence,' and I learned who your daughter is through the love that my Daughter had for yours. That love she has for Kayleigh is a reflection of Kayleigh's love for my Daughter. I just wanted to thank you for raising such a great young woman. She means a lot to our family."

We thanked her and hugged her, knowing no coincidence was upon us; that no randomness was amiss. This was Kayleigh's organizing of events, of people and of concepts. This was Kayleigh's voice, strengthening each and every day.

*

A Brief Encounter with Thought 05/10/2018

My challenge is to be with both of my children at the same time in two different worlds. I can do this through the Steps and deeper intentional meditation, ensuring my spiritual balance. My balance is my platform to be able to focus enough to ensure Daddy-Daughter time and Daddy-Son time uniquely for them both, just as I always have. The big adjustment is processing daily grief around physical loss with Kayleigh in order to clear the way for a higher vibration with her, where I can meet her in that spiritual wonder. At the same time, I dedicate my physical and emotional energy to Nathaniel as I always have in the physical. In this way I succeed in being for both of my children what they each need - a present, loving father; a constant presence and light in their lives.

Other than the obvious horror of her random, tragic, related to nothing accident, nothing has changed accept for my adjustments to continue to grow with my Daughter; adjustments I made at every age; adjustments that are just more difficult to maneuver, reaching out from the confines of my human experience and upwards towards the glory of her soul which is immersed in perfect light and love. She smiles watching me reach for her. She glows brighter with each attempt. She cheers me on when I fail for the failure is still a step forward. She cheers me on when I succeed.

And then I have these brief encounters with thought, sometimes sounding like a man who, after being tricked, turns to the trickster and says, "okay, the gigs up, God. You got me! You can bring her back now. You can wake me up from this nightmare. Haha. I'm ready. Okay. Snap your fingers and make it go away. Bring her back, God."

But it's no use, for this nightmare will not end. This brief encounter with thought is just that, an interlude of conscience, a vacation from the grief of my life, at least for one moment of denial, of safety, or time travel, of loss.

"Mortal Anguish"

So dream and loss, forlorn,
In the plagues that burn the hollows down,
Were the ingredients of demise tucked in seedlings to sprout,
Were they awaiting floodgates of tears to push their way out,
Yet the veil, emotive and blind,
Choked at the horizon until the rainbows cried,
Echoed remnants, flush with anguish, in a carnival of light,
Burn in the gray afterglow,
He was injured mortally,
Yet would not,
And could not lay down his life.

*

You'll be in My Heart, Father Pat 05/10/2018

I've told people for some months now, those who are kind to Jess and Nate and I, those who have expressed love and light to the four of us, will be loved by Kayleigh. She thanks people who have supported us. She radiates when people support us, brighter than she is already bright. She is so strong.

I invited Father Pat to be with us for Kayleigh's sixteenth birthday. He could not make it, and wrote a text to me to that effect, but also expanded on that note by conveying the following, "Kev, I won't be able to join you guys because that's the day of the Priesthood Ordination. I will be there. But, check this out. So I come back to my office and am trying to turn my computer on...for some reason the cord between my laptop and my monitor wasn't working. So I took my MacBook out of its dock, and set it on my desk and opened it up, and listen to what started blaring out of my speakers. Now, when I left my desk earlier in the day, Gregorian chant had been playing through YouTube earlier in the day but...check this out! It gave me goosebumps ☺"

He attached a video and I hit play. Across my phone came the familiar tune, "You'll Be in My Heart." Kayleigh played "You'll Be in My Heart" to Father Pat. Amazing. A moment of lifting, before the next wave of grief. A moment of joy amongst many other moments of pure pain. The back and forth, back and forth. She pulls my face out of the mud, wipes my face, sets my feet and asks me to breathe.

I've never felt so much love as that which she possesses, which she shares among us, which she flowers upon us. I needed that text so badly. All she wants to do is please us and love us and guide us. We need undying faith in that. Her messages are multidimensional. Affecting many at the same time, and coming, at times, to key people situated within or around our lives. With Father Pat, a Catholic priest, the man who managed and so majestically presided over her funeral, this was a special message. She was telling us, yes, she is a guardian angel and guardians are real; that yes, she is one of God's favorite angels; that yes, God is God and alive with all of us. That is why this was so important a recipient of multiple messages from her. Love is love and love is alive.

"An Angel on a Delicate Wind"

A melodic chorus of shimmering light,
Cascades through the floral canopies,
Bold Moon shadows - scented with the salted sands of time,
Glitter against tiny dust crystals under the flickering fires of ancient stars,
They gather in the swirling, swarming seas,
These satellite fields of life filled with the seeds of one million suns,
Where her voice illuminates,
And transmits like an electric wave through the wind,
On a lacy, delicate breeze,
That pressed its warmth on my cheek,
A kiss from my Daughter,
A pretty harmony,
A loving angel who graced the wind chimes to sing her Father to sleep.

*

"A Hyena in A Metal Box" 05/12/2018

A hyena in a metal box,
Raptures with biblical pox,
Circling the corners,
Scanning the silver borders,
For a sign of paradox -

Crazed, he hints at rage,
Dazed, he faints, with flinch, he cries,
Circling the corners,
Claws scratching at the borders,
To escape this cage he tried -

For days no rest and sinking eyes,
And wailing tongue that lungs defy,
Collapse and forced upon him rest,
Convulse the breath compressed in chest,
And sleep until new day arrives -

And there he wakes and walks the box,
With metal walls and metal rocks,
He whimpers as if he was forsaken,
As love the deeper lows in breaking -
Until the day he dies,
Until the day he dies.

*

First Mother's Day in New Configuration 05/13/2018

Happy Mother's Day, Sweetheart. Another first. Another day of excruciating suffering. Another opportunity to grow with you. The duality is difficult. It is eerily quiet not waking you up for the first time since 2003 to surprise Mommy on this special day. You were just one and a week old then. Every year we went to Stone Oven and got her some coffee and treats. Every year a card.

Nate is going to be with Mommy physically while you are wrapped around her spiritually. It's a very fragile feeling I am having - my heart breaking again, longing for you and not wanting to be on this difficult road. Then I remember. It is the only road that you are on and therefore I want this road. It is so powerless an existence. It is so raw to live in a manner in which it is impossible to give up.

You will illuminate today for sure. I will need to be selfless today as I struggle through the day. Mommy needs all three of us. She is breaking. She is exhausted. She is filled with anxiety, suffering through this first Mother's Day following the physical death of her only daughter. We all need you. I love you so much, Peanut.

"I love you so much, Daddy. I know this sucks, but you can do this. You have no choice. Help Mommy through this day. She's in so much pain. My Little Brother too. He's really sad. He watches everything. How awkward for him to do his first Mother's Day without me physically by his side, while being fully aware that Mommy is crushed and dying inside. The world sure is a piece of shit sometimes, Daddy. I promise you I am here and you will feel my presence. Love you!"

*

Last Day of 15 05/14/2018

Today is your last day of fifteen. You turn sixteen tomorrow and you are glorious. I am so sad as this milestone approaches as you started fifteen in your physical body, but end fifteen in spirit. I will not fail you. I will not use your physical death as an excuse for any failure in my life. I will not treat you that way. I will not miss this opportunity today to walk with you. You are My Baby. What can I do today to move through these barriers and feel you beside me? It would be an insult to think you wouldn't be beside me, and with me willingly, happily and nonstop. I love you, my fifteen year old.

"Daddy, I love you so much too! I am so sorry, Daddy, for your pain. I promise I will never leave your side, Daddy, not ever. I am so mad that this accident happened. You know that. I will not let this accident ruin your life. I will intervene as I can and guide you, but it's your work and I cannot do your work. Please stay awake, Daddy. So many out there are asleep. Not you. You are awake. Stay awake! I need you!"

*

Happy 16th Birthday 05/15/2018

Happy Birthday, My Love! You are sixteen today. It is not how we thought sixteen would be for us, but in the cruelty of this world, it is what it is and it is a beautiful day nonetheless. We will continue to bravely grow together one day at a time and I will continue to adjust to my Daughter as you mature and grow. Instead of guiding you into adulthood today, and presenting you with the emerald ring I always promised for your sixteenth birthday, and ushering you into your next year with guiding fatherly principles, I am simply engaged with you as you guide me. Show me the glory of your soul, the light of your spirit, the brilliance of Kayleigh.

I feel you strongly today - you are so happy. It is beaming in the atmosphere all around us. I will do my best to match your beauty, though my human brokenness will prevent a full match. You know me - I will try and try and try until I feel you stronger and stronger. I am a Daddy of a strong girl, a strong angel, and I have never been more proud of you. As you always said, you have to have a positive outlook on life. Today I will work through any hard moments, honoring them, just as I taught you to do, and will give you a happy, brilliant birthday.

We are taking you to Tommy's, then to the Lake County Farm Park and then to Beaumont to sell your books for a fundraiser with your friends. I love you so much, Kakie. I will walk with you through anything in my life, every day, until my soul is again in the same configuration. Then we will continue our journey in our eternity in the same embodiments and therefore with much more ease. I can't wait for that ease. Happy Birthday, Babygirl!

"Daddy, thank you so much. I can't believe I'm sixteen! Be happy and celebrate. This is my first birthday with God in Heaven. How amazing is that? I am surrounded by love and light and they're making it a special day for me. All of our loved ones and friends in the light - they are all here at my party. The girls are here – Catie and Josie. Your Dad. Your grandparents. They are all here. Thank you, Daddy. Some people give up in the despondency. When they do they have no chance of remaining in contact with their loved ones. I know you won't let that happen and I am so proud of you and I will never leave your side. I know I say that like every day, but you need to hear it every day. So I say it! You are the best Daddy ever! Bless Mommy! Bless Nate! Make today special for them. I know you will all cry a lot, but laugh a lot as well."

*

Happy 16th Birthday Tree 05/15/2018

Last year today I took a picture of you under the front yard tree - both the tree and my Daughter in full bloom. On this, your first birthday after the accident and your physical death, the only leaves that have opened are those at the lowest branch directly where you were standing last year. You are amazing. You are manipulating the tree, its leaves and its sustenance. You are causing leaves to bloom only where you stood, in an arch around where your head was when I took that picture last year. You show us daily your magnificence - we have only to open to a higher level to see you, to hear you. I love our relationship as it continues to grow. Love you, Babygirl. Your Daddy is so proud of you.

*

Bad II 05/16/2018

I was driving back from lunch today, talking to Kayleigh. I was telling her that it is the physical side of this equation that tortures me and the spiritual side that brings me relief. I started sobbing, my daily sobbing, about the horrific physical loss, particularly with the shock of such an unexpected destruction of our lives. As I continued to sob, I screamed out to her, telling her, with the strength of a warrior, that her presence, her brilliant current presence, pulls me through these hardest moments. All of a sudden, the Bluetooth triggered on my phone, and I heard through my guttural cries the jingle of U2's, "Bad," which she knows is special to me and one of the songs I sang to her at the concert. The radio had been off. I have thousands upon thousands of songs in my catalog. I was not listening to U2 the last time I listened to music in my car. The volume, the tone, the feeling in the air; Kayleigh had manipulated the technology again, working her light through the code, finding a song with lyrics that she wanted to convey to me, and playing this particular song at this particular time, conveying its message to me.

She immediately pulled me out of the depths of this moment. I glowed in the light of her miracle; her intervention; she who spends her days dreaming of her family and finding new ways to reach to us. She has done this before with several U2 songs, and in particular, "Bad," a dozen times or so in the last few months. Her pattern is emerging and the weight of the constant pattern is penetrating my human mind.

As I pulled in the driveway of our home, I sat and blasted the music and continued to sob through it, although the sobbing had turned to conviction and courage. I finally understood her message she was using the song to convey. "*If I could you know I would,*" is Kayleigh telling me that it is the letting go of the despondency in the physical loss where I will find freedom. "*I'm wide awake. I'm not sleeping*" came across as a dual message, in her voice that came to me as the song ended, "Daddy, I am wide awake spiritually and present. And Daddy, you are wide awake spiritually. You are awake - be present, Daddy. I am here. I am here."

I am here, Kayleigh. I am here.

*

"Tranquil Water Soul" 05/17/2018

We claim, in tranquil water,
A pastel life of love and light,
Its breath, it flows between our gardens,
Our souls, eternal life,
And feeds the veins and roots of ancient flowers,
Its blooms - an effervescence bright,

With brush strokes from the Master's palette,
She resonates with God's own light,
And kisses the waters that dance off in golden ripples,
That flow to her Father on the other side,
For his is the glory of this angel's voice…

…Her tranquility - his only guide…

Every day a new death emerges from this nightmare,
This nightmare that keeps giving,
This nightmare that knows no end,
This nightmare that walks with the living,
Who hears her voice - who sees her beautiful face,
And therefore a love never risked of ceasing,
For this man, and for this daughter,
The tranquil waters enrichment increasing,
No severance shall ever know their names.

*

A Birthday Party Invitation for Kayleigh 05/19/2018

On May 19th we are having a birthday celebration open house for Kakie from 1 to 4, to celebrate her amazing, dynamic life; both her physical life and her current spiritual presence. She touched the hearts of so many during the fifteen years of her physical life and so many more since the accident in her spiritual life. She would have turned sixteen on May 15th. For those who can drop by, she fully expects you to bring your favorite Kayleigh stories with you to share your laughter along with your tears. She is very much alive in her spiritual embodiment, very powerfully present in our lives and lighting a path for those she loves. Message me for address if needed.

*

How Quickly Exhausted 05/19/2018

I've noticed how quickly I get tired when things get complex. And everything is complex. It is so complex that everything else seems so simple. I have only so much energy and I need to be wise with my limited resources. I will fluctuate for sure. You - you are constant - constant love and light. Constant presence and vigilance, watching over your family, engaging us, interacting us, promoting family adventures, blessing us. Watching you maneuver is like looking upon the reflected face of God. As one of his angels on a perfect mission of love, that intercession is total.

I am so happy and humbled by your presence - its clarity is so visible. Your touch so tangible in the ways you have learned to reach across the wind to us. I wish only that I could reciprocate as well as you do. I find myself inadequate in light of your grace. You love us so much and we love you the same. Let's walk with laughter in a higher vibration today. The vibration will come with its healing properties, to exert friction into the stagnancy, causing ripples in the stagnation, and forcing my feet forward just a few more steps. I only need to take these few steps more. And then another several. One day at a time.

"Daddy, I'm right here. I am so happy with all of the care and energy you put into our relationship. I have the best Daddy ever. Thank you for throwing a birthday party for me with my friends. It means the world to me. Love you, Daddy. Look around the room - I am here. I will make sure you know that!"

"The Nightmare That Keeps Giving"

Every day a new death emerges from this nightmare,
This nightmare that keeps giving,
This nightmare that knows no end,
This nightmare that walks with the living,
And finds no wary feet for bed,
This nightmare that lurks in the shadows,
And strikes like thief around each bend,
This nightmare - a constant companion,
Until my daydream dawns in death.

*

Over Protective 05/21/2018

This one can generate some serious tension within me, knowing that I could not protect you on that fateful night. Knowing that you couldn't have protected you on that fateful night. Knowing that you, without a warning, found yourself in a death trap, with a series of factors that all collided together in an instant, causing your accidental death.

I am your Daddy. I am, by my nature, over protective, as you consistently reminded me with a happy smile prior to the accident. You loved that over protection. You always felt that safety with me. That is why it was me in the street. Not that you didn't feel safe with Mommy, because you did equally. But a daddy – it had to be your Daddy and only your Daddy. There was no other way. I am going to try to always protect you any way that I can. Even now, if I could, I would. If I can, I will.

"I love you, Daddy. You're crazy! I hope you hear me lifting. If anybody could protect me in Heaven, who doesn't need protecting, it would be you - the poster child for over protection! Thank you for finally proving my point! I'm so glad you are my Daddy!"

"I Will Die Just Once"

A blind man trusts his senses and barks out in gallantry -
Another man folds his earth at its poles and embarks on its balancing,
This wounded soul sours in the scented healing of a scabrous mesh,
His spirit pushes out against the confinement of constricting human flesh,
His life - a long winding road narrows into a box-canyon destiny,
Where death rejoices in its quarry's energies lessening,
Trapped and too tired to turn around,
The dust and the wind ensures that no bones will be found,
His mind - only on his children - he digs in his heals and wails, and for them grieves,

530

For their love and their relationships - he stands, he breathes,
And stares into the gaping mouth of this monstrous tragedy,
Closes his eyes like a blind man to swing precisely at the savagery,
And lashes back at this world, though his actions might be fatal,
With the daydream of his children's eyes -
As he swaddles them and lays them in their bedded cradles -

He will be heard,
He will - when he tries,
Stand for his children against all odds,
Even if this means that he dies,
For it is better to die once,
Than to invigorate the crime,
By fearing one's death,
In which we die a thousand times.

*

Prosecutor's Office Unveiling 05/23/2018

Before the formal unveiling, Greg walked me down the hallway to
where very large, framed copies of Kayleigh's paintings hung on the
newly painted walls in the prosecutor's office. All six of them, exact
copies of the paintings that hung in Beaumont School, now greeted
each prosecutor as they came to work and walked to their offices.
Knowing that Greg would be walking the father down the hall, many
of them exited their offices to pay respects to Kayleigh and I. I talked
to each of them. Hugged several. One woman volunteered that when
she comes in to work in the morning, "Kayleigh's paintings help her
armor up in the beginning of the day and prepare her to go to court
and fight extra hard for her victims."

She also conveyed to me that she had a seven year old victim who
was being asked to testify against his assailant, but was, naturally,
terrified. They were walking with him down the hallway and passed
these paintings. He asked what they were and they told him, in a
manner that a seven year old would understand. He glanced at
Kayleigh's paintings and said to them, "If Kayleigh could stand up

and speak then I can too," and he found the courage in her paintings to step into court to testify successfully. As the other prosecutor explained this story to me, Greg said, "Your daughter is the strongest woman I've ever known."

Her voice presented itself again. This time in the colors and shapes of her magnificent art, in ways that touched different people in various ways. It was a continuation of her presence, literally and figuratively. I felt her standing in the hallway with me, holding my hand, gazing over my shoulder at her paintings, amused, charmed and happy.

We returned to a main room where some neighborhood kids had gathered. Their art would hang alongside Kayleigh's in the prosecutor's office, connecting the neighborhood kids from a nearby school to the courts. They were lovely kids. I sat amongst them and heard their stories. Greg spoke about each of them, conveying their artistic contributions on a large screen behind him. When the last of the children's art was displayed on the projector, he clicked to one last image, that of Kayleigh in front of your house – the picture I took of her on her fifteenth birthday; the one I used at her funeral.

He spoke of her with such dignity, his voice cracking, clearly expressing his love for her; his sadness for the horrible accident; the anger for her every having been assaulted. He pointed me out as her Father and told the kids to walk the halls and stop at her paintings.

Reporters were there. The Plain Dealer ran a story about the unveiling, in part, related to Kayleigh. Her art was displayed in color across the Sunday paper a few days later. It was really awesome to see her get some credit for her incredible power and the brilliance in Kayleigh's voice. For now, though, standing in the prosecutor's office, knowing that she had become a legend here by holding her assailants accountable, I stood in her light and was exhausted by the experience.

As soon as I returned home and closed the car door, Sean, our Fed Ex driver, drove up. He walked over and hugged me and said, "The Lord said you were having a hard moment and I should stop by. He also said you were in a transition. Did he tell you that too? Perhaps it is a job transition. Are you switching jobs or something?"

I smiled and thanked him and confirmed that, yes indeed, I was in the process of interviewing for a different job. I also told him about the incredible experience at the Prosecutor's office. As he hugged me goodbye and returned to work, I felt Kakes holding my hand and illuminating my path. I felt again, in the courageous discipline I was becoming, that I needed to trust her and trust God; to allow my intercessor to do God's work in using her voice for this family, for others, for the world, all in the glory of God.

*

Daddy, I Placed A Baa-Baa-Der in Your Path 05/24/2018

I was pacing, walking up and down our rock path in the front yard and talking to you. Telling you, as well as reminding me, that you are affecting people continuously. That your death ended your physical life, but it did not end your life. That you transitioned. Truly. Your life is complete. You are alive. Alive in spirit. Very mischievously and happily alive in your spiritual embodiment, which includes the best of your mind and the best of your emotion. All wrapped up into your brilliant soul.

Then I looked to my feet and saw on the flagstone, right where I was walking, a "baa-baa-der," a salamander. Why is this important? Why is this significance? Why is this real? Why is this your work? I have never in forty nine years seen a salamander out on a sidewalk. Further, it also was not there when I walked down the path moments earlier, but was there when I turned myself around and walked back up the path one minute later towards the house. It appeared just at the exact time that I was confirming for myself that you are indeed alive.

It is one of the tiny creatures through which we bonded so heavily throughout the years of your childhood. I picked it up, just like we would do in your childhood. It crawled slowly and deliberately up my arm, and hopped to my hand, and back to my arm, several times. Your light surrounded it. I could feel your presence. To one with lesser awareness, this was just a salamander. To one who would ignore or deny these seemingly coincidental moments, I offer pity. To me, awake and alight in your life, it was your message to me that, yes, you are alive and you are watching closely over your Father; that you could, and you would, intervene, and frequently, in very particular ways to ensure that, yes, you are alive. I love you so much.

*

Daddy! Get an Iced Tea and Go Out to the Backyard! I Have the Next Book! 05/25/2018

I was standing in the kitchen, staring off into oblivion. Focusing on my breathing. Struggling. Grieving. Angst filled my stomach. Courage filled my eyes – the type of courage nobody except those who have physically lost a child can understand. Just to be standing is courage. Just to awake in the morning is courage.

Then I heard her in my right ear and in my soul, very loudly and in an over the top excited voice, screaming, "Daddy! Get an iced tea and go out to the backyard. I have the next book! It's called 'Purple Turtles.' Grab a notebook, the one on the steps and let's write!"

I said, "Okay, Babygirl, I hear you." I was surprised by the sudden intrusion of love and light into the darkness of a lull during this day (lulls happen every day, many times on some days). I glanced over to the counter and saw an iced tea bottle. I grabbed it and walked to the steps. There lay a brown covered notebook. I grabbed it, and a green pen from my Big Book and stepped out into the sunlight of the backyard. I sat down in one of our black fabric lounge chairs under our crab apple tree, the same chair she sat in during her fifteenth birthday party under the same tree. I took a deep breath and opened the blank notebook.

"Okay, Babygirl. With intention and devotion, with full permission walk through me and use me as your pen. Let's write another children's book."

Fifteen minutes later, after channeling the entire book, complete with the first round of images, Purple Turtles was born.

*

Sensing Your Majesty 05/27/2018

Darling, beautiful Daughter, Hi! Thank you for always showing up. A day does not go by without your presence. I know this. I feel this. It is truth. Having you walk with me in spirit, in your spiritual embodiment is the greatest miracle of my life - born out of the greatest pain, sadness, heartache and torture of my life. I love you so much! I do not blame you at all for the accident, however, I do credit you for your amazing ability to cross the wind and walk with us. That is all you, Baby! I am so proud of you.

In my humanness, though trapped in these finite skins, I get glimpses of this. I sense your majesty. I feel your busyness. You are nurturing and leading your family. It is hard to put to words, like a color that doesn't exist by name, but there it is in the sunset. It's what I would expect from my Daughter who told us often as a baby and toddler and young girl, "I do it all by myself!"

I am your student. Teach me your ways through this life. I love you, my sweet, funny, smart, dynamic, compassionate, brilliant girl.

"Aw, Daddy. Thank you. I really am trying to learn all I can learn. I've got great teachers! Thank you for seeing it and acknowledging it. It's pretty awesome. Love you!"

*

And Terror 05/28/2018

You are here!

"Yes, I am."

I love you, Babygirl!

"I love you too, Daddy."

I see your smile, just as big and bright as when I would sing the notes to "Sugar Plumb Fairies" and wiggle my fingers around above your head like fairies and dance my fingertips across your face to the beat of the song, like fairies touching your cheeks and forehead with their magical feet.

"I'm smiling for you. You are the best."

So are you, Sweetheart. I am so scared.

"I know, Daddy. I know. I've got you and know that I'm not scared. You are going to be okay. Trust me."

Okay, Babygirl, but I can't breathe.

"Breathe my light."

Okay, Babygirl.

"Okay, Daddy. Sshhh. I love you."

I didn't get a chance for you to revive and recover. I didn't get a chance to save you.

"You held me and guided me into God's light. What more could a father do? You did more than save my physical life, Daddy."

Thank you. I have to live the rest of life without you in your physical body. It is so much to bare. Too much to bare.

"I know, Daddy. I hate what you and Mommy and Nate have to face. It is so unfair. But you can do this, Daddy. We can do this. We can do hard things. There is nobody like you and me."

*

Kayleigh Physically Died In A Simple Accident 05/30/2018

After a recent interaction where a person had false information about Kayleigh's physical death I find it necessary to clear this up. The rumor I was told is that my Daughter was raped, and so devastated by the rape, that she committed suicide by throwing herself in front of a car. That's just stupid. Nothing can be further from the truth. I held my Daughter as she physically died - she having no idea that she had been hit by a car. It was a simple accident. Nothing more. It wasn't even a mistake. This occasional rumor has caused harm to a great family who is already suffering horribly daily.

Kayleigh was indeed raped ten months before the accident. Before and after that event Kayleigh's life, in general, was a happy brilliant life up to the moment of the accident, dealing with age appropriate teenager angst and ups and downs and growth and learning how to be a young woman. Yes, also, she was deeply harmed by the rape, but she never let the rape define her - courageously stepping up against sexual violence at fourteen immediately after the event took place - something factually most victims don't do. She used the event to make her voice stronger, conquering the assault and giving her even more self-confidence and internal peace. She embarked on her hard, healing process telling me often to encourage herself, "Daddy, we can do hard things, right?" She prosecuted. She advocated for other girls. She cried. She laughed. She played. She lived. She forgave her rapists. She was a legend to countless women who watched her use her voice. She was on top of the world and living an empowered happy life, continuing to press forward to define her life when the accident, in the blink of an eye, happened.

Then, in a totally unrelated event, on that horrible night, she was clipped by a car as she stepped out from behind a telephone pole that spun her down, where she hit her head on the street and physically died in my arms several minutes later. She had no idea she had been hit. She was not in any pain. She listened to my voice and acknowledged she could hear me as she passed. She was not drunk. She was not distracted. She did not enter the street to get hit. She was not trying to get hit. She did not throw herself in front of a car. She was actually never in front of the car, the car colliding with her at its front right bumper as she simply stepped off the curb to cross the street to innocently retrieve her shoes on the other side of the street to come home. Obscured by the telephone pole, the driver didn't see her. Obscured on the other side of the pole, she didn't see the car. That's it. Simple. Innocent. Tragic. Horrific. Completely unrelated to the rape. Unrelated to anything. It was not a suicide. Not a mistake. It was a simple accident. And my baby physically died.

As Kayleigh did with her rapists, so I do with whoever started this disgusting rumor. I forgive you. If anyone has spread this rumor, you have an obligation to my Daughter to correct the misinformation. Kayleigh deserves the truth and the truth again is so sad and simple - my beloved baby, one of the two loves of my life, physically died in a tragic accident at the most empowered, happiest point in her wonderful life. It rips my breath away in its simplicity. I love you, Kakie, and am so completely proud of you.

"She Dances In a Sea Of Stars"

She wears galaxies for her gowns,
Liquid light - liquid gold,
And rainbow stars like glittering fabric,
Spiral forth from her sparkling soul -

She dances aloofly on the winds aloft,
And presses her feet like rose petals soft,
Upon my fields of earthly firmament,
Where, with her, the hours of my days are spent.

*

A Million Things in the Physical World I Miss 05/30/2018

The way we would laugh so hard together - which elevated the other's surprise and laughter, until we would both be convulsing with tears, our heads turned up with mouths wide open and not breathing, lunging forward towards each other. Crying so hard in the laughter. Then a long breath as our laughter simmered down. It was usually something rather stupid that would trip up one of us; making fun of somebody lightheartedly or egging each other on; watching Japanese commercials on YouTube; falling off the bed while doing art projects. I've never cried as well as with you at these moments, usually resulting in that boisterous bombastic explosion of a cackle you would let out. Brilliant. Beautiful. And my laugh tuning higher and higher until I sounded, myself, like a teenage girl. I miss a million things, one of the most prominent of which are those moments where we laughed until we cried. I have to bare these accumulating losses in order to stay in contact with you, Sweetheart. Your fingerprints are everywhere. I am learning to leave mine on the windows of Heaven, looking in, searching for my elevation. I live in the duality. I strive for our laughter.

*

And Confusion 05/30/2018

The confusion comes frequently. Throughout any given day I experience every type of emotion a multiple of times per day. I was on top of the world. We just had a great vacation. You were feeling incredibly strong and had reinforced your voice. You were well equipped for life. You had never stopped living after the assault. You used it to become stronger. We laughed through our days, and huddled up for hard moments. I had not a fear for you in your life. School was starting. I was going to maybe change careers and maybe make a little more money for us. Then the accident happened, the worst thing the world could ever have thrown at me, and my life was destroyed. What happened to my life? Just like that, the horror visited and a nuclear bomb went off in a breadbox.

I miss you so much in your physical form. It is indescribable to those who haven't suffered like this. Please help me stay where you are - centered in spirit - and help me find you where you are, not where you are not.

"Daddy, I am here. Don't give up. Keep pushing though. We can do hard things, Daddy. I love you so much!"

"Always By My Side"

There are times that I cannot feel you,
These are truly dire times,
Though the timeframe cannot steal you,
I search nervously for signs,
Though I need not fret if I can't see you,
For your presence by design,
Is more radiant than this dimension,
And more brilliant over time,
And though in moments I cannot feel you,
And there are moments when I feel blind,
I know that you are holding my hand,
And standing by my side.

*

Using My Voice 05/31/2018

Hi, Babygirl. I am proud of myself for using my voice and advocating for you. I resisted for many months, knowing that I owe, and you owe, no explanation to anybody for anything that happened during the accident. It is only one in a thousand who have misinformation and I have only been questioned a few times by those few who did not have the correct information about what happened to you. Some actually wanted different facts, I am sure, because if an arbitrary accident could happen to you, then it can happen to their kids too, and they wouldn't want to think about their children being physically killed in an innocent flash. It is much easier on these selfish people to spin up a gross gossipy lie that somehow you precipitated the accident, and in that way, it wasn't arbitrary, and in that way, their kids are safe. It is the arbitrary nature of this accident, the unpredictability that causes people to want you to have some deeper issue that caused the accident. It is so cruel. So heartless. So heart wrenching for us.

Yet the accident was simple. And innocent. With no extra spice. With no drama. With nothing except an amazing child suddenly caught in ten or eleven factors that all crushed into the same space at the same time to create an almost instant fatality. Yet with these people - God, these people! It became important for me to use my voice - not to change anybody's opinion, no matter how irregular or incorrect - but just for the sake of using my voice. That's what I always taught you. It continues to come full circle, the lessons I taught you to empower, you are now teaching me to empower. I love you, Babygirl. I miss you tremendously in your physical form and am so grateful that you are present in your spiritual embodiment, growing with me each day.

"Good job, Daddy. Use your voice. You did always teach me that and because of you I used my voice and because of you I found my voice. These people who came up with this rumor are bullshit people. They are actually bullshit. And they are nothing compared to you. And they are lost in their assumptions and totally wrong. Thank you, Daddy, for watching over me as you always have. I guess you aren't over protective!"

It was infuriating. Their rumor actually would attempt to take away from the glory of who you became in your strength. It was so wrong - somebody trying to guess that you were a broken child who committed suicide, rather than a happy, empowered girl full of life who just happened to have been physically killed in a horrible accident, not unlike an innocent kid walking down the street and being struck by a falling brick, or a child being killed by a shark while swimming. I was not going to let this go any further. And what I realized is that the vast majority of people around us and in the community never heard the rumor - that only a few had spun it up, and that a few others who had heard it, did not believe it; some even coming to your aid and setting the record straight. At long last, not one person who actually knew you believed the rumor. It was several in the community who never met you. How stupid. How perfectly low vibrational and human. I want to burn down the earth.

"Now let them go, Daddy. We have bigger things to accomplish. The anger only gets in the way."

*

Your Needs Today 06/04/2018

I need to determine your needs today, just as I always have assessed your needs, with both of my children. Every morning I think through what Nate needs and also what you need. I have done this since before both of you were born. How can I do better; what did you both need at any given moment. That has not changed for both of my children need different things at different ages. Now, both of my children need different things from me at different ages, and in different body types and worlds.

For you, Kakes, what do you need from your Daddy today? How can I build our relationship; how can I warm your soul; put a smile across your angelic face; cause you to gush with love for your Father.

"Daddy, you already have. Just by writing this and acknowledging that I need my Daddy, that's it. I need my Daddy. You are perfect in my eyes. I love you so much!"

*

Beautiful Day 06/05/2018

I ended today's morning prayer and meditation with you as I normally do – with a statement from the heart: "Kakes, I can't have you in your physical form today, but I can have you in your spiritual embodiment today. I am not going to miss out on our relationship today. You and me together. It's going to be a wonderful, beautiful day. God bless us as we walk together today and fill up the day with our relationship."

Then I jumped into the Pilot and drove off to work, listening to myself eat a power bar. Then listening to a few minutes of sports talk radio. Then the Bluetooth came on by itself. I heard the sonic slow beat of a very familiar song and just couldn't believe that you turned on my phone and overrode the radio, cycled through it and found this song and played it. Although, it is exactly what I can believe and do believe. It is what you do. U2's "Beautiful Day." Of course.

I could see you laughing, sitting next to me in the car, very pleased with yourself, and knowing the multiple meanings of the song. Not only is this a song I used to sing to you and Nathaniel beginning when you were seven or eight, but it was substantially identical to the words I had just prayed with you several minutes earlier. Further, it was an incredible song and spectacle when they played this for us in July at your last concert in your physical form at Browns Stadium, standing beside your Father, arm in arm, amazed by the power and energy emanating from the stage; aglow in the rainbow lights that illuminated the summer atmosphere.

"Daddy, look what I played for you. U2! Remember, Daddy, this was my first concert at the Rock and Roll Hall of Fame with Aunt Tricia when I was little, and U2 was my last physical concert with you forty five days before the accident. It is a beautiful day, Daddy. Any day with you is a beautiful day and I am so grateful I get to walk with you and you get to walk with me. I will always walk with you. I will always show you little clues and leave you messages. I always did and I always will. I am so grateful that you are so awake. You are amazing with the work you are doing, Daddy. It's really beautiful. That's why I chose this song, Daddy, because the words remind me of what you are doing – *"it's a beautiful day - don't let it get away – touch me, take me to that other place..."* That is what you are doing with me, Daddy, with your daughter. You refuse to lose the day. Don't ever lose this day because I am here. I'm right here."

It is a simple miracle, but spectacular in its execution. I've learned already in these months that you always pick the right song at the right time, manipulating the technology that is at your disposal. You also will only pick U2 at very particular times, using very particular messages to reach me just at the times when I am feeling the lyrics in my life. You explain what I am going through with specific lyrics.

You watch over me and work to offer me these gifts, ever loyal, ever present. I owe you my continued dedication and you know you have it. You are my Daughter and we are living a miracle of breaching the two worlds of Heaven and earth to be together as well as we can until we are both in the same body type and on the same plain again. You have proven the existence of the soul, of God, of Heaven, of a guardian angel – not proof that I needed, but proof nonetheless for those that may need it or want it.

It's a beautiful day, Kakie, made more powerful and beautiful because of you – your light, your soul, your presence, and your gifts. I take myself to a higher vibration today, with you, and I promise I will not let this day get away from us. I love you.

"You Helped to Raise the Sun Today"

Today you helped to raise the morning,
Unveil the light of day,
And through the mist with clear intention,
Your fingers spread the golden lace,
That moistened the edges of awakening,
That shone like a million flames,
Whose kiss set steam upon the grass,
That greets the sun with your embrace.

*

Intuitive Interaction with Kakie 06/06/2018

I led a meeting on the east side. I left an empty chair next to me with a card with Kayleigh's name on it on the table so the audience could see her name. I ended my lead talking about Kayleigh, her accident, our devastation and our continued journey together, strengthening my sobriety each day with her guidance.

When we stood to do the Lord's Prayer the young secretary held my hand and pulled it close against her stomach almost feeling like she was cradling me. Like I needed the extra love. As we began to recite the prayer I began to cry again and she pulled my hand even tighter just to embrace me in my grief.

After comments and the meeting was turned back over to her, she shook my hand and held it in both of hers and said she was just overwhelmed and didn't know what to say, but thank you. She closed down the meeting. Afterwards she said, "My sponsor makes me nervous. She doesn't really understand when another is on the other side." She seemed like she wanted to tell me something. She gave me an "in" as we stepped outside into the parking lot.

Assuming her intentions correctly, I turned to her. "Kayleigh is here," I said, "She is present. She shows up every day."

She was relieved but also drawn in and nervous. "Oh yeah," she said, her eyes wide and seeming overwhelmed. She struggled and giggled to explain that, yes, Kayleigh was very present. During the lead inside. Here outside standing in front of her. She gestured in circles with her hand, stating, "In the empty chair you left for her, she was there. Out here right now. She's here. I mean, like really right here."

Referring to the empty chair I said, "Did you see Kayleigh?"

She said, "oh yeah. She was sitting right there at her seat with the card. She wasn't doing acrobatics or anything, but she was present the whole time. A very big presence. She is here right now. It's overwhelming as she's right in front of my face. I can't see her full human form - I see like a blonde platinum full body but blurred, like emanating in waves of light, and she is right here standing in front of me. Like right here."

She seemed joyous, a little manic with her laughter, but awe struck overwhelmed. "What's going on here is huge. What went on in there while you led and with you two - it's massive."

"She's very present," I said meaning always with me as our relationship grows.

"Kayleigh loves, loves, loves her Daddy," I said.

She smiled nervously. "Oh yes!" she said forcefully and with purpose. "Very much so. She's not going anywhere. She's not leaving. She's right here." She said it in a way that made me think that Kayleigh had just told her to convey that, or she could see Kayleigh's permanence surrounding me and holding me and she got that overwhelming feeling of loyalty and eternal devotion. Like Kayleigh's presence was a million sunrises surrounding me.

"It's hard for me in a way," she said struggling for the words, "My son and I don't have a good relationship. He wasn't wanted, but then I had him anyway and we've struggled. But you two. This. What's going on here? You two. What went on while you led? What's going on here (motioning in circles and motioning in front of her with her arms opened wide) it's beyond human words and beyond human understanding. I don't even have the words. I'm going to have to pray on it. It is huge. What you have is huge. I wish I had that with my son."

It wasn't like she felt threatened since Kakes is never threatening and has always been so sweet and gentle, especially after she shed her humanness, but it was like she felt vulnerable due to the immense power that Kayleigh could wield as a guardian angel. Not just a normal angel, but an elevated, high order angel. I felt a little strange hoping she didn't say anything weird - my own prejudices or humanness emerging illogically and ignorantly in that sacred space.

I felt her energy as she was uncomfortable in Kayleigh's presence. Not from fear but in awe. She was awe struck by Kayleigh's spirit. She could see her and I think the fact that this was the first time she saw a soul so big and bright, that it was hard for her to contemplate Kayleigh's magnitude. I felt on the day of her funeral, as I was thunder struck, that my God, we knew Kayleigh was always amazing, but could it be that this whole time we had one of God's favorite angels. I heard in my soul God respond with a resounding, "yes!" Now this young woman was seeing what one of God's favorite angels looks like to an intuitive human. And it blew her away.

I held my right hand up, palm down, where I felt my Daughter's energy, at about 5 foot 11, looked to my right, assessed where my hand naturally would go, and said, "She's right here."

She looked under my hand and smiled in acknowledgment to confirm my statement.

I said "we are a great family. Kayleigh is all about family. She loves her Mommy. She loves her Brother and she loves her Daddy. Family is everything to her. She protects us."

She said "oh yes. Oh yes," while looking downward and around. She finally looked ahead under my hand and said, raising a hand to gesture to the air with reverence in front of her, almost in an embarrassed voice, "Kayleigh, I'm not trying to ignore you, honey - really I'm not." She turned back to me, and laughed nervously, "She's right here."

"You can feel her" I said, "Kayleigh is pure light and pure love. She's incredibly powerful and she walks with me every day."

"Yes it's huge. It's overwhelming. She's right here."

It seemed like, and knowing Kakes, I wouldn't be surprised if she was jumping up and down and so excited that this woman could see her energy - not a full human form as she explained, but a bright, radiating blurry presence. I imagined Kakes being Kakes and deliberately rambling off a series of orders to her like, "Sweetie, you can see me! You're a good girl. Tell my Daddy I'm right here. Make sure he knows. He's had a hard day. Make sure you tell him..."

And it seemed like she was on the receiving end of this and having a hard time receiving since it was so powerful and filled with energy.

I hugged her and told her Kayleigh was proud of her. She was happy I said that. Almost like Kayleigh's presence was clearly a force protecting me and it was overwhelming. She opened up to me and because she did, I could sense even deeper Kayleigh beside me in that sacred space. The electricity was amazing. I could feel my baby where this wonderful young woman was looking - right to my right, where Kayleigh spends a lot of her time.

She continued, "Most of the time when I see souls it is in the corner of your eye or a gray figure that you can't really see. But Kayleigh is the closest I've ever come to seeing a full apparition. She is full light like the color of when a girl bleach blondes her hair but it resonates. Like the resonance of sound. Like light vibrating and pulsing out from her."

She continued, "Most souls, after transition, there is little incentive to stay on this side because the afterworld is so amazing. I've seen a few times souls that will linger with loved ones. But with your Kayleigh, this isn't a linger. She is intentionally with you and so powerful. She isn't leaving you all the way through your own transition. It is so cool and overwhelming that I can see your Kayleigh. During your lead I was looking out to my sponsor who is also intuitive, and was like, with my eyes, 'hey sponsor, do you see this. My sponsor just smiled, nodding her head all nonchalant and told me afterward that she sees full bodies like Kayleigh all the time. I'm not going to sleep tonight. I'm just buzzing having met your Kayleigh."

When I left the meeting for the drive home, I gave her a hug and as I did I said to Kakes in my heart, "Kakie pleases give her a hug through me to thank her."

The woman shot up straight in my arms and said, "Oh okay! Okay" and smiled. I told her what I had just prayed with Kakes and she said, "Yep, so that's what that was when you hugged me. Yes, I felt that."

I drove home amazed. With all we suffer daily, these high moments of rejoicing in God's mystery was a saving grace.

"Seat of Soul"

These truths are guiding credo,
This fabric of woven light,
It fits together in perfect union,
The four of us - across our lives;

And as her life ushered into transition,
From the physical to the spiritual realm,
She, with devotion, intended her position,

And assumed for the family her angelic helm;

She walks as she has always,
With light beside my eyes,
She moves about across my aura,
And protects the earth, my seas, my skies,
For she loves her family - is loyal - and bold,
And blesses our days from the Seat of the Soul,
Right here - right here - by my side.

*

Daddy, I Mean What I Say 06/07/2018

"When I tell you that you are the best Daddy in the world - I mean you are the best Daddy in the world. When I tell you I love you so much I mean I love you so much. When I tell you I will never leave your side I mean I will never leave your side. Don't doubt that. I know you are still in shock and it has to be hard trusting all that you cannot see.

I came to you through Savannah last night to show you that I mean what I say. It's all real, Daddy, and I am me! Sweet, funny, loud, slightly irreverent, faithful, loving, crazy-Kakes! I love you so much, Daddy. The seat of my soul is with you. I am never leaving your side."

Thank you, Kayleigh, so much. I love you so much. Let's sit on your bed and do some writing tonight. I love doing this nightly.

"Every Nighttime on Your Bed"

In your window, nighttime framed,
Branches and the streetlights play,
Whistling, the wind bares its stream of breath,
A scent of lavender - sparkling jade,
And Father stretched across her bed,
Where bedtime books once were read,

A million pains and grief's barbed kiss,
What he mostly misses is what he is yet to miss,
And Father stretched across her bed,
Meditates to mend his heart and head,
He talks to her - they reminisce,
They live the miracle that persists,
And Father stretched across her bed,
Knows their bond has conquered death,
And feels her there because she is,
And she is there for there she lives.

*

Kayleigh Kakes Release 06/07/2018

Off to the big ocean. She was feisty, waiving her flippers around as if she was already in the water. Active. Dynamic. Vocal. Focused. Dead set on her return. Headstrong and deliberate. Gentle yet belligerent in the arms that held her just above the water. She had her mind calculated on executing her task and she was going to accomplish her goal - return to the ocean. If the turtle could talk she would have said, "Baby do it - all by myself!"

Of course this marvelous Kemps Ridley has the same dynamic qualities as my Kayleigh. This is, after all, as we like to say, my Daughter's endangered sea turtle. Kayleigh flowered this sea turtle with love and covered it with her healing light every day since my Daughter's accident. It glows with her light. Its shell reflects Kayleigh's guardian golden light in its greenish gray shell. Its eyes sparkle with Kayleigh's soul. It arrived at the Georgia Sea Turtle Center on August 12th, having suffered a boat strike just north of Jekyll Island as we drove past that section of Georgia on our way back to Cleveland on that same day, five days before Kayleigh's accident. From the night of the 17th on, following her physical death in that horrible car accident, my Kayleigh has never left this sea turtle's side.

There is no coincidence that this sea turtle was named after Kayleigh soon thereafter, representing the massive outpouring of love and sadness resounding around the hearts of thousands who mourned our baby in the aftermath of the accident. She is a special turtle - the most endangered type of sea turtle - one more rarely received by the Georgia Sea Turtle Center. Their love and compassion, their persistent interaction with us throughout these months, their care for this special turtle should never be underestimated. We owe them a great deal and I know my Kayleigh will touch each of them individually with special blessings. She always does to those who show love to her three loves - Mommy, Daddy and Little Brother.

And so it is today - the Georgia Sea Turtle Center workers slowly immersing Kayleigh Kakes into the surf, Jess beside her as she entered the water. She immediately put her head down and splashed off in through the waves. Just like Kayleigh. Persistent. Loyal. Dedicated. Friendly. Laughing. Joyful. Grateful. Energetic. Free. It was just a minute or so and she was out of sight and off to live her days, to return to her beach to lay her eggs and to perpetuate the Kemps Ridley line - now imbued with the light of an angel in its spirit and around its beautiful life.

She swims again in the open ocean, nearly ten months after her accident. She swims with Little Phil, the baby Loggerhead that Kayleigh saved on August 6th. She swims in pure love and light, mixed with the salty waters of the Atlantic. My Kayleigh is surely swimming alongside her, laughing with her, talking to her, encouraging her, protecting her, kissing her with love - guiding her forward with a special liquid light that lay a road through the ocean for her to pass. Kayleigh Kakes - swim in Kayleigh's light. She will never leave your side.

"The Ocean"

The full moon blossoms orange and breathes,
And exhales a golden mist out over the sea,
While I stand silently on a silvery beach,
Under rustling palm trees with purple leaves,
Heeding the voice of the Ocean,
That speaks in the rumble of the waves,
That speaks to the soul,
That speaks in dreams,
On a humid breeze...

*

With An Unbreakable Bond of Devotion - An Eleventh Step Addition, A.M. 06/09/2018

With devotion and intention I awaken to you, open to you, uplift myself to you, reach higher in my life to you and for you and towards you. You are here. You are smiling. You are safe. You are free. You are happy. You are with me. It is my job, my gift, my challenge, my opportunity to lift myself towards your realm and there commune with you. You continuously reach across to me; and I to you. We are unbreakable. We are love. We are truth. We are a Daddy and Daughter combination the likes of which the world has rarely seen.

We know you never meant this severance, this untimely physical separation. We know you long and desire to be with me, Mommy and Nate and you do everything in your power to be as present as you can be. Likewise, we will do the same, building bridges over the breach, lifting ourselves to you, incorporating you in all that we do - for our interactions together are not a concocted sentiment just to make us feel better or to comfort us or a bend of life in the crooked corridors of denial. We are alive, the four of us and share, as we always have, our thoughts, words and actions. Among the four of us, this family, are these truths. It is true. You are here. Kayleigh, whether you are in your physical form or your spiritual form you are still Kayleigh, you are still the same kid, and always will be. Thank you for your loyalty and devotion to your family. Thank you for your unending gifts, your presence, guidance and abundance of light and love.

"No, Daddy, thank you! I'm so grateful you know that I am alive and you get it. I am right here. Literally right here! Right here, and I am never leaving your side."

I know, sweet Babygirl, thank you so much. I love you.

"Me too, Daddy!"

*

"Daddy, We Wrote Another Book" 06/11/2018

"Daddy, you always listen to me. I was so happy you heard me, but of course you heard me. You always do. It's who we are and we are amazing! And, after my transition, you are now my pen. I have so much to write!

I think it's hilarious that people don't know that I wrote this with you nine months after the accident and my transition. It freaks them out! But I did. You will never forget that I called out to you while you stood in the kitchen on May 25, 2018 and said, 'Daddy! Daddy! Let's go sit outside in the backyard and write another children's book. It's called 'Purple Turtles.''

You heard me. You smiled. You knew a blending of the dimensions was happening. Immediately you grabbed a notebook, an iced tea and a purple pen and sat in the backyard in a lounge chair in the sun. You said to me, "okay, Babygirl (I love that you call me Babygirl), what do you want to write? Write through me."

And I sat with you. And we wrote. Fifteen minutes later you and I had finished scribbling out "Purple Turtles." I wanted people to use their voices and fight back like I did. Thank you so much, Daddy, for listening and hearing. And for including some of my friends in illustrating it. You heard me ask you to include them. It was amazing drawing with them and hanging out with them around our dining room table. I love them. They knew I was there. I'm always there. You know that. You and Mommy see me and feel me and hear me every day. Because I am. And we are.

Daddy, I just love you so, so much! And now our book is finally finished and I love it! Let's write another!"

*

Another Day 06/12/2018

Another day closer to Heaven, living as I go and gifting My Three Loves with my light no matter the suffering or pain or heartache. We press forward. We grow. We live. She is so strong. When the four of us are all together in one room we can feel the four corners resonating at its greatest power. It's amazing. I will not miss this opportunity to be with all three of My Loves for anything.

Please help me embrace Kayleigh where she is. Not where she isn't. She isn't in her physical body. She is, however, in her spiritual form and spiritual life, as strong as ever and as present as she always has been.

"Meditation with You, My Darling"

I see you - your magnificence,
Standing strongly in long white gowns,
Laced in sun flares and sunrises,
And swirling galaxies hemmed into the fabric of sky,
And oceans of stars flowing out from your open palms,
That spiral slowly around me,
Twinkling like brilliant diamonds a million tiny flashes at a time,
Enveloping me with pure love in its energetic flow,
Wrapping me with the wonder and the wisdom of Heaven,
That penetrates the fabrications of the mind,

And washes through my soul,
You were smiling, ever vigilant,
In a way that your Father knows,
Your love is eternal - your love so safe and inviting,
I come to rest in its glow.

*

A Woman Who Met Spirit When He Was Randy 06/13/2018

We were swimming at the Hamptons where Jess' parents live. Jess. Nate. Me. Kayleigh. I sat in the hot tub with a woman and her daughter. After some time, small talk discussion evolved to talking about our pets. She is a dog groomer. I explained we had two - Rosie the pedigree blue tick beagle and Spirit the street dog, half Rottweiler and half Besengi.

She surmised that I had bought him from a pound. I explained that the city kennel had him, but then they were going to put him down. Instead, the Parma Animal Shelter took him in, even though they were at capacity.

I explained how my Daughter and I went to the shelter to see a different dog and after spending time with it my Daughter asked if she could see the smaller one in the first cage as we walked in. As we originally passed she said, "oh Daddy! He's so cute. Can we look at that one?"

I explained to this woman that I looked at him and he looked like a beaten up street dog. Typical black with little tufts of brown above his eyes. I said, "Let's look at the one we came to see first."

"Okay," she said as we passed. Now it was fifteen minutes later. She was done with the first dog and ready to meet her soulmate. They brought the street dog out to the fenced yard to meet Kayleigh who sat in the grass. Of course he ran across the grass and dove into her arms, licking her a hundred times. "Oh Daddy, I love him. Can we get this one?" And that was that. I then told this woman that he had

555

the worst name ever, "Randy! Randy?! Horrible right? Who would name a dog Randy?"

"Randy?" She said and smiled. "And you said he was half Rott and half Besengi, right? And the Parma Animal Shelter?"

"Yes," I confirmed.

"I met your dog," she said, beaming with excitement, "when he was still at the shelter. I very distinctly remember seeing his name and thinking - who names a dog Randy? It was about a year and a half to two years ago, right?"

"Yes it was."

"Small world," she said, "I met your dog right before you and your daughter brought him home to your family."

Small world. Or just Kayleigh making the world a spirited world. There is no coincidence. Kayleigh arranged the whole thing somehow. We meet a stranger, a woman, swimming at Jess' parent's complex, who knew Kayleigh's dog, while it was in a shelter, right before we bought him from that shelter. Of course.

*

First Father's Day in New Configuration I 06/17/2018

Today we celebrate you making me a Father, to be followed and doubled by your wonderful brother a few years later. You. Because of you and Nate I am a Father. It is what I had always wanted more than anything - my sobriety opened the path for this miracle. I sit here today - a Father forever, and ever have I been - to two brilliant souls. I am so lucky I am yours. On this first Father's Day since the accident, I hold you and your brother in reverence, although there is a part of me that wants to hold my breath until my breath fails me. The duality is my only hope - my only balance. I feel utterly hopeless and overwhelmed by the magnitude of your physical loss in my life. The horror is so rich and vibrant, in full color, and in my face, every hour

556

of every day. Yet your spiritual presence - the breath of wind that just soothed me; the warmth across my back when you cradle me; the way you touch the top of my head because you know, as tactile as I am, that I would always know when it is you; the electricity around me from your brilliant, white light; your voice - in many forms that comes in through the ears or the brain or my flesh, that gets translated somehow within my soul. You. It is you always that picks my face up out of the mire, out of the bog, and sets my feet upon a rock - like Psalm 40 (of course, made famous by U2).

No matter the challenges, we keep writing our song, our story - a life I cannot document if I am buried in sadness, even though the sadness is inescapable. I refuse to lose contact with my babies and so I will cry, I will wail, I will suffer the reconciling, walking and skulking and stalking that metal box of powerlessness if I must; in order to properly process; in order to open to the fullness of you, Sweetheart, and to my beloved Nate.

I will never stop. I will pick myself back up. As always, you each have your own set of needs and I bring myself to each of you to open to and determine each child's desires. I love you, Babygirl, with all of my heart. What are your needs today? What is our prayer today?

"Daddy, I love you so much. I am so sorry this is so hard. You are the best Daddy in these worlds and I don't want you to second guess decisions or my life or if you could have prevented this. It was a horrible accident. Even I couldn't have prevented. Nobody could have. Anybody standing there would have had the same outcome. I am so, so sorry I am not there physically, but you hear me and feel me and know that I am holding you. You are my Daddy! My Daddy!

Do you know how many of my friends always wished that you were their daddy? A lot! But you're not! You are mine! Mine and Nathaniel's! He loves you so much too and really needs you. He's going to feel the burden for carrying both of us to you today, in his own way and his own understanding. Be extra gentle to be aware of this today. I'm right here, Daddy. I've got you. Hear that Cardinal out over your right shoulder? Just a little extra something. I am alive, Daddy, my life and journey continuing. Meet me in my life - I have so much cool stuff to show you. Happy Father's Day, Daddy, our first with me in Heaven watching over you and blessing the man I love most on Earth and in eternity. Love you, Daddy, love you!"

*

First Father's Day in New Configuration II 06/17/2018

Happy Father's Day to my two magnificent Loves. For you I am your blessed Father. For you I continue to grow each day with each of you at the same time in two different worlds. We are unbreakable. I love you with my soul. - Daddy.

"A Love Song to My Baby"

I have words that press deeply to soul,
Like the stone from the sun is spun into gold,
They are your words in your lovely voice,
Deliberately spoken and offered by choice,
Wrapped in cloud paper and sealed with a kiss,
That lessen the burden of a lifetime's abyss,
My Little Girl,
Thank you, thank you, thank you for this,
My Little Girl -

Our lives were so full - effortless and bright,
Until the toll of an accident on an August summer night,
And in your last breath as I cried out your name,
You entered your death and I entered this pain,
In a shock and a tragic suddenness,
My Baby, My Child,
With all that I miss,
I miss mostly -

Everything,
Everything,
Everything.

*

U2 D.C. Father's Day 06/18/2018

On 07/03/2017, I took my kids to U2 at Cleveland Browns stadium where I sang "One" to them, arm in arm, Nate on my right and Kayleigh on my left. Forty six days later, the unthinkable happened when Kayleigh was blindsided by a car. This night, Kakie returned to a U2 concert with me for the first time since the accident where I serenaded her with "One" while she strengthened me with her light and held her Daddy upright through my convulsing sobbing and tortuous tears. I am so grateful that I have always sung to my children and pray that others do with theirs.

My brother, Tim, and his wife, Irene, and my sister Tricia were with Kakes and I at the concert, while Nate was with his sister and their cousins at one of our family homes in DC. Jess was with Kakes in Cleveland. She is where we are – in many places at once.

I thank these three for taking a courageous step with me and Kayleigh at this U2 concert. They were perfect support. What most people have a hard time understanding is that our lives have literally been destroyed and the simplest tasks are near impossible at times. The restless waves of grief are endless since Kayleigh, my child, naturally follows me in time, and is therefore supposed to be physically living when I physically die. Time does not heal the wounds of the physical death of a child - it actually makes it harder in certain respects. My siblings and Irene caught a tiny glimpse of every day of my life after this horrible tragedy as the waves go up and down. My message to them was this: to please know that this pain will never end and there should never be an expectation that it will. Further, this doesn't mean Jess and I are not growing. We reconcile bravely each day and face each next surprise around every new corner with intention and devotion to Kakes and Nate and continue to boldly grow with both. The physical loss of Kayleigh - my sweet dynamic Kayleigh – the physical death of a child in childhood I it is one of those places that never exists until you've been there. I pray Jess and I are the only ones we know who ever suffer like this. Thank you again for holding me while I crumbled at a concert. I love you each very much.

"No Matter Cloud or Clear Night Sky"

Even through the gray cascading,
It's cloth that dims the night,
Cannot its haze - its imperfections,
Dampen all dancing shards of light,
For there, deep - amidst the quieting sky,
No severance befalls the bond between you and I;

Even when clouds, like oceans,
Roll forth and tumble onward, above,
And try it may to wash the moon beams,
Cannot its tide eclipse our love,
For there, it may, through the sleepy, silent midnight sky,
The moon, although I cannot see it,
Radiates in constant praise, My Love,
For you and I.

*

My Family of Four 06/24/2018

It Amazes me. We amaze me. And we don't amaze me, knowing this
is just who we are. Nurturing each other effortlessly. Every day. It is
the fabric of this family that we have created through energy, love,
dedication, the disrobing of each ego, the defining of priorities and
importance - God, family first - everything else in any other order.

Still, amongst the fallout of this tragedy are thousands of trapdoors,
barriers, surprises and heartache around every corner of every each
day. It is daunting to be spinning through this life knowing that in the
next five minutes, or hour or evening, I will see something or feel
something that reminds me of what once was or what would have
been or what has been lost, or what will never be, all resulting from
the accident. Some are memories and reality. Some are not reality -
seeing a girl that looks like Kayleigh at what would have been her
current physical age; seeing her friends driving and working and

going to and from school; getting prepped for college and life and marriage and children; the robbery of my Daughter physically. The simultaneous robbery of my grandchildren from Kayleigh that will never be – holding a little blonde baby girl that is my adult daughter's child – all wiped away; Kayleigh, in her fifties, standing with her brother, holding my hand and smiling at me as my eyes dim and I physically die as an old man. It is all so very overwhelming if taken in one chunk of human life and experience. This is a spiritual death trap for me. I take these moments one at a time through Steps 10, 11 and 12 more than I ever have, and process as I go. Otherwise, it would be each of the waves of trauma that overwhelm and destroy me, over and over again. The waves nearly kill me, yet the waves I manage one at a time.

We need to search for the beauty in our lives or there will be none. The searching is key. The connection is vital. We each know the consequences of lethargy or complacency or despondency - knowing that each has a part to play to continuously develop this unique family unit and interconnecting each of our spirits together in this joyous cross-stitching of four strands of light, bound in one brilliant interwoven blanket of life. We wrap ourselves in this blanket. We are shielded by this blanket. We share this blanket with others in need of comfort or protection.

We are all four of us learning our new configuration. We are all taking things one step at a time, particularly the three of us in our human condition, taking direction from Kayleigh who is ensuring her presence and holding us up in her light. My family of four amazes me - each of us has been doing such incredible work to show the resilience of unbreakable love.

"Amongst All Angels"

You are charmed, and charismatic, little child,
Amongst all angels you are honored, special, chosen,
You stretch your golden wings to the tallest trees tops,
And fill with light the basin where my heart's backbone was broken,
Calling me forth,
Calling me gladly,
Calling me forward,

Calling out to your Daddy -

And I cry,
And my tears are as deep as the universe is wide;

Among all angels you are the brightest,
You are pure innocence and grace,
You, my brave child, are ever present,
I see your eyes within my eyes within my face,
You are exactly who you are,
The moon and its aura that laced with light the fields of brilliant stars,
We transcend everything,
Every scene,
Every dream,
Every scream,
To dance and we dance and we dance in each other's arms…

…And I smile,
With a heart that is as deep as the universe is wide.

*

Verbal Pages 06/25/2018

Part of writing this book are reducing to writing the verbal, person to person exchanges, in the stories we share of Kayleigh; from her physical life; from her spiritual life. Her totality in what we share to the world. These are part of her book, these very personal interludes among people we meet as we share our daughter and Nate's sister. It is one method by which she helps tie the world together in a tapestry of light. She, by the way, loves this interpersonal interchange one on one with people that she brings into our sphere. She has a plan and executes on those plans. She picks people. She picks people who will understand. She picks those who will love her family.

"Celestial Silvery Dawn"

She, the Ancient, the great eternal soul,
Illuminates the darkness that midnight claimed to hold,
Dancing fires that glitter atop the fields of ocean foam,
Reflects her majesty in each wave's pitch and roll,
She tucks the night time clasped within her hold,
Lighting up the beachfront with her great celestial glow,
She is promise - that one day we shall know,
The dawn of the heavens - and its eternal gold.

*

Daddy I Was Holding Your Hands 06/26/2018

"Daddy, I hate seeing you so sad and troubled. Your body beaten down by the stress. You keep getting sick, though you are doing incredible work moving forward with the transition. In both hands, one each of sad and happy. I am so proud of you. Yet I am so worried about you, Daddy.

I leave you messages. I give you signs. You know that. You are so in tune with me and it makes me so happy. I'm actually impressed with how much you're picking up. I always find it hilarious with some things I think you'll see that go right by you. It cracks me up and I am stunned because I make it so easy sometimes. But mostly there you are with a head turn or looking into the wind but looking right into my eyes, and knowing it. Or leaning towards the wind that rustles through the trees beside you and holding me.

But you are so tired. Your body nearly broken. It is amazing because you are doing such incredible grief work. You are facing this trauma head on and as you say, Daddy, in full color. But it's still taking a toll on you. I am worried about you. You know that.

I couldn't resist the opportunity today. You looked so peaceful - so tired - so in need of my light. So, while you took a nap this Saturday afternoon, your hands both facing up and laying alongside your resting body, I slipped my hands into yours and squeezed.

'Kayleigh!' you said, 'Kakes you're holding my hands. Sweetheart, you are holding my hands. Okay. Okay. I'm going to just rest here and feel you holding my hands.'

Your words were so pure and innocent, Daddy, as you trusted me and took my lead. You had such a wondrous smile. I knew I had put that spark in your face. I closed my eyes and I passed my light and my energy to you as you rested, sitting on your left hand side with my head bowed down, my long blonde hair shaping my face, my eyes closed in honor of my Father. My beloved loyal Father. The best. I honor you so much, Daddy.

I was glad to sit with you. You know I always do. Sometimes I can generate more energy than at other times, but even when my energy is not seeming constant, I am constant. I am always with you and Mommy and my baby brother.

'We love you too,' you said, acknowledging my words to you and the feeling of my angelic palms resting in yours, not much unlike the way we would hold hands, Daddy, when I was a little girl and you would walk me into a room.

'Thank you, Babygirl, for holding my hands. You held my hands. You really held my hands. It is real. You are amazing,' you said.

I only wish that you could see my full smile. Soon, Daddy, as you successfully maneuver this life, no matter the days or years - for me it will be a blink of the eye. Someday, it will be that for you too. For now take it a day at a time and know that your little girl is a guardian angel of the highest order and always with you, Daddy. I just wanted you to know that."

Thank you, Kayleigh. I accept that I don't get to watch you grow up physically behind me in time. Spiritually I get to watch you grow up in front of me. We will transcend this great robbery of our lives and emerge daily stronger and stronger. I have two choices. Be destroyed

in the horror of your physical death or rise to a higher level hand in
hand with you. Rise with me. Rise with you.

"My Love Song to You"

My love song to you is simply my life,
The days ahead,
The flows and ebbs,
The gardens tending,
Wounds amending,
Through the triumph and the strife,
My love song to you is how I treat my life -

A thieving grievance bites to shun me,
A forbearance scores my earth,
A poison fills the lowlands and leads to my sea,
I will tend to that also because,
My Love, you see,
My love song is the condition of my life,
To which I have bequeathed,
My gift of me to you -

I will not leave this human skin,
Leaving a debris field of my country within,
Leaving a wretched wreck on the shores of your soul,
No, no - I will not dishonor you,
I will offer you light, and love to behold,
By churning my spirit into luminous gold,
By each step that I take here,
With intention - with this goal,
I write my love song to you,
As we walk the remainder of my road.

*

31 Years This Morning 06/28/2018

"Happy Anniversary, Daddy! This one is special. This one was earned more than others. I am so proud to call you my Daddy. I am with you and I'm not going anywhere. I love you so much and will direct you as much as I can. I am still your daughter and always will be. I love that I am both your daughter and your guardian angel. How lucky am I, Daddy?"

How lucky am I, Babygirl? Ever since you were a baby I said the same prayer to you each night, and to your brother as well once he was born; one prayer outside your bedroom and one outside of his bedroom. It has always been the same prayer nightly: "Every single day of your life through today I have given you the greatest gift I can give you - the gift of my sobriety. And I promise you my sobriety until the day that I die. This is a promise I will never break."

Since the accident, sitting on your bed, with my hand on your pillow, it goes like this: "Every single day do your physical life and every single day of your spiritual life after you transitioned, I have given you the greatest gift I can give you - the gift of my sobriety. And I promise you my sobriety until the day I physically die and transition into your arms. This is a promise I will never break." Then I step outside of your room and place my hand on Nate's door and say the old version for him, modified slightly, "Every single day of your life through today I have given you the greatest gift I can give you - the gift of my sobriety. And I promise you my sobriety until the day that I physically die and transition into your sister's arms. This is a promise I will never break." Two children in two different states of being at the same time. This is my life today and today is my first day of year thirty two.

"Yeah!"

*

31 Years This Evening 06/28/2018

Today is 31 years of sobriety, my first such anniversary since my Kayleigh's tragic accident. I love you my Kakie, Jess, Nate - my sobriety is not my gift - it is yours. It is not mine to ruin. It is not mine to throw away. It is yours. And yours. And yours.

I cried steadily today. I wept for you. I wept for each of us. I lost ten things today with you in the physical. I gained ten things with you in the spiritual. At one point, while driving, my mind zeroed in on that most important and poignant part of our journey together, that critical moment that I held my child and gave you permission to transition. I recalled that brilliance in the trauma, somehow not even understanding the trauma, but understanding clearly the power I was feeling as God placed a globe of light around you and I, that nobody could penetrate, and we locked into each other in an unbreakable, firm and immortal manner, and I graced you with that bridge of permission, as you held on to your physical body, just long enough for me to be by your side, holding you, crafting the air with my love and light into the shape of an eternal cradle of my soul.

As I took deep breaths, as a I sobbed once again in pure thanks for the beauty that mixed with the worst possible thing that could ever have happened in my life, suddenly my Bluetooth triggered, and out of thousands of songs on my phone, you played U2's "Bad," just as you had been doing purposely at critical times along this road. It was you. The feeling in the air confirmed your miracle, speaking through U2 to speak to your Father; to convey messages; to confirm your presence. "If I could, through myself, set your spirit free - I'd lead your heart away, see you break, break away - Into the light and to the day....I'm wide awake...I'm wide awake...I'm not sleeping..."

I am wide awake, Kakie. I am wide awake.

"A Bridge Across The Breach"

A new dawn is cast upon us,
No different, though changing are the roads,
We are growing through transition,
We are taking on different roles,

We are transforming our relationship,
In the sacred beauty of our souls,
For you the light illuminates the everything,
For me, I have before me much growth,
And as the dawn with its shifting light,
As the new dawn's sun takes hold,
Our love expands across the breach,
Enriched, empowered, aglow.

*

Harmonize 07/02/2018

Hey Babygirl, every day has its challenges. Every day has its traps. Help me harmonize. If the accident hadn't happened, I would be harmonious in my life with a sixteen year old in your physical life. Instead, I have a sixteen year old in spirit, whose current life is amazing and I get to and want to harmonize with you. I just don't always know how. I am with you and your brilliant present life both as your Daddy and also as your student. I am here. I will never leave your side.

"I am here, Daddy, too. I will never leave your side. Never. Thank you for never giving up on being with me and doing things with me. It means the world to me. You hear me! You feel me! You see me! All you are experiencing is true and helping you build into a Higher Life. It's all real. I love you so much!"

"A Lifeboat Planked in Poetry"

Muse, your music - it dances on the tongue,
You were stolen from my earthly presence,
Far too young,
Both of us - much too young;

Muse, your magic - it harvests the birthing sun,
And brings a million sunrises in the flash of every dawn,

Still, the steps forward from this tragedy are daunting,
My Daughter, for which I have called only one;

I am drowning in a sea of traumatic consequence,
When then the poetry - a lifeboat - emerges from the fog,
And offers me the platform of momentary sanctuary,
Just as my breath dips beneath the ebony water,
I hear the lovely chorus of my indigo daughter,
Laying on my heart the offering of her healing song;

My Child, please walk in my soul from end to end,
Cleanse me, my fields and streams, the purple hills and heather river bends,
I trust you like no other on this spirit road,
Only one may enter and freely roam my soul,
You, my Muse, we write together the words of my feet,
And hand in hand - and sometimes in your hands, lessening the load,
I find the sacred cradle of your love is the framing of this boat.

*

And Despondency 07/03/2018

Despondency attempts to steal the faith I have before me like a thief with no moral compass; a psychopath with total disregard for the slightest grievance of decency. I see and experience your miracles and somehow, a few days later, I slip back into the void. Help me fight off this thief. It steals reality - something so unique between us that most do not experience. It is. It is not only for you and I that I need to do my work and remain in the miracle, but for Nate and Mommy and countless others who are watching or who will hear our story; my story; your story. A guardian angel of the highest order - my Kayleigh - I am humbled to be your Daddy. I love you, Sweetheart.

"Good work, Daddy. That's exactly right. Grow with me and don't look back or turn away. You'll get confused. How could you not get confused? I've got you, Daddy, fiercely. I love you!"

"The Hyena Returns to His Metal Box"

The silence can be a curse,
And something much worse,
To seethe on the fuel of grief;

A hyena it clawed,
At its metal four walls,
Spinning in circles and grinding its teeth,
In a box from which there is no escape...

...and in defeat,
His energy collapses and he falls,
Curling into a bloody corner,
Into a powerless fetal ball,
Laying on his face,
And on his blistered paws...

...when will this nightmare cease,
When will he capture release,
If no option exists but to sleep,
And to rise again to his wounded feet,
Just to circle this box once again.

*

One Year After U2 Concert 07/03/2018

I did not remember this. It was Sunday. Ninety six degrees. Humid. Scorching. I was struggling, feeling like that hyena in a metal box again. The image comes daily at some time or another. In fact, not one day has gone by since the accident without its emergence. It hits sometimes out of nowhere. It is the most powerless feeling I've ever suffered - worse than the mental obsession of my alcoholism before I sobered up. A thought rang through my mind to drive out to the north coast beach of Mentor Headlands. Neither Jess nor Nate wanted to go. Alone, but for Kayleigh. She and I would have Daddy-Daughter time together at the beach that she would love to go to with me.

During my drive I reminded us that I was aware of the fact that when I get stuck in the horrific tragedy of her physical death then I cannot easily hear her spiritually or be with her spiritually. In those moments, I already can't have her in her physical life, and these distractions prevent me also from having her in her spiritual life. So I get neither. I talked to my sister Tricia on the highway while I drove. I did a Tenth Step. I cried. I arrived.

The goal to remember and keep as a credo on my heart is this: if I can't have her in her physical life I am going to do everything in my power to have her in her spiritual life. I work at this daily. I defend this vow daily. Through everything I push and I push and I push. I will do everything in my power to build my relationship with both of my children and so I do. Stopping at nothing to grow with and love my babies. I reset. I re-opened. I was awake.

Then I realized that this was the one year anniversary of the last time she and I were at Mentor Headlands together. With Tricia. Tim and Irene and their kids were with us too. We walked up and down the beach looking for white rocks for Tricia's yoga students.

So that was it. Kayleigh brought me to Mentor Headlands for our one year anniversary of our last time being there together in the same body types on the same plain. To celebrate, we would walk up and down the beach and collect white rocks for Tricia and mail them to her, and thank her for all she had done since the accident. So we did.

As I stood in waist deep water and picked up white rocks among the millions of colorful rocks, others walked by or splashed in the surf. An old Indian man saw me collecting stones. Seeing they were white rocks he leaned down and collected some for me and without a word placed them in my hand and walked away. Humanity at its finest. Karuna - The quivering of one's own heart in response to another's suffering.

Ten minutes later two young men walked by me. One of them walked up to me and asked, "Are you a rock collector?"

"I'm collecting rocks for my Daughter," I said and smiled.

He reached into his pocket and handed me 6-7 white rocks he had in his pocket that he had collected during their stroll down the beach. I told him that he just did a great deed and he'd be blessed for it - that it was a year anniversary since my Daughter and I walked this beach collecting white rocks and soon after last year's visit she was physically killed. The two men stood there with tears in their eyes, saddened and true in their hearts. I thanked them again and told them they were really good guys - that there stones were now part of her collection.

Then, and only then, I realized it was also the one year anniversary of our famed U2 concert. My mind is just like this these days, failing to recall moments from ten minutes ago. And yet, having failed to realize that it was the one year anniversary of one of the happiest days of my life, Kakes laughed, dragged me out to Mentor Headlands alone, and presented me, when the timing was perfect, that memory.

Then she clearly said to me, "Daddy, I can come to the beach whenever I want. But I can't go to the beach with you if you don't go. When you go, I love it as we are there together. I love when we spend time together doing great things. It's what we always did and we will always do. Just make the effort and I will provide. I will be there always by your side. Let's see the world together, Daddy. I see it whenever I want, but not with you unless you participate. So Participate. You've got to get up and come and I will always come with you, wherever we want to go."

I returned to the car, amazed by this experience, and turned on the car. After a moment, the Bluetooth triggered, and of all of the songs that could have played on my phone, of the thousands of options, with no album set to play, Kayleigh played, "One" by U2 and blew me away. As the first chords began my eyes burst with light. I turned to her sitting in the passenger seat and laughed out loud, thanking her over and over. I sang with her, screaming down the highway, tears of joy and sadness and frustration and faith and unconditional love flowing over my face.

"I Miss"

Everything - simply everything,
Tip toe dancing - princess dresses,
Chasing butterflies - making messes,
The way you studied my eyes when we talked,
The bedtime stories - and chalks and paints,
And cooking dinners - and dreams we chased,
The way the beach sand printed out our walks,
I swallow the emptiness,
I breathe distress,
And hit a wall,
Thinking of all of this,
All of us,
You know, my Love,
What I miss...

...I miss it all,
I miss it all,
I miss it all.

*

Robbery and Tenth Step 07/04/2018

Ten: I don't get to direct or discipline or redirect or think through guidance and make corrections with my Daughter anymore. None of it. Empty handed. Robbed of one of my greatest attributes, being a great, thoughtful father. I miss everything. It is like being ripped to pieces from the inside out. And to make it even worse, I see an occasional father out there who is not paying any attention to his daughter; who is annoyed constantly by his daughter; who takes his daughter for granted. 4 - Selfish? No. Dishonest? No, which is what is so hard. I see the truth in full color. But yes, in that, I am looking for ways to go back in time. Resentment? Yes. Fear? Yes. 5 - Share with who? Carly. 6 - Willing to have God remove? Yes. 7 - Ask God to remove? God and Kayleigh I place this on your altar. Please remove my defects and explain to me why shitty fathers and shitty daughters walk by my path daily and Kayleigh who is amazing and me who is amazing have this permanent physical fracture. 8 – Willing to change? Yes. 9 - Change? Breathe. I do my work. Expect: being ripped apart daily. Attitude: hold the line. Perspective: Kakes' silver lining is that I can reconcile with an angel and harmonize with my Daughter who is bigger than any human. 12 - Nate, Jess now, and my Mom and Dave are coming from out of town in an hour.

Carly responded, "I think one thing you can focus on is how incredible of a relationship you had when she was physically here and how unbelievable you have that connection now. Those shitty fathers would never connect how you did or do. They are lost to each other. You have each other constantly. Doesn't make the pain go away, but you need to see how amazing you are as a father and how in love she is with you. Right here. Right now."

Keep reminding me. It gets lost in the translation of life.

"Miracles at Her Fingertips"

She disperses the night,
Like a tight, thin silken veil,
Releases to a knife;
She immerses us with light,
Like fire hail,
Sets ablaze the big country,
Until it's haze is blinding white,
Yet we stare amazed in spite,
Of our human limitations,
And through our lamentations,
She asks us to enter,
Like a sunrise enters night,
Handing us the tools of our salvation,
To cut to a higher ground,
Armed with her light.

*

574

Kathy and Iris 07/04/2018

She was missing the point. I would say something like, "I'm so tired from our stress (with grief)," and she would de-minimize it and avoid the true topic, Kayleigh's accident, and say, "oh, you work so hard." And I would say, "Mom, it's not about work. It's the stress from the physical loss of my Daughter." Or I would say, "This bag has her shoes, shirt and shorts she was running to get when she was hit. We've never opened it," and she said, "Did you put more rocks on the altar?" After that exchange I said to her, "that doesn't help. I brought up something really intense and personal and you changed the subject."

It was frustrating. I used my voice pleasantly. I redirected her three times. I told her how I felt. Then I walked into the kitchen to be alone and do a Tenth Step. She was okay, and a little confused as she walked into the TV room, leaving her phone on the dining room table next to Kayleigh's ashes.

Then a minute later, out of nowhere, my Mom's phone started playing a song. She had never had that happen before, the phone just playing all by itself. Jess thought it might be her ringer for an alarm going off and so walked over to it and picked it up.

"Kathy, is this your ring tone," Jess asked.

"Oh, yes," my Mom said, and then she thought about it and said, "actually, no. I've never heard that before. Kev, what is this?"

I walked in from the kitchen and over to Jess, who handed me the phone, having looked on its face and seeing what was playing. Jess was smiling in that spiritually amazed smile so I knew something was afoot. I looked down at the phone and I stood there amazed too. She did it again. Right on point. Specific to the human interaction between my Mother and I into which she intervened.

"Iris" was playing on her phone - a special song by U2. It was Kayleigh reminding me to use my voice, but to be respectful and gentle to my Mother while I do it - and also reminding me that Kayleigh was like a different version of Iris guiding me through my life in this physical world that is but an illusion of true life - the

Afterlife being the true life. "*Iris*" is Bono's song to his mother who is in spirit and watching over him and guiding him - a belief he held so strongly that he wrote this song about it. When this album came out U2 pushed the album in a contract with Apple to every iPhone for free, the "Songs of Innocence." My Mother had no idea it was even on her phone and had never accessed it. Not ever. She had never heard this song. Yet Kayleigh found it on my Mom's phone, which was sitting dormant on the dining room table near her ashes, and blasted it in the house for everyone to hear, right after I was frustrated with my Mother. Proving another miracle. Proving her strength, her love, her powerful enduring light.

It is really gigantic how she works across the wind and across two worlds to remind us to have faith no matter what. That her life truly is only in transition, that she is alive and needs her parents to interact with her just like before the accident. That she has the ability to redirect me and gently push me in different directions, if only I can open my soul enough to rise in that higher vibration. When I pause and think about that, it resets everything in my life.

I hate what's happened to us, Kakes, but I love what you've been able to do with it. I hate missing out on everything we planned. I hate the losses that accumulate. The plans between us, however, have changed, Babygirl. Please help me change with the plans. Please help me accept this challenge of Fatherhood – to stop at nothing to continue to grow with my children, no matter what, no matter the situation, no matter the worlds in which I must traverse to do so.

*

Daddy, You Saw Me - You Did 07/05/2018

It was raining. Very hard. I was standing along the edge of the house under the lip of the roof in the darkness screaming at the dogs to go pee-pee in the yard. They were scared and did not want to go pee-pee in the yard and hid under the house and under the chairs at the back of the yard where they continued to get wet. A huge storm was coming – even heavier rain for hours. I wanted them to get it over with now before the heavy rain. Silly dogs - somehow they didn't understand their human telling them to stand in the middle of the yard under thunder and lightning and pouring rain for no reason.

The rain was streaming passed me off of the gutters on the roof; a steady bubbling flow of water. Suddenly, a dull, yet long, stick of light passed by me. It is the only way I can describe it. To my left. A foot or so away from me. From about twelve feet up in the air as its origin and straight down – it was like the rain illuminated and lit up; the flesh of the rain in a long rope of light, vibrating in the water reaching down from the air and disappearing about two feet off of the ground. A quick few seconds of bright and then faded light. A flash. A stick of light traveling through the rain – a traveler working her way through the rain, working with the rain. Kayleigh.

I immediately said, as if expected, "Kayleigh! Hey Sweetheart." I thought to myself - I just saw my Daughter.

She told me in that quick flash, "Daddy, be gentle with the puppies. They're scared."

"Okay, Babygirl," I said and called over to Rosie and Spirit, stepping out into the rain with them to help them.

It was the most inviting, warm and gentle experience. She was as she always is – ever compassionate; non-threatening, loving; content; direct. I imagined she was angry because I was yelling at her two dogs to get drenched in the rain so they wouldn't pee on the dining room floor in front of her ashes like they will do sometimes. Then I thought, not Kakes. She doesn't get angry. She wasn't angry. She was just concerned for them and knew I needed support. She was sweet in her redirection. Perpetually calm. A guiding force.

"Awakening"

In the distance, the ringing flashes of musky lightning,
Ignite against the flak of sprinkling rain - swallowed by the sea,
Above wispy opaque cloud ceilings the star fields bloom,
Twinkling lavender, sapphire and bright ruby green,
Awaken - and spin in the glitter spirals of the galaxies,
That she spreads out with her fingers just for me.

*

U2 – Kayleigh Played U2 Again, Gloria! Gloria! 07/07/2018

For months, almost on a daily basis, knowing how to manipulate the material world around you, like a cast away uses stones to write big letters on a beach, you have used consistently music to convey messages to me. You started this so early on that by the time we came upon the thirty day mark in this new configuration, you had mastered this clay.

A week or so ago, out of nowhere, while driving around and talking to you, you switched on the Bluetooth and flipped my music over to U2 and played "Gloria." I listened intently that day and thought I understood the entire message of the song; a song for God; for the glory of God, as Bono sang, "the door is open, you're standing there, you let me in…" What was amazing about this day, ten days ago, is that, as I drove, the music just continue to play the "October" album, the first song of which is "Gloria." When I parked ten days ago, and returned to my car, expecting to pick up on the fourth song, you started it over on "Gloria." You did that five straight times I turned off the car and returned to the car. And then on the sixth time, you did not start it over, just to let me know that it wasn't a trick of the code in the phone; it wasn't the phone at all. Then on the next time back in the car, "Gloria" began again.

You have done this, even when I have switched to another album while in the car and even when just sitting at home or at work. Yet, you will return to "Gloria" and I always know why. So for ten days now, almost every time I turn on the car, no matter what is on the current play list, you change the music to U2's "October," and I hear the opening drum and guitar of "Gloria," and its lyrics of absolute glory for God, "Oh Lord, if I had anything, anything at all, I'd give it to you…"

And so I come to today, finally documenting the last ten days of constant messaging from my Daughter in her life of light; in her body of light. Everything you do you do for the glory of God. Everything you are, you are for the glory of God. Every breath of light you breathe, you breathe for the glory of God. Every ounce of love that you have and that you are, you are for the glory of God. You want me to be that glory, that light, that love, all engaged to you and through you, ultimately for the glory of God. God has gifted us with this relationship that has defied the bounds of physical humanity, and has touched the brilliance of Heaven in your palm, to which you pass its joy to your Father. You do this in the glory of God and in God's love. Thank you, Kayleigh. I understand. I walk with purpose. I walk holding your hand, listening to your words, seeing your angelic smile.

"Gloria, Daddy! I knew you would get it!"

*

Interwoven Tapestry of Light 07/07/2018

Individual threads of light, interwoven into God's tapestry of love; one person to another, and those that each have loved, affected or embraced; my Daughter, who never met in her physical life a son of a friend of her Father, who likewise physically passed in childhood – their light, through the two fathers, interweaves, interlocks, links in the crisscross of eternal light. They met each other through their love for their own fathers, who were two men, friends, bound together in this physical world.

There are some strings that are thin and some relations that make those interconnections much thicker, melding and blending such light into stronger and stronger bonds. A tapestry of light. God's blanket.

Your Great, Great, Great, Great Grandfather, Michael, for whom your middle name is derived – you have spent over a year with him walking through his immortal memory, through the harvests of his youth and the memories and his stories of the horror of the Great Hunger as the family, all but him, perished in its genocidal storms of disease and starvation. You have walked with him in the streets of Cleveland in the second half of the 19th century, when the roads were paved in gold and money grew on trees and he built this family into a powerful force in the city from his bare hands. You have seen the Fenian Brotherhood in action, as spoken through his words. He loves you. He has always loved you. For you and your brother were the future he dreamed of yesterday. You, and your brother, you were the dream he held onto as he slumped off down the pocked roads filled with bodies; starving, sickened, tired and alone, trudging away from death and towards the coastline and passage to Americay in a space twenty inches for four feet high in the belly of a Black Ball Line packet ship – a coffin ship. And now, in your body of light, you get to spend time with this man, and he with you. I cannot say that I am not jealous.

"Thy Sea That Scourged This Heart"

And then as the sea,
Alive as it seems,
Unleashed its waves,
That flooded the seams,
Seething and foamed,
Its watery teeth,
Bite off the dunes,
Protecting the beach,
And swallow the sand,
And drag it beneath,
Leaving a scar,
As far as its reach,
As such as the sea,
Alive as it seems,
Have thee no heart,
Remaining in me.

*

My Kayleigh Love, the Counter-Balancer 07/08/2018

Energized in those dynamic days of youthful passion and joy - your carefree nature abounds; filled with life enough to fill the sea, a week before the accident. Your life now is a thousand fold of what it was in the physical, elevating you from a happy life to a higher happiness - present with me daily in the most miraculous ways. I hold that miracle in a sacred space as I watch you continue to mature. I hold onto that sacred place when the torture strips my skin.

For on each day, like the oceans, the tides are sure to rise. There is no preventing this; no way to control the waves. The waves, by their nature, defined by their surroundings and their intrinsic elements, roll upon the sea, pitch and break, smooth out and ruffle into white foam. There is no escaping them. They are grief. They are strange storms of denial, but not what one might think. The denial is, not that my child has physical died, but the occasional lapse of thought of knowing that she is actually right here beside me. They work together, grief and denial, and block me from seeing her, feeling her and interacting with her in these heavier moments.

The human physical life, its own ocean, is a life unto the earth. It lay on the earth's land and contours about its valleys and mountains. It is physical. It has a spirit, however, the spirit of the sea. It speaks. It breathes. It remains, in part, associated with the flesh of the ocean in which it sings, yet it is an entity unto itself. It resides, at least temporarily, in the shell of water that encases it, yet it lives both within and without the waters, both under and above the water line. It is light. It is alive.

Kakie, an innocent accident, your physical death, a child in childhood, bares no name for such tragedy. It remains its own unique cross to wear; to carry; to manage, that nobody can come close to understanding unless they too have suffered the same fate of the physical death of a child in childhood. Unlike any other death, this type of death, backwards in time to the parent, does not heal; nor which is its intention. It remains unhealed for the parents for the remainder of the parents' physical days. There is no "moving on," nor any "getting over 'it'," nor "being okay with it," nor "this too shall pass." These sentiments may work with general human challenges, but not for something like this.

The loss, each day away from the accident, accumulates upon the prior day, day over day, lost experience over lost experience, birthday after birthday, holiday after holiday, over time. Time is not an ally of this type of physical death, but an exponentially increasing burden through the parents' lives.

A counterbalance must be created, teased from the suffering, in a manner that permits breathing and living and functioning and moving forward, for us, as a family of four, in this new configuration. This counterbalance prevents drowning in the waves; permits the soul and emotional state to rise and fall with the waves, like seaweed at the surface that floats where the ocean takes it.

And that is where your miracles are critical - you have never left our side and live abundantly, interacting, growing and strengthening with us. Together we counterbalance the rising tide of loss each day with equal and opposite courageous gains in your spiritual body. I am learning to reconcile stronger to counter the rising losses as the days away from your physical life accumulate and the days of your spiritual life increase. And so it goes, as go the waves on the ocean, never ceasing, always changing, always constant and ever enchanting. I am so in love with you.

"Denial's Feast"

Sometimes like a familiar friend,
The denial presents at my kitchen door,
It is hungry - hasn't spoken for hours,
And opens up just like infected soar,
I deceive the thunder,
I see arid sky, although it rains,
I recede asunder,
When it escalates - this hollow pain,
And in these thoughts,

I cannot believe,
This happened to you?
And I cannot breathe,
What is this about?
Upon which the mind feeds,
This happened to you,
No this cannot be -

My Love, my Little Girl,

At the center of my world,
Your Daddy sees you in the garden playing,
Holding rocks and chasing squirrels,
Your Daddy sees you now at fifteen,
With high heels as a woman unfurls,
Your Daddy sees you on the verge of adulthood,
And then the accident destroys my world,
My Love, my Little Girl,
This cannot be,
Please, oh God, please,
Please, please, please, please...

...And then this release, daily,
After the feast,
Denial recedes,
Denial retreats,
Until the next time,
It hungers for me,
And slaves on my mind,
And strangles my feet.

*

What is the Riddle 07/10/2018

I know you. You would prefer to be able to communicate directly. You would have preferred that the accident had never happened, although you are swimming in the eternal warmth of love and light and joy.

I know you. In your dynamic and boisterous mind, in your funny and witty nature, you would just throw the words out for me to hear. Yet crossing the veil, penetrating the physical world from the higher vibration of Heaven, living on both sides of this sacred veil, but here in the physical in your body of light, this is no easy feat. You are left to finding modalities and channels that work, getting stronger and stronger over time. And you do this work for you are pure dedication to your family and to God.

The communications come across sometimes in code; sometimes in song; in nature or the wind; sometimes blotchy; sometimes in pieces; frequently in my right ear. Each seems to my human mind to be like a riddle that you lay before me to figure out - because you must. There is no other way to fully directly communicate. And when I do figure out what you are saying to me, you do a fist pump and jump up and down, knowing your Daddy is cued in, trying, searching, fearlessly listening, yearning and trying to match your communication with that of his own. You know that I am firing away at attempting to find modalities and channels as well, and sometimes we hit the same channel at the same time, opening up a domain in which I know, beyond any doubt, that I am holding your hand or you are kissing my forehead or working on opening up my third eye. That your love for me is a mirror of my love for you, a symbiotic dance of two equal souls with the deepest of unshakeable, unbreakable love. A pink, unbreakable cord of immortal love binds us.

Our light combines; blends; expands into and through the other. It never retreats. It always empowers. We offer each other ourselves to the other; our light and are warmth; our trust and our courage; soul to soul, with no real need for our human bodies when the annals of time have been written with the quill of God's light. This holds true as between each of the combinations of the four of us – Mommy, Nathaniel, Kayleigh, and Daddy. We are complete.

So I get clues that you leave in this physical reality set. I get pieces left here or there, with a knowledge that I need to do my part in attempting to jigsaw it together and test it. We are quite the team in our two different worlds; me, mostly anchored in this physical world but able to lift, although this human vibration is heavy, into a higher spirit slightly; and you, the magnificent one, fully empowered in Heaven and also fully engaged and strong in this physical world, even though you have been severed from your physical body, transitioned out of that body and elevated into your complete body of light.

So what is the riddle today? I find it in deep meditation. In the silence. In the grace. In your voice that calls down a hallway in my right ear and gives me the instinctual leaning to investigate the wind. Your voice, the voice of courage; the lovely angelic voice of My Daughter. My Daughter. My Daughter.

*

A Place That Never Exists 07/11/2018

This is a place that "never exists 'until you've been there" - with the worst suffering of physical loss and the highest spiritual light with My Daughter transcending beside me. For the two of us I speak. I do not need to wait until I physically die and we are on the next plain in the afterlife to be together. We are together now, albeit on different channels. As such a transition is so personal, no one on earth has a right to tell me as it relates to my beautiful Kayleigh how I should feel, how I grieve, how I should reconcile. And I have no right into another's process, not even my wife's process. We will each have our own unique perspective - as unique and brilliant as each of our children. That holds true even for my wife and I and our shared child who made this physical transition - and the support and respect we place in each other for each of our individual paths. It is, from my perspective, individual suffering, even when situations with other families may be substantially similar. Individual healing. Individual paths or life and recovery - or destruction. How any individual represents his or her path with the sacred physical death of a child I

585

will honor - with no criticism and no judgment? I am in my unique shoes and walk the road that lay before me. I walk beside you as you walk in your shoes as well. I know that not all experience what Kayleigh and I are experiencing; what Jess and Kayleigh are experiencing; what Nate and Kayleigh are experiencing. Yet here it is. Real. True. Amazing.

The dialogue is important – the word choice, in this sacred situation, may lead one down a road; another choice of words down another. Our truth is simple – physical death and transition, transferred her life into her spiritual body. She is alive in Heaven and here on earth on the physical plain in that elevated body of light; the same kid; still Kayleigh, but heightened in God's palm. No, I do not need to wait to physically die to be with My Daughter. I am with her right now.

"Daddy, I Would Never..."

The unbreakable line she's holding - indelible and bold,
Connects the sky fields between the lanterns of our souls,
She with turquoise oceans of diamonds in her sky blue eyes,
Walks beside me as I trudge forth in human toll,
She with flurries of stars like hurricanes in her palms,
Watches over me as my life continues to unfold,
And I hear her in a warm wind that bows across my aura,
Daddy, Daddy - I will never, I will never,
I will never leave you here to suffer alone.

*

Stand Beside You - Stand Beside Me 07/19/2018

I stood beside you and you gazed to me in moments of doubt - moments of fear, trusting me; trusting my judgment; trusting my words and my emotion. And I stood beside you and carried you through, supporting you, loving you, crying with you, sighing with you and ultimately laughing with you when afterwards we realized we'd crossed another threshold. It is what we do for each other. You have been doing that for me for eleven months now. Holding me. As

586

I gaze into your angel eyes, I trust you. When the fear comes with a crushing finality, I force myself to breathe and turn to your strength. You stand beside me and I believe in you and you carry me through. Then we laugh. And we cry. And we stare into each other's eyes knowing we are one - we are a union like no other; a Daddy and a Daughter.

We always support each other. Yet now, not unlike me with the empowerment when you were just a few days old, I feel like I am now that baby just days old and you are the full empowerment of a parent showering her infant with love. Our relationship has so drastically shifted as you have illuminated in your glory a thousand fold - from an amazing fifteen year, empowered, strong young woman into a guardian angel that knows no bounds.

"Singing Through a Broken Heart"

I am singing through a broken heart,
It sounds different these days,
When the words are loud and scratchy and fall apart,
And disintegrate;

Yet I am singing - though with broken heart,
I am singing for you, my Love,
For all that was,
And all of the loss,
For all that is,
And all that is to come;

We have purity, a poetry between us,
An effortless manner,
A father and daughter, in love,
Gentle happiness, respect and honor,
We speak a thousand languages, and always between us,
The fresh river flows -
"The road is not over, no,
Straighten the backbone, Father Dear,
Dear Father know - oh, Dear Father know,
I love you,
I love the song that, like our river, flows."

The Little Miracles 07/19/2018

"Daddy, be content with the little miracles. Sometimes that's all I'm able to do. I try daily to show myself to you guys. It's really cool and really fun. I love all that we do together."

Thank you, Sweetheart. Please help me not get complacent with your miracles. I don't want to take for granted the slightest hint of you in my life, Babygirl. I do not want to minimize any time you cross through the wind and touch us or sing to us or watch over us or make your presence known, even in the slightest breeze or smallest kiss on my cheek. I love you, little Peanut. You amaze me.

"And you call them miracles, Daddy! That's so cute! We will call them miracles. It's just me saying hi."

"This Shitty World…We Are Stronger"

There is no other way that the world could have hurt me more,
As if it knew how best to harm me,
And, without conscience, slashed my soul to the floor;

There is no other way that the world could cut me so,
As if the world in its psychosis,
Attacked a great family with a deadly blow;

Yet what the world, in its ignorance, didn't know,
We are four spirits that are unbreakable,
We are four souls that continue to grow,
Despite the world's best intentions,
To destroy the seat of our home.

*

God, You Know…07/20/2018

Every time I want to chastise you; every time I want to rake you for your belligerence, for your callousness, for turning your back on us, I am reminded quite quickly that you have enabled Kayleigh with the true power of an intercessor, a guardian angel, who flows freely with your light and love both in Heaven and here on Earth. She is sitting with me with a smile on her face, correcting my words, making me capitalize Your Name (thank you, Kakes). How can I hate you? How can I blame you? How can I hold onto my grudge against you – well, I mean, let's review: on the day of this perfect, innocent accident, I was over thirty years sober, had helped thousands of alcoholics, am deadly loyal to my wife and kids, am the poster child to how you want your children to love you and live an effortless, great, balanced, incredible life; always placed you first, followed by my sobriety, then my two kids and my wife; always with You and the love of family at the center of all that I was and am. And then my beautiful daughter, in the blink of an eye, is physically killed!

"The Struggles and the Storms"

As God as my witness and God as my target,
With anger and angst and a heartache now guarded,
I am throwing unpolished antidotal stones,
Raptured in the apocalyptic storms,
Drowning in channels of the marrow of antiquities' scattered bones,
This tragic simplicity becoming my norm,
As I grieve,
As I mourn…

…As I retrieve the reality that new life is upon you,
Just like the sacred day you were born,
I circle my cage looking for escape,
But know the search is forlorn…

…Yet always emerge with my breath to release,
Knowing you are alive and you are the peace,
That conquers all storms,
You are the light that eclipses my norm,

You are the strength,
From my arms you were torn,
Only to rest in them simply again,

- In the moment you were reborn.

*

Dear Families 07/21/2018

It came to this. we had explained to both families what we needed; had expressed our frustration that certain members of both families has simply vanished; that we wanted to express what we needed to feel supported to two families that had never suffered the physical death of a child. It came to this letter to convey this clearly and succinctly. Nobody needed to support us, naturally. Yet, one would think that family would bend over backwards to lend that love and light. Some just never seemed to get over themselves enough to support us. We were not surprised in some, but aghast, when some of our family made this letter about themselves, and found insult in it, rather than just supporting us in the voice that we explained we needed. And the circle gets smaller…

"To begin - we love you. We cherish our relationships and intend to continue to grow with each of you. In order to facilitate that we find it necessary, as we have absorbed unnecessary frustrations at times, to provide you with helpful suggestions that will lead to the support we desire. Without such guidance some have unintentionally made that intimate sharing about our children challenging. With Kayleigh's tragic physical passing, our circles of trust have been radically redefined and we are continuing to determine who in our lives with whom we feel safe. As Kayleigh is our child, and this is our sacred experience, we want to avoid this feeling of frustration and feeling unsafe by stating clearly what we need.

1. Seat at the table. When there are family dinners and we are invited, we are a family of four and request that there be a place set for

Kayleigh. This is a very simple request that we have made several times.

2. Conscientious about word choice. Please do not try to build bridges concerning other deaths. A death of a child is not the death of a parent or friend or cousin. When this happens we are pushed further away. Please do not avoid talking about Kayleigh. If you are someone who has a hard time with your own emotions in speaking about her, selflessly consider us for a moment and find the courage to talk about her. We need this. Please do not say you "understand" since, unless you have experienced the death of a child in childhood, you do not understand. When we hear this it de-minimizes our tragedy rather than making a bridge which is typically intended. It is infuriating. We don't need advice. We need you to listen. Some helpful questions may be, "How are you reconciling with Kayleigh today? How can I support you? I am here to listen."

3. Do not (incorrectly) assume our individual reconciling processes are pathological. The death of a child in childhood is the only death that does not heal. This is not open to debate. There is nothing more unnatural than a child predeceasing a parent. There is also nothing unnatural with never healing from such a blow. There is no healing as one might expect in the deaths of parents or grandparents. There is, however, reconciling with this truth on a daily basis. We have accepted this truth - that an open wound will remain for all of our days. In this acceptance we know how to reconcile this daily in order to function in this world. We are, unfortunately, the experts in this arena and really do not need words of wisdom, platitudes or encouragement. We just need you to listen and to incorporate Kayleigh into our discussions. Too many times we feel as though, with the avoidance of talking about her, it is like she never existed. This causes us tremendous pain.

4. Kayleigh is alive. This is also not open to debate. Kayleigh is a powerful guardian angel who walks with us daily. This is not something we tell ourselves to comfort us and is not a statement of denial because we can't accept our child is physically dead. We clearly understand that her body is dead. What we would like you to understand, regardless of your own spiritual beliefs or lack thereof, is that Kayleigh truly, in reality, and in full color, is alive. She has

transitioned from her physical body to her spiritual body, but make no mistake - she is here and she always will be.

These are our truths and this is our child. We all love Kayleigh, but no one loves her like us. We all mourn Kayleigh, but no one mourns like us. We are the experts related to our children and this is our request for the support we require."

*

Footprints 07/22/2018

She just told me this very clearly in a very deep meditation where my mind was wide awake and my body asleep:

"Daddy, you taught me about God and used Footprints and that resonated with me. I took that and as I learned more at Beaumont about God being a great Father I thought, well I have a great Father, and since I believe in you and your love and your safety I felt with you, then it was easy for me to believe in God as a great Father. Because of your example in our lives and how we interact, I was able to accept and have faith in God - because I have faith in you."

*

Orange Swirl Kayleigh Stone 07/22/2018

My God, as the weight of this grief nearly strangled me, she just did it again. Thank God. We needed this. Where we meditate in the backyard today I found this Kayleigh stone, a stone the type of which we have not seen since the last house. These stones were packed away at the last house, at 3035, in 2016. That box was never opened at the new house. Yet here is one of these stones, lying in the dirt and the grass, where we meditate with Kakes, at my feet. I remember specifically buying this bag of stones with her when she was like six at Joann Fabrics since it had an orange swirl in it, the only such type

592

of bag of stones we purchased that looked like these. Just lying in the dirt securely imprinted and barely visible to our eyes, but our heads were turned downward, to the side, directly catching it in our site. Then as I walked into the house and stepped across the kitchen I turned back around towards the back door and thought I saw for two seconds a quarter size ball of light float into the room - so calming and powerful - like she was following me into the house with a smile on her face, and my human eye was only capable of catching a few of the points of light that flesh in her beautiful body, a body constructed of millions of points of galaxy light.

"She and This Silvery Sea"

A full moon leans out over a silvery sea,
No fire for the water without celestial stream,
It radiates and it softens resistance,
Altering worlds - a deep, black thickness,
Melts,
Touched by the glowing torch of the heavens;

The waves lick at the air to drink its flame,
The air lifts itself into its illuminated domain,
And there, there amongst the angels,
She smiles, aglow, in love, in spite,
Of our physical separation,
She showers me with light.

*

Glass Turtle, Glass Pumpkin 07/24/2018

In was August 11, 2017, the day before we returned to Cleveland after a wonderful two week family vacation. I needed to buy a frog figurine for one of my secretaries. I asked you to come with me to the Jekyll Island craft stores. We went into the collectibles store along the main road and found a blue soap stone frog. It now sits next to your ashes. Then we went to the next store, stores we shopped in together constantly on each of our trips to Jekyll Island, perhaps twenty five vacations in your fifteen years.

"Daddy, let's get an iced lemonade," you said, "I know we always do that with Nathan, but he's at home with Mommy. You snooze you lose," she laughed.

"Yeah, screw him," I said, "had he put down his phone and come along he would have had the chance to get one. Come on!"

We walked under the majestic pines along the oyster concrete road towards the Shack where we always got our iced lemonade. We bought Jess a bottle of salad dressing in the store. We bought Nate a candy bar.

We sat outside on a park bench and watched a horse drawn carriage pass us. A Daddy and his Daughter. A Daughter and her Daddy. In love. Effortless. Chatting - our conversations, whatever the topics, free flowing, easy and engaging. Loving each other's presence, really truly loving each other's company, we sucked down the icy drinks on a very sweaty August Georgia day.

"Daddy, can we go to the glass blowing art store? Just one more store. We always go there. I love that store," she said and smiled at me, and nodded off behind the bench to the store, "come on, Daddy..."

There is no way I could resist that smile. She needn't have, however, tried to sway me. I loved hitting little shops with her and spending time doing whatever with her. We had bought a few necklace pieces over the years from the glass blowing store. I knew something magical would await us. So we went in.

We scanned up the left side of the glass showcase and back down the right, enamored with the beautiful pieces. She noticed loggerhead sea turtle glass figures on the right side of the store. "Oh Daddy," she said, "look how cute. Can we buy one of these little glass turtles to commemorate me saving my baby sea turtle?"

"Absolutely," I said without hesitation, as we started comparing the colors on about a dozen different glass sea turtles. There were subtle differences with each and we settled on about five. Then three and then two. Finally she picked one, happy with her choice. Happy to be spending valued time with her man.

She crossed back over to the left side of the store and was drawn to more figurines. They were pumpkins made of swirling glass; some the size of a softball; others much smaller. Her eyes twinkled. "Daddy, Can I get a pumpkin also? You know how much I love pumpkins. And I have a credit card."

I smiled. "Well, you've worked hard this summer and I know you still have money in your account so, yeah, okay, Sweetheart. If you want to buy an extra pumpkin you can."

"Great!" She said as her eyes went directly to a wonderfully beautiful little pumpkin, "I do want to buy one. I think this one." Always the frugal shopper, although her eyes were also drawn to a bigger glass pumpkin, she knew the cost would be prohibitive from what she had in her account. She elected this small one that fit within her budget without a word from her Father.

As we approached the woman at the back of the store to purchase the two figures she said, "Oh, Daddy, I don't have my purse. I forgot my credit card at home. I promise I will pay you back. Can we still get them both?"

I laughed. "Of course you did," I said, "and it's okay. You can get both."

The woman behind the counter laughed, hearing the entire conversation, and knowing that a sweet child had just convinced her Father to buy several things for her. "She forgot her credit card," I said to her and winked.

"Oh course she did!" said the manager as she smiled upon Kayleigh with an expression of joy. I knew what she was thinking - what a sweet girl. She also seemed to relate to Kayleigh. I concurred with a smile.

On the way home I told her I was so happy to buy her both the turtle and the pumpkin and it was my little treat; that she didn't have to pay me back; that I was so proud of how responsible she was and proud of the young woman she had become. Truthfully, I loved leading on my kids, as in this situation, knowing I was going to pay for it, only to surprise them. What was so surprising was that after all these years they were still surprised.

When we returned to the beach house she sat with Mommy. She was ablaze, beaming from ear to ear. She sat Jess down, humbled and happy with our trip to the stores. She explained how we shopped for my secretary; how we snuck an iced lemonade without Nathaniel; how we went to her favorite store and Daddy bought her glass figurines. Jess told me later that night all about it. I was happy. Happy like I was familiar being happy, having consistently given her special treats and thousands of moments like that.

Those two figurines would be the last gift I bought for Kayleigh. Both sit atop her ashes.

*

Night 07/24/2018

As I peeled back the layers of the night, there was another, and another; sheets of black rain; veils of dark smoke; velvet blankets that held stars in their stitches, stacked against the morning and melting one by one into the next layer, as if attempting a stoic permanence, an inescapable field of loss, of pain, of confusion - of night;

Yet I face it - this night, I face it - I lean into it and peer into the darkness to look through it; I am blind in its wake, in the waves of coal colored waters and ebony smeared air that crash against my soul, my soul - this mooring firmly steeped in the sands of time; rooted in faith and fearing not the onslaught I preside in; no, night knows no conquering - it only knows the mirage of that conquest and tells its tail to the willing ear, an ear that once bent, will drown in its fury;

596

Yet it is just a night as it dreams into another shadow of night; it is not forever, no matter the eternity in the slow seconds that tick off of the clock on the wall; we cannot see it for it is night; though we can hear it's toll in the darkness; we swallow it's tone if we must and sing to its rhythm if we summon the courage of song;

For there will he morning and that morning will radiate, just after the long night of this life; and then I will peel back the sheets of the light of morning, and another, one at a time, a continuous radiance of light and love, washed in tranquility and sternly feeling the warmth of her soul upon my face; she will kiss me then, on my cheek, on my forehead, and pull me into her smile, jumping for joy in the sunrise, spinning her Father around in dancing circles in her arms, for she will have finally walked me through the insidious sheets of night and into my salvation of eternal life I touch for the first time when next, on the same plain once again, in the same body types, I hold her hand.

"Recognized Only By His Stain"

Now my life -
It is so complex - it doesn't make sense,
With a million moving parts - all with consequence,
Out of order,
Maligned of sequence,
Out of the blue,
With a steady frequency,
Comes a nightmarish rues,
Bereft of all decency,
With the hardships aligned in my ragged eyes -

I see others unaware of how lucky they are,
Others who bare not the likes of this scar,
And then there is me and now my life,
Like a beautiful garden after meeting the knife,
Where but roots and mere stripped stalks remain,
And a space where once a great garden stood,
Now bares the shape of a good man,
Recognized only by his stain.

*

"The Voice of the Sea, Daddy, Speaks to the Soul" 07/25/2018

Soft ethereal strands of sea oat,
This, her blonde hair, rustles in the sea breeze,
She is tender and sweet like honey gold,
And rooted in the dunes,
That slope into the sea;

This is her sun soaked playground,
A peaceful home, another home,
She radiates and the wind, her voice,
Like a wave on the sand unfolds,
Like nothing has changed at all,
Like days of memories old.

*

Great Despondency 07/25/2018

It is so easy to do nothing; to lay down and die; to crawl into a corner
and wilt away. Yet, I will not sink into the mire of despondency for
you are not found there. I will rise and sing my life in your name, and
in so doing, will be able to continue to build our relationship with you
in Heaven and on Earth simultaneously, while continuing to build a
relationship with your brother here on Earth. You are pure happiness.
Please help me reflect back to you that happiness, a gift from a Father
to his children.

My gift to you in not despondent grief. My gift to you is living,
despite immense grief. It is reconciling through the darkness that
hawks the sky in my eyes a hundred times a day. I will actively and
currently change with you, Kayleigh, for you too are continuing to
learn and grow and shine brighter. I will not permit passive
despondence or assuming you are here but not acting like you are
here. I will take an active role in your life, just as I always have,

learning from and with my child, adjusting with my child, just as I always have done with you and your brother. I will take the long view on this challenge, knowing that I will get in the way; life will get in the way; grief will get in the way. I will need to process through it each time to get closer and closer to you. We have so much growth, love and light in front of us, Sweetheart. Help me harness it. Help me remain active when the heart is so heavy it wants to lie down in quicksand and suffocate into sleep.

Instead, show me how to walk in your life. Show me how to actively participate in your life in an active, current relationship. I participated at every age, in every month and every day with you – when you were two and throwing paint around the living room; making blogs at eleven; collecting shells and rocks and bugs at three, five, seven, nine; shoe shopping at thirteen; practicing driving (illegally) at thirteen, fourteen, fifteen to help you become an amazing driver by the time you turned sixteen. And now at sixteen, where you don't need to drive, but where you continue to change and mature in your spiritual life, I am here and I am present. I am here. I want to walk in your life. Show me and I will be there in the way you need your Daddy. I will never leave your side.

"Mask"

Pursue the mask and fate may bate the nascent pain,
Fueling hurricanes with barbed wire and spiral flames,
That lick the metal into liquid,
Within the heart that can't keep pace,
And breed the torture like fields plowed with rusty nails,
That etch their claws that rake their trenches into the fleshy face,
Until the man cannot find himself,
Not at all,
Not a trace.

*

The Challenge of a Lifetime 07/26/2018

My challenge now, following the total destruction of my life, is to be with both of my children at the same time in two different worlds; with Nathaniel in his physical body and Kayleigh in her spiritual body; with one in the physical world and the other in both Heaven and the physical world. This new combination is not an easy feat and requires focus, dedication, intention and devotion. It is exhausting, yet there is no other path I would or could take. It is the single most rewarding and important journey of my life. Yet its elements are simple and clearly within my wheelhouse. Nothing more could be clear to me. I engage both as I always have; just in a different manner. I need to be ever creative in my approach, adjusting as I go, and striving forward with both through courage, love and light. I love you both, My Babies, and know that it is the easiest thing in the world to love you. Let's go live today. Remember our rallying cry from your childhoods, "Nothing stops the Mooney's!" Let us go do this and accept the unacceptable challenge before us. For you, Kayleigh, we will take all efforts to ensure that you are incorporated into everything we do. We cannot have you in your physical body, yet we can have you in your spiritual body. You are alive and present, our dimensions intact and crossing each other like two cords of electricity, each second of every day. I just have to adjust and send that love down a different channel. I meet you here in the present and grow with you.

"Courage"

Just to rise in the morning,
That, in itself, is a miracle,
Just to rise in the morning,
And facilitate the strain,
Though slumber has forsaken me,
The sun has come again,
And twisted its light like a dagger in the eye,
And forces my hand though it aches with pain,
With courage I remove the knife,
And mend my soul with the ointment of the day.

*

The Last Time I Ran My Fingers Through Your Hair
07/26/2018

It should have been as I reached up to you, laying on a bed at eighty eight, you fifty five, me transitioning and physically dying, an old crumpled body, a soul prepared for it's safe travels; staring into your eyes; running my fingers in your half a century old silvery blonde hair, knowing that I fulfilled my promise and privilege to be your Daddy on this plain. That should have been the last time I ran my fingers through your hair, but it was not.

The last time I ran my fingers through your hair, you were laying in a casket. Jess and Nate and I before you, as the funeral home employees began to lower you in the casket, as my last glimpse of your physical body ended with the lid closing down over you. A few days earlier, in the hospital, was the second last time that I ran my fingers through your hair, laying on a hospital bed in room #41, sitting for three hours with you, not wanting to leave the room. I ran my fingers through your hair from your forehead back. I wept on you. I kissed your cheek, your forehead. After the Last Rights, I made a sign of the cross on your forehead with my tears – my tears that soaked into your skin and became part of your body. Just hours before I had kissed you on your forehead as you sat on the couch with Mommy as I said, "Love you," to which you smiled and said back to me, "love you." Then I went to my A.A. meeting and you went out with your friends – we would meet next in the street where our souls locked into a connection that was unbreakable, as you listened to your Daddy's voice and physically died in my arms.

It seems like just a few hours before that I sat in a rocking chair with a tiny bottle, not much longer than my fingers in my left hand, with you cradled in my right arm, feeding you and kissing your forehead and promising you that I would always watch over you and take care of you and keep you safe. Yet fifteen years later I was running my fingers through your hair for the last time.

"Kayleigh Guide"

Alight, my darling Daughter,
The brilliance of your life,
Compassionate and friendly,
This deep thinker full of light,
A moment of accidental consequence,
An innocence in flight,
My Darling, how my soul hurts,
Since that tragic summer night,
And the wind holds your voice,
And your essence and grace,
You have bloomed like a million suns,
From the smile on your face;

Kayleigh, your Father mourns you,
Yet joins you here daily,
Walking hand in hand,
With my beautiful Kayleigh,
My heart is filled with trauma,
Yet also filled with gold,
I reconcile these counterpoints across the void,
Guide by your soul,
For you are alive here,
If there is nothing else I know,
You are alive,
In a vibrancy, aglow.

*

The Great Distinction 07/27/2018

Kayleigh lost her physical life, this is true. Yet she is here in the physical world, now in her embodiment of light, rather than in her human skin to which we had become accustom. So I have not suffered a loss of Kayleigh in this physical world. I have suffered the loss of my Kayleigh in her physical form. This is a critical distinction as

Kayleigh is not lost. Kayleigh is not gone. Kayleigh is not absent. Kayleigh is transformed from the beauty to which we were familiar to a much higher beauty to which we need to adjust. She resonates in unhindered light and unbreakable love. She sits with me just as she always has, yet radiating in her higher self. She is laughing with me and singing with me and dancing beside me. Just because most can't see her there, it doesn't mean she isn't here. She is. I am adjusting, honing my human senses, arming my sixth sense, and in so doing, am continuing to fulfill the grace of being her Daddy.

Kayleigh, we do not get you in physical form today, and I accept this brutality and reconcile with this fact daily. However, we get this today with you in your spiritual form and we are not going to miss out on our relationship today. Our love conquers all distance of time, space or worlds. We are together for sure – your presence a miracle I embrace.

Bring me to your life today with all of its majesty and splendor and joy. I want to engage in your life, to be there with my Daughter. Kayleigh, help me be present in your life. You are living in the Light. You are very much alive, stronger and happier and more alight as you ever have been in your happy human life. Take me by the hand and walk me into your life; to see what you see; to feel what you feel; to hear what you hear; to experience what you experience, as much as I can on this plain while tucked within my human flesh.

*

I Am A Proud Wall 07/28/2018

I want you to be proud of me at the end of each day. My poem "Best of Me" encapsulates this: "I give you this light, which flows from this soul...and leads to your spirit, where the best of me grows..." It was my open and vibrant admission that my kids made me better. In my daily activity; my actions, thoughts, words; in how I treat others and in how sacred I make the bed of my life; all of these moments are presented to you, to Mommy, to Nate and to myself as a gift of which I pray is worthy of this majestic family of four. I pray that this gift of

603

my life is worthy of our love. I pray that the way I live my life is something that you are proud of at the end of each day while we are in different body types on different plains.

The interaction between us is magical. You had certain power during your physical fifteen years. You had a higher power prior to your birth as well, every present with each other in this dancing of our souls throughout time. I alluded to this power of yours all the time in my poetry throughout the years. I made me better by being with you and your brother closely and deliberately. I become better by staying close to you both with that same deliberate searching of the soul. It is true – I am always better because of you two.

So I ask, Sweet Daughter, what gift do you bring today to the world? How can I assist you in bringing that gift to the world, and specifically, to whom? I am your Servant Father. I know you think that's hilarious!

"You Are Here"

Your fingers approach and press through the wind,
Leaving trace on the air of your loving prints,
Resonating your presence,
Illuminating your essence,
That prevails and pushes its way in;

Your fingerprints bless this quiet wind,
It waxes, it blossoms, in wisdom it wanes,
It forces out the worst suffering one can never think possible,
That has staked within me its claim,
That has stalked my life, my name,
That has come with its pain,
To scorch a beautiful land,
Only to be eclipsed in a wind,
My heart triaged by your loving hands,
With sparkling traces left behind as witness,
Of your fingerprints.

*

God 07/30/2018

God, Kayleigh is brilliant, compassionate, loving, funny, a little edgy, artistic, logical, smart as hell, wise, selfless and sweet, empathetic and kind to others, beautiful inside and out, a little sassy and incredibly loyal - the full package.

There was no challenge in life that was going to stop her. She was battle tested, firm, confident, fully empowered and fully engaged to enter adulthood and have a successful long life. She was still fifteen, of course, and dealing with fifteen year old issues, but in a way that others were not or could not process. She was mature beyond those years, not because anybody harmed her, but simply because she is. Following the assault she absorbed, she used it to become stronger; to believe in You further; to embrace life even more lovingly than she already had been doing. Who, God, who does that? Kayleigh Mooney does that.

Everything does not happen for a reason. This is a silly notion that people like to state when the stakes are manageable. Someone loses a job – oh well, everything happens for a reason. A marriage dissolves – oh well, everything happens for a reason. Somebody else has a tragedy on the news – oh well, everything happens for a reason. Yet it does not. Sometimes arbitrary things happen. Sometimes great things happen to terrible people and sometimes terrible things happen to wonderful people – for no reason.

There could be no plan that included stripping a child of her future; a child from her parents. Yet somehow You will work this tragedy into the overall plan, after the fact. I thank You for permitting Kakes to be a guardian angel who walks with us and intervenes and plays with us daily. Yet her physical loss of presence is catastrophic. This is my little girl, God. At times I think - what have You done, yet I know You didn't do this. It was an arbitrary accident. And I know You cried with me in the street holding her as she physically passed to You, promising to turn this tragedy into gold. Kayleigh is gold. You need look no further for gold. She is right here. In Your palms. Sacred. Beautiful. My girl.

"Death"

I am grief - I am thunder,
I am wave that pulls you under,
I am thief that chipped the diamond from its crown,
I am the meaning of life that you have found,
In the darkest of hours,
I have darkened your hours -

I am clearly arbitrary,
A disruption in your pretty sanctuary,
I am nothing, nothing really,
But still you must fight,
I beg you to fight -

I have claimed your deepest feelings,
I have floored your highest ceilings,
And leveled your home,
And washed with barbed wire your eyes,
Yet confused I pirouette,
There are few like you I've met,
You respond here to conquer me?

There is wind once a hurricane,
It can no longer lift a grain,
I can't lift a grain,
No, no longer, not in your name -

So I came to steal your daughter's sacred breath,

I am finality - I am Death,
Yet you pivot and adjust right through my pain,
As she crosses earthly barrier and walks it's plain,
Holding her Father's hand, in song,
A guardian who is brighter than I am strong,
And so defeated,
I recede,
A dream away.

*

Rocks from Jekyll Wall 07/31/2018

We have returned again without you physically. Yet we do nothing without you in your spiritual presence. You grew up here, along this stretch of beach, where the engineer's wall keeps the high tide out of the dunes. Kakes, show me what rocks we should take back to your room. I will be your physical hands. Just point them out. I will be your physical eyes. Just direct me. I am listening.

"Daddy, can I just stop you for a minute and tell you how much I love you. I'm so grateful for you. For your love. You love me so much and it makes me feel so good. I just love you and I love walking on the beach with you. Can you believe that we are walking the beach together? After the accident, Daddy, we are still together."

I find a spike of courage despite the massive grief I feel; a yearning, sometimes hollow yearning, to embrace life and find joy, even though the horror remains in our veins every day and will never wash out. Then I glance out to our ocean. Two pelicans wing to wing, gliding passed us just now about one hundred feet above our heads. "That's us, Darling, always in sync with each other," I said, as they continued, then turned on a dime and banked into the wind and hovered above us for twenty seconds, then dipped their wings to the left, caught the wind and flew off down the beach.

"The Higher Life"

There is a place that is higher,
Inside of us all,
A place as long as the universe is wider,
From end to end - wall to wall,
In which the spirit flourishes,
Spreading rainbows of galaxies tethered,
With all of the souls we have touched in our days,
A tapestry of light interwoven together,
That take us to a higher ground.

*

Jekyll Closing 08/01/2018

Two days ago as we left Cleveland, we did several things, which still are so hard to believe that we do. First, we hid your ashes in the house, trying to find the safest place for your ashes while we are out of town. This is one of the most frantic exercises in my life. Secondly, we drove down to the bench so that we could physically look upon this site prior to driving to Georgia. As we approached, the Bluetooth turned on and the phone found "Safe and Sound" from Hunger Games, which clearly, you played for us, one of your favorite songs as a tween, and so hauntingly sad. It is exactly what we were feeling as we were packed into our car, but without your physical body in one of the seats, begrudgingly going on vacation.

I walk through quicksand while breathing concrete, missing your physical presence. Your love is an engine for this family; it drives us, propels us forward. You have more courage than I have ever had and it flows through my veins as we continue to live together in our new configuration in a healthy, brilliant family of four, courageously facing the daunting task of that new configuration.

As we are now back at Jekyll Island, the last time in our family home before it is sold off in a month, I am reminded of your glory. I see you at every age running through the hallways; sitting on the couches; sleeping on the beds; running on the dunes, your blonde hair like long sea oat dancing in the wind. I see your unabashed life. That is one of the colors of your amazement, Kayleigh, this the ability to live and love and naturally find your center and happiness despite the troubles in the world. No matter the obstacle, no matter the level of fear or discomfort, you walked, head high and forward into and through it. My God, Babygirl, I am in awe of you.

I am learning this important and perfect method of imparting miracles. You are so sweet and gentle and all knowing - holding God's secrets and letting them out in bursts. You follow the rules, for sure, ever the compliant one, now in the glory of God's playgrounds.

We see these little teasers release all the time, like tiny riddles wrapped in the material world. You blew us away today when we were driving and Mommy asked me, incredibly randomly, "When the band Genesis broke up were they friends?"

I said, "oh yeah..." and then took a few minutes to tell her the quick story of Peter Gabriel leaving the band and then Steve Hackett leaving the band. Then my phone tuned in through the Bluetooth and flipped to a thirty minute interview of Genesis talking about their relationships as Peter and Steve left the band!!!!!!

Kayleigh!

"Daddy! Ha!"

*

Key Largo, My Promise 08/03/2018

It was a promise I kept. Taking her to Key Largo. The prior year the boys had gone to Key Largo while the girls went to New York, a consequence of different school vacation schedules. We texted back and forth the whole time. She could not wait to go to Key Largo. This was one of my promises.

"With My Daughter, Sitting"

Watching the sun set,
Blossoming light, bright burning light,
We sit in the sea,
Our laughter - like sparks through the waves,
That ripple away,
In living, glistening golden streams,
That create new dreams,
That we weave into the day,
While still we have this day,
Today...

*

Unnatural, the Human Condition 08/03/2018

A spiritual being no longer stuck in the unnatural human condition. Now she is a spiritual being released into her natural state of her spiritual life, empowered, unhindered by the constraints of humanity, a guardian angel who can traverse Heaven and earth whenever she wants, more vibrant and alive as ever. While my son, like me, and their mother, remain in our physical bodies, separated only by our skins and the body types in which we live. All of us, someday, to be freed of this constraint. In the meantime, it is painful, grief stricken, a difficult life. I watch my baby boy and I see the strain in his eyes, the toll of the last year, the losses, the desperate confusion in this complicated world – all conspiring to cloud him. Yet he watches me and his mother, and talks to his sister. Through it all, he dares to dream. He dares to believe.

"My Children"

Two earths spin about their very own star,
Bright sky fire - eternal spark,
A lantern aglow - merged from two souls,
No darkness can this light part,
She, within her palms, holds,
A little boy and all he knows,
Of sister too young in life called home,
(And he cries for he loves her so),
He buries the cross lodged in his throat,
And hunkers down under heavy coat,
He sheds his tears to clear his eyes,
He dreams of her right by his side,
Daring her presence and her peace,
That destroy the barriers thrown up by grief,
And she, because it's what she does,
Showers her brother with her love,
He glances over shoulder to catch,
A glimpse of the present or of the past,

And though the human eye is thin,
He sees her there…

…Right beside him.

*

An Angel on a Golden Turquoise Reef 08/06/2018

I knew by the reef reports that it would be rough, but told the others we'd be okay. They said maybe one to two foot waves and maybe ten to fifteen knots. I knew it would be three to four foot waves and perhaps fifteen to twenty knots. Having Jess, who had never snorkeled before and who could barely float, let alone swim, and Nate, who panicked the last time I took him on a reef who may do likewise again, but knowing it was our last day, and knowing I could keep them safe if they listened to my instructions, we went out on the snorkeling boat with Kayleigh. Kayleigh and I decided that what Jess and Nate didn't know ahead of time would likely not hurt them.

With twenty others on the boat we left the canal. As we tracked a few miles out, the spray gave warning to the roughness that lay ahead. No matter. It would be less tranquil, but still manageable. I instructed Jess and Nate to keep their heads up and eyes fixed on towers back on the island as the fixtures shrank smaller and smaller, further and further away.

After twenty minutes the engine simmered down and the boat slowed. There it was - just one hundred yards in front of us, curving for a few hundred yards to both the left and right, a crescent moon shaped reef. The reef unfolded into a white sandy bottom that stretched towards the boat and beyond. It was three to five feet below the surface, looking green and dark brown from the boat, with an open ocean blue behind it; a stark, bright turquoise water in front of it. The boat was pitching in the three foot waves. The waves were crashing on the deep ocean side and over the reef and swelling behind it towards the boat. There was a steady current drifting off and away from the boat. Not ideal, yet we were here and it was time.

There was an ethereal sunlight on the reef that afternoon - a golden sun; golden wind; golden air. A peculiar glow set itself through the turquoise waters. An essence of something magical - much bigger than the reef. It conveyed a perfect sense of peace in the atmosphere. I could not wait to jump into the water to fulfill my promise to Kayleigh. She was on the edge of the boat with me in her bikini, not needing a snorkel mask.

Jess entered first so that one of us was in the water to help coax Nate in. As I gave Nate a pep talk and helped him face his fear, I looked back over my shoulder to Jess who was floating half way to Cuba, resting on her noodle and not moving her feet. "Jess, you're floating the wrong way. You have to kick your legs, Honey," I said as Nate and I both laughed. She started to kick. She looked hilarious, quite comical and so Jessica. That big snorkel mask swallowed her face and her feet raised up and down in the water like she was a camel trying to swim. To my surprise she made ground back towards the boat, smiled up at me and continued on towards the reef.

As Nate and I followed, we swam over to Jess and Kayleigh. Though distracted by the height and the strength of the waves more than I would have liked to have been, I tried to stay present with my three loves as we tracked in the waters. A ray swooshed below us on a breath. Reef fish scattered and gathered, released into the shifting current and waving this way and that. Gold shimmered under water as if sheets of transparent brilliant lights radiated in these fields of life.

It hit me later that night when I was able to finally articulate it, although I was keenly aware of this while the experience was unfolding. I had attained in the water what I had never been able to manage before - an unblemished, perfect mantle of courage. It was effortless - much like the effortlessness that I experienced with Kayleigh and our family before the accident. Yet never have I felt more fearless. For once, in that afternoon, I felt a total, complete absence of even a trace of fear, which is extra amazing considering the ocean conditions and a few sickening gulps of sea water. A total relaxed state. Breathing regulated in a meditative state. Swimming in the glow - the glow of Kayleigh spreading out a golden shield of protection over and around us.

Jess felt it too. As did Nate once he worked through the jitters of jumping off of a perfectly good boat into the middle of the ocean; once the panic subsided and he was able to regain his trust in himself and me; once he was able to swim over to his struggling Mother who was drifting off towards Cuba. As he dragged her back closer to the reef and helped her swim back to it several times, he was energized with courage. We continued to swim in the golden glow. Kayleigh. She enveloped the entire reef.

"I illuminated a reef, Daddy. Think about that! I illuminated an entire reef while we swam together in the sea. When it gets heavy with my physical absence and you hate not watching me grow up anymore as a young adult in my physical body, remember what you actually get to see me grow up in the present. And look what I can do! Your daughter lit up a reef. An entire reef! It was magical and I am amazing!"

"In Angel's Clothing"

I imagine your white dress -

Long silky sky hemmed into star gowns,
A thousand shades of blue and green alight with golden white,
And flowing like the Milky Way with a wispy sound,
Radiating against the blackness of night,
Sparkling in resonance,
And bending all light with your eyes.

*

19 Year Anniversary 08/08/2018

Nineteen years ago today I married my soul-mate. A brilliant marriage to date, having suffered the most horrendous loss a parent can face, we continue to support and nurture each other and grow one day at a time in ways that bring us closer together. We are the pillars for our children, the captain of our family's boat in which the four of us travel. I love you, Jess. From this marriage came two of the world's most amazing gifts - our baby girl, Kayleigh and our baby boy, Nathaniel. You two are our central light. We love you with a thousand lives and grow with you each in the daily celebration of the four of us.

Kayleigh, tonight is the first wedding anniversary without you in your physical body and with you in your spiritual body. So sullen, the days. So difficult the journey. So heavy the tears. For fifteen anniversaries, we have celebrated with you in your physical form. Today is different. Days that used to be filled with easy joy and now filled with joy upon much brickwork and labor.

*

Jekyll Golfing and Kake's Video Played in My Pocket 08/09/2018

I went golfing with Kayleigh. As I was swinging my driver and prepping for hole number two on the Great Dunes Course, I suddenly heard a lovely voice singing. I looked around to see where it was coming from. It was coming from me. From Kayleigh. In my pocket. On my phone.

"Think of me, think of me fondly when we've said goodbye. Remember me once in a while, please promise me you'll try..." I heard her voice and these words, and looked to my phone, where a video was playing on my phone, yet my phone was locked and the screen was black. It had been locked for fifteen minutes and in my pocket the same amount of time. I pressed the button to light up the screen and unlocked the phone and saw her beautiful presence in this video; a video she had self-recorded in our house.

My God. Of course. There is no question. I don't even need to promise my belief. It just is. And always will be. And not once in a while. I literally think about you all day long. And you literally think about me all day long; thinking of ways to reach across to touch me;

ways that I will understand are not coincidence. Ways like this. You played a video on my phone while my phone was locked in my pocket. Kayleigh! My God, My Love! I am here. I see. I witness. I feel. I touch you in this space.

*

Kayleigh and Daddy Fly In 1940 Bi-Plane 08/11/2018

One year ago today, six days before the horrific accident that stripped my baby of her physical life and transitioned her into spirit, I promised Kayleigh we would go flying the next time on Jekyll Island. We were at the pool, watching the bi-plane fly overhead. We called to see if we could fly on our last day at Jekyll. He had no appointments. So I promised, the next time we were at Jekyll and he was flying, she and I would fly.

Today she and I went flying and soared together through the sky - a glimpse of both the amazing, fun, dynamic life she was living when the accident happened, and the greater beauty she has become in spirit - laughing her Kayleigh laugh the whole time we were in the air. We glanced on the air, banking in the breeze. Phil, our pilot, knowing the story, knowing my mission with Kayleigh, watching the purple ribbon I tied around my wrist fly in the breeze above the islands, piloted the plane with purpose; with passion; with tears in his eyes.

I Love you, Babygirl. We did it. We went flying in this bi-plane, just as I promised we would do. The passing of your physical body does not pass your life. I embrace your life. I embrace you as I can. And I can. So I do. And we grow. So we do. Let us keep growing, Sweet Kayleigh.

*

615

Kayleigh's Transition Anniversary 08/16/2018

Dear Friends,
We will be gathering at Kayleigh's Bench (at the corner Euclid Heights Blvd and Edgehill) on Friday August 17 at around 10 PM. We will be having a candlelight vigil and at 10:45 PM Kayleigh's Mommy, Daddy and Brother will walk over alone to the island where she was physically transitioned for a few moments of total silence. It is imperative that, if you are coming to support us, that you hold this moment sacredly and not be late. Also we do not want anybody walking over to the island with us as this is a sacred moment strictly for the four of us. Thank you for understanding and for your continued love and support. Message me with any questions.

"The Day I Was Dropped On Another Planet"

The day I was dropped on another planet,
With no oxygen reservoirs,
And a barren, foreign landscape,
An alien in an alienated place,
A companion to grief and trauma,
It fills the every crack of this porous space,
While I walk through quicksand while breathing concrete,
And feeling the arbitrary nature of life strip my footing from my feet,
A heart once broken works little at all,
Cannot in defeat catch the floor with the fall,
I miss you so horribly - your physical presence,
As I learn this new planet,
And its untamed resonance.

*

Today is One Year 08/17/2017

Sweet Kakie, beautiful Babygirl, I grieve horribly this one year anniversary of the blindsiding accident and your transition and all the daily suffering that comes with it. I also celebrate with you your vibrant spiritual life. We do not get you in your physical form today

616

and I accept and reconcile this. We do, however, get this today with you in your brilliant spiritual embodiment and we are not going to miss out on our present, active relationship today. Our love conquers all distance of time, space or worlds. We are together - your presence a miracle I embrace. I love you, Kayleigh. I am the luckiest Daddy in the world. ❦○🐀◗

"In Your Spirit Clothes"

I cannot meet you where you are not,
I cannot have what I cannot,
Yet I can meet you where you are,
I can touch the light of your guiding star,
And feel its radiance humming in my aura,
Like the forest holds electricity in its flora,
Spiking through the roots of all that grows,
In the endless frontiers of our souls,
Where we can have what we can,
And I meet you, Daughter, where you stand,
In the present - in your spirit clothes,
In your life lit up with light aglow,
Our love as endless,
As the universe is known.

*

One Year in Heaven (Daddy's Reading at Candlelight Vigil) 08/17/2018

Kayleigh is all about family. She loves her Daddy. She loves her Mommy. Mostly, she loves her baby brother, Nathaniel. More than anybody she loves you, Nate. Tonight is also about you. Kayleigh wants you to know what a treasure you are.

One year ago, our beautiful Kayleigh's life was transitioned from her physical body to her spiritual embodiment. We daily grow in our relationships with her. In this new life Kayleigh has been thriving and affecting people's lives in miraculous ways – always with us, walking with us, touching us, speaking to us, blessing us daily. In one sense, tonight is a celebration of new life for Kayleigh and she is standing here with that bright face and her boisterous laughter shouting out, "come on guys! Heads up! Celebrate with me my one year anniversary of being with God! This is awesome!"

In all, we live on two sides of a coin at the same time, every day. On one side of this coin is the most exhausting, tremendous grief we could not have ever imagined. The physical death of a boy's only sibling is an unbearable pain for Nathaniel to bare. For Jess and I, the physical death of a child in childhood, the only type of death that does not heal, there is nothing more unnatural to bare. We break a dozen times a day and process hundreds of moments every day. There is no healing as one might expect in the deaths of parents or grandparents. There is, however, reconciling with this truth on a daily basis in order to function in this world - that an open wound will remain for all of our days.

The other side of this coin is Kayleigh's current life - the highest spiritual highs we have ever experienced – Kayleigh leaving us stones from her funeral in specific places; she plays with our Bluetooth and changes songs for us; she sings through the wind-chimes; she kisses our cheeks; when we sit in silence with her, she will sometimes lay her angel hands across our foreheads, run her fingers through my hair or hold our hands. Kayleigh is a powerful guardian angel who can cross two worlds to be both with God in Heaven as well as walking with us here on earth. Of course she can – its Kayleigh after all. I'm sure no one here would be surprised to know that, if anybody could do that, it is Kayleigh. Part of her legacy is her dynamic presence – here with us now and always.

Her lessons remain from her physical life as well - remember that, after she was violently assaulted ten months before the accident, she used the event to make her voice stronger, conquering the pain and giving her even more self-confidence and internal peace. She embarked on her hard, healing process telling me often to encourage herself, "Daddy, we can do hard things, right?" She prosecuted. She advocated for other girls. She cried. She laughed. She played. She lived. In the ultimate display of empowerment, she forgave her rapists. She is a legend to countless women who watched her use her voice. She was on top of the world and living an empowered happy life, continuing to press forward to define her life when this arbitrary and horrific accident, unrelated to anything, happened. She wants us all to remember that 99% of her life was amazing with an amazing family and amazing friends – the other 1% of difficulty she faced she used to make herself stronger – what an example. She also wants us all to know that she's a little pissed off that this unexpected accident happened to her as she was centered and happy and ready for her next phase of life – though she is extremely happy now, going from that raw happiness in her physical life to a much higher happiness unhindered by human restriction.

My Kayleigh Mooney – our dynamic, artistic, compassionate, selfless, funny, giving, strong and courageous, slightly edgy, deep thinking, passionate bright girl, one of the two loves of our lives, the strongest girl I've ever known, I am so grateful that you transitioned at the most empowered, happiest point in your wonderful life. It was a perfect transition – emotionally you did not intend the accident and did not know that you had been hit by a car and therefore you were not afraid; physically you felt no pain, thank God; yet spiritually and slightly mentally you knew that your Daddy was talking to you and you were eternally comforted as you were asked, "Kayleigh if you can hear your Daddy's voice, squeeze my hand," and you did several times before you passed your light right through me. We love you, Kakie and are so completely proud of you. Continue to shine brighter than a million suns; and we promise to Look to the Moon if we are lost, for you hold all power." We see you. We feel you. We hear you. We love you.

*

"Thank You, Daddy, For My One Year Transition Anniversary"
08/18/2018

"Daddy, that was amazing. All of these people came out to celebrate me. Me! I am so happy. Daddy, I can't thank you enough. You and Mommy and Nate love me so much. We really are unbreakable. It was amazing to see everyone gathered together from my old friends and new friends, to Angela and Colleen who were with us on the street in the night of my transition, to all of your A.A. friends, neighbors, strangers, and the police, including the Chief. I really like her. She's a very strong woman.

Little Nathaniel. He is really special, Daddy, as you know. He's really hurting. He misses me so much. I miss him the way we were on the same plain too, even though I walk with him every day and won't ever leave his side. He doesn't always feel it but in his heart he knows it's true.

You were my voice tonight, Daddy. I am so proud of you. You stood there and fired away, using your voice to tell my story and to touch a huge crowd. In the rain. Did you notice the times I stopped the rain. And yes, that was me. That candle near the telephone pole was lit for 24 hours and as things wound down and people started leaving I asked you to look over to it, which you did, and watched it flicker out. That was me. Because I'm awesome. And because I wanted to thank you by letting you see what I can do. For you. For Mommy. For my little Nate. I love you so much, Daddy!"

"The Transition"

Like the moon and every cycle - rise,
You renew and hold me here,
Like the sun too bright for human eyes,
You are just beyond my fear,
Like the stars that mark the traveler's tide,
You the chart - the ship to steer,
Like the galaxies you plant in my skies,
Are all proof that you are here,
Lighting up a pathway home,
To a higher atmosphere.

*

Find Me in the Light 08/19/2018

Daddy, find me in the light. It is there where I am. It's simply the truth. Find me in the light. This year two is different than last year. The first year was the first year and full of confusion and grief. Now this is year two of my spiritual life and we are going to take this to a higher level. You will still grieve in a very familiar manner. Every day. Yet your resilience will kick in quicker and stronger, because Daddy, you will find me in the light. Not in depression or despondency or excruciating pain. But in the light. It's the same message over and over, day after day. The duality is your constant. Reach higher, Daddy. Find me in the light of your life and in Nate's life and in Mommy's life and in my spiritual ongoing beautiful life. I am right here, Daddy, walking in your light. Walk in mine. Find me in the light.

"Light Bending"

Bending the light - I blend the night with bleeding morning sun,
Into a holy union - burdened not and together, into one,
Fires clash with the darkest rash and flicker yellow flames in coal like shadows,
Lighting up the atmosphere that floods like footlights through the shallows…

…Where I lay.

*

A New Game to Play 08/26/2018

"Oh my God, Daddy, that's a great idea. Okay, let's do it. We will find each other in the light in that way."

Right, since I've been struggling with the physical side of the coin and all that we've lost in that space, and I don't doubt you are here with me, but I've had trouble at times tapping into that spiritual space, let's make it a game like hide and seek and we will look throughout the days for times when we find each other in the light. Leave me bread crumbs. Leave me riddles. Leave me little signs, Honey.

"I've always loved playing games with you, Daddy. This one is brilliant."

Thank you, Sweetheart. It sounds pretty fun and a way to keep my human brain engaged and focused on you in the light rather than in all of the loss. The losses accumulate day after day but I can't stay just in that. I have to counterbalance. In that way, you are constantly in the light and with me.

"Yep, and you know I'll show up. It'll be a competition and I think I have a clear advantage. It's almost unfair. Ha! See you in the light, Daddy."

See you in the light, Baby.

"A Man's Shadow of Light"

Like his shadow but only of light,
That casts spray of radiance,
She passes her energy in waves of life,
With variant frequencies and varying gradient,
An arm wrapped around her Father,
While he wanders in the halls of disbelief,
She sings to him - she whispers - she speaks,
She radiates, emblazoned - empowered she seeks,
To shine a radius of love about him,
That only the rare eye can see,
She comforts his broken heart,
In his waking hours - while he sleeps,
For she is every minute, every minute that he keeps,
She is every moment, every moment that he breathes.

*

Never A Day 08/26/2018

We never missed a day. Not one. Waking you in the morning and you flinging your toddler arms around me; bouncing in the wagon going around the block; you and your brother as little children; stopping to get rocks and leaves and sticks and acorns; buckling his buckle to keep him safe; being ever compliant and staying seat-belted in; laughing and exploring the world. Exploring the world in a new way every day even on the same path around the block. We never missed a day.

That scenario was true every day at every age all the way to fifteen, three months and two days. We always told each other we were going to find something new, even though we tracked across the same path a thousand times. Something different. And we did. Always. A new bug. A new bird. The way the clouds moved. A breeze. Water bugs in the pond. A turtle. A fish. We never missed a day.

"Milky Dark Mirages"

Grief, a darkness,
Like the milky blackness of a moonless, midnight sea,
Laps against my body - it washes over me,
As I search through the endless mire, aimlessly,
I must remember,
Hold on,
Its mirage comes to claim my reality;

For in the next breath,
A turn from the flood,
When all seems hopeless,
A line opens up,
Horizon - it glows - a golden light grows,
And as the bright light breaks through,
I know…

…It is you…

…You've come to where you always are,
As bright as the ocean birthing a star;

The Moon is rising yet the Moon is always here,
The Moon is constant in its angelic atmosphere,
In those moments when the eyes cannot capture it,
Worry not - she whispers…

…"I am here."

*

No Permanent Scar 08/30/2018

Kayleigh has no permanent scar. She was free light before the accident and so she is now. I am grateful for her majesty and her power - a guardian angel of the highest order packed into my little girl. She tells me to find her in the light - a soul that shines a thousand percent of pure light, breaching Heaven and earth daily. She told me she is taking me higher and walking me home. She is so in love with me and I am in love with her. I have never felt such strength and sorrow that no one can understand unless they experience this. It is a million times worse than anyone can imagine. Yet it brings me to my promise to reach a million times higher to be with her each day in her higher calling.

I, too, have a higher calling. I am beginning to accept that truth. I am peeling back the gloss of this life to uncover the true life beyond. I am not afraid. I am curious and full of faith. I am between both worlds - with my boy in this physical space – and on the doorstep of the heavenly realm with my Daughter - with, both of my children at the same time - the two equal loves of my life. I shift from pole to pole along this axis of my physical life wanting to be in both worlds, for how could I not. My soul pulls to my boy and my girl and to my beloved wife standing at this axis with me. We are a dynamic true family of four. Four lights. Four perfect lights. We rotate about each other's orbit. We thank God for our eternity together.

Kakes told me this morning on the way to work, "Daddy, you don't know how beautiful you are," and I started crying, like it was hard to believe. She tried to encourage me further as she said, "you are the Daddy of a guardian angel. How cool is that, Daddy?" She wants me to know I'm special. I forget how gushy she gets with me because I can't physically look in her eyes and see her smile and feel those physical cues. Yet it is there. She is timeless in her love, so when the feeling comes, it is dynamic and powerful and never ebbing.

"A Painting for Your Father"

You were painting the night with shooting stars,
Streaks of light that left their scars,
Like thin valleys of flame through a shadow terrain,
Like flashes of fire and meteor rain,
You were painting the night sky above the sea,
In radiant strokes - just for me.

*

The Last Picture I Took Of Kayleigh (08/11/2017) 09/07/2018

This photo tells a hundred tails. So simple. So ordinary. The last. One of us was always placing the bar a little higher. This time it was Nate, jacking up his shorts as high as he could to try to get reactions from strangers as we walked into FlashFoods on Jekyll Island.

You can see it on his face, egged on by his Father to keep a straight face as people noticed him. He was ready and in character. His mother, happy and slightly surprised, but not really - this is what we do with our children. Daily. Kayleigh, amused, brushing her golden blonde hair out of her eyes and stepping into the scene in order to get a front row view.

So effortless. Simple. These are the days of the four of us prior to the accident. Earlier in the day it was me dressed up as the Pink Nightmare. Later in the day, Kayleigh, placing Saran Wrap over the entrance to Nate's door. Pushing the envelope. Getting each other to laugh. Supporting this family, each of us, in an interwoven cradle of love and light.

I would have no way to know I only had six more days in this configuration when I took this picture. Six more days of love and laughter with all of us together in the same body types on this physical plain. A great family engaged in what was the ordinary for each.

Everything is different now. Much more quiet. Our configuration consists of three on the physical plain and one on the spiritual plain; together, a strong family of four, even more in love with each other. Empowered above us all, Kayleigh has a front row seat to all that we do and participates in the funny moments when we can wrestle up the strength to engage. It is extremely difficult to do at times. The physical laughter, however, must continue - the energy, well, it's not quite always there, taking on average of three times the energy it used to take just to get through a day.

We all need our laughter. Nathaniel in particular. At such a young age, he has been through so much with this accident and all that it has stripped from us. And so we laugh and act and push each other to engage. In fact, we press forward as four, living in and finding Kayleigh in the light. The higher we rise spiritually the more profoundly we feel her and hear her and see her fingerprints around the house and our lives. She constantly reminds us of her brilliant immediacy, as profoundly alive and present now as on this hot August afternoon in 2017 when I took the last picture I ever took of my beautiful daughter, Kayleigh. I miss you horrifically in your physical form and those pains will last this lifetime. Thank God for your life in your spiritual embodiment as you are here right now helping me write these words.

"One Hour"

One hour without you is like a month without breath,
An ocean without water,
One hour without my Daughter,
A night that never sets,
A day that never rises,
A thousand, thousand deaths,
One hour, you are centuries,
To claw through with barren voice upset,
A bird without wings,
And sleep without rest,
Air with no oxygen,
A life without breath.

*

Would You Ever Leave My Side 09/08/2018

"Daddy, I would never leave your side. Would you ever leave my side if the tables were turned? No. So why would you ever think that I would leave your side? You are my Daddy. You need me. I need you. I love you so much, Daddy. So much. It's the grief talking when you forget how much I need and love you. When you laugh, I light up brighter. When you engage with life, Daddy, I seem even closer. I resonate and my light and love and my energy radiates stronger when you take yourself higher."

Kakes, you always know how to comfort me. I was in the TV room seemingly alone, laying on couch on my left side with a migraine. Thinking of you. Always thinking of you. All of a sudden, I felt you rest your hand across my right side, your fingers along my ribs. You were sitting beside me. Watching me suffer. And rested your angelic palm on my body to give me rest - to let me know that you were here. Your hand, when you somehow touch me, feels like it transfers a storm of golden butterflies that enter my body and flutter around, their golden wings blessing my flesh as they bounce along on their flight paths. I sit in wonder and amazement, knowing that a miracle is upon me. An angel - my angel, my Daughter in my midst. My baby soothing my pain. I am sensing this more and more as I key in more and more. Keep reaching me, Babygirl, in patience. I am coming to you, Honey, I am here.

"The Star Muse"

She sprinkles in the fertile night air,
The seedlings of crystal stars,
That radiate as they spire into place,
And root in flame like fire scars,
That sing, their voices, the sound of light,
Enchant the canvas of the night.

*

One: Truth and Protection 09/09/2018

Today I turned to Kayleigh in the car, recycling my furious anger at a few people in the neighborhood who rumored about Kayleigh and her tragic passing to fit their own narrative. We never should have been placed in a position where anybody was making up stories about such an over the top horrific tragedy as the physically death of a child. That they conjectured, that they guessed, that they never knew my Daughter, it was so disgusting. So I turned to her in the passenger seat and said, "Baby, I will make sure the truth is always told about you. I will always protect Mommy and Nathaniel and you, Babygirl, from any mistruths."

"Thank you, Daddy," she said very clearly, "because if someone tries to say I committed suicide it de-minimizes the power and strength that I became. It doesn't really, but it seems to take away from all the work I did and how empowered I was and how much I healed. These people are stupid and ignorant and really sick. Those few people who spread that rumor never even met me, Daddy! What a ridiculous type of person. Thank God it was only a couple. It was a simple car accident. You know that, Daddy. Make sure people know."

As soon as her voice faded out the song "One" by U2 blasted in the car out of nowhere, picked by Kakes in that moment to remind me that she and I are one; that we never became the hurt in that song, that we were and always will be the love in that song, carrying each other, we carry each other.

You are a miracle, Kayleigh.

"You are too, Daddy. Love you."

*

Others Changing the Narrative So They Can Manage Their Lives 09/10/2018

Every once in a while a person will find their comfort only by changing the story to fit their narrative - if your accident was an arbitrary act, they might subconsciously think, then their children too could end up physically killed in the blink of an eye; but if the story was different, if only they can make up a different story, like you being distraught and throwing yourself in front of a car, then they can feel comforted knowing that their children would never do that - that the world has order and there is nothing arbitrary within it. Yet nothing from this can comfort their misguided eyes. For arbitrary accidents do happen.

I will never permit their lie as a narrative as long as I am here to confront it. Thank God it is one in a thousand and usually someone who doesn't know you and hasn't spoken directly to me or Mommy about the accident. It really shows the immaturity and narrowness of certain adults who walk around with the aspirational levels of toddlers, hiding, ducking, failing to feel the full impact of randomness and arbitrary forces of life. With us, with you, Honey, with this horrible accident, we confront it daily and in full color. I remind myself due to its shocking simplicity – blindsided in a car accident; trying to get you shoes; happy and vibrant life; not a high risk child; not a terminally sick child; not a child with a hidden disease; a fully perfectly happy and healthy child trying to come home to her family. So simple. So tragic. So arbitrary.

*

Room 41 09/11/2018

I just had a flashback to University Hospitals, sitting for three or four hours with Kayleigh's physical and spiritual bodies. I told a doctor, near the end of that sitting, that I needed her to walk out of room #41 with me because I couldn't do it by myself - I couldn't stand up and leave my baby's body. I needed a doctor to hold my hand, help me stand, and slowly walk me from the room.

What I did not remember until now, and now I see it and hear it so clearly, is that I now remember Kakes telling me in the most comforting way, in a gentle whisper, with her arm around my shoulders, "Daddy, its okay. We have to leave my body here and go home to Mommy and Nathaniel. My body is safe. I am here with you. Come on, Daddy...it's time for us to get up to go home. Let's go home, Daddy. Let's go home."

Then the doctor walked in and I asked her to give me a few more minutes, but to come back to walk with me from the room. Which she did. I was hearing my baby from the very, very beginning. In the street moments after her transition. Hours later in Room #41. Those initial minutes, hours, days and weeks – they set the stage to our current connection. There is such comfort in that, even though the trauma is suffocating.

"Like A Cement Truck Pores Cement Down Your Throat"

And then, trapped in hours of breathing cement,
Feeling suffocated in my own lungs,
A coating of stony mesh,
No, it is not panic - it is not anxiety,
It is raw grief that coagulates, strangulates and eviscerates the flesh,
I am struggling, though falling forward,

630

Sometimes just breathing is doing my best,
Just to squeak out a little life from the concaving of the chest,
Until the texture lessens,
And opens once again.

*

"*My Son, A Warrior Child*" 09/13/2018

This road of grief - so long and so hard,
And sacred ground so deeply scarred,
I watched the pain that gouged your heart,
As all of us - we fell apart,
A chisel with a concave blade,
And torture that this angle made,
And triage comes, and bandages,
And little boy, he manages,
And every day we walk with you,
Your Sister, me and Mother too,
Cradle you in outstretched hands,
The baby of the family understands,
That everything - we do for you,
And sap our strength to pull you through,
For like your Sister's special gold,
You are the equal of her soul,
With strength in you - don't let it go,
And know that we…

…We love you so...

*

Like A Galaxy Spinning On My Third Eye 09/14/2018

While I lay on her bed in meditation today, I asked her humbly, as I do every day, if she could reach out to me and touch me. If she could kiss me on my forehead like I used to do to her when she'd go to sleep at night as a little girl.

I suddenly felt a swirling light on my third eye, like a hurricane of energy without the wind, a calming circular motion, counter clockwise on my forehead. It felt like a galaxy with all of its amazing tiny sprinkles of warm, sharp light spinning, spinning, spinning.

After a few minutes, she then ran her fingers in a circle around the top of my head and down my ear and on my cheek, caressing me lovingly.

"The Star Muse II"

Her gowns are layers of atmospheric thread,
Sheets of flowing wind across her frame - loosely spread,
Like silky white cloth emblazoned with a million tiny gems,
Crystals and stardust and solar flares upon the hems,
Alight her shimmering sundress with a billion rising suns,
Reflecting in her ocean eyes -
The promise of eternity - its brilliance has begun.

*

Cannot Fade Away 09/15/2018

I promise continued growth of our incredible relationship. You cannot fade away. It is impossible. However, my contact with you, and therefore as a consequence, our relationship, could fade and blur away due to an overload of consistent despondency, depression and grief. It must be processed. Passed. It is up to me to take action to ensure the processing of grief to ensure that fading does not occur between us - and it is up to you to continue to light my path and carry me when I need it. We are a true partnership bound by unbreakable love.

I have nothing but adoration, respect, honor, humility and love for you. That is what my poem was about (The Best of Me), written a month before the accident. Whether then or now, that respect and adoration does not change, save for it increasing as you mature in spirit. The more I engaged with you (before the accident) the better I become. That was one of the core meanings of that poem. It holds true following the accident as well. The more I engage with you, the more whole I become. I just need to engage with you in more creative ways in order to feel you and see you and hear you. It is hard; actually nothing in life is harder than a parent physically losing a child. Through the torment I will walk. If it means being together, then we can do hard, and I will walk. We can stretch our souls. We can.

"Embrace the day, Daddy. Remember you always used to tell me to embrace the day."

Yes I did, My Love. Embrace the day. Full circle, my Love, for you are now my teacher. Full circle.

*

Not Both, but One 09/16/2018

I can't have both, but I can have one. And one I can't have anymore, leaving me with the opportunity for only the other. I will take the only option I have every time, even if I long for and grieve for the first. I will not fail you. I will not fail to be with you.

I, of course, wish and long for you in your physical body. I can no longer hold you in that form and laugh with you in that form, a form to which I had become so innately accustomed. I can, however, following the transition, hold you in your spiritual embodiment, laugh with you and hang out with you in your spiritual body as you continue your life and continue to mature. If I can't have you in your physical state, I am going to do everything in my power to have you in your spiritual body. I promise you that.

*

One Year Ago Kayleigh Dropped God in Jess' Soul 09/17/2018

Today is the one year anniversary of Jess accepting and finding God. You, Kayleigh blasted "You'll be in My Heart" after changing out our Bluetooth and turning up the car stereo today last year, changing Mommy forever. The texture of the relationship between you and Mommy is so strong and sacred that you were able to lead Mommy to God. That is a higher truth more than anything, proof of your ongoing life. You led Mommy to a relationship with God at the lowest point in her existence. You proved both your power and presence, as well as God's ultimate presence. I remind Mommy to always use this miracle when the days are hard. And all days are hard. No greater miracle exists than one pulling God into one's heart and you did that. You did that. Revel in your light. Dance in your light.

"Thank you, Daddy, Mommy really needed that. She really needed that. I studied how to do it and just went for it. Hey, by the way, do you hear me in the wind chimes?"

Yes. You are either playing with the chimes with your fingers or singing through them and the sound of light is translating through the air and also the chimes in a beautiful melody; one of the ways your voice resonates on this plain in pure light and love. You're amazing. I love the way you channel your voice. I am listening. I hear you. I am here.

"With Interconnecting Light Forever"

All tied together with strings of love,
A relation to one bound by another,
To another, though she did not know enough,
The lights combine - sister and brother,
Sister, a daughter, to father and mother,

The light intersects in a thread of illumination,
Even when one of us touched another,
Whom the others did not know,
If our loved one loves this other one,
Then we are tied together,
Like a credo etched in stone,
Tied with interconnecting lights across the many,
Forever,
Thread by threaded soul.

*

Physical Life and Spiritual Life 09/16/2018

Here it goes, and it is hard to write with you. There are benefits to both your physical and spiritual lives. Certainly, the familiarity of us with each other on the physical plain, in physical bodies, made the journey simple and freeing, filled with the full dynamic of a strong relationship, including all emotion and physical cues. On the physical plain I could see you, hear you, and touch you; literally, standing in front of me or sitting next to me. Yet only when we were together or on the phone or video chatting could we be together. There were long hours at work when I was not with you or your brother or mother, thinking of you and wishing to be with you, excited to know that, when work was over for the day, I would come home and there you would be.

That is tragically no longer the case. However, in the spiritual life, I can be with you 24/7 and I am. I still think of Nate and Mommy, and can't wait to get home to them and can't wait for the three of us on the physical plain to be in the same room, because I know when we three are all in the same room together, that actually all four of us are together resonating amongst each other.

When we were both of the physical plain in physical bodies, we had everyday opportunities and challenges to grow together and it was quite simple to build a bridge with each other; growing, laughing, work things out. We would find ways to continue to grow with each other and it was mostly effortless, very rarely challenging, but always with positive, forward momentum. Now in your spiritual life, it is much more fruitful for it is much more challenging since it is so hard, at least for me in my human capacity, to try to push through to Heaven; though easier for you, I suspect, as a guardian angel, to be able to push through from Heaven to the physical world, but what do I know? Perhaps it is harder. It is a greater challenge of crossing over the worlds to be together than it is to go to lunch in our physical states at Los Arcos. But we do it. And the rewards are even greater. Each aims for the other. Each investigates and learns new techniques to push through to the other. Each has the other in heart and mind. Each offers light and love to the other. Each resonates in each other, lifting the other to a higher ground.

For me, the center of our communion begins in morning meditation and prayer. Nightly meditation and prayer. A hundred moments a day to break from the world - a world I let go of a little more each day with its frivolous nonsense. I live in between two worlds - certainly not shed of my humanness so not in Heaven, but aiming in that direction and lifting myself, because that is where my older baby is. And living with my feet on the ground on earth and striving each day to dig through this life, for that is where my little boy is. I process great watershed moments of grief - each day. It is exhausting yet I persist and push on.

I am a Father that will stop at nothing to be with both of my children, and so I do. Regardless. Nonetheless, it is not a path that mainstream Americans are accustomed to and for them, but only secondarily, I will blaze this trail. Those who want to believe will believe. Those who do not want to believe will not believe. Neither is my affair. My focus, my job, my goal is to be the best Father I can be to both of my children and neither of my children will be fatherless on any day of our existence.

You are sitting with me right now. You are sitting with Mommy right now. You are sitting with Nate right now. And we are in three separate rooms. Your current experience is timeless and boundless, for you and your heart always flutters with the excitement and love you have for us. You gush for us in that sweet Kayleigh voice and your sweet Kayleigh eyes. You are heightened and cleansed and sacred in emotion, emotion that is tied with light to your heightened mind and your soul at the core of who you now are. That is comforting in many ways. I know you are safe. I know you are happy. I know you are one of God's favorite angels. I know your current life is wonderful and amazing. I find total peace in that.

My heart does both - I flutter with a troop of butterflies for my Daughter the way I always have and used to before the accident - excited to be with you, to introduce you to people, to be in your presence, to be honored to just spend time with you. I flutter for you. I also ache in my humanness and the weakness of this physical life, particularly when I fall into looking at this physical life as if I was looking at life through a keyhole. Everything else is everything else. All that is within view on the physical plain is so tiny in comparison. Yet I am here in this flesh and mind and emotion and the excruciating pain in your accident and the daily aftermath is overwhelming at times.

You are like one of your kid paintings; hands clasped together, eyes wide open with a hundred hearts flying out of you representing your love for us. You are always in that state. That is one of your great lessons for us. I want to be in that state with you and Mommy and Nate. Always. Yet the three of us wane because that is part of the human experience your brother, Mother and Father are still stuck in the limited dimension and sticky glue of being human. Then we pick ourselves up. Things get in the way. Then we remove them. All the while you gush nonstop for us - a hundred hearts flying out from you to us. You amaze me, Sweet Love.

"Your Light Body"

One million points of God's own light,
One million vibrations of your loving life,
When the great transition shed your human skin,
Your light body emerged...

...Empowered on the wind.

*

A Black Rock 09/18/2018

So, yesterday she hid one of her funeral stones in a pile of bills lying on the counter in the kitchen. It fell to the floor when I picked up the stack of bills. It was positioned right in the middle of a dozen bills. Think about that. A tiny, black stone, one of Kayleigh's stones, the likes of which were passed out to a thousand people at her funeral, was tucked into a stack of bills. We kissed it and thanked her and placed it on the ledge above the counter in the kitchen.

If that special contact was not enough, today she hid this black rock again for us to find. Jess was in the kitchen and opened up all twelve envelopes, and as she paid the bills, she placed the paper on one of the stools tucked under the counter. One at a time she placed the paper on the stool. After she was done paying all of the bills, Jess walked away, leaving the stack of papers on the stool,

Two hours later, we picked up the stack of paper from the stool in the kitchen and there, on the bottom of that stack, was this black rock. . Underneath the stack of papers sat this black rock. It clearly was not there when Jess lay the first bill on the stool. Kakes! That makes eight for the year – eight funeral stones left for us, including, now, one black rock. Thank you for your intervention.

"Garden of Light"

And it grows, in a garden streamed with light,
And the flora, it glows, celestially bright,
For you and me,
Like stars crushed into liquid light and illuminating the sea,
Where the stardust glitters on the leaves,
And the fires bloom, like sunrise,
Blazing flowers in your eyes,
Fill my gardens with pure life,
And our love, it grows,
And grows.

*

Daydreams 09/20/2018

I had a daydream today, interspersed between the multiple paths I seem to walk. I was in the Pilot at lunchtime. I see Kayleigh in all that she does not get to do. Driving to school. Dances. Dinners. Graduating high school. Sleeping in. I even noticed earlier in the day a Thule atop a car and was reminded that we purchased a Thule - Kakes help pick it out, and used it for several years when we traveled since we had four long skinny people in the car. The Thule was purchased primarily to carry the teenage daughter's suitcases. Now we do not need a Thule, yet there it is in the garage leaning up against the back wall, in the same position it was in when I took it off the Pilot five days before the accident.

Yet now, adrift in daydream, stolen moments from one of the hundred dreads I face daily, it is both fantasy and therapy, reality of what isn't, and the non-reality of my heart aching to create that which will not be. In the dream Nate was seventeen. He was driving Mommy and Daddy out to a beach. Kakes was twenty and away at college. She drove herself from college and met us there, getting to the beach house before us. I knew she was there as we drove down the highway. I couldn't wait to see her as we drove down the last road towards the beach.

She was tracking us on her phone, becoming more excited to see us as the miles shrank in distance. When we pulled in the sandy gravel drive, she came bounding out onto the porch and bee-bopped down the stairs and I screamed, "Kakie! Hey baby!"

She was wearing a black sleeveless top and cute shorts, her long blonde hair flowing in the wind, her big blue eyes like two bright galaxies reaching out to greet us. She jumped in my arms. "Hey Daddy! I missed you!"

"Oh, my Love! I missed you too! It's been like four months. Far too long since I've seen you!"

Then the daydream washed in and out with a whitish haze. I sat deeply in the seat of my Pilot - and wept. And wept. And wept. In that daydream, in that realization, I was reminded of how much has been robbed from us; reminded of a simple greeting that will never now be. Over and over again. Each day. The text that no longer comes. The voice over the phone. The hug. The yell. The laughter. The physical presence on the couch, in the yard, at the dinner table, in the car, meeting me at the beach in her twenties, with her children, in the everywhere – now a physical and brutal void.

Then she picked me up and in her spiritual embodiment, clasping her hand in mine, reminding me that through the process I understand the next world more and more; I become more in tune to her voice and presence; I rise higher where we can meet. She reminded me that no four months will ever separate us - even though in the physical plain years will separate us horrifically; in spirit not one second has been lost, misplaced, or unattended. For she is here. She is alive. She is in her body of light, even stronger and more aware. And she told me so. Again. And hugged me in my pain.

After a longer pep talk, and simmering back down from the emotional mountain climb, I sighed and prepared to go back inside to work. Armed with my Daughter by my side. And so we did.

Those who have not experienced this type of tragedy - love each simple greeting, each opportunity, each mundane moment. How many do not find gratitude in a simple passing through the house with a loved one, who in the moment, is cranky or dispassionate or quiet or meek. How many times is a loved one taken for granted in the course of a twenty four hour cycle? The choice of direction is at hand - the power to engage in the moment upon each and every one of us. Whether it is the distance of a loved one knowing they are physically alive somewhere else in another city, or sitting beside you, or even for me, with Kakes sitting beside me in her body of light rather than in her human form, treat it as a gift of the highest order. I never missed a moment with her in her physical body. I never miss a moment now.

"If I Could Change Places"

If I could just change places,
If the night could have seen me pass,
I hesitate in thought,
In grief,
I would not wish this pain upon you,
No, I cannot bare you mourning me,
But I ache for your physical life,
Yes, I would trade places on that night,
Yes - oh no, oh no –

I do, but I don't,
I would, but I won't,
And in the paralysis - it is here I persist,
In unadulterated powerlessness,
I cling, I claw - a wraith, I resist,
And I want to,
But in this vacuum I remain,
For it is all that I can do,
Alas, My Love, I would not change places,
For I cannot bare you baring this pain.

*

Nuclear Bomb in a Breadbox 09/20/2018

Tenth Step. I saw a twenty five year old mom who looks just like
Kakes walking hand in hand with a two year old boy right passed me.
Kakes will not have children. I will not have grandchildren from
Kakes. Robbed of thousands of treasures - not only my child but my
grandchildren. The impact of her physical death is like a nuclear
bomb in a breadbox. 4: Selfish? Not really. Just a punch to gut. Trying
to not internalize it. Dishonest? Yes. The future that won't happen is
true, but the future is fantasy. Resentment? Yes. Fear? Yes. And
angry with the world that someone so beautiful and wonderful and
hopeful and happy could be cut down. 5: Share with someone? My

sister. 6: Willing to have God and Kakes remove? Yes. 7: Prayer: god and Kakes please help me reconcile and remove these defects. This sucks. Worst of the worst. Please help me continue to transition into this horrible new un-normal. 8: Willing to change? Yes. 9: Change? Breathe. Expect these moments. Attitude I can be kind. Perspective - I don't get grandkids from Kakes, but I have Kakes right here in a different form. 12: Turn to someone I can help? One of my workers who needs direction and my focus.

"Every Stitch of Clothing"

Every stitch of clothing I packed away broke my heart,
Every of your belongings stacked away ripped me apart,
I have twenty bins of yours on the shelf,
Stuffed animals, your shoes, bags and clothes and jewels and art,
A physical life represented in tangible possessions,
That leaves upon the soul its powerful impressions,
And also represents the losses in future tension…

…Like a stitch of cloth - each stitch apart.

*

Your Voice 09/24/2028

And other queues. All of the physical queues that are now absent - I ache in the void. I yearn in the emptiness. It is every day. Every hour here.

Your presence. Your voice. Your lovely voice. It was so articulate. Mature. Silky. It pulled on my heart strings. I tuned in when I heard your voice coming around the corner or calling down the stairs. I listened intently when you were sad or upset, or happy and boisterous, prepared to support you or jump into the laughter with you. I ache for your human, physical voice. Yet it is gone. Though it has been replaced with your many voices in spirit, and I love your spirit voice,

I miss your physical voice. These two truths co-exist and each have standing in this day.

The texture of your voice now flows in many languages: of the wind, of the air, of the sea, of the trees, of music, of flowers, of light, of the moon and the stars, of the birds, and alas, your central spirit's voice that comes from your soul and rings true in my right inner ear. You talk to me and I to you. Some of our conversations are as they always have been. Some are very new. All connect to the wonder of our relationship. Please help me continue to grow in learning to listen.

"Butterfly Eyes"

Awake, and open, wide and true,
Brilliant crystals, diamond bible blue,
With butterflies in her belly,
That rise and flock in her eyes,
The way she looks at me,
So innocently,
So trusting and so wise -

These butterflies - they grace your gardens,
These butterflies - they range in your skies,
Soft butterflies with wings of silk rainbows,
I see as you dream in my eyes.

*

The Owl and the Earth Walkers 09/26/2018

In angst and pure pain, I sat outside in the darkness and stillness of the night attempting to balance, attempting to contact my baby, and ask, "May I see you? Can you touch me? Can you talk to me, Sweetheart?"

I sat in the silence taking slow breaths, recalling the murderous moments I clawed my way through this day. I noticed then, as I glanced out across the yard, that there were two deer up the street at

643

our old house, just seven properties away. They were walking my way. I sat quietly attempting to blend in so they could walk close by as they passed. And waited.

They stopped on the next door neighbor's lawn, foraging in peace near the sidewalk. A streetlight hung in the trees above them as one walked to the median strip of grass between the two one way streets. The other stood on the tree lawn.

"Kayleigh," I whispered, "aren't they beautiful? We used to always do this together. I could always count on you sitting and being patient long enough for nature to unfold."

"Oh, Daddy, they are so cute," she said, "I love them."

I was reminded of the effort that was required of me to punch through these dimensions, raising my vibration and staying close to her, and said to her, "you can see the deer whenever you want, but you can't see them with me if I'm not out here looking. I've got to be out here looking. Remember, that's one of the things you've been telling me this last year."

Suddenly a majestic white and brown barn owl landed on a thick branch above the deer in the median strip, just beside the lantern, magnified under the powerful lamp. She was staring down at the deer below her. And the other. Back and forth - seemingly watching over them with a delicate, yet watchful eye.

Kayleigh. She had come. I felt it. I sat in a deeper quiet and watched the owl watch the deer. Intentionally.

After five minutes she stretched her wings, and on a breath, bound into the air and over our lawn, across the open yard of our neighbor to the right and into the trees in the following yard.

I jumped up from my front steps and walked across the grass and slowly stepped under the trees where I thought the owl would be. I sensed her sensing me. I knew she could see me even though I could not see her.

Content with the power of the moment I turned back to our yard and a sudden figure caught my eye - a third deer, one I had not seen, had stepped towards me from across the street. The other two were where they had been - in the now far neighbor's yard and the median strip. I walked back to my yard and it followed me. Sitting in the grass momentarily so I could observe it and pray for it and talk to it, the deer soon indicated that it wanted to cross my yard and hesitated. I moved back to the steps so he could pass.

It was then that I fully realized, now with the third deer - the owl had been tracking along the branches and following the three deer all the way down the street; guiding them and protecting them. As they moved, so did she. As they entered a new yard, so did she. A guardian. An apex guardian. One winged, white and bright spiritual creature - a spirit in the night, and of the moon, watching over three earth walkers, tracking through the yards and the grasses, the days and the hours. Kayleigh. Nathaniel. Jessica. Me.

She had arranged that I witnessed this. She had lined the pieces together. She felt my pain. My anger with God. My equal gratitude for God. My confusion and loneliness. My request that she sit with me. It was all there in a cauldron of human emotion. And she came. As an owl, guiding three earth walkers through a night. I remained in the yard and watched the three deer meander down the long street until they were out of view, the owl flying above them, tracking their paths into the night.

*

Watching a Warrior Rise 10/01/2018

And then I watched a warrior rise. In those first days after the assault, she was not eloquent in her throws of emotion nor a sweet melody of acceptance, yet she was fiercely determined to love herself. Someone had left a mess at her feet in her yard and she understood that it was incredibly unfair not only to have been harmed, but also to have to then do extra work to deal with the trauma; that she would need to care for herself even more than she already did; she would need to do the work to heal, no matter how unfair the situation and how illogical it seemed.

She started on a multi prong attack - therapy; and putting therapeutic tools in action, by example, art, long walks, journaling, prosecuting. All at once. Such pressure. Such pain. At fourteen. Yet in its midst, a warrior rose to the occasion and she defined the moment in the manner she intended. I watched her draw a line in the sand and advocate for herself and for others. I watched a fourteen year old turn into an ancient sage. I watched a young girl turn into a wise and brutally strong woman. I watched a warrior rise. And now she is asking me to follow her lead, and likewise, rise as a warrior.

"Honey, I am Coming!"

My Daughter, she is calling,
But no strain eclipsed her voice,
She on the near other side of the wind,
Cheering her Daddy forth,
Studying the air I find,
I shall not be deterred,
I will shred any barrier,
And claw through any wind to get to her,
Tearing down the barricades,
Ripping down the breeze,
Like they were heavy wooden sidings,
Blocking her from me,
And with my fingers bleeding,
And hands swollen from the pain,
I rested to regain my strength,
And then I tried again,
Yet for my Daughter,
Across the all the while,
Filled with golden light,
And her gorgeous golden smile,
Knowing the Kingdom her Father scurried for,
Its entrance - requires a life to live,
Then simply cross right through its door,
Yet I have thrown myself against a mighty hurricane,
Honey, I am coming,

I am coming,
I am coming,
Until I exhaust the links of these human chains,
And break forth - break forth - in your name.

*

The Shallows and an After Movie Communication 10/04/2018

It was the last Daddy-Daughter genre movie we watched together before the accident. This night we watched it again. The Shallows. Stupid shark movies - that was the special movie type for the KMMs. We relished in it. Nate and Jess, well, they ignored us in this genre and just did something else when we settled into bad shark movies.

Tonight, as I watched Blake Lively on the screen with Kayleigh, I talked to Kayleigh about the two sides of this mortal coin - how she looked so much like Blake; that she would have looked like her in her twenties had the accident not happened. And we talked about the miracle of her sitting on the couch with me watching this movie like nothing ever happened. Two sides of the coin - physical horror and spiritual life.

When we finished watching The Shallows, she told me to go outside and stand in the front yard and watch for her. Listen for her. Be with her. It was quiet. Perfect. I sensed her direction. I walked slowly down our walkway towards her big tree and to the sidewalk. Talking to her. Listening for her. Being.

"Remember last year, Kake, around this time. You gave me a salamander. Just after the accident. Sitting on this narrow stone walkway with grass on either side of it," I said, "they don't do that. They don't just pop out of the grass like that and sit on the walkway. I've never seen that before. It was you. It was a miracle and you made it for me."

We were very present in each other's embrace. Standing, looking up at the tree and the streetlight where she showed herself just days ago as a huge white owl. Now she was talking through the wind. She was touching my hair like electric currents sizzling across water. She was reviving my spirit that had slipped agnostically under the weight of despondency over the previous several days. She was lighting a fire. Restarting my eyes.

I talked to my Dad also and thanked him again for his never ending presence with Kayleigh, remarking how much these two loved each other - how they would never be separated, and how that love continues presently. I walked back up the walkway slowly. I gazed down at my feet. And there it was - a salamander.

Just like last year at this time, I knew immediately by the tone in the air and the words that glanced in my soul that this was Kayleigh leaving me a salamander. They don't live in the grass and on stonework like that. They live underground. Under rocks. Not in our grass. They just don't. Kakes. She did this. She brought me this spirit guide. I scooped him into my hands and delicately carried him closer to the house and lay him on the rock wall along the garden that hugged the house. He scampered off below the rock and found a moist, cool place.

Then I stood there dumbfounded. I had just mentioned her miracle last year, not thinking another would come again like this. But it has. Several other times. I am surprised I was surprised. I should be surprised by nothing anymore. Particularly as it relates to my Babygirl.

And so, with my spirit renewed, and this Daddy and this Daughter continuing to grow closer in an already amazing relationship, I dragged myself to bed where, instead of sleeping, I rejoiced in this miracle and wrote it all down. Bless you, Babygirl. I love you.

*

Intention 10/08/2018

It came up again in my heart today like a chunk of poisoned meat stuck in my throat. You did not intend to get hit. You did not try to get hit. You did not kill yourself. You did not intend harm to yourself in any manner. To the contrary - your intention was simple and innocent; clear and radiating. In your final intention you were meaning to come home to your family, to your comfort, to the seat of love in your soul. My anger in the very few who weaved together this disgusting rumor rises at times, filling my heart with vengeance, hatred, disgust and a waste of time. Their thoughtless behavior is a waste of time. Lastly, once those few were actually told of the truth of your accident, being blindsided by a car in an innocent manner, they understood and retracted their words, some in embarrassment and utter disgrace. What is left here is that likely nobody thinks the accident was more than just that – a horrible, simple accident. Finally, these few found their way to the truth. Why, on top of everything else, I had to go through that, I will never understand.

Your intention was to cross the street. Your intention was to gather your shoes. Your intention was to enter the street to cross the street and only for that sole purpose. Then you were to jump into a car and drive home. Your intention was life. Your intention was gentle. Your intention was happiness. Your intention was to spend time with Mommy and Daddy. Your intention was to come home. And that is it - the last intention of your physical life was magical, beautiful, authentic and sweet.

*

Today A Feather 10/08/2018

I opened my laptop at my desk in our TRW building this morning, plugged it into the network and worked through the morning. Nearing lunch, and knowing I was working in our Brecksville location for the afternoon, I turned it off, closed it up and placed it in my computer bag.

After meeting my Information Security team for lunch, I drove out 271 to 77 to Brecksville. As is our norm, Kakie and I talked and she picked music for me. There were some dead on picks and I listened intently to her voice in my ear, or in the music, or in the atmosphere of our relationship. We love driving and singing together. Always have. Always will.

Then she played "Devorzhum" by Dead Can Dance which I originally was going to use with her six minute recovery-with-art video. As I listened to it, I could see her artwork in my mind and the images of her as a sweet little girl, an older girl, a tween and a young beautiful teen just before the accident.

I thought in an angry, but powerless, protective yet shocked manner, neither of these unrelated events should ever have happened to you, Kakes. I thought about my little girl - compassionate, friendly, dynamic, sweet, hilarious and breathtaking, that most were drawn to naturally - harmed by a rape, from which she empowered herself like a warrior to become even more beautiful, but then struck down in an unrelated, simple and innocent yet horrifically tragic car accident. It was all such horseshit in this horseshit filled world.

I screamed, "Kake! Kake! My little baby!" and burst into shredding high pitched garbled shrieks and barbed wire tears, slurring into bubbling words chopped up in the sobbing. The noises I make in these moments sounds like a banshee being skewered by a tree.

I sobbed with screams of torture as I continued to drive down the highway, screaming out to her over and over again, "Kakie! My little Kakes! This should never have happened! Not to you! My little girl! My little girl!"

The shock, the longing, the physical absence - it hits me like that at times, a complete guttural powerlessness, the perpetual hyena in a metal box, scratching insanely in circles at the barrier edges and finally, with bloodied paws, screaming and collapsing in exhaustion.

She held my hand. She asked me to breathe with her. Just breathe. She mimicked the depth of the breath she wanted from me. I listened.

I tried. I breathed. She turned to me and said, "Daddy, I am right here, Daddy. Right here." She comforted me back into my breath as my tears slowed and I once again could talk at my normal pitch and voice. She sat there in the passenger seat smiling at me and nodding to me with her sweet smile - so proud of me and so thankful for our devotion to each other.

I reached work just in time to find an office and start a conference call. I pulled out my computer, opened it, and turned it on. And there it was - a white silky feather, about an inch long, laying on the keyboard near the top keys. Penetrating the physical matter of this physical dimension, she placed a white feather where one had earlier not existed, in a way that I would know was a special gift from her, and in a way that I would know was a real miracle and truthful proof of her divinity and everlasting love and devotion she has for her Daddy.

And from there, the day proceeded forth...until the next wave - each of which she will never permit me to face alone.

"Daddy, as Things Come I Will Be There"

And the day - it's time, a toll,
As the weight caves in the soul,
And caverns scavenged by the blue buzzards,
A spirit nearly smothered,
Gangrene,
And bones picked clean,
Worry, wanting, suffering,
And they squawk and belch and groan,
And shit upon the sacred stones,
Jewels and gems,
Lodged into the firmament,
And cold in a darkness -

For the light that never enters,
There is nothing more to steal,
For the light to never enter,
A soul would be found sealed,
For the light to never enter,

A soul could not feel,
All that it would need,
For life to appeal,
To its hidden springs.

*

Dear Fathers and Friends 10/10/2018

My name is Kevin Michael Mooney. My family was exiled from
Ireland during The Famine in January 1847. My GGG Grandfather,
Michael Mooney, at the time 21, the only survivor. Our cottage was
a small hovel somewhere within a one mile radius or so of Knock
Cross I believe on the road to Roscrea. Our family's story is posted
on roscreathroughtheages.org under Michael Mooney.

I have been planning to come home to Ireland to visit for a long time
as the family has never returned to Knock Cross. This trip has become
even more important as one of my two children, my beloved
daughter, Kayleigh Mickayla Mooney, was struck by a car and
physically killed and spiritually released at the age of fifteen, on
August 17, 2017 in our hometown of Cleveland, Ohio. Our heartache
is immense, but Kayleigh's enduring spirit and presence is larger,
miraculously walking with us daily.

I am writing to you to ask if we can meet to conduct a candle lighting,
or prayer service or a simple blessing at St. Patrick's at Knock Cross,
the parish grounds from which our family emigrated. We arrive in
Dublin early morning on the 24th and will be in and around Roscrea
and Knock between October 24-27th.

In advance, God bless you and thank you for considering this
incredibly poignant opportunity for our family to pray for and with
its most cherished daughter in the grounds where once our family
prayed.

*

Time 10/15/2018

It is a truth that must be accepted to catch a mere glimpse into the lives of families who have suffered the physical death of a child in childhood, the awful truth of time. I have had people tell me some quite horrible things in attempts to cheer me up, which, by the way, I do not need. Things like, "you're still young, maybe you can have another child," or "maybe you can adopt," or "at least you have another child," or "this too shall pass," or "time heals all wounds," or "give time time." Each of these, every last one of them, and all other variations of these sentiments, are catastrophic, abysmal failures of an individual to get out of his or her own way and just listen. All of these statements are just stupid, which causes, not a closeness, but a pushing away and an isolation to the grieving parents. Whomever you are in my life – who have not suffered the physical death as I have – think clearly – do you really think that I need a misguided platitude to keep my life from falling apart. It is really quite silly. What we need is for others to just listen. To allow us the space and safety to collapse and cry and rise again. Over and over, every day if need be. If this does not seem appropriate to you, whomever you are, you are free to exit my life. In the long run, you will end up causing more harm to me and my family, and it is better that we part ways now.

Time is not an ally. It does not get better. The cruel truth and answer is – it doesn't get better – not ever; it actually gets worse over time as we get further from her physical days. The complexity is vexing. Also, what we define as "it" does not matter. In many ways it incrementally gets worse day after day. Time is a thief of the worst magnitude. Time is – all of the things she doesn't get to do; all that I don't get to do, including stealing potentially being a grandfather away from me. Two things grow and get stronger: (1) the losses as they accumulate, and (2) our resilience – after we suffer one thousand times over, we get used to the lashes. And my relationship with Kakes, withstanding that type of pain, and still standing, gets stronger.

"Breath Thief"

The gravity has compressed,
My backbone to my chest,
And travelers they pass on by,
Unaware and none the wise,
They never can unless they too,
Have lived within these tortured shoes,
And scabs that rip and shred awake,
Each time I yearn the breath to take,
These wounds, alive, they never heal,
I reconcile, but don't congeal,
And this - this is as this should be,
A Father's love and Father's grief,
It may take my breath, this thief,
But it can never take from me,
My Daughter, for her brilliant soul,
Has grown at least a thousand fold,
And pushes breath back into chest,
Each time I face another threat.

*

"Every Breaking Wave" 10/14/2018

You did it again today. Kayleigh, you are my saving grace. I was playing U2. Mommy and I were talking and she said, "Remember when your Mom was here and Kayleigh played a U2 song on her phone. Your Mom didn't even know she had the album on her phone and it just started playing all by itself." We laughed at Nana's expense.

"Yeah, I remember for sure. She played 'Iris' which is a song Bono wrote about his mother and she played it right after I was frustrated with my Mom and Kakes was telling me to be gentle with my Mom. Remember in DC at the U2 show right before she came to town, when they played "Iris" I hit the floor sobbing thinking about Kayleigh.

And then a few weeks later Kakes played it on Nana's phone all of sudden while it sat alone near Kayleigh's ashes."

We then played Iris while I made French toast. I sobbed all the way through it, my chest convulsing to the tears, standing beside Mommy who listened to every word and sang along somberly. You had already picked me off the floor five or six times this morning and it was only ten am. It would end up being twenty times by the time the day closed.

A half hour later I went to get a new phone and received a text from my Mom. You knew I needed your comfort. You always know how to comfort me. Her text read simply, "I was brushing my teeth in the other room this morning and your Kayleigh played some song called "Every Breaking Wave" on that U2 album on my phone. It was just sitting there on the table, just like when I was at your house, and she played it all by itself."

Of course you did. I talk to others about the waves of grief that catch and crash and crack along the beaches of my soul; the hurricanes, the thunderstorms, the misty foggy mornings, the rainbows in a tropical storm, the tidal waves that drown me nearly. Your choice today was incredibly on point, as usual, as you watched me stand in the shallows and absorb a tiger wave, and another and another, pouncing, shredding. Wailing. Sobbing. Anguishing within my skin. Breathing out the horror and turning to be knocked off of my feet yet again, only to stand up again and turn back towards the tumultuous tide and the storms raging over the ocean that looms above my eyes.

You do not want me to get caught in the waves. Just let them pass. They are real, but they are just waves. I hear you Kayleigh. I promise you I will "stop chasing every breaking wave..."

You are the promise. You lost your physical body and in the transition gained your spiritual body. You have also gained the glory of Heaven in the spiritual world while retaining your presence in the physical world. You are the light that graces two worlds, the link between this life and the next, higher life; between God and those of us still captured in our human condition. Your miracles and blessings abound. Sing your truth, Honey - we are listening. We are watching. We believe.

"Riding the Rainbow Home"

Beachcomber come breach the doorway with a collection of unique treasures,
Stranded on the high tide when the ocean took its measure,
Your selections of salty jewels - deliberate and judgment free,
Purple shells, like shining purple roses,
Sparkle on the doorstep of the sea,
As the rain, it hydrates my eyes - these eyes that have seen too much,
A rainbow burns through the mist with a colorful brush,
And alights my pathway home.

*

Laugh Until We Cry 10/16/2018

We used to laugh until we cried - now I cry until I laugh. After you have been punched in the face a thousand times you get used to the sting. You get accustomed to it. Even though the sting is the same, its impact reduces. The acclimation to the pain is a pivotal component. Without that socialization to the unthinkable, life would be unbearable.

I think fondly on moments when we laughed so hard, our eyes locked, further egging on the other to open our mouths wider, until the convulsions burst through the seams and we literally started sobbing from pure hilarity. It would roll on for a few minutes until we caught our breath. Almost falling out of chairs. Off of couches. Off of beds. Out of swing sets. These are by far my favorite moments between us - this unbridled happiness and laughter.

The inverse seems to occur now, although I do find myself in new situations with you where I start laughing my ass off. Those occasions are rare, however. Mostly the tears come. And come. It is not pathological or me not "doing my work." It is just grief. Grief for its own sake. A deep wave amongst smaller waves, all ever present in this new un-normal life thrust upon me. It is healthy. It is processing.

These are very hard and emotive cries. Shoulder bouncing, guttural, full impact cries, combined with shrieks of words that pitch around in my mouth as they try to make sentences. And then a heavy, heaving breath. And laughter. And a shake of the head - the, my God, what the hell happened to my life, yet knowing clearly and cruelly exactly the what.

Worry not, Babygirl, you did nothing wrong, Sweetheart. It was just an accident. Let it not take away our laughter. It is up to me to ensure the laughter emerges from the cries. Empower me with your light. Lift me higher. Laugh with me, My Love.

"Exhaustion"

And the thunder captured in the lungs,
A king's ransom, a bandage and a drum,
Blisters manage adhesion to the heels,
Skins have thinned him as he is overcome;

With a weak voice expelled without a sound,
Feet rake the hinterland and ashen, absent grounds,
With a makeshift walking stick he comes,
Stagger through the sagebrush and dragging chafing tongue;

Still, devotion, it stirs him to carry forth,
He dreams of his children and never breaks his course,
They are dancing in his eyes and in his heart and light,
They are two mornings - rise in two worlds,
Divisible by night.

*

Right There - Kayleigh is Right Here 10/18/2018

We were watching Expedition Unknown tonight about near death experiences. Participants on the show told their stories. One told if being immersed in perfect light - with only two emotions - pure love and pure peace. Then they showed a frame with bright golden, warm light on the program. It reminded me of what Kayleigh described to me after the accident. I was sobbing. Soft sobs.

I turned to Spirit and pet him and said through my tears, "I'm so happy for my girl that she lives in that light, but I am also so sad as I miss her physically so much." Kissing him, I turned to Jess and said, "That's what Kayleigh saw as she transitioned - a sudden warm, golden flash that blasted down all of the streets out from where she lay. She told me and showed me that. She told me, 'Daddy, that's where I met Heaven.'"

I looked down at my phone. A message on Facebook had just come through while we were watching the story and talking. It was Michelle from Beaumont who had just commented on one of my posts stating her thanks for being affiliated with our family and quoting the words, "right there."

I scanned up to see what picture she had posted on and it was a piece I called, "This is Where I Met Heaven, Daddy." I knew exactly what was happening and turned down into the words to see where Michele was quoting from and read, "And then this brilliant blinding light appeared through this incredible doorway. Right there, Daddy, in the street."

Michele had also just sent me a friend request. She's never posted anything on my wall before. Just this one. Just this piece. Right there. Right now.

We are listening, Kakie. We hear you. We believe.

*

658

This Life Is Just A Keyhole 10/25/2018

I had been thinking about this for quite some time. It took me a bit to articulate it. Looking at this physical life is really like looking through a keyhole and missing the grand splendor of all we have in our lives. Everything not captured in this lens is, by its nature, surrounding this lens and much bigger and deeper than this narrowing scope. We miss the bigger life, that life beyond human skins.

Kayleigh's life continued on August 17, 2017 as she, through a horrific accident, burst through the confines of that keyhole and opened her beautiful life up to the fullest beauty of her higher life. Some may call this the afterlife, but I do not. For how does something come after that which never ends? Heaven is the higher life - a soul's full expression of perfect peace and love.

While I live this life, I am in the keyhole. Kayleigh is not, cheering me on to bend and break the mold, to push out from the human cage, to permeate the space beyond the keyhole. Far too many people stare down the barrel of the keyhole, and in the collective human experience, it becomes the glittering light, the shiny object, the center of the combined gravitational pull towards the finite bounds of a human life measured from birth, upon first breath, to physical death, with the last breath. That is the keyhole. That is the lie. That is the trap to true growth and understanding. At the same time, it is also the reality of this plain and so it must be treasured. It does not, however encompass the totality of life as life truly has no horizon. So live this life to the fullest, but know that it is not an end to itself.

My child is not stuck within the flurry of the keyhole, although I do, in my selfishness and in my grief, wish the accident had never happened. She is a million times bigger and stronger than its grip, which has its hold on me. I will live to the fullest as I have strived to do most of my life. In so doing I honor myself, Kayleigh, Nate and Jess. At the same time, I look out passed the barrier of the keyhole and know beyond its tunneled limits a vast world of God's light and love awaits.

"Your Light Body II"

One million points of God's own light,
One million vibrations of your current, loving life,
Radiates;

When the great transition shed your human skin,
Your light body bloomed and emerged from within,
And resonates -

You are rainbow brilliance dancing on a diamond's face,

One million stars lighting up and sparkling galaxy lakes,
You are the guardian in this physical world,
An angel, my companion,
A constant presence, my Little Girl,
Guiding safe passage through random waves and rash of storms,
From end to end - life through life - shore to shore.

*

Knock 10/29/2018

In January, 1847, my GGG grandfather and his parents and sisters, victims of the Great Hunger, were evicted from their cottage in Knock Cross on the road to Roscrea, Tipperary. All died except for my Michael. 171 years later, this last week, the family gathered again for a prayer service in our Knock Cross church for Kayleigh Mickayla, my Daughter of Knock/Roscrea, whose middle name bares Michael's in his honor. 171 years between visits to this church - for you, Kayleigh, My Love. We are unbreakable.

*

Awakening 10/30/2018

There are many. For some, there are none. Awakenings come at different junctures of ones journey - but for the untrained eye, or the untried heart, these junctures may pass them by. It is innately human to choose one's openness and one's ability to become awake. It is entirely possible for someone to live their days completely unaware. And that is sad.

I do not want to miss the mission; the moments when they come. I have had several. One in particular that is dearest to me. To become awake one must first learn how to become unawake. This is easy. It is, at its crux, being unaware. Unaware of one's own defects and assets. A total lack of self-awareness. I see men and women like this constantly. They are usually managing others, which I find quite fascinating. They are frequently managing their direct reports in ways that are not conducive to moral or building leaders. They are clueless. They the blind.

Sometimes they will, in the depths of being unaware, have a golden moment and emerge with a renewed sense of vigor, attempting to recapture their lost time, lost lives or lost dreams. Some will claw out a new name for themselves - in the furtherance of helping others. For me, awakenings have become a way of life for three decades. This latest awakening, the active engagement of Heaven, much earlier than I ever dreamed I would need to, is the hardest and most important awakening of my soul.

*

Newgrange 10/30/2018

Five thousand year old Irish passage tomb, surrounded by ninety seven stones. We are here. On the winter solstice at 8.58 hours, the sun will catch through the roof box and illuminate the burial chambers within. Yet here in October, we are here; we are home; together. I held your hand, sweet Daughter of Ireland, and carried your funeral stones through the passage, watching your eyes glimmer in the fascination of walking these grounds with your family.

*

Nate 11/01/2018

Gladly, I fulfilled a promise to you, my Little Love, and to your sister, on our journey through the homeland of Ireland. I am in love with you, my strong yet gentle boy - and my heart breaks for you - at such an early age, as our lives were singing along effortlessly, you have lost so much in this tragedy; have been stripped of your sister's physical presence, who's love you share so tenderly; have watched your parents crumble and crumble and rise again and again. I have showed you how to live, to grieve, to laugh, to be confused, to anguish, to be angry, to reconcile, to breathe, to be human and to stand again. You and your sister - you are our everything. I hold you in one hand and Kayleigh in the other, being with both of my children at the same time in two different worlds, in two different body types. I am me because of you two, and I will lead you through the maelstrom and down this road that became so treacherous after the innocence of Kayleigh's horrific accident. My Son, the best Son in the world, we will walk through this nightmare together illuminated by Kayleigh's beacon of brilliant light. She holds us. She loves you like no other. Mommy, Daddy, Nathaniel, Kayleigh - we are an unbreakable family of four.

"This Boy"

He with the wounding thorough,
He with the banshee cries,
He with the soul wrapped golden,
He with the gentle eyes;

Then in a moment arbitrary,
Then when his sister simply tried,
Crossing the street to gather shoes,
Yet then his sister died;

Shocked into sudden horror,
Shocked outward from the inside,
He with the soul wrapped golden,
Ripped out from his side,
He with the strength and promise,
He with the love he hides…

…See this warrior of light,
You can see it in his eyes,
He will grow stronger,
And wealthy wise.

*

In the Flesh of Light 11/02/2018

Transitioned into the flesh of pure light and love, these millions of points of radiance, you are. In your presence, in awe, I rest, I breathe, and I embrace my child. When this tragic accident stole from all of us your physical life, as you took your final breath in your physical body and in my arms and within my aura, you blasted through this transition in a blinding innocence, shedding your human body to which we had become accustomed, and were replaced with your new body fleshed with light.

This light body existed prior to your birth; remained within you during your physical life; released in your physical death and transition. In that moment, this flesh of light persisted from within - reaching out from the center of the soul and filling in the space where once the physical flesh was framed, replaced it with dazzling galaxies of brilliant light - a million sparkling rainbow suns and golden stars illuminating and pouring into the mold and outline of your physical form, and standing beside me as if no physical death had removed your presence. It is you, my dear Kayleigh, stronger and more wonderful than ever. I will enhance our relationship any way I can. I will stretch and mold my mind and soul around your needs and your Brother's needs just as I have always done. I am listening.

"A Higher Mission"

Tears, whether wet or weathered dry,
Claw the walls of my insides,
Every day, My Love, wishing for you -

Never more across the yard,
And in an instant my life is hard,
My very heart explodes from missing you –
The Lord, He cried at the impact zone,
And filled your spirit with an angel's gold,
Heaven's Father in the act of gifting you -

Yet your Earthly Father, in love with you,
Asked to do the hardest thing a Daddy can do,
Hold your body as your light lifted from you -

And I see the glory of this today,
For I see the morning rises with your face,
I feel the rising of your love and your grace,
As you wrap your arms around the day,
And pull it towards me,
You wrap your arms around the day,
And lift it for me;

I have memories and photos of your blue eyes,
Feed me the energy of the skies,
Our mission now is stronger than this plain,
Remind me of this, please, a million times.

*

Linda Reading 11/03/2018

Jess and I sat with an intuitive woman. Immediately Linda stated that
she felt two extra presences. One with blonde hair, a girl. Kakes. The
other was taller. She said it was my Dad. Brilliant light flowed in.

Kakes showed her massive light. Linda has never seen that type of angelic light so brightly in a reading.

Through Linda, Kakes turned to me and said that I was brilliant. She thought I was the brilliant one when I told Linda that Kakes was brilliant. Kakes then showed her hands like they were my hands holding her – - that I am her protection. She was safe always. She felt safe always with me and Mommy. She was safe in life and during the transition. She relies on us equally, Kayleigh said through Linda, but in different ways. Like two different kinds of hands pulling her up. One was firm and one was soft.

I was the humor. Kayleigh told us through Linda, do not let it die. It is a healing agent. She loves our laughter and I shared that Kakes plays with the Bluetooth and I joke that I threaten to sing to her in my awful singing voice. Linda said that Kakes wants that to continue.

She then said that Kakes was falling, but was then picked up. Linda suggested that Kayleigh was saying that Mommy is currently falling, and then Linda said that Kayleigh had just corrected her; that Jess was not falling, but was drowning. There is a distinction. Kakes kept clarifying her, trying to get Linda to say the right words.

Kakes is worried about Jess - wants her to just be and take care of herself. She loves Jess massively. Doesn't want Jess to question it. During physical life they had such a strong and gentle bond. Kayleigh was telling us that strength continues.

She said she had the most amazing physical life. Would never have made it through tough events without our support. That there were nit-picky things like in any relationship, but very, very few negative moments. That her life was filled with love. With light. We are incredibly special and strong. That there are no parents out there like us. She is blessed. Lucky. Grateful. Couldn't have had better parents.

Linda said she felt a situational heavy feeling in her chest, transferred from Kayleigh through this channel of communication. We explained that Kakes, when she went through puberty, had a shift of chemistry and some depression and that she conquered it. Then she was assaulted, and likewise, stood tall and conquered it. Linda said that makes sense.

I said that we, as her parents are Kayleigh's Cradle of life – Linda said that Kakes had just interrupted and said that it was much more than that.

I told Linda about the car accident and how Kayleigh passed. Kakes then said her Transition was perfect, that it couldn't have been better being in her Daddy's arms. There's a reason it was me. I permitted or allowed her that moment because I was on point and focused on her transition and she is so amazed and thankful that I was so strong. Kakes said her heart breaks for me for having to suffer through that but she is so happy - her heart breaks for us for losing her physically but she is so happy. That it was meant to happen. It was going to happen. If not that night the next. Like Mommy says, when it's your time it's your time. And it was her time. But it was perfect because she was in Daddy's hands and Daddy passed her to God and into the light. No one is at fault said Kakes. It was not even a mistake on either part. It just happened. A perfect accident where neither the driver nor Kayleigh saw the other at the exact same time.

Linda said to us, translated from Kayleigh, not to underestimate us and our beauty and amazement. Kakes wants us to know we aren't just good people. We are way beyond that. We are pure light like her. We are strong. We are great souls. When Linda would use a qualifier word in this conversation, Kayleigh would correct her and use a higher level word. Like good people to amazing people. We had never met Linda before. Kayleigh picked her. Kayleigh knew she could communicate through her. And she did.

*

A Prayer of Healing 11/03/2018

Avenge only the truth. Let revenge reverberate and vibrate into itself until it transforms into ribbons and echoes of blinding light. Let the soul wounds incapable of healing be respected and revered as such, and their owners reconcile this loss daily in the reconstruction of their lives. If there be a weapon, let it be love, pounding like a hammer against the pliable edges of a credo firmly entrenched in the finite spaces of the human mind. Think deeper - bigger - with the mechanism of the soul rather than the mechanically limited and often defective brain, into which the higher self will rise into others for the mutual joy and prosperity of life. True life. Higher life. Love and rise higher. Let this message unfold....

*

Begrudgingly 11/04/2018

Begrudgingly everything we do we do now without you in your physical form. But gratefully, everything we do now we get to do with you in your spiritual form. We do nothing without you. It is our family of four. Our creed.

*

Love Is All We Have Left 11/05/2018

On Saturday I was listening to U2's "Achtung Baby." It was not on shuffle. I was listening to "The Fly," which was midway through the song as I was trying to turn right into a department store driveway and realized that five cars in front of me was dead, blocking the turning lane with an island on either side. All the cars were stuck behind it. I shot around to the left in the other lane and took a right into that second turn lane and glanced at the driver as I drove passed. A man.

I drive on and Kayleigh said, "Daddy, it's you. Nobody else is going to help. But you do. So do."

I drove up and into the parking lot of Beachwood Place and parked. I ran across the parking lot and down the narrow driveway to his side and said, "Hey man, let's get this car moving. Put it in park and push from the door and I'll push from behind."

He was quite surprised, but grateful. We started pushing this car up the slight incline, yearning and scratching our way out of the driveway until we cleared the neck of the parking lot and we swung his dead car into the lot. He thanked me. I smiled, knowing it was a higher calling.

As I ran back to my car I hear Kayleigh say to me, "it's all about love. Daddy, that's what we have. That's why we are here. You loved this man and he knows a stranger helped him."

I turned on the car expecting to hear "The Fly," as that was what I was listening to, and was surprised that she had changed the music, as she frequently does, but specifically to "Love Is All We Have Left," by U2. Not only did she shuffle it away from "Achtung Baby," she deliberately moved it to another U2 album, and specifically to this song about love - lyrics of which she was just sentimentally speaking into my ears as I ran back to the car.

She did it again and again that day. I went to the store and it reset and started freshly on that song. She played it a dozen times. The last time I drove that night I listened through the first four songs.

Then on Sunday. I was with Jess as we jumped in the car to go to Tommy's and it started over again, even though it was three songs further on that album from the night before. We drive to the transition site after breakfast. When we jumped back in the car, it reset again even though it was on the next song, "Lights of Home." It happened again and played through and to the next song again, "Lights of Home" which played half way by the time I got home. Then I was leaving to go to the cemetery to my Dad's plot, and I thought, I hope she doesn't play it again because I don't want to get sick of it. "Kakes, no I didn't mean that," I said, "I don't want you to not do a miracle. I was just thinking I don't want the miracle to diminish." I really, however, did not want it to stop. She is amazing.

When I turned on the car, it did not turn back and I was a little bummed, instead playing "Lights of Home" and continuing from there as I drove. After my visit to the cemetery I jumped in the car and she reset it to "Love is All We Have Left" and I smiled and I heard her laugh. She was picking and choosing when to play it and ensuring she was manipulating the music enough that I knew it could not be a coincidence. It was so clearly deliberate and intentional. It wasn't an electrical issue or a string of code on the phone. It was Kayleigh, in her flesh of light, in the spirit dimension that overlay the physical dimension. It is real.

Today's biggest lesson: we are building our relationship and adding songs as we go, adding to our memories, adding to our relationship even though her physical body has ended. Her spiritual body is. Kayleigh is. She is right here. She is alive. She is pure white light. She is love, more than I could possibly understand. And she is in love with me. Me. How lucky am I, living in the presence of a guardian angel and it is my beloved daughter.

She then decided to push the message home and played it for a week. Over and over for 7 days and then it stopped...

"In The Moon..."

Shockingly bright,
She is no passive light,
That hangs over the night,
Just pleased with her glow,
Not this one, no -

She is active in flight,
And engaged in this life,
And heals the ways of this soul,
For she lovingly knows...

...The fields of glittering silver that glow upon my sea,
These rivers of stars that flow within me,
Entangled in my galaxies,
That loom in luminescence in her palm -

669

She is courageous and powerful,
Centuries strong,
She has learned to bridge two worlds and its wound,
She is the glowing reflection of God's own light,
That pools with love's perfection,
And radiates in the moon.

*

Word Thief 11/07/2018

Sometimes I can't find words. Or there are no words. And I just sit with you. Sometimes, My Love, I sit still and quietly like flowers in a vas, nourished by depleting water. My body stretched out over your bed. Longing for your arms. Your touch. Your voice. Cycling memories. Mourning. Grieving. Numb.

"Your Pen"

My fingers await you, Author,
My hand your willing pen,
My soul an open country,
For you to walk from end to end,
My heart, though bombed and broken,
It's bones in shards but not condemned,
My life a channel for your calling,
Your voice that has no end,
And so the words await you, Daughter,
My hand your willing pen.

*

Look Up, Daddy 11/08/2018

I have been the main speaker at over a few dozen A.A. meetings since the accident. I am not a dumb man. I know the significance of my journey with Kayleigh to those in A.A. struggling, those who think they could not stay sober under stressful situations and those that need a lift. After I led I was sheepish listening to comments. People were telling me I saved them - I impacted them - I was a power of example.

Kayleigh put her arm around me and hugged me. "Daddy, look up. Look up, Daddy. Look at these people. They are saying you saved them or helped them through the years. Its okay, Daddy. Listen to them. Take it in. Own it. They are telling you that you affected them greatly. So wear it and be proud. You did this, Daddy and they are acknowledging you. I am so proud of you."

*

She Played the Ocean for Me 11/08/2018

I had three browser windows open earlier today. Early in the day I was listening to the ocean on a three hour YouTube feed. It had been turned off for a few hours. As the day was ending, I opened up another browser and checked my LinkedIn account. After a few minutes I went to pick up a document on the printer and thought about Kakie and thought, my God I can't believe my Little Girl was physically killed! Kayleigh!

She said in my ear, "breathe. It's okay. I'm right here," as I walked back to my office. As I stepped in my office, I heard a noise and looked at my computer. The browser to LinkedIn was open as I had left it a few minutes earlier. However, the ocean browser was playing in the background - that YouTube video had begun playing while I was out of the office. She turned on the ocean for me.

"Upon the Winds Aglow"

We are, as if the wind were fleshed in light,
Waves of luminous energy alive in silky flight;
She holds in her palms a thousand galaxies, ignite,
They rise in the beauty of her eternal life;
And in this frenzied bouquet of suns and stars alight,
She transforms into morning a mourner's darkly night;
Washing through this earthly plain upon the winds aglow,
Illuminating those she loves with the presence of her soul.

*

November Reading 11/14/2018

Jess sat for a reading today with a woman who knows nothing about us. Within the first few minutes, Kayleigh presented herself to the woman and told her, and she turned and told Jess, "my funeral was amazing - you guys pulled out all the stops. When Daddy was up at the podium I had my arms wrapped tightly around him. When Mommy and my Brother were at the podium I did the same with them."

Only those at her funeral would know that I went up to eulogize Kayleigh, just after Mommy and Nate did a reading together. It was supposed to be Mommy alone, but Nate stood by her side, and took over for Jess when she could not read.

Kayleigh continued to tell this woman that she loved the big pictures at her funeral, but she would have picked several different pieces. That, "when Daddy sits quietly that's when he is in the most pain" (like what I do each night on her bed), that "it was an accident and she felt like she was suddenly thrown out of her body; that she felt tingling but no pain; that she wasn't alone and all of a sudden Jesus was holding her hand!!" (Like footprints on her wall). That "she is kind of frustrated that it happened like that as she didn't see it coming - she thought that she was supposed to get sick and die slowly from

672

it, but this accident changed that - but she's so alive and happy" that "she wants Mommy to make strawberry shortcake - when a loved one makes a special dish an angel can taste it and it tastes the best that way" (Jess used to make strawberry shortcake for the kids two or three times a week for years before school).

Kayleigh kept redirecting the lady while she sat on her healing bench. She kept throwing her head back laughing and the lady said what they all say - that she is really powerful and full of pure light. She also said she saw her holding fancy shoes and they were in a special place and she sometimes moves them, "it's not an animal - it's me and on purpose," said Kayleigh (like her high heeled shoes under her altar holding her ashes). That she comes to little Brother all the time, but he can't feel her much and he doesn't know how to be open, so she comes to him in his dreams.

She told this intuitive woman that, I sings with my family and mess around with the radio all the time! I'm literally with my family all the time. Please tell them to never doubt it."

The woman told Jess that Kayleigh conveyed to her that Kayleigh is not ever leaving us, stating that she will be present as long as we want her to be present, which is forever. So she is forever present. Jess then asked Kayleigh is Kayleigh felt that she was a good mom and Kakes laughed out loud and said, "I knew she was going to ask me that! Yes, Mommy, you are amazing!"

She continued the conversation by telling this woman that she is picking out her calling still - maybe helping kids pass in war torn areas or working with dogs. This lady has never met Jess and they did the reading over the phone, a referral from someone we met In Ireland two weeks earlier.

*

Daddy, Yes! Yes! - It's Me! 11/16/2018

Back and forth day after day, these two albums…throughout the months she will play different songs, mostly by U2. They are deliberate. Disconnected in any manner other than the meaning within the songs. She is using the lyrics to talk. Now I am in a wonderful cycle where she is shifting back and forth between the "October" album, playing "Gloria," and the "Songs of Experience" album and playing "Love is All We Have Left." Even when I turn off the Bluetooth, or change it to sports radio, or put it on another album by a different band, she will bring it back, as she has been doing now for days upon days, to these two songs in particular. I understand the meaning to both, Honey. Keep rolling. Keep shining brightly.

When she illuminates and blesses us, in any channel she can manage, it doesn't take away the trauma, but it balances it out. We have the chance to stay balanced. She knows what we need and provides it just in time to keep us balanced; like walking across a footbridge and there is a plank missing, but before my foot presses into the empty space, she quickly slides a new board into that opening to catch my foot. Over and over again. If she can balance out the trauma a day at a time, that's as good as it'll get, but that level of good is far better than the alternative. It's quite amazing. That level of good is living in a modern miracle. Thank God for that balance.

"Always Was"

Always with you - always with me,
Always loving - endless living,
Always lively - always loved,
Always is - always was.

*

U2 – We Get to Carry Each Other... 11/16/2018

"Daddy, I picked U2 because it's one of the many things we share and love. My first concert was beside you, Daddy, at nine at U2. My last concert before my Transition was beside you, Daddy, at fifteen at U2. And we've seen them together twice now since the Transition and I love that we do that! I love all we used to do and I love all that we do now! Thank you for the special songs – I know they are so hard now – when you hold my picture up at concerts now and sing to me for "One" and when you scream my name at the end of "There is a Light," it makes me so happy, Daddy.

It's been fifteen months now and you know I learned how to manipulate your Bluetooth so quickly to communicate with you – remember, it was like my second week! I'm getting better and better at it too! It actually cracks me up watching your reactions. But you always know that I pick the songs on purpose and the words are in them that I want you to hear. And, you're right – the other day when you were listening to U2's album, "Boy" and the song, "I Will Follow," when it switched over right in the middle of the song to the album, "October" and the song, "Gloria," that was me. The best part – you knew it was me, laughed, thanked me and talked to me about it! How awesome are we!

Then as you continued to listen to the "October" album in the car we got to the fifth song singing together and you turned off the car. I couldn't wait until you got back in the car and turned it on, thinking you'd hear the fifth song, and instead I reverted back to "Gloria" again – five different times over the course of the day, until you wondered, fear against truth, if somehow it was the setting on the phone – so the next time you turned the car on, I didn't flip it on. Haha! Then the time after that I did! Then I didn't again. Then I got tricky and the phone read that it was playing the song, "I Fall Down" but I was actually playing "Gloria" And you heard "Gloria" pounding through the speakers. After doing that three more times with three different songs showing, but actually playing "Gloria," you clearly understood. It is me. It is always me. *The door is open, You're standing there, You let me in - Glory in You, Lord / Glory, exalt..."* – pretty cool, huh, Daddy?

And how did you like last week when you were crying and listening to U2's "Achtung Baby" and singing "One" in the car, and in the middle of it I changed it to their album, "Songs of Experience" and the song, "Love Is All We Have Left," and you laughed the same way and knew it was me! I know it can be easy with grief to forget, but I literally did the same thing last week, Daddy, as the songs played in the car on the "Songs of Experience" album, when you parked and then got back in I flipped it back to "Love Is All We Have Left." Remember, I did that almost a dozen times and when you had the same fear, your human mind playing tricks on you, I chose not to flip it back to that song and it kept playing where it left off. But then the next time I got in the car you played "Love Is All We Have Left" yet again! I understood that meaning immediately as I listened to your voice strumming along with Bono as he sang, *"Now you're at the other end of the telescope, Seven billion stars in her eyes, So many stars, So many ways of seeing - Hey, this is no time not to be alive....Love and love is all we have left, a baby cries on the doorstep, love is all we have left..."*

It's amazing that we communicate in so many ways and this is just one of them. I love it. I see how anguishing the grief is for you and how it beats you down – and how amazing your spiritual highs are as you lift your spirit to resonate higher to be with me. It works. You have, what you tell people all the time - an active, current relationship with me even though I am no longer in my physical body and am in spirit. You are the best Daddy ever and you are mine!

So, Daddy, it was again this lunchtime today while you were taking the elevator to the garage and telling your worker about how I've been playing with the Bluetooth again, but this time specifically with U2, and you showed him that the phone was set on the album, "The Unforgettable Fire" and the song, "Pride," which you had been listening to when you drove into work. That "Pride" should play when you two jumped in the car and started to drive. And when you turned on the car, with a witness beside you, what did I play, Daddy? – *"GLORIA!!"* Haha! I love you, Daddy!"

*

676

Counter-Balance 11/18/2018

Before the accident I really felt centered and empowered. Everything was clicking along. I was confident. I used my voice. I changed the world in little ways. Even facing a difficult pain as we did when Kayleigh was assaulted, we had the energy, the reserves, the hope to push forward and conquer the adversity. And we did, led by my magical daughter who showed the strength of a thousand women wrapped up into one in her season of enlightenment.

The best I can hope for now, daily, is my spiritual connection and ongoing relationship with Kayleigh as a counterbalance to the immense grief that I suffer daily. And it is immense.

Most do not stop to think and cannot put themselves in the shoes of a parent who has suffered such a grievous physical loss. The grief is literally around every corner and in each step; not because we are stuck in it or in self-pity or are pathological, but because this is the raw nature of the physical death of a child in childhood. She is always behind me in time - the physical death backwards to nature. I see her friends filling out college papers, visiting colleges, driving, going to dances, watching their siblings play basketball, working at grocery stores - I see cute outfits advertised for girls on TV and think, 'she'd look so cute in that' - every blonde young woman looks like her - every step has a resemblance to what I have lost. And it is immense. I stand there at the doorway of fatherhood each day with outstretched, giving, loving, yet empty hands, yearning to hold her, physical to physical, eye to eye, laughter to laughter, tear to tear. Yet she has been physically killed. In her physical - all is empty handed.

So I can be swallowed by this grief or I can do my work, sometimes a lot of work (meditation, prayer, journaling, Daddy-Daughter walks, etc.) in order to counterbalance the grief and reduce the pain to neutral. I turn to where my Daughter is instead of to where she is not. To the spirit and away from the physical. A pivot. A Daddy searching to be with his child. It is so worth it, but not without incredible exhaustion. It is the hardest work (to penetrate two worlds) and the easiest work (effortlessly loving my children) I've ever done. I do my work and counter the grief down to a manageable cubes of time and space, manageable states of living. And this is about the best that can be expected.

I will never live so effortlessly or freely, the way I did before the accident, again. That is something I need to continue to accept. All of my soul does not want to accept it - does not want to accept the innocence and tragedy of the accident - does not want to accept that my little baby's physical life was destroyed in one horrible, epic moment of tragedy. But I must, or the grief will swallow me. So I grow with my baby, who is brilliant and strong and powerful, and she leads me through the darkness and the numbing pain of daily life, giving me just enough strength to breathe and make this life an okay life - a neutral life in constant counterbalance of this physical loss to the light and glory of this spiritual gain. This permits me to continue to be a great father to both of my children - and to, specifically, engage with Kayleigh as she matures in her spiritual life; to guide Nate through his epic tragedy and on an ongoing basis; to support my beloved wife through her epic tragedy and to nurture myself through the great, unfair robbery of my life. To strengthen as a family of four through the tragedy. How amazing are we.

Kayleigh and I are magic, and Nate and Jess have the same magic with Kayleigh. We both intentionally and devotionally walk with the other. Hand in hand. Right now, though one is in human flesh and the other in the flesh of light. Eventually the spiritual journey she and I are on together will prevail - my physical life will end and we will continue to walk as we do now - yet both in a spiritual embodiment - both in the flesh of light. And in that moment she will hug me and say, with no boundaries of worlds to work through to get to the other, smiling in her brilliant blue eyes, "Daddy, you did it. You did it. I knew you could do it."

*

678

Interwoven Blanket of Light 11/19/2018

We do this together. We all have a part to play. All of us. Kayleigh.
Nathaniel. Mommy. Daddy. Spirit. Rosie. Tiger. Felix. Our family's
other angels. Our angel pets. All of us. Light. Love. Eternity.

"Grief Traveler"

In the blinding light of morning,
Just as the sea blazed silver white,
As the sun comes with its promise,
And obliterates the black, thick veil of the night,
God has opened up,
The broken with a flood,
The grieving parent,
Star gazers,
Grief grazers,
Grief travelers with their faces in the mud;

We are here intending,
We are here in love,
We are here for our children,
We travel this road because…

…There is no other road to travel.

*

When the Lion King Roars 11/20/2018

One of the most resonating pieces of grief work I have absorbed
relates   to the Lion King. To paraphrase, when a gazelle hears the
roar of the Lion King near the river, it instinctively runs in the
opposite direction, and straight into the waiting teeth and claws of a
half dozen lionesses. In traumatic grief we are reminded, that when
we hear the roar of grief, the Lion King, we run straight at it.

And so, my little Babygirl, as nothing will keep me from my children - I lean forward with fury and run dead straight towards the dangerous growl of grief that pitches every day. In full color. Wide awake. In love. Spiritually fit. Battle tested. In pure anguish. With clear intention. With hope and joy and communion in mind. With you, my Daughter, in my eyes, motivating the forward movement of my exhausted, wailing steps. Empowering my soul, you wait for me when the grief comes to block our path, for it is my work - not yours, to be done.

When the Lion King roars I run straight at him, never breaking eye contact. If he can, surprised, he scurries to my side, but I always throw him back before me. If he does not scurry and stands his ground - I tackle him, and in the scuffle - as I crash through the grief and tussle nose to nose in the dirt, eye to eye with the Lion King, I step through him and it becomes a part of my history. Pushing through its trauma, going right though the Lion King, like separating branches to open thick wood to a pleasant clearing, on the other side of its grief I find you there in your glory, alight in your spiritual embodiment, in flowing white gowns sprinkled with galaxies; long, flowing golden sparkling hair; brilliant golden blue eyes and a transcendent smile acknowledging, yes, Daddy, yes...You would run through anything for me. Thank you, Daddy. I am right here. Right here.

*

The Stars on Your Ceiling 11/22/2018

"You're at the other end of a telescope, seven billion stars in her eyes; So many stars - so many ways of seeing...this is no time not to be alive..."

I don't recall how much time it took over how many days. I clearly remember the effort. Mostly I recall the magic of its completion. An entire ceiling covered spatially with perhaps a few thousand glow in the dark stars that looked like the night sky without any light pollution. This included the hundreds of stars I placed on the four blades of her ceiling fan, that when still, gave it a deeper dimension; and when spinning made it look like a flurry of stars in the heavens.

This was your room from age four through nine. We would lay there together, on many nights, across the ages, as I put you to bed at night, staring up at the stars and picking out constellations. I purposely mapped out some of the constellations on the ceiling for you to find. Under the stars. Spending quality time together. While some other fathers were off drinking at bars with their workmates or watching TV or out of town on business for a career they chose, I was lying next to my Kayleigh and my Nate, engaging with my children through their eyes, building our relationships, enchanted by the environment we create.

*

"God's Wheel-barrel" **11/24/2018**

His grace wrapped in a honeycomb,
A sheath of knowledge we are not to know,
A wreath of wisdom where the angels flow,
Why, oh God, and how...

- "No" -

"Do you believe I can cross this river's peril,
On a tightrope pushing a wheel barrel,
Have you the faith that I can traverse...

...Then get inside the barrel first -

And I will cross you to the other side,
While you stare into the dark,
From which you cannot hide,
I will take you where the angels sing,
Deeply, my son, deep inside;"

But the rope, the rope is razor thin,

Across the canyon, a shredding wind,
Walker, is there no other road you see,
If I don't - then what becomes of me,
And if I do - what becomes of me;

The Walker's smile emitted trust,
A spark to eyes of eternal love,
Whatever I was thinking,
He knew what it was -

And so, with trembling, faithful eyes,
As big as this river is deeply wide,
I take my place in the metal barrel,
And I faced the fear that I defy.

*

Kayleigh's Transcending and Nate's Growth 11/25/2018

I have an active current relationship with both of my children. With you, Kakes, it transcends two worlds, Heaven and earth, and is amazing. It is real. It is transcending.

I only need to be in one world for Nate, but because of our relationship transcending two worlds, it lifts mine with Nate even higher. So you continue to have a profound effect upon Nathaniel's life and who he is and who he is becoming. He watches. He struggles. He wants to believe. He is very selective with his grief. Very protective of you. He grieves. He is draped in confusion and anger and sadness. Then he turns to you and somehow he finds his smile.

"Floods of Liquid Light"

The golden waters explode from the fabric,
Flood into a glorious light,
Streams of purple lightning spark,
And horizons expand and ignite,
Farewell to the human condition,

Its cycles of midday and night,
And welcome, Sweet Child, to perfect peace,
The love that flows in your Higher Life;

Your Father - with vision - with senses,
Feels that which he cannot yet see,
His Daughter loves and embraces him,
And his aura - it bursts at the seams,
She is steady and constant,
She with her guidance and grace,
She is the hope that sinks in his skin,
While the grief ploughs new lines on his face;

He lifts his heart and his weary eyes,
Yet battered - he still stands for the fight,
He senses that he is ever surrounded,
In streaming floods of her liquid light,
And Daughter - he gave you the ocean,
He gave you the stage for your dreams,
Dear Father, Dear Father she gives you now,
A glimpse from the kiss of her lips…

…of The Everything.

*

Butterfly 11/27/2018

As a caterpillar I can only walk and I can't fly. But as a butterfly
Kakes can fly and walk. Until my transformation I can only walk.
You can fly and you can walk. Flight is in the spiritual dimension.
Walking in the physical world. I can only lumber in the physical
world. I wish for that day to take flight.

The transformation gave you double the ability while I, still hampered
by my human shell, which withholds my angel wings, am limited to
the slow gate of the caterpillar. I can look upward. I can emulate the

butterfly. I can look forward to the day that my wings too unfurl, but for now, I cannot breach my skin. So I walk. For I must.

"Butterfly with Wings of Light"

Sparks and crystal glitter, a thousand shooting stars in the draft,
Trail behind her fire wings as she floats upon the air,
Like the ocean, rolling waves, holds a raft,
And God - her wind, her effortless breeze,
She swims upon the clouds, her seas,
In a perfect sunrise of perpetual peace,
She, alive - yes, and no, not I,
For if the wind my face to kiss,
Would I, wingless and remiss,
Find the strength to blaze across the sky,
While hampered with the weight of thieving human cries,
While she,
She is, with wings of blinding, golden light,
The melodic flight of the butterfly,
Who has awakened the truth of the ages,
And asks her Father to take her hand,
And rise, rise, rise...

*

Tenth Step: This Is the Shittiest Thing in the World 11/28/2018

The ripple effects concuss across each other and through each other. We are three survivors who are traumatically throwing up on and over each other at times. We are a family of four, a car with four tires, who has lost one of its tires, flying down the highway rattling, swerving, bumping, banging and dangerously close to recklessly being out of control and somehow we are asked to continue to drive. Thank God Kayleigh is driving or we would all be sunk.

Nate is sobbing in the car and can't get out to go to school. He is afraid of people asking him questions and feeling like a loser. If he doesn't go to school, the trauma defeats him. I told him he can have a few hours of reconciling, but needs to get back in the game and that it sucks that I have to push him to do that. That he shouldn't have to face such odds, but it is what it is and there's little we can do about it - that he can avoid school and fall further behind and be more traumatized or he can cry it out and salvage as much of the day as he can. The grief has stolen so much from him and it slaps him in waves that are truly overwhelming for him. This pattern in particular, where he doesn't want people treating him differently because his sister was physically killed. IT SUCKS LIKE A MILLION SUCKS!!!! Selfish? No. I am doing the hard work of parenting under the worst of conditions. Dishonest? No. Resentful? Yes, re-feeling the pain. Also, yes, my God, my God why have you forsaken us. Fear? Yes, that it will always be like this. The unfortunate reality is, that in some form, it will be. 5: Share with someone? Yes. 6: Willing to have God and Kayleigh remove defects? Yes. 7: Prayer? God and Kakes please remove defects and help me continue to hone my skills. 8: willing to change? Yes. 9: Change? Breathe. Do the work I am asking Nate to do. Expect horror. Attitude quiet. Perspective Kakes is ever present and although this is immensely unfair and always will be, we have no choice but to continue to walk through the valley of the shadow of death. 12: Turn thoughts to who? To Nate and Jess. Then Kakie time.

"Accept Some Things Are Unacceptable"

Sometimes I accept that some things are unacceptable,
The grief, like forest torched, breaks the sky,
I cannot see my beautiful little girl and I struggle not to question why
-

So many horrible people polluting the world with their filth,
So many self-inflicted wounds - the worship of greed and of guilt,
Then she comes with compassion to wrap her sweet arms around this world,
And a simple, innocent accident takes away my little girl -

Some things in this world are unacceptable to accept,
Yet I accept the unacceptable,
And onward, in the inequitable…

I press…

*

Spiritual Accelerant 11/29/2018

Kayleigh and I intended spiritual acceleration in the street, not death of a relationship, and so we live. Together, our partnership is unbreakable. We face this reality set in full color. The joy of her amazing physical life; the grief of her physical death; the glory of the transition into a higher spiritual life; and the miracle of our continued journey together.

At times, knowing your presence, I may feel empowered; beyond this limited earthly, human experience. As a body of light securely locked within a much smaller frame, I sometimes take flight against the cage, feeling the centuries before this one, the yearning to shed this temporary skin. In the most peaceful way, you have proven God, the higher life of Heaven and the existence and reliance of Guardian Angels.

At any given moment, on any given day, the waves may shift; the grief may grow ugly. In those moments the mechanism of the human mind wants answers it cannot have. The breath, it changes. The only way through is through.

"Without You"

I long for you as if you are my breath,
That without you, with no air through my chest,
I would die one thousand times,
One thousand deaths,
In each second without you,
Without my breath.

*

Wait Until I Die - Why Would I Do That?! 11/30/2018

I read where a woman, trying to be helpful to a mother who had physically lost her child, told her, to paraphrase, that her daughter was gone, was part of eternity, that she would be there someday too, but for now stop merging with her daughter and be with those around her who were still alive since you only get one short life. And the grieving mother thought that was okay.

I was stunned, both by the suggestion and the reception. I honor the variances of perspective of grieving parents, however, for me I could not disagree more with a multitude of the issues raised in that interchange. Number one: my Daughter Kayleigh, who physically died and whose life transitioned spiritually into her body of light in a horrible car accident at fifteen, is alive. Number two: this is not a denial state or failing to grasp our situation- we face it daily in true, full color, part of which is the absolute certainty of Kayleigh's elevation and current presence, albeit shifted in body type. Number three: I actually find higher true life in merging with Kayleigh right here and now - for eternity is in the now - it doesn't impede my life to engage with my children, but only helps this life to grow. And being present with her helps me be present with others. True hell would be a full absence of that relationship. Number four: when people say they find comfort in seeing their loved one after they die, meaning their relationship is over until then - I believe that the former is true and comforting, but the latter is tragically flawed. The bigger question is this - why wait until I die?! I have two children - one in his physical body and one in her body of light. I see and feel and hear my Kayleigh every day, differently than I did before the accident, but these new channels we have developed together evolve our relationship similarly to how we changed our relationship from two to five to seven to eleven to fourteen. Without that connection to both of my children, and particularly this special heavenly bond with Kayleigh, my life would be torture. Number five: how horrible would it be for Kayleigh to be beside me, but me denying her presence until I too physically died. That defies the selfless sacredness of parenting. And I will not deny my Daughter.

We hold horrible grief in one hand and brilliant radiant miracles in the other. It is not easy. Quite frankly, to be daily present with each other, it takes energy and work and discipline and opening up specifically and spiritually to a higher and higher vibration. And it is the most amazing reward - the glory of being with my children - both of them - right now, regardless of the horrible accident. It is the most courageous thing we have done. So we continue as a family of four in everything we do since she is right here, present and accounted for, transitioned, of course, out of her physical body and elevated into her beautiful body of light. If anything, with her empowerment in her current state, we set our eyes to taking our relationship even further, even deeper, ever higher. No, we will not abandon our relationship until I physically die to be somehow reassembled at that point in time. Soul to soul, regardless of our body types, we are today together. Whether she is in her physical or spiritual body, she is alive. Whether I am in my physical or spiritual body, I am alive. We carry each other...carry each other...

"The Night of the Soul"

No clear path underfoot,
And thickly the woods,
Wrap roots and branches around my feet,
And I struggle through vines,
Through thorns and their spines,
Though blind,
I follow your voice home,
Through this night - the night of the soul;

Pains embed in the scarred bark,
And trees cry in the dark,
But they whisper relief for me,
For their grief weaves light into the air,
And weakens the fear,
As your voice grows stronger,
In this night of the soul...

...Time like a mountain of smoke,
The illusion of time takes its toll,

And I let it go again and again,
Traveling through the black veils of light,
Knowing morning will come to this soul,
On the other side - one the other side of this night...

*

Isolation – Abandonment 12/01/2018

People look at me like I went through a tragedy a year and half ago, and so therefore, it was in the past and I should be better by now. Not all people, but some. As if I had a hamster that died. What they do not understand and cannot understand is that it is a year and a half since my tragedy *began*. A daily tragedy. A daily struggle. A daily triumph of our relationship led by Kake's soul.

Based on the way people generally interact with us, it is clear that what is true is what we have been saying all along. That this situation is a place that never exists until you've been there; that there is no human possibility for anybody to come close to understanding the trauma unless they too have suffered the physical death of a child in childhood; that the isolation comes, not always intentionally, but it comes nonetheless.

For me, k know our truth. I remind myself of it daily. I reject the injections of those in this world who think that somehow we are "stuck" or there is "something wrong because we are not healing." I reject the silliness in their affect. In reality, there is no healing from the physical death of a child in childhood. And if by stuck they mean I am in a relationship with Kayleigh, then, okay, I am stuck, for I am in a relationship, but I would not call it being stuck. I call it being in love; being a Dad; having a relationship with my child that knows no border and no barrier. Largely, I grow in the most courageous part of my soul's journey, building a relationship with both of my kids. For you, Kakes, I revert to this modification of the Serenity Prayer whenever I need the uplift:

God grant me the serenity to accept the things I cannot change:

To embrace, horrifically, the fact that I have to, against my will, live the rest of my life without your physical body by my side.

The courage to change the things I can:

To embrace the fact that I get to live the rest of my life with your spiritual body right by my side.

And the wisdom to know the difference:

To always counterbalance and lean towards what we are, not what we were; to find you where you are, in your spiritual body of light in the present, not where you are not, in your physical body to which we are so accustomed.

*

The Grief and the Glory 12/04/2018

The grief and the glory. They flow alike, two streams of colorful ribbon within and without; coiled; merged; released into separate streams yet gravitating in the spiral of emotion, time, faith and love to melt into one, like the splashes of nameless colors, spectral rainbows emitted from the sun on its descent over a stormy ocean.

They are opposing forces. They are so different that they tend to resemble the other, at least in power and tenacity, in tenderness and presence. Yet there the resemblance fails. For grief is a shadowy character, a thief of ill regard, with no conscience and a total disregard for anything but collecting tears and pain in a constant wheeled mechanism that will take as much as one will give.

Glory is glory. It is its own reward and its own beauty. It is the essence of spiritual centeredness and communion with God's intention. It is golden white light that sets its blinding glow upon the earth in the first sparks of sunrise, blasting away the night and setting the comfort and the calm for the day to rest within.

"A Mouth of Flowers II"

...Now a bright wreath of flowered stars,
Slowly drifts into view,
A bouquet that flashes like a stormy, healing front,
Approaches the wounds that dwell in this heart,
And I, rejoicing, know it is you -

And its mouth, gently toothed with a million suns,
Opens up widely to swallow me whole,
And I fully submit,
Knowing in its glowing waters where the spirits dance,
That is the place where you are,
In this mouth of stars,
That is the place of your soul,
Smiling with a radiance,
That lights my way...

...My way home.

*

The Weak Link 12/05/2018

I fully understand that I am the weak link in this equation of how to reach higher and build our relationship courageously in its new configuration. Stuck in my humanity, if I accepted its cage, I would forego the glory of who we are. I will not do that. Stuck in my humanity, I will push on the edges. Thank you for your patience. I promise you I will do my work and I will be with you. And although we will be together in the kingdom of Heaven, I do not need to wait until I physically die for us to be together. We are together now. Show me how to activate in your life. Guide us with that spark to engage us.

I bring myself to you. Show me how your Daddy can engage in your current life. Teach me the ways of the spirit to lift me higher so I can be with you more presently, which also helps me be more present with Nate and Mommy. Draw me into your light. Teach me how to rise. Show me what I need to do to be aware. Show me how to awaken further.

*

Catastrophic 12/06/2018

What we are going through is catastrophic. It is not an event, but a lifetime. It cannot be healed, yet we can resolve each moment just as we express each breath in our lungs. With some moments the breath will seem empty; in others like bags of jagged glass; yet onward each moment, tied to the last and tied to the next, lurches on. In each lives a lifetime of this tragedy, a longing, a heartache so unique there is no name for it, centered on my child, my Babygirl, My magnificent Daughter, who sits beside me encouraging each breath - who empowers me with her beautiful life in spirit, proving the duplicity and giving me just enough hope to breathe.

"Faith"

Your laughter lights a galaxy,
Your smile that heals the great divide,
Fools fumble in fictions and fallacies,
Into which their derelictions hide,
Failing in their higher responsibilities,
While you with divine dexterity,
Penetrate the veil with God's intent,
And then when all of their logic is spent,
You dream across their eyes,
You stream across their eyes,
You breathe across their eyes,
Yet do they see,
My Darling,
My Love…

…They are not me.

*

Higher Life 12/07/2018

I believe in you and know my little girl is also a brilliant angel of the highest order; a radiant light, a blinding light, a beacon of hope and faith for her family, friends and for those longing for the light.

There is no "afterlife," as what would come after that which does not end? Life does not end. It transforms. After the transition it is a continuation into a Higher Life. So what is truly meant is, following physical death, one enters the Higher Life; one continues into the Higher Life, or Heaven, if the reader prefers. It matters little what it is called as long as we understand that it is not an "afterlife." We need to change our earthly dialogue to match what is truly occurring - life in a continuous, unbreakable light.

The transition of physical death is an amplification of life into the true, higher spiritual life. There is no death, except for physical death, the death of a shell, a temporary shell at that, encasing our true selves that are actualized upon transition.

My Darling is in the Higher Life, very much alive, just not in a physical manifestation. I can find her presently in the light that shines upon this earth as well as simultaneously finding her light in Heaven, in the Higher Life. Kayleigh has proven this.

"Your Million Lights"

Darkness like cotton blankets - silence,
Deafening the atmosphere,
A moment when the mind loses sight,
And slips out of its gears,
Well, it's late and the day has died,
And the midnight song has come to the eyes,

It breaks like waves on the hazy rocks,
That line the beaches in this metal box;

Curl up with me now, Darling, will you,
To range this country of my dreams,
When you were just a toddler,
And a tenth the size of me,
Wrapped in my arms,
Safe and secure,
With your protector,
Watching over his girl,
And as I wake now,
Crumpled across your bed,
A million Lights of your aura,
Swirled around my head,
A million Lights of Aurora,
Wrapped me as I wept,
A million Lights - like wild flora,
Cradle me, though I lay here bereft,
Your million Lights,
My Darling,
Wash away this dread.

*

Harmonize My Life with Yours 12/07/2018

Infuse me with your light. Empower me today with your light. Share
with me your light in order to harmonize my life with your life; lifting
my spiritual life, no matter its limits in my human condition, to a
higher level where you flourish in your brilliant spiritual existence.

"She Paints the Wild Clouds"

And, indelible, we pry,
Through the halls of waking eye,
In hopes of glance that preys on the darkness,
For we need the breath of light,

For it teaches us, in spite,
Of the moments in this life we find to be heartless -

She rises, and rises - smiling on the halo of the sun,
She paints wild rainbows into the ribcage of clouds,
As the clouds, in their thunder run,
Explode with echoes off into the horizon -

And, incredibly, we try,
Through the halls of drying eyes,
To emerge from the surge of grief and its darkness,
For with this, the bread of life,
We may see, though not with sight,
But with knowledge of the sky,
And the strength to impart this -

She is here - call us to this higher ground,
To where the angels gather round,
Where only love and light and found,
Where she paints the wild clouds for her family...

*

I Have Two Children... 12/11/2018

You asked me if I had any children and the answer always is, "yes, I
have two children - Nate and Kayleigh. Nate, one of the loves of my
life, is in his physical body and Kayleigh, my other love of my life,
in August 2017 was tragically physically killed in a car accident and
transitioned into her spiritual life. She's here with me right now."

Just because one is with God, that is subjectively just a formality. It
does not mean I have one child. It also does not mean I only have one
living child. I have two living children, continuing to mature in their
respective lives. The reality is that I have, and always will have, two
children. Always.

"Alive"

No barricade, no bitter wall,
Nor cage, nor barrier to crawl,
No other world or other place,
No fields to cross to see your face,
No waiting for the end of life,
No waiting for my death,
For what comes after that,
Which does not end -

It permeates the present air,
As I feel you standing here,
No greater love exists,
Than the likes of the love that we share,
When I held you there,
My Girl,
And my arms grew heavy with your last breath,
You exploded right through my soul,
As you conquered your own human death -

And I miss you with a broken heart,
And pain that raged and ripped me apart,
No greater horror can exist,
Than a parent having to go through this,
Yet we can laugh and we can sing,
And we can do just about anything,
For you are here and thus we strive,
And you are very much alive,
Empowered in your flesh of light,
Continuing the journey of your life.

*

Envelop Me in Your Presence 12/08/2018

Let us look today to what the other needs and brashly continue to
build and develop our relationship, My Love. You long to spend time

with me just as much as I long to spend time with you. If the tables were turned, I would be right there on your every word wanting to engage with you, willing to do anything to engage - ever willing, in perfect love and peace, to interact with you all the time. With the tables turned the other way, I believe you do the same for me. You love me so much. As much as I love you.

Please, therefore, envelop me in your presence - teach me your ways and God's direction. Surround me with your light, Darling, so that I breathe your light in my daily activity, saturated by your millions of points of light and radiant love. With you by my side I can do anything.

*

Grief Blocking Relationship 12/08/2018

I wonder if sometimes parents leave their children behind in the grief. That it is too hard for them emotionally so they move on. I see it sometimes in dialogue. I don't know how others handle this unless they express this to me from their position, but for me, the wording is critical. I will not and have not left My Girl behind in the grief, in her physical life, in the life changing tragedy of her accident. I have pulled myself forward with her, as she is pulling me forward with her, in our relationship as it has heightened and transitioned. I don't agree with words such as "moving on." They seem to indicate they are actually moving on from their children, which they may not mean, but may occur unintentionally just by the use of the words. So I will never use these words. We are current. Present. Active. Alive. Awake. You are not dead. You are not left behind in your physical life. You are alive in your spiritual body of light, more alive than ever, and you were happy and alive and living a full life on the day of the accident. You are now capable of being in Heaven and here on the physical plain at the same time, with God and with us - in both places you belong; in our presence, loved and cherished. I love you, Sweetheart. Let us grow. Let us push forward. Let me learn from my child who is now a thousand times stronger than me. Teach me. Your student opens to you with intention and devotion.

"You Are Taking Me There..."

Daughter, we had so many dreams to dare,
Sitting upon my lap in a nursery chair,
Daughter, now a bright, young woman,
Just after birthday of your fifteenth year,
It was everything I ever wanted,
With you, with purpose, these days to share -

Then alone, when the sirens ceased the bluish strobe,
When the chalk it marked your place in the road,
And then the tragedy - it spoke,
It showed me misery,
And all the days that now will never be,
And all the Saints, they came to lecture me,
And yes, I took their audience,
For if I fall apart,
If I let concrete harden in the heart,
It would block me from your brilliant soul,
And also, also from my own -
I ask you now to hold me while I cry;

Footprints - your feet press gently into ocean sands,
Carrying me - for I no longer have the strength to stand,
Understand, I have a vow that I shall defend,
Charmed in our relationship that has no end,
And then, I feel the weight of body under feet,
And feel your hand in mine as you walk beside me,
And everlasting love, My Love,
My Babygirl,
Your voice - it overlays this earthly world,
And nudges me through my grief,
And the moments of disbelief -
Where you hold me while I scream and cry;

You reach across the threshold of eternity,
And convey a calming atmosphere,
A dancing light spiraled from your fingertips,
And touched my head and lifted my hair,

Daughter, we had so many dreams to dare,
And now My Girl, you are taking me there...

*

100% of the 50% for Each 12/08/2018

I hear people say to us things like, "she is gone but your love lives in;
keep her memory alive; you have lost her, how tragic, but you have
your memories," things of this nature. And they are all wrong.
Kayleigh is not gone. She is actually very present. Of course our love
lives on, but not because it is a time barred entity of the past that
carries forth in my heart due to my longing - rather, our love grows
because we both currently invest in the relationship. Her memory
alive? That's the dumbest of the bunch - I have my memories before
her physical death, but I also have memories every day since her
transition together as well, including today's activities with her that
become a memory tomorrow morning. Okay, maybe the last one is
the dumbest - I have not lost Kayleigh - she is right here. Presently.
Currently. Actively. She's amazing and more beautiful than ever. I
am so proud of all she is showing me and all she strives to become.

Kayleigh experienced a physical body loss, but not a loss of life; but
a transition of life from one form, in the physical, of which we are
incredibly familiar and accustomed, to her spirit body of light, to
which we are learning to become more accustomed day by day. That
is the key. Kayleigh is alive - just in another embodiment and Nate is
learning that as a primary lesson. That, for me and Jess with Nate, is
the most important piece of this. His relationship with his sister, as
that with our daughter, is a continuum through her physical life and
every day since the accident in her spiritual body.

We have two children. We don't "had" two children. We don't have
currently one child. We currently have two children. So, as always,
they each get 100% of their 50% from their parents and Nate loves
that fact that he does not get the energy and time we reserve for
Kayleigh. He is learning from us how to continually incorporate
Kayleigh, who is very active and present. A family of four not broken

by the transition of one of us from body to body. That is the courage he is witnessing and experiencing. That is the great challenge and the great leap of faith he is encountering. It is big. It is complex. It is beyond the normal synthetic thought of the human mind. It branches out beyond the normal thought process and reaches for something greater; something higher; something sacred; something eternal.

Of course we suffer the sadness and grief of her physical passing every day. This was her container, the type of which the other three of us are still within and through whose lens we feel and see and speak and reside. We are human and she has shed her human, physical body. The pain is excruciating. The pain is unbearable at times. The pain, by itself, is impossible to bare. Yet, it is not and should not be taken by itself. With it comes Kayleigh's second life - a Higher Life, where she walks with God in Heaven, however that translates for the reader, while still walking with us and connecting to us every second of the day on the physical plain. This is what we call the Second Truth. That raw fact, that my child in her spiritual body is searching to connect wherever she can to me, gives me breath, hope and determination. The counterbalance to the grief, therefore, is Kayleigh's ability to angelically touch us with an abundance of guidance and love and light. She is alive. Her life pulls us through her physical death, like a hermit crab abandons one shell for a newer, roomier shell. Her current presence replaces her physical presence and it comes, not without suffering, but it comes also with God's glory.

So if I failed to acknowledge the Second Truth, and I failed to understand the Second Truth, and I failed to believe in that Second Truth and address that and invest in that Second Truth, no matter how hard the road and how exhausting the process, would I not be a father who has failed his child? Would I not be a father who has abandoned his child due to my own inability to strive higher, or due to despondency and grief, or due to my self-imposed limits that truncate the ultimate expression of faith and love? No. I am not that father. I will not be that father. My babies both need me, granted, in different ways now. I will continue to be a great Daddy who creatively continues to find new ways to love his children and be with his children and embrace his children's lives. I am a warrior father and my children are God's gold.

"My Children"

It is where the silky rainbows merge,
Where warm, sparkling waters converge,
Where one million blazing shades of gold,
Flow like blinding rivers aglow -

It is the ocean fields of stars,
Indigo beacons in an endless heart,
It is carved in the softer features of my face,
When I live within my children's grace.

*

You Need Me to Want 12/09/2018

Right now you don't need me to carry you, but you need me to want to carry you. And I do. And I am here. It is a critical distinction, one which I breathe. My children simply need me, just as they always have. Our situation now is no different. My son needs me and my Daughter needs me. At times I can support Nate in certain ways and guide him and nudge him in certain directions. I did this for you until that fateful night, but following the accident quickly learned that, although you did not need my guidance as a teenage girl in your physical life after that moment, you find great strength, warmth and light in knowing that I want to support you; I desire to support; I am intentionally supporting you any way I can, even though you don't technically need my guidance like you did before the transition. But who knows - maybe you do. That is the brilliance of our relationship. That is what makes you smile. My presence. My desire.

At the same time, your support of me has grown a thousand fold, you now knowing the grace of the heavens and the keys to the kingdom. Prior to your transition, you were adept and wise, and instinctually someone who could ironically be a thoughtful companion and adviser to your Father, despite your youth. In the transition, ironically, you were catapulted now into an omniscient power and the ability to know which way I should turn; which direction I should go; which decision is best to make. So that instinct is now omniscient. It is one of the silver linings that, of course I wish never was upon me, but since it is, I embrace with open arms.

"A Winter Storm Outside Your Window"

Your light, like volcanoes packed in flakes of snow,
Every crystal, a fireball of ice,
Every frozen orb holds a piece of your soul,
Shift in sheets of blizzard under haze of streetlight,
A million snowflakes - all your own,
A million sparks that set the night aglow,
Dancing in the flurry of tiny diamonds,
That refract in sparkles as the wind blows,
Singing for you in the spotlight with reverence,
And I, in your window, know there is no severance,
As long as eternity springs with hope.

*

An Abdomen's Squatter 12/10/2018

I have a living entity in my gut. It gurgles. Spits. Sleeps. Stabs. Aches. Punishes. Bleeds. Cries. Shrieks. Pleads. Holds its breath. Rages like a hurricane. Just below my rib cage. In the fleshy soft material of my abdomen. It resides. It has taken up residence. It slashes with fury. It begs my fight back and resilience for it itches for battle, never wanting total subservience or surrender. It craves toying with my emotions. It wants to dangle my life before my eyes. It pulses trauma. It gleams with tears. It screams for my soul. It taps into my bloodstream and it sucks on the light that transcends my human flesh.

Yet a North Star obscured by clouds is still a North Star.

"These Ripples"

These ripples, like a wave unleashed in space,
Spreading nebulous rainbows,
And concussion bands,
That rattle the universe,
That plough grooves across God's face;

These ripples, like none other, thunder and roar,
And rip the crystal veils and Heaven's milky, sparkling lace,
Burning holes in the galaxies,
And wounding the soul with its deepest ache,
Yet even still, I lift my eyes from its many shores,
And stare into an angel's eyes,
My Daughter and that smile on her face.

*

Keenly Aware (of the First Truth) 12/13/2018

I am keenly aware of all that I have lost, all that I am currently losing, and all that will be lost in the future related to this tragedy. I have now, for sixteen months, with the opportunity of feeling it every minute over that period of time, suffered. The suffering never goes away. That is the first point of acceptance. The counterbalance, therefore, is key. My counterbalance with Kayleigh is magical, but not the subject here. I will focus on just one side of the coin. Today, without the counterbalance, the First Truth of devastation.

In any given day of our lives together, for instance, at the day do this writing she would be sixteen and a half in her physical life, and this morning I would have felt calm knowing she was physically alive and heard her in her room; getting ready for school; grabbing a bite to eat and jumping in the car with me; driving to school; quick kiss on the head and off with, "I love you." A text in second or third period. A quick one from me. Another after school. Knowing she is here or there and thinking of her occasionally, drifting back and forth between my kids and my wife throughout the day. Feeling grateful for a great family. Effortlessly loving the four of us. Dinner plans. Getting home. She's sitting at the table doing homework. Or filling the rooms of the house with her laughter or singing or behaving with wild boisterousness. Or fighting with her brother. Family things. Chit chat. Maybe a moment of redirecting. Dinner. Then walking the dogs and contemplating the day or a challenge or getting ready for college trips or tests. Then she borrows the car or I send her off to get us some groceries and tell her to get herself something. Or she's off with a boyfriend or girlfriend. Then I have to wait for the bathroom as she's taking her nightly shower. I sit on the couch waiting for her to finish her shower watching TV. Then she bounces downstairs and I say, "Hey Baby."

"Hi Daddy, goodnight."

"Goodnight, Babygirl. Have a great sleep. May God put a golden shield of protection around your mind, body and soul."

"Thank you. You too, Daddy."

Then I reflect before I go to bed on what a great family I have. How proud I am of Nate and Kakes and Jess. How everything is secure. How grateful I am that we are all together and physically alive. Give or take a few moments here or there, and in a nutshell, that is one day in our lives between just two of us. Blending all four of us together and multiplying these interactions out, a complex family beauty emerges. And that is one day. Lost. Forever. Multiply that by every day that has passed and every day that will come. This is the true accumulation of the loss as every day is added over time to the suffering. This is why the second Christmas is worse than the first and the tenth is worse than the seventh. This is the backwards nature of a child physically passing in childhood. This is hell on earth.

We live in the counterbalance, therefore. In the glory of Kayleigh's light and love. And in that balance we find the breath to live. We are breathing. Barely.

"Encasement of Light"

This shell, like black sheets, stretched out across the night,
A backdrop for one million points of blazing golden light,
Stars sing within my pores,
Suns burst within my soars,
Radiating my soul against my fleshy skin,
Pushing through the surface the glow that lies within.

*

Empty Handed - Fill These Empty Hands 12/13/2018

Had looked forward to your mid and late teen years. The conversations. The thoughtfulness. The guidance. The imprint into your decisions with suggestions and my wisdom. All of that. Stripped from me. Stripped from you.

Now with empty hands I open palms raised and ask to receive your light. Fill these empty palms with something more magical. Something more incredible and even more meaningful - a continued relationship with my Daughter on a much grander scale where you breach Heaven and earth and walk with me and with the heavens at the same time. That is more powerful than our midnight conversations when you would have had an issue with a boyfriend or been too excited about a part of your future to go to sleep. If I cannot have the first, but can have the second option, and the second option is all I have, I will take it with both hands.

"Lavender Seas"

Radiance - grace,
Lavender lace,
It blooms on the sea,
And her spirit, embrace,
She illuminates,
The waves that comfort me -

Sparkling crystals of rainbow liquid light,
Embody her current life,
No, not a dream;

She is present, aware,
She is truth - she is here,
With her arms wrapped around me,
Like the earth is wrapped -
By the Lavender Seas.

*

The Un-Corruptible Power of Love 12/14/2018

Within you, breathing through you, embodying you is an unbridled power, the power of light and love that cannot be corrupted or used selfishly. The more power You provide to Kayleigh, God, the brighter she shines in Your name. The more she resonates her light in our lives the brighter she shines, ultimately in Your name and light. It is untarnished, uncapped love. It is not corruptible. It is purity. Authentic light. Its only purpose is peace. Its only mission is love. Its only manifestation is light.

You walk amongst us as you always have, having shed your physical human body in an unfortunate and tragic traffic accident that ripples through me and echoes across the big country of my soul in a constant vibration. Within the tragedy of that moment is the glory of this – you immediately transitioned into your powerful body of light, gaining not only your body of light, but also the true fullness of Heaven in the Higher Life, while also gaining the ability to remain with us on the physical plane. That is amazing.

For your Father, still cocooned into his physical body, must walk the physical world while I reach higher for that spiritual world of which I can glimpse, into which I cannot quite press my feet. I reach. I see you. I call to you and you come. You are here. You are. Your voice crosses all hinterlands. Your words collapse all barriers. Your presence expands my world far beyond the tactile physical world on

706

which I currently reside. However, I am truly and actually between worlds as you have given me the window into the bigger light, a window into the highest of us – the window into our spirits and our eternal journey. This life is a mere keyhole, the space outside the keyhole, the everything else.

Your circle of influence is getting bigger, Kake. I will show Nathaniel the way through the pain and heartache. As I always have been, Mommy and I will continue to be his North Star. And yours. He will look back as an adult and say his Daddy and Mommy were there as his guide through the trauma while we were also going through our own trauma. Likewise, you are a part of that North Star, and he will also claim that his sister pushed him, led him, comforted him and was present with him every day of his life. Help us all rally in your light, Kakie.

"A Sunrise Over a Silver Sea"

A band of light we cannot see,
Though it flows in steady stream,
Know the earth holds this glow,
Like water holds an ocean,
And the clouds of liquid gold,
Radiate a daughter's devotion -

Oh sweet, thine angel, sing alight,
A higher, Higher Life,
And grace, this is, the mouth of miracles,
From which the riches flow;

In that moment when the sun with blinding light,
Captures the hope of day from the darkness of night,
That is my baby shining,
That is my baby smiling,
That is my baby rising,
That is my baby - my little girl;

And I see her, though not with human sight,
Sitting here beside me in her body of light,
A river's mouth of miracles - rejoice,

And breathe in the golden sunrise,
From which her riches flow.

*

The Moon Is Not a Passive Light 12/15/2018

The moon is ever present. Even when not visible. The moon is never
passive. The moon is ever active. The moon influences the tides and
the sway of the great oceans. The moon illuminates the darkness and
cycles the accord of man. The moon creates ambiance and mystery,
mystique and passion. The moon is indirect light, a reflection of the
sun. The moon is to the sun as an angel is to God, a reflection of the
true light. The moon is you Kayleigh, reflecting God's light, ever
present, ever active, always loving, forever light.

"The Soul Harvest"

It isn't lagging or logical,
Clearly not pathological,
It is just emotion that hardly conceals,
Some things just don't reconcile,
Some things just don't heal,
Biting acres off by the mile,
And the soul harvest bends to its yield,
For there is no death that rings like this,
And this death does not heal,
My child, I ache, I love you,
As the harvest accumulates,
Days, like stalks that populate,
These acres and miles of fertile fields,
Are caught in the illumination that echoes in its bloom,
Are caught in the illumination of a spirited full moon.

*

Our Beads 12/16/2018

Each night I take our Mala beads that I wear through the day and tell you, "Babygirl, here is a gift for you today packed into our beads. I've put my light and my love into these beads as a gift for you in the way that I lived my life today. I tried to fill these beads with my life and love and my gold. I pray that this gift is worthy of our love."

On some days I may say, "Today was hard. I may not have given you as strong a gift today, but I really tried. I hope that this gift is still worthy of our love."

On other days I may say, "Look at the colors I've added to the beads - the golds, the light blues, the greens. You can see my soul's love and light. We were really clicking today. I felt your presence and I was fully engaged and empowered. I feel like today's gift is worthy."

And I lay our Mala beads on your pillow and kiss your pillow where your head lay each night for sleep. You thank me each night. I feel you. I hear you. Almost like you are saying, "Oh, Daddy, for me? Thank you so much for giving me your light and love. I will wear these while you sleep and embrace your love and light. While you are sleeping I will use your light and love to help propel me in my life. And while you are sleeping I will add my light and love to these beads so you can pick them up in the morning when you wake and wear my light and love all day tomorrow to help propel you in your life."

With a healthy Eleventh Step, and sometimes meditating with you, Kakes, this is how I end each night. Knowing you are here, knowing you will faithfully and intentionally bring your light and love to bare while I sleep, I find comfort in you and wrap myself within your arms as I lay my head on your pillow and stare off to your ceiling or your walls or your stuffed animals in the corner.

In the morning I can't wait to come into your room, turn on your light, wish you a good morning, sit upon your bed where I always have and begin the new day. "Thank you, Baby, for bringing your light and love to our beads," I say each day as I lift our beads into my outstretched palms, "you always do and it is always worthy. Thank you so much."

"You're welcome, Daddy. Wear them today knowing my light and love is always with you. Our beads are blended with our light and filled with our love, Daddy."

They change color. Depending on my mood and the emotion that flourishes through me, it stagnates in my veins, the beads will grow warm or cold, icy blue in color or gold or green or opal. They are an extension of our magical relationship that, like our love, transcends the constructs of this earthly plain. Thank you, Kakie, for the interaction captured in our beads. They energize my every breath.

"Blending Souls"

Blend aura flesh,
And spiritual mesh,
Our streams of liquid light,
Weave together thread by thread;

Converge pink and white,
And become golden bright,
More together we are,
Than separate we are less...

...Divinity breathe us - we are home,
We in the cradle of light,
We in the blending of souls.

*

Kayleigh, You Emailed Me 12/16/2018

As I sat down to eat breakfast this morning at First Watch, I opened my phone to my email and noticed at the top of the inbox an email from...you. Received at 12:23 AM last night, nine hours earlier, while I was sitting on your bed talking to you, with my phone away for the night.

You sent an email. Sixteen months after your physical death. An email. You, My Love, my Little Girl. Of course you did. You sensed our grief, how I was slugging through the day; how Nate now hates Christmas; how Mommy is struggling. You always provide, we have come to learn, in ways we don't always understand.

You are strong today. Biblically powerful. As I sat staring at my phone and trying to wrap a human mind around this miracle, I also accepted it as readily as I did my own breathing. It is not beyond your abilities as a true guardian angel, aligned with God's wishes for us in this moment, delivered by you in His name. It is certainly a part of your DNA to be ever protective and vigilant of your family. You teach me new methods and miracles every day. And here is another – you sent me an email.

After a few minutes of staring at my inbox, I checked the email itself, reviewing that, yes indeed, this was sent from your personal email account. I noticed an attachment. I clicked the attachment and saw that it was a breathing exercise document with a quote at the top, "Listen. Are you breathing just a little and calling it a life?" - Mary Oliver.

It was a method for "Breathing Practices to Support Wellness During Life's Challenges and Transformations." It lay out a plan of breathing joy. Receiving an email from my Daughter sixteen months after her physical death, was already amazing, but then you became even more amazing than amazing you are. I scanned to the bottom of the document. It was a document pulled from my sister Tricia's website, something she sent to you in October, 2016, just after the assault. However, this email was not forwarded from that email. It was not sent years ago. It was a stand-alone email into which this pdf was attached, sent to me nine hours ago from your account. You, sixteen months after your physical death, when I desperately needed it, sent me an email from your account about better breathing practices through grief from my sister's website!

This is the path forward. To become stronger and even further open; to cast out despondency; to open further my third eye and blast free from my crown chakra. Whatever the world and its individual's choose to call it, it matters little. This is spiritual empowerment. This is other worldly; Higher worldly. This is you - pure love and light that transcends everything.

I am stunned yet energized; amazed yet just simply content; a proud Daddy and a student to the majesty of my child; an equal soul to my Daughter who shows me daily true devotion, intention and glory. Gloria, Kayleigh, Gloria...

"My Beautiful Daughter"

She is hugging her Father,
She, with intention, and adoration, fluttering,
Smiling with her ocean blue eyes aglow,
Her head resting on my shoulder,
She takes me by the hand,
I close my eyes and see her with my soul -

An angel's silky robe - alight with golden galaxies,
A silver universe of stars imbed each feather's fleece,
Of brilliant wings that radiate with elation,
Love, that illuminates the soul in this higher vibration,
Calls me in her warmth,
To gather myself in a blinding white light,
And carried forth in her perfect calm,
That, like the stars themselves, glitter with delight,
In the pulse of her perfect song,
And her lovely voice of life.

*

The Sand Dollar 12/17/2018

You are teaching the world that our dimensions overlay each other; that these dimensions crisscross and are blended; that life is not just contained within the days and years of a human condition, but are only partly representative of those days and years; that you are currently alive in the streams of love and light, where they merge in

712

a perfect peace. That you are on our beach of perfect Heaven, what we call Exuma Infinite.

You have mastered certain skills; have practiced and learned new ways of communication, some of which are astounding to the human mind, yet perhaps are part of a larger fabric beyond our human consumption. They say the soul is eternal. This is true, and if true, then this is fact and therefore factually you are alive, just on another channel. A channel of pure joy. Many do not get to experience the sensation of what you have been able to accomplish. This is partly the mission of this book - to journal your voice in its many beautiful tones and to convey that message to the world. And so I do.

It was with this in mind on the winter evening of this writing that I spoke to one of my guys in A.A. about your brilliance and ability to manipulate technology in order to talk to your Daddy as you continue to change my Bluetooth. You flipped to "Beautiful Day" when I drove to work this morning and later in the day, you changed it to "Gloria," and then again to another U2 song on another album. Sometimes you do this when others are in the car. They have heard. They have seen. They believe. They know. Countless others do as well.

Shortly afterward, my little sister sent a text and needed to talk to us immediately. She said that you showed up big time for her just minutes earlier and she had visual proof of your stamp on her day. She explained how she had a Sand Dollar that she had collected while vacationing with us when you were five on Jekyll Island. She had it laying in the dirt for years in a flower pot and had decided to give it to a friend. She cleaned the dirt off of it, and while drying it, looked down and was stunned to see an imprint of your face in a more pronounced part of the Sand Dollar's eleven year old dried, mossy shell.

She texted the photo to us and, to our amazement, there it was - clearly a print of your face, etched into the velvety texture of the Sand Dollar, like a laser etched an image into glass. Two things immediately occurred when my eyes first fell upon this miracle image: I heard you say, "Daddy! Look what I can do!" I smiled and felt such pure pride. Simultaneously, I saw clearly that you were sixteen and a half in the image, not fifteen and three months and two days, as you were on the day you physically passed. You have aged sixteen months in the last sixteen months after your body physically died. Your body of light is sixteen and a half years old.

We took a side by side picture of you with the image and it was startling. Even my mind, becoming much more accustomed to your miracles, was having trouble understanding the how, as I forgot not to worry about the "how" and just simply embrace the "is." As I say to people, your life is not a "was," it is an "is." You are here. You are alive. And this miracle – it simply, is.

And so, proving once again, you are here. Right now. As I lay stretched across your bed jotting down this most incredible miracle of showing yourself so profoundly to my sister who desperately needed a Kayleigh moment. A perfect child of God, child of light, child of love. Shine on, my Babygirl, your mission, in God's name, continues to illuminate this earthly plain and that dimension which overlay this one. I am so proud. And humbled. A Sand Dollar, Kayleigh. Of all things in the material world that you could have used to explode upon this plain; of all things you could have used from the scraps of this material world, you used a perfect symbol of God's peace. Also a personal family symbol of our many walks on the beach - as I taught you as a little girl, 'when you find a Sand Dollar at the shore that is alive we gift it back to the sea, and if we do, the sea will honor us and gift us a special bleached Sand Dollar that had died that we can take with us.' Eleven years later, this special Sand Dollar became part of your platform today, a heavenly canvas, to call out to us with glory and joy; to remind us to rejoice in your current life of light and love; in the eternity of the now. Amazing.

"Kayleigh Paints a Sand Dollar"

As with God, so God has ordained with us,
Offering what is to continue,
From the human flesh that was,
Bathed in the birth of earthly cells,
Ornate with poinsettia and Christmas bells,
A canvas illuminates angelic paint,
Across this Sand Dollar's organic face;

Through the trials of life and its unpredictable weather,
The soul, like diamonds, resulting from pressure,
Expands as it breaches its human skin,
And exchanges one body for the one held within;

And this Sand Dollar, itself beseeched,
Proclaims a miracle that no human hand can speak,
And was chosen after careful inspection,
To bare this soul's beautiful impression,
And humbly, and not unlike His resurrection,
She stands on this heavenly beach,
In the glory of God's light...

...With a mission, she holds dearly, to teach...

*

Kayleigh's Voice 12/18/2018

Sixteen months after her transition, she placed her golden hand on a Sand Dollar and emblazoned her face on it. She is telling us very clearly that life just transitions. I can't explain how comforting it is. The whole point of this book, of your voice, Kayleigh, is very clear to me. The world is asleep. The world is blocked. There are many ways that this world can align itself with light and love.

Some souls are as mature as you and others are not. Significantly, in this two-way street, most souls still trapped in human conditions are just blocked – blocked by their own ego and fear and despondency, or just blocked by not knowing. Many more could access their loved ones in the Higher Life if they could only yearn to believe, and strive to truly wake up. I know that our connection, my devotion and intention with you, brings light and joy to you in a magnificent way. You are proud. You know your Daddy is not asleep; that your Daddy will stop at nothing to open himself up to a higher vibration to be with you. Always.

"Playing For Something Bigger Than Flesh and Blood"

Just beyond the veil of the wind from our eyes,
In the courage that explodes from the deepest pools of my cries;

We are playing for something bigger,
Bigger then flesh and blood,
Everything that now is,
Is everything that then was,
I call out - I cry out, for you, My Love,
For you, my shrieks that echo us,
Your Father grieves the great thief of,
A young physical life - a brilliance and grace,
Yet relishes the glory,
Of a spiritual body that took its place,
I fight for you and push my way through,
Just to catch an angelic glimpse of your face,
For you are here, my Little One,
On a mission blessed with God's embrace,
Brighter than one million suns;

So angle now for something bigger,
Bigger than flesh and blood,
Everything that now is, My Girl,
Is everything that then was…

*

Denial 12/20/2018

There is an abysmal denial in situations like ours cast upon the
western world. Sometimes from ignorance. Sometimes from
dogmatic individuals who may believe differently, and so therefore,
attempt to deny my faith. Some are forcefully in denial, finding better
comfort in the not knowing, than going through the strenuous process
of walking a spiritual road.

Fortunately for us, it isn't us who are in denial. I know you are here. You are touching my hair as I write this to confirm that truth. Some in the human race simply don't realize they don't need to deny their loved ones who have physically died, by denying they are still alive, for whatever reason. Based on the linguistics of death, with how they approach death, with how they avoid death, with how they avoid their feelings and through misinformation and misplaced ideas, they are in denial. Gone? Lost? Memories? No, not you. You are not gone. You are not lost. You are not a memory. Like a hermit crab leaving one shell for another, you have left your human body and your life has transferred and transitioned into another shell, this one being one of light rather than flesh. Anyone who denies this is in denial. We get to change the dialogue of death.

"Change the Dialogue of Death"

A hundred winds that howl of loss,
A mine field that we dream across,
And sleep with death,
Under crooked cross,
And midnight shade that colored thoughts,
Release the pain and bleed the pause,
For everything that once there was,
And understand - the heavy cost,
But know that all - all is not lost –
All roads they lead to you,
All roads they lead to truth,
Broken path, a wilderness,
A blizzard squall of bitterness,
Invades my ears and singes soul,
They don't know what they don't know,
But there they are with shallow words,
And selfish thoughts - and so absurd,
For they don't know what they don't know,
Why not just listen to my road;

The words are so important,
They shape the scene lest we forget,
The right words map experience,
With no room left for variance,

They are purposeful, meaningful,
Into which this sacred stage is set,
And there she stands - full of life,
Stronger in her frame of light,
And so it comes at my request -

We must change,
We must change,
We must change the dialogue of death.

*

"The Secret of the Water Road" 12/23/2018

Opal foam webbing glistens, as the emerald sea, it pulls,
On the lacy sunset curtains that spread out over the flow,
Of warm tropical waters that draw the sunlight below,
Sparkling against the coral, shining up in purple, dreams and gold,
And wreathed in tranquil waters - I see my Daughter's soul,
She is reaching for my spirit as if only she knows,
How to teach her Father,
The secrets of the water road...

...She opens up the sea door,
On the beaches of Exuma Infinite,
And through its floral glow,
We swim the loving moons of affection,
That rise within our souls...

*

Our Love Songs to Each Other 12/25/2018

Our poems are love songs to each other. Our words, individual strings of white and pink light that attach us by our hearts and souls. My life, your life – these lives stream like poetry in a melody that emotively stamps a moment of time with its flavor, its color, its feeling - sometimes quite tearfully - sometimes full of unbridled joy - sometimes with no breath - sometimes with an exhale like a tidal wave.

My soul is ripped out from the inside daily; and repaired just the same. Lurching and heaving back and forth; never healing but always reconciling; never advancing but never retreating from the full color of this catastrophe nor from the brilliant spiritual experiences that take us together to higher ground, the likes of which most will never know. But we do. Its vibrancy resonates pure light between us. It's life, illuminating from our love that we share, expands and intensifies as we dance around the edges of these two worlds looking for channels and connectors to the other; modules to everlasting love, light and life. We find them. We embrace. We communicate. We expand. How lucky am I in you; and you in me. Merry Second Christmas in our new configuration, Honey.

"Leaning Into the Next Wave Together..."

Collapse of curled wave,
Explode with a spray,
Just you and me -

As we brace in towards,
The sea's tidal door,
Digging in our feet...

...We lean...

...And the waters recede under knees,
To gather again in the deep,
To gather again to sweep us away,
Yet it never can sweep us away…

…And comes the next wave,
To crash in the wake,
Of the last water dream…

…Our souls as our tether,
We lean in together,
And tame the wild sea...

...You and me…